Augsburg
George Sverdrup Library
Minneapolis, Minnesota 55404

CO-BWQ-975

WITHDRAWN

THE RISE OF URBAN AMERICA

ADVISORY EDITOR
Richard C. Wade
PROFESSOR OF AMERICAN HISTORY
UNIVERSITY OF CHICAGO

A BIBLIOGRAPHY
OF
MUNICIPAL PROBLEMS
AND
CITY CONDITIONS

Robert C. Brooks

ARNO PRESS
&
The New York Times
NEW YORK · 1970

Reprint Edition 1970 by Arno Press Inc.

Reprinted from a copy in The State Historical Society of Wisconsin Library

LC# 78-112527
ISBN 0-405-02439-8

THE RISE OF URBAN AMERICA
ISBN for complete set 0-405-02430-4

Manufactured in the United States of America

MUNICIPAL AFFAIRS.

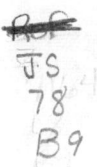

ISSUED AT QUARTERLY INTERVALS BY THE
Reform Club Committee on City Affairs, New York.

Vol. V, No. 1.   *MARCH, 1901.*   Whole No. 17

A BIBLIOGRAPHY OF MUNICIPAL PROBLEMS AND CITY CONDITIONS.

By ROBERT C. BROOKS.

SECOND EDITION—REVISED AND ENLARGED

Complete to January 1st, 1901.

NEW YORK:
Reform Club, Committee on City Affairs,
52 William Street.
LONDON: P. S. King & Son, Orchard House, Westminster, S. W
PARIS: Société Nouvelle de Librairie et d'Édition, 17 R. Cujas.
THE HAGUE: Martinus Nijhoff.

Entered at the Post Office at New York, and admitted for transmission through the mails as second-class matter.

Copyright 1901, by the Reform Club Committee on City Affairs.
All Rights Reserved.

INTRODUCTORY.

"Knowledge is of two kinds. We know a subject ourselves or we know where we can find information upon it. When we enquire into any subject, the first thing we have to do is to know what books have treated of it."—
SAMUEL JOHNSON.

In any rapidly developing literary or scientific field, an absolutely complete bibliography is an impossible ideal. No argument is needed to show that municipal government in the present stage of public interest presents such a field. Since the publication of the first edition of this work in 1897, the literature on cities has grown so rapidly that from three to four times as much space is now required to list it adequately. Amid such a flood of materials, it is unavoidable that some errors and omissions should occur. In spite of the exercise of the utmost caution, the bibliographer therefore can only hope that such as may be found in the present work will not prove to be of a serious character.

However, it is believed that the materials presented will prove sufficient in all cases either to open up any portion of the field to the thorough investigator, or to answer the chance question of the casual seeker for information. In order that the lists might answer such diverse ends as these, many titles of apparently ephemeral and local interest have been included. There is no widespread interest, so far as the compiler is aware, in the water works of Kowloon, nor can it be claimed that a German *Doktorarbeit* on the population of some obscure fifteenth century market-town touches a burning question of the day. Yet among those into whose hands the bibliography may fall there perhaps will be some to whom such subjects are of professional or local interest, and it is certainly a legitimate purpose of a work of this nature to facilitate access to the information they seek. For while there is undoubtedly great need among students for a systematic guide to the *best* literature on the subject of municipal government, the purpose of a bibliography, like that of a dictionary, is wider and more catholic. It cannot afford to be exclusive, it cannot profess to present the best only, it must seek to be comprehensive.

Accordingly the present edition has retained the same ambitious scope proposed for the work of 1897, and aims to include the books, pamphlets and periodical literature on municipal affairs of the United States,

Great Britain and Colonies, Germany, France, Italy, Spain and other European countries. It is a pleasure to note in this connection that the collections made by American librarians in the meantime—notably that of the Reform Club Committee on City Affairs—have greatly lightened the labor of the bibliographer and assured it a degree of comprehensiveness before impossible of attainment. All the materials published in the first edition of the bibliography and in the fifteen quarterly supplements prepared by Dr. Maltbie, and appearing subsequently in MUNICIPAL AFFAIRS, are included in the present work. A great number of references gathered by special investigators in English, German and French libraries have also been added. Especially useful were the briefer bibliographies covering one part or another of the field, which have been issued by various organizations since 1897.

So far as public documents are concerned, the aim of the present bibliography is the same as that of its predecessor. Formal accounts and routine reports of cities or of organizations following municipal ends have not been indexed except where specially important matter justified mention. On the other hand an attempt has been made to include all the more important special reports, national, state and local, on municipal topics. This distinction may perhaps be made clearer by a few illustrations. Routine reports—those omitted—include, for instance, Municipal Registers, City Documents or Year Books of American cities, the *Verwaltungsberichte* and *Haushaltsetats* of German cities, etc. To have cumbered the bibliography with such titles would have added enormously to its bulk and practically nothing to its value.

Special reports—those indexed—include such as appear at irregular intervals, often from sources outside the city. Thus our own Consular Reports contain much valuable material, and have been indexed in detail, since otherwise the only access to them would be through the numerous indexes and tables of contents in the Consular Reports themselves. The investigations of special legislative committees, as the Lexow Committee, the Parliamentary Commission upon Municipal Trading now in session in Great Britain, also belong to this category. State administrative departments sometimes publish the results of investigations of great municipal interest, *e. g.*, the recent reports of state labor bureaus on municipal ownership. Studies of this sort are somewhat out of the line of the regular work of these departments and consequently might be overlooked unless special reference were made to them. Sometimes city councils or administrative officials make investigations of special topics not usually included in their regular reports, as the report of the special committee of the City Council of Chicago on street railway franchises and operations in that city. Valuable special reports are also made from time to time by business men's associations, municipal leagues and other similar organizations.

While attempting to note materials of the above description, the bibliography can make no claim to completeness in this direction. But it represents the results gleaned from a few of the most thoroughly equipped libraries in the country, and will perhaps serve better to point out the meagreness of our resources in this field than to indicate its real extent and richness.

A few words regarding the arrangement of references may facilitate use of the work. The bibliography is divided into two main parts, a Subject Index (p. 1) and an Author List (p. 313). The Subject Index includes not only the principal topics of municipal administration—a partial list of which is given on page VII., but cities and countries as well, all arranged alphabetically. In the arrangement of the references the following plan has been followed: All relating to any one city have been grouped under that city. Thus references on Sewage Disposal in Berlin are found under BERLIN, subhead Sewage Disposal. The same is true as to countries. The references on Water Supplies in the United States, for instance, are under UNITED STATES, subhead Water Works. In each case, cross references to the city and country have been placed under the main topics. Thus, for example, immediately following the head LIGHTING there is a list of the cities and countries under which will be found additional material on lighting, but which is not general in character, relating only to the city or country referred to.

In the division of topics the compiler has aimed at a greater degree of centralization than in the first edition. For example, such topics as "Special Assessments," "Municipal Bonds," "Municipal Finance," "Octrois" and "Taxation," which were before given separately, are combined in the present work under the single heading "Finance." Cross references under the former separate headings indicating all such changes will speedily set students familiar with the old arrangement on the right track. The advantage gained by the bringing together of all the separate subdivisions of a given topic will, it is hoped, more than compensate for the initial annoyance involved.

One other feature of the Subject Index needs special mention. Upon classifying the material according to this plan a small number of unclassifiable titles were found which resisted every device of the bibliographer's art, titles referring neither to any particular city, nor country, nor single topic. These, together with the important general works, have been given special prominence by being grouped at the beginning of the Subject Index

(p. 1) under the rubric "CITY GOVERNMENT, GENERAL AND UNCLASSIFIED." A similar plan has been followed in each country and city.

In order to keep the bibliography within reasonable limits of size, titles of works were not repeated in the Author List (p. 313). By means of the figures following the names of authors, full reference to their works may readily be found in their appropriate places in the Subject Index. Thus the notation "2—12" refers to title 12 on page 2, and "237—78" refers to title 78 on page 237. The same system is followed in cross references in Subject Index. Whenever one finds the phrase "see 1—4b," or a similar symbol, it means consult reference 4b on page 1; the first number indicating the page and the second the paragraph.

The abbreviations adopted are those in common usage, and are so simple as to be easily understood and to render unnecessary the publication of a long and cumbersome list of magazines. If desirable, the reader may refer to any previous issue of MUNICIPAL AFFAIRS, where a considerable number are listed.

Altogether, this edition contains about 12,000 different entries in the Subject Index. In the Author List there are some 8,000 titles referred to under the names of nearly 4,500 authors. By far the larger proportion of the titles are in the English language, but Germany, France, Italy, Austria, Spain, Russia, Holland, Switzerland and many other countries are well represented.

The compiler desires to express his deep sense of obligation to Dr. Milo Roy Maltbie, editor of MUNICIPAL AFFAIRS, who has prepared the quarterly bibliographies appearing since 1897, and without whose assistance the appearance of the present edition would have been subjected to even greater delay than the unexpected magnitude of the work rendered unavoidable. Special mention is also due to the courteous and efficient library staffs of Cornell and Columbia universities.

Ithaca, N. Y., May 30, 1897.

PRINCIPAL TOPICS IN THE SUBJECT INDEX.

	Page.
City Government, General Works and Unclassified	1
Art, Municipal	12
Baths	17
Bossism	26
Building Laws	35
Burials, Cemeteries	36
Charities	40
Church and Municipal Conditions	50
Civil Service	52
Councils and Boards of Aldermen	57
Direct Legislation	60
Elections	63
Electrolysis	67
Engineering, Municipal	68
Finance	70
Fires and Fire Departments	75
Garbage and Refuse Disposal	83
Home Rule	98
Housing Problem	99
Libraries	116
Lighting	116
Liquor Problem	125
Municipal Control, Municipal Ownership	157
Parks, Playgrounds, Squares	212
Parties and Party Politics	216
Pavements, Paving	218
Police	226
Population, Growth of Cities	227
Proportional Representation	230
Sanitation	240
School Systems	244
Settlement Movement	247
Sewage Disposal	248
Streets, Street Building, Street Cleaning	257
Transit Facilities	262
Unemployed	271
Water Supplies	302

PRINCIPAL CITIES AND COUNTRIES IN SUBJECT INDEX.

	Page.		Page.
Albany	10	Hamburg	94
Amsterdam	11	Holland	98
Australia	14	Italy	109
Austria-Hungary	14	Leeds	115
Baltimore	15	Leipzig	115
Basel	16	Liverpool	127
Belfast	18	London	128
Belgium	18	Manchester	149
Berlin	19	Massachusetts	151
Berne	23	Michigan	153
Birmingham	24	Milwaukee	154
Boston	26	Minneapolis	155
Bradford	32	Munich	156
Bremen	32	New Jersey	172
Brussels	33	New Orleans	172
Budapesth	33	New York City	174
Buffalo	34	New York State	200
California	37	Ohio	204
Canada	39	Paris	206
Chicago	46	Pennsylvania	221
Cincinnati	51	Philadelphia	222
Cleveland	53	Pittsburgh	226
Columbus	55	Rome	235
Constantinople	56	Russia	236
Denver	59	St. Louis	237
Detroit	59	St. Paul	238
Dresden	61	San Francisco	238
Dublin	62	Spain	255
Edinburgh	63	Switzerland	259
France	77	Toronto	261
Frankfort-on-the-Main	82	United Kingdom	274
Geneva	85	United States	288
Germany	85	Vienna	298
Glasgow	91	Washington	301

SUBJECT INDEX

INCLUDING CITIES, STATES AND COUNTRIES.

City Government, General Works and Unclassified.

[Note.—The literature of city government, and especially the part produced in America, is of such a nature that to distinguish between works that are systematic and those that are propagandist is practically impossible. Under the above general heading, therefore, are included all materials which in the Bibliography of 1897 were placed under the topics "Administration" and "Reform," together with all similar titles of more recent date. In current discussion, the terms "city government," "municipal administration," etc., are used interchangeably. Articles bearing such titles are grouped below. In arranging articles dealing with special cities and countries, the same division into topics has been followed as in the Bibliography as a whole. The list of cities and states under each topic indicates that articles dealing with that subject in these cities and states may be found under their names. One exception to the general alphabetical arrangement has been made by placing the titles of works dealing with municipal government, general city conditions, or which are otherwise unclassifiable, at the head of the lists under the name of separate cities and states.]

Short list of cyclopedias and other works frequently referred to by number:

"Cyclopedia of Political Science, Political Economy and of the Political History of the United States." Lalor, John J. Chicago, M. B. Carey & Co., 1883. 3 vols. $7.50 each.   **1**

"Dictionary of Political Economy." Palgrave, R. H. Inglis. London, Macmillan, 1894, 1896, 1899. 3 vols. 8vo, 798, 848, 757 pp. Cl. $6.50 each.   **2**

"Encyclopedia of Social Reform, Including Political Economy, Political Science, Sociology and Statistics, etc." Bliss, W. D. P. (Editor). London and New York, Funk & Wagnalls Co., 1897. 8vo. 1439 pp. Cl. $7.50.   **3**

"Historic Towns Series, American." Powell, Lyman P. (Editor.) 3 vols. New York, Putnams, 1898, 1899, 1900. 8vo. 597, 439, 528 pp. Cl. $3.50 each.
  Historic Towns of New England.   **4a**
  Historic Towns of the Middle States.   **4b**
  Historic Towns of the Southern States.   **4c**

"Municipal Government in Continental Europe." Shaw, Albert. New York, Century Co., 1895. 8vo. 500 pp. Cl. $2.   **5**

"Municipal Government in Great Britain." Shaw, Albert. New York, Century Co., 1895. 8vo. 385 pp. Cl. $2.   **6**

"Social Statistics of Cities." (History, description and statistics of principal American cities in 1880.) Waring, Geo. E. Pt. I, New England and Middle States, 915 pp. Pt. II, Southern and Western States, 843 pp. Washington, Government Printing Office, 1886.   **7**

"Statesman's Year Book." Keltie, J. Scott, Editor. London, Macmillan, issued annually. $3 per year.   **7a**

"The State." Wilson, Woodrow. Boston, D. C. Heath & Co., 1889. 686 pp. $2.   **7b**

"Handbuch der Politischen-Oekonomie." (Volkswirtschaftslehre in zwei Bänden, Finanzwissenschaft u. Verwaltungslehre im dritten Band). Schönberg, Gustav. (Hrsgbr.) Tübingen, H. Laupp, 2 Auflage, 1885. 734, 1007, 1015 pp. 50m.   **8**

City Government, General Works and Unclassified—*Continued*.

"Handbuch des öffentlichen Rechts der Gegenwart in Monographien." (References to local organization indexed under separate countries.) Marquardsen, Heinrich. (Hrsgbr.) Freiburg i. B. J. C. B. Mohr, 1887-1889. Bd. I, II, III, (2 Halbbände), IV, (2 Halbbände). Subscr. Pr. n. 97 m. — 9

"Handwörterbuch der Staatswissenschaften." Edited by Conrad, Elster, Lexis and Loening. Jena. Gustav Fischer, 1st edition 6 vols. 8vo, 1890-1894. 1046, 1007, 1105, 1276, 885. 959 pp. Index 82 pp. issued 1895. Two supplements, 904 and 1076 pp., 1895-1897. n. 120 m. geb. n. 135 m. Four volumes of the second edition issued. — 10

"Constitutions Européennes; les parlements, les conseils provinciaux et communaux et l'organization judiciaire dans les divers Etats de l'Europe." Demombynes, Gabriel. Paris, Larose et Forcel, 1881, 2d ed. 1883. 2 vols. 8vo, 1600 pp. 1st ed., 18 fr.; 2d ed., 24 fr. — 11

"Dictionnaire des Finances." (Important articles on Assistance Publique, Le Budget Communal, Communes, Octrois, indexed separately.) Say, Leon. Paris, Berger, L. & Co., 1889, 1894. 2 vols. 1562, 1571 pp. 87 fr. 50 c. — 12

"Nouveau Dictionnaire d'Economie Politique." Say, J. B. Leon. Paris, Guillaumin, 1891-1892. 2 vols. 1448, 1345 pp. 55 fr. — 13

"Administration, The Study of." Wilson, Woodrow. Pol. Sci. Q. 2:197 (1887). — 14

"Administrative Law, Comparative." Goodnow, Frank J. New York and London, Putnam, 1893. 2 vols. 8vo, 338 and 327 pp. $5. (Book III. Vol. I. on Local Administration in the United States, England, France and Prussia). — 15

"Advantages of City Life." Halstead, Leonora B. Soc. Econ. 4:219 (1893). — 16

Bibliography. "Reference List of Works Relating to Municipal Government." Woodward, Frank E. Malden, 1887. 4 pp. — 17

———. "References on Municipal Government in the United States." Hodder, Frank H. Cornell University Library Bulletin, Vol. II, 1888. — 18

———. "Bibliography of Municipal Government in the United States." Hodder, Frank H. Kansas University Quarterly 1:179-196 (1893). — 19

———. "Bibliography of Municipal Government and Reform." Pp. 341-81. Pro. First National Conf., 1894. See 6-18a. — 19a

———. "Reference List on Municipal Government." (Chiefly since 1894.) Monthly Bulletin of the Providence (R. I.) Public Library. The Bulletin of the Providence Public Library for Feb., 1895 (pp. 14-16), contains an earlier list on the same subject referring principally to works appearing since 1890. These lists are based upon a bibliography prepared by Miss Mary S. Cutler, of the New York State Library School, Albany, N. Y. — 20

———. "Bibliography of Municipal Administration and City Conditions." Brooks, Robert C. New York, Reform Club, 1897. 8vo, 224 pp. 50 cts. (Published as No. 1, Vol. I. of Municipal Affairs. Subsequent numbers of this quarterly contain bibliographies of the municipal literature for the preceding quarter, all of the material thus published being collected in the present work.) — 21

———. For references to bibliographies on various special municipal topics see "Bibliographies," or the sub-head bibliography, under the several topics.

City Government, Municipal Government, Municipal Administration.

"American Political Ideas and Institutions in their relation to the Problem of City Government." Rowe, Leo. S. Municipal Affairs 1:317 (June, 1897.) — 22

"Business Men in Municipal Government." Real Estate Rec. and Guide, Feb. 23, 1895. — 23

———. "The Business Man and His Interest in City Government." Young, John F. Proceedings of the Convention of the League of Wisconsin Municipalities, Bulletin No. 3, p. 30, June 26-27, 1899. — 24

———. "Relation of the Business Man to the Municipality." Freud, J. Richard. Cal. Mun. 1:15 (Aug., 1899.) — 25

Business Theory of City Government, etc. "Municipal Government, a Corporate, Not a Political Problem." Morison, Frank. Forum 13:788 (1892.) — 26

———. "Government of Cities, the Need of a Divorce of Municipal Business from Politics." Storey, Moorfield. Proc. Natl. Civil Service Reform League, Buffalo, 1891. p. 47. — 27

"City Government." Bradford, Gamaliel. Vol. II, Chs. XXIV, XXV, XXVI, XXXIII. "The Lesson of Popular Government." New York, Macmillan, 1899.

BIBLIOGRAPHY. 3

City Government, General Works and Unclassified—*Continued.*

2 vols. 8vo, 520 and 590 pp. $4. 28
"City Government." Raemelin, C. Paper read before the American Association for the Advancement of Science, at Ann Arbor, Mich., Aug. 1885. Summary of the paper, p. 508 Proceedings of the Association for 1885. 29
City Government, Municipal Government, Articles on. Conkling, Alfred R. Mun. & Ry. Rec. 4:18, 57, 104 (Jan.-March, 1899); Davis, J. DeP. Arena 2:506 (1890); Eaton, Dorman B. Am. J. Soc. Sci. 5:1 (1873); Garrison, W. P. Nation 55:197 (1892); Gladden, Washington. Cent. 49:155 (1894); Godkin, E. L. Nation 13:188, 333 (1871); Hale, E. E. Old and New 7:249 (1873); Ivins, W. M. Pol. Sci. Q. 2:291 (1887); Jordan, David Starr. Mchts. Assoc. Rev. p. 1, May, 1897; Parton, James. Chaut. 8:203 (1888); Picton, J. A. Contemp. 34:678 (1878); Shaw, Albert. Our Day 13:472 (1894); Stevenson (Mrs.) Cornelius. Good Govt. 13:123 (1894); anon. Nation 4:434 (1867), 13:183 (1871); Albany Law Journal 4:263 (1871); Christian Register, Nov 17, 1892. 30
"City Government, Past, Present and Future." Chamberlain, Joseph. New R. 10:649 (1894). 31
"Commissioner Plan of Municipal Government, The." Young, W. E. City Govt. 6:24 (Feb., 1899). 32
"Considerations on Municipal Government." Conder, F. R. Fraser 95:34 (1877.) 33
"Democracy, City Government and." Curley, E. A. Leslie's Wkly. 74:40, 126 (1892), Cosmopol. 14:737 (1893.) 34
——. "Great Cities and Democratic Institutions." Pickard, C. E. Am. J. Pol. 4:378 (1894.) 35
"Development of an Efficient City Government." Stewart, Gilbert H. Public Policy 3:359 (Dec. 8, 1900.) 36
"Duties of Citizens in Reference to Municipal Government." Nichols, Wm. I. Municipal League of Philadelphia Pubs. 1892. 12 pp. . 37
"Europe, Municipal Government in." Hudson, Richard. Ann Arbor Studies in Finance and History, Michigan Univ., Vol. II, No. 4. 25c. 38
——. "Comparative Sketch of municipal institutions in France, Belgium, Italy, Prussia and Austria, with the addition of an outline of local self-government in England." (In Russian.) Wtoroff, Nicholas. St. Petersburg, 1864. 8vo. 39
——. "European Town Life." Shaw, Albert. Chaut. 9:519 (1889.) 40
——. See under names of various European countries. Also especially 1-5.
"Evils of Municipal Government." Black, William Nelson. Engng. M. 3:73 (1892.) 41
"Failures in Municipal Government, Our." Bradford, Gamaliel. Ann. Am. Acad. Pol. Sci. 3:691 (1893). Separate, 15 cts. Same subject, Scrib. M. 2:485 (1887.) 42
——. "Municipal Government, Why It Fails." Cooley, Stoughton. Am. J. Pol. 3:178 (1893.) 43
"Federal Plan of Municipal Government." Black, Samuel L. City Govt. 6:27 (Feb., 1899); Gladden, Washington. Prog. Age 15:557 (Nov. 15, 1897.) 44
Good City Government. (See under Reform of City Government, Reform Organizations below.)
"Government of Cities." Hoffman, Frank S. Chap. XI, p. 187, "Sphere of the State." London and New York, Putnam, 1894. 275 pp. $1.15. 45
——. "Government of Cities." Hosmer, James Kendall. Pp. 298-307 "Short History of Anglo-Saxon Freedom." New York, Scribner, 1890. 419 pp. $2. 46
——. "Government of Cities." Hotchkiss, Wm. Horace. Address before the Liberal Club, Buffalo, Feb., 1893. 47
——. "Government of Cities." Storey, Moorfield. Address before Citizens' Association of Buffalo, Sept. 30, 1890. Article on same subject, New Eng. M. n. s. 6:432 (1892.) 48
——. "Government of Cities." Walthew, George W. (Chapter V, in "The Philosophy of Government."). New York, G. P. Putnam's Sons, 1898. 12mo, 207 pp. Cl. $1.25. 49
"Government of Municipalities." Eaton, Dorman B. New York, The Macmillan Co., 1899. 8vo, 526 pp. Cl. $4. 50
"Great Cities, Government of Our." Godkin, E. L. Nation 3:312 (1866.) 51
——. "Government in Great Cities." Jenkins, H. M. American 6:8 (1883.) 52
Local Government, including municipal government. Pp. 624-627. Vol. II. Palgrave. See 1-2.

City Government, General Works and Unclassified—*Continued.*

——. "Books on Local Government." Gomme, G. L. Bibliographer 1:116, 149; 2:45 (1882).   53

——. "Local Government Among Different Nations." Dilke, C. W. J. Statis. Soc. 37:313 (1874).   54

——. "Local Government at Home and Abroad." Porter, Robert P. Princeton Rev. n. s. 4:172 (1879.)   55

——. "Local and Municipal Government." Axon, W. E. A. British Almanac Com. 1885, p. 56.   56

——. "Local Government and Taxation." Probyn, J. W. Cobden Club Essays. London, Paris and New York. Cassel, Petter & Galpin, 1875. 454 pp. 5s. (Contains articles which have been indexed separately on local government and taxation in England, Scotland, Ireland, Australian Colonies and New Zealand, Belgium and Holland, France, Russia, Spain and Germany.)   57

——. "Local Self-Government and Centralization, the Characteristics of Each and its Practical Tendencies as Affecting Social, Moral and Political Welfare and Progress." Smith, J. Toulmin. London, Chapman, 1851. 8vo. Cl. 5s.   58

"Municipal Administration." Mathews, Robert. Rochester, N. Y., 1885. 16 pp.   59

"Municipal Government." Bellamy, Francis. Address before Baptist Congress, New Haven, Conn. 1890.   60

——. "Municipal Government." Fisher, Wm. R. Philadelphia Social Science Association Publications. 1883. 28 pp.   61

——. "Municipal Government." Harrison, Carter H. Address before Nineteenth Century Club, New York, Nov. 23, 1886.   62

——. "Municipal Government." Lea, Henry C. A letter to the Municipal Commission of Pennsylvania, Jan. 4, 1877.   63

——. "Municipal Government." Low, Seth. Address delivered Feb. 19, 1885. Same subject, address before the Philadelphia Committee of Fifty, Jan. 25, 1892.   64

——. "Municipal Government." Moffett, S. E. Chapter VII, p. 86, "Suggestions on Government." Chicago, Rand, McNally & Co., 1894. 200 pp. $1.   65

——. "Municipal Government." Sterne, Simon. Pp. 257-74 in his "Constitutional History and Political Development of the United States." New York, Cassell, 1883. 575 pp. $1.25.   66

——. "Municipal Government." Williams, Leighton. Address before Baptist Congress, New Haven, Conn. (1890.)   67

——. "Municipal Government as it should be and as it may become." Rowe, Leo. S. P. 111 Proc. First Natl Conf. for Good City Govt., 1894. See 6-18a.   68

"Notes on Municipal Government." Rowe, Leo S. and Allen, W. H. A special department in the Annals of the American Academy of Political and Social Science since Nov., 1894.   69

"Political Organization of a Modern Municipality." Lewis, Wm. D. Ann. Am. Acad. Pol. Sci. 2:458 (1892.)   70

——. "De l'Organisation Communale et Municipale en Europe, aux Etats Unis et en France. Pascaud, Henri. Paris, Guillaumin et Cie., 1877. 3 fr. 50c.   70a

"Problem of Municipal Government." Cooke, Frederick H. Am. J. Pol. 3:58 (1893.)   71

——. "Problems of City Government." Godkin, E. L. Address before the American Acad. of Pol. and Soc. Sci., March 16, 1894. Ann. Am. Acad. Pol. Sci. 4:857 (1894). Separate paper, 26 pp. 25c.   72

——. "Problem of City Government." Janes, L. G. New York, D. Appleton & Co., 1892. 40 pp. 10c.   73

——. "Problem of City Government." Low, Seth. Notes to J. H. Univ. Studies No. IV.   74

——. "Problem of Municipal Government." Low, Seth. Address at Cornell University, March 16, 1887. Printed by the University. Same subject, Civil Service Reformer, April, 1889.   75

——. "The Municipal Problem." Wilder, A. P. New Haven, 1891. Printed for the New Haven Chamber of Commerce. 78 pp.   76

——. "Problem of City Government." Will, T. E. Am. Mag. Civics 7:231 (1895.)   77

——. "Why We Must Solve the Municipal Problem." Larocque, Jos. and others. New York, Published by the City Club, 1896. 12 pp.   78

"Property and Good Municipal Government." Real Estate Rec. and Guide, Feb. 24, 1894, p. 292.   79

City Government, General Works and Unclassified.—*Continued*.

"Recent Books on City Government." Judson, H. P. Dial 18:147 (1895.) — 80

"Responsibility in Municipal Government." Hyslop, James H. Forum 28:469 (Dec., 1899); Kelley, F. W. Am. J. Pol. 4:449 (1894.) — 81

"Some Neglected Points in Municipal Government." Rowe, Leo S. Address before the American Acad. of Pol. and Soc. Science, Dec. 20, 1893. Same subject, Public Opinion 19:810 (1895.) — 82

"Study of City Government: An Outline of the Problems of Municipal Functions, Control and Organization." Wilcox, Delos F. New York, Macmillan Co., 1897. 12mo, 268 pp. Cl. $1.50. — 83

——. "Study of the Science of Municipal Government." Prichard, Frank P. Ann. Am. Acad. Pol. Sci. 2:450 (1892.) Also in California Municipalities 1:73 (Oct., 1899.) — 84

——. "Studies in Municipal Government." Mead, E. D. Lend a H. 4:352 (1889.) — 85

Syllabi. "City Government." Commons, John R. Syllabus of a course of six lectures delivered at Indiana University, 1895. Paper, 29 pp. — 86

——. "City Government." (Outline of ten lectures.) Commons, John R. Albany, Extension Department University of New York, May, 1898. 12mo, 69pp. — 87

"Unofficial Government of Cities." (Assumption of municipal functions by private citizens or organizations, bossism, charity.) Wheeler, Everett P. Atlan. 85:370 (March, 1900.) — 88

"Cities as Units of Our Polity." Martin, William R. No. Am. 128:21 (1879.) — 89

"Civic Outlook, The." Waite, Henry Randall. Arena, Aug. 1897. — 90

"Civic Renaissance, Our." Shaw, Albert. R. of Rs. 11:415 (1895.) — 91

Civilization of the City. Férrero, G. Revue des Revues, Jan. 1, 1897. — 92

——. The City and Civilization. Adams, Alva. City Govt. 1:130 (Dec. 1896.) — 93

"Coming City, The." Commons, John R. Our Country 5:123 (April, 1897.) — 94

"Commercialism, The Capture of Government by." Chapman, John Jay. Atlan. 81:145 (Feb. 1898.) — 94a

——. Causes and Consequences. Chapman, John Jay. New York, Scribner, 1898. 12mo, 166 pp. $1.25.

Consolidation of Cities, Incorporation of Suburbs. "Municipal Co-operation vs. Municipal Consolidation." Baker, M. N. Mun. Aff. 3:18 (March, 1899); anon. Engng. News 41:104 (Feb. 16, 1899.) — 95

"Continuing City, A." Jordan, David Starr. Ind. 51:1340 (May 18, 1899), 51:1406 (May 25, 1899), 51:1545 (June 8, 1899.) — 96

Corporations, Law of Municipal, Powers of.

"Cases on Selected Topics in the Law of Municipal Corporations." Smith, J. Cambridge, Harvard Law Review Pub. Ass'n, 1898. $1.25. — 97

"Commentaries on the Law of Municipal Corporations." Dillon, John F. Boston, Little, Brown & Co., 4th ed. 1890. 1516 pp. $12. — 98

"Company Law, Commentaries on the Law of Public Corporations, including Municipal Corporations and Political and Governmental Corporations of every kind." Beach, Chas. F. Jr. Indianapolis, Bowen, Merrill & Co., 1893. 2 vols. 1692 pp. $12. — 99

"Constitutional Law of the United States, The." von Holst, H. Chicago, Callaghan & Co., 1887. 369 pp. (Sec. 102, pp. 329-36 on Cities.) — 100

"Constitutional Limitations." Cooley, Thomas M. Boston, Little, Brown & Co., 1896. 6th edition, 885 pp. $6. (Chapter VIII, pp. 223-310, on "The Several Grades of Municipal Government.") — 1

"Constitutional Restrictions on Municipal Corporations." Berryman, J. R. Am. Law R. 22:403 (1888.) — 2

"Liability of Municipal Corporations as upon Implied Contracts." Thompson, Seymour D. Am. Law R. 33:707 (Sept.-Oct. 1899.) — 3

"Municipal Corporation Cases." Michie, T. J. Charlottesville, Va., R. B. Michie & Co., 1899. 8vo, 796 pp. Cloth, $5. — 4

Local Government, Including Municipal Government. (See under City Government, etc., above.)

MUNICIPAL AFFAIRS.

City Government, General Works and Unclassified.—*Continued.*

"Powers of Municipal Corporations." Goodnow, F. J. City Govt. 2:182 (June, 1897); Pro. of the Louisville Conf., 1897. See 6-18d; Pingrey, D. H. Central Law Journal, 22:318 (1886). 5

"Management of Cities." Butts, I. Galaxy 13:173 (1872). 6

"Misgovernment of Great Cities." Crandon, F. P. Pop. Sci. Mo. 30:296, 520 (1887). 7

——. "Municipal Misgovernment." Compton, Lenox. Belford's M. 5:903 (1890). 8

——. "Municipal Misrule." Parkhurst, Charles H. Homilectic Review May, 1892. See also Christian at Work Feb. 2, 1893. 9

——. "Municipal Misrule: Its Causes and Remedies." Baldwin, F. Spencer. Self-Cult. 9:145 (April, 1899). 10

——. "Mayor Harrison on Misgovernment." Harrison, Carter H. City Govt. 7:35 (Aug. 1899). 11

——. "Remedies for Municipal Misgovernment." Fiske, Amos K. Forum 3:170 (1887). 12

——. "Why Cities are Badly Governed." Fassett, J. Sloat. No. Am. 150:631 (1890); anon. City and State 7:215 (Oct. 5, 1899). 13

"Modern City Life." Spectator No. 3680, p. 45 (Jan. 14, 1899); Mun. & Ry. Rec. 4:61 (Feb. 15, 1899). 14

Municipal Corporation, Law of. (See under Corporations above.)

Municipal Government, Municipal Administration. (See under City Government above.)

"Municipal Progress." Quincy, Josiah. Coming Age Jan. 1899. 15

Municipal Reform, Reform Organization, etc.

"The City." (General reform). Ch. V. Washington Gladden's "Social Facts and Forces." New York, Putnam, 1897. 235 pp. $1.25. 16

"The City, A Study with Practical Bearings." Stevens, Charles E. New York, J. J. Little & Co., 1885. 13 pp. 17

City and Social Reform. Pp. 278-295 Encyc. Soc. Ref. See 1-3.

"Closing Work of the Nineteenth Century." (Municipal Reform.) Capen, Samuel B. Indianapolis Conf. p. 116, 1898. See 6-18e. 17a

"Commercial Organizations and Municipal Reform." Ritchie, Ryerson. Pp. 118-128, Louisville Conference, 1897. See 6-18d, also under Business Men above. 18

Conferences. "Proceedings of the First National Conference for Good City Government." Held at Philadelphia Jan. 25 and 26, 1894. Philadelphia, published by the Municipal League, 1894. 386 pp. (With an extensive Bibliography of "Municipal Government and Reform," p. 341.) 18a

——. "Proceedings of the Second National Conference for Good City Government." Held at Minneapolis, Dec. 8-10, 1894; and of the First Annual Meeting of the National Municipal League and of the Third National Conference for Good City Government, held at Cleveland, May 29, 30 and 31, 1895. Philadelphia, published by the National Municipal League, 1895. 1 vol. 544 pp. 18b

——. "Proceedings of the Third National Conference for Good City Government and of the Second Annual Meeting of the National Municipal League." Held at Baltimore May 6, 7 and 8, 1896. Philadelphia, National Municipal League, 1896. 308 pp. 18c

——. "Proceedings of the Louisville Conference for Good City Government and of the Third Annual Meeting of the National Municipal League, May 5, 6, 7, 1897." Philadelphia, National Municipal League, 1897. 8vo. 294 pp. $1. 18d

——. "Proceedings of the Indianapolis Conference for Good City Government and the Fourth Annual Meeting of the National Municipal League, held November 30, December 1-2, 1898." Philadelphia, National Municipal League, 1898. 8vo, 273 pp. Cloth $1. 18e

——. "Proceedings of the Columbus Conference for Good City Government and the Fifth Annual Meeting of the National Municipal League, held Nov. 16, 17, 18, 1899." Philadelphia, National Municipal League, 1899. 8vo. 280 pp. Cloth, $1. (Papers in above volumes indexed separately.) 18f

——. "Cleveland Conference for Good City Government." Woodruff, C. R. Am. Mag. Civics 7:167 (1895). 19

——. "Letters from Mayors and Councilmen Regarding a National Conference of City Officials." City Govt. 3:9, 45 (July, Aug. 1897). 20

City Government, General Works and Unclassified.—*Continued.*

"Cosmopolis City Club." (A story of municipal reform). Gladden, Washington. New York, Century Co., 1893. 135 pp. $1. (The "Cosmopolis City Club" may also be found in the Century Magazine 45:395, 566, 780.) (1893.)   21

"Good Citizenship." Essays on "Social, Personal and Economic Problems and Obligations," separately indexed.) Edited by J. E. Hand. London, George Allen, 1899. 474 pp.   22

Good Government of Cities. Lea, Henry C. Hrprs. Wkly. 38:79 (1894); Welsh, Herbert. Am. J. Pol. 5:67 (1894); Woodruff, C. R. Pub. Opin. 18:536 (1895).   23

"Good Government and Good Citizenship, For." Giles, William A. Chicago, 1894. 18 pp.   24

Ideal City, The. "La Cité Idéale." Fournière, Eugene. Rev. Soc. 28:263 (Sept. 1898).   25

"Improved Municipal Government." Fitzgerald, T. J. City Govt. 1:40 (1896).   26

——. "Municipal Government, Improvement in." Ely, R. T. Christian Union Oct. 9, 1891.   27

"Key to Municipal Reform." Godkin, E. L. No. Am. 151:422 (1890).   28

——. "Municipal Problems: A Discussion of the Model Charter of the National Municipal League." Baldwin, Henry De Forest. Mun. Aff. 3:3 (March, 1899); anon. Engng. News 40:344 (Dec. 1, 1898).   29

"Local Government, Christian Socialism and." Russell, George W. E. p. 236 "Good Citizenship." See 7-22.   29a

"Model Charter for American Cities, Elements of a." James, Edmund J. p. 154, Proc. Second Natl. Conf., 1895. See 6-18b.   29b

"Modern Municipal Reform." McKelway, St. Clair. J. Soc. Sci. No. 34, p. 126 (Nov. 1896).   30

——. "Municipal Government, How Corrupted and How Reformed." Independent, Sept. 13, 1891, p. 1-13. Also published in pamphlet form by the Independent, 1894. 64 pp. (Papers by Otto Kempner, W. Harris Roome, Chas. A. Schieren and others.)   31

Municipal Reform, Articles on. Adams, Charles Francis. Springfield (Mass.) Weekly Republican March 13, 1893; Bemis, E. W. Dial 16:175 (1894); Bridgman, R. L. New Eng. M. 11:698 (1895); Brown, George Morgan. New Englander 45:152 (1886); Crehore, C. F. Lend a Hand, Extra No., Vol. IV, March, 1889; Field, David Dudley. Albany Law Journal 48:355 (1893); Garvin, L. C. F. Arena 10:570 (1894); Hart, T. N. and others. No. Am. 153:580, 591 (1891); Hatton, Joseph. Cent. 46:155 (1893); Kasson, John A. No. Am. 137:218 (1883); Pingree, H. S. Arena 17:707 (April, 1897); Strong, W. L. Gunton's 13:327 (Nov. 1897); Teall, O. S. Cosmopol. 10:564 (1891); Tolman, Wm. Howe. Arena Oct. 1896; Will, T. E. (with a brief bibliography) Arena 10:555 (1894); anon. Our Day 8:291 (July 8, 1891); Other Side 1:9 (July 8, 1899).   32

"Municipal Reform Needed." Parkhurst, Charles H. No. Am. 158:197 (1894).   33

——. "Municipal Reform in the United States." Devlin, Thomas C. New York, Putnams, 1896. 174 pp. 75 cents. (Chapter I, p. 3, Reform Efforts; Chapter II, p. 19, American Conditions; Chapter III, p. 45, Elections; Chapter IV, p. 63, Municipal and State Politics; Chapter V, p. 85, Civil Service Reform in Cities; Chapter VI, p. 105, Cost of City Government; Chapter VII, p. 135, Officers, Their Powers and Duties; Chapter VIII, p. 155, The Official, the Press and the People.)   34

——. "Municipal and Federal Reform." Nation 31:454 (1880).   35

——. "Municipal Reform Projects." Gardner, Rathbone. Advance Club Pubs. Providence, R. I. 1891.   36

"The New Patriotism—A Golden Rule Government." Jones, Samuel M. Mun. Aff. 3:455 (Sept. 1899), Public Improvements 1:231 (Oct. 1, 1899), Prog. Age 17:427 (Oct. 2, 1899), Other Side 1:214 (Nov. 4, 1899).   37

Obstacles to Municipal Reform. Low, Seth. Forum 5:260 (1888); Macomber, J. K. Midland Monthly March, 1898.   38

Organizations, Municipal Reform. "Constitutions and By-laws of the Municipal League of Philadelphia; City Club of New York; Citizens' Association of Boston; Baltimore Reform League; Civic Federation of Chicago; Good Government Club of San Francisco; Law Enforcement Society of Brooklyn, and Civic Club of Philadelphia." Phila. Pubs. of the Natl. Mun. League. Pamphlet No. 4. 1895. 36 pp.   39

——. "Proposed Constitutional Amendment." (Committee of Ten of the National Municipal League). Pro. Indianapolis Conf., p. 16, 1898. See 6-18e.

MUNICIPAL AFFAIRS.

City Government, General Works and Unclassified.—*Continued.*

——. "Proposed Municipal Corporations Act." (Committee of Ten of the National Municipal League.) Pro. Indianapolis Conf. p. 25, 1898. See 6-18e.

——. "Report of the Committee on Municipal Reform." (Committee of Ten of National Municipal League.) Pro. Indianapolis Conf. p. 1, 1898. See 6-18e.

——. "Law Enforcement Societies." Elliott, George Frederick. p. 482, Proc. Second Natl. Conf. for Good City Govt., 1895. See 6-18b. 40

——. "Law and Order Leagues." Pamphlet prepared and published by the Citizens' Law and Order League of Connecticut. New Haven, 1892. 16 pp. 41

——. "Law and Order Leagues of Connecticut." Prince, Walter F. Pamphlet, reprinted from the "Connecticut Citizen." 1895. 22 pp. 42

——. "Law and Order Movement and the Citizen." Wilder, A. P. Lend a H. 12:437 (1894). 43

——. "Work of Law and Order Leagues." Lend a H. 12:295 (1894). 44

——. "Movement for Municipal Reform." Woodruff, Clinton Rogers. No. Am. 167:410 (Oct. 1898). 45

——. "Municipal Reform Movements in the United States." Tolman, Wm. Howe. New York, Fleming H. Revell & Co., 1895. 219 pp. $1. 46

——. "Municipal Government and Young Men's Municipal Clubs." Shaw, Albert. p. 5, New Series No. 1. Publications of the American Institute of Civics. New York, 1895. 21 pp. 20 cents. 47

——. "Municipal Leagues and Good Government Clubs." Welsh, Herbert. p. 146, Proc. Second Natl. Conf., 1895. See 6-18b. 47a

"Party Politics, Municipal Reform as Related to." Boyeson, I. K. Address. Chicago, 1893. 48

"Practical Municipal Reforms." Gunton's 16:388 (May, 1899).

"Problem of Municipal Government, The." Batten, J. H. Arena 24:589 (Dec. 1900). 49

"Programme of Municipal Reform." MacVeagh, Franklin. Am. J. Sociol. March, 1896. 50

——. "A Municipal Program, Report of a Committee of the National Municipal League. (Contains the Model Charter—see above—and papers in its support. Part of the same material appeared in the report of the Indianapolis Conference.) New York, Macmillan, 1900. 8 vo. 246 pp. Cl. $1. 51

——. "Need of a Positive Programme of Municipal Reform." Williams, Leighton. Arena 9:644 (1894). Also published as Municipal Programme Leaflet No. 1. New York, 1894. 10 pp. 5 cents. 52

——. "Positive Programme Progress." Scudamore, William. Municipal Programme Leaflet No. 7. New York, 1895. 11 pp. 5 cents. 53

"Progress of Municipal Reform." Woodruff, C. R. Outlook 49:958 (1894), Mun. Aff. 1:301 (June, 1897). 54

"Proper Standard for Municipal Affairs, The." Etting, Theodore M. Municipal League of Philadelphia Pubs, 1894. 55

"Reforms in State and City Government and Their Relation to Practical Politics." Cowen, John K. Taxpayers' Association of Baltimore. Addresses, 1889. 85 pp. 56

"Social and College Settlements of America and Their Relation to Municipal Reform." Alden, Percy. Outlook 51:1090 (1895). (See also **Settlements.**) 57

"Social Reform and the Church." Commons, John R. New York, T. Y. Crowell & Co., 1894. 176 pp. 75 cents. (Municipal Monopolies, pp. 121-51.) 58

"Some Suggestions for Municipal Reformers." Wilby, Chas. B. Address at Cincinnati, March 8, 1891. 59

"State, Relation of the, to Reform in Municipal Government." Bowles, Samuel. Am. J. Soc. 9:140 (1877). 60

"Step Toward Municipal Reform, A Definite." Welsh, Herbert. Forum 17:179 (1894). 61

"Voluntary and Temporary (Reform) Movements, Results Obtained by." Low, William G. p. 136, Proc. Second Natl. Conf., 1895. See 6-18b. 62

"Unorganized Municipal Reform." Cent. 41:789 (1891).

"Women, Relation of,—to Municipal Reform." Mumford, (Mrs.) Mary E. p. 135, Proc. (First) Natl. Conf., 1894. See 6-18a. 62a

——. "Relation of Women to Municipal Reform." Welsh, Herbert. Printed by the Civic Club of Philadelphia, 1894. 63

City Government, General Works and Unclassified.—*Continued.*

"Municipality, Old and New, The." (Comparison of English and American municipalities.) Baxter, James Phinney. New Eng. M. 17:469 (Dec., 1897.) 64
"Needs of the City, The." Ely, R. T. Address before the Evangelical Alliance, Dec. 4, 1889. Published by the Alliance. 65
"Patriotism, Municipal." Barrows, John H. A sermon preached at Plymouth Church, Chicago, Nov. 27, 1890, 22 pp.; Fortune, William. Other side 1:25 (July 22, 1899). 65a
"Problem of the City, The." Woodruff, Clinton Rogers. Am. M. Civics, Dec., 1896. 66
"Problem of Next Century's City." Strong, Josiah. No. Am. 165:343 (Sept., 1897.) 67
Self-Government. "Die Selbstverwaltung in politischer und juristischer Bedeutung." Hatschek, Julius. Staats- und Völkerrechtliche Abh. Bd. 2, Hept. 1, 1898. 8vo, 236 pp. 68
———. "Principles of Self-Government, Applied to Townships, Cities and Villages." Matteson, Andre. Chicago, 1893. 48 pp. 30 cts. 69
"Social Failure of the City, The." Rogers, [Mrs.] Emma Winner. Bib. Sac. 55:143 (Jan., 1898.) 70
"Social Problems of Great Cities." James, L. G. Unitarian R. 39:309 (1893.) 71
"Social Waste in a Great City, The." Seaman, Louis L. Science 8:283 (1886.) 72
"Work of Cities, The." Low, Seth. Lend a H. 4:255 (1890.) 73

Aachen, Germany. (Aix la Chapelle.)

City Plan. "Aachens Bebauungsplan und Bauliche Zukunft." Stübben, J. Deutsche Bauz., p. 100, 1880. 74
Plan for Laying Out of Northern Aachen. "Konkurrenz für Pläne zur Bebauung des Nördlichen Theils der Stadt Aachen." Deutsche Bauz., pp. 90, 290, 1878. 75
Water Works of Aachen, Extension of the. "Die Erweiterung des Wasser Werkes der Stadt Aachen." Zeitschr d Ver Deutscher Ing. Sept. 11, 1898. 76

Abattoirs, Public.

See also Biarritz (France), Birmingham (Eng.), Germany, London, Paris.
"Abolition of Private Slaughter Houses." Cridlan, J. J. Land M. Feb. 1899. 77
"Advantages of Public Abbattoirs." Littlejohn, Harvey. San Rec. 20:167 (Aug. 13, 1897.) 78
Compulsory Slaughter Houses. "Ueber obligatorische Schlachthausanlagen." Brandau, L. Kassel, Kessler, 1883. 1m. 79
———. "Wesen und Wirkungen d. Schlachthauszwanges." Mascher, H. A. Dortmund, Köppen'sche Buchh., 1888. 1m. 20 pf. 80
Municipal Abattoirs and Their Mechanical Equipment. "Städtische Schlachthöfe und deren Maschinelle Einrichtungen." Witz, Gustav. Zeitschr. d. Oest. Ing. u. Arch. Ver. 52:437 (July 13, 1900.) 81
"Municipal Authorities and Public Slaughter Houses." Parkes, E. Sanitarian 42:97 (Feb., 1899), J. San. Inst. 20:23 (April, 1899.) 82
"Municipal Slaughter Houses." London, The Fabian Society, 1900. 4pp. Pamphlet, 1d. 83
"Public Slaughter Houses." Richardson, B. W. New R. 8:631 (1893). 84
"Public Slaughter Houses Considered from a Humane and Hygienic Standpoint." May, J. San. Rec. 9:419 (Nov. 10, 1899). 85
"Report by the Architect upon Public Slaughter Houses in Continental Cities visited by him. Photographs and Plan of Abattoir." 4d. L. C. C. Doc. 405 (1900). ....
"Slaughter Houses and Slaughter House Inspection." Anderson, G. H. San. Rec. Sup. No. 31, p. 9 (Aug. 1899). 86

Aberdeen, Scotland.

"Electric Tramways, The Aberdeen Corporation." Ty. & Ry. World 9:5 (Jan, 11, 1900). 87
"Water Supply, Aberdeen and Its." San. J. 4:545 (Jan., 1898.) 88

Accounting, Municipal. (See under Finance.)

"**Acton, England,** Sewage Treatment at." Fuertes, James H. Engng. Rec. 41:418 (May 5, 1900.) 89

Adelaide, Australia.
" City of Adelaide." Mun. J. 9:237 (March 30, 1900.) 90
" Municipal Extension in Relation to Greater Adelaide." Pp. 7-13 in "Municipal Extension and Other Essays." Ellery, T. George. Adelaide, W. K. Thomas & Co., 1899. 12mo, 51 pp. Pamphlet. 91

Advertising.
"A Beautiful World: Journal of the Society for Checking the Abuses of Public Advertising." (Contains proceedings of the Society, articles on the abuse of public advertising, drafts of bills to regulate such abuses, etc.) London, printed by John Bale & Sons. Distributed gratis.
" Advertising Run Mad." Warner, John DeWitt. Mun. Aff. 4:267 (June, 1900), 4:772 (Dec., 1900.) 92
"Age of Disfigurement." (Against Abuses of Public Advertising.) Evans, Richardson. London, Remington & Co., 1893. 8vo., 112 pp. 1s. 93
"Checking Bill Board Nuisance." Olmsted, Frederick Law, Jr. City Govt. 9:6 (July, 1900). 94

" **Africa**, Street Railway Affairs in South." Stowe, J. G. St. Ry. J. 16:415 April 28, 1900.) 95

Aix la Chapelle. (See Aachen.)

" **Alameda, Cal.** Referendum." Dodson, G. R. Ann. Am. Acad. Pol. Sci. 13:131 (Jan. 1899). 96

Albany, N. Y.
" Municipal Condition of Albany." Thacher, John Boyd. p. 137 Proc. Third Natl. Conf., 1898. See 6-18c. 97
Description and Statistics of Albany, N. Y., in 1800. Census. See 1-7
" History of the City of Albany." Weise, A. J. Albany, Bender. 1884. 4to, 520 pp. $5. 98
———. " Albany Fifty Years Ago." Lossing, Benson J. Harper's M. 14:451 (1857). 99
———. " Collections on the History of Albany from Its Discovery to the Present Time." Munsell, Joel. Albany, N. Y., 1865-71. 4 vols., 8vo. $30. 100
———. History of Albany, N. Y. Battershall, W. W. See 1-4b., 1-7. 1
" Water Filtration Plant, The Albany." Hazen, Allen. Pro. Am. Soc. Civ. Engs. 26:528 (April, 1900); Engng. Rec. 41:317 (Apr. 7, 1900); Mac Harg, Martin. Engng. Rec. 42:516 (Dec. 2, 1900); J. N. E. W. W. Assn. 14:291 (June, 1900); Engng. News 39:191 (Feb. 10, 1898), 40:254 (Oct. 20, 1898), 43:31 (Jan. 11, 1900), 44:88 (Aug. 9, 1900); Engng. Rec. 40:622 (Dec. 2, 1899); Sci. Am. 88:182 (Mar. 24, 1900); Mun. Engng. 18:297 (May, 1900.) 2
———. " Albany's Water Supply and Her Neighbors." Featherstonhaugh, J. D. Sanitarian 43:318 (Oct. 1899.) 3
———. " Notes on the Albany Water Works." Engng. Rec. 40:98 (July 1, 1899).

" **Aldershot [Eng.]** Sewage Disposal at." Dennis, Nelson F. Engng. Rec. 40:603 (Nov. 25, 1899). 4

" **Alexandria**, The Electric Railway of." St. Ry. J. 13:8344 (Dec., 1897.) 6

" **Algiers [Africa]**, Electric Railway in." St. Ry. J. 15:209 (April, 1899); Ry World 7:133 (May 5, 1898.) 7

Allegheny City, Pa.
" Municipal Condition of Allegheny." Kennedy. Wm. M. p. 336 Proc. Second Natl. Conf., 1895. See 6-18b. 8
" Street Railways of Allegheny City and Pittsburg." St. Ry. Jour. May, 1890, p. 254, Oct., 1891, p. 1.
" Water Supply of Allegheny City and Pittsburg." Harlow, James H. Proceedings of the Engineers' Society of Western Pennsylvania, March, 1883. 9
———. " Filter Crib of the Allegheny Water Works." Engng. News 43:328 (May 17, 1900). 10

" **Alliance, Ohio,** Sewage Disposal at." Engng. Rec. 41:31 (Jan. 13, 1900.) 11

BIBLIOGRAPHY. 11

Allotments. (See **Vacant City Lots, Cultivation of.**)

Altoona, Pa.

"Sewage Disposal Plant at Altoona, Pa." Linton, Harvey. Mun. Engng. 13:11 (July, 1897); Engng. News 38:50 (July 22, 1897), p. 339, xiiith Annual Report of the State Board of Health * * * of Pennsylvania, Harrisburg, 1898.   12

"Water Works. Flood Water Channel, Altoona Reservoirs." Knight, Charles W. Engng. Rec. 40:386 (Sept. 23, 1899).   13

Amballa (India), Water Works. Goument, Charles E. V. Engng. Rec. 39:473 (April 22, 1899).   14

Amiens France. "Les Tramways Electriques d'Amiens." L'Electricien May 13, 1899.   15

Amsterdam, Holland.

"Civic Institutions in Amsterdam: How the City is Kept Clean." de Jong, E. W. Elsevier's Geillustreerd Maandschrift July, 1898.   16

Lighting. "The Amsterdam Gas Works." Salomons, Henry H. Gas World (London) May 8, 1897; Am. Gas Lgt. J. 67:202 (Aug. 9, 1897).   17

"Prison of Amsterdam, The Municipal." Wines, Frederick Howard. Char. R. 9:282 (Sept. 1899).   18

"Sanitary Service in Amsterdam." Eckstein. Am. Arch. 28:84 (1890.)   19

Sewage Disposal. "Das Liernur System in Amsterdam." Gl. Annalen (March 1, 1898).

——. "Sewerage of Amsterdam." Downes, Edward. U. S. Consular Reports, Vol. xlvii, No. 173, p. 160 (Feb., 1895.)   20

"Telephones of Amsterdam, Municipal." Falkenburg, Ph.; Van Zanten, J. H. Mun. Aff. 4:24 (Mar., 1900); Mun. J. 9:441 (June 8, 1900); J. Nat. u. Stat. 20:79 (July, 1900.)   21

Amusements, Municipal.

"Amusements for the People." Spec. 67:220 (1891.)

"Amusements of the People." pp. 1-28, "Methods of Social Reform," by W. Stanley Jevons. London and New York, Macmillan, 1883. 383 pp. $3.   22

"Recreation for the People." Wingate, Chas. F. Lend a Hand, Jan. 1897.   23

Theatres, Municipal. (See **Theatres, Municipal.**)

Ancient Cities. (See under **History, Municipal.**)

"**Annapolis, Md.,** History of." Shafer, Sara Andrew. See 1-4c.   24

Antwerp, Belgium.

Charity. "Abandoned Children in Antwerp." Van Geert, Prosper. p. 16 "International Congress." Vol. V, 1893. (See under **Charities.**)   25

Appointment of Municipal Officers. (See under **Civil Service.**)

Architecture. (See also **Art, Building Laws, Housing.**)

See also **Birmingham** (Eng.), Boston, Cardiff, Dundee (Scotland), Edinburgh, Glasgow, **Northampton** (Eng.), Oxford (Eng.), Padua, Sheffield.

"Ancient Town Halls of Europe, The." Anderson, Rowand. Builder (London.) (Dec. 19, 1896), Arch. & Buil. 26:31 (Jan. 16, 1897.)   26

"Architectural Annual for 1900." Kelsey, Albert, Editor. Phila., Architectural League, 1900. 4to, 292 pp.   27

"Architecture and Citizenship." Hamlin, A. D. F. Pub. Imp. 2:265 (April 16, 1900).   28

"Arrangement of American City Architecture." Gardner, E. C. Engng. M. 4:201 (1892.)   29

"Beautiful Cities." (Architecture.) Lethaby, W. R. Ch. II. p. 45 of "Art and Life and the Building and Decoration of Cities." (London.) Rivington, Percival & Co., 1897. 12mo, 260 pp. $2.40.   30

"City Hall Architecture in America." Ferree, Barr. Engng. M. 4:201 (1892.)   31

Architecture—*Continued.*

"Civic Architecture from Its Constructive Side." Lamb, Chas. R. Mun. Aff. 2:46 (March, 1898). 32

"Color in the Architecture of Cities." Ricardo, Halsey. Ch. V. p. 211 of "Art and Life and the Building and Decoration of Cities." (London). Rivington, Percival & Co., 1897. 260 pp. $2.40. Article by same author on this subject in Builder (London) Dec. 12, 1896. 33

"Decoration of Public Buildings." Crane, Walter. Ch. III. p. 111. of "Art and Life and the Building and Decoration of Cities." (London.) Rivington, Percival & Co., 1897. 260 pp. $2.40. 34

"Government Buildings, Architecture of Our." Aiken, William Martin. Engng. M. 12:815 (Feb. 1897). 35

——. "Grouping of Public Buildings." Bush-Brown, H. K. Report of National Convention of Architectural Societies, p. 45, June 2-3, 1899. 36

——. "Interior Decorations of Public Buildings." Hayes, H. H. Our Day 16:311 (July, 1898). 37

"Municipal Buildings, Architecture of." Gardner, E. C. Engng. M. 8:609 (1895.) 38

"Restraints upon the Practice of Architecture." Robinson, John B. Engng. M. 11:307 (1896). 39

"School and School House Architecture." Gardner, E. C. Engng. M. 10:478 (1895). 40

"Street Architecture." Statham, H. H. Architect (London) Dec. 11, 1896. 41

Town Architecture. Stübben, J. Vom Fels zum Meer Nov., 1897. 42

"Value of Good Architecture in Cities." Ferree, Barr. Engng. M. 10:671 (1895). 43

"**Argentina,** Electric Railway Practice in." Manville, E. St. Ry. J. 15:693 (Oct., 1899); anon. same 15:69 (Feb., 1899.) 44

Art, Municipal. (See also **Architecture, Building Laws, Parks.**)

See also Belgium, Camberwell, Edingurgh, Italy, London, Netherlands, New York, St. Louis.

"Art Commission, The National." Sewall, Frank. Am. Arch. 52:6 (1896). 45

"Art and Labor." Starr, Ellen Gates. Chapter IX, p. 165, "Hull House Maps and Papers." 46

"Art League of the United States, The Public." Am. Arch. 51:86 (1896). 47

"Art and Life and the Building and Decoration of Cities. A Series of Lectures by the Members of the Arts and Crafts Exhibition Society, Delivered at the Fifth Exhibition of the Society in 1896." London, Rivington, Percival & Co. 1897. 12mo, 260 pp. $2.40. 48

"Art in Municipal Affairs." Other Side 1:14 (July 15, 1899). 49

"Baltimore Municipal Art Conference." Hrprs. Wkly. 43:1332 (Dec. 30, 1899); Mun. Aff. 3:706 (Dec. 1899). 50

"Beautiful Public Life, A More." Mead, Edwin D. New Eng. M. May, 1894. 51

Brussels Conference. (See Proceedings below.)

"City Æsthetics." Buls, Ch. Mun. Aff. 3:732 (Dec. 1899). 52

"City Beautiful, The." Kriehn, George. Mun. Aff. 3:594 (Dec. 1899). 53

"Color, Civic Treatment of." Lamb, Frederick S. Mun. Aff. 2:110 (Mar. 1898). 54

"Civil Law Development." (Municipal Æsthetics from a Legal Standpoint.) Holbach, F. Mun. Aff. 3:715 (Dec. 1899). 55

"Development of Æsthetics in Cities." Boulden, Jane Long. Arena Q. 1:108 (June, 1900). 56

"Embellishment of Cities, The." Hrps. Wkly. 42:282 (March 19, 1898). 57

"'Garden Cities,' The Coming of." Mun. J. & London 8:928 (Aug. 18, 1899). 58

"Government Buildings, A Suggestion for Grouping; Landscape, Monuments and Statuary." Brown, Glenn. Arch. R. 7:89 (Aug. 1900). 59

"Ideal City, The." Ricardo, Halsey. Builder 78:613 (June 23, 1900), Am. Arch. 69:29 (July 28, 1900). 60

"Improvement in City Life, III." Robinson, Charles Mulford. Atlan. 83:771 (June, 1899.) 61

"Matters that Suggest Themselves." Warner, John DeWitt. Mun. Aff. 2:123 (March, 1898). 62

Monuments and Decoration of Cities. pp. 403-439. J. Stübben's "Städtebau."

Art, Municipal—*Continued.*

Darmstadt, Bergsträsser, 1890. 8vo, 561 pp. 32m.   63

Municipal Art. Bell, Edward Hamilton. Hrprs. Wkly. 38:401 (1894); Blashfield, Edwin Howland. Mun. Aff. 3:582 (Dec. 1899); Caffin, Charles H. Harper's 100:655 (April, 1900); French, Lillie H. Hrprs. Wkly. 37:371 (1893); Lamb, Frederick S. Mun. Aff. 1:674 (Dec. 1897); same reprinted in Mun. Engng. 14:61 (Feb. 1898); Loring, Charles M. Park & Cem. 10:61 (May, 1900); Sargent, C. S. Garden & F. 8:501 (1895); Tryon, Thos. Public Improvements 1:98 (July 15, 1899); anon. Garden & F. Jan. 15, 1896; Mun. J. and London 8:515 (April 28, 1899).   64

"Municipal Conditions Improving." Church, William G. Public Improvements 2:121 (Jan. 15, 1900).   65

"Municipal Improvement." Meade, Edwin D. Park & Cem. 10:92 (June, 1900.)   66

"Municipal Memorials." Stübben, J. Mun. Aff. 3:724 (Dec. 1899).   67

"Municipal Sculpture." Bitter, Karl. Mun. Aff. 2:73 (March, 1898).   68

"Mural Decoration." Reid, G. A. Canadian M. 9:501 (April, 1898).   69

"Mural Painting." Blashfield, Edwin Howland. Mun. Aff. 2:98 (March, 1898).   70

Museums. "Our Public Art Museums: A Retrospect." Robinson, Sir Charles. 19th Cent. Dec. 1897.   71

"Planning of Cities, The." See, Milton. Public Improvements 2:51 (Dec. 1, 1899), 2:75 (Dec. 15, 1899).   72

——. "The City's Plan." Harder, Julius F. Mun. Aff. 2:25 (March, 1898).   73

Proceedings of First International Congress on Public Art, Brussels, September 24-29, 1898. "Œuvre de L'Art Public. Premier Congrès International de L'Art Public tenu à Bruxelles du 24 au 29 Septembre, 1898." Liège, Aug. Bénard, 1900. 4to, 196 pp. Paper.   74

"Public Art in American Cities." Mun. Aff. 2:1 (March, 1898).   75

Public and Art, The. Obrist, H. Kunstgewerbeblatt Feb. 1900.   76

Schools, Art in. "Pictures for Our Public Schools." Van Rensselaer, M. G. Hrprs. Wkly. 41:1295 (Dec. 25, 1897). (See also under **Schools.**)   77

"Stained Glass, A Plea for." Parkhurst, Henry L. Mun. Aff. 3:694 (Dec. 1899).   78

"Street Lighting, Art in." Foote, Allen, Ripley. Elec. Eng. 24:330 (Oct. 7, 1897), Prog, Age 15:465 (Oct. 15, 1897).   79

Ashland, Wis.

Water Works. "Masonry Covered Sand Filter Beds at Ashland, Wis." Wheeler, Wm. Engng. News 38:338 (Nov. 25, 1897).   80

——. "The Ashland Water Pollution Case." Engng. Rec. 39:67 (Dec. 24, 1898).   81

Asia.

Market Towns on the High Asiatic Plateaux. "Villes de Marchés sur les hauts Plateaux Asiatiques." Monstier, J. Science Sociale 28:464 (Dec. 1899).   82

Assessments, Special. (See **Finance.**)

Athens, Greece.

"City Government of Athens." Wilcox, Delos F. Ind. 49:1200 (Sept. 16, 1897).   83

History. "Stadtgeschichte von Athens." Curtius, Ernst. Berlin, Weidman, 1891. 8vo, 391 pp, 16 m.   84

Atlanta, Ga.

History, Description and Statistics of Atlanta, Ga., in 1880. See 1-7.

"Municipal Condition of Atlanta, Ga." Davis, A. H. p. 96 Proc. Third Natl. Conf., 1896. See 6-18c.   85

"Sewerage System of Atlanta." Hering, Ruolph. Engng. Rec. April 4, 1891 p. 294; Engng. News April 4, 1891, p. 328.   86

"Street Railway Move at Atlanta, Ga., An Important." Elec. W. & E. 34:224 (Aug. 12, 1899).

——. "Street Car Transfers in Atlanta, Ga." Mun. Rec. & Ad. July 31, 1897.   87

"Water Works at Atlanta, Ga." Engng. Rec. March 31, 1894.   88

——. "The Results of the Meter System in Atlanta." Hillyer, George. Engng. Rec. 38:292 (Sept. 3, 1898).   89

"**Atlantic City, N. J.** Some Passing Notes on American Gas Works."
Am. Gas Light J. 68:660 (April 25, 1898). 90

Austin, Tex.

"Municipal Ownership at Austin, Texas." Hornaday, W. D. Elec. W. & E. 34:575 (Oct. 14, 1899), Other Side 1:198 (Oct. 28, 1899). 91
———. "The Austin, Texas, Argument against Municipal Ownership." Ind. 52:844 (April 5, 1900).
"Sewerage System, Austin, Texas." Engng. Rec. 37:429 (April 16, 1898). 92
Water Works. "The Failure of the Austin Dam." Parker, R. D. Engng. Rec. 41:372 (April 21, 1900); von Rosenberg, Wm., Jr. same 41:468 (May 19, 1900); anon. same 41:340 (April 14, 1900); Engng. News 43:250 (April 19, 1900). 93

Australia.

Charities. "Care of Children in Australia." Spence, Catherine H. p. 27 "International Congress," vol. V, 1893, see 43-99. 94
"City Government, Australian." Mun. J. & London 9:33 (Jan. 12, 1900). 95
———. "Australian Municipal Progress." Plummer, John. Mun. J. 9:583 (July 27, 1900). 96
Communistic Villages in South Australia. "Les Villages Communistes de l'Australie Méridionale." Vigouroux, Louis. R. Municipale 3:2063 (April 21, 1900), 3:2078 (April 28, 1900), 3:2092 (May 5, 1900). 97
Finances. "Local Government and Taxation in the Australian·Colonies and New Zealand." Dilke, C.; Ware, Thomas Webb; Archer, W. H.; p. 233 "Local Government and Taxation." J. W. Probyn, editor, New York, Cassell, 1875. 5s. 98
"Referendum in Australia and New Zealand." Tomn, Lillian. Contemp. 72:242 (Aug. 1897). 99
"Social Experiments in Australia." Burgess, H. T. Arena 23:132 (Feb. 1900). 100

Austro-Hungary.

See also Budapest, Vienna and other principal Austrian cities.
Charities. "Armenpflege in den österreichischen Städten und ihre Reform." Mischler, Ernst. Wien, Deuticke, 1890. 2 m 1
———. "Poverty and its Relief in Austria." Menger. p. 224 "International Congress," vol. I, 1893, see 43-99. 1a
———. "Sketch of the Organization of Public Poor Relief in Austria." Probst, Friederick. p. 230 "International Congress," vol. I, 1893, see 43:99. 1b
———. "The Austrian Poor Law System." Sellers, Edith. p. 216 "International Congress," vol. I, 1893, see 43-99. 1c
Finances of the Larger Austrian Cities. (See under Statistics below).
Local and Municipal Government in Austro-Hungary. Demombynes. Vol. II. pp. 199-219, 258-284. See 2-11. 2
———. "Die Selbstverwaltungskörper." Ulbrich, J. VI. Kap. pp. 82-87. Vol. IV, 1, 1-3. Marquardsen. See 2-9. 2a
Pawnshops. "Story of a Philanthropic Pawnshop." (The Imperial Pawn Offices of Austria). Sellers, (Miss) Edith. National No. 170:243 (April, 1897). 3
Population. "Die Bevölkerung Oesterreichs." (Chs. V., VI. and VII. on Cities. Census of 1890). Rauchberg, Heinrich. Vienna, A. Hölder, 1895. 8vo, 530 pp. 3a
Statistics. "Oesterreichisches Städtebuch, statistische Berichte von grösseren österreich. Städten." Hrsg. durch die k. k. statis. Centralkommission, edited by Karl Theodor v. Inama-Sternegg and Josef Freih. v. Friedenfels. Biennial seventh issue, Vienna, 1897, 708 pp. 12 m. Each issue contains statistics on Vienna, Wiener-Neustadt, Salzburg, Marburg, Laibach, Trient, Prag, Aussig, Brüx, Budweis, Eger, Gablonz a. N., Jicin, Karlsbad, Pilsen, Reichenberg, Tetschen a. d. Elbe, Brünn, Iglau, Olmütz, Troppau and Krakau. 4
———. Statistics of Occupation and Social Condition. "Das Sociale Connubium in den österreichischen Städten. Inama-Sternegg, Karl Theodor. Statistiche Monatschrift 24:69 (Feb. and Mar. 1898). 5
Transit Facilities, Municipal. "Electric Railway Practice in Austria-Hungary." Ziffer, E. A. St. Ry. J. 15:685 (Oct. 1899). 6

Bahia. Electric Street Tramways. "Das Elektrische Strassenbahn in Bahia." Braun, Gustav. Elektrotech. Zeitschr. Sept. 8, 1898; anon. St. Ry. J. 15:207 (April, 1899). 7

"**Bakeries,** Municipal." Fabian Society Tract No. 94 Dec. 1900. 1d.

Baltimore, Md.

City Government, General References and Unclassified.

"Baltimore in Her Centennial Year." Logan, Charles T. Frank Leslie's Popular Monthly June, 1897. 8

"City Government of Baltimore." Bonaparte, Charles J. p. 87 Proc. (First) Natl. Conf. for Good City Govt., 1894. See 6-18a; Latrobe. F. C. Taxpayers' Assoc. of Baltimore, Addresses, 1898, p. 148. Thomas, Thaddeus P. J. H. Univ. Studies XIV:7 (1896). 25 cts. 9

"New Charter for Baltimore." Hollander, J. H. Ann. Am. Acad. Pol. Sci. 11:425 (May, 1898); anon. 12:307 (Sept. 1898); Nation 66:201 (March 17, 1898). 10

"Crisis in Baltimore, The." Bonaparte, Charles J. Good Govt. 15:27 (1896). 11

Description and Statistics of Baltimore, Md., in 1880. Census. See 1-7. 12

"The New Baltimore." Bonsal, Stephen. Harper 92:231 (1896). 13

"Court House, Baltimore's New." Arch. & B. M. 1:189 (March, 1900). 14

Economic and Financial History. (See under History below.)

"Elections, Report of the Committee on." Publications of the Reform League, 1895. 11 pp. 15

Finance. "Application of the Single Tax to Baltimore." Ogden, William J. Taxpayers' Association of Baltimore. Addresses, 1889. p. 122. 16

——. "Report of the Committee on Municipal Taxation." Publications of the Baltimore Reform League, 1895. (See also under Transit Facilities below.) 17

Fire Department. (See under Police below.)

"Future of Baltimore." Ely, R. T. pp. 157-62 and 178-88. "Problems of To-day." New York, Crowell, 1890. 296 pp. $1.25. 18

History. "The Chronicles of Baltimore, Baltimore Town and City from the Earliest Period." Scharf, J. T. Baltimore, Turnbull, 1874. 8vo. $1.50. 19

——. "Economic History of the Baltimore and Ohio R. R." Reizenstein, M. J. H. U. Studies, xvth series, Nos. 7 and 8. Baltimore, 1897. 87 pp. 50 cts. 20

——. "Financial History of Baltimore, The." Hollander, J. H. Baltimore, Johns Hopkins University Press, 1899. 8vo, 397 pp. Cloth, $2. 21

——. History of Baltimore, Md. Sioussat, St. George L. See 1-4c; anon. Census, see 1-7. 22

——. "The Monumental City, Past History and Present Resources." Howard, George W. Baltimore, 1873. 8vo. $1. 23

Housing. Slums of Baltimore. See the Seventh Special Report of the Commissioner of Labor on "The Slums of Great Cities." 1894. 24

"Libraries of Baltimore." Adams, Herbert B. Nation 34:116 (1882). 25

Lighting. "The System of the Brush Electric Company of Baltimore." Elec. World 31:267 (Feb. 26, 1898).

—— "Preliminary Report of the Lighting Commission of the City of Baltimore." Hollander, Jacob H., Phelps, Charles E., Jr., and Baetjer, Edwin G. Baltimore, 1900. 8vo, 20 pp. 26

"Markets of Baltimore." Lathe, Agnes M. Chaut. Dec. 1896. 27

"Park, Druid Hill." Robbins, M. C. Garden & F. 7:233 (1894). 28

"Police, Our, History of the Baltimore Force." Folsom, De Francias. Baltimore, Ehlers, 1888. 546 pp. 29

——. "Reform in the Police and Fire Departments of Baltimore." Good Government 18:6 (July-Oct. 1900).

"Revolt in Baltimore, The Recent; its Results and Lessons." Howard, Charles Morris. p. 75 Proc. Third Natl. Conf., 1896. See 6-18e. 30

"Rule of the Criminal Classes in Baltimore." White, H. Nation 44:159 (1887). 31

"Sanitation of Baltimore." Billings, John S. Forum 15:727 (1893). 32

"Schools of Baltimore, Public." Rice, J. M. Forum 14:145 (1892). 33

——. "Public Educational Work in Baltimore." Adams, Herbert B. J. H. U.

Baltimore, Md.—*Continued.*

Studies xviith series, No. 12. Baltimore, 1899. 58 pp. 25 cents.   34

——. "Report of the Committee on Public Schools." Publications of the Baltimore Reform League (1895).   35

"Sewerage of Baltimore, The." Allen, Kenneth. Proc. Am. Soc. Mun. Imp. (5th yr.), Pt. II. p. 57 Oct. 1898. City Govt. 5:227 (Dec. 1898); Mun. Engng. 16:20 (Jan. 1899); anon. Engng. Rec. 37:53 (Dec. 18, 1897); 40:291 (Aug. 26, 1899).   36

——. "Report of the Committee on Sewers, etc." Publications of the Baltimore Reform League (1895).   37

Statistics. "Vital Statistics of the District of Columbia and Baltimore covering a period of six years ending May 31, 1890." Billings, John S. Washington, Government Printing Office, 1893. 241 pp. Eleventh Census of the United States.   38

"Streets, Opening and Closing of." Publications of the Baltimore Reform League, 1895. 9 pp.

——. "McCulloh St. Opening. A Misfit Improvement." Brown, Frederick J. Baltimore, Cushing & Co., 1891. 10 cents.   39

——. "Streets and Slums, a Study in Local Municipal Geography." Brown, Frederick J. Baltimore, Cushing & Co., 1892. 21 pp. Maps. 35 cents.   40

Taxation, Single Tax. (See under Finance above.)

Transit Facilities. "Electric Street Railways in Baltimore, Md. Notes from the Field." Fairchild, C. B. Elec. Eng. 25:569, 742 (May 26, June 30, 1898); anon. St. Ry. J. Feb. 1894.   41

——. "Attempt to Increase Taxes and Regulate Transfer Privileges in Baltimore." St. Ry. J. 16:51 (Jan. 6, 1900).   42

——. "Rapid Transit in Baltimore." P. 51. "Rapid Transit in Foreign Cities." Parsons, W. B. New York, 1894.   43

Unemployed. "How Baltimore Banished Tramps and Helped the Idle." Gould, E. R. L. Forum 17:497 (1894).   44

——. "Problem of Tramps in Baltimore." Briscoe, M. S. M. Chr. Lit. 6:458 (1892).   45

"**Bandora**, The Sanitation of." Wallace, John. Ind. & East. Eng. 2:275 (April 1898).   46

Barcelona, Spain.

Competition for plans for a city park and the extension of Barcelona. "Konkurrenz für Anlage eines Stadtparkes und der Stadtweiterung zu Barcellona." Deutsche Bauz. p. 128, 1871.   47

"Electric Railways in Madrid and Bercelona." Armstrong, F. C. St. Ry. J. 15:75 (Feb. 1899); anon. Ry. World 8:1 (Jan. 5, 1899).   48

"**Barking Town [Eng.]**, Its Progress and Public Work." London 6:956 (Dec. 9, 1897.)   49

Basel, Switz.

Finance. "Progressive Taxation as levied in Switzerland, cantons Basel-Stadt, de Vaud, and Uri." Palgrave, R. H. T. Journal of the London Statistical Society 51:225 (1888).   50

Financial History. "Finanzverhältnisse der Stadt Basel in XIV. und XV. Jahrhundert." Schönberg, Gustav Fr. Tübingen, Laupp, 1879. 8vo, 821 pp. 18 M.   51

Housing. "Die Wohnungsenquête in der Stadt Basel." Bücher, Karl. Basel, Georg & Co., 1891. 8vo, 356 pp. 5 M.   52

Transit Facilities. "The Basle Electric Tramway." Schweiz. Bau. Oct. 30, Nov. 6, 13, 20, 1897; Ry. World 6:328 (Nov.1897).   53

Unemployment, Insurance against v. Heckel, Max, Jr. Nat. Stat. 64:107-122 (1895); Jay, Raoul. R. Econ. Pol. 9:368-386 (1895); von Welck, A. Jr. Gesetz. Ver. Volks. 24:1005 (Heft 3, 1900); anon. Schweiz. Bl. 1:134 (1895); Yale R. 9:86 (May, 1900.)   54

——. "Die Gesetzgebung d. Schweizerkantone Bern, St. Gallen u. Basel bet. eine Versicherung gegen Arbeitslosigkeit." Garrelts, Fr. Goettingen, L. Horstmann, 1896. 2 S. m. 1 Tab. in Imp. Fol. 1 M.   55

Water Works. "Das Wasserwerk der Stadt Basel." Markus, A. Schweizerisches Bauwesen (Zurich) Oct. 8 and 10, 1896.   56

BIBLIOGRAPHY.

Batavia (Java), The Electric Tramway in. "Die Elektrische Strassenbahn in Batavia." Elek. Zeit. Oct. 26, 1899. — 57

Bath (Eng.). "Municipal Roman Baths." Mun. J. & London 8:1187 (Nov. 3, 1899.) — 58

Baths, Laundries and Lavatories, Public. (See also **Public Comfort Stations.**)

See also Bath, Berlin, Bilston, Birmingham, Boston, Brookline, Brighton (Eng.), Buffalo, Chicago, England under United Kingdom, Glasgow, Great Britain under United Kingdom, Harrogate, Liverpool, London, Munich, New York, Paris, Philadelphia, Pirna (Ger.), Pittsburgh, St. Pancras, St. Paul, Vienna, Yonkers.

"Arrangement of Public Baths, The." Engng. Rec. 39:383 (March 25, 1899.) — 59
"Baths for the Poorest." Court, W. R. Arch. Sept. 29, 1899. — 60
"Baths and Gymnasia, Playgrounds." Quincy, Josiah. City Rec. 1:517 (Sept. 3, 1898), Santarian 41:303 (Oct. 1898), Ann. Am. Acad. Pol. Sci., 12:444 (Nov. 1898), N. Y. Educa. 2:135 (Nov., 1898.) — 61
"Baths in the Slums." Mun. J. & London 8:1103 (Oct. 6, 1899.)
"Baths and Wash Houses." Faure, John P. Municipal Program Leaflet No. 5, New York, 1894. 7 pp. 5 cts. — 62
Bibliography. (See nos. 70 and 83 below.)
Civilizing Mission. "Die Culturaufgabe der Volksbäder." Lassar, O. Berlin, Hirschwald, 1889. 8vo, 44 pp. 30 pf. — 63
"Free Public Baths." Sanitarian 38:424 (May, 1897.) — 64
"Free Water for Private Baths." Case, L. N. Engng. Rec. 38:51 (June 18, 1898), City Govt. 4:211 (June, 1898), Mun. Engng 15:25 (July, 1898.) — 65
"Lavatories." Tolman, Wm. Howe. Municipal Program Leaflet No. 6, New York, 1895. 10 pp. 5 cts. — 66
"Municipal Free Bath, The." Stewart, Jane A. Our Day 19:11 (Jan., 1900.) — 67
"Municipal Public Baths." Williams, Mary B. H. Citizen 1:251 (1896.) — 68
"People's Baths." Gerhard, William Paul. Public Imp. 1:191 (Sept. 15, 1899.) — 69
"People's Baths, The." Publications of the New York Association for Improving the Condition of the Poor. With Bibliography on Public Baths. 16 pp. 1896. — 70
Plans for Public Baths, Prize. "Preistentwürfe für Volksbäder." Loewenstein, Franz. Gesund. Ing. 23:156 (May 31, 1900), 23:171 (June 15, 1900.) — 71
"Private Initiative in Furnishing Public Bath Facilities." Kirkbride, Franklin B. Ann. Am. Acad. Pol. Sci. 13:280 (March, 1899.) — 72
Public Baths. Brown, Goodwin. Char. R. 2:143 (1893); Foster, E. San. Plumb 17:25 (Sept. 1, 1899); Morris, Moreau. Sanitarian Sept. 1896; Tolman, Wm. H. Yale R. 6:50 May, 1897); anon. Outlook 52:545 (1895). See also p. 47, Report of the Tenement House Committee (N. Y. State), 1894. — 73
———. "Public Baths and Cheap Baths for the People." Vachee, Francis. London, 1879. Pamphlet, 22 pp. — 74
———. "Plea for Public Baths, with an Inexpensive Method for their Hygienic Utilization." Pamphlet, 45 pp. Reprinted from the Dietetic Gazette, May, 1891. — 75
———. "Public Baths in Europe." Hartwell, Alfred M. Washington, Bulletin of the Department of Labor, No. 11, July, 1897, p. 434. — 76
———. "Public Baths and Laundries." Donald, Robert. Outlook 53:285 (1896). — 77
———. "Public Baths and Lavatories." New York Citizens' Union, Pamphlet No. 1, May, 1897. 12 pp. — 78
———. "Public Baths and Wash Houses." Allsop, Robert Owen. New York, Spon and Chamberlain, 1884. 93 pp. $2.50. — 79
———. "Public Baths and Wash Houses." Tiltman, Hessell. Builder 76:139 (Feb. 11, 1899). Jour. Roy. Inst. Brit. Arch'ts. Feb. 11, 1899, Am. Arch. 64:5 (April 1, 1899), 64:11 (April 8, 1899), 64:21 (April 21, 1899); Arch. & Buil. 30:123 (April 22, 1899), 30:131 (April 29, 1899), 30:159 (May 20, 1899), 30:167 (May 27, 1899.) — 80
———. "Public Baths and Washhouses." Tiltman, A. Hessell. London, 1899. Pamphlet, 12 pp. — 81
Public Comfort Stations. (See under **Public Comfort Stations**).
"Public Rain Baths in America." Fisk, Harvey E. Sanitarian 36:404 (1896); Morris, Moreau. Sanitarian, July, 1896. — 82

Baths, Laundries and Lavatories, Public—*Continued.*

"Report on Public Baths and Public Comfort Stations." (With an extensive Bibliography.) Tolman, William Howe, Moreau Morris and William Gaston Hamilton, Committee. New York. Published by the Mayor's Committee on Public Baths and Public Comfort Stations, 1897. 195 pp. Ill. Cloth, $1; paper, 50 cts.   83
——. "Preliminary Report of the Sub-Committee on Baths and Lavatories, Committee of Seventy." New York, 1895. 15 pp.   84
"Social Arrows." Brabazon, Lord. (Parks, Play Grounds, Public Baths). London, Longmans, G. & Co., 1887.   85
"Systems of Public Baths." Brown, Goodwin. Public Imp. 3:314 (May 15, 1900).   86
"Why Public Baths are Essential to Public Health." San. Rec. 20:36 (July 9, 1897)   87

Battersea. (See also London.)

"Municipal Workshops, Battersea's." London 7:3 (Jan. 6, 1898), 7:49 (Jan. 27, 1898.)   88

"Battle Creek, Mich., Electrolysis in." Brigden, W. W. Engng. Rec. 39:446 (April 15, 1899.)   89

Belfast, Ireland.

"Gas Engine Plant, The Belfast." Railroad Gaz. 29:728 (Oct. 15, 1897.)   90
Housing. "Workmen's Dwellings in Belfast." Munce, James. J. San. Inst. 19:41 (April, 1898.)   91
Lighting. "Cost of Illuminating Gas in Belfast." Taney, J. B. U. S. Consular Reports 53:516.   92
——. "Gas at 60 cents, Illuminating." Taney, James B. City Govt. 2:102 (April, 1897), Engng News 37:271 (April 29, 1897), Prog. Age 15:191 (May 1, 1897).   93
——. "The Belfast Municipal Electric Plant." (Editorial.) Elec. World 32:504 (Nov. 12, 1898.)
Transit. "Belfast Tramways." Ry. World 8:194 (May 11, 1899.)

Belgium.

City Government, General and Unclassified.
Cities. "Les Villes en Belgique." R. Municipale 3:1889 (Feb. 3, 1900).
Local and Municipal Government in Belgium. Vol. I. pp. 252-274, Demombynes. See 2-11.   94
——. Provincial Organization. "L'Organisation Provinciale en Belgique." R. Municipale 3:1871 (Jan. 27, 1900.)
Municipal Government in Belgium. Palgrave 2:831-832. See 1-2.
——. "The Provincial and Communal Institutions of Belgium and Holland." de Laveleye, Emile. p. 245 "Local Government and Taxation." See 4-57.   95
——. "Gemeinde- und Provinzialverfassung. Vauthier, Maurice. V. Abs. pp. 102-149. Vol. IV., 1, 4-6. Marquardsen. See 2-9.   96
Municipal Law. "Commentaire sur la loi du 30 mars, 1836, et les lois qui l'ont modifiée." Bivort, J. B. Bruxelles, Larcier. 9e edit. 278 pp. 1882. 5 fr.   97
——. "Loi Communale du 30 mars, 1836, Coördonnée avec les lois subsequentes." Larcier, Ferd. Bruxelles, Larcier, 1884. 1 fr. 50c.   98
——. "Responsibilité des Communes et de leurs Administrateurs." Peeters, L. J. Bruxelles, F. Larcier, 1888. 6 fr.   99
"Municipal System of Belgium." Shaw, Albert. Chap. III, p. 210, "Municipal Government in Continental Europe." See 1-6.

"Art in Belgium, Public." de Wolf, Bradford Colt. Self-Cult. 11:132 (April, 1900); anon. Mun. Aff. 2:14 (March, 1898.).   100
——. "Art in the Belgian Parliament." Wiart, Carton de. Mun. Aff. 3:742 (Dec. 1899.)   1
"Charity in Belgium." Van Geert, Prosper. p. 198 "International Congress," vol. I, 1893, see 43-99.   1a
——. "Charity in France and Belgium." Valleroux, Herbert. p. 135 "International Congress," vol. III, 1893, see 43-99.   1b

Belgium—*Continued.*

Elections, Municipal. "Code Electoral belge, Supplément contenant les Lois de 11 avril et du 12 septembre, relative aux Elections Communales" Scheyven et Holvoet. Bruxelles, E. Bruylant, 1895. 161 pp. 8vo. 3 fr. 50c. 2
———. "Commentaire de la Loi relative aux Elections Communales." Biddaer et Somerhausen. Bruxelles, imprimerie J. Janssens, 1895. 3
———. "Loi Electoral Communale, Commentaire de la Loi relative à la Formation des listes des Electeurs Communaux." Henri, Albert. Bruxelles. Société belge de Libraire, 1875. 75c. 4
Finance. "Traité des Taxes Communales." Bollie, J. Bruxelles, Larcier, 1881. 334 pp. 6m. 5
———. "City Taxes in Belgium." Roosevelt, George W. Consular Reports 58:438 (Nov., 1893.) 6
History. "Les Libertés Communales." Wauters, Alph. Bruxelles, Office de Publicité, 1878. 2 vols. 14 fr. 7
Housing. "Les Habitations ouvrières en Belgique." Royer de Dour, Hippolyte de Brussels, Société Belge de Libraire, 1890. 314 pp. Plates and diagrams. 7 fr. 50c. 8
———. "Logement de l'ouvrier et du pauvre en Belgique." Bertrand, Louis. Bruxelles, chez l'auteur, 1888. 3 fr. 50c. 9
Markets. "Le Colportage et les Marchés Publics en Belgique." Heins, Maurice. R. Municipale 3:1724 (Nov. 25, 1899.) 10
Municipal Control, Etc. "Expériences de Municipalisation de Services Publics en Belgique." Heins, Maurice. R. Municipale 3:1901 (Feb. 10, 1900.) 11
———. "La Politica Comunale dei Socialisti Belgi." Vinck, Emilio. Critica Sociale 10:9 (Jan. 1, 1900), 10:29 (Jan. 16, 1900). 12
Pensions. "Institutions de Prévoyance, Belgique." Duboisdenghien, L. (Paris Exposition series, Group XVI., Class 109.) Brussels, Bruylant-Christophe & Co., 1900. 8vo, 214 pp. 12a
Population. "La Belgique et ses grandes Villes au XIX. Siècle, La Population." Heins, M. Ghent, Ad. Hoste, 1897. 8vo. 1 fr. 13
"Proportional Representation and the Debates upon the Electoral Question in Belgium." Mahaim, Ernest. Ann. Am. Acad. Pol. Sci. 15:381 (May, 1900.) (See also Elections above.) 14
———. "La Représentation Proportionnelle en Belgique." Dumont, Hermann. R. Pol. e. Par. 22:524 (Dec. 10, 1899.) 15
———. "Le Mécanisme de la Représentation Proportionnelle dans le Nouveau Système Electoral Belge." Vanlaer, Maurice. R. Pol. e. Par. 25:67 (July 10, 1900.) 16
Referendum. "A Letter on the Referendum in Belgium." Van den Heuvel, J. p. xxxix. in "The Referendum in Switzerland," by Simon Deploige. London, Longmans, 1898. 8vo, 334 pp. 7s. 6d. 17
Taxation. (See under Finance above.)
Transit Facilities. "Belgian Tramways and Light Railways." Ry. World 7:101 (April 7, 1898.) 18

Bellary Water Supply—Copper Hills Scheme." Nowroji, Hormusji. Ind. Engng. Sept. 25, 1897; Oct. 9, 1897. 19

Bergen. "Die Elektrische Strassenbahn der Stadt Bergen." Die Schmal Spurbahn, Nov. 1, 1897. 20

Berlin.

City Government, General and Unclassified.
"Berlin." Burbank, Emily M. Chaut. 26:355 (Jan., 1898); Ely, R. T. Nation 34:145, 245, 267 (1881); Spielhagen, Fr. Cosmopol. 14:515 (1893.) 21
———. "Berlin in 1889." Edwards, W. H. U. S. Cons. Rep. No. 120, 1890, pp. 165-76. 22
"Berliners." Spielhagen, Frederick. Cosmopol. 14:724 (1893.) 23
Festschriften. "Die öffentliche Gesundheits- und Krankenpflege der Stadt Berlin." (Contains not only descriptions of sanitary service, hospitals, asylums, etc., of the city, but also of water works, baths, sewerage, lighting, abattoirs, food inspection, markets, parks, street cleaning, and burial in Berlin.) Hrsg. v. den städt. Behörden. Festschrift d. Stadt Berlin dargeboten X. Internation-

Berlin—*Continued.*

alen Medizinischen Kongress. Berlin, August Hirschwald, 1890. 4to, 362 pp. 10m. 23a

——. " Beleuchtung, Wasserversorgung und Kanalisation der Stadt Berlin." Festschrift d. deut. Vereins v. Gas u. Wasserfachmännern. Berlin, 1883. 8m. 23b

——. " Die Stadt Berlin, Festschrift der Stadtgemeinde f. d. Teilnehmer am VII., internationalen Geographen-Kongress." (Particularly valuable for its accounts of the history, pp. 41-78, administration, pp. 99-114, and statistical offices of the city, pp. 267-277. Contains also much valuable scientific information regarding Berlin.) Buseman, M., editor. Berlin, 1899. 12mo, 371 pp. ill. map. 23c

" Government of Berlin." Gneist, Rudolph. Contemp. 46:769 (1884); Rowe, Leo S. Nation 55:221 (1892.) 24

——. " Berlin, A Study of Municipal Government." Baxter, Sylvester. Bulletin of the Essex Institute, Vol. XXI., 1889, Salem, Mass. Printed in pamphlet form by the Baltimore Taxpayers' Association, 1891. 25

——. " Report on the Government of Berlin." Coleman, Chapman. Foreign Relations Report No. 294, p. 478, 1881. Consular Reports, Nov. and Dec., 1888, p. 413 26

Abattoirs. (See under Festschriften above.)

Art. " Famous Monuments of Berlin." Park and Cem. 7:140 (Aug. 1897). 28

——. " Das Kaiserdenkmal auf der Schloss Freiheit zu Berlin." Deutsche Bauz. March 20, 27, 1897. 29

Asylums. (See under Festschriften above.)

Baths. " Die Stadt Badeanstalten Berlins." Gesundheits-Ingenieur, March 15, 1899. (See also under Festschriften above.) 30

Building Laws and Regulations. " Bauordnung für die Stadt Berlin." Berlin, Julius Sittenfeld, 1877. 56 pp. 31

——. " Baupolizei in Berlin, Denkschrift über die Handhabung der." Parey, Karl. Berlin, Toeche, 1886. 29 pp. 1m. 32

——. " Berlin und seine Bauten." Bearbeitet und Herausgegeben vom Architekten Verein zu Berlin und der Vereinigung Berliner Architekten. Berlin, Wilhelm Ernst u. Sohn, 1896. 2 Vols., 873 and 680 pp. 33

Burial System. (See under Festschriften above.)

Charity. "Asyl für Obdachslose in Berlin." Spindler, Will. Berlin, Rubenow, 1870. 34

——. " Die Organisation der Privatwohlthätigkeit in Berlin." Breslauer, Bernhard. Berlin, Mamroth, 1891. 27 pp. 60 pf. 35

——. " Die Wohlfahrtseinrichtungen Berlins und seiner Vororte." Berlin, Hrsg. v. d. Auskunftsstelle d. deutschen Gesellschaft f. ethische Kultur, Verlag Julius Springer, 1899. 8vo, 427 pp. 3m. 36

——. " How Berlin Provides for its Destitute Children." Sellers, Edith. Econ. R. 10:35 (Jan., 1900). 37

——. " Sociale Elend der Grossstädte Wien u. Berlin." Deutsch, Ed. Wien, Mayer u. C., 1878. 38

——. " Waisenpflege der Stadt Berlin." Fischer, A. Berlin, Oehmigke, 1892. 6m. 39

Council. " The City Council of Berlin." James, Edmund J. Am. J. Sociol. 6:407 (Nov., 1900.) (See also under Elections below.) 40

Dust-Burning, The Berlin Investigation of. Oesterr. Monatschr. f. d. öffent. Baudienst, February, 1898. 41

Elections in Berlin, Municipal. Artibal, J. R. Municipale 3:1615 (Oct. 7, 1899); Brooks, R. C. Ann. Am. Acad. Pol. Sci. 15:480 (May, 1900). 42

Elevated Railways. (See under Transit Facilities below.)

" Finances, Berlin City." James, Edmund J. Ann. Am. Acad. Pol. Sci. 15:478 (May, 1900). 43

——. " Comparison as to Cost of Administration in Berlin and New York." Real Estate Rec. and Guide, Nov. 10, 1894, p. 673. 44

——. " Aufgaben der Berliner Communalverwaltung und die Erhöhung der Städtischen Steuern." Eberty, E. Berlin, Carl Heymann, 1878. 29 pp. 1m. 45

——. Comparison of Berlin and Paris. Ann. Am. Acad. Pol. Sci. 12:311 (Sept. 1898). 46

——. " Die Gemeindefinanzen von Berlin und Paris." Rowe, Leo S. Jena, Gustav Fischer, Pubs. Economic Seminary at Halle, 1893. 236 pp. 47

Berlin—*Continued.*

Fire Insurance in Berlin, Municipal. "Société d'Assurance Municipale Obligatoire contre les Risques du Feu à Berlin." Artibal, J. R. Municipale 3:2011 (March 31, 1900), 3:2030 (April 7, 1900). 48

Fire Protection. "Handbuch des Feuerlösch-Rettungswesens Berlins." Doehring, W. Berlin, Parey, 1881. 8vo, 310 pp. 10m. 49

Food Inspection. (See under Festschriften above.)

Garbage Disposal. "The Disposal of Garbage and Refuse—Berlin, Germany." Hering, Rudolph. Engng. Rec. 36:532 (Nov. 20, 1897). 50

———. "Der Neue Müllschmelzofen in Berlin." Häntzschel, W. Gesundheits-Ingenieur June 15, 1899; anon. Engng. M. 17:851 (Aug. 1899). 51

"Higher Life of Berlin, The." Soden, Herman von. Outlook 57:307 (Oct. 2, 1897). 52

History. "500 Jahre Berliner Geschichte." Streckfuss, Adolf. Berlin, A. Goldschmidt, 1899. 8vo, 807 pp. 12m. 53

———. "Berlin during the Barricades." de Circourt, Comte A. Revue de Paris June 15, 1897. 54

———. (See also under Festschriften above.)

Hospitals. (See under Festschriften above.)

Housing. "Berliner Wohnungsverhältnisse." Braun, Ad. Berlin, Verlag Vorwärts, 1893. 80 pp. 35 pf. 55

———. "Zur Berliner arbeiter Wohnungsfrage." Freund, Rich. u. Malachowski, Herm. Berlin, J. J. Heines Verlag, 1892. 52 pp. 1m. 60 pf. 56

———"Die sociale Lage d. arbeitenden Klassen in Berlin." Hirschberg, Ernst. Berlin, Liebmann, 1897. 8vo, 311 pp. 5m. 50 pf. 57

———. "Die Wohnungsfrage und die Bestrebungen der Berliner Baugenossenschaft." Nathan, Paul. Berlin, Simon, 1890. 84 pp. 2m. 58

———. "Die Wohnungsverhaltnisse in Berlin, insbesondere die der ärmeren Klassen." Berthold, G. pp. 199-235 Hft. 31, Schr. d. Ver. f. Socialpolitik. 59

———. "Housing of the Working Classes in Berlin." Surveyor 18:566 (Nov. 16, 1900).

———. "Tenement Houses in Berlin." de Kay, Charles. U. S. Consular Reports Vol. XLVIII., No. 178, p. 382-386 (1895), Am. Arch. 49:49 (1895). 60

———. "Les Habitations Ouvrières à Berlin." Nérincx, Alfred. Ref. Soc. Jan. 1, 1899. 61

"Insane Asylum, Berlin." Edwards, W. H. Cons. Rep. No. 130, 1891, p. 595-600. 62

Kaiser Wilhelm-Strasse. "Die Bebauung der Kaiser Wilhelm-Strasse in Berlin." Centralbl. d. Bauverw. p. 53, 1885. 63

Lighting. The Municipal Gas Works of Berlin. "Die Städtische Gaswerke Berlins." Gesun. Ing. 23:145 (May 15, 1900). 64

———. "Regulations for Acetylene Lighting at Berlin." Prog. Age 16:11 (Jan. 1, 1898). 65

———. "Street Lighting of Berlin." Edwards, W. H. Cons. Rep., No. 128, 1891, pp. 47-54. 67

———. (See under Festschriften above.)

Markets. (See under Festschriften above).

Mayoralty Contest of 1898-9. "Berlin without an Oberbürgermeister." Brooks, Robert C. Ann. Am. Acad. Pol. Sci. 14:94 (July, 1899), same 15:294 (March, 1900). 68

Moabit Quarter, Development of. "Die Entwickelung des Stadttheiles Moabit und die Bauten auf dem Gelände der Baugesellschaft am kleinen Thiergarten." Deutsche Bauz. p. 413, 1885. 69

Parks. (See under Festschriften above.)

"Police of Berlin." Nation 59:140 (1894.) 70

———. "Le Police, la Crime et le Vice à Berlin." Raffalovich, Arthur. Rev. d. deux Mondes 119:156 (1893). 71

———. "Die Verbrecherwelt von Berlin." Berlin, Jacobsthal, 1886. 2m. 72

Prostitution. "Die Verbreitung der Syphilus in Berlin." Blaschko. Berlin, 1892. 8vo, 32 pp. 80 pf. 73

Public Comfort Stations. "Zur Frage Errichtung öffentlicher Bedürfnissanstalten für Frauen und Männer in Berlin." Deutsche Bauz. p. 261, 1875. 74

"Sanitary System of Berlin." Murphy, Geo. H. Cons. Rep. No. 129, 1891, pp. 265-72. 75

Berlin—*Continued.*

——. " Die Einwirkung hygienischer Werke auf die Gesundheit der Städte mit besonderer Rücksicht auf Berlin." Weyl, Th. Jena, G. Fischer, 1894. 2m. **76**

——. " Oeffentliche Gesundheitspflege in Berlin." Albu, J. Berlin, J. Schröder. 1877. 6m. **77**

——. (See also under Festschriften above).

Savings Banks. " Die städtische Sparkasse zu Berlin, in ihrer Einrichtung und Geschäftsführung dargestellt." Thiele, L. Berlin, Rosenthal, 1887. 3m. **78**

School System. "Das gemeinde Schulwesen der Stadt Berlin." Bertram, Heinr. Berlin, Oehmigke, 1878. **79**

" Sewage Disposal in Berlin." Anon. Am. Arch. 20:126 (1886); Engng. News Oct. 7, 1885; Annales des Ponts et Chaussées, Sept. 1895; Gesund. Ing. 23:213 (July 15, 1900). **80**

——. " Die Canalisation von Berlin. Im Auftrage d. Magistrats ausgeführt." Hobrecht, James. Atlas, 57 plates and tables. Berlin, Ernst u. Korn, 1887. 75m. **81**

——. Sewage Farms of Berlin. Edwards, W. H. U. S. Cons. Rep. No. 130, pp. 462-7 (1891), same p. 164, Vol. XLVII., No. 173 (Feb. 1895); Fuertes, J. H. Engng. Rec. 40:30 (June 10, 1899); Hazen, Allen. Engng. News 38:178 (Sept. 16, 1897); Roechling, Herman. Proc. Inst. Civil Engineers 109:179-269 (1892); anon. Engng. Rec. p. 157, Aug. 6, 1892; Engng. News, Aug. 27, 1896; Gesund. Ing. June 15, 1898. **82**

——. "Operation of the Berlin Sewerage System and Sewage Farms for the Year 1898-9." Hazen, Allen. Engng. N. 43:848 (May 24, 1900.) **83**

——. (See also under Festschriften above).

Smoke Prevention. " Das revorstehende Verbot des Schornsteinrauchens in Berlin." Häntzschel, W. Gesund. Ing. June 30, 1899. **84**

Statistical Offices. (See under Festschriften above).

Street Cleaning of Berlin. "Das städtische Strassenreinigungswesen Berlins." (Methods and cost of cleaning the streets of Berlin). Gesund. Ing. Feb. 28, 1897. **85**

——. " Berlin Street Cleaning." Edwards, W. H. Cons. Rep. No. 128, 1891, pp. 116-119. **86**

——. " Street Cleaning in Paris and Berlin." Grimshaw, Robert. Engng. M. 13:99 (Apr. 1897). **87**

——. (See also under Festschriften above.)

Street Lighting. (See under Lighting above.)

Street Ordinances. "Strassenordnung für den Stadtkreis Berlin." Berlin, A. W. Hahn's Erben, 1900. 8vo, 36 pp. 30 pf. **88**

——. " Le Nouveau Règlement de la Voie Publique à Berlin." Artibal, J. R. Municipale 3:2107 (May 12, 1900). **89**

Transit Facilities. Combination Trolley and Conduit Electric Tramway. Martin, Henry. Le Genie Civil Nov. 5, 1898; anon. Engng. News 42:70 (Aug. 3, 1899); Zeitschr. f. Klein u. Strassenbahnen May 1, 16, 1900. **90**

——. " Electric Tramways of Berlin and Vicinity." Krieger, H. Gartenlaube Hft. 7 (1900); anon. Ry. World 6:261 (Sept. 1897); Schweiz. Bau. Oct. 22, 29, 1898; St. Ry. J. 16:619 (July 7, 1900); Ty. & Ry. W. 9:217 (June 7, 1900). **91**

——. History. " Berlin und seine Eisenbahnen, 1846-1896." Royal Prussian Minister of Public Works. Berlin, Julius Springer, 1896. 2 vols., 4to, pp. I, 375; II, 491. **92**

——. " Berlin City Railway." Appendix, "Report to the Rapid Transit Commissioners of Massachusetts." Fitzgerald, John E. Boston, 1891. **93**

——. " Elevated Railways in Berlin, Projects Submitted for." Deutsche Bauzeitung, Feb. 2, 1895, et seq.

——. " The Berlin Electric Elevated Road." St. Ry. J. 16:960 (Oct. 13, 1900).

——. Introduction of Electric Power upon the Berlin City and Belt Railway. "Einführung des Elektrischen Betriebes auf der Berliner Stadt und Ringbahn." Anon. Elek. Zeit. Nov. 16, 1899; St. Ry. J. 16:152 (Feb. 3, 1900); Elec. W. & E. 35:171 (Feb. 3, 1900); Glaser's Annalen Aug. 15, 1900.

——. " Metropolitan and Belt Railways of Berlin, The." Engng. News. 40:213 (Oct. 6, 1898).

——. " Rapid Transit in Berlin." p. 41 "Rapid Transit in Foreign Cities." Parsons, W. B. New York, 1894. **94**

——. " Street Railway Policy in Berlin." James, Edmund J. Ann. Am. Acad. Pol. Sci. 15:437 (May, 1900). **95**

Berlin—*Continued*.

———. "Tramways of Berlin." Glasers Annalen March 1, 1897.

———. "Tramway Projects in Berlin." Macgowan, D. B. Ty. & Ry. World 9:15 (Jan. 11, 1900). 96

———. Underground Railway. "Berliner Untergrundbahn." Zeitschr. f. Klein u. Strassenbahnen Dec. 1, 1899.

———. Underground Railways in London and Berlin. Silberstein, L. Die Zeit March 26, 1898.

Taxation (See under Finances above.)

Tenement Houses in Berlin. (See under Housing above.)

Theatres, Berlin. Poppenberg, Felix. Cosmopolis 11:282 (July 1898); von Zobelnitz, H. Velhagen und Klasings Monatshefte Jan. 1898. 97

* "Water Works of Berlin." Edwards, W. H. Cons. Rep. No. 129, 1891, pp. 265-72; Fuertes, James H. Engng. Rec. 38:320 (Sept. 10, 1898). 98

———. "The Filters of the Berlin Water Works." Ch. XIV., p. 230. "Purification of Public Water Supplies." Hill, John W. New York, Van Nostrand, 1898. 304 pp. 8vo. $3.00. 99

———. "Filtration of Water, City of Berlin." Frankel, Carl. Zeitschrift für Hygiene 8:1 (1890). 100

———. "Sale of Water by Meter in Berlin." Gill, Henry. Proc. Inst. C. E. 107:203 (1892); 119:236 (1895). 1

———. (See also under Festschriften above.)

"Workhouse, Berlin Municipal." Edwards, W. H. Cons. Rep. No. 132, 1891, p. 153. 2

Berne, Switz.

Extension of Berne. "Die rationelle Vergrösserung der Stadt Bern." Eisenb. 15:139 (1899).

History. "Finanzwesen und Bevölkerung der Stadt Bern im 15 Jahrhundert." Schindler, K. Zeitschrift für Schweizerische Statistik, 1900. 3

Municipal Government of Berne. Demombvnes. Vol. II., pp. 367-384. See 2-11. 4

"Unemployed in Berne, Aid for." Germain, Eugene. U. S. Cons. Rep. No. 167, 1894, p. 607. 5

———. "Die Gesetzgebung d. Schweizerkantone Bern, St. Gallen u. Basel, bet. eine Versicherung gegen Arbeitslosigkeit." Garrelts, Fr. Goettingen, L. Horstmann, 1896. 2 S. m. 1 Tab. in Imp.-Fol. 1m. 6

———. "Die Arbeitslosemersicherung in St. Gallen und Bern." Hofmann, E. Ar. Soz. Gesets. Stat. 13:85 (1 Heft, 1898). Schartlin, G. Schweiz, Bl. June, 1894. 6a

"**Berwyn, Pa.**, Water Company, The Slow Sand Filtration Plant of the." Ledoux, J. W. Engng. News 41:150 (March 9, 1899). 7

Bethnal Green. (See under **London**).

Betterment. (See Assessments, Special, under **Finance**).

"**Biarritz [France]**, The Abattoir of." Cumming, Alice L. Public Health July, 1900. 8

Bibliographies.

"Bibliography of Municipal Administration and City Conditions." (Published as Vol. I, No. 1 of Municipal Affairs) Brooks, Robert C. New York, Reform Club Committee on Municipal Administration, 1897. 224 pp. 50 cts. Quarterly supplements, Mun. Aff. 1:400 (June, 1897), 1:580 (Sept., 1897), 1:781 (Dec., 1897), 2:155 (March, 1898), 2:320 (June, 1898), 2:557 (Sept., 1898), 2:800 (Dec., 1898), 3:172 (March, 1899), 3:371 (June, 1899), 3:555 (Sept., 1899), 3:766 (Dec., 1899), 4:240 (March, 1900), 4:426 (June, 1900), 4:625 (Sept., 1900), 4:790 (Dec., 1900). Materials contained in supplements and bibliography of 1897 collected in present volume. 9

Housing of the Poor, Bibliography. pp. 127-132 in Marcus T. Reynolds' "Housing of the Poor in American Cities." New York, Publications Am. Econ. Assoc. Vol. VIII, Nos. 2 and 3, 1893. 132 pp. $1. 9a

"Municipal Government, Reference List of Works Relating to." Woodward, Frank E. Malden, 1887. 4 pp. 10

———. "Bibliography of Municipal Government and Reform." pp. 341-81, Pro. of

Bibliographies—Continued.

the First National Conf. for Good City Govt., 1894. See 6-18a.

——. "References on Municipal Government in the United States." Hodder, Frank H. Cornell University Library Bulletin, Vol. II., 1888. 11

——. "Bibliography of Municipal Government in the United States." Hodder, Frank M. Kansas University Quarterly 1:179-196 (1893).

——. pp. 95-103 "Mayor vs. Council." Univ. of Wisconsin. Madison, 1897. Paper, 50 cts.

"Municipal Reform, Bibliography of." Will, Thomas E. Arena 10:555 (1894). 12

Parks. (See Henry Sargent Codman on "The Art of Landscape Gardening" in Garden and F. 3:131 (1890) for references to the literature of Parks.) 13

——. "Bibliography of Parks and Play Grounds." Will, Thomas E. Arena 10:274 (1894). 14

"Political Corruption, Bibliography of." Will, Thomas E. Arena 10:845 (1894).

"Reader's Guide in Economic, Social and Political Science." Bowker, R. R. and George Iles. New York, Society for Political Education, 1891. 169 pp. 50 cts. (Bibliography of Workingmen's Dwellings p. 89. Municipal Government, p. 118.) 15

Settlements. "Bibliography of College, Social and University Settlements." Jones, M. Katharine. 1895. 54 pp. Paper, 10 cts. 16

United Kingdom, Bibliography on British Municipal History. (See under **United Kingdom**.)

Bilston, Eng.

"Baths of Bilston, Staffordshire, England, The Public." Fuertes, James H. Engng. Rec. 41:61 (Jan. 20, 1900). 17

"Water Works of Bilston, England." Fuertes, James H. Engng. Rec. 41:250 (March 17, 1900). 18

"**Binghamton, N. Y.**, Electric Railroad, The." Gardner, Harry N. Elec. Engng. 24:345 (Oct. 14, 1897). 19

"**Birmingham, Ala.**, The Street Railway of." St. Ry. J. 16:528 (June 2, 1900). 20

Birmingham, Eng.

City Government, General and Unclassified.

"The Best Governed City in the World." Ralph, Julian. Harper's M. 81:99 (1890). 21

"Birmingham. il comune modello." Bettocchi, C. Napoli, N. Jovene e C., 1893. 47 pp. 22

"Birmingham, its Civic Life and Expansion." Chap. VI, p. 168, "Municipal Government in Great Britain," by Albert Shaw. 23

"Birmingham Caucus." (Liberal Political Organization.) Marriott, W. T. 19th Cent. 11:949 (1882). 24

"Birmingham and Mr. Chamberlain." Porrit, Edward. Leslie's Wkly. 81:74 (1805). 25

"English Municipal Institutions Studied at Birmingham." MacDonald, J. A. 19th Cent. 20:234 (1886). 26

"Municipal Government of Birmingham, Manchester and Liverpool." Sharpless, Isaac. Haverford College Studies No. 11. 27

"Municipal Government, An Object Lesson in." Parker, Geo. F. Cent. 53:71 (1896). 28

"Municipal Institutions in America and England" (Comparison of Birmingham and Boston). Chamberlain, Joseph. Forum 14:267 (1892). See also Our Day 11:123 (1893). 29

"Municipal Progress in Birmingham." London 7:617 (Sept. 29, 1898). 30

Abattoirs. "New Municipal Slaughter-Houses at Birmingham." London 6:941 (Dec. 2, 1897). 31

"Architecture of Birmingham, England, The." Builder Nov. 27, 1897. 32

"Baths, Birmingham (Eng.)" Arch. & Cont. Rep. 58:166 (Sept. 10, 1897); City Rec. 1:597 (Oct. 20, 1898). 33

Finance. "Municipal Expenditures of Birmingham." Avery, T. J. Statis. Soc. 29:78 (1866). 34

——. "Municipal Finance as Illustrated by the City of Birmingham." Smith, E. O. J. Statis. Soc. 58:327 (1895). 35

Birmingham, Eng.—*Continued*.

"History of the Corporation of Birmingham, with a sketch of the earlier government of the town." Bunce, J. T. Birmingham, published for the corporation, 1878-85. 2 vols. Birmingham, Cornish. 8vo. 10 S. For other references on the history of Birmingham see p. 169 of Gross' "Bibliography of British Municipal History." ... 36

Lighting. "Centenary of Gas-Lighting in Birmingham, Eng." Arch. (London) Supp. p. 23 (Sept. 2, 1898). ... 37

Municipal Control, Ownership, etc. "Birmingham Municipality at Work." Dolman, F. New R. 17:74 (1894). See also Chap. I., p. 1, in his "Municipalities at Work." ... 38

Sanitation. "How Birmingham Keeps Healthy." Mun. J. 9:905 (Nov. 16, 1900). ... 39

"Sewage Farm at Saltley, Birmingham, Eng." San. Eng. Oct. 7, 1886. ... 40

——. "Sewage Works at Birmingham and Edmonton." Cole, T. Van Nostrand's Elec. Eng. Mag. 27:42 (1882). ... 41

——. "Death Rate, Birmingham's Abnormal: Is the Sewage System to Blame?" San. Rec. 20:280 (Sept. 10, 1897). ... 42

Transit Facilities. Tramways. Ry. World 7:162 (May 5, 1898); Mun. J. & London 8:205 (Feb. 16, 1899); Ann. Am. Acad. Pol. Sci. 14:143 (July, 1899). ... 43

——. "The Electric Railway in Birmingham." Halstead, Marshal. Elec. R. 37:224 (Sept. 5, 1900), Cons. Rep. 64:311 (Nov., 1900). ... 44

——. "Birmingham, Report of the Sub-Committee on Tramway Traction." (Brief reports on systems in use in Bristol, Blackpool, Paris, Rouen, Brussels, Vienna, Buda-Pesth, Dresden, Berlin, Hamburg and Bremen.) Birmingham, April, 1897. 50 pp. ... 45

——. "Birmingham, Report of the Public Works Committee on Tramways, presented to Council June 29, 1897." Birmingham, 1897. 66 pp. Commented on in St. Ry. Rev. 7:451 (July 15, 1897). ... 46

"Water Supply of Birmingham." Sat. R. 72:349 (1891), R. Technique, May 25, 1898; Eng. (London) 86:243 (Sept. 9, 1898); London 7:601 (Sept. 22, 1898). ... 47

——. "The Future Water Supply of Birmingham." Barclay, Thomas. Birmingham, Stanford, 1898. 3d ed. 8vo. 170 pp. 4s. ... 48

——. "History of Birmingham's Water Supply." Barclay, Thomas. London 7:603 (Sept. 22, 1898). ... 49

"Waterworks, City of Birmingham Corporation." Crespi, Alfred J. H. New Cent. R. 8:358 (Nov., 1900). Davey, Henry. Mechanical World 22:100 (Aug. 27, 1897), J. Gas Lgt. 70:682 (Sept. 28, 1897); anon. Arch. June 11, 1897; Mun. J. & London 8:1386 (Dec. 29, 1900). ... 50

——. "The Construction of the Elan Aqueduct, Birmingham." Lapworth, Herbert. Engng. Rec. 42:292 (Sept. 29, 1900). ... 51

Births, Deaths and Marriages. (See under Statistics.)

"**Blackpool** [Eng.], The Trolley Problem at." Elec'n, (London) 43:474 (July 28, 1899). ... 52

Boards, Municipal.

"Boards, Single-Headed Commissions or Council Committees." Evans, F. V. City Govt. 5:71 (Aug. 1898), Prog. Age 16:405 (Sept. 1, 1898); Young, W. E. Prog. Age 16:404 (Sept. 1, 1898). ... 53

——. (See also **Councils**.)

Bochum, Germany.

Housing. "Die Arbeiterwohnungen des Bochumer Vereins für Bergbau und Gussstahlfabrikation." Bochum, 1876.

——. "Wohnungsverhältnisse der ärmeren Volksklassen in Bochum." Lange. pp. 73-105 Hft. 31, Schr. d. Ver. f. Socialpolitik. ... 54

Bolbec, France.

Housing. "Cités Ouvrières de Bolbec." Nouv. Annales de la Const., p. 162, 1878. ... 55

Bolton, Eng.

"Electric Lighting at Bolton, Eng." Lomas, Harold, and Gunton, Herbert C. Elec. W. & E. 30:5 (July 3, 1897); Elec. R. (London) 46:101 (Jan. 19, 1900). ... 56

"Sewage Filtration Works at Bolton." San. Rec. 24:306 (Oct. 6, 1899). ... 57

"Tramways in Bolton, Municipal." Mun. J. & London 8:1335 (Dec. 15, 1899). ... 58

Bombay, India.

"Electric Works in Bombay." Fee, William T. Cons. Rep. 64:91 (Sept., 1900). 59
"Tramways in Bombay." Fee, William T. Cons. Rep. 61:561 (Dec., 1899); anon. St. Ry. R. 9:600 (Sept. 15, 1899). 60
"Water Supply of Bombay." San Rec. 26:299 (Oct. 5, 1900). 61

Bonds, Municipal. (See under **Finance**.)

Bordeaux, France.

Municipal Exchanges for Apprentices at Bordeaux. "Bourses Municipales d'Apprentissage pour les Garçons à Bordeaux." Peytoureau. R. Municipale 3:1760 (Dec. 9, 1899). 62
Sanitation. "Hygiène urbaine, l'assainissement de Bordeaux." Mauriac, Jean E. Bordeaux, Feret et Fils, 1890. 2 pp. 63
"Sewage Disposal, Bordeaux." Wiley, J. M. U. S. Cons. Rep. Vol. XLVII, No. 173, p. 164 (Feb., 1895). 64

"**Borsbeke, Belgium**, Co-operative Electric Lighting in the Village of." Schoentjes, H. Elec. Eng. April 28, 1897. 65

Bossism in City Politics. (See also under **Elections**, Tammany under **New York**.)

"American Boss, The." Lowell, Francis C. Atlan. 86:289 (Sept., 1900). 66
"Are the Bosses Stronger than the People?" Bishop, J. B. Cent. 54:465 (July, 1897). 67
"The Boss." Moffett, S. E. Chapter XV, p. 184 " Suggestions on Government." Chicago, Rand, McNally & Co., 1894. 200 pp. $1.00. 68
"The Boss,—An Essay Upon the Art of Governing American Cities." Champernowne, Henry. New York, Geo. H. Richmond & Co., 1894. 243 pp. $1.25. 69
"Boss Rule in Old English Municipalities." Porrit, Edward. No. Am. 164:125 (1897). 70
"Civil Service Reform in the United States and Bossism." Harris, J. A. Penn. Mo. 12:524 (1881). (See also under **Civil Service in Cities**.) 71
"Essence of Boss Government, The." (Editorial.) Nation 68:308 (April 27, 1899). 72
"Growing Impudence of the Bosses." Cent. 52:154 (1896). 73
"Price of Peace, The." (Bossism.) Bishop, J. B. Cent. n. s. 26:667 (Sept., 1894). 74
"Rule of the Boss." Godkin, E. L. Nation 13:236, 286 (1871) 75
"Why the Ward Boss Rules." Addams, Jane. Outlook 58:879 (April 2, 1898). 77

Boston, Mass.

Government, general references and unclassified. "Boston." Chap. VI. in "The Land of the Dollar" by G. W. Steevens. New York, Dodd, Mead & Co., 1897. 12mo, 316 pp. $1.50. 78
"Boston at the Century's End." Baxter, Sylvester. Harper's M. 99:823 (Nov., 1899). 79
Description and statistics of Boston, Mass., in 1880. Census. See 1-7.
"Government of Boston." Sprague, Henry H. Lend a H. Extra No. Vol. IV., March, 1889. 80
——. "City Government of Boston." Bugbee, J. M. J. H. U. Studies V:3 (1887). 25 cts. 81
——. "City Government of Boston." Matthews, Nathan, Jr. (Valedictory Address to Members of the City Council, Jan. 5, 1895.) Boston, Rockwell & Churchill, 1895. 8vo, 289 pp. 82
——. "Government of Boston." Storey, Moorfield. p. 61, Proc. First Natl. Conf., 1894. See 6-18a. 83
——. "Government of Boston; its Rise and Development." Sprague, Henry H. Boston, W. B. Clark & Co., 1890. 53 pp. 50 cts. 84
——. "The Organization of the City Government of Boston." Quincy, Josiah. Prog. Age 15:457 (Oct. 15, 1897), City Govt. 3:199 (Dec. 1897). 85
——. "Proposed Charter for the City of Boston." Bradford, G. No. Am. 123:1 (1876). 86
"Greater Boston." Atkinson, E. New Eng. M. 13:377 (1895). 87
——. "Greater Boston, a Study for a Federalized Metropolis." Baxter, Sylvester. Boston Herald, 1891. Leslie's Wkly. 80:348 (1895). 88

BIBLIOGRAPHY. 27

Boston, Mass.—*Continued.*

"Municipal Boston." Mun. J. & London 8:782 (July 7, 1899).
"Municipal Institutions in America and England." (Comparison of Birmingham and Boston.) Chamberlain, Joseph. Forum 14:267 (1892), Our Day 11:123 (1893). 89
"Municipal Progress in Boston." Quincy, Josiah. Ind. 62:424 (Feb. 15, 1900). 90
"Municipal Service of Boston, The." Lowell, Francis C. Atlan. 81:311 (March, 1898). 91
"Possible Boston, The." Hale, E. E. Lend a H. 4:263 (1899). 92
Record, City. (Beginning with Jan. 1, 1898, the City of Boston published weekly until 1900 an official gazette containing the more important city records. This paper was called "The City Record.") 93

Andover House, now South End House. (See below, under Settlements.)
"Architecture in Boston, Municipal." Engng. Rec. 39:133 (Jan. 14, 1899). 94
——. "Recent Boston Architecture." Cobb, Albert Winslow. Arch. & Buil. 26:235, 27:3, 47 (May 15, July 3, Aug. 7, 1897). 95
"Baths in Boston, Free Municipal." Cole, William J. City Govt. 7:43 (Aug., 1899), Mun. Rec. & Ad. 3:838 (Oct. 15, 1898); Engng. News 41:174 (March 16, 1899). 96
——. "Baths Statistics for the Period 1866-1898, Public." City Rec. 1:730 (Dec. 29, 1898.) 97
——. "Dover Street Bath House." City Rec. 1:594 (Oct. 20, 1898.) 98
——. "Public Playgrounds and Baths in Boston." Engng. Rec. 38:331 (Sept. 17, 1898.) 99
"Board of Estimate and Apportionment." Ann. Am. Acad. Pol. Sci. 11:423 (May, 1898.) 100
"Building Department of Boston, Mass., The." Engng. Rec. 40:119 (July 8, 1899.) 1
——. "Abstract and Discussion of Building Laws of Boston and New York." Am. Arch. Nov. 21, 1892, p. 97. Engng. Rec. Aug. 6, 1892, p. 159. 2
——. "Height of Buildings at Copley Square." City Rec. 2:713 (Nov. 2, 1899); Mun. Aff. 3:720 (Dec., 1899.) 3
——. "Limitation of Heights of Buildings." An. Am. Acad. Pol. Sci. 14:139 (July, 1899.) 4
"Burial Places of Boston and Vicinity, Historical." Merriam, John M. Proc. Am. Antiquarian Society n. s. 7:381-417 (Oct., 1891.) 5
"Business Men in Civic Service." Brooks, R. C. Mun. Aff. 1:491 (1897.) 6
——. "Municipal Representation of Business Organizations." Boston, Pamphlet reprinted by Rockwell and Churchill, from N. Y. Evening Post of Jan. 8, 1897. 10 pp. 7
Charities of Boston. Cole, William I. New Eng. M. 18:233 (April, 1898); Wines, Frederick H. Char. R. 6:41 (March, 1897.) 8
——. "Directory of the Charitable and Beneficent Organizations of Boston." Boston, Damrell & Upham, 1899. 12mo, 475 pp. Cloth, $1. 9
——. "The Public Charitable Institutions of Boston." Cole, Wm. I. A series in the New England Magazine, 1897-99. 10
——. "Relief of Poor in Boston." Lend a H. 5:696 (1890), 12:368 (1894.) 11
——. "A Study of Beggars and Their Lodgings." Sanborn, Alvan F. South End House Bulletin, No. VII, 1895. 12
——. (See also under Schools, Settlements, Women's Work below.)
"Concerts, Municipal." Baxter, Sylvester. Ann. Am. Acad. Pol. Sci. 13:125 (Jan., 1899.) 13
Conduits. "History of the Solution of the Wire Problem in Boston." Brophy, William. City Govt. 5:26 (July, 1898); anon. Mchts. Assoc. Rev. Vol. III. No. 31, p. 3 (March, 1899); Elec. W. & E. 31:224 (Aug. 12, 1899.) 14
——. "Municipal Wiring a Failure in Boston." Adams, Alton D. Elec. W. & E. 35:365 (March 10, 1900); Prog. Age 18:171 (April 16, 1900.) 15
"Department Store in the East, The. Confusion from Cheapness in Boston." Wright, John Livingston. Arena 22:165 (Aug. 1899.) 16
Direct Employment. (See under Labor below.)
"Drainage of Greater Boston, The." Twelvetrees, W. N. Surveyor 17:644 (June 15, 1900.) 17
"East Boston Tunnel." City Rec. 3:205 (April 5, 1900.) 18

Boston, Mass.—*Continued.*

Elevated Railway. (See under Transit Facilities below.)

"Finances of Boston, City." City Rec. 3:158, 173 (March 15, 22, 1900). (See also No. 89 above.) 19

"Fire Department and What It Consists of, The Boston." Grady, John. Fire & W. 24:323 (Sept. 24, 1898.) 20

Foreign Element. "Italian Immigrants in Boston." Bushée, Frederick A. South End House Bulletin No. X, 1897, Arena 17:722 (April, 1897.) 21

Garbage Disposal. "Utilization of City Refuse in Boston, Mass." Engng. Rec. 39:277 (Feb. 25, 1899.) 22

"Harbor Defects, Boston's." Seaboard (New York) June 3, 1897.

"Higher Life of Boston." Hale, E. E. Outlook 53:554 (1896.) 23

"History of Boston, Mass." Higginson, Thomas Wentworth and Hale, Edward Everett. See 1-4a; anon. Census. See 1-7. 24

——. "History of Boston, 1630-1880, Memorial." Winsor, Justin. Boston, Osgood, 1881. 4 Vols. $25. (The fourth volume covers the history of Boston during the nineteenth century.) 25

——. "Historic Towns—Boston." Lodge, Henry Cabot. London and New York, Longmans, G. & Co. (Historic Town Series) 1892. 242 pp. $1.25. 26

——. "The Story of Boston." Whiting, Lillian. St. Ry. Rev. 8:513 (Aug., 1898); anon. St. Ry. Rev. 8:500 (Aug., 1898.) 27

——. (See also Burial Places above.)

Housing. "The Anatomy of a Tenement Street." Sanborn, Alvan F. South End House Bulletin No. VI (1895), Forum 18:554 (1895.) 28

——. "Civilization's Inferno, Studies in the Social Cellar." Flower, B. O. Boston, Arena Co., 1893. 237 pp. $1. 29

——. "Moody's Lodging House, and Other Tenement Sketches." Sanborn, Alvan F. Boston, Copeland & Day, 1896. 30

——. "Model Lodging Houses in Boston." Norton, C. E. Atlan. 5:673 (1860.) 31

——. "Some Slums in Boston." Estabrook, Harold Kelsey. Boston, Twentieth Century Club, 1898. 23 pp. Pamphlet. See also Char. R. 8:242 (July, 1898.) 32

——. "Tenement House Census of Boston." Wadlin, H. G. Report of the Mass. Bureau of Labor Statistics, 1891 and 1892. Comment on the above, Tunis, J. Lend a H. 12:56 (1894.) 33

——. "Tenement House Districts of Boston, Report on a Sanitary Inspection of." Porter, Dwight. Boston, Rockwell & Churchill, prs., 1889. 76 pp. 34

——. "Tenement House Life in Boston." Swaffield, Walter J. Arena 9:668 (1894); anon. Mass. Labor Bulletin No. 11, p. 75 (July, 1899.) 35

——. "A Study of Boston's Tenement Houses." Flower, B. O. Arena 4:37 (1891.) 36

"If Jesus Came to Boston." Hale, E. E. New Eng. M. 11:402 (1894.) 37

Italian Immigrants in Boston. (See Foreign Element above.)

Labor and the Municipality. "Public Work. A Boston Argument in Favor of Direct Municipal Employment." Baxter, Sylvester. R. of Rs. 15:435 (April, 1897.) 38

Lectures. "Free Municipal Lectures in 1899." City Rec. 2:417 (June 1, 1899.) 39

"Legislative Interference." Baxter, Sylvester. Ann. Am. Acad. Pol. Sci. 14:142 (July, 1899.) 40

Library, Boston Public. Baxter, Sylvester. Hrprs. Wkly. 38:903 (1894); Sullivan, T. R. Scrib. M. 19:83 (1896); Swift, Lindsay. City Govt. 1:6 (1896); Wilson, Philip W. Temple Magazine Aug, 1899; anon. Hrps. Wkly. 39:251 (1895.) 41

Lighting. "Gas Supply of Boston, The." Gray, John H. Q. J. Econ. 12:419 (July, 1898), 13:15 (Oct., 1898), 13:292 (April, 1899), 14:87 (Nov., 1899); anon. J. Gas Light 76:82, 149, 213, 274 (July 10-31, 1894.) 42

——. "Boston's Big Gas Project." Am. Mfr. & Ir. Wld. 61:625 (Oct. 29, 1897.) 43

——. "Boston's Gas Atmosphere Cleared." (Editorial.) Prog. Age 15:595 (Dec. 15, 1897.) 44

——. "Gas Street Lighting in Boston." City Govt. 7:19 (July, 1899.) 45

——. "Public Lighting Contract." Quincy, Josiah. City Rec. 1:505 (Sept. 1, 1898); anon. Engng. Rec. 38:375 (Oct. 1, 1898.) 46

——. "A Municipal Failure in Boston." City Govt. 8:119 (May, 1900.) 47

Lodging Houses. (See under Housing above.)

Boston, Mass.—*Continued.*

"Markets of Boston." Lincoln, (Mrs.) Mary J. Chaut. Dec. 1896. 48

Mayoralty. "Administration of Mayor Quincy. A Progressive Administration." City Govt. 2:101 (April, 1897.) 49

———. "Mayor Quincy of Boston." Hooker, George E. Am. Mo. R. of Rs. 19:575 (May, 1899.) 50

"Municipal League of Boston." Capen, Samuel B. Address, Boston Transcript, Feb. 23, 1894. Same subject, Am. J. Pol. 5:1 (1894.) 51

Municipal Control, Ownership, Etc. "An Insolvent Utopia." Copeland, Guild A. Hrprs. Wkly. 44:549 (June 16, 1900.) 52

———. "City Ownership in Boston." Quincy, Josiah. Cal. Mun. 1:136 (Dec., 1899.) 53

———. "Municipal Socialism in Boston." Douglas, Francis T. Arena 20:545 (Nov.-Dec., 1898.) 54

———. (See also under Printing Plant below.)

"Organ Recitals in Boston, Free Public." Cole, Wm. I. Am. M. R. of Rs. 16:579 (Nov., 1897.) 55

Parks, Parkways, Etc. "Architectural Features of the Boston Parks." Baxter, Sylvester. Am. Arch. July 16, 1898. 56

———. "Metropolitan Park Commission." Ann. Am. Acad. Pol. Sci. 14:138 (July, 1899).

———. "Metropolitan Park Movement." Baxter, Sylvester. Garden & F. 5:62, 421 (1892.) 57

———. "Neighborhool Pleasure Grounds in Boston." Olmsted, F. L., Jr. Hrprs. Wkly. 41:1290 (Dec. 25, 1897.) 58

———. "Park System of Boston." Baxter Sylvester. Garden & F. 7:23 (1894), Cent. 54:952 (Oct., 1897); Eliot, Chas. New Eng. M. Sept., 1896; Pierce, William T. Park and Outdoor Art Assoc. p. 63, 1897; Pullen, Clarence. Hrprs. Wkly. 34:44 (1890); anon. Garden & F. 6:61 (1893), 8:171 (1895), 10:241 (1897); Engng. Rec. 40:618 (Dec. 2, 1899.) 59

———. "Playgrounds in Boston." City Rec. 1:357 (June 9, 1898.) 60

———. "Report of the Board of Metropolitan Park Commissioners." Charles Francis Adams, Philip A. Chase and William B. de las Casas. House Doc. No. 150, Jan., 1893. 147 pp. 61

———. "Topographical Surveys of Metropolitan Park Reservations of Massachusetts." Bryant, Henry F. J. Assoc. Engng. Soc. 18:252 (April, 1897.) 62

———. "Vegetation and Scenery in the Metropolitan Reservations of Boston." Eliot, Charles. Boston, Lamson, Wolffe & Co., 1898. 8vo, 80 pp. 63

"Pavements in Boston." Engng. News, May 12, 1892. 64

"Penal Institutions. Boston's." Cole, William I. New Eng. M. 17:613 (Jan. 1898.) 65

Play Grounds. (See under Parks above.)

"Population of Boston, Growth of the." Bushée, Frederick A. Am. Statis. Assoc. 6:239 (June, 1899.) (See also under Vital Statistics below.) 66

"Printing Plant, Boston's Municipal." Whalen, Thomas A. City Govt. 8:88 (April, 1900.) 67

———. "Municipal Printing in Boston." Chase, Harvey S. Mun. Aff. 4:774 (Dec., 1900.) 68

"Public Convenience Station, Boston Common." City Rec. 2:720 (Nov. 2, 1899.)

"Public Works, Municipal Government of Boston, with Especial Reference to." Jackson, Wm. J. Assoc. Engng. Soc. March, 1892, p. 123. 69

———. "Boston, Public Work in 1899." Mun. Engng. 19:381 (Dec., 1900.) 70

Quincy, Mayor. (See under Mayoralty above.)

Rapid Transit. (See under Transit Facilities below.)

"Real Estate Values in Boston." Whitmore, Henry. Am. Statis. Assoc. 5:1 (1896.) 71

Sanitation. "Health of Boston and Philadelphia." Billings, John S. Forum 17:595 (1894.) 72

"Schools in Boston, Public." Rice, J. M. Forum 14:753 (1893.) 73

———. "The Boston Schools: A Sanitary Investigation." Pearmain, Alice Upton. Mun. Aff. 2:497 (Sept., 1898); Domestic Engineering, June, 1896. 74

———. "A Study of Boston Evening Schools." Clark, William A. South End House Bulletin No. VIII, 1896. 75

———. "Table Showing the Distribution of Pupils in the Public Schools in Respect

MUNICIPAL AFFAIRS.

Boston, Mass.—*Continued.*

both to Age and to Grades, Jan. 3, 1899." City Rec. 2:297 (April 20, 1899.) 76
Settlements—College, Social and University. "Andover House Association." Woods, Robert A. Andover R. Jan., 1892. 77
———. "Ben Adhem House, Work of." Manning, Helen L. Journal of Practical Metaphysics, Boston, Nov., 1896. 78
———. "City Wilderness: A Settlement Study by Residents and Associates of the South End House, Boston." Woods, R. A., Editor. Boston, Houghton, Mifflin & Co., 1898. 12mo, 311 pp. Maps and plans. 79
———. Denison House. (See no. 80 below.)
———. South End House, Formerly Called Andover House, Articles on. Cole, W. I. New Eng. M. July, 1896; Tucker, Wm. J. Scrib. M. 13:357 (March, 1893); Woods, Robert A. Lend a H. 11:183 (1893), Char. R. 2:160 (1893); anon. Lend a H. 16:142 (Feb., 1896.) 79a
———. "Women's Work in Boston Settlements." (Denison House.) Dudley, Helena S. Mun. Aff. 2:493 (Sept., 1898.) 80
"Sewerage System, The Boston Main Drainage." Clarke, Eliot C. Engng. News, May 8, 1880, p. 159. 81
———. "The End of the Boston Sewer Assessment System." Engng. News 40:229 (Oct. 13, 1898); Engng. Rec. 39:585 (May 27, 1899.) 82
———. "Handling Boston's Sewage." Young, Henry G. Boston J. of Commerce, March 27, 1897. 83
———. "The Moon Island Sewage Reservoir, Boston." Engng. Rec. 40:530 (Nov. 4, 1899.) 84
———. Metropolitan Sewage Board. (See Sewage under **Massachusetts.**)
———. "New Law Regarding Sewage Works in Boston." City Rec. 1:547 (Sept. 29, 1898.) 85
———. "The New Massachusetts Metropolitan Sewerage Project." (Editorial.) Engng. Rec. 39:345 (March 13, 1899.) 86
———. "Studies for a High Level Gravity Sewer for Boston and Vicinity." Engng. News 41:166 (March 16, 1899.) 87
Slums. (See under Housing above.)
———. "Vital Statistics of Boston and Philadelphia, covering a period of six years, ending May 31, 1890." Billings, John S. Washington, Government Printing Office, 1895. 269 pp. Eleventh Census of the United States. 88
Statistics. "Boston's Department of Municipal Statistics." Minot, Lawrence. Pro. Indianapolis Conf. p. 254, 1898. See 6-18e. 89
"Street Cleaning in Boston, Cost and Methods of." J. Assoc. Engng. Soc., Aug., 1892, p. 433. 90
"Street Department, Report of the." City Rec. 1:673 (Dec. 1, 1898.) 91
Street Railways. (See under Transit Facilities below.)
"Street Work in Boston." Wood, Henry B. and others. J. Assoc. Engng. Soc. 11:427 (1892.) 92
Subway, Boston. (See under Transit Facilities below.)
"Sweating in Boston." p. 97 et seq. "Report of the Committee of Manufacturers on Sweating." H. R. Report No. 2309, 1893. John DeWitt Warner, chairman. 93
———. "Tenement House Workers in Boston." Hicks, W. L. Am. J. Soc. Sci. 30:103 (1894.) 94
Tenement Houses in Boston. (See under Sweating, Housing above.)
Transit Facilities. "The Erection of the Boston Elevated Railway." Fowler, Charles Evan. Engng. News 43:179 (March 15, 1900.) 95
———. "Cost of Boston Elevated Street Railways, Estimated." Railroad Gaz. 29:537 (July 30, 1897.) 96
———. "The Boston Elevated Railroad." (Important features of the new franchise.) Railroad Gaz. 29:472 (July 2, 1897), 29:517 (July 23, 1897.) 97
———. "The Elevated Structure of the Boston Elevated Railway." Engng. Rec. 41:245 (March 17, 1900.) 98
———. "Proposed Route of the Boston Elevated Railway." Engng. News 39:263 (April 21, 1898.) 99
———. "The System of the Boston Elevated Railway Company." Fairchild, C. B. St. Ry. R. 10:121 (March 15, 1900), 10:185 (April 15, 1900), 10:246 (May 15, 1900.) 100
———. "The Boston Elevated Railroad." Railroad Gaz. 30:291 (April 22, 1898);

Boston, Mass.—*Continued.*

St. Ry. Rev. 8:525 (Aug., 1898); St. Ry. Jour. 14:501 (Sept., 1898); Engng. News 41:303 (May 11, 1899.) 1

———. "Rapid Transit, Boston." Manley, Henry. J. Assoc. Engng. Soc. 8:280 (1889.) 2

———. "Report of the Rapid Transit Commission to the Massachusetts Legislature, April 5, 1892." Rice, Geo. S., Chief Engineer. 3

———. "Street Railway Consolidation." Baxter, Sylvester. Ann. Am. Acad. Pol. Sci. 11:119 (Jan., 1898.) 4

———. "Street Railway Lines." Rowe, Leo S. Ann. Am. Acad. Pol. Sci. 11:142 (March, 1898.) 5

———. Street Railway System, Conditions and Financial Results in Metropolitan Boston. St. Ry. Jour. April, 1895, 14:268, 471 (May-Sept., 1898.) 6

———. Subway, Boston. Beal, B. L. Mun. Aff. 4:219 (March, 1900); Kleinschmidt, F. City Govt. 1:72 (1896); Stewart, Jane A. Chaut. 28:568 (March, 1899); Talbot, J. E. Elec. World 30:295 (Sept. 11, 1897); Varney, Geo. J. Nat. M. 12:272 (July, 1900); Wright, John Livingston. Self-Cult. 9:439 (June, 1899); Public Improvements 1:120 (Aug. 1, 1899); anon. Engng. Rec. Jan. 23, 1897, 39:210 (Feb. 4, 1899); Engng. News 37:76 (Feb. 4, 1897); 39:74 (Feb. 3, 1898); Elec. R. 31:274 (Dec. 8, 1897); St. Ry. Rev. 85:544 (Aug., 1898); St. Ry. Jour. 14:493 (Sept., 1898); Ann. Am. Acad. Pol. Sci. 12:445 (Nov., 1898); Elec. World 33:165 (Feb. 11, 1899); City Rec. 2:293 (April 20, 1899.) 7

———. "The Completion of the Boston Subway and New Arrangements of Street Cars." Railroad Gaz. 30:759 (Oct. 21, 1898.) 8

———. "Erfolge und Erfahrungen mit der Bostoner Unterflasterbahn." v. Emperger, Fritz. Zeitschr. Oesterr. Ing. u. Arch. Ver. Oct. 5, 1900. 9

———. "Lease of the Boston Subway." Railroad Gaz. March 5, 1897. 10

———. "Opening of the Boston Subway." Hrprs. Wkly. 41:934 (Sept. 18, 1897.) 11

———. "Roof Shield in the Boston Subway, The." (Technical Description.) Railroad Gaz. Feb. 12, 1897. 12

"Unemployed, Boston's." Estes, Edith Perry. Hrprs. Wkly. 38:197 (1894.) 13

———. "The Unemployed in Boston." South End House Bulletin No. II. By residents and associates of the House, 1894. 14

Vital Statistics. (See under Statistics above.)

Water Supply. "The Chestnut Hill Pumping Station of the Metropolitan Water Works." Flinn, Alfred D. Engng. Rec. 42:345 (Oct. 13, 1900), 42:367 (Oct. 20, 1900), 42:390 (Oct. 27, 1900.) 15

———. "The Clinton, Mass. Dam." Fire and W. Dec. 12, 1896. 16

———. "Ice Water Fountains, Boston's." Fahey, J. H. Public Imp. 2:242 (April 2, 1900.) 17

———. "Nashua Aqueduct." Engng. News 37:114 (Feb. 25, 1897.) 18

———. Reservoirs. "Greater Boston's New Reservoir." Bemis, Charles H. Hrprs. Wkly. Jan. 16, 1897; Reservoir No. 5, Engng. News 37:130 (March 4, 1897); Wachusett Reservoir, Engng. Rec. 41:50 (Jan. 20, 1900.) 19

———. "Salt Water Pipe System of Boston." City Govt. 6:45 (March, 1899.) 20

———. "The Wachusett Dam for the Metropolitan Water Supply, Boston, Mass." Flinn, Alfred D. Engng. News 44:174 (Sept. 13, 1900); anon. Engng. Rec. 42:218, 242 (Sept. 8, 15, 1900.) 21

———. Metropolitan Water Supply. Noyes, Albert F. Jour. New Eng. Water Works Assoc. 10:117 (1895); Osgood, Fletcher. New Eng. M. June, 1896; anon. Engng. Rec. March 2, 1895, Engng. News March 7, 1895, Fire and W. Dec. 25, 1897. 22

———. "Report of the Massachusetts State Board of Health upon a Metropolitan Water Supply." Numerous maps and plans. 232 pp. Feb., 1895. 23

———. Water Works, Metropolitan. Stewart, A. J. Sci. Am. Nov. 4, 1899; anon. J. Assoc. Eng. Soc. 18:207 (April, 1897); Engng. Rec. 37:314 (March 12, 1898), 39:585 (May 27, 1899.) 24

———. (See under Water Supplies, **Massachusetts**.)

Women's Work. "Some Ways of Benefiting a City." Lincoln, Alice N. Mun. Aff. 2:483 (Sept., 1898.) 25

Bradford, Eng.

"Advance, Bradford!" Mun. J. & London 9:1 (Jan. 5, 1900).   26

"Garbage Cremation at Bradford, England." McTaggart, John. Engng. Rec. 42:297 (Sept. 29, 1900).   27

——. Spl. Cons. Rep. 17:13-221, 1899. (See **Consular Reports.**)

——. "The Disposal of House Refuse in Bradford." McTaggart, John. Elec. R. (Lond.) Sept. 14, 1900, Surveyor 18:312 (Sept. 14, 1900), San. Rec. 26:247 (Sept. 21, 1900), Engng. (Lond.) 70:383 (Sept. 21, 1900); pp. 23-30 in Pro. of the Assn. of Cleansing Superintendents of Great Britain, Sept. 6-9, 1899. Rochdale, James Clegg, 1900. 8vo. 63 pp.   28

"Housing Scheme, Bradford." Mun. J. & London 8:1201 (Nov. 3, 1899).   29

Lighting. "Bradford Corporation Electricity Supply," Porter, Robert. Jour. of Gas. Lgt. (Nov. 30, 1897).   30

Sewage Disposal, Bradford. Meeker, Claude. Cons. Rep. 47:173 (1895); another report in Cons. Rep. 17:13-221 (1899); Richardson, F. W. Engng. Rec. 42:544 (Dec. 8, 1900); anon. San. Rec. 26:289 (Oct. 5, 1900); Surveyor 18:467 (Oct. 19, 1900),   31

Transit Facilities. "Electric Tramways, Bradford Corporation." Elec. Eng. (London) Aug. 26, 1898; St. Ry. J. 14:532 (Sept. 1898); Ry. World 7:317 (Oct. 13, 1898).   32

"Water Works, The Bradford." Watson, James. Engng. (Lond.) 70:349 (Sept. 14, 1900).   33

Brandeis, Austria.

Housing. "Kolonistenhaüser des Kohlenwerks Brandeisl in Böhmen." Allg. Bauz. p. 86 (1856).   34

——. "Colonie Ouvrière des Mines de Houille de Brandeisl." Nouv. Annales de la Const. p. 25 (1870).   35

"**Brandon, Vermont.**" Kellogg, Augusta W. New Eng. M. 17:293 (1897). 36

Bremen, Germany.

Harbor Works. "Die Neuen Hafenanlagen in Bremen und Bremerhaven." Oesterr. Monatschr. f. d. Oeffent. Baudienst Nov. 1897.   37

History. "Geschichte d. Stadt Bremen." Bippen, Wilh. Bremen, C. E. Mueller, 1892. Bd. I, 293 pp. 1 m. 80 pf.   38

"Sewage Disposal, Bremen." Keenan, George. Cons. Rep. 47:77 (1895).   39

Brescia, Italy, The Municipal Palace at. "Vom Palazzo Municipale zu Brescia." Eicholz, P. Zeit. für Bildende Kunst 11:234 (July, 1900).   40

Breslau, Germany.

"Construction of Streets and Buildings in Breslau." Erdman, C. W. Cons. Rep. 61:390 (Nov. 1899).   41

"Electric Railways in Breslau." Erdman, C. W. Cons. Rep. 60:254 (June, 1899).   42

Garbage. Spl. Cons. Rep. 17:13-221. (See **Consular Reports.**)

Bridges.

See also Budapest, New York.

"Art in Modern Bridges." Schuyler, Montgomery. Cent. 40:12 (May, 1900).   43

"Artistic Side of Bridge Design, The." Engng. News 42:401 (Dec. 21, 1899).   44

"Bridges and Art." Warner, John De Witt. Public Improvements 2:97 (Jan. 1, 1900).   45

"Esthetic Design in European Bridges." Grimshaw, Robert. Engng News 37:371 (June 17, 1897).   46

Brighton, Eng.

"Brighton, Progress of." Mun. J. & London 3:611 (May 19, 1899).   47

"Baths at Brighton, Cottage." Mun. J. & London 8:805 (July 14, 1899).   48

"Brighton Municipal Tramways." Mun. J. 8:712 (June 16, 1899); 9:687 (Sept. 7, 1900).   49

"Brisbane, [Aus.], Tramway System of." Brown, S. Herbert. St. Ry. Jour. 14:528 (Sept. 1898).   50

Bristol, Eng.
"Bristol, The City of. A Glimpse of the Old and New Municipality." Mun. J. 9:121 (Feb. 16, 1900).   51
"Charities of Bristol, The." Sturge, Elizabeth. Char. Or. R. 3:233 (May, 1898).   52
——. "Condition of the Bristol Poor, Report of the Commissioners to Inquire into the." London, P. S. King & Son, 1884.   53
——. "La Misère en Angleterre—Condition du pauvre à Bristol." Raffalovich, A. Paris, Guillaumin et Cie, 1885. 1 fr.   54
History. "Bristol." Hunt, William. London, Longmans, 1887. Historic Towns Series. 8vo. 3s. 6d. (For other references on the history of Bristol see p. 176 of Gross' "Bibliography of British Municipal History.")   55
Transit Facilities. "Tramways, Bristol." Ry. World 7:89 (March, 1898), 8:85 (March 9, 1899); Ty. & Ry. 9:563 (Nov. 8, 1900).   56

Brockton, Mass. "Operation of the Sewage Filter Beds of Brockton, Mass., in 1896." (Report of F. Herbert Snow) Engng. News 37:307 (May 20, 1897); Felton, Charles R. Engng. News 43:213 (March 29, 1900).   57

"**Bromley [Eng.]**, Public Libraries." Brady, C. E. London 7:15 (Jan. 6, 1898).   58

"**Brookfield [Mo.]** Sewerage System." Garrett, R. P. Engng. Rec. 42:590 (Dec. 22, 1900).   59

Brookline, Mass.
"Bath House, Brookline's Model." Crosby, William B. Self-Cult. 9:314 (May, 1899); Stewart, J. A. Am. J. Sociol. 5:470 (Jan. 1900); anon. Eng. Rec. March 6, 1897.   60
"Brookline: A Model Town Under the Referendum." Flower, B. O. Arena 19:505 (April, 1898).   61

Brooklyn. (See under **New York City.**)

Brooklyn Idea of City Government. (Concentration of power in the hands of the Mayor. See under **Mayor.**)

Brünn, Austria.
Hospital. "Die Epidemie-Spital in Brünn." Gesund.-Ing. Feb. 28, 1897.   62
Statistics of Brünn. (See Statistics under **Austria.**)

Brussels.
Housing. "Tenement Houses in Brussels." Roosevelt, Geo. W. U. S. Consular Reports Vol xlviii., No. 178, p. 386-398.   63
Parks, etc. "Monuments and Parks of Brussels." Park & Cem. 8:74 (June, 1898).   64
Sanitation. "La Salubrité Publique à Bruxelles." d'Esmenard, E. R. Municipale 2:1596 (Sept. 30, 1899).   65
"Sewage Disposal, Brussels." Roosevelt, Geo. W. See 56-40a, 40b.   66
——. "Sewerage System of Brussels." Thompson, Gibson. Paving and Municipal Engineer, Nov. 1894.   67
——. "Etudes sur les Egouts de Londres, Bruxelles et de Paris." Tenier, Charles. Paris, Delahaye et Cie., 1897. 1 fr. 25 cts.   68
Streets. "L'Entretien de la Voie Publique à Bruxelles." R. Municipale 3:2099 (May 5, 1900).   69
Transit Facilities. "Brussels' Electric Tramways." Ry. World 7:88 (March, 1898).   70

Budapest.
"Budapest." Freson, J. G. Revue Generale (Brussels) May, 1897; Shaw, Albert. Cent. 22:163 (1892). See also his "Municipal Govt. in Continental Europe." pp. 435-468; Terhune, Everitt Bogert. National M. 11:655 (March, 1900).   71
Bridges. "Die Franz-Josefs-Brücke in Budapest." Zeitschr. d. Oesterr. Ing. u. Arch. Ver. Feb. 26, 1897; Engng. May 15, 1897.   72

Budapest.—*Continued.*

Sewerage. "Pumpmaschinen der Budapester allgemeinen Kanalisationwerke." Zeitschr. d. Ver. Deutscher Ing. Jan. 2, 1897; Mueller, O. N., Jr. Engng. News 38:280 (Nov. 4, 1897). 73

Transit Facilities. Crépy, P. Le Revue Technique Aug. 10, 1898; Dubsky, Alfred O. Cassier's 16:91 (June, 1899); Kollman, J. Electrician Nov. 6, 1896; anon. Transport (London) Jan. 29, 1897; Ry. World (London) April, 1897; Schw. Bauz, April 10, 17, 1897; St. Ry. Rev. 7:301 (May 15, 1897). 74

—— "Electric Street Railways of Budapest, an Object Lesson for American Cities." R. of Rs. 11:287 (1895). 75

Water Works. "Der Donautunnel des Wasserwerkes von Budapest." Deutsche Bauzeitung Oct. 24, 1896; Le Génie Civil July 31, 1897.

Buenos Ayres.

"The City of Buenos Ayres." Curtis, William Eleroy. Chaut. 29:249 (June, 1899); Public Improvements 1:146 (Aug. 15, 1899); Ebelot, A. Monde Moderne (Nov. 1897). 77

Housing. Workmen's Dwellings in Buenos Ayres. "Les Logement Ouvriers à Buenos Ayres." Gache, Samuel. Paris, Steinheil, 1900. 78

"Street Railway System of Buenos Ayres." St. Ry. J. 13:395 (July, 1897). 79

Buffalo, N. Y.

City Government, General Works and Unclassified.

"City of Buffalo." Shepard, F. J. New Eng. M. 14:237 (1893). 80

"Government of Buffalo with especial Reference to Public Works." Guthrie, E. B. J. Assoc. Engin. Soc. March, 1892, p. 123. 81

"Municipal Buffalo, or How a Model Municipality is Governed in the United States." M. & C. 4: Nos. 6, 7 and 8, 22 pp. (Aug. 1897).

"Municipal Condition of Buffalo." Loomis, Frank M. p. 344, Proc. Second Natl. Conf., 1895. See 6-18b. 82

"Well Governed Buffalo." Ralph, Julian. Hrprs. Wkly. 39:812 (1895). 83

"Bath House, Buffalo Free." Engng. Rec. Sept. 19, 1896. 84

"Building Operations, Statistics of, Buffalo, Rochester and Syracuse." B. Labor Stat. New York 1:170 (Dec. 1899). 85

——. "Building Ordinances of Buffalo, N. Y., Criticism of." Engng. Rec. July, 11, 1896. 86

Charities. "Outdoor Poor Relief in Buffalo." Richardson, A. C. Ann. Am. Acad. Pol. Sci. 14:275 (Sept. 1899). 87

"Garbage Disposal at Buffalo." Drake, M. M. City Govt. 7:150 (Dec. 1899). 88

"History of Buffalo, N. Y." Mahany, Rowland B. See 1-4b.

Lighting. "Electric Lighting Progress in Buffalo, N. Y." Elec. R. 31:75 (Aug. 18, 1897). 89

——. "The Sale of the Buffalo Gas Interests." (Editorial.) Prog. Age. 15:424 (Oct. 1, 1897). 90

"Park and Parkways on the South Side of Buffalo." Olmstead, Frederick Law. Buffalo. Pamphlet, 1888. 91

"Schools of Buffalo, Public." Rice, J. M. Forum 14:293 (1892). 92

Settlements. Westminster House, Articles on. Brush, E. H. Ind. 48:1001 (July 23, 1896); anon. Outlook Nov. 16, 1895, 56:420 (June 12, 1897), Commons (June, 1896). 92a

"Street Cleaning in Buffalo." Municipality and County, April, 1895. 93

"Street Paving in Buffalo." City Govt. 1:50 (1896); Guthrie, Edward B. Pro. Am. Soc. Mun. Imp. 5th yr., pt. II, p. 123 (Oct. 1898). 94

Transit Facilities. "Street Railways of Buffalo." St. Ry. Jour. Aug. 1894, Dec. 1896. 95

Water Works. Guthrie, Edward B. Engng. Rec. 38:362 (Sept. 24, 1898); Knapp, Louis H. J. N. E. W. W. Assoc 14:240 (March, 1900). 96

Building Laws. (See also **Architecture, Fires, Housing, Sanitation.**)

See also Berlin, Boston, Brooklyn, Buffalo, Chicago, Dresden, Edinburgh, England, France, Germany, Leipsic, Mainz, New York, Zurich.

"Building Departments and Building Materials." Arch. & Buil. 30:121 (April 22, 1899). 97

"Building Laws, Comparison of Municipal." Phillips, H. A. Am. Arch. 35:38 (1892), 39:26, 40:115 (1893). 98

——. "Die Wohnungsgesetzgebung." Kalle. Gegenwart 32:433 (1899). 99

——. "Comparative Municipal Building Laws." Am. Arch. 33:66, 150 (1891). 100

——. "The Enforcement of Building Laws." Arch. & Buil. 28:25 (Jan. 15, 1898). 1

——. "Need of Uniform Building Laws." Fryer, William J. Engng. M. 5:756 (1893). 2

——. "The Building Code as Influencing Municipal Improvements." Hill, Geo. Public Improvements 2:99 (Jan. 1, 1900). 3

——. "Building Regulations." Chapter VI, pp. 91-130 Eighth Special Report of the Commissioner of Labor on "The Housing of the Working People," by E. R. L. Gould. 4

——. Annotated Building Regulations. "Normale Bauordnung nebst Erläuterungen." Baumeister, R. Wiesbaden, 1880. 5

——. "Fire and Building Regulations in Foreign Countries." (Reports from 146 foreign countries and cities.) U. S. Spl. Consular Reports Vol. viii., 543 pp. (1892). 6

Building Reform in Cities. Schmidkunz. Oesterr. Monatschrf. d. Oeffent. Baudienst Feb. 1898. 7

"High Buildings." Himmelwright, A. L. A. No. Am. 163:580 (1896). 8

——. "Arguments for and against Tall Buildings." Huss, Geo. Martin and Ernest Flagg. Arch. & Builder, Jan. 18, 1896. 9

——. "High Building Bill, Discussion of the." Arch. & Buil. May 23, 1896. 10

——. "The High Buildings of the Ancients." Sci. Am. Sup. 46:18917 (Aug. 13, 1898); Arch. & Buil. 29:70, 87 (Aug. 27, Sept. 10, 1898). 11

——. "Against High Buildings." Fire and Water Dec. 5, 1896. 12

——. "High Buildings." (Objections presented in discussion before the New York Board of Trade). Fire and Water Dec. 26, 1896. 13

——. "Dangers from Tall Office Buildings." Goetz, Henry A. Engng. M. 2:792 (1892). 14

——. "Dangers of the Sky-Scrapers." (Chief Bonner's explanation of his opposition to high buildings.) Arch. and Buil. Dec. 12, 1896. 15

——. "A Defence of High Buildings." Blackall, C. H. Brick Builder, Feb. 1896. 16

——. "Different Interests Involved in the Sky-Scraper." (Editorial.) Arch. and Buil. 26:37 (Jan. 23, 1897). 17

——. "Electric Plant of the Modern Tall Building." Pattison, F. A. Engin. M. 13:782 (Aug. 1897). 18

——. "Elevators, High Buildings and Safe." Engng. News Nov. 26, 1896, Dec. 3, 1896. Quoted at length in the Sanitarian 38:44 (Jan. 1897). 19

——. "Tall Buildings and the Speed of Elevators." Hill, George. Engng. Rec. Feb. 6, 1897. 20

——. "Engineering Problems of Tall Buildings." Brown, C. O. Engin. M. 13:406 (June, 1897). 21

——. "Fire Risks on Tall Office Buildings." Atkinson, Edward. Engng. M. 3:149 (1892). (See also under **Fires.**) 22

——. "The Heights of Tall Buildings." Engng. Rec. 42:217 (Sept. 8, 1900). 23

——. "Limitations to Height of Buildings." Ball, Robt. S. Engng. T. July, 1899; Engng. Rec. Jan. 18, 1896; Real Estate Rec. & Guide, Jan. 16, 1892, p. 66, Feb. 1, 1896, p. 173; Feb. 22, 1896, p. 298; March 7, 1896, p. 383. 24

——. "Regulation of Tall Building Construction." (Regulations in force in Continental European Cities.) Engng. Rec. Jan. 2, 1897. 25

——. "Maisons Hautes en Angleterre et en Amerique." Calonne, Alphonse de. Rev. d. deux Mondes 122:855 (1894). 26

——. "The Modern Business Building." Steffens, J. L. Scrib. M. 22:37 (July, 1897). 27

Building Laws—*Continued.*

——. " The Modern Tall Building." Brainard, Owen. Chaut. 26:131 (Nov. 1897). 28
——. " Planning and Construction of High Office Buildings." Birkmire, William H. Arch. and Buil. 25:271; 26:27, 99, 135, 199, 259, 295; 27:39 (1896-97). 29
——. " How to Make High Buildings Safe." Clarke, Christopher. Fire and Water, Feb. 6, 1897. 30
——. " The Sky-Scraper up to Date." Schuyler, Montgomery. Arch. Rec. 8:231 (Jan.-March, 1899). 31
——. " Two Sky-Scrapers, and a Moral." Real Estate Rec. and Guide May 18, 1895, p. 824. 32
——. " The Tall Business Building." Adler, D. Cassier's M. July, 1897. 33
——. " Tall Office Buildings, Past and Future." Adler, Dankmar. Engng. M. 3:765 (1892). 34
——. " The Tall Building from an American Point of View." Hamlin, A. D. F. Engng. M. 14:436 (Dec. 1897). 35
——. " The American Tall Building from a European Point of View." Capper, S. H. Engng. M. 14:239 (Nov. 1897). 36
——. " Weighing of Tall Buildings." Waters, Theodore. Southern Architect (Atlanta.) May, 1897. 37
" Inspection of Buildings." Franklin, Benjamin. Pro. Eng. Club, Phila. 15:77 (March, 1898). 38
——. " How Can Better Inspection of Buildings Be Secured?" Engng. News Oct. 1 1896. 39
——. " Police des Constructions, etc." Lukomski, T., Périn, J. Paris, 1869. 40
——. Baupolizei. Loening, Edgar. Vol. II. pp. 515-531 Conrad, 2d ed. 1898. See 2-10. 41
" Municipal Control of Buildings, The." Longstaff, G. B. Builder, Nov. 30, 1895. 42
" Paris Fire and the Building of Temporary Structures, The." Statham, H. Heathcote. Engin. M. 13:504 (July, 1897). 43
" Public Squares, Buildings on. Attorney-General v. Williams et al." Mun. Aff. 3:720 (Dec. 1899). 44
" Restraints upon the Practice of Architecture." Robinson, John Beverly. Engng. M. 11:307 (1896). (See also under **Architecture.**) 45
Sky-Scrapers. (See High Buildings above.)
" Theatern, Circusgebäuden und öffentlichen Versammlungsraümen, Polizeiverordnung betreffend die bauliche Anlage und die innere Einrichtung von." Berlin, Carl Heymann, 1891. 44 pp. 46

Bulgaria, Local and Municipal Government in. Demombynes Vol. I. pp. 783-795. See 2-11. 47

Burial in Cities, Cemeteries, Cremation, Etc.

See also Derlin, Boston, Camden (N. J.), Coventry (Eng.), France, Germany, Italy, London, Milan, New York, Paris, San Mateo (Cal.), United Kingdom, Zürich.
Burial. "Sanitary Mausoleum Company's System." J. Frankl. Inst. 129:306 (1889). 48
——. " Die Bestattung der Todten in Bezug auf Hygiene, geschichtliche Entwickelung u. gesetz. Bestimmungen bet." Wernher, Adf. Giessen, Ricker, 1880. 2m. 49
——. " Beerdigungswesen." Rahts, C. Vol. II, pp. 538-544 Conrad; 2d ed. 1898. See 2-10. 50
——. " Cemeteries." Garden & F. 5:231, 242, 253, 301 (1892). 51
——. " God's Acre Beautiful or the Cemeteries of the Future." Robinson, W. L. London, Garden Off. 1883. 8vo. 7s. 6d. 51a
——. " Graveyards as a Menace to the Commonweal." Windmüller, L. No. Am. 167:211 (Aug. 1898). 52
——. " La Question des Cemetières. Etude sur les sources, sur la jurisprudence." Ashman, Henri, et van den Heuvel, Jules. Bruxelles, Larcier, 1897. 8vo. 2 fr. 53
——. " The Modern Cemetery." Farmar, A. Overland n. s. 29:440 (April, 1897). 54
Cremation. Cameron, G. Scot. R. 10:1 (1887); Chadwick, J. W. Forum 1:272 (1886); Cobb, A. G. No. Amer. 135:266 (1882); Coxe, A. C. Forum 1:64 (1886);

BIBLIOGRAPHY.

Burial in Cities, Cemeteries, Cremation, etc.—*Continued.*
Gordon Cumming, C. F. Contemp. 43:858 ((1882); Gould, S. B. Chambs. J. 69:428 (1892); Miller, O. T. Pop. Sci. Mo. 37:763 (1890); Newman, A. S. Westm. 139:654 (1892), Ecl. M. 121:130 (1893); Thompson, H. 19th Cent. 23:1 (1887). 55

——. Cremation. Pp. 396-399 Encyc. Soc. Ref. See 1-3.

——. "Christianity, Cremation and." Mancini, I. Dub. R. 106:384 (1889); Bigelow, A. G. No. Am. 143:353 (1886); Shinn, G. W. Church R. 47:73 (1885). 56

——. "Crematories." Am. Arch. 12:22 (1890), Current Literature 24:494 (Oct. 1900). 57

——. "Crime, Cremation as an Incentive to." Horden, F. S. J. Soc. Arts. 41:21 (1893). 58

——. "Desirability of Cremation for Infected Bodies." Smith, J. H. Arena 15:603 (1895). 59

——. "Hygiène, Inhumation, Crémation ou Incineration des Corps." Cadet, A. Paris, Germer, Bailliere et Cie., 1881. 12mo. 2 fr. 60

——. "Incineration of the Dead." Holmes, Howard M. Modern Crematist, July, August, 1887. Also printed separately in pamphlet form. 11 pp. 61

——. "La Crémation et ses bienfaits." Bonneau, Alex. Paris, Dentu, 1886. 12mo. 3 fr. 62

——. "La Crémation devant l'Histoire la Science et le Christianisme." de Hornstein, Edouard. Paris. Dentu, 1886. 8vo. 6 fr. 63

——. "La Crémation, Histoire, Hygiéne Technique." Reber, B. Geneva, Burkhard, 1888. 8vo. 1 fr. 50c. 64

——. "Les cimetières et la crémation, étude historique et critique." Martin, F. Paris, J. B. Bailliere et fils. 1881. 8vo. 5 fr. 65

——. "L'Incineration aux points de vue hygienique et historique." Golde (Mlle.) Paris, Maloine, 1896. 4to. 3 fr. 66

——. "Modern Cremation: its History and Practice." Thompson, H. pp. 108-136, Vol. vi, Woods, Medical and Surgical Monographs. New York, William Wood & Co., 1890. 67

——. "Opinions on Cremation." (Letters from one hundred prominent persons.) New York. Collected and published by the United States Cremation Company, Limited, 1889. Pamphlet. 55 pp. 68

——. "Ueber Feuerbestattung." (Diagrams, bibliography of French and German works). Goppelsroeder, Friedrich. Mülhausen, Wenz & Peters, 1890. Pamphlet. 108 pp. 69

Burlington [Iowa], The New Sewer Outfall at." Mun. Engng. 19:267 (Oct. 1900). 70

Bury, Eng.
"Housing Problem at Bury." San. Rec. 26:202 (Sept. 7, 1900). 71
"Sewerage and Sewage Disposal at Bury." Surveyor 18:648 (Dec. 7, 1900). 72

Business Men in Municipal Government, Business Theory of City Government. (See under **City Government, General Works and Unclassified.** 2-23, et seq).

"**Cairo, Egypt,** Electric Street Railroads in." Elec. World 32:716 (Dec. 31, 1898); Ry. World 8.245 (July 6, 1899). 73

Caisses d'Epargne. (Municipal Savings Banks. See under **Savings Banks.**)

Calbe [Ger.] Water Works. "Das Wasserwerk der Stadt Calbe." Zeitschr d. Ver. Deut. Ing. (Berlin) March 13, 1897. 74

Calcutta [India] Drainage Scheme. Indian Engineering (Calcutta). Jan. 28, 1897. 75

California.
"Conditions in California, Municipal." Phelan, James D. Arena 17:989 (June, 1897). 76
"Department Store in the West: 'America's Grandest' in California." Carlin, Eva V. Arena 22:330 (Sept. 1899). 77

California—*Continued.*

Elections. "Primary in California, The." Nye, A. B. Nation 34:74 (Jan. 26, 1882). 78
——."California Primary System." Stratton, F. S. N. Y. Conference on Practical Reform of Primary Elections, p. 137. Chicago, Hollister, 1898. 8vo, 150 pp. Paper. 79
Finance. "Municipal Indebtedness." Mason, H. W. City Govt. 8:135 (May, 1900); Cal. Mun. 2:161 (June, 1900). 80
——."General Property Tax in California." Plehn, Carl C. Publications of the American Economic Association. Economic Studies. Vol. II. No. 3. New York, Macmillan, 1897. 198 pp. 50 cts. 81
——."Mortgage Tax, the California." Plehn, Carl C. Ind. 50:143 (Feb. 3, 1898). 81a
——."Uniform Municipal Accounting, Report of the Committee on." Breed, A. H. Cal. Mun. 3:145 (Dec. 1900). 82
"Laws, The Work of the Code Commission in Relation to Municipal." Bulla, John N. Cal. Mun. 1:70 (Oct. 1899). 82a
"League of California Municipalities, The." Phelan, James D. Cal. Mun. 1:3 (Aug. 1899). 83
"Local Improvements within Municipalities, Proposed Act to Provide for." Cal. Mun. 3:108 (Nov. 1900). 84
"Water Works, Experience of [California] Cities with Municipal." Cal. Mun. 1:211 (Feb. 1900). 85

"**Calumet [Mich.]**, A Unique Municipality." Curtis, William Eleroy. Chaut. 29:33 (April, 1899). 86

Camberwell. (See under **London.**)

Cambridge, Eng.

History. "Township and Borough." (Early History of Cambridge.) Maitland, Frederic William. Cambridge, University Press, 1898. 8vo, 220 pp. Cl. 10s. 87
Lighting. "Electricity Supply Works." Elec. Eng. (Lond.) 25:42 (Jan. 12, 1900). 88
"Sanitary Engineering Refuse Disposal Plant at Cambridge, Eng." Fuertes, James H. Eng. Rec. March 20, 1897, Engng. Rec. 38:290 (Sept. 3, 1898). 89

Cambridge, Mass.

Description and Statistics of Cambridge, Mass., in 1880. Census. See 1-7.
"History of Cambridge, Mass." Eliot, Samuel A. See 1-4a; also anon. Census. See 1-7.
Liquor Problem. "A City without Saloons." Foxcroft, Frank. Ind. 49:635 (May 20, 1897). 90
"Non-Partisan City Government, A." Douglas, Francis J. Outlook 58:963 (April 16, 1898). 91
——."Non-Partisan Municipal Elections: Work of the Library Hall Association, Cambridge, Mass." Wright, Geo. G. Mun. Aff. 4:363 (June, 1900). 92
Parks. "A Feature of Park Development in Cambridge, Mass." Park & Cem. 7:266 (Feb. 1898); Park & Cem. 10:29 (April, 1900). 93
"Record of the City Government, 1898." Library Hall Ass'n, Cambridge. Cambridge, Mass., Library Hall, 1898. 8vo, 43 pp. Pamphlet. 94
Settlements. "Prospect Union at Harvard." Berry, Louis F. Outlook 63:691 (Nov. 18, 1899). 94a
"Water Works of Cambridge, Mass." Hastings, L. M. J. New Eng. Water Works Assoc. Dec. 1896; Fire & W. March 20, 1897, 22:434 (Dec. 4, 1897). 95

Camden, N. J.

Cemeteries. "Camden, N. J., Harleigh Cemetery." Park & Cem. 7:138 (Aug. 1897). 96
"Water Works of Camden, N. J." Fire & W. 22:300 (Aug. 21, 1897); Engng. Rec. 39:520 (May 6, 1899); Engng. News 41:297 (May 11, 1899). 97

Canada.

Finance. Local Indebtedness in Canada, Part III. "Public Debts in Canada." Perry, J. Roy. Toronto, University of Toronto Studies: Economic Series No. 1, 1898. 8vo, 88 pp. Paper, 50 cts. 98
———."A Provincial Municipal Auditor." Municipal World 7:67 (April, 1897).
"Local Government in Canada." Bellot, H. H. L. Westm. 140:281 (1893); Bourinot, J. G. J. H. Univ. Studies V: 5 and 6 (1887), 50 cts.; Wickett, S. M. Pol. Sci. Q. 15:240 (June, 1900). 99
"Municipal Amendment Act, The." Mun. World 7:116 (June, 1897). 100
Sewage Disposal. See 56-40b.
"Telephone Service in Canada." Bittinger, John L., and Sewell, William L. Cons. Rep. 50:341 (June, 1899). 1
"Water Works Expropriations in Canada." Chipman, Willis. Toronto, Canada, 1899. 8vo, 10 pp. 2

"**Canterbury [Eng.]** as a Civic Center." Mun. J. & London 8:1261 (Nov. 24, 1899). 3

"**Canton, O.**, Sewage Disposal Works at." Chapin, L. E. J. Assoc. Engin. Soc. 13:115 (1894); Engin. News, June 1, 1893, pp. 520, June 10, 1893, pp. 27, July 20, 1893, pp. 60, Sept. 14, 1893, pp. 217. 4

Cape Cod Towns.

"History of Cape Cod Towns." Bates, Katherine Lee. See 1-4a. 4a
"Town Government on Cape Cod." Hart, A. B. Nation 56:343 (1893). 5

Cape Town.

"Local Government, Cape Town." Mun. J. & London 8:1070 (Sept. 29, 1899); Mun. J. & London 9:137 (Feb. 23, 1900). 6
"Sanitary Works in Cape Town." Cowie, Alexander. San. J. 4:612 (Feb. 1898). 7

Cardiff, Wales.

"Architecture of Cardiff, Wales." Builder March 13, 1897. 8
"Sewage Disposal and Sewage Farm, Cardiff." Howells, Anthony. See 56-40a. 9
Transit Facilities. "Tramway Traction." Surveyor 17:452 (April 27, 1900); 17:476 (May 4, 1900); 17:510 (May 11, 1900); Mun. J. 9:262 (April 6, 1900). 10
"Water Filtration at Cardiff Wales." Engng. Rec. 38:94 (July 2, 1898). 11

Carlisle, Eng.

History. "Carlisle." Creighton, Mandell. London, Longmans (Historic Town Series), 1887. 8vo. 3s. 6d. (For other references on the history of Carlisle see p. 188, Gross' Bibliography of British Municipal History). 12
"Lighting, Carlisle, Electric." Burnet, Charles D. Surveyor 17:594 (June 1, 1900). 13
"Public Works in Carlisle, Some of the." Marks, Henry C. Surveyor 17:589 (June 1, 1900). 14
Transit Facilities. "Electric Tramways." Ty. & Ry. World 9:477 (Oct. 11, 1900). 15

"**Catania**, Electric Tramways in." Brühl, Louis H. U. S. Consular Reports 56:53 (Jan. 1898). 16

Caucus System. (See under **Elections.**)

Cemeteries. (See under **Burial in Cities.**)

Census Reports of the United States. The following volumes and bulletins of the Tenth, Eleventh and Twelfth Censuses of the United States (1880, 1890, 1900) are cited as bearing most directly upon the subject of municipal administration.

TENTH CENSUS, 1880.

"Defective, Dependent and Delinquent Classes, Report on." Wines, F. H. Wash-

MUNICIPAL AFFAIRS.

Census Reports of the United States—*Continued*.

ington, Government Printing Office, 1888. 581 pp. — 17
"Mortality and Vital Statistics." Billings, J. S. Washington, Government Printing Office. Part I, 767 pp. 1885. Part II, 803 pp. 1886. — 18
"Population at the Tenth Census, Statistics of the." Washington, Government Printing Office, 1883. 961 pp. — 19
"Social Statistics of Cities." Waring, Geo. E. Part I, New England and the Middle States, 915 pp. Part II, The Southern and Western States, 843 pp. (Sketches giving history, description, maps and statistics for 1880 of 123 larger American cities.) Previously listed among works of reference. See 1-7. Washington, Government Printing Office, 1886.
"Valuation, Taxation and Indebtedness." Porter, Robt. P. Washington, Government Printing Office, 1884. 909 pp. — 20

ELEVENTH CENSUS, 1890.

"Crime, Pauperism and Benevolence." Wines, F. H. Washington, Government Printing Office, 1895. 1085 pp. — 21
"Social Statistics of Cities." Billings, John S. Washington, Government Printing Office, 1895. 137 pp. — 22
"Statistics of Cities." Part II of the "Report on Manufacturing Industries in the United States." — 23
"Transportation Business in the United States." Adams, H. C. Part I, pp. 679-867 on Street Railway Transportation. — 24
"Vital Statistics of Boston and Philadelphia, covering a period of six years, ending May 31st, 1890." Billings, John S. Washington, Government Printing Office, 1895. 269 pp. — 25
"Vital Statistics of the District of Columbia and Baltimore, covering a period of six years, ending May 31st, 1890." Washington, Government Printing Office, 1893. 241 pp. — 26
"Vital Statistics of New York City and Brooklyn, covering a period of six years, ending May 31st, 1890." Washington. Government Printing Office, 1894, 529 pp. — 27
"Wealth, Debt and Taxation." Upton, J. Kendrick. Washington, Government Printing Office, 1892. 890 pp. — 28

TWELFTH CENSUS, 1900.

"Population of Cities having 25,000 inhabitants or more in 1900." (Gives figures for 1890 and 1880 for comparison; covers whole U. S.). Census Bulletin No. 11, Twelfth Census of the U. S. Washington, D. C., Oct. 25, 1900. 15 pp. — 29

"**Central Falls, R. I.**, Sewage Disposal Plant at." Keene, W. F. Engng. Rec. April 24, 1897; anon, Engng. News 40:133 (Sept. 1, 1898). — 30

"**Chamberlain, Joseph,** Municipal Career of." Dolman, F. Fortn. 63:904 (1895). — 31

Charities, City. (See also **Church and Municipal Conditions, Settlements, Unemployed in Cities.**)

See also Antwerp, Austria, Australia, Bavaria under Germany, Belgium, Berlin, Boston, Brooklyn, Buffalo, Chicago, Cincinnati, Detroit, France, Germany, Glasgow, Hamburg, Hartford, Holland, Italy, Leipsic, London, Madgeburg, Milan, New Haven, New Jersey, New York, Ohio, Oxford (Eng.), Paris, Philadelphia, Russia, San Francisco, Turkey, United Kingdom, United States, Vienna.

"Administration, Charity." Cosmopol. Aug. 1896, p. 446.
"American Charities." Warner, Amos G. New York, Thos Y. Crowell & Co., 1894. 430 pp. $1.75. — 32
"Aspects of the Social Problem." Bosanquet, Bernard. London and New York, Macmillan, 1895. 344 pp. $1. — 33
Associated Charities. (See under Organization of Charities below.)
"Causes of Pauperism and the Relation of the State to it." Wright, A. O. P. 146 "International Congress," vol. i, 1893, see 43-99. — 34
Charities, General. "Armenwesen," by Aschrott and others. (With sketches of the poor laws of Germany, Austria, Hungary, Belgium, Denmark, France, Great

BIBLIOGRAPHY.

Charities—*Continued.*

Britain, Italy, Netherlands, Sweden, Norway, Switzerland, and the United States.) "Obdachslose," by Loening. Vol. I, pp. 1052-1210, 2d ed. '98 and Vol. V, pp. 47-8, 1st ed. '93, Conrad. See 2-10. **34a**

"Charities of Cities, A Draw for Beggars." Chambers, W. Chamb. J. 51:337 (1874), 55:273 (1878). **35**

Child Problem in Cities.

"Baby Farming." Burt, F. P. Lend a H. 10:7 (1893.) **36**

"Bibliography on the Care of Destitute, Neglected and Delinquent Children." Folks, Homer. Char. R. 10:217 (July, 1900.) **37**

"Care of Children, The." Vol. V, Reports of the International Congress of Charities at Chicago, 1893. Baltimore, Johns 3 (Dec., 1899—July, 1900.)

"Care of Destitute, Neglected and Delinquent Children." Folks, Homer. Char. R. 9:459, 516, 564; 10:36, 89, 129, 213, (Dec. 1899—July, 1900.) **38**

"Child and the Community, The." Campbell, Helen. Chaut. 9:458 (1890.) **39**

"Child Labor." Kelley, Florence. Char. R. 6:221 (May, 1897.) **40**

"Child Life Insurance." Waugh, B. London, Kegan, Paul & Co., 1890. 24 pp. **41**

"Child Problem in Cities, The." Finley, John H. R. of Rs. 4:683 (1892.) **42**

"Children of Charity." (Children's Aid Society, New York.) Sherman, Alma Seymour. Am. M. Civics 7:177 (1895.) **43**

"Children of the Other Half." Hull. W. I. Arena 17:1039 (June, 1897.) **44**

——. "Children of the Poor." Riis, J. A. New York, C. Scribner's Sons, 1892. 300 pp. $1.25. **45**

——. "Children of the Poor," "Genesis of the Gang," "Justice for the Boy." Riis, Jacob A. Scrib. M. 11:531 (1892), Atlan. 84:302, 637 (Sept., Nov., 1899.) **46**

"Children of the State." Hill, Florence D. and Fowkes, Fanny. London and New York, Macmillan, 1889. 2d edit. 362 pp. $1.75. **47**

"Children of the Town." Kingsmill, Esther T. Canadian M. July, 1897. **48**

"Criminal Children, Homes for." Fowkes, Fanny. Lend a H. 5:527, 607 (1890.) **49**

——. "Value of Discrimination in Dealing with Juvenile Offenders." Putnam, Elizabeth C. P. 100 "International Congress," vol. v, 1893, see 43-99. **50**

"Curfew for City Children." Townsend, [Mrs.] John D. No. Am. 163:725 (1896.) **51**

"Dependent Children and Family Homes." Letchworth. William P. Char. R. 7:577 (Sept. 1898); Sanitarian 11:3 (Jan. 1898). **52**

"Family Life for Dependent and Wayward Children." Folks, Homer. Pp. 69-80, 112-128 "International Congress," vol v, 1893, see 43-99. **53**

"Foundlings and Illegitimate Children." Wilson, Anna T. P. 57 "International Congress," vol. v, 1893, see 43-99. **54**

"George Junior Republic, The." Commons, J. R. Our Country 4:247 (Jan., 1897); Am. J. Sciol. 3:281, 433 (Nov., 1897, Jan., 1898); Hull, Wm. I. Ann. Am. Acad. Pol. Sci. 10:73 (July, 1897); Humphreys, Mary G. McClure's 9:735 (July, 1897.) **55**

"History of Child Saving in the United States, Report of the Committee on the." Twentieth National Conference of Charities and Corrections in Chicago, June, 1893. Boston, Geo. H. Ellis, 1893. 321 pp. $1.50. **56**

"Importation of Dependent Children from other States." Randall, C. D. P. 24 "International Congress," vol. v, 1893, see 43-99. **57**

Kindergartens. (See under **Schools**.)

——. "Our Toiling Children." Kelley, Florence. Chicago, Woman's Temperance Publication Association, 1889. 40 pp. **58**

"Physical and Mental Condition of Children in Charitable Institutions and Public Schools, Notes on two Recent Inquiries into the." Morse, Francis R. P. 152 "International Congress," vol. v, 1893, see 43-99. **59**

"Placing-Out System in the Light of its Results." White, Francis H. P. 81 "International Congress," vol. v, 1893, see 43-99. **60**

"Poor Law Children, Conference on." London 6:653 (July 29, 1897.)
——. "Poor Law School Children." Harston, Frederick. Mun. J. & London 8:1387 (Dec. 29, 1899.) **61**

"Protection of Neglected and Abused Children." Fay, Frank B. P. 129 "International Congress," vol. v, 1893, see 43-99. **62**

"Protection of Children." McCallum, M. Ch. IV., p. 46. Bosanquet's "Aspects

Charities—*Continued.*

of the Social Problem." London, Macmillan, 1895. 343 pp. $1.   63

——. " Reform of the Law Affecting the Labor of Women and Children." R. Pol. et Parl. May 10, 1897.

" Social Responsibility towards Child-Life." Spencer, Anna Garlin. P. 6 " International Congress," vol. v, 1893, see 43-99.   64

" The State of Prisons and of Child Saving Institutions in the Civilized World." Wines, E. C. Cambridge University Press, 1880. 8vo, 719 pp. 25s.   65

" State Adoption of Street Arabs." Samuels, [Mrs.] A. Fortn. No. 373, p. 111 (Jan. 1898).   66

" Street Children." Waugh, B. Contemp. 53:825 (1890.)   67

" What Shall be Done with Dependment Children." Williams, H. S. No. Am. April, 1897.   68

Churches, Charity and the. "Signs of the Times and the Churches." Strong, Josiah. Char. R. 6:5 (March 1897.) (See also under **Churches**.)   69

" Colonization as a Remedy for City Poverty." Peabody, F. G. Forum 17:52 (1894.)   70

" Crime, Pauperism and." Weber, John B. P. 131 " International Congress," see 43-99.   71

" Darkest England and the Way Out, In." Booth, Charles. London, Published by the Salvation Army, 1890. 285 pp. 3s. 6d. (See also **Church and Municipal Conditions**.)   72

" Dispensary Charity, Abuse of." Roosevelt, Theodore. Char. R. 3:127 (1894.) (See also under Hospitals below.)   73

——. " Municipal Dispensaries." Sanders, C. Public Health, June, 1900.   74

" Elberfeld System of Poor Relief." Münsterberg, Th.; Thoma; Seyffardt, L. F. Pp. 187, 200, 207 " International Congress," vol. iii, 1893, see 43-99.   75

——. " Reports on the Elberfield Poor Law System and German Workmen's Colonies." Parliamentary Papers, London, Eyre and Spottiswoode, 1888. 137 pp. 9d.   76

Employment Bureaus. (See under **Labor and the Municipality**.)

" Financial Problems of Private Charities." Charities 4:1 (May 26, 1900.)

" Fresh Air Charity in the United States." Ufford, Walter Shepard. New York, Bonnell, Silver & Co. Thesis presented at Colum. Univ 1897. Pamphlet, 144 pp. Cl. $1; paper 50c. Also article by same author, Char. R. 6:230 (May, 1897.)   77

——. " Verhandlung des Internationalen Kongresses für Ferienkolonien, etc. in Zürich am. 13 u. 14 August, 1888." Hamburg u. Leipsic, Voss 8vo, 115 pp. 2m. 2m.

" Friendly Visiting." Chant, L. O. Lend a H. 11:431 (1893); Clews, Elsie. Char. R. 6:247 (May, 1897); Hamlin, Leonora. Char. R. 6:322 (June, 1897); Wolcott, (Mrs.) Roger. P. 108 " International Congress, vol. iii, 1893, see 43-99.   78

" Future of City Charities." Hunter, R. Nineteenth Cent. 27:72 (1890.)   79

" Future Problem of Charity and the Unemployed." Brooks, J. G. Ann. Am. Acad. Pol. Sci. 5:1 (1894.) Separate pamphlet, 27 pp. 25 cts.   80

George Junior Republic. (See above.)

" Hindoo Charity." Char. R. 6:302 (June, (1897).

History. Mutual Aid in the Mediaeval City. Kropotkin, P. Humanité Nouvelle (Oct., 1898.)   81

" Home Making, Charity and." Richmond, Mary E. Char. R. 6:118 (April, 1897.)   82

Hospitals. (See also Dispensaries above.)

Ambulance Service. " Le Service des Prompts Secours." Strauss, Paul. R. Municipale 3:2105 (May, 1900.)   83

" Burdett's Hospitals and Charities, the Year Book of Philanthropy and Hospital Annual." (British, American and Colonial.) Burdett, Henry. London and N. Y., Scribners, published annually. Edition for 1899. 8vo, 1002 pp. 5s.   84

" Public Hospitals." Folks, Homer. Mun. Aff. 2:271 (June, 1898.)   85

" Construction of Hospitals." Henman, William. (Deals principally with the design of large town hospitals.) J. Roy. Inst. of Brit. Archts. (London), May 6, 1897.   86

" Handbook for Hospitals." (List of books of reference, p. 265.) Worlsey, Abby Howland. New York, G. P. Putnam, 1895. 267 pp.   87

BIBLIOGRAPHY.

Charities—*Continued.*

"Hospitals and Asylums of the World." (Vol. I Asylums, Vol. II. Asylum Construction, Plans and Bibliography, Vol. III. Hospitals, History and Administration, Vol. IV. Hospital Construction and Bibliography.) Burdett, Henry C. London, J. A. Churchill, 1891, '93. 8vo, 701, 337, 944, 463 pp. 168s. — 88

"Hospitals, Dispensaries and Nursing." Edited by John S. Billings and Henry M. Hurd. Balto., Johns Hopkins Press (Intl. Conf.), 1894. 8vo, 718 pp. — 89

"Hospitals, Dispensaries and Nursing." Hurd, Henry M. Char. R. 10:298 (Sept., 1900.) — 90

"Isolation Hospitals, The Value of." Hill, Alfred. San Rec. 24:34 (July 14, 1899.) — 91

"Medical Charity, Its Extent and Abuses." Westm. 101:174 (1874.)

"Municipal Hospitals." Fabian Soc. Tract No. 95, Dec. 1900, 1d.

"The Plumbing, Water Supply and Drainage of Hospitals." Gerhard, William Paul. New York, 1898. Pamphlet, 37 pp. — 92

"Tuberculosis Hospitals, Municipal." (Editorial.) Sanitarian 43:74 (July, 1899.)

———. (See further under International Congress below.)

"How to Relieve the Poor and Prevent Poverty." Terrell, Ada K. Midland Mo. April, 1897. — 93

"How Should a City Care for Its Poor." Peabody, Francis G. Forum 14:474 (1892.) — 94

"Improvement in City Life." (Charity.) Robinson, Charles Mulford. Atlan. 83:524 (April, 1899.) — 95

"Incidentals of Quasi-Public Charities." Johnson, A. Char. R. 1:152 (1892.) — 96

"Industrial Condition of the Poor: Prolems of Poverty." Hobson, J. A. London, Methuen & Co., 1891. 227 pp. $1.25. — 97

"Inebriate Pauperism, The Problem of." Crothers, T. D. P. 140 "International Congress," vol. i, 1893, see 43-99. (See also under **Liquor Problem in Cities**). — 98

"International Congress of Charities, Reports of the,—Chicago, 1893." Baltimore, Johns Hopkins University Press, 1894. 5 vols. $1.50 each. Vol. I, Public Treatment of Pauperism; Vol. II, Hospitals, Dispensaries and Nursing; Vol. III, The Organization of Charities; Vol. IV, The Insane, Feeble Minded, Criminals; Vol. V, Care of Children, Sociology in Institutions of Learning. — 99

"International Treatment of Charity Questions." von Reitzenstein, Baron. P. 185 "International Congress," vol. iii, 1893, see 43-99. — 100

"Literature of Philanthropy." (Papers on Settlements and other Philanthropic subjects.) Goodale, Francis A. (editor.) New York, Harper & Bros., 1893. 12 mo, 205 pp. $1. — 1

Medical Charities. (See under Dispensaries, Hospitals above.)

"Midnight in a Great City." (Sermons on poverty and vice in cities.) Myers, Cortland. New York, Merril & Baker, 1896. 12mo, 252 pp. $1. — 2

"Missions and Mission Philanthropy." Goldie, John. London and New York, Macmillan, 1895. 212 pp. $1.50. — 3

———. "City Missions and Social Problems." North, F. M. Meth. R. 53:228 (1893.) — 4

———. "Missions in Workhouses." Mun. J. & London 8:762 (June 30, 1899.)

———. (See also under **Church and Municipal Conditions**.)

"Modern Charity Worker, The." Peabody, Francis G. Char. R. 6:17 (March, 1897.) — 5

"Municipal Charities." Folks, Homer. City Govt. 7:69 (Sept., 1899), Mun. Aff. 3:516 (Sept., 1899), Public Improvements 1:281 (Oct. 1, 1899); Other Side 1:181 (Oct. 21, 1899); pp. 32-36 in Proc. of the 3d annual convention of the League of Am. Municipalities, 1899. Low, Seth. Lend a H. 3:498 (1890.) — 6

———. "Municipal and County Charities." (Report of Standing Committee to the 25th National Conference of Charities and Correction, New York, May 18-25, 1898.) Folks, Homer, Chairman. Boston, Geo. H. Ellis, 1898. Pamphlet, 79 pp. — 7

"New York Conference of Charities." Folks, Homer. Char. R. 6:346 (June, 1897.) — 8

Organization, Charity.

"Address on Organization of City and County Public Charities." Wylie, James R. Proc. Nat. Conf. Char. and Cor., held in Toronto, Ont., July 7-14, 1897. — 9

"Associated Charities in Cities." Indiana Bulletin of Charities and Correction, June, 1898.

Charities—*Continued.*

——. "The Value of Associated Charities in Small Cities." Henderson, Charles R. Ind. Bulletin of Char. and Correction. June, 1900, p. 10.   10

"Charity Organization and Jesus Christ." Marson, C. L. London, Scientific Press, 1897. 60 pp. 1s.   11

"Charity Organization Societies." pp. 219-225. Ency. Soc. Ref. See 1-3.

"Charity Organization System of To-day." Leppington, C. H. d'E. Econ. R. Jan., 1897.   12

Defense and arraignment of Organized Charities. Gunton's M. April, 1897, 12:397 (June, 1897.)

"Development of Organized Charities." Pullman, J. M. Lend a H. 11:421 (1893.)   13

"District Charity Organization." Brackett, Jeffrey R. Char. R. 7:595 (Sept., 1897.)   14

"Growth and Character of Organized Charity." Schurman, J. G. Char. R. 1:191 (1892.)   15

"Handbook of Charity Organization." Gurteen, S. Humphreys. Buffalo, Published by the author, 1882. 8vo, 254 pp.   16

"Labor Bureaus, Charity Organization and." Hyslop, J. H. Char. R. 4:1 (1894.)   17

"Organization of Charities." Loch, C. S. London, Swan S. & Co., 1892. 106 pp. $1.   18

"Organization of Charities." Buzelle, Geo. B. Char. R. 2:3 (1892); Townbee, H. V. Longm. 21:409 (1893); White, H. C. New Englander 46:206 (1887.)   19

"Organization of Municipal Charities." Char. R. 6:501 (July & Aug., 1897.)

"Organized Charities in Small Cities." Rein, Carrie. Indiana Bulletin of Charities and Correction, Indianapolis, p. 106 (Sept., 1899.)   20

"Organized Charity from the Point of View of a Municipal Officer." Warner, Amos G. Lend a H. 9:403 (1892.)   21

"Social Philosophy of Charity Organization." (Reviews Bosanquet's "Aspects of the Social Problem," see above.) Hobson, J. A. Contemp. Nov., 1896. Reply to the foregoing. Bosanquet, H. and B. Contemp. 71:112 (Jan., 1897.)   22

"Southern Cities, Charity Organization in." Ayres, P. W. Char. R. 4:259 (1895.)   23

"The True Aim of Charity Organization." Lowell, Josephine Shaw. Forum June, 1896.   24

"What a Charity Organization Society can do and what it cannot." Bonaparte, Charles J. Char. R. 1:201 (1892.)   25

"Pauperism: Its Causes and Remedies." Fawcett, Henry. London, Macmillan, 1871. 8vo, 270 pp. 5s. 6d.   26

"Pauperism in Great Cities, its Four Chief Causes." Paine, Robert Treat. Boston, 1894. 42 pp. Also articles by same author, p. 1 International Congress. (See above.) Vol. I. 1893. Lend a H. 12:196 (1894.)   27

"Pauper Problem in America." Booth-Tucker, F. de Latour. Char. R. 6:127 (April, 1897).   28

"Philanthropy and Social Progress." Adams, Henry C. New York, T. Y. Crowell, 1893. 268 pp. $1.50.   29

"Police, Department of, as a Means of Distributing Charity." Campbell, A. F. Open Court 11:333 (June, 1897.)   30

"Politics in Public Institutions of Charity and Correction." Henderson, Charles R. Am. J. Sociol. 4:202 (Sept., 1898.)   31

"Poor in Great Cities: Their Problems and What is Doing to Solve Them." New York, Chas. Scribner's Sons, 1895. 400 pp. $3. (A collection of papers by R. A. Woods, W. T. Elsing, Jacob A. Riis, Walter Besant and others contributed to Scribner's Magazine during the years 1891, '92 and '93.)

"Poorhouses, Location, Construction and Management of." Giles, H. H. Mun. World 7:169 (Aug., 1897.)   32

"Poor Relief in Large Cities." Greenwood, F. Nineteenth Cent. 25:737 (1889.)   33

"Poor Relief Questions, Some." Lubbock, Gertrude. London, John Murray, 1895. 329 pp. $3. Chapter III, p. 194 on "The Provision of Meals at Public Schools."   34

——. "Relief and Care of the Poor in Their Homes." Devine, Edward T. Char. R. 10:119 (May, 1900.)   35

"Problems of Poverty. Industrial Condition of the Poor." Hobson, J. A. Lon-

BIBLIOGRAPHY. 45

Charities—*Continued.*
don, Methuen & Co., 1891. 227 pp. $1.25. 36
"Public Aid to Private Charity." Sturgis, F. R. Charities Vol. III, No. 13, p. 2
(Aug. 26, 1899.) 37
——. "Co-operation between Public and Private Poor Relief." Böhmert, Victor
and Alex. Johnson. Pp. 114-210 "International Congress, vol. iii, 1893, see 43-99. 38
——. "Public Funds and Charitable Institutions." (Editorial.) Outlook 62:468
(July 1, 1899.)
——. "Public Subsidies to Private Charities." Warner, Amos G. P. 120 "International Congress," vol. iii, 1893, see 43-99. 39
——. "Relation of State, City and Individual to Modern Philanthropic Work."
Warner, Amos G. J. H. Univ. Publications, 1889. 5 cts. 40
"Public Outdoor Relief." Devine, Edward T. Char. R. 8:129, 186 (May, June,
1898.) 41
"Reform and Public Charities." Folks, Homer. Outlook, March, 1897. 42
"Registration of Charitable Relief." Morse, Francis R. P. 99 "International Congress," vol. iii, 1893, see 43-99. 43
"Rescuers and Rescued, Experiences among Our City Poor." Wells, J. London,
Hodder, 1890. 3s. 6d. 44
"Rich and Poor." Bosanquet, [Mrs.] Bernard. London, Macmillan & Co., 1896.
12mo, 216 pp. $1.50. 45
"Shiftless and Floating City Population." Devine, E. T. Ann. Am. Acad. Pol. Sci.
10:149 (Sept., 1897.) 46
Slums. (See Slums under **Housing**.)
"Smoky Pilgrims." (A study of pauperism and crime in a small town.) Blackmar,
Frank W. Am. J. Sociol. 2:485 (Jan., 1897.) 47
"Social Evils and Their Cure." Wines, F. H. Char. R. 6:193 (May, 1897.) 48
"Statistics, A Story of Charity." Labor Bulletin, Mass., No. 12, p. 120 (Oct., 1899.)
"Sympathy and Reason in Charitable Work." Jones, Edward D. Char. R. 6:289
(June, 1897.) 49
"Training of Charity Workers, The." Richmond, Mary E. Char. R. 6:308 (June,
1897.) 50
Tramps. (See Vagrancy below.)
Unemployment. (See under **Unemployment**.)
"Unofficial Government of Cities." (Charity, etc.) Wheeler, Everett P. Atlan.
85:370 (March, 1900.) 51
Vacant City Lots, Cultivation of. (See under **Vacant City Lots**.)
"Vagrancy." Wright, A. O. P. 108 "International Congress," vol. i, 1893, see 43-99. 52
——. "Vagrancy and Public Charities in Foreign Countries." United States Special Consular Report, 1893. 350 pp.

Charleston, S. C.
Description and Statistics of Charleston, S. C. in 1880. Census. See 1-7.
"History of Charleston, S. C." Snowden, Yates. See 1-4c; Census. See 1-7. 53
"Municipal Condition of Charleston, S. C." Ficken, John F. Pp. 188-191, Pro. of
the Louisville Conf., 1897. See 6-18d. 53a

"**Charlottenburg, [Germany]**, A Sewerage Pumping Engine at."
Engng. News 39:126 (Feb. 24, 1898.)

"**Chateau-Gontier, [France]**, Etudes sur la prostitution dans la ville
de, suivie de considerations sur la prostitution en général." Homo, H. Paris,
1872. 8vo, 5 fr. 54

Chatham, [Eng.]
"Chatham, [Eng.]." Mun. J. & London 9:21 (Jan. 21, 1900.)
"Town Hall, Chatham." Surveyor Supp. March 23, 1900.

"**Chatham [N. J.]**, Artesian Wells for the Water Supply of." Tribus,
Louis L. Engng. News 42:92 (Aug. 10, 1899.) 55

"**Chatham [Ont.]**, Municipal Lighting Plant." Can. Elec. 8:57 (April,
1898.)

Chattanooga, Tenn.

History, Description and Statistics of Chattanooga, Tenn., in 1880. Census. See 1-7.
"Municipal Condition of Chattanooga, Tenn." Ochs, George W. P. 397 Proc. Second Natl. Conf., 1895. See 6-18b. 56
"Water Works Question in Chattanooga." (Editorial.) Engng. Rec. 39:201 (Feb. 4, 1899).

"Chautauqua [N. Y.], Sewage Disposal at." Engng. Rec. June 24, 1894.

"Chemnitz i. S.," Die Wahrnungsverhaltnisse in." Dittrich. Pp. 107-127 Hft. 31, Schr. d. Ver. f. Socialpolitik. 57

"Chesterfield [Eng.], and Electric Light." Mun. J. & London 8:773 (June 30, 1899).

Chicago, Ill.

Government, General References, Unclassified.

"Chicago." Flinn, J. J. Chicago, Flinn and Sheppard, 1891. 543 pp. $1.50. (Part I, History; Part II, Government, Educational Institutions, Water, Sewerage, Population, etc.) 58
"Chicago." Chap. XVII in "The Land of the Dollar," by G. W. Steevens. New York, Dodd, Mead & Co., 1897. 12 mo, 316 pp. $1.50. 59
Chicago, General Articles on. Canby, Noble. Chaut. 15:323 (1892); Gage, Lyman J. Open Court 11:193 (April, 1897); Mason, Edward G. Atlan. 70:33 (1892); St. Ry. R. 9:634 (Oct. 15, 1899). 60
"City Government of Chicago." MacVeagh, Franklin. P. 80, Proc. First Natl. Conf., 1894, see 6-18a; Sweet, Ada C. Bedfords Nov. 1892. 61
"Civic Life of Chicago." Stead, F. H. R. of Rs. 8:178 (1893). 62
Description and Statistics of Chicago, Ill., in 1880. Census. See 1-7.
"How to Govern Chicago." Anon., signed "By a Practical Reformer." Chicago, Chas. H. Kerr & Co., 1895. 118 pp. 25 cts.
"Municipal Misgovernment in Chicago." Gifford, O. P. Our Day 11:59 (1893). 63
"Municipal Progress in Chicago, Notes on." Smith, Edwin Burritt. Pro. Indianapolis Conf. p. 269, 1898, see 6-18e; Vischer, J. Lend a H. 14:439 (1895). 64
"Problems of Municipal Government for Chicago." Shorey, Daniel L. Chicago, 1885. 16 pp. 65
"Two Babylons, London and Chicago." Stead, W. T. New R. 10:560 (1894). 66
"Western Modes of City Management." Ralph, Julian. Harper 84:709 (1892). 66a

---

Almanac. "Chicago Daily News Almanac and Political Register." Chicago, Published annually by the Chicago Daily News. Edition for 1899, 484 pp.
"Baths, Chicago, The Wentworth Avenue Free." Engng. Rec 37:35 (Dec. 11, 1897).
"Building Problem in Chicago." Bramhall, John T. Leslie's Wkly. 83:91 (1896); Arch. & Buil. 28:121 (April 9, 1898). 67
"Charities in Chicago, Summer." Char. R. 9:266 (Sept. 1899).
——. "Poor of Chicago." Kirkland, Jos. Scrib. M. 12:3 (1892). 68
"Charters of the City of Chicago: Pt. I, The Early Charters, 1833-1837." James, Edmund J. Chicago, The University of Chicago Press, 1898. 8vo. 76 pp. Paper. 69
——. "Charters of the City of Chicago: Part II, The City Charters." James, Edmund J. Chicago, University of Chicago Press, 1899. 8vo. 191 pp. Paper. 70
——. "Special Charters in Chicago." Hodder, F. H. Seminary Notes, p. 31, Nov. 1892. 71
Civil Service. "The Chicago Civil Service Commission. Law, Rules and Regulations Governing Examinations, Appointments, Promotion and Removal in the Classified Service." Chicago, 1895. 71pp.
——. "Civil Service Reform." Partridge, Newton A. Ann. Am. Acad. Pol. Sci 12:307 (Sept. 1898); Phelps, E. J. Good Govt. 14:137 (1895), 15:80 (1896); Ralph, Julian. Hrprs. Wkly. 39:812 (1895); Rowe, Leo. S. Ann Am. Acad. Pol. Sci. 11:140 (March, 1898). 72
——. "Civil Service Reform, Chicago since the adoption of." Starr, Merritt. p. 162 Proc. Third Natl. Conf. for Good City Govt., 1896. See 6-18c. 73

Chicago, Ill.—Continued.

Conduits. "Proposed Plan for Chicago Subways." W. Elec. 27:100 (Aug. 18, 1900).
"Constitutional Convention and other Legislation." Chicago, Address by the Citizens' Association, 1895. 12 pp.
"Council Reform in Chicago: Work of the Municipal Voters' League." Smith, Edwin Burritt. Mun. Aff. 4:347 (June, 1900). 74
"Day Labor, Municipal Tunnel Driving by, Chicago." Brown, Paul G. Engng. Rec. 41:97 (Feb. 3, 1900). 74a
"Department Store in the West, The: The Struggle in Chicago." Handy, William Matthews. Arena 22:320 (Sept. 1899). 75
Drainage Canal. (See under Sewage Disposal below.)
"Electrolysis Problem in Chicago, The." Ellicott, Edward B. W. Elec. 26:87 (Feb. 10, 1900). 76
Engineering. "Recent City Engineering in Chicago, Ill." McGann, L. E. Engng. News 43:30 (Jan. 11, 1900); anon. Eng. Rec. Nov. 21, 1896; Public Policy 2:51 (Jan. 27, 1900.) 77
"Finances of the City of Chicago and Constitutional Amendments." Chicago. Address by the Citizens' Association, 1896. 8 pp.
——. "Financial Statement of the Sanitary District of Chicago." Engng. News 38:309 (Nov. 11, 1897).
——. Taxation in Chicago. Bemis, Edward W. Bib. Sacr. 54:746 (Oct. 1897); Commons, John R. J. Pol. Econ. 3:434 (1895); Whitten, W. H. J. Pol. Econ. (March, 1897). 78
Foreign Element. "Italians in Chicago, The." Bulletin Dept. Labor No. 13, p. 691 Nov. 1897; Kelley, Florence. Ar. Soz. Gesetz. Stat. 13:291 (2 Heft, 1899). 79
"Garbage Burning, Chicago." Lane, M. A. Hrprs. Wkly. 38:82 (1894). 80
"Gentler Side of Chicago, The." Ralph, Julian. Harper M. 87:286 (1893). 81
Grade Crossings, Track Elevation in Chicago. Cloverdale, W. H. and others. Jour. W. Soc. Engs. Dec. 1898; anon. Railroad Gaz. 30:20 (Jan. 14, 1898); Engng. News 40:22 (July 7, 1898), 43:18, 24, 122 (Jan. 11, Feb. 22, 1900). 82
"Higher Life of Chicago." Stone, M. E. Outlook 53:326 (1896). 83
History. "Chicago Antiquities." Hurlbuts, H. H. Chicago, 1881. 670 pp. 84
——. "Chicago." Colbert, E. Chicago, 1868. 210 pp. 85
——. "Chicago—Past, Present and Future." Wright, John S. Chicago, The Author, 1870. 2d ed. 8vo, 435 pp. $4. 86
——. "Early Chicago." Wentworth, John. Chicago, 1876 and 1881. 87
——. History to 1880. Census. See 1-7.
——. "History of Chicago." Andreas, A. T. Chicago, 1888. 3 vols. 657, 740, 875 pp. 88
——. "History of Chicago." Bross, William. Chicago, 1876. 126 pp. 89
——. "History of Chicago: Its Commercial and Manufacturing Interests and Industries." Guyer, I. D. Chicago, 1862. 196 pp. 90
——. "History of Cook County, Chicago." (To 1857.) Andreas, A. T. Chicago, published by author, 1884. 4to, 490 pp. $14-$18. 91
——. "Municipal History in Chicago." Hodder, F. H. Seminary Notes, p. 74. (Dec. 1891). 92
——. "Municipal History and Present Organization of the City of Chicago." Sparling, Samuel Edwin. Bulletin of the University of Wisconsin, No. 23, May, 1898, Madison, Wis. 8vo, 188 pp. Paper, 75 cts. 93
——. "The Great Conflagration, Chicago, Its Past, Present and Future." Sheahan, J. W. and Upton, G. P. Chicago, 1891. 458 pp. 94
——. "The Story of Chicago." (To Dec. 1894). Kirkland, Joseph. Chicago, 1892. 12mo, 511 pp. $3.50. 95
"Housing of the Poor in Chicago, The." Embree, Frances Buckley. J. P. E. 8:354 (June, 1900); Stevens, Alzina P. Arena 9:662 (1894); anon. Char. R. 10:292 (Sept. 1900). 96
"Hull House Maps and Papers, a presentation of nationalities and wages in a congested district of Chicago, with comments and essays on problems growing out of the social conditions." Addams, Jane, and others. New York, T. Y. Crowell & Co., 1895. 230 pp. $2.50. (For articles on Hull House itself see under Settlements below.) 97

Chicago, Ill.—*Continued.*

"If Christ came to Chicago." Stead, W. T. Chicago, Laird and Lee, 1894. 472 pp. 50 cts; Reviewed, Goldwin Smith, Contemp. 66:380 (1894). **98**

"If the Devil came to Chicago." A plea for the misrepresented by one who knows what it is to be misrepresented himself." Granville, Austyn and W. W. Knott. Chicago, Bow-knot, 1894. 352pp. **99**

Italians in Chicago. (See under Foreign Element above.)

Library, Chicago Public. Crissey, Forest. Outlook 57:279 (Oct. 2, 1897); Hrprs. Wkly. 41:934 (Sept. 18, 1897); Dial 23:207 (Oct. 16, 1897). **100**

Lighting. "Electric Lighting in Chicago, Municipal." Meyers, W. J. Pol. Sci. Q. 10:87 (1895); Mikkleson, M. A. Ann. Am. Acad. Pol. Sci. 2:715 (1892); Elec. Eng. 26:314 (Sept. 29, 1898). **1**

——. "Chicago Gas War." Prog. Age 18:471 (Nov. 1, 1900).

——. "Gas Companies of Chicago." Part III of Ninth Biennial Report of the Bureau of Labor Statistics of Illinois, 1896; Prog. Age 15:59 (Feb. 1, 1897).

——. "Park Lighting Plant, A Public." (Description of the plant in Chicago which supplies current for the chain of parks and boulevards on the West Side.) Heldt, P. M. American Electrician April, 1897. **2**

Liquor Problem. "Saloon Question in Chicago." George, John E. New York, Macmillan, Publications of the American Economic Association, April, 1897. 110 pp. 50 cts.; Melendy, R. L. Am. J. Sociol. 6:289 (Nov. 1900), Commons No. 52, p. 1 (Nov. 1900); Moore, E. C. Am. J. Sociol. 3:1 (July, 1897). **3**

Logan Monument, Dedication of the." Hrprs. Wkly. 41:777 (Aug. 7, 1897).

"Markets of Chicago." Wakeman, (Mrs.) Antoinette V. H. Chaut. Dec. 1896. **4**

Parks, Playgrounds, etc. Bramhall, John T. Leslie's Wkly. 80:337 (1895); Pullen, Clarence. Hrprs. Wkly. 35:413 (1891); Robbins, M. C. Garden & F. 6:403 (1893); Sly, Mary E. Kindergarten M. 10:141 (Nov. 1897); Zueblin, Charles. Am. J. Sociol. 4:145 (Sept. 1898); anon. Am. Arch. 26:185 (1889); Hrprs. Wkly. April 3, 1897. **5**

——. "Public Parks, their effect upon the moral, physical and sanitary conditions of the inhabitants of large cities, with especial reference to Chicago." Rauch. John H. Chicago, S. C. Griggs & Co., 1869. **6**

"Pavements of Chicago." Fox, E. A. Engng. News Jan. 10, 1878, p. 14; Engng. Rec. 39:45 (Dec. 17, 1898). **7**

"People's Institute and Home Salon, The Chicago." Bramhall, John T. Leslie's Wkly. 80:240 (1895). **8**

"Population of Chicago, Mixed." Ridpath, J. C. Chaut. 12:483 (1891). **9**

——. "The Wonderful Growth of Chicago." Shumann, Andrew. Leslie's Wkly. 70:58 (1890). **10**

Reform Organizations. "Civic Federation of Chicago." Baker, R. S. Outlook 52:132 (1896); Small, A. W. Am. J. Sociol. 1:79 (1895). See also p. 474 Proc. Second Natl. Conf., 1895. See 6-18b. **11**

——. "Voters' League of Chicago, The." Outlook 60:130 (Sept. 10, 1898); Smith, Edwin Burritt. Atlan. 85:834 (June, 1900). **12**

Saloons. (See under Liquor Problem above.)

"Sanitary Condition of Chicago." Ingals, E. F. Forum 15:585 (1893). **13**

——. "Sanitary Inspection Service." Anon. Sanitary News Oct. 10, 1885; Bemis, E. W. Nation 44:230 (1887). **14**

Schools, Public. School System of Chicago. Andrews, E. Benjamin. Educa. 20:201 (Dec. 1899); Milliken, O. J. Am. J. Sociol. 4:289 (Nov. 1898); Rice, J. M. Forum 15:200 (1893). **15**

——. "Kindergarten in Chicago School System." Vandewalker, Nina C. Kindergarten M. 9:679 (May, 1897). **16**

Settlements. Chicago Commons. Gavit, John P. Our Day Feb. 1897; Hegner, Herman F. Outlook Aug. 31, 1895; anon. Char. R. 4:102 (Dec. 1894). See also monthly issues of "The Commons" published by the Settlement. **17**

——. Hull House. Addams, Jane. Forum 14:226 (Oct. 1892), Atlan. 83:163 (Feb. 1899); Brodlique, Eva H. Chautauquan Sept. 1890; Heyer, Edith. Altruist 5:14 (Oct. 1897); Kelley, Florence. New Eng. M. 18:550 (July, 1898), Living Age 218:138 (July 9, 1898); Laves, Kurt. Allgemeine Zeitung, München, Beilage March 9, 1896; Learned, Henry B. Lend a H. 10:318 (May, 1893); Miller, Alice. Char. R. 1:167 (Feb. 1892); Moore, Dorothea. Am. J. Sociol. April, 1897; Muzzey, A. L. Arena 16:432 (Aug. 1896); Stevens, A. P. Self Culture 9:42

BIBLIOGRAPHY.

Chicago, Ill.—*Continued.*

(March, 1899); Stone, Melville E. Outlook 53:327 (Feb. 22, 1896); anon. Atlan. 77:118 (Jan. 1896). 18

——. " Art Work done by Hull House." Addams, Jane. Forum 19:614 (1895). 19

——. " Social Settlements in Chicago." Embree, Francis Buckley. Gunton's 19:452 (Nov. 1900). 20

Sewerage. "Drainage Channel and Water Way: A History of the Effort to Secure an Effective and Harmless Method for the Disposal of the Sewage of the City of Chicago." (Description, Bibliography.) Brown, G. P. Chicago, Donnelly, 1894. 8vo. 480 pp. 21

——. " Drainage Channel." Baker, M. N. Outlook 64:357 (Feb. 10, 1900); Brown, G. P. Engng. M. 7:654 (1894); Clement, F. Leslie's Wkly. 80:7 (1895); Colby, B. H. J. Assoc. Engng. Soc. 24:137 (Feb. 1900), Sci. Am. Sup. 49:20356 (May 5, 1900); Guthrie, Ossian. J. Assoc. Eng. Soc. 9:77 (1890); Jordan, Edwin O. Am. R. of Rs. 21:56 (Jan. 1900); Phillips, Hiram. Sanitarian 42:339 (April, 1899); "Quondam." Our Day 18:65 (Feb. 1898); Raddin, Charles S. Overland 35:301 (Oct. 1899); Randolph, Isham. Jour. of W. Soc. of Engs. (Dec. 1897); Skinner, Frank W. Eng. (London) 84:125 (Aug. 6, 1897); Smailey, E. V. Ind. 51:3292 (Dec. 7, 1899); Smith, Joel W. Ind. 49:433 (April 8, 1897); Stewart, J. A. Sci. Am. 82:105 (Feb. 17, 1900); anon. Hrprs. Wkly. 38:827 (1894); Engineering (London) Jan. 1, 1897; Engng. News 38:214 (Sept. 30, 1897); Engng. Rec. 37:407, 39:259 (April 9, April 21, 1898); Engng. News 40:375, 41:127, 41:270 (Dec. 15, 1898, Feb. 23, April 27, 1899); Engng. Rec. 39:489, 40:241 (April 29, Aug. 12, 1899); St. Ry. R. 9:18 (Oct. 18. 1899); Engng. Rec. 40:537, 617 (Nov. 4, Dec. 2, 1899); Engng. News 42:379, 43:22 (Dec. 7, 1899, Jan. 11, 1900); Engng. Rec. 41:26 (Jan. 13, 1900); Surveyor 17:65 (Jan. 26, 1900); Engng. Rec. 41:265 (March 8, 1900); Engng. N. 44:97 (Aug. 9, 1900). 22

——. " Power Development of the Drainage Canal at Joliet." W. Elec'n Sept. 22, 1900.

——. " The Chicago Main Drainage Channel." (Machinery used, methods adopted.) Hill, Charles Shattuck. New York, Engng. News Pub. Co., 1896. 8vo. 129 pp. pl. ill. Cl. $1.50. 23

" Street Cleaning, Toronto and Chicago compared in the matter of" Hooker, George E. R. of Rs. 15:437 (April 1897). 24

" Sweating in Chicago." p. 66 et seq. "Report of the Committee of Manufacturers on Sweating." H. R. Report No. 2309, 1893. John DeWitt Warner, Chairman. 25

——. " Sweating in Chicago." Kelley, Florence Chapter II, p. 27 "Hull House Maps and Papers." 26

Taxation in Chicago. (See under Finance above.)

" Telephone Traffic in Chicago." Elec. R. 31:236 (Nov. 17, 1897).

Track Elevation. (See under Grade Crossings above.)

Transit Facilities. Allen and Humphrey Bills. anon. Railway Age April 23, 1897; St. Ry. J. 13:442 (July, 1897); St. Ry. Rev. 7:428 (July 15, 1897); Elec. World 32:718 (Dec. 31, 1898); City and State 5:406 (Dec. 29, 1898).

——. Cable Traction. Anon. St. Ry. J. p. 213. May, 1890; Ry. World 7:111 (April 7, 1898).

——. " Chicago Railway Problem." (Terminals, Rapid Transit, Marine Commerce and Related Interests.) J. Assoc. Engng. Soc. May, 1892, p. 223; Sept. 1892, p. 470. Abstracts in the Engng. Rec. June 4, 1892; Engng. News June 9, 1892.

——. " Discipline on Chicago City Railway." St. Ry. Rev. 8:254 (April 15, 1898).

——. Electric Traction. Anon. Ry. World 7:111 (April 7, 1898); 8:53 (Feb. 9, 1899); St. Ry. J. 15:613 (Oct. 1899).

——. Elevated Roads. Bramhall, John T. Leslie's Wkly. 80:380 (1895); Gerry, M. H., Jr. Engng. News 38:179 (Sept. 16, 1897), R. R. Gaz. 29:674 (Sept. 24, 1897); Sperry, Henry M. Railroad Gaz. 31:186 (Mar. 17, 1899); anon. St. Ry. J. Feb. 1895, 14:763, 766 (Dec. 1898); St. Ry. R. p. 263, May 1895; 9:675 (Oct. 1899); Elec. Eng. p. 433, .May 15, 1895, R. R. Gaz. p. 364, June 7, 1895; Elec. R. p. 32, July 12, 1895; Power, p 1. Aug. 1895: Western Electrician March 27, 1897, 21:199 (Oct. 9, 1897); Engng. News 38:210 (Sept. 30, 1897); Ry. Age 24:602 (July 23, 1897). 27

——. " History of the Yerkes System." St. Ry. Rev. 8:273 (April 15, 1898), 9:62 (Jan. 15, 1899).

——. " Questions of Street Railway Policy." Maltbie, Milo Roy. Public Policy 3:347 (Dec. 1, 1900). 28

Chicago, Ill.—*Continued.*

——. "Rapid Transit in Chicago." p. 53 "Rapid Transit in Foreign Cities." Parsons, W. B. New York, 1894. 29

——. "Rapid Transit in Chicago." Speed, John Gilmer. Hrprs. Wkly. 39:377 (1895). 30

——. "Report of Special Committee of the City Council of Chicago on the Street Railway Franchises and Operations, etc." Chicago, City Council, 1898. 8vo. 313 pp. Commented on in Engng. News 40:246 (Oct. 20, 1898).

——. "Report of the Street Railway Commission of the City Council of the City of Chicago." Sikes, George C., Secretary. City Council, Chicago, 1900. 8vo. 136 pp. Paper. 31

——. Street Railways in Chicago, Articles on: Gray, John H. Q. J. E. 12:83 (Oct. 1897); Partridge, Newton A. Ann. Am. Acad. Pol. Sci. 12:305 (Sept. 1898), 13:124 (Jan. 1899); Tanner, John R. City Govt. 6:19 (Jan. 1899); anon. St. Ry. J. Aug. 1894, 13:163 (March, 1897); Elec. Eng. Dec. 2, 1896; St. Ry. R. April 15, 1897, 9:649 (Oct. 15, 1899); Elec. World 32:718 (Dec. 31, 1898); City and State 5:406 (Dec. 29, 1898); Economist 21:69 (Jan. 21, 1899). 32

——. "Street Railways of Chicago and other Cities." Schilling, George A. Chicago, Committee of One Hundred against the Humphrey Bills, 1897. 8vo, 73 pp. 33

Unemployed, The. "The Distress in Chicago." Lane, M. A. Hrprs. Wkly. 38:38 (1894). 34

"Upward Movement in Chicago, The." Fuller, Henry B. Atlan. 80:534 (Oct. 1897). 35

"Water Supply of Chicago." Engng. News May 11, 1893, p. 438; Engng. Rec. 37:538 (May 21, 1898), 39:431 (April 8, 1899).

——. Water Supply Tunnels of Chicago. Atwood, Wm. G. Trans. Assoc. Civ. Engs. of Cornell Univ. June, 1897; anon. Engng. News 44:259 (Oct. 18, 1900), 44:306 (Nov. 8, 1900). 36

"Wide-Open Chicago." Matthews, Franklin. Hrprs. Wkly. 42:88 (Jan. 22, 1898). 37

"Women's Work for Chicago." Addams, Jane. Mun. Aff. 2:502 (Sept. 1898). 38

"**Chichester [Eng.]**, Sewage Disposal at." Fuertes, James H. Engng. Rec. 41:129 (Feb. 10, 1900). 39

Child Problem in Cities. (See under **Charities**.)

"**Chillicothe** Water Works Case, The." Wollman, Henry. Engng. Rec. 37:208 (Feb. 5, 1898), Engng. Rec. 38:530 (Nov. 19, 1898). 40

"**China**, Village Life in." Smith, A. H. New York, F. H. Revell & Co., 1899. 8vo, 360 pp. Cloth, $2. 41

"**Chiswick [Eng.]**, Rising Suburbs." London 6:753 (Sept. 16, 1897).

Christian Endeavor Societies, etc. (See **Church and Municipal Conditions**.)

Church and Municipal Conditions. (See also under **Charities, Reform, Municipal Settlements**.)

"Christian and Civic Economy of Large Towns." Chalmers, Thomas. Henderson, Charles R., editor. New York, Charles Scribner's Sons, 1900. 12 mo, 350 pp. Cl. $1.50. 42

"Christian Endeavor Societies, The Work of, in Behalf of Better Citizenship." Baer, John Willis. p. 517 Proc. Second Natl. Conf. for Good City Govt., 1895. See 6-18b. 43

"Christianization of our American Cities." Buchtel, Henry A. The Christian City 10:763 (Dec. 1898). 44

"Christian Citizenship Movement." Martyn, Carlos. Homiletic. R. 34:397 (Nov. 1897). 45

——. "Christian Citizenship League." Lawson, Albert G. p. 275 Proc. Third Natl. Conf. for Good City Govt., 1896. See 6-18c. 47

——. "The Christian Citizen and the Municipality." Maxon, W. D. Am. M. Civics 7:543 (1895). 46

——. "Power of the Church in City Politics." Coler, Bird S. Outlook 63:634 (Nov. 11, 1899). 48

"Civic Church, The." Stead, W. T. R. of Rs. 8:438 (1893). 49

Church and Municipal Conditions—*Continued.*

"Civic Function of the Church." Bean, L. S. Our Day 13:215 1894). 50
"Darkest England and the Way Out, In." Booth, William. London, Published by the Salvation Army, 1890. 285 pp. 3s. 6d. 51
——. "'Darkest England' on the Wrong Track." Bosanquet, Bernard. London, Swan, S. & Co., 1891. 1s. 2d. 52
——. "Darkest England Social Scheme." (Report of first year's work.) London, Salvation Army Publication Department, 1891. 157 pp. 30 cts. Also same subject by Lowell, J. S. Char. R. 1:219 (1892). 53
——. "General Booth's Panacea." Ashley, W. J. Pol. Sci. Q. 6:537 (1891). 54
——. "General Booth's Scheme and the Municipal Alternative." Roberts, W. H. London, Simpkin, 1891. 6d. 55
——. "General Booth's Social Scheme, Criticism of." Loch, Bosanquet and Dwyer. London, Swan, S. & Co., 1891. 272 pp. $1. 56
——. "Salvation Army as a Social Reformer." Walsh, G. E. Chaut. 17:328 (1893). 57
——. "Social plans of General Booth." Woods, R. A. Andover R. 14:485 (1890). 58
——. "Social Scheme of the Salvation Army, The." Vincent, Geo. E. Am. J. Pol. May, 1893. 59
"Endowment of City Churches." Hamlin, Teunis S. Ind. 49:1225 (Sept. 23, 1897). 60
"Modern Cities and their Religious Problems." Loomis, S. L. New York, Baker and Taylor, 1887. 219 pp. $1. 61
"Modern Methods in Church Work, the Gospel Renaissance." Mead, Whitefield. New York, Dodd, Mead & Co., 1896. 363 pp. Cl. $1.50. 62
"Municipal Reform and the Churches." Strong, Thomas N. Pp. 261-267 Pro. of the Louisville Conf., 1897. See 6-18d. 63
"Our Country: its possible future and its present crisis." Strong, Josiah. New York, Baker & Taylor, 1886. 8vo, 229 pp. 60 cts. 64
"Primary and the Prayer Meeting, The." Clarke, Francis E. City and State, Vol. I, No. 24, p. 5. 65
"Problems of the City in Terms of Theology." Nash, H. S. Open Church 2:282 April, 1898). 66
"Problems of the Modern City Church." Dickinson, C. A. Andover R. Oct. 1889. 67
"Relation of the Church to Municipal Politics." Slicer, Thomas R. Mun. Aff. 4:385 (June, 1900). 68
"Settlements and the Church's Duty." Starr, Ellen Gates. Boston, Church Social Union, 3 Joy St., n. d. pamphlet 10 cts. 69
——. Relation between Churches and Settlements, Articles on. Gavit, John P. Commons 2:3, 3:3 (Feb. May, 1898); Gordon, Clarence. Commons 2:1 (Nov. 1897); McGinley, A. A. Catholic World 71:145, 396 (May, June, 1900). 70
"Social Economics and City Evangelization." Commons, John R. The Christian City 10:767 (Dec. 1898). 71
"Social Reform and the Church." Commons, John R. New York. T. Y. Crowell & Co., 1894. 176 pp. 75 cts. (Municipal Monopolies, pp. 121-151.) 72
"The New Era, or the Coming Kingdom." Strong, Josiah. New York, Baker & Taylor, 1893. 277 pp. 75 cts. 73
"Twentieth Century Churches." Ch. VII, p. 131. "The Twentieth Century City." Strong, Josiah. New York, Baker & Taylor Co., 1898. 16 mo, 181 pp. 50 cts.
"Work in Great Cities, Six Lectures on Pastoral Theology." Ingram, Arthur F. Winnington. London, Gardner, Darton & Co., 1897. 3d edit. 12 mo, 194 pp. 3s. 6d. 74

Cincinnati, O.

City Government, General Works, Unclassified.

Description and Statistics of Cincinnati, O., in 1880. Census. See 1-7.
"Fair Cincinnati." Logan, Charles T. Leslie's Pop. M. Jan. 1898. 75
"Municipal Condition of Cincinnati." Wilby, Chas. B. p. 313 Proc. Second Natl. Conf. for Good City Govt., 1895. See 6-18b. 76
"Plain Municipal Lessons from Cincinnati." Chaut. 12:383 (1891).

"Art in Cincinnati, Public. Decorations for the Main Entrance of the New City

Cincinnati—*Continued.*
Hall." Hrprs. Wkly. 41:696 (July 10, 1897).
Charities. "Thirty-five Years Among the Poor and the Public Institutions of Cincinnati." Emery, Jos. D. Cincinnati, G. E. Stevens & Co., 1887. $1.25. 77
"Cincinnati Southern Railway, a Study in Municipal Activity, The." Hollander, J. H. J. H. Univ. Studies XII, 1 and 2. 50 cts. 77a
"Garbage Utilization at Cincinnati." Engng. News Oct. 8, 1896; Hermann, August. Engng. Rec. 40:465 (Oct. 14, 1899); Mun. Engng. 17:333 (Dec. 1899); Engng. News 43:271 (April 26, 1900). 78
"Gas Works, Franchise." May, Max B. Ann. Am. Acad. Pol. Sci. 14:141 (July, 1899). 79
History to 1880. Census. See 1-7.
"Indebtedness, Bonded." May, Max B. Ann. Am. Acad. Pol. Sci. 14:262 (Sept. 1899). 80
Paving. "Maintenance of Asphalt Streets in Cincinnati, Ohio." Harper, J. M. Engng. Rec. 40:627 (Dec. 2, 1899). 81
"Schools of Cincinnati, Public." Rice, J. M. Forum 14:293 (1892). 82
Settlement, Cincinnati Social. Commons, May, 1897.
"Sewer Repairs, Cincinnati, Ohio." Harper, J. W. Engng. Rec. 39:447 (April 15, 1899). 83
"Street Railway Company, The Chester Park Shops of the Cincinnati." St. Ry. Jour. 14:77 (Feb. 1898).
Water Supply. "Water Supp'y and Typhoid Fever, Cincinnati." Sanitarian 36:404 (1896); Engng. Rec. 36:561 (Nov. 27, 1897); Fire & W. 23:13 (Jan. 8, 1898); Engng. News 41:159 (March 9, 1899); Engng. Rec. 39:323 (March 11, 1899); City Govt. 6:68 (April, 1899); Fire & W. 25:135 (April 29, 1899).

Cinque Ports. (See under **United Kingdom.**)

"Citizens' Union." (See under **New York.**)

Citizenship, Civic Duty, Etc. (See under **Elections.**)

Civil Service in Cities.

See also Boston, Brooklyn, Chicago, New York, San Francisco, United Kingdom, United States.

"Appointment of Municipal Officers." Press, John. Cambridge (Mass.) Civil Service Reform Association Publications, 1884. 84
"Bibliography of Civil Service Reform and related topics." (pp. 5-7 bibliography on the Civil Service in Municipal Government, the remainder of the bibliography being devoted to references on the other phases of the subject.) New York, Published for the Women's Auxiliary to the Civil Service Reform Association, 1900. Pamphlet. 14 pp. 10 cts.
"Citizenship and the Civil Service." Walbridge, C. P. Proc. Natl. Civil Service Reform League, 1894. p. 68. 85
"Civil Service in Great Britain: a History of Abuses and Reforms, and their bearing upon American Politics." Eaton, Dorman B. New York, Harpers, 1877. $2.50 86
"Civil Service in Municipal Government." Freud, J. Richard. Outpost 1:3 (Aug. 5 and 12, 1899); Richardson, Charles. Good Govt. 13:65 (1893); Webb, Sidney. Mun. J. & London 9:77 (Jan. 26, 1900). 87
Civil Service Reform in American Cities, Articles on. Davis, Horace. Mchts. Assoc. R. p. 2, May, 1897; Eliot, Charles W. Forum 12:153 (1891); Low, Seth. Good Govt. 13:29 (1893); Patterson, C. Stuart. Penn. Mo. 13:295 (1882); Schurz, Carl. Good Govt. 13:93 (1894); Shaw, Albert and Horace Deming. Proc. Natl. Civil Service League, Cincinnati, 1897, p. 120, also published separately by the League, gratis; Wilby, Chas. B. same, 1894, p. 79; anon. Outlook, March, 1897. 88
——. "Civil Service Reform in Cities." Chapter V, p. 85, "Municipal Reform in the United States," by Thomas H. Devin. New York, Putnam, 1896. 174 pp. 75 cts. 89
——. "Relations of Civil Service Reform to Municipal Reform." Schurz, Carl. p. 123 First Natl. Conf. for Good City Govt., 1894. See 6-18a. 90
——. "Growth of Civil Service Reform in States and Cities." (pp. 521-559, Fifteenth Report of the U. S. Civil Service Commission, 1896-7.) Also printed sepa-

Civil Service in Cities—*Continued*.

rately, in pamphlet form, to be had by addressing Clerk of the Senate Document Room, Washington, D. C.

———. " Civil Service in States and Cities." Shepard, Edward M. Am. J. Soc. Sci. 20:98 (1895). 91

" Competitive Tests and the Civil Service of States and Cities." Shepard, Edward M. New York, Putnams, 1885. (Economic Tracts No. 11.) 25 cts. 92

" Examinations, Civil Service." Bowker, R. R. New York, Society for Political Education, 1886. 45 pp. 15 cts. (National, State and Municipal Examination Papers.) 93

Finance and Civil Service Reform, Orations on. Vol. IV, " American Orations: Studies in American Political History," edited by Albert Johnston and James A. Woodburn. New York, G. P. Putnam's Sons, 1897. $1.25. 94

" Influence of the Spoils Idea upon the Government of American Cities." Welsh, Herbert. New York, National Civil Service Reform League, 1894. Gratis. 95

" Merit System of Civil Service." Pp. 469-473 in "The City for the People or the Municipalization of the City Government and of Local Franchises." Parsons, Frank. Philadelphia, C. F. Taylor, 1900. 8vo, 597 pp. Cloth, $1. 96

———. " Merit and Party Systems." (Editorial) Ind. 50:53 (Jan. 13, 1898).

" Municipal Misgovernment, One Remedy for." (Civil Service Reform). Eliot, Charles W. Forum 12:153 (1891). 97

" Poison in the Civil Service." Ralph, Julian. Hrprs. Wkly. 40:131 (1896). 98

" Police and Fire Department Civil Service of Cities." New York Civil Service Reform Association, 1884. Report made at the request of the Civil Service Commission of the State. 24 pp.

" Prize Essays on Municipal Reform." Pense, T. H., John Prentiss and Henry T. Terry. Published by the Cambridge, Mass. Civil Service Reform Association, 1884. 74 pp. 99

" Proceedings at the Annual Meeting of the National Civil Service Reform League." New York, Published annually by the league, 1882-1900. 8 cts. per number.

" Theory and Practice of Getting Jobs." Alvord, J. W. Public Policy 2:282 (May 5, 1900). 100

Working Men and Civil Service. " Civil Service Reform in its Bearings upon the Interests of Workingmen." Welsh, Herbert. P. 116, Proc. Natl. Civil Service Reform League, Washington, 1895. 1

———. " The Application of the Civil Service Rules to Public Laborers." Russell, Charles Theodore, Jr. P. 49, Proc. Natl. Civil Service Reform League, Buffalo, 1892. 2

———. (See also under **Labor and its Relation** to the **Municipality**.)

Cleveland, O.

City Government, General Works, Unclassified.

" Civic Problems of Greater Cleveland, A Few." (I. An Extensive Dock System. II. A New Union Railway Station. III. Sewage Disposal. IV. A Cleveland "Court of Honor." V. The Mediterranean and Great Lakes Compared.) Bolton, C. E. Cleveland, O., 1897. Pamphlet. 40 pp. 3

Description and Statistics of Cleveland, O. in 1880. Census. See 1-7.

" Federal Plan of Municipal Government as Illustrated by the City of Cleveland." Avery, Elroy M. South Bethlehem, Pa., 1892. 15 pp. Reprinted from the Lehigh Quarterly, June 1892, Vol. 2, No. 3. 4

———. " Cleveland's Federal Plan." Ralph, Julian. Hrprs. Wkly. 39:829 (1895). 5

———. " Municipal Government of Cleveland." Blandin, E. J. p. 112 Proc. Second Natl. Conf. for Good City Govt., 1895. See 6-18b. 6

" Chamber of Commerce, Annual Report of, for 1896." p. 132, "The Business Management of a Great City," by Mayor William L. Strong, of New York. p. 142, " Civic Pride," by Mayor Robert S. McKisson, of Cleveland. 7

Garbage Disposal. Mun. J. & Eng. 9:157 (Dec. 1900); Engng. N. 43:358 (May, 31, 1900).

" History of Cleveland, Chapter on the." Burton, C. M. Detroit, Burton, 1895. 31 pp. 8

———. History of Cleveland to 1880. Census. See 1-7.

Cleveland, O.—*Continued.*

"Library of Cleveland, Public." Brett, W. H. Mag. Western His. 7:55 (1888).   9
"Municipal Service, Cleveland's." Cleveland Leader, Jan. 22, 1896.
"Parks of Cleveland, Ohio, The." Park & Cem. 10:5 (March, 1900).
"Sanitary Needs of Cleveland, O." Engng. Rec. Feb. 15, 1896.
"Settlement, Goodrich Social." Cadwallader, Starr. Commons 2:1 (Oct. 1897); anon. Ann. Am. Acad. Pol. Sci. 11:134 (Jan. 1898).   10
Sewage. "Bacterial Sewage Disposal at East Cleveland." Engng. Rec. 41:128 (Feb. 10, 1900).
Street Paving. "Pavements of Cleveland." Richie, James. J. Assoc. Engng. Soc. March, 1895; Sargent, J. H. J. Assoc. Engng. Soc. Sept. 1888.   11
"Street Railway Problem in Cleveland." Hopkins, William Rowland. Am. Econ. Assoc. Economic Studies Vol. I, Nos. 5 and 6, 1896. 376 pp. 75 cts.   12
——. "Street Railway Franchises, Cleveland." Fanning, M. J. Ann. Am. Acad. Pol. Sci. 14:380 (Nov. 1899), 15:121 (Jan. 1900); Short, S. H. St. Ry. J. 14:43 (Jan. 1898); Wilcox, Delos F. Ann. Am. Acad. Pol. Sci. 13:127 (Jan. 1899).   13
"Suburban Village, A Model." Bolton, C. E. Am. Mo. R. of Rs. 20:573 (Nov. 1899).   13a
"Telephone Co., The New Exchange of the Cleveland." Elec. Eng. 25:175 (Feb. 17, 1898).
"Water Works, of Cleveland, O. The New Lake Tunnel and Cribs for the." Schulz, C. F. Engng. Rec. May 22, 1897; Engng. Rec. 37:492 (May 7, 1898).   14

Clichy, France, Housing. "Habitations Ouvrières Cité Jouffroy-Renault à Clichy." R. Gen. de l'Arch. p. 158, 1867.

Clinton, Mass.

Sewage. "The Clinton, Mass., Sewage Disposal System." Engng. Rec. 39:136 (Jan. 14, 1899); Engng. Rec. 41:196 (March 3, 1900).

Coal Yards, Municipal. (See also under **Municipal Control, Municipal Ownership.**)

"Municipal Fuel Bill Pronounced Unconstitutional." New Nation 2:310, 328 (1892).
"Municipal Fuel Yards." Parsons, Frank. New Nation 2:325 (1892); anon. New Nation 1:421 (1891); To-day 3:453 (1891).   15
"Opinions of the Justices of the Supreme Judicial Court as to whether cities and towns have right to establish and maintain municipal coal yards." (Massachusetts.) Doc. 519. 1892. 13 pp.

"**Cohoes [N. Y.]**, The Sewerage of." Engng. Rec. 37:533 (May 21, 1898).

Colchester, Eng.

"Colchester's New Town Hall." Surveyor Supp. Jan. 12, 1900.
History. "A Town with a Past." Benham, Charles E. Mun. J. & London 8:1379 (Dec. 29, 1899).   16
——. "Colchester." (History.) Cutts, E. L. London, Longmans, 1888. Historic Towns Series. 8vo. 3s. 6d. (For other references on the history of Colchester see p. 193 Gross' Bibliography of British Municipal History.)   17

"**Colne [Eng.]**, The Slums." Mun. J. & London 8:1251 (Nov. 17, 1899).

Cologne, Ger.

Buildings. "Köln und seine Bauten." Köln, 1888.
Improvement of Cologne. "Die Stadterweiterung von Köln." Stübben, J. Wochbl. f. Arch. u. Ing., pp. 25, 41, 1879.   18
Library of Cologne, The Town. Algermisen, J. L. Zeitschrift für Bücherfreunde (Jan. 1899).   19
Sewage. The Purification of Sewerage at Cologne. Geshundheits-Ing. Nov. 15, 1897.

"**Colombo**, Municipal Lighting." Ind. Engng. July 16, 1898.

"**Colorado Springs** Water Works." Lakes, Arthur. Engng. M. 10:273 (1895).   20

Columbus, Ga.
"Electrical Equipment of a Southern City, The." Boileau, W. E. Elec. World 30:275 (Sept. 4, 1897).   21

Columbus, O.
"City of Columbus, The." City Govt. 3:81 (Sept. 1897).
"Condition of Columbus, O., Municipal." Williams, D. E. p. 323 Proc. Second Natl. Conf. for Good City Govt., 1895. See 6-18b.   22
Council. "Dr. Gladden's Election." Outlook 64:855 (April 14, 1900).
Description and statistics of Columbus, O. in 1880. Census. See 1-7.
"Garbage Reduction at Columbus, Ohio." Engng. N. 44:47 (July 19, 1900).
History of Columbus to 1880. Census. See 1-7.
"Lighting at Columbus, Electric." Leitsch, W. C. Municipality 1:32 (April, 1900).   23
Municipal Control. "Franchise Discussion in Columbus, Ohio." St. Ry. J. 16:1224 (Dec. 29, 1900).
Street Railways. "Railway Company, Operating Methods of the Columbus." St. Ry. J. 16:789 (Sept. 1, 1900).
"Water Supply of Columbus, O., Proposed Storage Reservoir and Infiltration Conduit for the." Engng. News 38:346 (Nov. 25, 1897); Griggs, Julian. Engng. Rec. 40:9 (June 3, 1899); Engng. News 42:8 (July 6, 1899).   24

Compulsory Education. (See under Schools.)

Compulsory Voting. (See under Elections.)

Concerts, Municipal.
"Report on Outdoor Concerts." Drohan, John. City. Rec. 1:546 (Sept. 29, 1898).   25

"Concord [Mass.], Sewage Pumping and Electric Station, The." Engng. Rec. 42:320 (Oct. 6, 1900).

Concord, N. H.
History. "Concord, History and Life." Cooke, George Willis. New Eng. M. 18:425 (June, 1898).   26
——. "History of Concord, N. H." Sanborn, Frank B. See 1-4a.   27
Lighting, etc. "Concord Municipal Lighting and Sewerage Plant." Am. Gas Light J. 72:124 (Jan. 22, 1900).
"Water Department of Concord." Fire and Water March 13, 1897.

Conduits.
See also Berlin, Boston, Chicago, Glasgow, London, New York, Paris, St. Louis.
"Advantages of Tunnels in Large Cities." Parsons, William Barclay. Engng. Rec. 40:672 (Dec. 16, 1899).   28
"Architecture, Subway." Arch. & B. M. 1:185 (March, 1900).
City Subways for Pipes and Wires in Cities. Bryant, Henry F. Cosmopol. 26:439 (Feb. 1899); anon. Engng. News 43:176 (March 15, 1900); Engng. Rec. 40:14 (June 3, 1899); same 41:585, 601 (June 23, 1900).   29
"The Systematic Location of Gas Mains and other Pipes in the Streets." McDonald, Donald. Prog. Age 18:260 (June 15, 1900); anon. Engng. News 38:264 (Oct. 21, 1897).   30
"Underground Conduits for Telephone, Telegraph and Electric Light Wires." United States Consular Report No. 139, 1892. pp. 739-810.
"Underground vs. Overhead Wires." Webb, Herbert L. Engng. M. 1:677 (1891).   31

Congestion of Population in Cities. (See under Population.)

Connecticut.
"Ballot Law, Connecticut." Harrison, L. New Englander 51:401 (1890).   32
"Beginnings of Connecticut Towns." Andrews, Charles M. Ann. Am. Acad. Pol. Sci. 1:165 (1890).   33
"Sewage Disposal in Connecticut." (Report of the Sewage Commission.) Hart-

Connecticut—*Continued.*

ford, Conn., 1899. 8vo, 88 pp. Commented on in Engng. News 41:107 (Feb. 16, 1899), Engng. Rec. 39:249 (Feb. 18, 1899).

Transit Facilities. "Electric Railways in Central Connecticut." St. Ry. J. 15:430 (July, 1899).

———. "Operating Expenses of Connecticut Railways." St. Ry. R. 8:81 (Feb. 15, 1898).

Constantinople.

"Constantinople." (Historical and descriptive.) Grosvenor, Edwin A. (With an Introduction by Lew Wallace.) Boston, Roberts Bros., 1895. 2 vols. 8vo, 413, 411 pp. Cl. $6.   34

"Constantinople." Hutton, William Holden. New York, The Macmillan Co., 1900. 8vo, 341 pp. Cl. $1.50.   35

"Constantinople as an Historic City." Ch. XI, pp. 309-340 in Frederic Harrison's "The Meaning of History." New York, Macmillan, 1894. 8vo, 482 pp. $2.25.   36

"Constantinople, The Story of the Old Capital of the Empire." Hutton, William Holden. New York, Macmillan (Mediæval Town Series), 1901. 16mo, 341 pp. $1.50.   37

Street Life in Constantinople. Gottwald, J. Deutscher Hausschatz Heft 5, 1897. 38

"Turkish Syphons at Constantinople." Wegmann, Edward. Engng. Rec. 40:549 (Nov. 11, 1899).   39

Consular Reports of the United States.

The following list indicates the more important volumes in the Consular Reports of the United States which have a more or less direct reference to municipal affairs in foreign countries. The shorter reports have been indexed under each city and country.

"Fire and Building Regulations in Foreign Countries." U. S. Spl. Consular Reports Vol. VIII, 1892. 543 pp.

"Gas in Foreign Countries." Special Consular Report. Washington, Government Printing Office, 1891. 260 pp.

"Local Transportation in Foreign Cities." Cons. Rep. No. 139, 1892. pp. 597-728.

"Public Works of German Municipalities." Washburn, Albert H. pp. 202-214 U. S. Consular Reports, No. 149, Feb. 1893.   40

"School Gardens in Europe." U. S. Spl. Consular Reports, Vol. XX, pt. II, pp. 163-224. Washington, Government Printing Office, 1900.

"Sewerage in Foreign Cities." U. S. Consular Reports No. 173, 1895. pp. 145-245. (Systems of Amsterdam, Berlin, Bordeaux, Bradford, Bremen, Brussels, Cardiff, Constantinople, Copenhagen, Dublin, Edinburgh, Florence, Frankfort, Glasgow, Hamburg, Leeds, Leith, Liverpool, Lyons, Manchester, Marseilles, Munich, Rome, Rotterdam, St. Petersburg, Stettin, Stockholm, Trieste, and Vienna.)   40a

———. "Disposal of Sewage and Garbage in Foreign Countries." U. S. Special Consular Reports Vol. XVII, pp. 13-221, 1899. (Systems of Amsterdam, Antwerp, Berlin, Bradford, Brussels, Canadian Towns, Ghent, Glasgow, Gothenburg, London, Lyons, Manchester, Nice, Nottingham, Nuremberg, Rotterdam, St. Gall, Trieste, Zürich and other cities.)   40b

"Streets and Highways in Foreign Countries." Special Consular Report, 1891. 592 pp.

"Underground Conduits for Telephone, Telegraph and Electric Light Wires." U. S. Consular Report No. 139, 1892. pp. 739-810.

"Vagrancy and Public Charities in Foreign Countries." U. S. Special Consular Report, 1893. 350 pp.

Copenhagen, Denmark.

Housing Workingmen's Building Societies in the Suburbs of Copenhagen. Westergaard, Niels. Ar. Soz. Gesetz. Stat. 14:716 (Dec. 1899).   41

"Sewage Disposal of Copenhagen." Kirk, Robert J. See 40a above.   42

———. "The Place of the Council and of the Mayor in the Organization of Munici-

"Small Gardens for Tenement Dwellers in Copenhagen." Loeb, Morris. Char. R. 10:445 (Dec. 1900).   43

"Tramways, Fares and Earnings of the Copenhagen." Faber-Madsen, V. St. Ry. Jour. 14:425 (Aug. 1898).   44

BIBLIOGRAPHY. 57

Cork, Ireland.
Electric Tramways, Cork. St. Ry. J. 14:6 (Jan. 1898), 15:35 (Jan. 1899); Ry. World 7:108 (April 7, 1898), 8:23 (Jan. 5, 1899); St. Ry. R. 9:5 (Jan. 15, 1899).

Corporations, Municipal. (See under Government, General References and Unclassified.) p. 1.

Councils and Boards of Aldermen. (See also Mayor.)
See also Berlin, France, Germany, London, New York, Philadelphia.

"Aldermen and their Appointment." Godkin, E. L. Nation 38:158 (1884). 45
——. "Aldermen and Municipal Corporations." (England.) Spectator 58:1398 (1885).
Council Committees. "Boards, Single-Headed Commissions or Council Committees." Evans, F. V. City Govt. 5:71 (Aug. 1898); Prog. Age 16:405 (Sept. 1, 1898); Young, W. E. Prog. Age 16:404 (Sept. 1, 1898). 46
Council Government vs. Mayor Government. (Favors council government.) Durand, E. Dana. Pol. Sci. Q. 15:426, 675, (1900). 47
——. "Mayor vs. Council: The Twenty-seventh Annual Joint Debate of the University of Wisconsin." Madison, George B. Nelson, 1897. 103 pp. 50 cts.
——. "Outgrown City Government." (Against the council.) Parton, James. Forum 2:539 (1887). 48
——. "Problem of City Government. Where to Locate Municipal Powers, The Council and the Mayor." Mchts. Assoc. Rev. p. 5, June, 1897.
pal Government—The Necessity of Distinguishing Legislation from Administration." Goodnow, Frank J. Pp. 74-88 in "A Municipal Program." New York, The Macmillan Co., 1900. 8vo, 246 pp. Cl. $1. Also in Proc. Indianapolis Conf. of the National Municipal League p. 71, 1898. See 6-18e. 49
Evolution of Council. See Stubb's "English Constitutional History." Vol. I, p. 419. Oxford, Clarendon, 1874-8. 50
"Legislature in City and State, 1797-1897, The." Deming, Horace E. Pp. 89-102 Proc. of the Louisville Conf. for Good City Government, 1897. See 6-18d. 51
——. "Decline of Legislatures." Godkin, E. L. Atlan. 80:35 (July, 1897). 52
"Organization of Town Councils." Williams, Sylvester G. Public Improvements 2:174 (Feb. 15, 1900). 53
"Reform of our Municipal Councils." Williams, Henry W. p. 236 Proc. Third Natl. Conf. for Good City Govt., 1896. See 6-18c. 54
"Representative Robbery." City and State, Vol. I, No. 21, p. 5 (1895).
Salary of Council Members. "Should Municipal Legislators receive a Salary." Pryor, James W. p. 263 Proc. Third Natl. Conf. for Good City Govt., 1896. See 6-18c. 55
"Single or a Double Council." Butler, John A. p. 252 Proc. Third Natl. Conf. for Good City Govt., 1896. See 6-18c. 53
——. "Shall we have One or Two Legislative Chambers." Capen, Samuel B. Proc. Third Natl. Conf. for Good City Govt., 1896. See 6-18c. 57
"Work of City Councils, The." Bird, Albert. Citizen 1:206 (1895). 58

Coventry, Eng.
"Crematory, Coventry's Municipal." City Govt. 7:24 (July, 1899).
Electric Tramways of Coventry. Ty. & Ry. World 8:327 (Sept. 7, 1899); St. Ry. R. 10:137 (March 15, 1900); Elec. W. &E. 35:504 (April 7, 1900).
History. "Life in an Old English Town: A History of Coventry, from the Earliest Times. Compiled from Official Records." Harris, Mary Dormer. New York, Macmillan Co., 1898, 8vo, 307 pp. Cl. 17s. 6d. 59

Crefeld [Ger.] "Die Wohnungsverhältnisse der arbeitenden Klassen in der Stadt Crefeld." Seyffardt, L. F. pp. 153-156, Hft. 31, Schr. d. Ver. f. Socialpolitik. 60

Cremation. (See under **Burial in Cities.**)

Crime, Criminals in Cities. (See under **Police.**)

Croker, Richard.

"Mr. Richard Croker and Greater New York." Appendix to "Satan's Invisible World Displayed," by W. T. Stead. New York, R. F. Fenno & Co., 1897. 12mo, 300 pp. $1.25. Also article by same writer, Mun. Rec. & Ad. Vol. I, No. 19, p. 6 (Oct. 16, 1897). (See also **New York.**) 60a

"Secret of Croker's Influence, The." Gunton's 17:161 (Sept. 1899).

"What Croker Is and Means." Hrprs. Weekly 43:832 (Aug. 26, 1899).

Cronenberg [Ger.], Housing.
"Krupp's Arbeiter-Colonie, Cronenberg." Haarmann's Zeitsch. f. Bauhdw. p. 171, 1877.

Crossness [Eng.], (See under London).

Crowding of Cities. (See under Population.)

Croydon, Eng.

"Electric Traction for Croydon." Monkhouse. Ty. & Ry. World 8:486 (Dec. 7, 1899). 61

"Street Lighting by Electric Lamps—with Special Reference to the Systems in Use at Croydon, England." Minshall, F. H. Am. Gas Light J. 73:968 (Dec. 17, 1900). 62

Cuba.

A Brief Study of Cuban Municipal Government. "Breve Estudio sobre * * los Asuntos Municipales en la Isla de Cuba * * ." Carrera y Jústiz, Francisco. Habana, Los Niños Huerfanos, 1900. 12mo, 86 pp. 63

Cultivation of Vacant City Lots (Pingree Plan.) See under Vacant City Lots.)

"**Cumberland [Md.]**, The Pollution of the Water Supply of, by a Paper Pulp Mill." Hungerford, Churchill. Engng. News 39:90 (Feb. 10, 1898). 64

Cumulative Voting. (See under Proportional Representation.)

"**Curfew for City Children.**" Townsend, (Mrs.) John D. No. Am. 163:725 (1896). (See also Child Problem in Cities under **Charities.**) 65

Danville, Ill.

"Water Works Decision, The Reversal of the Danville." Engng. Rec. 39:417 (April 8, 1899).

Day Labor and Contract System on Municipal Works. (See under Labor and Its Relation to the Municipality.)

Dayton, O.

"Electrolysis of Cast Iron Water Pipes at Dayton, Ohio." Brown, Harold P. Pro. Am. Soc. Mun. Imp. (5th yr.) Pt. II, p. 215 (Oct. 1898), Elec. Eng. 26:441 (Nov 3, 1898), St. Ry. Rev. 8:817 (Nov. 15, 1898), St. Ry. J. 14:785 (Dec. 1898), Mun. Engng. 16:84 (Feb. 1899); Rowe, Chas. E. Engng. Rec. 38:422 (Oct. 22, 1898). 66

"Street Railways of Dayton, O." St. Ry. Jour. 14:119 (March, 1898).

Death Rate in Cities. (See under Statistics of Cities, also under Population.)

Debts and Loans, Municipal.(See under Finance.)

"**Deerfield [Mass.]**, History of." Sheldon, George. See 1-4a. 67

Defences of Cities.

"Defence of Our Great Cities, The." "C. E." Mun. Rec. and Ad. 1:6 (Nov. 20, 1897), 2:3 (Dec. 11, 1897), 2.33 (Dec. 18, 1897), 2:65 (Dec. 25, 1897), 2:97 (Jan. 1, 1898), 2:125 (Jan. 8, 1898), 2:189 (Jan. 22, 1898.)

Denmark, Local and Municipal Government in. Demombynes Vol I., pp. 219-229. See 2-11.

Denver, Col.

City Government, General Works, Unclassified.
"Denver City Government." Cochran, Charles W. City Govt. 2:12 (Jan., 1897.) 68
Description and Statistics of Denver, Col. in 1880. Census. See 1-7.
"Mayor McMurray's Veto of the Opposition Charter for Denver, Col." (Editorial.) Am. Gas Light J. 67:447 (Sept. 20, 1897.)
"Municipal Condition of Denver, Col." Rogers, Platt. p. 424 Proc. Second Natl. Conf. for Good City Govt., 1895. See 6-18b. 69

"Department Store in the West, The. Changes for the better in Denver." Meredith, Ellis. Arena 22:337 (Sept., 1899.) 70
History of Denver to 1880. Census. See 1-7.
Lighting. "The Offer of the Denver Consolidated Gas Company to the City." (Editorial). Am. Gas Light J. 67:449 (Sept. 20, 1897.)
"Sewers and Pavements of Denver, Col., Notes on the." Hardesty, W. P. Engng. News 40:295 (Nov. 10, 1898.) 71
"Water Supply of Denver, Col." Engin. News 37:125 (Feb. 25, 1897.)
———. "Sedimentation Tanks with Numerous Circular Overflow Weirs; Denver Union Water Co." Engng. N. 44:322 (Nov. 15, 1900.)
"Women's Work in Denver." Conine, Martha A. B. Mun. Aff. 2:527 (Sept., 1898.) 72

Department Stores in Cities.

See also Boston, Chicago, Denver, New York, Philadelphia.
"Department Store Question, The." Hirsch, Adolph. Business 19:605 (Oct., 1899.) 73
"Two Weeks in Department Stores." MacLean, Annie Marion. Am. J. Sociol. 4:721 (May, 1899.) 74

"**Depew, N. Y.**, The Sewerage System of." Engng. Rec. 38:120 (July 9, 1898.)

"**Derby, [Eng.]** and Ashbourne Electric Railway." Ry. World 6:344 (Nov., 1897.)

Des Moines, Ia.

History, Description and Statistics of Des Moines, Ia., in 1880. Census. See 1-7.
Lighting, Electric. "Taxpayers Protected." Public Policy 2:122 Feb. 24, 1900.)
"Roadside Settlement." Commons, Aug., 1897.

Detroit, Mich.

"City Government in Detroit." Kent, Charles A. Ann. Arbor, Studies in Finance and History, Michigan Univ. Article in Vol. I., No. 6 (Dec. 1895). 25c. 75
Description and Statistics of Detroit, Mich., in 1880. Census. See 1-7.
"Detroit: A Municipal Study." Pingree, Hazen S. Outlook Feb., 1897. 76
"Detroit an Interesting City." Mun. Engng. 15:69 (Aug., 1898.)
Detroit Plan, Pingree Plan. (See under **Vacant City Lots, Cultivation of.**)
"Municipal Condition of Detroit." McLaurin, Donald D. p. 382 Proc. Second Natl. Conf. for Good City Govt., 1895. See 6-18b. 77

Elections. "Working Digest of Registration and Election Laws." Detroit, McCrackan, 1895. 24 pp. 15 cts.
"Garbage Disposal in Detroit." Kempster, Walter. Mun. Engng. 15:159 (Sept., 1898); anon. Engng. Rec. 38:200 (Aug. 6, 1898.) 78
History of Detroit to 1880. Census. See 1-7.
Labor. "Municipal Employment Scheme Proposed for Detroit, Mich." Post, James A. Proc. Nat. Conf. Char. and Cor., held in Toronto, Ont., July 7-14, 1897. 79
Lighting. "Various Gas matters in Detroit and Toledo." Prog. Age 16:477 (Oct. 15, 1898.)
———. Municipal Electric Lighting in Detroit, Articles on. Fairlie, John Archibald. Mun. Aff. 4:606 (Sept., 1900); Fisher, Geo. E. Elec. Eng. 25:64 (Jan. 13,

Detroit, Mich.—*Continued.*

1898); Gonden, H. J. Mun. Ownership 1:9 (June, 1900); Moore, Chas. Am. Econ. Asoc. 2:539 (1888); Starring, Ford. Elec. Eng. 24:377 (Oct. 21, 1897); anon. City Govt. 1:35 (1896), 7:76 (Oct., 1899); Elec. Eng. 24:326, 329, 378 (1897), 25:61, 26:154 (1898); Engng. Rec. 38:221 (Aug. 13, 1898), 40:310 (Sept. 2, 1899); Engng. News 40:152 (Sept. 8, 1898); Public Policy 2:50 (Jan. 27, 1900); Public Improvements 2:152 (Feb. 1, 1900.)

" Parks of Detroit, Mich., The." Park & Cem. 9:77 (June, 1899.)

" Public Work, Methods in Detroit." Mun. Engng. 19:324 (Nov. 1900.)

" Telephone Company, The Detroit." Grace, S. P. Elec. Eng. 25:123, 153 (Feb. 3, 1898, March 15, 1898.

Transit Facilities. Articles on Detroit's experience with municipal street railways, three-cent fares, etc. Bemis, E. W. Mun. Aff. 3:473 (Sept., 1899); Brown, Thomas W. Am. Law R. 33:853 (Nov., Dec. 1899); Insull, Samuel. Elec. Rev. 35:28 (July 12, 1899); Moore, Chas. J. Q. J. E. 13:453 (July, 1899), 14:121 (Nov., 1899); Van Zandt, A. D. B. City Govt. 1:11 (1896); anon. City Govt. 6:68 (April, 1899); St. Ry. R. 9:224, 363, 452 (April, June, 1899), 10:218 (April, 1900); Public Improvements 1:61 (June 15, 1899); St. Ry. J. 15:447, 477 (July, 1899); Other Side 1:12, 15 (July, 1899); Ann. Am. Acad. Pol. Sci. 14:108 (Sept., 1899.)

——. " Experience of Detroit. The Public vs. the Street Car Companies." Boston, Leaflet issued by the Citizen's Committee of Boston, 1897.

——. " New Equipment for the Rapid Railway of Detroit." St. Ry. J. 16:119 (Feb. 3, 1900.)

——. " The Interurban Electric Railways around Detroit." St. Ry. J. 15:1 (Jan., 1899.)

" Water Rates, Detroit's Low." City Govt. 7:36 (Aug., 1899.) (June 29, 1899.)

——. " The Partial Abolition of Water Rates at Detroit." Engng. News 41:416

——. " Typhoid Fever and the Water Supply of Detroit." Williams, Gardner S. Pamphlet reprinted from the Proc. of Sanitary Convention held in Detroit, Dec. 9-15, 1897. 17 pp.

——. " The Equity of the Detroit Water Rates." Engng. Rec. 38:272 (Aug. 27, 1898.)

——. " The Record System of the Waterworks Department, Detroit." Engng. Rec. 37:230 (Feb. 12, 1898.)

Devonport, Eng.

" Municipal Devonport." Hunt, Fred W. Mun. J. 9:81 (Feb. 2, 1900.)

" The Progress of Devonport." Hunt, Fred W. Mun. J. 9:103 (Feb. 9, 1900.)

Dijon, France.

" La Municipalité de Dijon." Marpaux, A. Mouvement Soc. 2:385 (April 1, 1900), 2:162 (April 15, 1900.)

Socialism, Municipal. " L'Oeuvre des Municipalités Socialistes, Dijon." Marpaux, A. Le Mouvement Socialiste, April 1, 1900.

Direct Employment. (See **Day Labor and Contract System.**)

Direct Legislation. (See also under **Home Rule for Cities.**)

See also Alameda (Cal.), Australia, Belgium, Brookline, New England, New Orleans, New Zealand, San Francisco, Switzerland, United States, Victoria (Aus.)

" Arguments and Authorities for Direct Legislation or the Initiative and the Referendum." Dir. Leg. Rec. Vol. VII., No. 4 (Nov., 1900.)

" Direct Legislation." Pp. 255-386 in " The City for the People or the Municipalization of the City Government and of Local Franchises." Parsons, Frank. Philadelphia, C. F. Taylor, 1900. 8vo, 597 pp. Cloth $1.

" Direct Legislation in Switzerland and America." Commons, J. R. Arena 22:725 (Dec., 1899.)

" Direct Legislation, etc." (An extensive collection of arguments and digests of literature on the subject of direct legislation.) Washington, 1898. Senate Document No. 340, 55th Congress, 2d Session. 327 pp.

" Direct Legislation by the Citizenship through the Initiative and Referendum."

BIBLIOGRAPHY.

Direct Legislation.—*Continued.*

Sullivan, J. W. Ruskin, Tenn., The Coming Nation Press, 1896, 4th ed. 120 pp. Paper 10 cts. — 88a

"Direct Legislation by the People." Cree, Nathan. Chicago, A. C. McClurg & Co., 1892. 194 pp. 75 cts. — 89

"Direct Legislation Record." Eltweed Pomeroy, Editor. Published monthly at Newark, N. J. Devoted to advocacy of Direct Legislation. — 90

"Individualistic Argument for Direct Legislation, The." Pomeroy, Eltweed. New Time 1:288 (Nov., 1897.) — 91

"Poll of the People." (Referendum—General). Strachy, J. St. Loe. Cosmopolis 6:48 (April, 1897.) — 92

Referendum. Pp. 273-274. Vol. III. Palgrave. See 1-2. — 93

"Referendum Communal, Le." Sizeranne, Robert de la. Paris, Armand, Colin et Cie., 1893. 86 pp. 1 fr. — 94

Referendum and Initiative, The. Pp. 1178-1181. Encyc. Soc. Ref. See 1-3.

"Social Argument for Direct Legislation, The." Pomeroy, Eltweed. New Time 1:206 (Oct., 1897.) — 95

"Swiss Solutions for American Problems." McCrackan, W. D. New Eng. M. n. s. 11:448 (1894.) — 96

"The Doorway of Reforms." (Direct Legislation.) Pomeroy, Eltweed. Arena 17:711 (April, 1897.) — 97

"The Problem of the Cities." (Direct Legislation.) Pomeroy, Eltweed. Am. Fed. 1895. Reprinted, pp. 187. Senate Document on Direct Legislation. See above. — 98

"The Referendum in America together with some chapters on the history of the initiative and other phases of popular government in the United States." (Local referendum Ch. IX. et seq.) Oberholtzer, Ellis P. New York, Scribners, 1900. 8vo, 430 pp. $2. An earlier work by the same author on the same subject appeared in the publications of the University of Pennsylvania, Vol. IV., No. 12, 1893. 225 pp. $1.50. — 99

Direct Nominations. (See under **Elections.**)

Dispensaries. (See under **Charities.**)

"**Dolgeville, N. Y.**, Electric Light and Power Plant, The." Elec. Eng. 25:279 (March 17, 1898.)

"**Dortmund [Ger.]**, Die Arbeiterwohnungsfrage in." Arnecke. pp. 157-186 Hft. 31, Schr. d. Ver. f. Socialpolitik. — 100

"**Douglas, Isle of Man,** Municipal Works in." Prescott, A. Ernest. Surveyor, Supp. Aug. 31, 1900. — 1

Dover [Eng.]

Municipal Tramways. Carden, Edward. Ty. and Ry. World 9:10 (Jan. 11, 1900); Stilgoe, Henry E. Elec. Eng. (Lond.) May 7, 1897; anon. Elec. World 30:326 (Sept. 18, 1897); Mun. Eng. 17:30 (July, 1899.) — 2

Dresden, Saxony.

Buildings. "Die Bauten von Dresden." Hrsg. v. d. Sächs. Ing. u. Arch. Ver. und der Dresdener Arch. Ver. Dresden, Meinhold u. Söhne, 1878.

"Dresden, Saxony, A Case of Good City Government." Peabody, F. G. Forum 13:53 (1892.) — 3

"People's Club, Volkswohl, of Dresden; Its Evening Entertainments and Homes for the People." Böhmert, Victor. P. 223 "International Congress," vol. iii, 1893, see 43-99. — 4

"Sewerage of Dresden, Germany." Fuertes, James H. Engng. Rec. 36:514 (Nov. 13, 1897.) — 5

Statistics. "Jahresbericht des statistischen Amtes der Stadt Dresden." Dresden, appears annually, first edition, 1894. Also "Mitteilungen d. stat. Amtes d. Stadt Dresden," appearing irregularly since 1891. The 9th Heft (June, 1899) contains a bibliography of the city's statistical publications. Beginning in June, 1900, the city is publishing "Statistisches Jahrbuch für die Stadt Dresden." Erster Jahrgang, 1899, mit einer Chronik für 1899. Hrsg. v. Stat. Amt. 8vo, 127 pp.

Dresden, Saxony.—*Continued.*

Street Cleaning in Dresden. "Die Strassenreinigung Dresdens." Gesund. Ing. 23:107 (April 15, 1900.)

Water Supply. The New Water Works at Dresden. "Das Neue Dresdener Wasserwerk." Vacherot, Chief Engineer. Zeitschr. d. ver. Deutscher Ing. July 1, 1899; Engng. News 42:154 (Sept. 7, 1899); Fuertes, James H. Engng. Rec. 40:722 (Dec. 30, 1899.)   6

Dublin.

"Greater Dublin." Mun. J. & London 8:517 (April 28, 1899.)

History. For bibliography of municipal history of Dublin. See p. 211 Gross' Bibliography of British Municipal History.

Housing of the Laboring Classes. Cameron, Chas. A. Arch (London) Supplement, p. 21, Aug. 26, 1898; Russell, T. W. Mun. J. 9:38 (Jan. 12, 1900); anon. Mun. J. & London 8:952 (Aug. 25, 1899.)   7

——. "The Homes of the Working Classes in Dublin." Spencer, Edward. Paper read Oct. 1, 1884, before Congress of Sanitary Institute of Great Britain. Vol. VI. Transactions of Institute. Separate paper 24 pp.   8

Lighting. "The Supply of Water Gas in Dublin." Reynolds, J. Emerson. J. Gas Light 75:1124 (May 1, 1900.)   9

——. "Electric Lighting in Dublin." Wilbour, Joshua. Cons. Rep. 62:319 (March, 1900); anon. St. Ry. Rev. 8:160 (March 15, 1898.)   10

"Sewage Disposal in Dublin." Ashby, Newton B. Cons. Rep. 47:194 (1895).   11

Statistics. "Observations upon the Dublin Bills of Mortality, 1681, and the State of that City, Etc." Pp. 479-491, 493-498, Vol. II, "Economic Writing of Sir William Petty, edited by Charles H. Hull, Cambridge University Press, 1899.   12.

Transit Facilities. Electric Tramways. Bridge, Albert H. Elec. World 30:758 (Dec. 25, 1897); anon. St. Ry. J. 14:4, 203 (Jan., April, 1898); Ry. World 7:264 (Aug. 4, 1898), 8:165 (May 11, 1899.)   13

——. "Electric Traction in Dublin. The Tramway to Clontarf." Ry. World 7:1 (Jan., 1898.)

——. "The Ringsend Power Plant of the Dublin United Tramways Company at Dublin." Shaw, A. C. St. Ry. J. 16:421 (May 5, 1900.)   14

"**Dubuque [Ia.]** of To-day, the Key City; Historical, Descriptive and Biographical, Commercial and Industrial." 1897. 159 pp.

Duluth.

Duluth. In article "Capitals of the Northwest." Ralph, Julian. Harper 84:576 (1892.)   15

"The Municipal Water Works of the City of Duluth, Minn." Patton, W. B. Engng. News 39:282 (May 5, 1898.)   16

Dundee.

"Architecture of Our Large Provincial Towns, Dundee." Builder 75:139 (Aug. 13, 1898.)

"History of Dundee." Thomson, James. Dundee, 1874. 8vo. (For other references on the municipal history of Dundee, see p. 217 Gross' Bibliography of British Municipal History.)   17

"Sanitary Progress, Dundee." McGrady, Lord Provost. San. J. 4:345 (Sept., 1897.)   18

Düsseldorf, Germany.

"City of Düsseldorf, The Model." Mun. J. 9:979, 997, 1017 (Dec. 14, 21, 28, 1900.)

Public Comfort Stations. "Die Entwässerung und Reiningung der Städte auf der Gewerbe-Austellung in Düsseldorf: Oeffentliche Bedürfnissanstalten." Stübben, J. Gesund.-Ing. p. 741, 1881.   18a

Dwellings of the Poor. (See under **Housing.**)

"**East Orange, N. J.**, Sewage Works." Bassett, C. Ph. Trans. Am. Soc. Civil Engineers 25:125 (1891.)   19

Edinburgh, Scotland.

"Advertisement Act, Edinburgh." Mun. Aff. 3:719 (Dec., 1899.)
"Architecture of Our Large Provincial Towns, Edinburgh." Builder Jan. 1, 1898.
"Building Problem in Edinburgh." Arch. Oct. 1, 1897.
——. "Building Rules of Edinburgh." Arch. 61:20 (Feb. 3, 1899.)
City Government. "How Edinburgh is Governed." Gulland, John W. Edinburgh, Nelson, 1891. 8vo., 1s. 20
Garbage. "Refuse Disposal in Edinburgh." Engng. Rec. 38:199 (Aug. 6, 1898), 39:525 (May 6, 1899.)
History. "Old and New Edinburgh, its History, its People and its Places." Grant, James. 3 Vols. London, Cassell, 1881. 8vo. 9s. (For other references on the history of Edinburgh see p. 225 Gross' Bibliography of British Municipal History.) 21
——. "Town Life of Edinburgh in the XVIII. Century." Ch. III., p. 81, Vol. I. of H. G. Graham's "Social Life of Scotland in the XVIII. Century." London, Adam & Chas. Black, 1899. 2 Vols. 8vo, 265 and 272 pp. 22
"Housing of the Working Classes Act (1890) in Edinburgh, The." Bruce, William. San. Rec. 22:88 (July 22, 1898.) 23
——. "Housing Problem in Edinburgh." Mun. J. 9:701 (Sept. 7, 1900.)
"Improvement of Edinburgh, Civic. The Work of the Cockburn Asociation" Robinson, Charles Mulford. Mun. Aff. 3:664 (Dec., 1899.) 24
Lighting. "Gas Works at Edinburgh." Fleming, Rufus. Cons. Rep. 59:626 (April, 1899); Herring, W. R. Gas World Jan. 21, 1899. 25
——. "Electric Lighting of Edinburgh." Hewington, Frank A. Elec. Eng. (Lond.) 22:41 (July 8, 1898). 26
——. "Public Lighting in Edinburgh, London and Elsewhere." J. Gas Light 73:297 (Feb. 7, 1899).
"Sewage Disposal, Edinburgh." Macbride, Robt. J. Cons. Rep. 47:198 (1895); Fuertes, James H. Engng. Rec. 41:29 (Jan. 13, 1900.) 27
Transit Facilities. Cable Traction in Edinburgh. Colam, W. N. St. Ry. Jour. 14:542 (Sept. 1898); anon. Ry. World 6:323 (Nov, 1897), 7:268 (Aug. 4, 1898); Ty. & Ry. World 9:89, 608 (March, 8, Dec. 6, 1900); Mun. J. 9:401 (May 25, 1900). 28
"Water Works of Edinburgh." Fuertes, James H. Engng. Rec. 38:472 (Oct. 29, 1898). 29

Education. (See under **Schools**).

Elberfeld [Ger.] "Die Wohnungsverhältnisse der ärmeren Bevölkerungsklassen in der Stadt Elberfeld." Ernst. pp. 237-248 Hft. 31, Schr. d. Ver. f. Socialpolitik. 30

Elberfeld System of Poor Relief. (See under **Charities**).

Elections, Ballot Reform in Cities. (See also under **Proportional Representation, Parties and Party Politics**).

See also Baltimore, Belgium, California, Connecticut, England, France, Germany, Italy, Kentucky, Massachusetts, Milwaukee, New York, Pennsylvania, Philadelphia.
"Automatic Ballot, The." Pp. 488-491 in "The City for the People or the Municipalization of the City Government and of Local Franchises." Parsons, Frank. Philadelphia, C. F. Taylor, 1900. 8vo, 597 pp. Cloth, $1. 31
Ballot Laws, Ballot Reform. (See under Elections below).
Caucus System. Reform of the Caucus, Etc. "American Caucus System, its Origin, Purpose and Utility." Lawton, G. W. New York, Putnams, 1885. 107 pp. $1. 32
——. "Caucus Reform." Quincy, Josiah. N. Y. Conference on Practical Reform of Primary Elections, p. 102. Chicago, Hollister, 1898. 8vo, 150 pp. Paper. 33
——. "Caucus Reform, The sine qua non of." Easley, Ralph M. R. of Rs. 16:322 (Sept. 1897). 34
——. "A Word About the Caucus." Dallinger, F. W. New Eng. M. 8:754 (Aug. 1893). 35
——. "Caucus System, The." Whitridge, F. W. New York, Society for Political

Elections, Ballot Reform in Cities.—*Continued.*

Education, 1882. 27 pp. 10 cts. Also in Labor's Cyclopedia Vol. I, p. 357.   36

——. "Facts About the Caucus and the Primary." Green, G. W. No. Am. 137; 257-270 (Sept. 1883).   37

——. "Legalization of Caucuses." Sedgwick, A. G. Nation 8:86 (Feb. 4, 1869).   38

——. "Substitute for the Caucus." Terry, H. T. New Englander 34:734 (Oct. 1875). Reprinted in Cambridge Civil Reform Association's Prize Essays 58-70 (1884).   39

——. "Substitutes for the Caucus." Dana, R. H. Forum 2:491 (Jan. 1887).   40

——. "The Trouble With the Caucus." Means, D. M. New Englander 34:473 (July, 1875).   41

——. (See also under Primary, Primary Reform below).

"Citizen and His City, The." Thacher, John Boyd. Arena 17:847 (May, 1897).   42

——. "Citizen and the City, The." Bird, Albert A. The Citizen 2:100, 130, 167 (1896).   43

——. "The Trustworthy Citizen." Dole, Chas. F. Lend a H. Extra No., Vol. 4, March, 1889.   44

——. "Citizenship and Other Papers." Brinley, Chas. A. Philadelphia, Porter & Coates, 1893. 44 pp. 10 cts. Also New Series No. 3, American Institute of Civics, New York, 1895. 44 pp. 10c.   45

——. "Obligations of Citizenship." Goodale, W. H. Am. M. Civics Dec. 1896.   46

——. "Society for Promoting Good Citizenship." Crehore, C. F. Lend a H 4:489 (1890).   47

"Civic Church, The." Stead, W. T. R. of Rs. 8:438 (1893).   48

"Civic Duty." Bishop, J. B. Nation 57:4 (1893).   49

——. "Teaching of Civic Duty." Bryce, James. Forum 15:552; Contemp. 64:14; Ecl. M. 121:217 (1893).   50

"Civic Ideals." Harrison, Frederic. Ann. Am. Acad. Pol. Sci. 12:314 (Sept. 1898).   51

"Compulsory Voting as a Means of Correcting Political Abuses." Holls, Frederick William. Ann. Am. Acad. Pol. Sci. 1:586 (1891).   52

Corruption, Corrupt Practices, Etc. "Best Means of Overcoming Corruption." Pp. 492-504 in "The City for the People or the Municipalization of the City Government and of Local Franchises." Parsons, Frank. Philadelphia, C. F. Taylor, 1900. 8vo, 597 pp. Cloth, $1.   53

——. "Centralization the Cure for Political Corruption." Am. M. Civics Dec. 1890.

——. "Corrupt Practices Acts in England and America." Giles, William A. Chicago, Hamilton Club, 1899. Pamphlet. 10 pp.   54

——. "Ethical Survivals in Municipal Corruption." Addams, Jane. Int. J. of Ethics 8:273 (April, 1898).   55

——. "A Brief Review of Legislation Against Corrupt Practices at Elections." Sherman, Rogers. Chicago, Hamilton Club, 1899. Pamphlet, 7 pp.   56

——. "Money in Elections." Cent. n. s. 22:952 (1892).

——. "Money in City Elections." Bishop, J. B. Address before the Commonwealth Club, March 21, 1887. Reported in the Evening Post.   57

——. "Money in Elections, Machine Politics and." Ivins, W. M. New York, Harper Bros., 1887. 150 pp. 25 cts.   58

——. "Money in Politics, Corrupt Use of, and Laws for its Prevention." Gregory, C. Noble. Paper read before the Historical and Political Science Association of the University of Wisconsin, 1893. 25 pp. 25 cts.   59

——. "Money Power in Politics." Bishop, J. B. Nation 44:180, 204, 220 (1887).   60

——. "Money in Practical Politics." Jenks, Jeremiah W. Cent. 44:940 (1892).   61

——. "Municipal Corruption." Smith, Goldwin. See his "Our Situation Viewed from Without." No. Am. 160:552 (1895).   62

——. "Political Corruption, How Best Oppose." Will, T. E. Arena 10:845 (1894). (Brief Bibliography).   63

——. "Publicity as a Cure for Political Corruption." Welsh, H. Forum 14:26 (1892).   64

——. "Reform of Present Political Corruption." Rice, Allen T. No. Am. 148:82 (1889).   65

——. "The Morals of Municipal Corruption." Nation 66:297 (April 21, 1898).

Elections, Ballot Reform in Cities.—*Continued.*

——. "Utter Corruption in American Politics." Northcote, A. S. Nineteenth Cent. 35:692 (1894). 66

——. "Venal Voting, Methods and Remedies." McCook, J. J. Forum 14:159 (Oct. 1892). 67

——. "Alarming Proportion of Venal Voters." McCook, J. J. Forum 14:1 (Sept. 1892). 68

——. (See also following articles under Elections).

Elections. Ballot Law Reform. Bishop, J. B. Nation 46:46 (1888); Dana, R. H. Lend a H. 4:204 (1890); Grubb, E. B. No. Am. 155:684 (1892); Hoadley, G. Forum 7:623 (1889); Vassault, F. I. Overland n. s. 13:134 (1889); Wigmore, J. H. Nation 49:165 (1888); anon. Pub. Opin. 8:327 (1890).

——. "A Lesson in Electoral Reform." Deming, C. Nation 52:25 (1891). 69

——. "A Logical System of Municipal Elections." Clark, C. C. P. p. 524, Proc. Second Natl. Conf. for Good City Govt., 1895. See 6-18b. 70

——. "Ballot Reform Essential to Free and Equal Elections." Binney, Charles Chauncey. Philadelphia, Pennsylvania Civil Service Reform Association, 1889. 43 pp. 71

——. "Elections." Chapter III, p. 45 "Municipal Reform in the United States," by Thomas H. Devlin. New York, Putnam, 1896. 174 pp. 75 cts. 72

——. "Fraudulent Elections in the United States." Cook, J. Our Day 10:814 (1892). 73

——. "Genuine and Bogus Electoral Reform." Bishop, J. B. Nation 52:493 (1891). 74

——. "Juggling with the Ballot." Goff, John W. No. Am. 158:203 (1894). 75

——. "Municipal Voters." Richardson, Charles. Pp. 256-260 Pro. of the Louisville Conf. for Good City Govt., 1897. See 6-18d. 76

——. "Progress of Electoral Reform." Mather, F. G. Andover R. 16:492 (1891). See also Nation 48:460 (1889). 77

——. "Reform of Our Municipal Elections." Fisher, Francis. Philadelphia, 1866. 78

"Guilds, City Government by." (Election by social groups instead of geographical divisions). Cutter, John D. Cent. o. s. 34:157 (1887). 79

Money in Elections. (See under Corrupt Practices, etc. above).

"Machine Politics." Soc. Econ. 2:1 (1891).

——. "The 'Machine' Abolished and the People Restored to Power by the Organization of all the People on the Lines of Party Organization." Clark, Charles C. P. New York, Putnam's Sons, 1900. 12mo, 196 pp. Cloth, $1. 80

——. "The 'Machine' and City Government." (Editorial). Self-Cult. 9:475 (June, 1899).

——. "Machine Politics and Money in Elections." Ivins, W. M. New York, Harper Bros., 1887. 150 pp. 25 cts. 81

——. "The Machine versus the People." Cent. 44:154 (May, 1892).

——. "The Machine versus the Popular Will." Nation 54:390 (May 26, 1892).

——. "The 'Political Machine.'" Ind. 51:2490 (Sept. 14, 1899).

——. "Why the Machine Lives." Watson, Edward W. City and State Vol. I, No. 25, p. 6 (1895). 82

Nominating System. (See under Primary below).

"Ownership Vote, The." Wade, H. T. Westm. 143:316 (1895). 83

"Political Assessments." Roosevelt, Theodore. Atlan. 70:103 (1892); Whitridge, F. W. Lalor's Cyclopedia Vol. I, pp. 153-55. 84

Primaries, Primary Reform, Nominating Machinery, Etc. "Direct Nomination of Candidates by the People." Hopkins, John S. Arena 19:729 (June, 1898). 85

——. "A New Kind of Primary." Nation 66:161 (March 3, 1898).

——. "Futility of Primary Reform." (Editorial). Nation 65:431 (Dec. 2, 1897).

——. "How to Reform the Primary Election System." Insley, Edward. Arena 17:1013 (June, 1897). 86

——. "Legalization of the Primary." Commons, John R. N. Y. Conference on Practical Reform of Primary Elections, p. 18. Chicago, Hollister, 1898. 8vo, 150 pp. Paper. 87

——. "National Conference on Practical Reform of Primary Elections, held at the Rooms of the New York Board of Trade and Transportation Jan. 20, and

Elections, Ballot Reform in Cities.—*Continued.*

21, 1898." (Papers, addresses, discussions). Chicago, Hollister & Bro., Printers, 1898. 150 pp.

——. " Nominating Conventions." Godkin, E. L. Nation 22:240 (April 13, 1876). 88

——. " Nominations for Elective Office in the United States." Dallinger, Frederick W. (Harvard Historical Studies). New York, Longmans, Green & Co., 1897. 8vo, 290 pp. Cloth, $1.50. 89

——. " Nominations for Public Offices." Sulzberger, M. Penn. Monthly 12:177 (March, 1881). 90

——. " Our Nominating Machines." Green, G. W. Atlan. 52:323 (Sept. 1883). 91

——. " Primary Elections." Eaton, Dorman B. Lalor's Cyclopedia, Vol. III, pp. 343-50. 92

——. " Primary Elections." Remsen, Daniel S. New York, G. P. Putnam's Sons, 1894. 117 pp. 75 cts. 93

——. " Primary Election Laws, Report of the Special Committee of the Buffalo Republican League on." Buffalo, 1897. Pamphlet 23 pp.

——. " Primary Election Reform." Kies, W. S. Municipality Vol. I, No. 4, p. 21 (Oct. 1900). 94

——. " Primary Elections; Reform in the Delegate System of Nominations." Hoffman, E. F. Penn. Monthly 12:602 (Aug. 1881). 95

——. " The Primary and the Prayer Meeting." Clarke, Francis E. City and State, Vol. I, No. 24, p. 5. 96

——. Primary Reform, articles on. Field, D. D. Forum 14:189 (Oct. 1892); Record, Geo. L. Mun. Aff. 2:176 (June, 1898); Schurz, Carl. Hrprs. Wkly. 42:123 (Feb. 5, 1898); anon. Nation 33:486 (Dec. 22, 1881); Ind. 50:117 (Jan. 27, 1898); Outlook 58:261, 266 (Jan. 29, 1898); Gunton's 14:152 (March, 1898); Hrprs. Wkly. 42:218 (March 5, 1898). 97

——. " Regulation of Primaries." Record, George L. N. Y. Conference on Practical Reform of Primary Elections, p. 86. Chicago, Hollister, 1898. 8vo, 150 pp. Paper. 98

——. " Substitutes for the Primary." (Editorial). Nation 65:490 (Dec. 23, 1897).

——. " Tendencies in Primary Legislation." Branson, Walter J. Ann. Am. Acad. Pol. Sci. 13:346 (May, 1899). 99

——. " The Nominating Ballot." Brooks, F. M. Outlook 57:950. Editorial on same subject 57:943 (1897); McConachie, L. G. Outlook 58:176 (Jan. 15, 1898). 100

——. " The Nominating System." Ch. III, p. 48. " Unforeseen Tendencies of Democracy." Godkin, E. L. New York, Houghton, Mifflin & Co., 1898. 265 pp. $2. Also article by same writer, Atlan. 79:450 (April, 1897). 1

——. (See also under Caucus System above).

Property Qualifications. " Report of the Tilden Commission." Mun. Aff. 3:434 (Sept. 1899). (See also Elections under **Germany**).

Proportional Representation, Preferential Voting, Etc. (See under **Proportional Representation**).

Registration. " The American Ballot." Lusk, H. H. Forum 22.225 (Oct. 1896). 2

" Ross, Robert, The Life of." A Story of Patriotism calling for municipal reforms." Ross, James H. Boston, James H. Earle, 1894. 180 pp. 75 cts. 3

" St. Louis Election Schools, The." Saunders, William F. Am. Mo. R. of Rs. 17:326 (March, 1898). 3a

" Separate City Elections." Nation 40:333 (1885).

——. " Elections in Cities Separate from State." Bishop, J. B. Nation 58:422 (1894). 4

——. " Evils of Drawing Party Lines in Local Affairs." Speakman, Thomas H. 10 pp. 1873. 5

——. " Separation of Municipal from other Elections." Roome, W. Harris. p. 144, Proc. First Natl. Conf. for Good City Govt., 1894. See 6-18a. 6

" State Control of Political Parties." Pavey, F. D. Forum 25:99 (March, 1898). 7

" Suffrage in Cities." Sterne, Simon. New York, Putnam's, 1878. 41 pp. 25 cts. 8

——. " Right of Suffrage in Cities." Nation 25:285 (1877).

——. " Safeguard of the Suffrage." Gladden, Washington. Cent. 37:621 (1889). 9

——. " Suffrage and the Ballot." Remsen, D. S. New York, Appleton, 1892. 10

Three Class Election System. (See Elections under **Germany**).

Venal Voting. (See under Corrupt Practices above).

Electrolysis.

See also Battle Creek (Mich.), Chicago, Dayton, Kansas City, New York, Peoria, Providence, Reading (Pa.), Yonkers.

"A British View of Electrolysis." Irving, D. Engng. Rec. 42:41 (July 14, 1900). 11

"Cure of Electrolysis by Independent Returns." Newbaker, C. A. Am. Elec. 12:72 (Feb. 1900), Prog. Age 18:70 (Feb. 15, 1900). 12

"Effect of Joint Resistance on Railway Electrolysis." Knudson, A. A. Am. Elec. 12:119 (March, 1900). 13

"Electrolysis." Davis, F. A. W. Pp. 25-37 in "Third Annual Report of the Central States Water Works Association, Cincinnati, O. Sept. 5-7, 1899. Mun. Engng. 17:349 (Dec. 1899), Am. Gas Light J. 71:966 (Dec. 18, 1899); Knudson, A. A. Mun. & Ry. Rec. 4:54 (Feb. 15, 1899); Schaeffer, J. H. pp. 50-53 in report of Central States W. W. Assoc. quoted above; Jenkins, E. H. Am. Gas Light J. 72:652 (April 23, 1900), Prog. Age 18:189 (May 1, 1900), St. Ry. R. 10:260 (May 15, 1900). 14

"Electrolysis in the Cleaning of Metallic Surfaces." Burgess, C. F. Elec. World 32:445 (Oct. 20, 1898). 15

"Electrolysis Decision." Prog. Age 17:383 (Sept. 1, 1899).

"Electrolysis from Facts and Figures." Brownell, E. E. J. N. E. W. W. Assoc. 14:363 (June, 1900); Mun. Engng. 19:74 (Aug. 1900). 16

"Electrolysis from the Ground Return Current of Street Railways." Herrick, Albert B. St. Ry. J. 16:472 (May 5, 1900). 17

"Electrolysis from Railway Currents." Abbott, Arthur V. Cassier's 16:371 (Aug. 1899). 18

"Electrolysis Scare, The." (Editorial). Public Improvements 1:305 (Oct. 15, 1899).

"Electrolysis from the Standpoint of the Municipal Electrician." Wynkoop, H. S. Prog. Age 17:500 (Nov. 1, 1899), Mun. Eng. 17:270 (Nov. 1899). 19

"Electrolysis of Underground Pipes." Blake, Lucien I. Prog. Age 18:11 (Jan. 1, 1900). 20

"Electrolysis, an Unsolved Municipal Problem." Wynkoop, Hubert S. Pp. 119-142 in "Pro. Brooklyn Engineers' Club for 1899." 8vo, 233 pp. Paper, $2. Articles by same writer, Mun. & Ry. Rec. 5:10 (July 15, 1899), Fire & W. 26:388, 394, 400 (Nov. Dec. 1899); anon. Elec. W. & E. 33:543 (April 29, 1899). 21

"Fallacies Regarding Electrolysis, Some." Herrick, Albert B. St. Ry. J. 14:775 (Dec. 1898). 22

"Features of Electrolysis from Railway Work." (Editorial). Elec. Eng. 26:434 (Nov. 3, 1898).

Gas and Water Mains, Electrolysis of. Brown, Harold P. Prog. Age 17:13 (Jan. 2, 1899); Chamen, W. A. J. Gas Lgt. (June 7, 1898); Fleming, J. A. St. Ry. Rev. 8:807 (Nov. 15, 1898); Prog. Age 16:553 (Dec. 1, 1898); anon. Ry. World 8:67 (Feb. 9, 1899); Irving, D. J. Gas Lght. (June 5, 1900); anon. J. Gas Lght. 76:843 (Oct. 2, 1900). (See also under Water Mains below). 23

"Prevention of Electrolysis." Addams, Alton D. Mun. Engng. 18:1 (Jan. 1900); anon. Prog. Age 17:272 (July 1, 1899). 24

"Problem of Electrolysis." Engng. Rec. 39:465 (April 22, 1899).

"Railway Electrolysis Popularized." Am. Gas Light J. 70:609 (April 24, 1899).

"Underground Metal Structures, Electrolysis of." Maury, Dabney H. Engng. N. 44:38 (July 19, 1900), Am. Gas Light J. 73:165 (July 30, 1900), St. Ry. R. 10:433 (Aug. 15, 1900), pp. 121-135 in Proc. xxth Annual Meeting of Am. Water Wks. Assoc., Richmond, Va., May 15-18, 1900. 8vo, 216 pp. Cloth, $1. 25

Water Mains, Electrolysis of. Blake, Lucien I. Elec. W. & E. 34:934 (Dec. 16, 1899); Davis, F. A. W. City Govt. 7:144 (Dec. 1899). (See also under Gas and Water Mains above.) 26

——. "Electrolysis and Water Supply." Rowe, C. E. Pp. 17-19 in "Second Annual Convention of the Central States Water Works Association, Springfield, O., Sept. 27-29, 1898." 27

Elevated Railways. (See under Transit Facilities).

Elmira, N. Y., History, Description and Statistics of in 1880. Census. See 1-7.

Employment Bureaus, Municipal; Employment of Laborers by the Municipality. (See under **Labor and its Relation to the Municipality**).

Engineering, Municipal. (See also under **Conduits, Electrolysis, Garbage Disposal, Sanitation, Sewage Disposal, Streets, Transit Facilities, Water, Etc.**).

See also Germany, Illinois, London, Michigan, New York, Paris, Philadelphia, St. Louis.

" Appointment of Boards of Public Works and Engineers, and Checks Upon Their Action, The Method of." Brown, Chas. Carroll. Mun. Engng. 13:276 (Nov. 1897). 28

City Engineer. " Office of City Engineer." (Statistics). Engng. News Feb. 1, 1894.

——. " The Consulting Engineer in Municipal Affairs." Searles, Wm. H. J. Asso. Engng. Soc. 19:107 (Sept. 1897). 28a

——. " The Duties and Compensations of Municipal Engineers." Thompson, A. D. Mun. Engng. 16:1 (Jan. 1899). 28b

——. " Engineers as Commissioners for Public Works." Schurz, Carl. Engng. News Feb. 1, 1894. 29

——. " Fees of Consulting Engineers." City Govt. 6:37 (Feb. 1899).

——. " Notes from Reports of City Engineers." Engng. News Feb. 15, 1894.

" Contracts and Specifications, Engineering." Johnson, J. B. New York, Engineering News Pub. Co., 2d ed., 1898. $3. 30

" Electricity in Municipal Engineering." Owens, R. R. Elec. Eng. 25:131 (Feb. 3, 1898), Elec. World 31:151 (Jan. 29, 1898). 31

" Engineering and Architectural Jurisprudence." Wait, J. C. New York, Wiley & Sons, 1897. 8vo, 905 pp. Cloth, $6. 32

" Laying Out of Cities, Practical and Aesthetic Principles for the." Stübben, J. Trans. Am. Soc. Civil Engrs. 29:718 (1893). 33

——. " Der Städtebau." (Contains sections devoted to Housing, Streets, Parks, Gardens, Public Squares, Trees, Street Railways, Monuments and Decoration in their relation to the general plan of the city, with extracts from the building laws, regulations and forms of a number of German cities). Handbuch d. Architektur IV. Teil, 9 Halb-Band. Stübben, J. Darmstadt, Arnold Bergsträsser, 1890. 561 pp. 32m. 34

" Management of a City Engineer's Office." Kimball, Geo. A. Engng. Rec. Feb. 3, 1894. 35

" Management of Public Works. Municipal Government, with Especial Reference to the." J. Assoc. Engng. Soc., March, 1892, pp. 123-65. A description of the systems of the following cities: St. Louis, by Robert Moore; Boston, by William Jackson; New York, by F. M. Scott; Providence, by J. H. Shedd; Buffalo, by E. B. Guthrie; Philadelphia, by Dwight Porter; and Paris, by Henry D. Woods. See also Engng. News Feb. 27, March 5, 1892. 36

" Municipal Engineering." Anon. Engng. N. Jan. 16, 1886, and succeeding numbers; San. Rec. 20:445 (Oct. 22, 1897).

" Municipal Engineering Abroad." Hering, Rudolph. Engng. Rec. Sept. 26, 1891, p. 261. 37

" Municipal Improvements, a Manual of the Methods, Utility and Cost of Public Improvements for the Municipal Offices." Goodhue, W. F. New York, Wiley & Sons, 1900, 3d ed. 12mo, 216 pp. Cloth, $1.75. 38

" Municipal and Sanitary Engineer's Handbook." Boulnois, H. Percy. London, E. & F. N. Spon, 1892. 8vo, 445 pp. 15s. 39

" Planning the Site for a City." Haupt, Lewis M. Engng. M. 8:626 (1895). 40

" Plans and Specifications." Duryea, E. Jr., Cranford, W. V. Pp. 143-165 in " Pro. Brooklyn Engineers' Club for 1899." 8vo, 233 pp. Paper, $2. 41

" Present Problems in Municipal Engineering." Meade, Thomas De Courcy. Engng. Rec. 42:199 (Sept. 1, 1900); Mun. Engng. 19:289 (Oct. 1900); anon. Engng. Rec. 42:221 (Sept. 8, 1900). 42

" Problems in Municipal Engineering, Some." Hastings, L. M. J. Assoc. Engng. Soc. Nov. 1891, p. 549. 43

" Public Work Methods." Brown, Charles Carroll. City Govt. 2:14 (Jan. 1897). 44

" Public Works." Commons, John R. Our Country 5:76 (March, 1897). 44a

Engineering, Municipal—*Continued.*

——. " Public Works Abroad. Observations in London and Paris, City Methods Compared." (Article published first in the New York "Sun.") An extract describing City Works in Paris is published in City Govt. 2:78, 118 (March and April, 1897). Collis, C. H. T. New York, 1897. Pamphlet, 31 pp. 44b

" The Ideal City Engineering Bureau." Collingwood, Francis. Engng. M. 9:445 (1895). 44c

" Value of Engineering Services." (Editorial). City Govt. 6:34 (Feb. 1899).

England. (See **United Kingdom**).

Epernay [Fr.] Workmen's Dwellings. "Cité Ouvrière d'Epernay." Jemot & Levy. Nouv. Annales de la Const. p. 34, 1880. 45

Erfurt, Germany.

Lighting. " Benzolized Water Gas at Erfurt." J. Gas Light 76:1386 (Dec. 4, 1900).

Erie, Pa.

" Library, The Erie Public." City Govt. 8:114 (May, 1900).
" Water Works of Erie, Pa." Fire and W. March 21, 1896.

Essen, Ger.—Housing. " Die Arbeitercolonien der Gussstahlfabrik von Friedrich Krupp in Essen." Beyer. Deutsche Viert. f. Oeff Gesundheitspfl. p. 615, 1874. See also article, Glückauf, May 29, 1897; and Wiebe, pp. 187-197, Heft 31, Schr. d. Ver. f. Socialpolitik. 46

Europe. (See under **City Government, General Works and Unclassified,** especially 1-5, also under names of various countries in Europe).

" **Evansville, [Ind.]** The Potato Patch, Experience in." Hornbrook, R. S. Indiana Bulletin of Charities and Correction June, 1898. 48

Excise. (See **Liquor Problem in Cities**).

Exeter, Eng.

" Exeter." (History). Freeman, E. A. London, Longmans, 1887. Historic Towns Series. 8vo. 3s. 6d. (For other references on the history of Exeter see p. 231 Gross' Bibliography of British Municipal History). 49

" Sewage Treatment at Exeter, England, The Septic Tank System of." Crane, Albert S. Engng. News 39:18 (Jan. 13, 1898); anon. San. Rec. 20:584, 607 (Nov. 26, Dec. 3, 1897). 50

Expropriation.

See also France, Germany.

" De l'Occupation temporaire en vue de l'exécution des travaux publics, loi du 29 décember, 1892." Bourcart, G. Paris, Pédone, 1895. 8vo, 167 pp. 3 fr. 51

" La municipalisation du sol dans les grandes Villes." Einaudi, Luigi. Paris, Giard & Brière, 1898. Pamphlet 60 pp. (Extrait du Devenir Social 4:1, 127 (1898). 2 fr. 52

" Sanitary Purposes, Expropriation for." Ch. III, pp. 53-68. Eighth Special Report of the Commissioner of Labor on " The Housing of the Working People," by E. R. L. Gould. 53

Fall River, Mass.

" A Typical New England Factory Town, Fall River, Mass." Blatch, Harriet Stanton. Humanitarian April, 1899. 54

History, Description and Statistics of Fall River, Mass., in 1880. Census. See 1-7.
" Street Railway System of Fall River, Mass." St. Ry. Jour. April, 1893, p. 201.

" **Farmville, Va.,** The Negroes of: A Social Study." Du Bois, W. E. Burghardt. Bulletin Dept. Labor No. 14, p. 1 Jan. 1898. 55

Ferries. (See under **Transit Facilities**).

Finance, Municipal.

See also Adelaide, Australia, Baltimore, Basel, Berlin, Birmingham, Boston, California, Canada, Chicago, England under United Kingdom, Florence, France, Germany, Glasgow, Havana, Iowa, Ireland under United Kingdom, Issoire (Fr.), Italy, London, Martinique, Massachusetts, Naples, New Jersey, New York, New York State, New Zealand, Ohio, Omaha, Paris, Pennsylvania, Philadelphia, Prussia, Russia, San Francisco, Scotland under United Kingdom, Spain, Switzerland, United Kingdom, United States, Wales under United Kingdom, Washington, Wisconsin, Würtemberg under Germany, Wyoming.

General Works and Unclassified.

"Administration des Finances Municipales." Blanc, Charles. Paris, Cotillon, 1881, 5 fr. — 56

"Comparative Table Showing the General and Financial Condition of the cities of Detroit, Buffalo, Cincinnati, Louisville, St. Paul, Minneapolis, Cleveland, Milwaukee and Rochester. Blades, F. A., compiler. Detroit, 1899. 6 pp. — 57

"Contract System, A Municipal." Foote, Allen Ripley. Prog. Age 18:12 (Jan. 1, 1900). — 58

"Cost of City Government." Chapter VI, p. 105, "Municipal Reform in the United States," by Thomas H. Devlin. New York, Putnam, 1896. 174 pp. 75c. — 59

"Das Kommunale Finanzwesen." (England, France, Belgium, Germany, Austria). Reitzenstein, F. Frh. v. pp. 559-687 of Gustav Schönberg's "Handbuch d. Pol. Oekonomie." 3d Bd. Finanzwissenschaft. Tübingen, H. Laupp, 1885. — 60

"Debt and Local Taxation, Municipal." Wells, David A. Ed. R. 167:350 (1888). — 61

——. "Local Taxation, Debt and Government." Conder, F. R. Fraser 93:360 (1876). — 62

——. "Municipal Debt and Local Taxation." Ed. R. 167:350 (1888).

"Delusive Methods of Municipal Financiering." Ford, William F. Pubs. Phil. Soc. Sci. Assoc., 1879. — 63

"Dictionnaire des Finances." Say, Léon. Paris, Berger, L. et Cie., 1889. 2 Vols. 1562 and 1571 pp. 90 fr. (Important articles in Assistance Publique à Paris, Le Budget Communal, Communes, Octrois, etc., etc). — 64

"Economy, Municipal." Harris, D. L. J. Soc. Sci. 9:147 (1878). — 65

"Endowments and Municipal Property, Municipal." Pp. 44-51 in "Municipal Extensions and Other Essays." Ellery, T. George. Adelaide, W. R. Thomas & Co., 1899. 12mo, 51 pp. Pamphlet. — 66

"Essai sur les Finances Communales." Paul-Dubois, L. Paris, Perrin & Co., 1898. 12mo, 306 pp. — 67

"Extravagance, Municipal." Ellis, A. B. Atlan. 52:84 (1883); Harris, D. L. Penn. Mo. 7:913 (1876). — 68

"Finances Communales: Etude Theorique et Pratique." Acollas, René. Paris, Giard, et E. Brière, 1898. 12mo, 259 pp. Paper, $1. — 68a

"Finanzwesen der Selbstverwaltung in einigen Staaten." (England, Prussia, Austria, France, Belgium). pp. 110-130 of Adolph Wagner's "Finanzwissenschaft." Dritte Auflage. Leipzig, Winter, 1883. — 69

"Gemeindefinanzen." Eheberg, K. Th. Vol. IV, pp. 106-144 Conrad, 2d ed. See 2-10. — 70

"Municipal Finance." Boyden, H. P. Public Policy 2:62 (Jan. 27, 1900); Hall, C. C. Scrib. M. n. s. 3:33 (1888); Hirst, F. W. Econ. J. 9:384 (Sept. 1899); Ivins, W. M. Harper 69:779 (1884). — 71

"Municipal v. Private Financiering." Gemünder, M. A. City Govt. 2:109 (April, 1897). — 72

"Municipal Finance Statistics." Gardner,, Henry B. Am. Statis. Assoc. 1:254 (1889). Separate pamphlet No. 6. 75 cts. — 73

"Municipal Revenue in Europe." Ulrich, B. A. City Govt. 1:43 (1896). — 74

"Parish Finances." Blake, H. B. Boston R. 6:559 (1866). — 75

"Suggestions for the Study of Municipal Finance." Clow, Fred R. Q. J. Econ. 10:455 (1896). — 76

"Taxpayer in City Government, The Interest of the." Leitsch, W. C. Proceedings of the Convention of the League of Wisconsin Municipalities, Bulletin No. 3, pp. 38, June 26-27, 1899. — 77

"Valuation, Taxation and Indebtedness." Porter, Robert P. Washington, Government Printing Office, 1884. 909 pp. Tenth Census of the United States. — 78

Finance, Municipal—*Continued.*

"Wealth, Debt and Taxation." Upton, J. Kendrick. Washington, Government Printing Office. 1892. 890 pp. Eleventh Census of the United States.   79

"Accounts, Municipal and Other." Laing, J. B. Mun. World Vol. 8, No. 1, p. 4. (Jan. 1898).   80

———. "Classification of Municipal Receipts and Expenditures." Rowe, Leo. S. Ann. Am. Acad. Pol. Sci. 12:436 (Nov. 1898).   81

———. "Examinations of Public Accounts." Henderson, Harry B. Public Policy 3:213 (Oct. 6, 1900).   82

———. "Municipal Accounting." Cal. Mun. 1:35 (Sept. 1899).

———. "Municipal Economics." (Publicity of accounts, etc.) Commons Vol. 2, No. 6, p. 5 (Oct. 1897).

———. "Public Accounting." Rowe, L. S. Public Policy 2:126 (Feb. 24, 1900); Prog. Age 18:121 (March 15, 1900).   83

———. "Public Accounting under the Proposed Municipal Program." Rowe, Leo. S. pp. 104-123 in Proc. of the Columbus Conf. for Good City Govt., 1899. See 6-18f; also pp. 89-110 in "A Municipal Program." New York, Macmillan, 1900. 8vo, 246 pp. Cl. $1.   84

———. "The Financial Reports of Municipalities, with special Reference to the Requirement of Uniformity." Hartwell, E. M. pp. 124-135 in Proc. of the Columbus Conf. for Good City Govt., 1899. See 6-18f.   85

———. "Uniform Municipal Accounting." Baker, M. N. Public Policy 3:186 (Sept. 29, 1900).   86

———. "Uniform Municipal Accounts and Reports." Baker, M. N. Public Policy 3:183 (Sept. 22, 1900).   87

———. "Uniformity in Municipal Finance." Tooke, C. W. Mun. Aff. 2:195 (June, 1898), Prog. Age 16:436 (Sept. 15, 1898).   88

———. "Uniformity for Purposes of Comparison, The Importance of." Sparling, Samuel E. pp. 136-147 in Proc. of the Columbus Conf. for Good City Govt., 1899. See 6-18f.   89

"Bonds, Municipal." Dillon, John F. St. Louis, G. I. Jones & Co., 1876. 63 pp. Paper 75 cts.   90

———. "American Municipal Bonds as Investments." J. H. Rudall & Sons, editors. 1874.

———. "How Municipal Bonds Should be Issued." Dow, W. A. Cal. Mun. 2:75 (April, 1900).   91

———. "Law of Municipal Bonds." Burhans, J. A. Chicago, S. A. Kean & Co., 1889. 342 pp. $4.   92

———. "Municipal Bonds." Ford, W. F. J. Soc. Sci. 15:156 (1882); Green, G. W. Lalor's Cyclopedia, Vol. II, pp. 920-3.   93

———. "Municipal Bonds, a Consideration of the Various Classes of Municipal and other Bonds with a Comparison of their Relative Security." Gay, Eben H. Boston, Damrell & Upham, 1890. 43 pp. 50 cts.   94

Budget. "Le Budget Communal." de Crisenoy, J. D. Vol. I, pp. 467-485. "Dictionnaire des Finances." Say, Léon. See 2-12.   95

———. "Bulletin Annuel des Finances des Grandes Villes." Körösi, Jos. Budapest, 1876-84. 3m. each.   96

"Control over Municipal Receipts and Expenditures, Financial." Crosby, Albert F. pp. 148-154 in Proc. of the Columbus Conference for Good City Govt., 1899. See 6-18f.   97

———. "Financial Control: Capitalization, Methods of Accounting and Taxation." Coler, Bird S. Ann. Am. Acad. Pol. Sci. May, 1900, Supp. p. 21.   98

Debts, Municipal, Debt Limitation, etc. "Creditwesen der Staaten und Städte der Nordamerikan. Union in s. histor. Entwickelung." Plehn, Carl Copping. Jena, Fischer, 1892. 8vo, 93 pp. 2m.   99

———. "Constitutional Limitations of Municipal Indebtedness in Relation to Public Improvements." Tooke, C. W. Public Imp. 1:214 (Oct. 1, 1899), Other Side 1:162 (Oct. 7, 1899).   100

———. "Constitutional Limitation of the Financial Powers of Municipalities to Public Works, Relation of." Tooke, Charles W. Mun. Engng. 16:164 (March, 1899).   1

———. "Debts of Cities." Hale, C. Atlan. 38:661 (1876).   2

Finance, Municipal—*Continued.*

——. "Debts and Resources of the States, Cities and Towns." (Supplement to the Commercial and Financial Chronicle, issued quarterly.) New York, Dana Co., April 15, 1899. 4to, 188 pp. Paper, 25 cts.

——. "Limitation of Indebtedness of Municipal Corporations." Tooke, C. W. Mun. Engng. 18:243 (April, 1900). Pub. Policy 2:303 (May 12, 1900).   3

——. "Limitations on Municipal Indebtedness." Berryman, J. R. Central Law Journal 29:346, 364 (1889).   4

——. "Local Deficit Financiering." Pt. III, "Public Debts." Adams, Henry C. New York, Appleton's, 1887. 8vo, 407 pp. $2.50.   5

——. "Municipal Debt and Local Taxation." Ed. R. 167:350 (1888).

——. "Municipal Debts." Porter, Robert P. Bank. M. (N. Y.) 35:800 (1876).   6

——. "Municipal Debts Increasing—State Debts Decreasing." (Editorial.) Mun. Rec. & Ad. Vol. I, No. 14, p. 3, (Sept. 11, 1897).

——. "Municipal Indebtedness." Art. 8, Sec. 10, New York State Constitution of 1894.

——. "Municipal Indebtedness." Freud, J. Rich'd. Mchts. Assoc. R. Vol. 2, No. 2, p. 5 (Oct. 1897).   7

——. "National, State and Local Debts." Porter, Robert P. Lalor's Cyclopedia, Vol. I, pp. 725-34. See 1-1.   8

——. "Percentage Limitation, The Problem of the." Tooke, C. W. Mun. Engng. 17:198 (Oct. 1899).   9

——. "Population and Bonded Debt of Leading American Cities, The." (Editorial.) Mun. Rec. & Ad., Vol. I, No. 13, p. 3 (Sept. 4, 1897).

——. "Power to Incur Indebtedness, The City's." Coler, Bird S. City Govt. 7:152 (Dec. 1899).   10

——. "Power of Municipal Corporations to Borrow Money." Dillon, John F. Southern Law R. 6:663 (1881).   11

—— "Power to Incur Indebtedness under the Proposed Municipal Program." Coler, Bird S. Pp. 96-103 in Proc. of the Columbus Conference, 1899, see 6-18f. Also pp. 111-119 in "A Municipal Program." New York, Macmillan Co., 1900. 8vo, 246 pp. Cl. $1.   12

——. "Some Fallacies About Local Indebtedness." Beckett, J. Mun. J. & London 8:1097 (Oct. 6, 1899).   13

"Franchises, Taxation of." St. Ry. J. 15:381 (June, 1899).

——. "Franchises and Taxation." Ninth Biennial Report of the Bureau of Labor Statistics of Illinois. Springfield, 1896. 8vo, 320 pp.

——. "Shall Franchises be Taxed?" Vincent, Edgar L. Self Cult. 10:138 (Oct. 1899).   14

——. "Taxation of Corporation Franchises." Gunton's 16:417 (June, 1899).

——. "Taxation of Franchises." Marshall, Matthew. Prog. Age 17:471 (Oct. 16, 1899); Fletcher, William Meade. Chicago, Hamilton Club, 1900, 8vo, 38 pp; anon. Railroad Gaz. 31:190 (March 17, 1899).   15

——. "Taxation of Gas by local authorities." Carr, Isaac. Gas World (London) June 19, 1897.   16

——. "Taxation of Public Franchises." Ford, John. No. Am. 168:730 (June, 1899).   17

——. "Taxation of Street Railroad Franchises." Williams, Timothy S. Public Policy 3:299 (Nov. 10, 1900), St. Ry. J 16:1138 (Nov. 24, 1900).   17a

——. "Taxation of Street Railways for Purposes of Revenue and Control." Curtis, Charles E. Yale R. 8:173 (Aug. 1899).   17b

——. "Taxation of Public Service Corporations." Public Policy 3:403 (Dec. 29, 1900).

——. "The Franchise Tax." Theodore Roosevelt. Prog. Age 18:58 (Feb. 1, 1900).   18

"Octrois." Renouard, Alfred. Pp. 395-410, Vol. II Say's Dict. d'Econ. Politique; Martel, J. Pp. 663-686 Vol. II. Ibid. See 2-12.   19

——. "Impositions municipales en vue de la suppression des Octrois." Desplanques, A. Paris, Savine, 1893. 12mo, 97 pp. 2 fr.   20

——. "L'Octroi, pourquoi il est conservé." Block, Maurice. Paris, Berger, L. et Cie., 1878. 8vo, 40 pp. 1 fr. 50c.   21

——. "Les Octrois en France et à l' Etranger." d'Avenel, Georges. Paris, Guillaumin et Cie., 1881. 47 pp. 1 fr.   21a

Finance, Municipal—*Continued.*

——. Octrois. von Heckel, Max. Vol. V, pp. 50-53 Conrad. 1st ed. '93. See 2-10. 22
——. " Octrois en France et à l'Etranger." d'Avenel, Georges. Paris, Guillaumin et Cie., 1881. 47 pp. 1 fr. 23
——. " Octrois Municipaux." Turquey, Elie. Paris, Giard et Brière, 1899. 8vo. Cl. 7f. 24
——. " Question des Octrois." Berthélemy, H. R. d. Paris 6:880 (Feb. 15, 1899). 25
——. " Suppression des Octrois." Pey, J. B. Paris, Larose et Forcel, 1895. 49 pp. 1fr. 50c.; Weber, Adrien. Rev. Soc. 28:287 (Sept. 1898), 28:719 (Dec. 1898). 26
" Sinking Fund, Calculation of." Mogensen, Peter. Engng. News 38:259 (Oct. 21, 1897). 27
Special Assessments. (See under Taxation below.)
Taxation. "Assessment and Taxation, The Law of." Browne, William W. Rochester, 1887. 28
——. " Bonds, Taxation of City." Belmont, P. Internat. R. 6:463 (1879). 29
——. " City and Country Taxes." West, Max. Pol. Sci. Q. 14:305 (June, 1899). 30
——. " Essays in Taxation." Seligman, E. R. A. New York, Macmillan & Co., 1895. 434 pp. $3. 31
——. " Evils of Tax Administration." Bemis, Edward W. Ind. 50:140 (Feb. 3, 1898). 32
——. " Evils, The Three Fundamental." Seligman, Edwin R. A. Ind. 50:138 (Feb. 3, 1898). 33
——. " Exemption from Municipal Taxation." McLean, F. W. Canadian Monthly 4:388 (1873); 10:311 (1876). 34
——. " Exemption of Personalty: Discussed with Special Reference to City Conditions." Purdy, Lawson. Mun. Aff. 3:299 (June, 1899). 35
——. " Foreign Countries, Taxation in." U. S. Consular Reports Nos. 99 and 100. Pp. 259 to 791. 1888.
——. " Incidence and Administration of Local Taxation." Pell, Albert. National 1:442 (1883). 36
——. " Incidence of Urban Rates." Edgeworth, F. Y. Econ. J. 10:172 (June, 1900). 37
——. " Is an Ideal System Possible?" Means, D. McG. Ind. 50:139 (Feb. 3, 1898). 38
——. Kommunalabgaben. v. Herrfurth. Pp. 590-606, 1st supplement to 1st edition Conrad. See 2-10. 39
——. " Local Option in Taxation." Tuttle, Leonard. Mun. Aff. 2:395 (Sept. 1898). 40
——. Local Option. "Practical Effect of Advances in Tax Law." Bryan, George J. Cedar Rapids, Iowa, Frank Vierth, 1899. Pamphlet, 30 pp. 5 cts. 41
——. " Local Taxation in America, Theory and Practice." Wells, David A. Atlan. 33:59 (1874). 42
——. " Local Taxation and Public Extravagance." Minot, Wm., Jr. J. Soc. Sci. 9:67 (1879); Ecl. R. 79:313 (1844). 43
——. Municipal Taxation, Books and articles on. O'Meara, J. J. London, Cassell & Co., 1894. 310 pp. 7s. 6d. (The appendix shows the financial condition of a number of large municipalities); Palgrave, R. H. Macmil. 33:516 (1875); Commons, John R. Our Country 5:116 (April, 1897); anon. Can. Mo. 4:388 (1875); Arch. & Buil. 30:73 (March 11, 1899). 44
——. " Natural Monopolies and Local Taxation." Ely, R. T. Lend a H. 4:178 (1889). 45
——. " Natural Taxation." (Single tax.) Shearman, Thomas G. New York, G. P. Putnam's Sons, 1895. 239 pp. 75 cts. 46
——. " Principles of Taxation." Wells, David A. Pop. Sci. Mo. Serial beginning Sept. 1896. 47
——. " Rational Principles of Taxation." Wells, D. A. Am. J. Soc. Sci. 6:120 (1874). 48
——. " Reform of Local Taxation." Wells, D. A. No. Am. 122:357 (1876). 49
——. " Single Tax Applied to Cities." Holt, Byron W. Mun. Aff. 3:328 (June, 1899). 50
——. " Single Tax and Special Assessments." Brown, Edward Osgood. The

Finance, Municipal—*Continued.*

Standard 8:4 (1890). 51
——. Single Tax. "Taxation of Ground Values." Sargant, C. H. Contemp. 57:282 (1890). 52
——. Single Tax. "Taxation of Ground Rents." Moulton, J. Fletcher. Contemp. 57:412 (1890). (Reply to above.) 53
——. "Some Recent Books on Local Taxation." Seligman, E. R. A. Q. J. E. 11:201 (Jan. 1897). 54
——. "Taxation as a Partial Substitute for Borrowing to Cover the Cost of Permanent Municipal Improvements." Durand, E. D. Pub. Amer. Econ. Ass'n. 3rd Series 1:123 (Feb. 1900). 55
——. "Taxation, its Sum, Justification and Methods." Belmont, P. Forum March, 1897. 56
——. "The Tax Question." Ensley, Enoch. Public Policy 3:314 (Nov. 17, 1900). 57
——. "Treatise on the Law of Taxation, including the Law of Local Assessments." Cooley, Thomas M. Chicago, Callaghan & Co., 1886. 2d edition. 991 pp. $6. 58
"Special Assessments." Bouton, George T. Mun. Engng. 17:289 (Nov. 1899), City Govt. 7:136 (Dec. 1899). 59
——. "America, Betterment Tax in." Rae, John. Contemp. 57:644 (May, 1890). 60
——. "Assessments for Local Improvements." Weakley, John B. Jr. (Pp. 41-45 in "Proceedings of the 3d Annual Convention of the League of American Municipalities, 1899." 8vo, 148 pp. Also in Public Imp. 1:225 (Oct. 1, 1899), Other Side 1:169 (Oct. 14, 1899), City Govt. 7:95 (Oct. 1899). 61
——. "Betterment and Local Taxation." Quar. R. 178:185 (1894).
——. "Betterment Tax." Seligman, E. R. A. Chapter XI, p. 340, "Essays in Taxation." New York, Macmillan & Co., 1895. 434 pp. $3. Same subject, article by Webb, James Avery. Am. Law R. 33:347 (May-June, 1899). 62
——. Controversy on Betterment. Argyle, Duke of. Contemp. 57:911 (June, 1890); Reply to the preceding, Rae, John. Contemp. 58:133 (July, 1890); "House of Lords and Betterment." Hobhouse, Arthur. Contemp. 65:438 (1894); Reply to preceding by Argyle, Contemp. 65:483 (1894), Rejoinder by Hobhouse, 19th Cent. 65:704 (1894). 63
——. "Decisions on Assessments for Public Works, A Review." Tooke, C. W. Mun. Engng. 18:93 (Feb. 1900). 64
——. "General Taxation and Special Assessment for Municipal Improvements." Lewis, N. P. Mun. Engng. 13:268 (Nov. 1897). 65
——. "I Contributi Speciali per i Lavori di Migliora. Studio di Finanza." Dalla Volta, Da Ricardo. Florence, Bocca, 1896. 68 pp. 66
——. "Justice in Special Assessments." Quick, J. H. Public Imp. 2:49 (Dec. 1, 1899). 67
——. "Municipal Assessments." Simpson, J. Alexander, Jr. Philadelphia, 1891. 68
——. "Pavement, Assessment of the Cost of—in 27 American Cities." Paving and Mun. Engng. April, 1895.
——. "Principles of Betterment." Bellot, H. H. L. Westm. 141:405 (1894). 69
——. "Sewerage Systems and Assessments, Municipal." Bouton, George T. Engng. Rec. 42:268 (Sept. 22, 1900). 70
——. "Sewers and Water Mains, Assessment for." Brown, Charles Carroll. Mun. Engng. 15:215 (Oct. 1898). 71
——. "Special Assessment Systems." (St. Louis, Milwaukee, Denver, Boston, New York.) City Govt. 1:135 (Dec. 1896).
——. "Special Assessments, a Study in Municipal Finance." Rosewater, Victor. Columbia College Studies, Vol. II, No. 3, 1893. 8vo, 152 pp. 75 cts. (Contains a brief bibliography of special assessments.) 72
——. "Special Assessments for City Work." Johnson, J. A. Pp. 37-41 in "Proceedings of the 3d Annual Convention of the League of American Municipalities, 1899." 8vo, 148 pp. Paper. Also in Public Imp. 1:228 (Oct. 1, 1899), City Govt. 7:54 (Sept. 1899), Other Side 1:157 (Oct. 7, 1899). 73
——. "Street Improvement Purposes, Apportionment of Taxation for." Cal. Mun. 1:179 (Jan. 1900).
——. "Street Improvements, Methods of Paying for." Brown, Charles Carroll. Mun. Engng. 12:67 (Feb. 1897). 74
——. "Taxation by Special Assessments." Ch. XX, pp. 606-678 of "A Treatise

Finance, Municipal—*Continued.*
on the Law of Taxation," by Thomas M. Cooley. Chicago, Callaghan & Co., 1886. 991 pp. $6. 75
——. "Theory and Practice of Laying Assessments for Benefit." Lewis, N. P. Public Policy 3:349 (Dec. 1, 1900). 76
Uniform Accounting. (See under Accounts above.)

Finland. (See under **Russia.**)

Fires, Municipal Fire Departments, Insurance, Etc. (See also **Building Laws.**)
See also Baltimore, Berlin, Boston, France, Glasgow, London, Los Angeles, Michigan, New York, Paris, Pittsburg, Providence, Rome.
General Works and Unclassified.
"English and American Fire Services." Purroy H. D. Forum 2:299 (1886). 77
"European and American Fire Systems." Purcell, Thomas P. City Govt. 2:82 (March, 1897). 78
"Fire and Building Regulations in Foreign Countries." (Reports from one hundred and forty-six foreign countries and cities.) United States Special Consular Report. 1892. 543 pp.
"Fire Protection in Europe." Sachs, Edwin O. Engineering (London) Serial, 1st part June 18, 1897. 79
"Fires in American Cities." Peabody, Andrew P. Boston, Damrell and Upham, 1891. 27 pp. 20 cts.; International R. 1:17 (1874). 80
"The Prevention of Loss by Fire, Fifty Years Record of Factory Mutual Insurance, etc., with suggestions for the protection of cities from conflagrations." Atkinson, Edward. Boston, Damrell & Upham, 1900. Pamphlet 95 pp. 81
"Urban Fire Protection." Sachs, Edwin O. London, Batsford, 1895. 36 pp. 1s. 82

"Automatic Fire Alarm Systems." Brophy, William. City Govt. 7:92 (Oct. 1899); Burgher, Charles. City Govt. 9:123 (Nov. 1900). 83
——. "A Great Advance in Fire Alarm Telegraph Protection." Aydon, J. W. Elec. Eng. 26:176 (Aug. 25, 1898). 84
"Fire Department, The." Paige, J. D. Mun. World 10:52 (April, 1900). 85
——. "Equipment and Organization of a City Fire Department." Bonner, Hugh. Engng. M. 14:789 (Feb. 1898). 86
——. "Fire Departments in Europe in Comparison with American." Hosmer. Fire and Water Oct. 3, 1896. 87
——. "Fire Department Statistics." City Govt. 5:154 (Oct. 1898), 5:200 (Nov. 1898).
——. "Fires and Fire Departments." Bugbee, J. M. No. Am. 117:108 (1873). 88
——. "Practical Benefits of Gymnasiums to Fire Departments." Roberts, W. E. City Govt. 5:135 (Oct. 1898). 89
——. "What Fire Departments should have." Paige, J. D. City Govt. 8:35 (Feb. 1900). 90
"Fire Hydrants, The Care of, in Winter." Bailey, George I. Engng. Rec. 40:387 (Sept. 23, 1899). 91
Firemen. "Heroes Who Fight Fire." Riis, Jacob A. Cent. 55:483 (Feb. 1898). 92
——. Insurance of Firemen in case of Accidents. "Assurances des Sapeurs-Pompiers en Cas d'Accidents." R. Municipale 3:1967 (March 10, 1900).
"Fire Proof Construction and Recent Tests." (Tests made by the New York Department of Buildings.) Himmelwright, A. L. A. Engng. M. Dec. 1896. 93
——. "Fireproofing Tests." Am. Arch. May 8, 1897.
——. "Official Test of Fireproof Floor Construction Systems." Engng. Rec. May 29, 1897.
——. "Report of Progress of the Committee on Fire Proofing Tests." Am. Soc. of Mech. Engrs. Dec. 1896.
"Fire Protection." Stevens, Frank B. Ind. Jan. 1900. 94
"Fire Streams and their Handling." City Govt. 9:101 (Oct. 1900).
High Buildings. "Fire Risks on Tall Office Buildings." Atkinson, Edward. Engng. M. 3:149 (1892). 95

Fires, Municipal Fire Departments—*Continued.*

——. "How to Fight Fires in High Buildings." Fire & W. 26:275 (Aug. 19, 1899).

——. "Protection of High Buildings from Fire." Fire & W. 26:42 (Feb. 11, 1899).

——. "The Tall Building Under the Test of Fire." Parsons, H. deB. Engng. M. 16:767 (Feb. 1899). 96

Horses. "Style of Horse best suited to the Fire Service." Devine, James. City Govt. 5:137 (Oct. 1898). 97

——. "The Quick Horse and the American Fire Service." Dellenbaugh, F. S. St. Nicholas Feb. 1898. 98

"How Fires Are Extinguished." English Ill. M. 22:434 (Feb. 1900).

"Insurance, Municipal Fire." Donald, Robert. Contemp. 68:839 (1895); anon. Banker's M. (London) Feb. 1897; Mun. J. & London 9:25, 30 (Jan. 12, 1900). See also under **France**. 99

"The Ounce of Prevention." Affeld, A. O. City Govt. 9:121 (Nov. 1900). 100

"Stand Pipes for Fire Protection and Street Flushing." Tribus, Louis L. Engng. M. 10:1040 (1895). 1

"Street Railways, Fire Protection for." St. Ry. R. 7:305 (May 15, 1897).

"Waste by Fire." Thompson, Clifford. Forum 2:27 (1886). 2

"Water Works and Fire Protection." Freeman, John R. Jour. New Eng. Water Works Assoc. 7:49 (1892). Abstract in Engng. Rec. July 16, 1892. See also Journal of the New England Water Works Assoc. 7:152 (1892) for criticism. 3

"Florence [Colo.], Water Works." Garrett, R. P. Engng. Rec. 41:127 (Feb. 10, 1900). 4

Florence, Italy.

Finance. "De l'Impôt sur le Revenu à Florence au xve Siècle." Barboux, Henri. Rev. Pol. e. Par. 18:517 (Dec. 10, 1898). 5

History. "Forschungen zur Geschichte v. Florenz. 2 Tl. Aus den Stadtbüchern und Urkunden von San Gimignano." Davidsohn, Rob. Berlin, E. S. Mittler & Sohn, 1900. 8vo, 352 pp. 9 marks. 6

——. "The Story of Florence." Gardner, Edmund G. London, J. M. Dent & Co.; New York, Macmillan, 1900. 16mo, 436 pp. Cl. $1.75. 7

"Sewage Disposal, Florence." Bernardi, Spirito. Cons. Rep. 47:202 (1895). 8

Transit Facilities. "Electric Railways at Florence, Italy." St. Ry. J. 15:528 (Aug. 1899); Ry. World 8:295 (Aug. 10, 1899).

"Florida Gas Works, Some Random Notes upon." Am. Gas Light J. 67:931 (Dec. 13, 1897).

"Flushing [L. I.], Electric Light and Power Station." Elec. World 30:659 (Dec. 4, 1897).

Foreign Element in American Cities. (See also under **Elections**.)

See also Boston, Chicago, New York.

"Assimilation of Nationalities in the United States." Mayo-Smith, Richmond. Pol. Sci. Q. 9:426 (Sept. 1894). 9

"Control of Immigration." Mayo-Smith, Richmond. Pol. Sci. Q. 3:46, 197, 409 (March, June, Sept. 1888). 10

"Emigration and Immigration." Mayo-Smith, Richmond. New York, Scribner's, 1890. 12mo, 316 pp. $1.50. 11

Foreign Element in Cities. Census Bulletin 357 XIth Census of the U. S., 1890.

——. "Conquest of Our Cities by the Irish." Bocock, J. P. Forum 17:186 (1894). 12

"Mixture of races and nationalities. Theories of." Mayo-Smith, Richmond. Yale R. 3:166 (Aug. 1894). 13

——. "The Immigration Question." Senner, Joseph H. Ann. Am. Acad. Pol. Sci. 10:1 (July, 1897). 14

France.

General Works.

"Administration Communale, Petit Dictionnaire d' A, B, C des Municipalités." Souviron, Alfred. Paris, Berger, L. et Cie., 1880. 1 fr. 50 c. 15

"L'Administration locale en France et en Angleterre." Leroy-Beaulieu, Paul. Paris, Guillaumin, 1872. 8vo. 16

"Arrondissements et Pays de France." des Rotours, J. Angot. Ref. Soc. 6:469 (Oct. 1, 1898). 17

"Conferences sur l'Administration et le Droit Administratif." Aucoc, Léon. Paris, Dunod, 1885-7. 3d ed. 2 vols. 836 and 863 pp. 26 fr. 18

"De l'Administration des communes en France, origine, transformation, état actuel, Lois de 1867 et 1868." de Toulza, Etienne. Paris, Durand et Pedone-Lauriel, 1869. 12mo. 3 fr. 50 c. 19

"Dictionnaire de l'Administration Française." Block, Maurice. Paris, Berger-Levrault et Cie., 1891. 3d ed. 8vo, 2232 pp. (and 122 pp., supplements for 1892, '3 and '4.) (See particularly list of articles under headings: Internal Administration, Communal and Departmental Administration, Police p. viii; Charity, etc. p. ix; Education p. x; Sanitary Administration p. xii; Financial Administration p xii.) 20

"Dictionnaire des Communes (France et Algerie), avec indication des Perceptions dont chaque commune fait partie, etc." Paris, Berger-Levrault et Cie., 1899. 8vo, 755 pp. 6 fr. 21

"Die Oertlichen Verwaltungen." Lebon, André. V Abteilung pp. 56-63, Vol. IV, 1, 4-6. Marquardsen. See 2-9. 22

"Institutions municipales et provinciales comparées. Organisation locale en France et dans les autres Pays de l'Europe. Comparaison; Influence des institutions locales sur les qualités politique d'un peuple et sur le gouvernement parlementaire. Réformes." (Bibliography mainly on the subject of decentralization.) de Ferron, H. Paris, Alcan, 1884. 8vo, 570 pp. 8 fr. 23

"La Commune. Entretiens familiers sur l'Administration de Notre Pays." Block, Maurice. Paris, Hetzel et Cie., 1880. 1 fr. 50 c. 24

"La Réforme Administrative." D'Avenel, Georges. Paris, Guillaumin et Cie., 1892. 3 fr. 50 c. 25

Law of 1884. "Code des Communes; ou Commentaire de la nouvelle loi municipale du 5 avril, 1884." Taulier, A. Grenoble, Bureau du Repertoire, 1884. 208 pp. 3 fr. 26

———. "Code des Conseillers Municipaux contenant le texte complèt de la loi du 5 avril 1884, etc." de Mailhol, D. Paris, Libraire Speciale Parisienne, 1888. 2 fr. 50 c. 27

———. "Commentaire de la loi du 5 Avril 1884 sur l'Organisation municipale." Grelot, Félix. Paris, Berger-Levrault et Cie., 1888. 2d ed. 5 fr. 28

———. "Etudes sur la loi municipale du 5 avril 1884." Ducroiq, Th. Paris Thorin, 1886. 5 fr. 29

———. "Loi Municipale, Commentaire de la loi du 5 avril 1884 sur l'organisation et les attributions des conseils municipaux, suivies du commentaire de la loi du 22 mars 1890 sur les syndicats de communes." Morgand, Léon. Paris, Berger, L. et Cie., 1896. 5th ed., 2 vols. 8vo, 1191 pp. 15 fr. 30

———. "Manuel pratique d'administration communale ou commentaire de la loi du 5 avril 1884, etc." Lescuyer, P. Paris, Giard et Brière, 1891. 8vo. 8 fr. 31

"Le Gouvernement local en France et l'Organisation du Canton." Bellangé, Charles. Paris, H. Didier, 1900. 8vo, 466 pp. 9 fr. 32

"Les Communes et la Liberté. Etude d'Administration Comparée." Block, Maurice. Paris, Berger-Levrault et Cie., 1877. 3 fr. 50 c. 33

"Les Institutions administratives en France et à l'Etranger. Des réformes à apporter à notre législation sur la commune et le département." Ferrand, Joseph. Paris, Cotillon et Cie., 1879. 6 fr. 34

"Life in a French Commune." Donald, Robert. Contemp. March, 1897. 35

"Local Government in France." de Franqueville, Le Comte. P. 283 "Local Government and Taxation." Editor J. W. Probyn. London & New York, Cassell, 1875. 5s. 36

Local and Municipal Government in France. Demombynes, Vol. II, pp. 53-122. See 2-11. 37

Municipal Government in France. Pp. 832-834. Vol. II. Palgrave. See 1-2. 38

MUNICIPAL AFFAIRS.

France—*Continued.*

"Précis de Droit Administratif." Hauriou, Maurice. Paris, Larose et Forcel, 1891. 2d ed. 1900. 10 fr.   39

"Question des Sous-Préfets et la Réforme Administrative." R. Pol. e. Par. 25:330 (Aug. 10, 1900).

"Recueil annoté des Lois et Décrets sur l'Administration communale et departementale, comprenant les textes, spéciaux à l'administration de la ville de Paris et du département de la Siene." Souviron, Alfred and de Pontich, Henri. Paris, Muzard et fils, 1889. 8vo. 10 fr. 1893, 1328 pp.   40

"Art, Administration of, in France." Barthélemy, A. Am. Arch. 52:68 (1896).   42

Building Laws. "Manuel des Lois du Bâtiment." Lucas, Ach. Paris, Ducher et Cie., 1879. 5 vols. Part I, 738 pp.; Part II, 1516 pp. 40 fr.   43

Burial, Cemeteries, Cremation. "Les Cimetières au point de vue de l'hygiene et de l'administration." Bertoglio, L. Paris, Bailliere et fils, 1889. 12mo. 3 fr. 50 c.   44

——. "La Crémation en France 1797-1889." (avec 7 figures.) Salomon, Georges. Paris, Dentu, 1890. 8vo. 1 fr.   45

——. "Les Cimetières et la police des sepultures. Traité pratique de legislation." Fäy, Emile. Paris, Berger, Levrault et Cie., 1889. 2d edit. 8vo. 3 fr.   46

Charity. Articles on "Assistance." Chevalier, Emile. Pp. 69-83 Vol. I, pp. 449-455 Vol. II, Say's "Dictionnaire d. Economie Politique." D'Echérac et Nielly. Pp. 199-209 Say's "Dictionnaire des Finances."   47

——. "Administration et Comptabilité des Bureaux de Bienfaisance." Thorlet, Léon. Paris, Berger-Levrault & Cie., 1889. 8vo, 333 pp. Paper, 5 fr.   48

——. "L'Assistance publique dans le Commune." Lefèvre, André, R. Municipale 3:1934 (Feb. 24, 1900).   49

——. "L'Assistance publique en France de 1889 à 1900." Monod, Henri. R. Gén. D'Administration 69:129 (Oct. 1900).   49a

——. "L'Assistance publique relativement a l'enfance." Marie, J. Paris, Berger-Levrault, 1892. 8vo. 2 fr.   50

——. "Bureaux de Bienfaisance." Lucipia, Louis. R. Municipale 2:1577 (Sept. 23, 1899).   51

——. "Charity in France and Belgium." Valleroux, Herbert. p. 135 "International Congress," vol. III, 1893. See 43-99.   52

——. "Des Secours a Domicile dans la ville de Paris." des Cilleuls, Alfred. Paris, Berger-Levrault, 1892. 8vo. 2 fr. 50 c.   53

——. "Mecanisme, Statuts, Reglements des Institutions de Bienfaisance. Economiste Pratique." Cacheux, Emile. Paris, Baudry, 1884. 40 fr.   54

——. "Public Assistance of the Poor in France." Balch, Emily Greene. Am. Econ. Assoc. Vol. VIII, Nos. 4 and 5. $1.   55

——. "Public Provision for Children in France." Balch, Emily Greene. p. 49 "International Congress," vol. V, 1893. See 43-99.   56

——. "Relief by Work in France." Grosseteste-Thierry. p. 207 "International Congress," vol. I, 1893. See 43-99.   57

——. "The French Municipal Farm for Indigents." Connor, Edward. Mun. World 8:123 (Aug. 1898).   58

——. "Traité Theorique et Pratique d'Assistance Publique." Derouin, H.; Gory. A.; Worms, F. Paris, Larose, 1900. 8vo, 2 vols., 824, 628 pp. Paper, 28 fr.   59

——. "L'Unification de la Representation des Pauvres et de l'Administration des Etablissements d'Assistance." de Tinguy du Pouet, J. R. Municipale 3:1616 (Oct. 7, 1899).   60

Council and Central Power. "Der Pouvoir central et des conseils municipaux." Lavergne, P. R. Gén. l'Administration 67:385 (April, 1900), 68:18 (May, 1900).   61

"Decentralization." Dreyfus, F. Revue Bleue March 27, 1897.   62

——. "Administrative Centralization and Decentralization in France." Young, J. T. Ann. Am. Acad. Pol. Sci. 11:24 (Jan. 1898).   63

——. "De la Décentralisation Communale." De Gand, Emmanuel. Paris, G. Lebrocquey, 1877. 50c.   64

——. "Décentralisation et Liberté dans la Commune." Imbart de la Tour, Jean. R. Pol. e. Par. 22:82 (Oct. 10, 1899), R. Municipale 3:1664 (Oct. 28, 1899), 3:1679 (Nov. 4, 1899), 3:1694 (Nov. 11, 1899).   65

BIBLIOGRAPHY.

France—*Continued.*

———. "La Décentralisation." Deschanel, Paul. Paris, Berger-Levrault et Cie., 1895. 2 fr. 50c.   66

———. "La Décentralisation. Projet de Réforme de la loi municipale du 5 avril, 1884." De Marcère Edouard. Paris, Larose et F. 2 fr.   67

———. "Necessité de Restituer au Pays ses Franchises Municipales." Germain, Félix. Paris, Guillaumin et Cie., 1871. 1 fr.   68

Elections, Municipal. "Les Elections Municipales." Gay, Ernest. R. Municipale 3:1785 (Dec. 23, 1899).   69

———. "Elections Municipales, Jurisprudence du Conseil d'Etat. Lois des 5 avril 1884 et 22 juillet 1889." Juillet, Saint Laeger. Paris, Berger, L. et Cie., 1900. 5th ed. 1 vol, 8vo, 470 pp. 5 fr.   70

———. "Les Elections Municipales du 6 Mai 1900." Fournier, Marcel. R. Pol. e. Par. 24:357 (May 10, 1900).   71

———. "Manuel électoral. Guide pratique de l'électeur et du maire, comprenant les élections municipales, départementales, législatives, etc." de Guer, Guerlin. Paris, Berger-Levrault et Cie., 1898. 7th ed. 12mo. 3 fr. 50 c.   72

———. "Manuel Formulaire des Elections à l'Usage des Préfets." Paris, Larose et Forcel, 1892. 3 fr.   73

———. "Petit Manuel Electoral." Cohn, L., Pasquier, Lucien. Paris, Sagnier, 1876. 60 c.   74

Expropriation. "L'Occupation définitive sans expropriation." Sanlaville, Ferd. Paris, Berger-Levrault, 1891. 8vo. 4 fr.   75

Finance, Municipal. "Budget Communal, Le." de Crisenoy, J. D. Say's Dictionnaire des Finances. Vol. I, p. 467-485.   76

———. "De l'Avenir des Biens communaux en France, et particulièrement dans les pays sectionnaires." Juillet, Saint Laeger. Paris, Berger-Levrault, 1882. 8vo. 2 fr. 50 c.   77

———. "Budget Municipal." Desbats, A. Gabriel. Paris, Berger-Levrault et Cie., 1895. 8vo, 450 pp. Paper 7 fr. 50 c.   78

———. Commune. de Crisenoy, J. De. Pp. 1113-1124, Vol. 1, "Dictionnaire des Finances." Say, Léon.   79

———. "Emprunts Municipaux en France et en Angleterre." Puibarand, Louis. Paris, Berger, L. et Cie., 1879. 8vo. 1 fr. 25 c.   80

———. "Essai sur les Finances Communales." Paul-Dubois, L. Paris, Perrin & Co., 1898. 16mo, 306 pp.   81

———. "Etude sur l'Administration des Finances municipales. Le municipe romain en droit romain. Les finances de la commune et la question des octrois." Blanc, Charles. Paris, Pichon & Cotillon, 1880. 8vo, 216 pp. 5 fr.   82

———. "Finances Communales: Etude Théorique et Pratique." Acollas, Renè. Paris, Giard & E. Brière, 1898. 12mo, 259 pp. Paper, $1.   83

———. "Französische Gemeindefinanzen." Pp. 733-766 R. v. Kaufmann's "Die französichen Finanzen." Leipzig, Bibliographischer Institut, 1882. 8vo, 882 pp. 25 M. Cl. 30 M.   84

———. "Local (Departmental und Communal) Besteuerung, Die." Pp. 137-144 Ergänzungsheft to Adolph Wagner's Finanzwissenschaft, Leipzig. Winter, 1896. 8vo, 168 pp. Also pp. 862-916 of his Finanzwissenschaft. 3 Thl. Leipzig. Winter, 1889. 8vo, 916 pp.   85

———. Octrois. (See Octrois below.)

———. "Régime Financier et Comptabilité des Communes. Traité Pratique Destiné aux Maires, etc." Thorlet, Léon. Paris, Berger, L. et Cie., 1889. 8vo. 5 fr.   86

———. "Situation Financière des Communes et les Centimes Communaux." Callet, Albert. R. Municipale 2:1499 (Aug. 19, 1899).   87

———. "Taxation, French System of." Covert, John C. Cons. Rep. 43:150 (June, 1900).   88

Fire Insurance. "La Caisse des Incendiés du départment de la Meuse, apropos des Projets de Création des Caisses départmentales d'Assurances." Salmon-Legagneur, Paul. Ref. Soc. 6:334 (Aug. 16 and Sept. 1, 1898), 6:434 (Sept. 16, 1898).   89

History. "Histoire de l'Administration en France et des progrès du pouvoir doyal depuis de régne de Philippe Auguste jusque là mort de Louis XIV." Dareste de la Chavanne, Antoine C. Paris, Guillaumin, 1848. 2 vols, 8 vo, 390 and 424 pp.   90

France—*Continued.*

——. "L'Administration municipale en XIIIe siecle dans les villes de consulat." Ramalho, A. Revue Generale d'Administration 55:407, 56:151 (1896). In pamphlet form. Paris, Berger, 1896. 2 fr. 50 c.   91

——. "L'Administration provinciale et communale en France et en Europe, 1785-1870." Hesse, A. Amiens, Prévost-Allo, 1871. 8vo.   92

——. "Du passé, du présent et le l'avenir de l'organisation municipale de la France." Champagnac, Emile. Saint-Flour, Vidal Rovet, 1843. 2 vols. 8vo. 10 fr.   93

——. "Histoire administrative des communes de France." Dupin, Claude François Etienne. Paris, 1834. 8vo.   94

——. "Institutions communales et provinciales et les corporations des pays de l'ancienne France a l'avénement de Louis XI." Paquet, 1860. 8vo.   95

Housing. "Die Wohnungsfrage in Frankreich." Raffalovich, Arthur. pp. 1-72, Hft. 31, Schr. d. Ver. f. Socialpolitik.   96

——. "Etude sur les Habitations à bon marché en France et à l'Etranger." Lucas, Charles. Paris, Aulanier & Co., 1900.   97

——. "Etude sur le projet de revision de la loi concernant les Logements insalubres." Jourdan, Gustave. Paris, Berger-Levrault et Cie., 1883. 8vo. 2 fr.   98

——. "Les Habitations Ouvrières." de Nouvoin, George. J. Economistes 42:336 (June, 1900).   99

——. "La Question des Habitations Ouvrières en France et à l'Etranger." Cheysson, E. Paris, G. Masson, 1887. 1 fr. 50 c.   100

——. "L'Intervention des Pouvoirs Publics dans le Mouvement d' Amélioration des Habitations à bon marché." Rostand, Eugène. Ref. Soc. 10:353 (Sept. 1, 1890).   2

——. "Legislation sur les Logements Insalubres. Traité Pratique." Jourdan, Gustave. Paris, Berger, L. et Cie., 5th ed., 1900. 8vo, 564 pp. 6 fr.   3

——. "Les Logements Insalubres, La loi de 1850." Laurent, Emile. Paris, Picard, 1882.   4

——. "Pouvoirs des Maires en Matière de Salubrité des Habitations." Jourdan, Gustave. Paris, Berger, L. et Cie., 3d ed., 1900. 12mo. 2 fr.   5

——. "The Modern Movement for the Housing of the Working Classes in France." Willoughby, William F. Yale R. 8:233 (Nov. 1899).   6

Lighting. "Concessions de Gaz et d'Electricite devant la juridiction administrative, 1823-1894, Recueil d'arrêtés des Conseils de Préfecture et d'arrêtés du Conseil d'Etat." Garnier, Léon et Paul Dauvert. Paris, aux bureaux du Journal des Usines à Gaz, 1894. 525 pp. 1 fr.   7

——. "Essai sur les Concessions d'eclairage et notamment sur la concurrence electrique." Cruveilhier, Jean. Paris, Berger-Levrault, 1900. 8vo. 3 fr.   8

——. "Monopoles communâux. Eclairage au gaz et à l'électricité, distribution d'eau et de force motrice, omnibus, tramways." Pilon, E. Paris, Giard et Brière, 1899. 8vo. 4 fr. 50c.   9

——. "The Future of Water Gas in France." J. Gas Light 76:86 (July 10, 1900).

Liquor Problem. "Alcoholism in France from a Sociological Point of View." Legrain. Revue Scientifique April 17, 1897.   10

——. "Financial Study of the Drink Question in France." Boulanger, E. Revue Politique et Parlementaire Jan. 10, 1897.   11

Municipal Control, etc. "Du Régime des Etablissements d'utilité publique." des Cilleuls, Alfred. Paris, Berger-Levrault, 1891. 8vo. 1 fr. 50 c.   12

——. (See also under Socialism, Municipal below.)

Octroi. Pp. 31-32. Vol. III, Palgrave. See 1-2.   13

——. "De la suppression des octrois et de leur remplacement." Guignard, A. Paris, Guillaumin, 1888. 6 fr.   14

——. "L'Impôt Communal sur le Revenu: Application à la Suppression des Octrois et a la Suppression des Centimes Additionnels." Malzac, Miranda. R. Pol. e. Par. 26:472 (Dec. 10, 1900).   15

——. "L'Impôt Communal sur le Revenu: Reforme des Contributions Directes et Octrois." Malzac, Miranda. Rev. Pol. e. Par. 18:360 (Nov. 10, 1898).   16

——. "Les Octrois municipaux, fondement économique, organisation administrative et financière, jurisprudence." Turquey, Elie. Paris, Giard et E. Brière, 1899. 8vo, 410 pp. 7 fr.   17

——. "La Suppression des Octrois." (History, present status in Paris and the

France—*Continued.*

provinces.) Veber, Adrien. Paris, Giard et Brière, 1899. 8vo, 234 pp. Also article by same writer, Rev. Soc. 28:156 (Aug. 1898); Grillot, P. R. Pol. e. Par. 19:543 (March, 1899). — 18

———. "The Octroi System of France." Haussmann, Carl A. U. S. Consular Report No. 117, p. 314, 1890. — 19

Pawnshops. "Monts de Piété en France." Vanlaer, Maurice. Paris, Guillaumin et Cie., 1895. 2 fr. 50 c. — 20

Police. "Des Rapports des Municipalités et du Puvoir central en matière de Police." Miriel, Emile. Paris, Larose, 1897. 8vo, 130 pp. — 21

———. "De l'Organisation de la Police (étude historique, theorique, et pratique) (thesis)." Pelatant, Leopold. Dijon, Berthond, 1899. 8vo, 307 pp. — 22

———. "Manuel de Police administrative et judiciaire." Paris, Bureau du Journal des Commissaires de Police, 1877. 423 pp. — 23

———. "L'Office de Police Judiciare." Thiriat, M. Paris, Giard et Brière, 1894. 3 fr. — 24

———. "Repertoire de Police administrative et judiciaire. Législation et réglementation. Jurisprudence et Doctrine." Courcelle, Louis. Paris, Berger-Levrault, 1899. 8vo, 2793 pp. 60 fr. — 25

———. "Traité de Police administrative et de Police judiciaire." Thorlet, Léon. Paris, Berger-Levrault, 1891. 8vo, 713 pp. 10 fr. — 26

"Political Education in France and the Organization of the Republican Party." Fournier, M. R. Pol. e. Par. Jan. 10, 1897. — 27

Population. "Accroissement de la population urbaine en France." de Castelleux, Comte. J. Economistes, 2d series, 13:372 (1857). — 28

———. "Depopulation." Bernard, François. Pp. 692-697 Vol. I, Say's "Dictionnaire d'Economie Politique." — 29

"Prostitution au point de vue de l'hygiène et de l'administration en France et à l'etranger, La." Reuss, L. Paris, Baillière et Fils, 1889. 636 pp. Bibliographie. 7 fr. 50 c. — 30

———. "La Prostitution en France. Etudes morales et démographiques avec une statistique générale de la prostitution en France." Després, A. Paris, Bonchut, 1882. 8vo. 6 fr. — 31

Public Works. "De l'Occupation temporaire en vue de l'execution des travaux publics, loi du 29 decembre, 1892." Bourcart, G. Paris, Pedone, 1895. 3 fr. — 32

———. "Traite des Travaux communaux a l'usage des maires." Thorlet, Léon. Paris, Berger-Levrault et Cie., 1893. 8vo, 437 pp. 7 fr. 50 c. — 33

———. "Des Travaux Publics Communaux." Bourgeois, Léon. Paris, Maresc-quainé, 1877. 2 fr. 50 c. — 34

Sanitation. "Pouvoirs des maires en matière de Salubrité des Habitations." Jourdan, Gustave. Paris, Berger, L. et Cie., 3d ed., 1900. 12mo. 2 fr. — 35

———. "La Reforme de l'Hygiene Publique." Dejamme, Jean. Paris, Berger-Levrault, 1885. 8vo. 1 fr. — 36

Savings Banks. "Réforme des Caisses d' Epargne Francaises." Rostand, Eug. Paris, Guillaumin et Cie., 1891. 5 fr. — 36a

———. "Le Projet de Réforme des Caisses d' Epargne." Moireau, M. A. Rev. d. deux Mondes 111:879 (1892). — 37

Schools. "Les Ecoles et les Oeuvres municipales d'Enseignement (1871-1900). Lavergne, F. Paris, 1900. 4to. — 37a

———. "Des Obligations et des Droits des communes en matière d'Ecoles." Dejamme, Jean. Paris, Berger-Levrault, 1889. 8vo. 2 fr. — 38

Socialism, Municipal. "L'Oeuvre des Municipalités Socialistes." (Dijou, Paris Roubaix.) Marpaux, A. Le Mouvement Socialiste, April 1, 15, May 1, 1900. — 39

———. "Le Socialisme Municipale." Bourdeau, J. R. Mondes July, 1900. — 40

———. "Socialists in French Municipalities." Kerr, Charles H.; and Simons, A. M. Chicago, Charles H. Kerr & Co., 1900. 16mo, 31 pp. Paper, 5 cts. — 41

———. "The Socialistic Municipalities of Northern France." Rowe, L. S. Yale R. 7:363 (Feb. 1899). — 42

Streets. "Traité de la Voirie." Courcelle, Louis. Paris, Berger-Levrault, 1900. 8 vo. 7 fr. 50 c. — 43

———. "Voirie vicinale et voirie urbaine: Lois, reglements, etc." Delaunoy, Léon. Paris, Frameries Dufrane-Friart, 1895. 3 fr. 50 c. — 44

Transit Facilities. "L'Exploitation des Tramways en France." Jean, Charles.

France—*Continued.*

Génie Civil Nov. 4, 1899. 45
——. "Electric Railway Practice in France." Connett, A. N. St. Ry. J. 16:927 (Oct. 13, 1900). 46
——. "La Réglementation des Chemins de Fer d'Interest Local, des Tramways et des Automobiles." Doniol, A. Paris, Béranger, 1900. 8vo, 365 pp. Paper, 10 fr. 47
——. "Les Tramways, Législation et Jurisprudence les concernant." Guillaume, Eugène. Paris, Berger-Levrault, 1884. 8vo. 2 fr. 48
——. "Light Railways and Tramways in France." Ty. & Ry. World 9:146 (April 5, 1900).
——. "The Construction of Tramways in France." Conradi, H. Ty. & Ry. W. 9:594 (Dec. 6, 1900). 49

Franchises, Municipal. (See under **Municipal Control, Municipal Ownership** and **Finance.**)

Frankfort-on-the-Main.

Housing. "Die Wohnungen des Volkes zu Ende des 19 Jahrhunderts." Meissner, Alois. Allgemeine Bauzeitung 59:82 (1894). 50
——. Die Wohnungsverhältnisse in Frankfurt a. M. Flesch. pp. 57-93, Hft. 30, Schr. d. Ver. f. Socialpolitik. 51
Population. "Die Bevölkerung von Frankfurt a. M. in 14. u. 15. Jahrhunderts." Bücher, Karl. Sozial. stat. Studien, Tübingen, 1886. 8vo, 15 M. 52
"Sewage Disposal. Frankfort." Mason, Frank H. See 56-40a. Anon. Trans. Society of Engineers pp. 123-56 (1892). 53
——. "Sewerage of Frankfort-on-the-Main." Fuertes, James H. Engng. Rec. 41:347 (April 14, 1900). 54
Statistics. "Statistische Beschreibung der Stadt Frankfurt am Main und ihrer Bevölkerung." Bleicher, H. Frankfurt a. M. Hrsg. d. d. statistische amt, 1892. 4to, 288 pp. and many tables. A second volume was issued in 1893 containing statistics on the movement of population in 1891, 64 pp. and tables. 55
Street System. "Strassenanlage in Frankfurt a. M." Seestern-Pauly. Allg. Bauz. p. 287, 1868-69. 56
"Water Works of Frankfort, Germany, New." Fuertes, James H. Engng. Rec. 37:542 (May 21, 1898). 57

Frederick Town [Md.], History of. Shafer, Sara Andrew. See 1-4c. 58

Freiburg, Switz. Statistics of Population and Property. "Bervölkerungs-und Vermögensstatistik in der Stadt und Landschaft Freiburg (im Uechtland) um die Mitte des 15 Jahrhunderts. Buomberger, Ferdinand. Freiburg, Stämpfli & Co., 1900. 8vo, 147 pp. 59

Fresh Air Charities. (See **Charities**, also Charities under **New York.**)

"**Friendly Visiting.**" (See under **Charities.**)

"**Fulham [Eng.]**; Past, Present and Future." Mun. J. 9:343 (May 4, 1900).

"**Functions, Municipal;** A Study of the Development, Scope and Tendency of Municipal Socialism." Maltbie, Milo Roy. Mun. Aff. 2:577-799 (Dec. 1898). 60

Galveston, Tex.

History, description and statistics of Galveston, Tex., in 1880. Census. See 1-7. 61
"Harbor Works, The Galveston." Sherman, W. J. J. Assoc. Engin. Soc. Dec. 1896. Engng News 37:162 (March 18, 1897) 62
"Water Supply of Galveston, Texas, Artesian." Peek, R. H. Engng. Neys 39:138 (March 3, 1898). 63

Garbage and Refuse Disposal. (See also **Streets.**)

See also Amsterdam, Antwerp, Berlin, Boston, Bradford (Eng.), Brooklyn, Brussels, Buffalo, Cambridge (Eng.), Canada, Chicago, Cincinnati, Cleveland, Columbus, Detroit, Edinburgh, Ghent, Glasgow, Gothenberg, Halifax (N. S.), Hamburg, Leyton, London, Lyons, Manchester (Eng.), Moline (Ill.), New Brighton (N. Y.), New Orleans, New York, Nice, Nottingham, Nuremberg, Paddington, Richmond, Rotterdam, St. Gall, San Francisco, Shoreditch, Syracuse (N. Y.), Toronto, Trieste, Torquay, United Kingdom, Wilmington (Del.), Zürich.

General References.

Collection and Disposal of Garbage. General articles on. Andrews, H. A. City Govt. 3:161 (Nov. 1897); Carpenter, Thomas B. Sanitarian 40:395 (May, 1898); Foster, Wolcott C. Engng. News 23:243 (1890); Gonden, H. J. City Govt. 7:51 (Sept. 1899), Public Improvements 1:273 (Oct. 1, 1899), pp. 13-19 in " Proceedings of the Third Annual Convention of the League of American Municipalities, 1899," 8vo, 138 pp. Paper; Hering, Rudolph. Engng. M. 13:392 (June, 1897), Engng. News 38:301 (Nov. 4, 1897), Engng. Rec. 36:558 (Nov. 27, 1897), Sanitarian 39:485 (Dec. 1897); Hill, G. Everett. Public Improvements 1:39 (June 1, 1899); Hosmer, G. W. Hrprs. Wkly. 38:711, 750 (1894); Jackson, J. San. Rec. 24:476 (Dec. 1, 1900); Kohnke, Quitman. City Govt. 5:66 (Aug. 1898); Livache, Ach. Bull. de la Soc. d'Encour. May 31, 1900; M'Cannel, W. J. City Govt. 9:62, 108 (Sept. Oct. 1900); Morse, W. F. City Govt. 3:158 (Nov. 1897), Prog. Age 15:555 (Nov. 15, 1897), Sanitarian 43:481 (Dec. 1899); Munn, Wm. P. City Govt. 2:6 (Jan. 1897); Pierce, Walter S. Sanitarian 39:299 (Oct. 1897); Reynolds, Arthur R. City Govt. 5:180 (Nov. 1898), Pro. Am. Soc. Mun. Imp. (5th yr.), Pt. II, p. 173 (Oct. 1898), Mun. Engng. 16:31 (Jan. 1899); Scherer, H. P. Mun. Engng. 19:331 (Nov. 1900), Cal. Mun. 3:116 (Dec. 1900); Walker, F. A. City Govt. 5:67 (Aug. 1898); Williams, H. S. Hrprs. Wkly. 38:835 (1894); Williams, J. J. City Govt. 7:49 (Sept. 1899), Public Improvements 1:267 (Oct. 1, 1899), pp. 12-13 in "Proceedings of the Third Annual Convention of the League of American Municipalities, 1899," 8vo, 148 pp. Paper; anon. Mun. and County Oct. 1895; Engng. Rec. 36:494 (Nov. 6, 1897); Engng. News 38:347 (Nov. 25, 1897); Mun Engng. 13:348 (Dec. 1897).   63a

" Garbage Disposal in American Cities." Engng. N. July 18, 1891, p. 51.

——. " Unsatisfactory Condition of Garbage Disposal in America, The." Engng. News 38:313 (Nov. 11, 1897), reprinted in Sanitarian 11:20 (Jan. 1898).

" Disposal of Sewage and Garbage in Foreign Countries." Special Cons. Rep. 17:13-221 (1899), see 56-40b.   64

" Economic Disposal of Towns' Refuse." Goodrich, W. Francis. London, 1900. 8vo, ill. Cl. $4.20.   65

" European Garbage Removal and Sewage Disposal." White, W. Howard. Trans. Am. Soc. Civil Engineers Dec. 1886.   66

" The Proper Disposal of Household Refuse and the Care and Cleanliness of Cellars." Cabeen (Mrs.) F. Von A. Philadelphia, Publications of the Civic Club, 1895.   67

" Animal Refuse, Disposal of." Boobbyer, Philip. San. Rec. 21:67 (Jan. 21, 1898). 68
Barren Island Garbage Disposal Plant. (See Garbage Disposal under **New York.**)

Burns and Engle Systems. "The Garbage Question." City Govt. 1:140, 2:50 (Dec. and Feb. 1896).

Collection. "Excreta, Removal of." Maxwell, Wm. H. San. Rec. 20:548 (Nov. 19, 1897). 69

——. " Motor Vans for Dust Collection." Mun. J. 9:561 (July 20, 1900), 9:682 (Aug. 31, 1900).

" Contracts, Garbage." (Editorial.) City & State 4:259 (Jan. 20, 1898).

Cremation of Garbage." Morse, W. F. Am. Arch. 39:155 (1893); Sanitarian 43:323 (Oct. 1899).   70

——. " Cremation from a Sanitary Standpoint." San. Rec. 23:548 (June 23, 1899).

——. " Decarie Garbage Incinerator." City Govt. 4:137 (April, 1898).

——. " Destruction of Refuse." Anon. Engineer 35:55 (March 1, 1898); **Engng.** 67:458 (April 7, 1899).

——. " Garbage Crematories and the Destruction of Organic Matter by Fire." Kilvington, Samuel S. Pamphlet, Minneapolis, 1888.   71

Garbage and Refuse Disposal—*Continued.*

——. " Refuse Destructors." Maxwell, William H. San. Rec. 21:7 (Jan. 7, 1898), 21:33 (Jan. 14, 1898), 21:63 (Jan. 21, 1898), 21:88 (Jan. 28, 1898), 21:111 (Feb. 4, 1898), 21:137 (Feb. 11, 1898), 21:164 (Feb. 18, 1898), 21:193 (Feb. 25, 1898), 21:221 (March 4, 1898), 21:249 (March 11, 1898), 21:276 (March 18, 1898), 21:305 (March 25, 1898), 21:333 (April 1, 1898), 21:361 (April 8, 1898), 21:416 (April 22, 1898), 21:475 (May 6, 1898), 21:500 (May 13, 1898), 21:532 (May 20, 1898), 21:560 (May 27, 1898). 72

" Electric Supply and the Destruction of Town Refuse." Warden-Stevens, F. J. Architect (London) May 14, 1897. 72a

" Food of Plants and the Refuse of Towns, The Exact Relation Between the." Builder 30:817. 73

" Holthaus Garbage Disposal System." City Govt. 4:93 (March, 1898).

House Refuse: Collection and Disposal of. Kelso, W. W. San. Rec. 24:373 (Oct. 27, 1899); Maxwell, William H. San. Rec. 20:331 (Sept. 24, 1897), 20:382 (Oct. 8, 1897), 20:436 (Oct. 22, 1897); anon. Gesundheits-Ing. Oct. 31, 1898. 74

Incineration. (See under Cremation above, Utilization below.)

Lighting. Garbage as a fuel for electric light stations. (See under Utilization of Garbage below.)

" Municipalization of Waste." San. Rec. 20:635 (Dec. 10, 1897).

" Scavenging Disposal of Refuse." Mason, Charles. San. Rec. May 8, 1896. 75

" Sludge Destructor, The First." London 7:53 (Jan. 27, 1898).

Small Towns, Garbage Disposal in. Bishop, Edwin F. P. 61, Assoc. Ex. Hlth. Officers of Ontario xith meeting, 1894; Denham, Prierly. Eng. (Lond.) 90:192 (Aug. 24, 1900); Kelso, W. W. J. San. Inst. 6:338 (Sept. 1899); Kittilson, Edward. Mun. Engng. 18:160 (March, 1900); Maxwell, Wm. H. San. Rec. 20:604 (Dec 3, 1897); Watson, W. M. Can. Eng. Dec. 1897; anon. Engng. Times May, 1900, Elec. R. (Lond.) Sept. 21, 1900. 76

Street Cleaning, Garbage Disposal and." Woodward, W. C. Engng. Rec. 40:458 (Oct. 14, 1899). 77

——. " Street Sweepings, Utilization of." San. Rec. 22:559 (Nov. 25, 1898).

——. " Value of Street Sweepings." Oldham, Edward A. Mun. Engng. 15:80 (Feb. 1899). 78

Study of Refuse Disposal from a Municipal Standpoint, A Plea for the More Comprehensive." Woodward, William Creighton. City Govt. 7:50 (Sept. 1899), Public Improvements 1:264 (Oct. 1, 1899), pp. 19-22 in Proc IIId Annual Convention of the League of American Municipalities, 1899. 8vo, 148 pp. Paper. 79

Utilization of Refuse. Brookman, F. W. Rochdale, James Clegg, 1900. 8vo, 13 pp.; Morse, W. F. Sanitarian 42:221 (March, 1899), Mun. Engng. 16:303 (May, 1899); Terne, Bruno. J. Frankl. Inst. 136:221 (1893), Am. Arch. 41:185 (1893); anon. San. Rec. 20:282 (Sept. 10, 1897). 80

——. " Disinfection and Sterilization, The Utilization of City Refuse." Morse, W. F. Sanitarian 42:343 (April, 1899). 81

——. Electric Lighting, Garbage and. Campbell, A. H. Mun. Engng. 17:99 (Aug. 1899); Perry, N. W. Cassier's 13:99 (Dec. 1897); Tomlinson, Thomas. Engng. M. 7:522 (1894); anon. Engng. (Lond.) 64:19 (July 2, 1897); Engng. News 38:137 (Aug. 26, 1897); Mun. Rec. & Ad., Vol. I, No. 13, p. 5 (Sept. 4, 1897); Chambers, J. 14:588 (Oct. 1897). 82

——. Fuel, Use of Garbage as. Campbell, A. H. City Govt. 6:154 (June, 1899); de Segundo, Ed. C. Elec. R. (Lond.) 46:41 (Jan. 12, 1900); anon. Engng. Rec. 37:291 (March 5, 1898), 41:60 (Jan. 20, 1900). 83

——. House Refuse, Experience in the Municipal Utilization of. " Erfahrungen in der städtischen Hausmüllverwerthung." Koller, Theodor. Glaser's Annalen July 15, 1899. 84

——. " Is Dustbin Refuse a Fuel?" Humphreys, Norton H. Jour. Gas Lgt. 71:175 (Jan. 25, 1898). 85

——. Street Sweepings. (See above).

——. " Waste Liquids from Garbage Reduction, The Disposal of." Engng. Rec. 37:410 **(May** 7, 1898). 86

" Willoughby Refuse Destructor, The." Engineer 84:271 (Sept. 17, 1897).

Gas Works, etc. (See under **Lighting.**)

" Gateshead [Eng.], Overcrowded." Mun J. 9:741 (Sept. 21, 1900).

Geneva, Switz.

General References. "Higher Life of Geneva." Waurin, Louis. Outlook July 3, 1897. 87
Improvements for Geneva. "Die neuen Anlagen von Genf." Allg. Bauz. p. 325, 1858.
Municipal Government of Geneva. Demombynes. Vol. II, pp. 421-431. See 2-11. 88
Observations in Geneva, in Article, "The Swiss and Their Politics." Macy, Jesse. Am. J. Sociol. 2:25 (July, 1896). 89

Prostitution. "La Lutte contre l'exploitation et la règlementation du vice à Genève." Paris, 1900. 18vo, 322 pp. 3 fr. 90
Sanitation. "Rapports sur les Visites Sanitaires Instituée par le conseil Administratif de Genève pendant l'été 1884." Ferrière, F. Genève, H. Georg, 1885. 1 fr. 91
Transit Facilities. "Street Railways in Geneva." Ridgely, Benjamin H. Cons. Rep. 63:76 (May, 1900); anon. St. Ry. J. 16:695 (Aug. 4, 1900). 92

Genoa, Italy.

"Costituzione dell'Amministrazione Civica dell'Annesione dei Comuni Suburbani a tutto l'anno 1887: Contributo alla Storia del Municipio di Genova." Drago, Raff. Genova, Pagano, 1888. 103 pp. 93
"Genoa: The Superb City." Irish Monthly 27:119 (March, 1899).

George Junior Republic, The. (See Child Problem in Cities under Charities).

"Georgetown, Demerara, Electric Railway for." Swan, N.; Rankin, Norman S. St. Ry. R. 10:705 (Dec. 15, 1900). 94

Georgia.

"Street Railways in Georgia." Bennett, S. H. St. Ry. Jour. 14:82 (Feb. 1898). 95
——. "The Right of Consolidating Competing Street Railway Corporations in Georgia Upheld by the Supreme Court." St. Ry. J. 16:403 (April 21, 1900).

Germany.

Government, General References, Unclassified.
"German Cities." Ely, R. T. Congregationalist June 30, July 7, 1892.
——. "Government of German Cities." Shaw, Albert. Cent. 48:296, 380 (1894). (See also Chapters V and VI in his "Municipal Government in Continental Europe.") 96
——. "Handbuch der Verfassung und Verwaltung in Preussen und dem deutschen Reiche." Hue de Grais. Berlin, Springer 12th ed. 1898. 8vo, 584 pp. 97
——. "Lehrbuch d. deutschen Verwaltungsrechts." Loening, Edgar. Leipzig, Breitkopf u. Härtel, 1884. 8vo, 859 pp. 16 m. 98
——. "Lehrbuch d. deutschen Verwaltungsrechts." Meyer, Georg. Leipzig, Duncker u. Humblot, 2d ed. 1893. 2 vol. 669 and 428 pp. 16 m. 99
——. Local and Municipal Government in Germany. Demombynes. Vol. II, pp. 727-803. See 2-11. 100
——. "Municipal Activities in Germany." Hoffman, Frank S. Outlook 58:1063 (April 30, 1898). 1
——. "Municipal Government in Germany." Anon. Real Estate Rec. & Guide Dec. 28, 1895, p. 925; Mun. J. 9:977 (Dec. 14, 1900).
Bavaria. "Gemeinden und Gemeinde Verfassung." Seydel, Max, in III Abs. pp. 124-164, Vol. III. Marquardsen. See 2-9. 2
History of Administrative Law. (See under History below).
Prussia. "Handbuch der städtischen Verfassung und Verwaltung in Preussen." Steffenhagen, H. Berlin, Heine, 1888. II Bde. 317 and 320 pp. 7m. 60 pf. 3
——. "Die Organisations-gesetze der inneren Verwaltung in Preussen." (Especially p. 147 Städteordnung of 1853). Anschütz, Gerhardt. Berlin, Carl Heymanns Verlag, 1898. 657 pp. 4m. 4
——. "Die Preussischen Städteverfassungen." Kotze, Otto. Berlin, Gustav Hempel, 1879. 631 pp. 10m. 5
——. "Die Stadtverordneten. Ein Führer durch d. bestehende Recht." (Espe-

Germany—*Continued.*

cially Städteordnung). Jebens, A. W. Berlin, Springer, 1899. 294 pp. n. 3m. 6

———. " Die Städteordnung von 1853 in ihrer heutigen Gestalt." Zelle, R. Berlin, Springer, 3d ed. 1893. 86 pp. 1m. 7

———. " Die Städteordnung für die sechs östlichen Provinzen der preussischen Monarchie vom 30 Mai 1853. Mit Ergänzungen u. Erläuterungen." Oertel, O. Liegnitz, H. Krumbhaar, 2 Aufl., 1893. 460 pp. 8m. 8

———. " La Vie municipale en Prusse." Leclerc, M. Annales de l'Ecole Libre des Sciences Politique, Paris, 1888. 9

———. " Local Government in Prussia." Goodnow, F. J. Pol. Sci. Q. 4:648 Dec. 1889). 10

———. " Local Government considered in its historical development in Germany and England, with special reference to Recent Legislation on the Subject in Prussia." Morier, R. B. D. P. 357 " Local Government and Taxation." J. W. Probyn, editor. London & New York, Cassell, 1875. 5s. 11

———. Municipal Government in Prussia. pp. 834-836 Vol. II. Palgrave. See 1-2. 12

———. " Organization der preussischen Verwaltung nach den neuen reform Geset zen, historisch u. dogmatisch dargestellt." von Stengel, Karl Freih. Leipzig. Duncker u. Humblot, 1884. 8vo, 677 pp. 12m. 13

———. " Preussisches Stadtrecht: Verfassung u. Verwaltung d. preuss. Städte systematisch dargestellt." Leidig, Eugen. Berlin, Siemenroth u. Worms, 1891. 552 pp. 8m. 14

———. " Preussisches Verwaltungsrecht." (Pp. 113-179 Die Städteverfassungen). Bornhak, Conrad. Freiburg, Mohr, 1889-90. 2 vol., 498, 710 pp. Ergänsungsbd., 1893. 68 pp. 20m. 15

———. " Städteordnungen der preussischen Monarchie." Backoffner, R. Berlin, Marquardt u. Schenck. 250 pp. 2m. 16

Saxony. " Die sächsische revid. Städteordnung u. Städteordnung für mittlere und kleinere Städte v. 24 Okt. 1873." v. Bosse, H. A. 1898. 280 pp. 3m. 20 pf. 17

Württemberg. " Die Selbstverwaltung und ihre Organe." Gaupp, L. Abs. VI, pp. 171-198, Vol. III. Marquardsen. See 2-9. 18

" Abattoirs in German Cities, Municipal." Blashill, Thomas. Mun. J. & London 8:133 (Feb. 3, 1899). 19

Bavaria. (See under separate topics).

Building Laws. " Extracts from the Building Laws, Regulations and Forms of a number of German States and Cities." Pp. 516-562 J. Stübben's " Städtebau." Darmstadt, Bergsträsser, 1890. 561 pp. 32m. 20

———. " Das königlich sächsische Baupolizeirecht. Mit Erläuterungen." Leuthold, C. E. Leipzig, Rossbergsche Hof. Buchhandlung, 6th ed. 1895. 334 pp. 21

———. " Die Baupolizei, Ratgeber für das ganze Gebiet der Baupolizei nebst einem Anhang über Statik und Festigkeitslehre im Hochbau." Rau, Albert. Karlsruhe, Nemrisch, 1894. 121 pp. 4m. 50 pf. 22

———. " Polizeiverordnung betreffend die bauliche Anlage und die innere Einrichtung von Theatern, Circusgebäuden und öffentlichen Versammlungsräumen." Berlin, Heymann, 1891. 2d ed. 44 pp.

Burial, Cremation, etc. "Fortschritte der Feuerbestattung in Deutschland." Engerth, Karl. Vienna, M. Perles, 1892. 2d ed. Pamphlet 20 pp. 60 pf. 23

Charities. " Armenwesen." Loening, E. Pp. 855-925 of Gustav Schönberg's Handbuch d. Pol. Oekonomie. 3 Bd. "Finanzwissenschaft." Tübingen, H. Laupp, 1885. 24

———. " L'Assistance Publique en Allemagne. Législation, statistique en 1885." Le Roy, P. A. Paris, Berger-Levrault, 1889. 8vo. 3 fr. 50c. 25

———. " L'Assistance Publique en Prusse." Artibal, J. R. Municipale 3:1740 (Dec. 2, 1899). 26

———. " Count Rumford and his Work among the Poor in Bavaria." Gilman, Elizabeth. Char. R. 6:211 (May, 1897). 27

———. " Das Armenwesen in 77 deutschen Städten und einigen Landarmenverbänden." Böhmert, Victor. Leipzig, Duncker u. Humblot, 1893. 139 pp. 28

———. " Das Gestetz über den Unterstützungswohnsitz vom 6. Juni, 1870," (as amended March 12, 1894.) Koppe. Berlin, Carl Heymanns Verlag. 2 M. 29

———. " Ueberblick über d. Ergebnisse der Sommerpflege in Deutschland im Jahre, 1890. Erstättet von der Zentralestalle d. Vereins für Sommerpflege in Deutschland." Berlin, 1891. 30

Germany—*Continued.*

Civil Code, The Cities and the German. Schwartz, J. C. Preussische Jahrbücher Oct. 1898. 31

Conference of Municipal Officials, Prussian. "The Prussian Städtetag." Brooks, Robert C. Ann. Am. Acad. Pol. Sci. 13:264 (May, 1899). 32

Cremation (See under Burial above.)

"Department Stores in Germany, Special Taxation of." Mason, Frank H. Cons. Rep. 64:5 (Sept. 1900). 33

Elections. "Das Dreiklassensystem." Jastrow, Ignaz. Berlin, Rosenbaum u. Hart, 1894. 8vo, 157 pp. 3m. 34

——. "Die nationale Rechtsidee von den Ständen und das preussische Dreiklassenwahlsystem." v. Gneist, Rudolph. Berlin, Springer, 1894. 8vo, 272 pp. 4m. 35

——. "Die Staats und Gemeindewahlen im preussischen Staate." (Three class elections of 1893.) Evert, G. XVII Ergänzungshft. z. Zeitschrift d. kgl. preuss. statistischen Bureau, Berlin, 1895. 36

——. "La Loi Electorale municipale en Prusse." Le Mouvement Socialiste April 1, 1900.

——. "Political Clubs in Prussian Cities." Brooks, Robert C. Mun. Aff. 4:375 (June, 1900). 37

——. "Three Class Election System in Prussian Cities." Brooks, Robert C. Mun. Aff. 3:396 (Sept. 1899). 38

Expropriation in Saxony. "Die Gesetzgebung über Wegebau und Expropriation im Königreich Sachsen." Ludwig-Wolf, L. F. Leipzig, Rossbergsche Buchhandlung, 3d ed., 1892. 455 pp, 5m. 40 pf. 39

Finance. "Die deutschen Städte." Pp. 51-60 of Adolph Wagner's Finanzwissenschaft 3 Theil. Leipzig, Winter, 1899. 8vo, 916 pp. 40

——. "Einiges über die Einnehmenquellen der Städte des Regierungsbezirks Cassel." Straus, Carl. J. Nat. u. Stat. 19:62 (Jan. 1900). 41

——. "Local Government and Finance in Prussia." Rice, C. Spring. Diplomatic and Consular Reports of Great Britain, No. 487, Miscellaneous Series, 1899. 23 pp. 1½d. 42

——. "Municipal Economy in Prussia." James, E. J. Nation Oct. 23, 1881. 43

——. "Städtische Finanzen im Mittelalter." Stieda, Wilhelm. Jr. Nat. Stat. III Folge, 17 Band. Pp. 1-54 (Sept. 1899). 44

Finance: Taxation. "Die progressive Einkommensteuer im Staats u. Gemeinde-Haushalt." Neumann, F. J. Leipzig, Duncker u. Humblot, Schr. d. V. f. Sozialpolitik, 1874. 8vo, 238 pp. 4 M. 80 pf. 45

——. "Das Kommunalabgabengesetz." Nöll, F. Berlin, Heymann, 1894. 8vo, 405 pp. 8 M. 46

——. "Das Kommunalabgabengestez vom 14 Juli, 1893." Luks, W. Berlin, Valen, 1894. 8vo, 76 pp. 1 M. 60 pf. 47

——. "Das Kommunalabgabengestez vom 14 Juli, 1893. Ausführungsanw. u Uebergangsbestimm. vom 10 Mai, 1894." Strutz. Berlin, Carl Heymanns Verlag, 3 Auflage. 3 M. 48

——. "Das preuss. Finanzreform durch Regulirung der Gemeindesteuern." v. Gneist, Rudolph. Berlin, Springer, 1881. 6m. 49

——. "Die Besteuerung der Gemeinden: Finanzwissenschaftliche Erörterungen." Friedberg, Robert. Berlin, Püttkammer u. Mühlbrecht, 1877. 8vo, 107 pp. 2m. 40 pf. 50

——. "Die bayrische Gemeindebesteuerung seit Anfang des 19 Jahrhunderts." Tröltsch, Walt. München, C. H. Bech, 1891. 8vo, 145 pp. 3m. 51

——. "Die Communalsteuerfrage, Ausarbeitung eines Referats im Verein für Sozialpolitik; mit einem Nachwort, der Verein für Sozialpolitik und seine Verbindung mit dem volkswirtschaftlichem Congress." Wagner, A. H. G. Leipsic, C. F. Winter, 1878. 8vo, 68 pp. 2m. 50 pf 52

——. "Die Communalsteuerfrage. Zehn Gutachten und Berichte." (Schr. d. Ver. f. Soz. Pol.) Leipsic Duncker u. Humblot, 1877. 8vo, 302 pp. 6m. 60 pf. 53

——. "Die deutschen Städtesteuern insbesondere die städtischen Reichssteuern im 12. u. 13. Jahrhundert." Zeumer, Karl. Leipzig, Duncker u. Homblot, 1878. 8vo, 162 pp. 4m. 54

——. "Die Gemeindebesteuerung und deren Reform." Bilinski, Leon Ritter von. Leipzig, Duncker u. Humblot, 1878. 325 pp, 8vo. 55

——. "Die persönlichen Steuern vom Einkommen verbunden mit Ertrags oder mit

Germany—*Continued.*

Vermögenssteuern, mit besonderer Beziehung auf Württembergische Verhältnisse." Neuman, Fr. J. Tübingen, Laupp, 1896. 8vo, 281 pp. 4m. 60 pf.   56
——. " Oeffentliche Kinderfürsorge." Lammers, Berlin, 1885. Pamphlet. 1m.
——. " Die gegenwärtigen Communalbesteurung im preussischen Staate, erlautert." Zimmer, Berlin, 1889. 50 pf.
——. " Die preussischen Kommunalanleihen mit besonderer Rücksicht auf eine Centralisation des Kommunalkredits." Kähler, W. Jena, G. Fischer, 1897. 8vo, 121 pp. 4m.   57
——. " Städtefinanzen in Preussen." Gerstfeldt. Leipzig, O. Wigand, 1882.   58
——. " Studien über d. weitere Entwickelung d. Gemeindesteuerwesens auf Grund d. preussischen Kommunal-abgabengesetzes vom 14 Juli, 1893." (Aus: Ztschr. f. d. ges. Staatswiss.) Adickes, F. Tübingen, Laupp, 1894. 8vo, 125 pp. 2m. 60 pf.   59
——. " Zur Gemeindesteuerreform in Deutschland, mit besonderer Beziehung auf sächsische Verhältnisse." Neumann, F. J. Tübingen, H. Laupp, 1895. 8vo, 303 pp. 6m.   60
Fire Departments. "Die kommunale Besteuerung der Feuerversicherungspolicen u. d. Heranziehung d. Feuerversicherungs-Anstalten zu den Feuerlöschkosten in Preussen." Herrfurth, L. Berlin, Heymann, 1895. 8vo, 56 pp. 1m.   61
——. " Geschichte der deutschen Feuerlösch- u. Rettungs-Anstalten." Fiedler, Ottomar. Berlin, Springer's Verlag, 1873. 8vo, 5m.   62
" Garbage Cremation in Germany." Engng. Rec. June 20, 1896.   63
History. "Bilder aus dem deutschen Städteleben in Mittelalter." Pfalz, F. Leipzig, Klinkhart, 1869. 2 vols. 8vo.   64
——. " Chroniken der deutschen Städte." Edited by Karl Hegel, Leipzig, 1862-96. 25 vols.   65
——. " L'Evolution des institutions communaux en Prusse et en Angleterre." Paul-Dubois, L. Rev. Pol. et Par. Aug. 1897.   66
——. " Geschichte der Städteverfassung in Deutschland." v. Maurer, G. L. Erlangen, Enkes Verlag, 1869-71. 4 vols., 8vo, 45m. 70 pf.   67
——. " Geschichte des preussischen Verwaltungsrechts." Bornhak, Conrad. Berlin, Springer, 1884-86. 3 vols. 8vo, 434, 336 and 350 pp. 25m. 20 pf. (A number of chapters devoted to city government.)   68
——. " Life and Times of Stein." (Reform of City Government in Prussia, 1808.) Seeley, J. R. Cambridge, 1878. 3 vols. 8vo.   69
——. " Markt und Stadt in ihrem rechtlichen Verhältnis. Ein Beitrag zur Geschichte der deutschen Stadtverfassung." Rietschel, S. Leipzig, Viet u. Co., 1897. 241 pp. 6m.   70
——. Origin. "Die Entstehung der deutschen Stadtgemeinde." Jastrow, Düsseldorf, 1889. Same title, Below, G. v. Düsseldorf, Voss & Co., 1888. 8vo, 127 pp. 3m.   71
——. Origin of Large Towns. Oppenheimer, F. Neue Deutsche Rundschau June, 1899.   72
——. Rhine Cities. "Geschichte der rheinischen Stadtkultur ihren Anfängen bis zur Gegenwart." Boos, Heinrich. Berlin, J. A. Stargardt, 1889. 3d vol, 8vo, 483 pp. 6m.   73
——. " Niederrheinisches Städtewesen vornehmlich im Mittelalter." Liesegang, Erich. Breslau, Koelner, 1897. 8vo, 758 pp.   74
——. " Die Entstehung des deutschen Städtewesens." Hegel, Karl. Leipzig, S. Hirzel, 1897, 8vo, 192 pp. 7 marks. Same title, Sohm, Rudolph. Leipzig, Duncker u. Humblot, 1890. 8vo, 120 pp. 2m. 40 pf.   75
——. " Städte und Gilden der germanischen Völker im Mittelalter." Hegel, Karl. Leipzig, Duncker u. Humblot, 1891. 2 vols, 8vo, 457 and 516 pp. 20m.   76
——. " Ursprung der deutschen Stadtverfassung." Heusler, Andr. Weimar, Böhlau, 1872. 8vo, 252 pp. 4m.   77
Housing. "Etude sur la Concentration des Habitations dans les Maisons Urbaines d'Allemagne." Cacheux, Emile. Soc. Fran. Hab. à bon marché, No. 2, p. 67 (1900).   78
——. " Die Grossstädtische Wohnungsnot." Walcker, Karl. Hamburg, in Zeit. und Streitfragen, 1892.   79
——. " Die Wohnungsnoth der ärmeren Klassen in deutschen Grossstädten." (Contains papers on housing conditions in principal German cities, indexed separate-

BIBLIOGRAPHY.

Germany—*Continued.*

——, and propositions for reform.) Schriften d. Vereines für Sozialpolitik, Hft. 30, 31, 33. Leipzig, Duncker u. Humblot, 1886-7. 80
——. " Die Wohnungsnot in den Grossstädten u. d. Mittel zu ihrer Abhülfe." Albrecht, H. München, R. Oldenburg, 1891. 8vo, 127 pp. 2m. 50 pf. 81
——. " Die Wohnungsverhältnisse unserer ärmeren Klassen." Diestelkamp, L. Berlin, George & Fiedler (Soz. Zeitfragen.) 1885. 59 pp, 1m. 82
——. " Gebäudesteuer und Wohnungsfrage in Preussen." zur Nieden, Walter. Jahr. f. Gesetz. Ver. u. Volks. 24:1 (Erstes Heft). 83
——. " Homes of the German Working People." Smith, James Henry. U. S. Consular Report No. 98, pp. 173-257, 1888. 84
——. " Lösung der Wohnungsfrage, etc." Stolp, Hermann. Berlin, Rosenbaum and Hart, 1892. 8vo, 10 pp. 10 pf. 85
——. " Stadterweiterung in rechtlicher Beziehung." Meyer, E. Berlin, Heymann, 1893. 99 pp. n. 2m. 86
——. " Verbesserung d. Wohnungen." Schriften d. Zentralstelle für Wohlfahrtseinrichtungen Bd. I. Berlin, Heymann, 1892. 208 Abbildungen. 370 pp. 8 M.
——. " Wohnungsfrage vom Standpunkte der Armenpflege." Deutscher Ver. f. Armenpflege u. Wohlt. XI Heft. Leipzig, 1890.
——. " Wohnungsmietrecht und seine soziale Reform." Schneider, K. Leipzig, Duncker und Humblot, 1893, Staats u. Soz. wiss. Forschungen G. Schmoller, Hrsgbr. 170 pp. 3m. 60 pf. 87
Inns and Taverns. "Die Gast- und Schankwirtschaften in den deutschen Gemeinden mit mehr als 15,000 Einwohnern, November, 1898." Tenius, Gustav. Dortmund, 1899. 8vo, 109 pp. 88
Labor. "Sweating in Germany." Brooks, J. G. Am. J. Soc. Sci. 30:59 (1892). (See also under Unemployment below.) 89
Libraries. " Volksbibliothek u. Volkslesehalle eine kommunale Veranstaltung." Aschrott, P. F. Berlin, Leibmann, 1896. 66 pp. 1m. 90
Lighting. "Municipal Electric Light and Power in Germany." DuBois, James T. Consular Reports 56:546 (April, 1898). 91
——. " Photometry in Germany." Jour. Gas Lgt. 73:178 (Jan. 24, 1899).
——. " Statistik der Elektricitätswerke Deutschlands." Elektrotech. Zeitschr. July 7, 1898.
Local Independence in Prussia. "Les Libertés Locales en Prusse." Blondel, Georges. Ref. Soc. 8:776 (Nov. 16, 1899). 92
Paving. "Care of Asphalt Streets in Germany." Erdman, C. W. Cons. Rep. 15:686 (April, 1899.) 93
" Pawnbroking in Germany." Barnes, C. E. Cons. Rep. 61:371 (Nov. 1899); anon. J. Soc. Arts 47:860 (Oct, 13, 1899). 94
Police Administration. "Praxis der Polizei Verwaltung." Erdmann, Wald. Berlin, Heine, 1891. 12m. 95
——. " Die bestehende Organisation und die erforderliche Reorganisation der preussischen Polizeiverwaltung." Held, Otto. Berlin, F. Ludhardt, 1886. 228 pp. 96
——. " Sittlichkeitspolizei." Loening, E. Pp. 926-937 in Gustav Schönberg's Handbuch d. Pol. Oekonomie, 3 Bd. Finanzwissenschaft. Tübingen, H. Laupp, 1885. 97
Political Clubs in Prussian Cities. (See under Elections above.)
Population. "Growth of Cities in Germany and America." Hamilton, James H. Our Country 7:49 (March, 1898). 98
Prostitution. (See "Sittlichkeitspolizei" under Police above.)
Prussia. (See separate topics.)
" Public Works of German Municipalities." Washburn, Albert H. pp. 202-214 U. S. Consular Reports No. 149, Feb. 1893. 99
Sanitation. "Gesundheitswesen." Jolly, L. Pp. 805-855 in Gustav Schönberg's Handbuch d. Pol. Oekonomie, 3 Bd. Finanzwissenschaft. Tübingen, H. Laupp, 1885. 100
——. German Public Health Associations. Transactions of the, of Munich, Freiburg, Frankfurt and Strassburg. "Verhandlungen des Deutschen Vereins für oeffentlche Gesundheitspflege zu München, Freiburg i. B., Frankfurt a. M. and Strassburg." Deutsche f. Oef. Gesundheitspfl. p. 1, 1875; p. 10, 1886; p. 12, 1889; p. 20, 1890. 1

MUNICIPAL AFFAIRS.

Germany—*Continued.*

"Savings Banks in Prussia, Report on." Rice, Spring. British Diplomatic and Consular Reports No. 478, Miscellaneous Series. London, Eyre & Spottiswoode, 1898. 16 pp. 1d. 1a

——. "Das deutsche Sparkassenwesen." Seidel, Max. Berlin, Heymann, 1896. I. Bd. Deutsche Staaten mit Ausnahme Preussens u. Elsass Loth. 8vo, 472 pp. 6m. 2

——. "Die Sparkassengesetzgebung Deutschlands. Sammlung der die sparkassen betr. Gesetze, Erlasse, Verordnungen, Verfügungen." Heyden. Essen, 1892. 3

——. "Die Sparkassenverhältnisse im Königreich Sachsen." Trautmann, A. Leipzig, Würzner in Comm., 1882. 8vo, 40 pp. 60 pf. 4

Saxony. (See separate topics.)

Schools. "Das Schulwesen und seine Verwaltung. Reform, etc." Zródlowski, Ferd. Leipzig, Wigand, 1889. 2m. 5

——. Central Confirmation of Members Elected to School Boards. "Die Staatliche Bestätigung der Mitglieder städtischer Schul-deputationen nach Preussischem Recht." Preuss, Hugo. Ar. f. Oef. Rt. 15:202 (1900). 6

——. "Handbuch der Organisation und Verwaltung der städtischen Schuldeputation." Steffenhagen, H. Berlin, Heine, 1888. 7

——. "Preussisches Schulrecht." Leipzig, Osterwitz, 1890. 6m. 25 pf.

"Sewage Purification in Germany." San. Rec. 21:142 (Feb. 11, 1898).

"Small Holdings and Allotments in Germany." Tetley, William C. Land M. Feb. 1899. 8

"Statistisches Jahrbuch deutscher Städte." Breslau, Published yearly by M. Neefe and others. 1 Jahrgang, 1890, 247 pp.; 2 Jahrgang, 1892, 397 pp.; 3 Jahrgang, 1893, 378 pp.; 4 Jahrgang, 1894, 360 pp.; 5 Jahrgang, 1896, 360 pp.; 6 Jahrgang, 1897, 388 pp.; 7 Jahrgang, 1898, 416 pp.; 8 Jahrgang, 1900, 420 pp. Cost last annual edition 12m. 60 pf. (Principal topics discussed: Area, Location, Distribution of Space in cities, Meteorological and Natural Statistics, Land Ownership and Buildings, Building Operations, Dwellings and Separate Establishments, Water Supply and Water Works, Fire Protection, Savings Banks, Public and Private Pawnshops, Industrial Courts (Gewerbegerichte), Street Railways, Omnibusses, etc., Postal, Telegraph and Telephone Business, Employment Bureaus and Emergency Works, Cattle Yards and Slaughter Houses, Wages, Cost of Necessities of Life, Public Disinfection Plants, Street Cleaning and Watering, Sewage Disposal, Public Parks, Gardens and Show Places, Educational Statistics, Population, Municipal Taxes, Municipal Debts, Charity, Police and Justice, City Administration incl. Elections, Markets and Fairs.) 9

Theatres, Law of. "Deutsches Theaterrecht, unter Berücksichtigung der fremden Rechte, systematisch dargestellt." Opet, O. Berlin, S. Calvary & Co., 1897. 8vo, 519 pp. 10m. 10

Transit Facilities. Electric Tramways. Magee, Louis J. St. Ry. J. 15:647 (Oct. 1899); anon. Eng. (London) May 13, 1898. 11

——. "An Important German Rapid Transit Problem." St. Ry. J. 16:157 (Feb. 3, 1900).

——. "Statistik der Electrischen Bahnen in Deutschland." Elektrotech. Zeitschr. 19:12 (Jan. 6, 1898), 20:15 (Jan. 5, 1899), 21:14 (Jan. 4, 1900).

Water Supply. "Die Wasserversorgung der Städte im deutschen Reiche sowie in einigen Nachbarländern." Grahn, E. I Bd. Preussen, München, Oldenburg, 1898. 547 pp. 26m. II Bd. Bayern, same, 1899. 224 pp. 10m. 12

——. Bavaria. "Der Stand der Wasserversorgung in Bayern." Zeitschr. d. Ver. Deutscher Ing. Nov. 4, 1899.

——. "Filtration of Water in Germany, The." Beer, E. Engng. Rec. 42:416 (Nov. 3, 1900); Holman, M. L. J. Assoc. Engng Soc. 21:1 (July, 1898), Engng. Rec. 38:319 (Sept. 10, 1898), 40:32 (June 10, 1899). 13

Unemployment, Insurance against. "Grundzüge eines Reichsgesetzes zur kommunalen Versicherung gegen Arbeitslosigkeit." Sonneman, L. Ar. Soz. Gesetz. Stat. 10:800-805 (1897). 14

——. "Le mouvement économique et social en Allemagne; Statistique des sans-travail; les bureaux de placement; l'assurance contre de chômage." Block, Maurice. L'Economiste francais 2:241 (1895). 15

Württemberg. (See separate topics.)

Ghent. Sewage and Garbage Disposal. See 56-40b. 16

Gill City Schools. (See under **Schools**).

Glasgow.

Government, General References and Unclassified. " Administration of Glasgow." City Govt. 2:131, 169 (May, June, 1897), 3:52 (Aug. 1897).

———. " Glasgow." Gordon, W. J. Leisure Hour, Oct. 1899; Shaw, Albert. Cent. 39:721, 792 (1890). (See also his " Municipal Government in Great Britain, pp. 69 to 145). 17

———. " Glasgow, its Municipal Organization and Administration." Bell, James, and James Paton. Glasgow, MacLehose & Sons, 1896. 4to, 426 pp. maps. (Contains several chapters on the history of the city, also Ch. IX, The Corporation: its Wealth and Activity; Ch. X, Magistrates and Jurisdictions; Ch. XI, Police; Ch. XII, Streets and Bridges; Ch. XIII, Sewers and Sewage; Ch. XIV, Fire Brigade; Ch. XV, Public Lighting; Ch. XVI, Cleansing; Ch. XVII, Baths and Wash Houses; Chs. XVIII-XXI, Health Department; Ch. XXII, The Improvement Trust; Chs. XXIII-XXV, Water Supply; Ch. XXVI, Corporation Gas and Electricity; Ch. XXVII, Municipal Markets; Ch. XXVIII, Tramways; Ch. XXIX, Clyde Navigation; Ch. XXX, Public Halls and Entertainments; Ch. XXXI, XXXII, Parks; Ch. XXXIII, Science and Art, Art Galleries and Museums; Ch. XXXIV, Education, Libraries; Ch. XXXV, Education, Schools; Ch. XXXVI, Education, Charity; Ch. XXXVII, Public Charity; Ch. XXXVIII, Religion. Review of the above, J. Gas Light, March 30, 1897. 18

———. " Glasgow of To-day." Hammerton, J. A. Temple M. Sept. 1899. 19

———. " Glasgow, a Model Municipality." Fisher, W. E. Garret. Fortn. 63:607 (1895). 20

" Architecture of Our Large Provincial Towns; Glasgow." Builder 75:21 (July 9, 1898).

Ferries. (See under Transit Facilities below).

Finance. " Municipal Work and Finance of Glasgow." Smart, W. Econ. J. 5:35 (1895). 21

———. " Taxation in Glasgow." Rowe, L. S. City and State 4:210 (Dec. 30, 1897); anon. Sci. Am. 77:5 (July 3, 1897); Ann. Am. Acad. Pol. Sci. 11:430 (May, 1898). 22

" Fire Brigade, Glasgow." Surveyor, Supp. July 27, 1900.

Garbage Disposal. See 56-40b. 23

———. " Garbage Disposal: The Cleaning of a Great City." McColl, Donald. City Govt. 9:37 (Aug. 1900). 24

———. " The Cleansing of Glasgow." Murdoch. Pp. 14-18 in " Pro. of the Assn. of Cleansing Superintendents of Great Britain, Sept. 6-9, 1899." Rochdale, James Clegg, 1900. 8vo, 63 pp. 25

———. " The Glasgow Corporation Farms." McFarlane. Pp. 19-22 in " Pro. of the Assn. of Cleansing Superintendents of Great Britain, Sept. 6-9, 1899." Rochdale, James Clegg, 1900. 8vo, 63 pp. 26

Harbor Facilities. " Glasgow Harbor Tunnels." Engng. Rec. July 30, p. 138, 1892.

———. " The Development of the Clyde." Mun. J. & London 8:1043 (Sept. 22, 1899).

" History of Glasgow from the earliest period to the present time." MacGregor, George. Glasgow & London, 1881. 8vo. (For other references on the city of Glasgow see p. 239 Gross' Bibliography of British Municipal History). See also No. 18 above). 27

———. " Records, The City of Glasgow and its." Scottish R. 32:249 (Oct. 1898).

———. " Town Society of Glasgow in the XVIII Century." Ch. IV, p. 127, Vol. I of H. G. Graham's " Social Life of Scotland in the XVIII Century." London, Adams & Chas. Black, 1899. 2 vols, 8vo, 265 & 272 pp. 28

" Housing of the Poor Problem in Glasgow." San. Rec. 19:477 (May, 1897).

———. " Dwellings for the Poorest." Mun. J. 9:961 (Dec. 7, 1900).

———. " Lodging-House Experiment at Glasgow, A Mixed." San. Rec. 22:241 (Sept. 2, 1898).

———. " Municipal Homes, Glasgow." Moore, F. W. Econ. R. 10:333 (July 16, 1900); Shone, J .F. Puritan May, 1900. 29

———. " Tenement Houses in Glasgow." Morse, Allen B. U. S. Consular Reports, Vol. XLVIII, No. 178, pp. 398-408. 30

" Industrial Schools, Neerbosch and Glasgow." Dooley, M. A. Arena 7:714 (1893). 31

Lighting. " Electricity v. Gas in Glasgow." Gas Wld. Sept, 2, 1899.

Glasgow.—*Continued.*

———. "Electric Lighting of the City of Glasgow, The." Elec. Eng. (Lond.) 32:410 (Sept. 21, 1900).
———. "Electric Power Supply, Glasgow." (Editorial). Am. Gas Light J. 68:863 (May 30, 1898).
———. "Glasgow Corporation, Gas Supply." J. Gas Light. 76:103 (July 10, 1900).
———. "The Light of Glasgow." Mun. J. 9:737 (Sept. 21, 1900).
———. "The New Electricity Works of the Glasgow Corporation." Elec. (Lond.) 45:765 (Sept. 14, 1900).
Lodging Houses. (See under Housing above).
"Municipal Ownership in Glasgow." Other Side 1:7 (July 8, 1899).
———. "Cities and Public Works—The Correct Story of Glasgow's Achievements." Watt, Robert. Am. Gas Light J. 41:891 (Dec. 4, 1899). 32
———. "Glasgow and its Municipal Industries." Smart, W. Q. J. Econ. 9:188 (1895). 33
———. "Municipal Monopoly in Glasgow." Polk, Jefferson F. Mun. Rec. and Ad. 2:348 (Feb. 26, 1898). 34
———. "The Glasgow Experiment in Municipal Ownership." Porter, Robert P. St. Ry. Rev. 8:294 (May 15, 1898). 35
Population, etc. (See under Statistics below).
"Sanitation in Glasgow, Practical." Fyfe, Peter. Sanitarian, Dec. 1896. 36
"Savings Banks of Glasgow." Meikle, William. U. S. Consular Report No. 122, 1890, pp. 513 to 530. 37
Settlements. "Toynbee House." Woods, R. A. The Congregationalist May 28, 1891. 38
Sewage Disposal at Glasgow. Fuertes, James H. Engng. Rec. 39:563 (May 20, 1899); Morse, A. B. See 56-40a; anon. Engng. Rec. p. 460, Nov. 23, 1895; see also 56-40b. 39
"Smoke Prevention in Glasgow." Fyfe, Peter. San. Rec. 26:267 (Sept. 28, 1900). 40
Statistics. "Vital, Social and Economic Statistics of the City of Glasgow, 1851-1891." Nicol, James. Glasgow, Maclehose, 1891. 8vo, 447 pp. 41
———. "Vital Statistics of Glasgow." Cowan, R. J. Statis. Soc. 3:257 (1840). 42
"Street Cleaning in Glasgow." Engng. News Aug. 30, p. 97, 1884.
"Telephone Inquiry, The Glasgow." Elec. Eng. 24:580 (Dec. 16, 1897).
Transit Facilities. "Street Cars in Glasgow." Taylor, Samuel M. Cons. Rep. 64:344 (Nov. 1900). 43
———. "Accounts Glasgow Tramway." Ty. & Ry. W. 9:364 (Aug. 9, 1900).
———. "Car Factory, Glasgow's Municipal." Mun. J. 9:597 (Aug. 3, 1900).
———. "Data on Electric-Power Generation, Glasgow." Engng. Rec. 39:478 (April 22, 1899).
———. "Electric Cars for Glasgow Tramways, New." Ry. World 6:335 (Nov. 1897).
———. "Electric Equipment of Glasgow Tramways." Anon. Ty. & Ry. W. 9:343 (Aug. 9, 1900); Elec. R. 37:364, 400 (Oct. 10, 17, 1900).
———. "Electric Traction; Special Reports to the Glasgow Corporation on latest Developments in." St. Ry. J. 15:39 (Jan. 1899).
———. "Electric Traction, Transition from Horse to, Tramway System of Glasgow." Taylor, B. Feilden's M. May, 1900. 44
———. "Electric Tramway Contracts, Glasgow." Ty. & Ry. World 8:357 (Sept. 7, 1899).
———. Electric Tramways, Glasgow. Parshall, H. F. Ry. World 8:149 (April 13, 1899); anon. St. Ry. J. 14:728 (Nov. 1898), Engng. Rec. 38:508 (Nov. 12, 1898), Mun. J. & London 8:42 (Jan. 12, 1899), Eng. 87:142 (Feb. 10, 1899), Ry. World 8:108 (March 9, 1899), St. Ry. Rev. 9:165 (March 15, 1899), Ty. & Ry. World 7:327 (Oct. 1898), 8:357 (Sept. 7, 1899), 8:474 (Dec. 7, 1899), 9:10, 116 (Jan. 11, March 8, 1900). 45
———. "Ferry Steamer with an Elevating Deck." Sci. Am. 82:216 (April 7, 1900).
———. "Functions of Modern Tramways and what Glasgow is doing Toward their Fulfillment." Young, John. St. Ry. R. 10:391 (July 15, 1900), Ty. & Ry. W. 9:455 (Sept. 6, 1900). 46
———. "Glasgow Commission, Report of the." (On Street Railway Traction and

Glasgow.—Continued.

Operation in American Cities). Electricity (London). Dec. 8, 1896. St. Ry. Jour. 13:28, 32, 36 (Jan. 1897).

———. " Municipal Tramways of Glasgow." Maltbie, Milo Roy. Mun. Aff. 4:40 (March 1900); anon. London 6:575 (July 8, 1897), Ry. World 7:88, 305 (March, Sept. 1898), 8:303 (Aug. 10, 1899), Elec. Eng. 28:87 (July 28, 1898), St. Ry. J. 15:247 (April, 1899), Mun. J. & London 8:781 (July 7, 1899), 9:543 (July 13, 1900). 47

———. " Rapid Transit in Glasgow." P. 22 " Rapid Transit in Foreign Cities." Parsons, W. B. New York, 1894. 49

———. " Subway, Glasgow District." (First Financial Results). Ry. World 6:367 (Dec. 1897).

———. " The Glasgow Subway and Cable Traction." Engineering Nov. 6, 1896.

———. Underground Railway, The Glasgow. Slater, P. F. Good Words June, 1899; Taylor, Benjamin. Cassier's 14:459 (Oct. 1898); anon. Eng. & Buil. Rec. Dec. 15, 1888, Engineer (Lond.) Dec. 4, 1896, Ry. World Jan. 1897, 6:247 (Aug. 1897), 7:294 (Sept. 1898), St. Ry. Rev. 8:158 (March 15, 1898). 50

———. " Wisdom in Glasgow." (Street Railways). Boston, Leaflet issued by the Citizens' Committee, 1897. 2 pp.

" Washhouses, Glasgow Corporation." Mun. J. & London 8:1215 (Nov. 10, 1899).

" Water Supply of the City of Glasgow, The." Taylor, Benjamin. Engng. M. 17:937 (Sept. 1899). 51

———. " A Prosperous Water Year at Glasgow." Mun. J. & London 8:761 (June 30, 1899).

———. " Water Works, Glasgow." Fuertes, James H. Engng. Rec. 38:205 (Aug. 6, 1898); Gale, James M. J. N. E. W. W. Assn. 14:240 (March, 1900). 52

Gloucester, Eng.

" Development of Gloucester, The Municipal." Mun. J. 9:617 (Aug. 10, 1900).

Electric Lighting at Gloucester, Eng. Anon. Engineer 84:222 (Sept. 3, 1897), Mun. J. 9:580 (July 27, 1900), Elec. R. (Lond.) 47:181 (Aug. 3, 1900).

Good City Government, Good Government Clubs. (See under Government, General and Unclassified.

Görz, Austria, Workmen's Colonies at. "Die Arbeiter-Colonie bei Görz." Romberg's Zeitsch. f. Pract. Bauk. p. 161, 1872.

Gothenburg, Sweden.

Gothenburg System. (See under **Liquor Problem in Cities**).

Sewage and Garbage Disposal. See 56-40b. 53

" Street Railways in Gothenburg." Bergh, Robert S. S. Elec. Rev. 35:285 (Nov. 2, 1898); St. Ry. Rev. 8:794 (Nov. 15, 1898); Cons. Rep. 58:571 (Dec. 1898), 60:572 (July, 1899). 54

Grade Crossings.

See also Chicago, Newton (Mass.).

" Crossing of Steam Railroads and Street Railways." (Review of Court Decisions.) St. Ry. R. 7:683 (Oct. 15, 1897). 54a

" Grade Crossings." Mordecai, Augustus. St. Ry. R. 10:80 (Feb. 15, 1900). 55

" Modern Problems of Grade Crossings." Webber, William O. Engng. M. 9:1034 (1895). 56

" Railway Crossings in Europe and America." Locke, Franklin B. Cent. 56:92 (May, 1898). 56a

Grand Rapids, Mich.

" City of Grand Rapids." Howard, Wm. Willard. Hrprs. Wkly. 35:186 (1891). 57

Government of Grand Rapids. Champlin, John W. Ann Arbor Studies in Finance and History, **Michigan** Univ., Article in Vol. I, No. 6. Dec. 1895. 25c. 58

History, Description and Statistics of Grand Rapids, Mich., in 1880. Census. See 1-7. 59

Lighting. " Municipal Central Station." Hart, Edward James. Elec. W. & E. 34:973 (Dec. 23, 1899). 60

Water Works. " The Grand Rapids Reservoir Accident." Cutcheon, Lewis D. Engng. Rec. 2:26 (July 14, 1900); anon. Engng. N. 44:25 (July 12, 1900). 61

Great Britain. (See under **United Kingdom**).

Greece.
History. " City-State of the Greeks and Romans, a Survey Introductory to the Study of Ancient History." Fowler, W. Warde. London, Macmillan, 1895. 332 pp. 12mo. $1. 62
Local and Municipal Government in Greece. Demombynes. Vol. I, pp. 819-824. See 2-11. 63
" Street and Other Railways in Greece." Woodbridge, J. E. Elec. World, April 17, 1897. 64

Grenoble, France.
" The Municipal or Co-operative Restaurant of Grenoble, France." Ward, C. Osborne. Dept. Labor U. S. No. 12, p. 594 (Sept. 1897). 65

Growth of Cities. (See under **Population**).

" **Guayaquil**, Notes on the Public Lighting of the Town of." Guichard, Charles. J. Gas Light. 76:1019 (Oct. 23, 1900). 66

Gymnasia, Public. (See also **Baths, Parks**).
" Public Gymnasia." Rothery, Guy Cadogan. San. Rec. 21:9 (Jan. 7, 1898); Quincy, Josiah. City Govt. 1:517 (Sept. 3, 1898), Sanitarian 41:303 (Oct. 1898), Ann. Am. Acad. Pol. Sci. 12:444 (Nov. 1898), N. Y. Educa. 2:135 (Nov. 1898). 67

Hackney, Eng. (See Lighting under **London**).

Hague, The.
" The Hague, Capitals at Play." Robinson B. Fletcher. Cassell's p. 398 (March, 1898). 68

" **Hale, Eng.** Sewage Disposal at." Surveyor 17:455 (April 27, 1900).

Halifax, Eng.
Electric Tramways of Halifax, England. Wilmshurst, T. P. St. Ry. Jour. 14:444 (Aug. 1898); anon. Ry. World 7:207 (July 7, 1898). 69
———. " Halifax Tramway Deputation in America." Whitlay, J. H. Ty. & Ry. World 9:39 (Jan. 11, 1900). 70
" Municipal Enterprise at Halifax." Mun. J. & London 8:262 (March 3, 1899).

Halifax, N. S.
" Attractions of Halifax." Tupper, E. Sherburne. Canadian M. 13:347 (Aug. 1899). 71
" Electric Railway System of Halifax, N. S."Archibald, E. M. St. Ry. J. 16:433 (May 5, 1900). 72
" Garbage Collection and Disposal at Halifax, N. S." Engng. N. 38:115 (Aug. 19, 1897).

Halle a S., Germany.
" Government of a Typical Prussian City: Halle a S." James, Edmund J. Ann. Am. Acad. Pol. Sci. 15:313 (May, 1900). 73
" Municipal Lighting in a Typical German City: Halle." James, Edmund J. Mun. Aff. 4:574 (Sept. 1900). 74
———. " Die stadtische Gas und Wasserwerke zu Halle a S." Gesund.-Ing. 22:326 (Oct. 31, 1899).

Hamburg.
General Works and Unclassified.
" Hamburg." Halstead, Murat. Cosmopol. 14:35 (1892). 75
" Hamburg: A City on Sand." Purdon, K. F. Ludgate May, 1900. 76
" Manchester and Hamburg." (A comparison). The Local Government Journal 27:46 (Jan. 15, 1898).

Charities. " Principles of Public Charity and Private Philanthropy in Germany." (Poor relief in Hamburg). Münsterberg, E. Am. J. Sociol. 2:589 (Jan., March, 1897). 77

Hamburg—*Continued*.

———. (See also under Pauperism below).

Garbage Disposal. "The Disposal of Garbage and Refuse, Hamburg, Germany." Hering, Rudolph. Engng. Rec. 36:446 (Oct. 23, 1897). 78

History. A Collection of Plans of the Harbors, Quays, Ships, Public Squares, Markets, from the Eleventh Century to the Present. "Hamburg's Vergangenheit und Gegenwart: Eine Sammlung von Ansichten der hervorragendsten und historich bekannten alten und neuen Hafen, und Quai-Anlagen, Schiffen, Platze, Markte, vom 11 Jahrh. bis die Gegenwart." Hamburg, Wendt & Co., 1897. 4to, 400 pp. M. 25. 79

———. Plan of Hamburg Before and after Fire of 1842. "Situationsplan vom Stadttheil Hamburgs vor dem Brande 1842 und nach demselben." Allg. Bauz. p. 20, 1865.

Housing. "Ueber die Wohnungsverhältnisse Hamburgs und die Versuche zur Besserung dieser Verhältnisse." Koch, G. pp. 41-57, Hft. 30, Schr. d. Ver. f. Sozialpolitik. 80

———. "Die Wohnungsverhältnisse Hamburgischer Unterbeamten im Jahre 1897." Pfingsthorn, Carl. Hamburg, Gräfe and Sillem, 1900. 8vo, 41 pp. Paper, 50 pf. 81

Pauperism and Prostitution in Hamburg. "Beitrage zur Geschichte des Pauperismus und der Prostitution in Hamburg." Schönfeldt, Gustav. Weimer, Verlag von Emil Felber, 1897. 8vo, 274 pp. Paper, 5 marks. 82

Reconstruction of the Embankment. "Die Neugestaltung des Wall-Terrains zwischen dem Damm- und dem Holsten-Thor zu Hamburg." Meyer, F. A. Deutsche Bauz. p. 481, 1879. 83

Sanitation. "Hamburg's New Sanitary Impulse." Shaw, Albert. Atlan. 73:787 (1894). (See also Chapt. VII, pp. 378-410, in his "Municipal Government in Continental Europe.") 84

"Sewage Disposal, Hamburg." Robertson, W. Henry. See 56-40a. 85

Transit Facilities. Electric Street Railways of Hamburg. Pitcairn, Hugh. Elec. R. 35:158 (Sept. 6, 1899), Engng. News 42:167 (Sept. 14, 1899), Cons. Rep. 61:218 (Oct. 1899); anon. Ty. & Ry. World 8:403 (Oct. 5, 1899). 86

Water Works. "Das Wasserwerk der Freien und Hansestadt, Hamburg." Meyer, F. Andreas. Hamburg, Meissner, 1894. 36 pp. Plates and tables. 6m. 87

———. "Hamburg Settling-Basins and Filters." Ch. XIII, p. 208. "Purification of Public Water Supplies." Hill, John W. New York, Van Nostrand, 1898. 8vo, 304 pp. $3. 88

———. "Die Reinigung der Hamburger öffenen Sandfilter in der Frostzeit." Gesund.-Ing. May 31, 1897.

———. "Water Filters at Hamburg, Germany, The New." Engng. Rec. March 18 and 25, 1893.

Hamilton, O.

"The Hamilton System." Jones, Ed. H. Prog. Age 17:69 (Feb. 15, 1899). 89

"Municipal (Lighting) Plant, The Hamilton, O." Gray, W. N. Elec. Eng. 24:5 (July 8, 1897). 90

Hamilton, Ont.

Lighting Plant, Electric. Domville, Percy. Can. Elec. N. 15:210 (Nov. 1898); anon. Mun. World 8:187 (Dec. 1898). 91

"Sewage Disposal by Chemical Precipitation at Hamilton, Ont." Barrow, E. G. Engng. News 37:63 (Jan. 28, 1897); Watson, W. M. Can. Eng. 6:39 (June, 1898). 92

Hammersmith, Eng.

"Electric Lighting in Hammersmith, Municipal." London 6:785 (Sept. 30, 1897).

———. "Modern English Central Station." Elec. World 30:668 (Dec. 4, 1897).

"New Sanitary Conveniences and Street Refuge, Hammersmith." Building News 58:901.

"Town Hall, Hammersmith's (Eng.), New." London 6:619 (July 15, 1897).

"**Hampton-on-Thames, [Eng.]** Sewerage and Sewage Disposal Works at." Kemp. J. Surveyor 18:456 (Oct. 19, 1900); anon. San. Rec. 24:343 (Oct. 20, 1890). 93

Hanley, Eng.
" Bacillite Sewage Disposal at Hanley, England." Engng. Rec. 39:385 (March 25, 1899).

Hanover, Germany.
City Plan. " Bebauungsplan der Stadt Hannover." Bokelberg. Zeitschr. d. Arch.-u. Ing.-Ver. zu Hannover, p. 240, 1889. 94
———. " Die Durchbruchs-Projekte für die Altstadt Hannover." Wallbrecht. Zeitschr. d. Arch.-u. Ing.-Ver. zu Hannover, p. 491, 1879. 95
———. " Grossstädtische Grundpläne und Hannovers Ringstrasse." Unger. Zeitschr. d. Arch.-u. Ing.-Ver. zu Hannover, p. 192, 1877. 96
" Street Railway System of Hanover, Germany." Johnson, Woolsey McA. Elec. W. & E. 34:572 (Oct. 14, 1899). 97

Harrisburg, Pa.
History, Description and Statistics of Harrisburg, Pa., in 1880. Census. See 1-7. 98
Water Supply of Harrisburg. Fire & W. 23:114 (April 9, 1898), 23:122 (April 16, 1898).

Harrogate, Eng.
" A Municipal Spa." Mun. J. 9:537 (July 13, 1900).

Hartford, Conn.
" History of Hartford, Conn." Talcott, Mary C. See 1-4a. 99
———. History, Description and Statistics of Hartford, Conn., in 1880. Census. See 1-7. 100
" Objections to Public Work for Unemployed in Hartford, Conn." McCook, J. J. Char. R. 3:236 (1893). 1
Street Railway Co., The Hartford, Conn. Elec. Eng. 24:112 (Aug. 5, 1897).

" **Hastings** [Eng.], All About." Gray, George G. Mun. J. 9:199 (March 16, 1900). 2

Havana, Cuba.
" Financial Conditions of the City." Ann. Am. Acad. Pol. Sci. 16:159 (July, 1900).
" Gas Works of Havana." Am. Gas Light J. 68:10 (Jan. 3, 1898).
Sanitary Conditions and Improvement of Havana. Gould, E. Sherman. Engng. News 42:68 (Aug. 3, 1899); Ludlow, William. Engng. News 42:242 (Oct. 12, 1899); Sternberg, George M. Cent. 56:578 (Aug. 1898); anon. Engng. Rec. 39:114, 155 (Jan. 1899); 40:426 (Oct. 7, 1899); Engng. News 41:28 (Jan. 12, 1899); Sanitarian 43:66 (July, 1899); Hrprs. Wkly. 44:588 (June 23, 1900). 3
———. " Colonel Waring on the Sanitation of Havana." Hill, G. E. Forum 26:529 (Jan. 1899). 4
" Sewerage of Havana." Fire & W. 26:59 (Feb. 25, 1899), 26:70 (March, 4, 1899).
Transit Facilities. " Electric Railways of Havana." St. Ry. J. 16:724 (Aug. 4, 1900).

Haverhill, Mass.
" Gas Case, The Haverhill." Chase, John C. Ind. 52:479 (Feb. 22, 1900). 5
" Socialism in the Saddle." Mun. & Ry. Rec. 4:21 (Jan. 15, 1899).

" **Havre**, Sewage Disposal in." Chancellor, C. W. U. S. Cons. Reports; Vol. XLVII, No. 173, p. 148, Feb. 1895. 6

Heidelberg, Ger. Housing. " Die Heidelberger Wohnungsenquête." May, Max. Zeit. für Social. 3:123 (Feb. 1900). 7

High Buildings. (See Building Laws).

Higher Life of Cities. (A series of articles in the Outlook, 1895-7 on Boston, Chicago, New Orleans, New York, St. Louis, Berlin, London, Paris and Geneva. See under these cities. Also one article by Theodore Roosevelt on " Higher Life of American Cities." Outlook 52:1082, 1895).

Highway Improvements. (See under Streets).

BIBLIOGRAPHY.

History of Municipalities, Municipal Law, etc. (See also Population).

See also Albany (N. Y.), Annapolis, Athens, Atlanta, Baltimore, Basel, Belgium, Bern, Birmingham, Boston, Bremen, Brooklyn under New York, Buffalo, Cambridge (Mass.), Cape Cod Towns, Charleston, Chattanooga (Tenn.), Chicago, Cincinnati, Cleveland, Columbus, Concord (N. H.), Constantinople, Coventry (Eng.), Deerfield (Mass.), Denver, Des Moines, Detroit, Dundee, Elmira, England under United Kingdom, Fall River (Mass.), Florence, France, Frankfurt, Frederick Town (Md.), Galveston (Tex.), Germany, Glasgow, Grand Rapids (Mich.), Great Britain under United Kingdom, Greece, Hamburg, Harrisburg, Hartford (Conn.), Indianapolis, Jersey City, Knoxville (Tenn.), Leicester, Leipsic, Little Rock (Ark.), Lombardy, Louisville (Ky.), Lowell (Mass.), Lynn (Mass.), Manchester (Eng.), Manchester (N. H.), Memphis (Tenn.), Milwaukee, Minneapolis, Mobile (Ala.), Montgomery (Ala.), Nashville (Tenn.), Newark (N. J.), Newburg (N. Y.), New Haven (Conn.), New Orleans, Newport, New York, Norfolk, Omaha, Oxford (Eng.), Paris, Paterson (N. J.), Philadelphia, Pittsburgh, Plymouth (Mass.), Portland (Me.), Princeton (N. J.), Providence, Richmond, Rochester, Rutland (Vt.), St. Augustine (Fla.), St. Louis, St. Paul, Salem (Mass.), Salt Lake City, San Francisco, Saratoga (N. Y.), Savannah, Schenectady (N. Y.), Syracuse, Tarrytown (N. Y.), Toledo (O.), Topeka (Kas.), Troy (N. Y.), United Kingdom, Venice, Vicksburg (Miss.), Washington (D. C.), Wheeling (W. Va.), Williamsburg, Wilmington (Del.), Wilmington (N. C.).

"L'Administration muncipale au XIIIe siecle dans les villes de Consulat." (Cities having foreign merchant quarters under special regulation.) Ramalho, A. Paris, Berger, Levrault & Cie., 1896. 8vo, 2 fr. 50c. 8

City, Ancient, Mediaeval and Modern. Pp. 290-296, Vol. I. Palgrave. See 1-2.

"Economic Policy of Mediaeval Towns, The." Treub, M. W. F. Vragen des Tiids July, 1899. 9

"Evolution of Cities." Réclus E. Contemp. 67:246-264, Living Age 204:707 (1895). 10

Free Towns. Pp. 140-143. Vol. II. Palgrave. See 1-2. 11

Gilds. Pp. 209-213. Palgrave. Vol. II. See 1-2.

Hanseatic League. Pp. 281-286. Vol. II. Palgrave. See 1-2.

Municipal Law. "Droit Municipal dans l'antiquité." Bechard, Ferdinand. Paris, A. Durand, 1860. 8vo, 8 fr. 12

———. "Droit Municipal au Moyen-Age." Bechard, Ferdinand. Paris, Durand, 1862. 2 vol. 8vo, 15 fr. 13

———. "Droit Municipal dans les Temps modernes." (XVIe et XVIIe siècles). Bechard, Ferdinand. Paris, Durand, 1866. 8vo, 8 fr. 14

"Origin of Cities and Towns." de Molenari, G. Vol. 1, pp. 468-73. Lalor's Cyclopedia. 15

———. "L'Origine des Villages à Banlieue morcelée et des Domaines agglomérés." von Brandt, Alexander. Ref. Soc. 6:645 (Nov. 1, 1898). 16

———. "Théories des Villes. Comment les villes se sont Formées." Gén. de L'Arch. p. 292, 1854.

———. "Ueber die Entstehung der Städte der Alten." Kuhn, Emil. Liepsig, Trübner, 1878. 8vo, 10m. 17

———. "Die inneren Wanderungen und das Städtewesen in ihrer entwicklungsgeschichtlichen Bedeutung." Ch. IX, p. 349 in Karl Bücher's Entstehung der Volkswirtschaft. Tübingen, H. Laupp, 1898. 8vo, 395 pp. 5m. 60 pf. 18

Real Estate in Cities During Middle Ages. "Etude sur la Propriété Foncière dans les villes du Moyen Age." des Marez, Guillaume. University of Ghent, 1898. 8vo, 392 pp. 19

"The City: Ancient, Mediaeval, Modern, Ideal." Ch. VIII, pp. 222-251. Frederic Harrison's "The Meaning of History." New York, Macmillan, 1894. 8vo, 482 pp. $2.25. 20

"The Ancient City. A study on the religion, laws and institutions of Greece and Rome." de Coulanges, Fustel. (Trans. by Willard Small.) Boston, Lee & Shepard, 9th ed., 1896. 8vo, 529 pp. 21

"The City in History." Rowe, L. S. Am. J. Sociol. 5:721 (May, 1900). 22

"**Hoboken's** [**N. J.**] New Library Building." City Govt. 2:77 (March, 1892).

Holland.

General Works and Reference Books.

" Die Gemeindeverwaltung." Hartog, L. de. IV. Abtheilung, pp. 59-61. Vol IV. 1, 4-6. Marquardsen. See 2-9. — 23

Local and Municipal Government in Holland. Demombynes, Vol. I. pp. 295-319. See 2-11. — 24

" The Principal Cities of Holland." Ragan, H. H. Chaut. 27:227 (June, 1898). — 25

" The Provincial and Communal Institutions of Belgium and Holland." de Laveleye, Emile. P. 235, " Local Government and Taxation." J. W. Probyn, editor. London & New York, Cassell, 1875. 5s. — 26

" Art in the Netherlands, Municipal." French, Allen. New Eng. M. 18:267 (May, 1898). — 27

Charities. " Poor Colonies of Holland." Gore, J. H. Chaut. Feb. 1896. — 28

" Electoral Districts, Dividing Cities and Provinces into." (Holland). Van Gikie, J. A. Vragen des Tijds Nov. 1896. — 29

Lighting. " Prepayment Meters in Holland." Bolsius, P. J. Gas Light 76:766 (Sept. 25, 1900), Prog. Age 18:497 (Nov. 15, 1900). — 30

——. " Electrical Works in the Netherlands." Cons. Rep. 60:571 (July, 1899).

Savings Banks. " Les Caisses d'Epargne en Hollande." Riedel, J. B. Jour. des Economistes 47:394 (1889). — 31

" **Hollister, Cal.**, Water Works at." Grunsky, C. E. Engng. News 37:274 (May 6, 1897). — 32

" **Holyoke [Mass.]**, The City of." Kirtland, Edwin L. New Eng. M. 17:715 (Feb. 1898). — 33

Home Rule for Cities, State Administrative or Supervisory Boards, Special Legislation, Relation of City and State Generally.

(See also under **Referendum.**)

See also England, Iowa, Massachusetts, New York.

Home Rule for Cities, Articles on. Goodnow, Frank J. Pol. Sci. Q. 10:1 (1895); Hale, E. E. Cosmopol. 16:735 (1894); Hotchkiss, Wm. Horace. R. of Rs. 9:682 (1894); Low, Seth. Address at Brooklyn, Oct. 6, 1882; McMath, Robert E. Mun. Engng. 19:205, Am. Gas Light J. 73:448 (Sept. 1900); Miller, Joseph D. Am. J. Pol. 4:25 (1894); Palmer, Clarence S. Am. M. Civics 9:56 (1896); Parsons, Frank. Prog. Age 16:406 (Sept. 1, 1898). — 34

——. " Home Rule for Cities." Pp. 387-468 in "The City for the People or The Municipalization of the City Government and of Local Franchises." Parsons, Frank. Philadelphia, C. F. Taylor, 1900. 8vo, 597 pp. Cl. $1. — 35

——. " Home Rule for our American Cities." Oberholtzer, Ellis P. Ann. Am. Acad. Pol. Sci. 3:736 (1893). — 36

——. " Municipal Home Rule, a Study in Administration." Goodnow, Frank J. New York and London, Macmillan, 1895. 12mo, 283 pp. $1 50. — 37

" Referendum on City Charters." Ch. XIV. pp. 335-368 of Ellis P. Oberholtzer's "Referendum in America," edition of 1900; Ch. IV, pp. 86-104, edition of 1893. See 60-99. — 38

" Special Legislation Unconstitutional." Shauck, John A. Public Policy 2:114 (Feb. 24, 1900). — 39

——. " The Evils of Special Legislation and the Remedy." Garfield, James R. Public Policy 2:222 (April 7, 1900). — 40

State Boards. "A State Municipal Board." Jenks, J. W. Mun. Aff. 2:411 (Sept. 1898). — 41

——. " The Relation of the City and the State." Goodnow, F. J. Mun. Aff. 1:689 (Dec. 1897). — 42

——. " State Board of Municipal Control." Holls, Frederick William. p. 226, Proc. Third Natl. Conf. for Good City Govt., 1896. See 6-18c. — 43

——. " State Supervision for Cities." Commons, John R. Ann. Am. Acad. Pol. Sci. 5:865 (1895); Grant, John H. Ann Arbor Studies in Finance and History, Michigan Univ. Article in Vol. II, No. 4. 25c. — 44

" Uniformity of State Laws Pertaining to Municipal Governments." Johnson, J. A. Prog. Age 15:456 (Oct. 15, 1897); City Govt. 3:120 (Oct. 1897). — 45

" Unmixed Self Rule for Cities." Fassett, Jacob Sloat. Our Day 7:411 (1891). — 46

BIBLIOGRAPHY.

Home Work. (See under **Sweating.**)

"**Honduras,** The Mysterious City of." Gordon, Geo. Brydon. Cent. 55:407 (Jan. 1898). — 47

"**Hong Kong,** Sanitary Conditions in." Alford, Robert C. Engng. Rec. 42:370 (Oct. 20, 1900). — 48

"**Honolulu** and its Street Railways." Cicott, Frank X. St. Ry. J. 14:725 (Nov. 1898). — 49

Hornsey, Eng. (See under **London.**)

Hospitals. (See Hospitals under **Charities.**)

Housing of the Working Classes and of the Poor in Cities, Lodging Houses, Tenement Houses, Slums, Etc. (See also **Population.**)

See also Basel, Belfast, Belgium, Berlin, Bochum, Bolbec, Boston, Bradford, Brandeis (Aus.), Brussels, Bury (Eng.), Chemnitz, Chicago, Clichy, Copenhagen, Crefeld, Cronenberg, Dortmund, Dublin, Edinburgh, Elberfeld, England see under United Kingdom; Epernay, Essen, France, Frankfort a. M., Glasgow, Germany, Görz, Hamburg, Heidelberg, Hull, Italy, Küchen i. W., Leeds, Leipsic, Liverpool, London, Manchester, Marburg i. Steiermark, Merseburg (Ger.), Milan, Mülhausen, Munich, Naples, Newcastle, New York, Nottingham, Osnabrück (Ger.), Paris, Philadelphia, Richmond, Salford, Scotland, Shoreditch, Southampton, Strassburg, Stuttgart, Switzerland, Tours, Ulm, United Kingdom, United States, Vienna, Walthamstowe (Eng.), Washington, Weissenfels (Ger.), West Ham under London.

GENERAL REFERENCES.

Owing to the extent of the literature on housing, general and unclassified works and articles have been listed (1) according to language, (2) according to date of issue, as follows:
American and English Books and Pamphlets, 1866-1900; pp. 99-100.
American and English Articles, 1813-1900; pp. 100-2.
Foreign Books and Pamphlets (French, German, Dutch, etc.), 1879-1900; pp. 102-3.
Articles, 1863-1900; p. 103.

References on particular phases of the housing problem follow in alphabetical order.

American and English Books and Pamphlets, 1866-1900.

"Homes of the Working Classes, with suggestions for improvement." Plates and plans. Hole, James. London, Longmans, 1866. 8vo. Cl. 7s. 6d. — 50
"Dwellings of the Laboring Classes, their arrangement and construction." Plans, elevations, etc. Roberts, H. London, 6th ed., 1867. 8vo. — 51
"Report on Dwellings Characterized by Cheapness combined with the conditions necessary for health and comfort." Chadwick, Edwin. Pp. 239-317, Vol. III of Reports presented to Parliament on the Paris Universal Exhibition. London, Eyre and Spottiswoode. 1868. — 52
"Improved Dwellings for Laboring Classes, the need and way to meet it on strict commercial principles." White, Alfred T. New York, Putnams, 1879. 27 pp. Plans 30 cts — 53
"Artizans' and Labourers' Dwellings." Spencer, Edward. London, 1881. — 54
"Dwellings of the Poor." Loch, C. S. London, Longmans, 1882. — 55
"Social and National Influence of the Domiciliary Condition of the People." Rawlinson, R. London, 1883. — 56
"Housing of the Poor in Towns." Chamberlain, Joseph. Chapter IV, p. 62 of "The Radical Program." London, Chapman & Hall, 1885. 328 pp. — 57
"Re-housing of the Industrial Classes." Solly, H. London, Swan, S. & Co., 1889. 6d. — 58
"The Housing of the Poor." Millington, F. H. London, Cassell & Co., 1891. 8vo, 104 pp. 1s. — 59
"Examples of Labourers' Cottages. With plans for Improving the Dwellings of the Poor in Large Towns." Birch, J. Edinburgh, Blackwood & Sons, 1892. 65 pp. 30 plates. 7s. — 60

Housing of Working Classes, Etc.—*Continued.*

"White Slaves, or the Oppression of the Worthy Poor." Banks, Louis A. Boston, Lee & Shepard, 1892. $1.50.   61

"Housing of the Poor in American Cities." Reynolds, Marcus T. Am. Econ. Assoc. 8:139 (1893). Separate, paper, $1. (Valuable bibliography.)   62

"Dwellings of the Poor and Weekly Wage Earners in and around Towns." Worthington, T. Locke. London and New York, Swan, S. & Co., 1893. 104 pp. $1.   63

"Housing of the Working Classes." Bowmaker, Edward. London, Methuen & Co., 1895. 186 pp. 2s. 6d.   64

"Housing of the Working People, The." Gould, E. R. L. Eighth Special Report of the Bureau of Labor, prepared under the direction of Carroll D. Wright. Washington, Government Printing Office, 1895. 461 pp.   65

"Housing the People." Reid, H. G. Paisley, A. Gardner, 1895. 69 pp. 1s.   66

"Housing of the Laboring Classes." Boulnois, H. P. St. Bride's Press, 1896, 2d ed., 8vo, 72 pp. 15s.   67

"The Dwelling House." Poore, George Vivian. New York, Longmans, Green & Co., 1897. 12mo, 178 pp. Cl. $1.25.   68

"The Housing of the Poor." Beachcroft, R. Melville. L. C. C. pamphlet, 1899.   69

"The Housing of the Poor." Hand, J. E. p. 113 "Good Citizenship" edited by J. E. Hand. London, Geo. Allen, 1899. 474 pp.   70

"Better Homes for the Workers, and How to Obtain Them." Aldridge, H. R. Land Nationalization Society Tract No. 80, 1900.   71

"Housing of the Working Classes in Urban Districts." Cranfield, Sydney White, and Potter, Henry Ingle. London, B. T. Batsford, 1900. 4to. 10s. 6d.   72

"Houses for the Working Classes, How to Provide them in Town and Country." Seven essays by Edwards, Clement and others. London, P. S. King, 1900. 48 pp. 1s.   73

"Working Class Dwellings. Papers read before the Royal Institute of British Architects, April, 1900, with the Discussion thereon." I—Effects of Injudicious Legislation, by John Honeyman; II—Block Buildings, The Associated and Self-Contained Systems, by Henry Spalding; III—The Later Peabody Buildings, by W. E. Wallis; IV—The Rebuilding of the Boundary Street Estate, by Owen Fleming. London, P. S. King, 1900. Plans and Views. 2s. 6d.   74

"Working Class Dwellings." Honeyman, J. London, P. S. King & Son, 1900. 4to, 30 pp. Cl. 2s. 6d.   75

"The Housing Question." Smith, Alfred. London, Sonnenscheim, 1900. 1s.   76

American and English Articles, 1813-1900.

"Dwellings of the Poor." Howell, George. 19th Cent. 13:992 (1813).   77

"Organized Work Among the Poor." Hill, O. Macmillan 20:219 (1869), 26:441 (1872).   78

"Dwellings of the Poor in Large Towns." Hoole, E. J. Soc. Arts 23:968 (1875).   79

"Homes for the People." Paine, R. T. Am. J. Soc. Sci. 15:104 (1882).   80

"Laborers' and Artisans' Dwellings." Chamberlain, Joseph. Fortn. n. s. 34:761 (1883).   81

"Improvements now practicable in the Dwellings of the Poor." Hill, O. 19th Cent. 14:925 (1883).   82

"Laborers' and Artisans' Dwellings." Salisbury, Marquis of. National 2:301 (1883).   83

"Housing of the Poor in Towns." Fortn. n. s. 34:587 (1883).   84

"Workingmen's Homes." Bowker, R. R. Harpers M. 68:769 (1884).   85

"Housing of the Poor." Boulton, H. E. Fortn. 49:279 (1888).   86

"Housing of the Poor." Lymington, Viscount. Fortn. 49:279 (1888).   87

"Homes for the People." Mawson, Harry P. Hrprs. Wkly. 35:869 (1891).   88

"Housing of the Poor." Horseley, J. W. Econ. R. 3:50 (1893).   89

"Homes for the Poor." White, A. T. Chaut. 14:442 (1893).   90

"Improvement of Working Class Homes." Bompas, H. M. Fortn. 64:738 (1895).   91

"Dwellings of the Poor." Lend a H. 15:135 (1895).

"Housing of the Poor." Blackall, C. H. Am. Arch. 31:53 (1890), 52:23, 63 (1896).   92

"Municipal Dwellings for Artisans." (London.) Donald, Robert. Outlook 53:245 (1896).   93

Housing of Working Classes, Etc.—*Continued.*

"Need of Better Homes for Wage Earners." Graffenreid, Clare de. Forum May, 1896. — 94
"Housing of the Poor in Cities." Outlook 53:204 (1896).
"Homes of the People." Commons, John R. Our Country 5:13 (Feb. 1897). — 95
"Half a Century of Improved Housing." Tolman, W. H. Yale R. 5:288, 389 (Feb. 1897). — 96
"Housing of the Laboring Classes Problem, The." Boulnois, Percy. San. Rec. Feb. 19, 1897. — 97
"English Homes for Workingmen." Wood, Octavius Grant. Inland Architect March, 1897. — 98
"Housing Question and Scientific Reform, The." Caldwell W. Bibliotheca Sacra April, 1897. — 99
"Improved Housing for the Poor." Cooper, Ella H. Gunton's M. 12:416 (June, 1897). — 100
"Housing of the Working Classes." Beveridge, A. T. Gordon. San. Rec. 20:96, 121 (July 23, 1897), San. J. 4:302 (Aug. 1897). — 1
"How to Live with Comfort and Economy." Gardiner, Florence Mary. San. Rec. 20:379 (Oct. 8, 1897). — 2
"Houses for Industrial Communities During the Victoria Era." Gardiner, Florence Mary. San. Rec. 20:408 (Oct. 15, 1897). — 3
"How to House the Poor." London 7:35 (Jan. 20, 1898).
"The Housing of the Poor." San Rec. 22:459 (Oct. 28, 1898).
"Housing of the Working Classes." Meade, T. deCourcy. Sanitarian 42:3 (Jan. 1899). — 4
"Housing Improvements." Sykes, J. F. J. Sanitarian 42:13 (Jan. 1899). — 5
"Dwelling Accommodations in Large Cities." Sykes, John F. J. San. Inst. 20:1 (April, 1899). — 6
"The Housing Problem." Barnett. Mun. J. & London 8:1337 (Dec. 15, 1899). — 7
"Artisans' Dwellings." Brierley, J. H. San. Rec. 24:386 (Nov. 3, 1899), 24:410 (Nov. 10, 1899). — 8
"Housing of the Working Classes, The." Evans, W. Arnold. Public Health 11:481 (April, 1899). — 9
"Dwellings for the Working Classes Financially Considered." Fyfe, Peter. Brit. Arch. 51:248 (April 7, 1899). — 10
"Problems in Housing." Fyfe, Peter. Mun. J. & London 8:493 (April 21, 1899). — 11
"The Housing Problem." Gould, E. R. L. Mun. Aff. 3:108 (March, 1899). — 12
"Housing Problem, The." (Editorial). Mun. J. & London 8:957 (Aug. 25, 1899).
"Housing Problem, The." Sanitarian 43:337 (Oct. 1899).
"Labourers' Dwellings." Ilbert, Lettice. Econ. J. 9:605 (Dec. 1899). — 13
"Laborers' Cottages." Cochrane, Constance. Fabian Tract No. 101, pp. 7-9. London, Fabian Society, 1900. 8vo, 50 pp. 1d. — 14
"General Principles." Dodd, E. Lawson. Fabian Tract No. 101, pp. 32-43. London, Fabian Society, 1900. 8vo, 50 pp. 1d. — 15
"Housing Impressions." Hayter, Richard. Char. Or. R. 7:16 (Jan. 1900). — 16
"House Hunger." Mun. J. 9:56 (Jan 19, 1900).
"The Housing of the Working Classes." Loch. C. S. Char. Or. R. 7:82 (Feb. 1900). — 17
"Working Class Dwellings." Tew, J. S. Pub. Health Feb. 1900. — 18
"The Housing of the Working Classes." Wilson, Edmund. J. Soc. Arts 48:253 (Feb. 9, 1900); San. Rec. 25:136 (Feb. 16, 1900). — 19
"People and Houses." Bosanquet, Helen. Econ. J. 10:7 (March, 1900). — 20
"Housing the Poor." Donald, Robert. Contemp. 77:323 (March, 1900). — 21
"The Housing Problem." Mun. J. 9:249 (March 30, 1900).
"An Aspect of the Housing Problem." Taylor, Graham. Commons No. 44, p. 3 (March 31, 1900). — 22
"The Housing Problem in Great Cities." Gould, E. R. L. Q. J. E. 14:378 (May, 1900). — 23
"Housing of the Working Classes." Priestley, J. San. Rec. 25:379 (May 4, 1900). — 24
"Overcrowding and Re-Housing." San. Rec. 25:490 (June 8, 1900).
"Housing of the Poor, The." Ann. Am. Acad. Pol. Sci. 16:160 (July, 1900).

Housing of Working Classes, Etc.—*Continued.*

"Housing of the Laboring Classes." Horsfall, T. C. Char. Or. R. 8:128 (Aug. 1900). 25
"Homes for the Very Poor." Mathews, J. Douglass. Mun. J. 9:610 (Aug. 3, 1900). 26
"Housing of the Laboring Classes." Boulnois, H. Percy. Mun. J. 9:634 (Aug. 10, 1900). 27
"Municipal Housing Conference." Waterlow, Sir Sydney. Mun. J. 9:634 (Aug. 10, 1900). 28
"Housing of the Working Classes." Dudfield, T. O. Public Health, Sept. 1900. 29
"Elements of the Housing Problem." Fisher, Lettice. Econ. R. 10:434 (Oct. 15, 1900). 30
"How the Working Class Live." Pp. 91-103 in "Socialist Campaign Book, 1900." Chicago, Charles H. Kerr, 1900. 8vo, 149 pp. 31
"The Housing of the Poor." Horsley, J. W. Humanitarian 17:326 (Nov. 1900). 32

Foreign Books and Pamphlets, 1865-1900.

"Die Wohnungsfrage mit besonderer Rücksicht auf die arbeitenden Classen." Berlin, Hrsg. v. Centralverein f. d. Wohl. d. arbeitenden Classen, 8vo, 1865. 33
"Die Wohnungszustände der arbeitenden Klassen." Sax, E. Vienna Beck's Univ. Buchh., 1869, 8vo. 34
"Reform der Wohnungszustände in grossen Städten." Ratkowski, Math. G. Wien, 1871. 1m. 35
"Die Arbeiterhäuser auf der Pariser Weltausstellung." Wist, Joh. Wien, 1877. 36
"Die Arbeiterhäuser auf der Pariser Weltausstellung von 1876." Böniches, F. Vienna, 1878. 37
"Die Arbeiter Wohnhäuser in ihrer baulichen Anlage und Ausführung, sowie die Anlage von Arbeiter-Kolonien." Klasen, L. Leipzig, 1879. 38
"Habitations Ouvrières en tous Pays." Muller, Emile, and Cacheux, Emile. Paris, Baudry, 1879. With supplementary volume of plates. 8vo, 650 pp. 78 plates. 60 fr. 39
"Gesunde Wohnungen." Schülke, Herm. Berlin, Springer, 1880. 218 pp. 5m. 40
"Die Wohnung des Arbeiters, mit Rücksicht auf die neuern Bestrebgn. zur Förderg. d. Wohls der Arbeiter-familien, etc." Balmer-Rinck, J. Basel, Detloff, 1883. 8vo, 30 pp. 2m. 40 pf. 41
"Die Wohnungsverhältnisse in den grösseren Städten." (Sammlung v. Vorträgen). Hausen, P. Ch. Heidelberg, 1883. 42
"Anlage von Arbeiterwohnungen vom wirtschaftlichen, sanitären und technischen Standpunkte mit einer Sammlung von P.änen der besten Arbeitshäuser Englands, Frankreichs und Deutschlands." Manega, Rudolf. Weimar, 1883. 2d ed. 170 pp. 43
"Das Wohnhaus des Arbeiters." Schmöke, J. Bonn, Strauss, 1883. 2d ed. 8vo. 8m. 50 pf. 44
"Der Haushalt der arbeitenden Klassen, eine sozial statistische Untersuchung." Berlin, F. Luckhardt, 1883. 136 pp. 3m.
"Economiste Pratique: L'Habitations Ouvrières et Maisons d'Employés, etc." Cacheux, Emile. Paris, Baudry & Cie., 1884. 40 fr. 45
"Les Classes ouvrières en Europe. Etudes sur leur Situation, materielle et morale." Lavollée, René. Paris, Guillaumin et Cie., 1884. 2 vols, 8vo, 20 fr. 46
"Devoir Social et les Logements ouvriers." Picot, Georges. Paris, Levy, 1885. 47
"Grundzüge der Arbeiterwohnungsfrage mit besonderer Berücksichtigung der Unternehmungen, die Arbeiter zu Hauseigentümern zu machen." Reichardt, Erwin. Berlin, Püttkammer u. Mühlbrecht, 1885. 74 pp. 1m. 40 pf. 48
"Les Logements d'Ouvriers et le Devoir des Classes Dirigeantes." Delaire, A. Lyon, 1886. 49
"Le Logement de l'ouvrier et du pauvre." (United States, Great Britain, France, Germany, Belgium). Raffalovich, Arthur. Paris, Guillaumin et Cie. 1887. 486 pp. 3 fr. 50c. 50
"Zur Wohnungsfrage." Engels, Fr. Sozialdemokratische Bibliotek XIII, Zürich, 1887. 51
"Die Wohnungsnoth in den Grossstädten." Wiss, Ed. Viertaljahrschrift f. Volkswirtschaft, 1887. 52
"Die Arbeiterwohnungsfrage, und die Bestrebungen zur Lösung derselben." Trüdinger, O. Jena, 1888. 233 pp. 53

BIBLIOGRAPHY. 103

Housing of Working Classes, Etc.—*Continued.*

"Congrés International des Habitations à bon marché, tenu à Paris les 26, 27 et 28 Juin 1889." Rouillet, A. Paris, 1889. 54
"Die städtischen Wohnungen." Pp. 5-31. J. Stübben's "Städtebau." Darmstadt, Bergsträsser, 1890. 561 pp. 32m. 55
"Etat des Habitations Ouvrières à la fin du XIXe Siècle." Cacheux, Emile. Paris, Baudry, 1891. 184 pp. 18 plates. 4 fr. 56
Wohnungsfrage. Lehr, J. Vol. VI, pp. 727-752 of Conrad, 1st ed., 1893. See 2-10. 57
Stadterweiterungen. Adickes. Vol. V, pp. 847-850, Conrad, 1st ed., 1893. See 2-10. 58
"Städtische Bodenfragen." Eberstadt, Rud. Berlin, M. Heymann, 1894. 8vo, 127 pp. 2m. 59
"Die wirtschaftlichen Aufgaben d. modernen Stadtgemeinde." Bücher, Karl. Leipsic, Seele & Co., 1898. 30 pp. 60
"De l'Amelioration de l'Habitation à bon marché." Beret, Auguste. Marseilles, Barlatier, 1899. 8vo, 303 pp. 61
"Weiträumiger Städtebau und Wohnungsfrage. Darstellung und Kritik darauf Einführung weiträumiger Bauweise im Städteerweiterungsgebeit gerichteten Bestrebungen." Abele. Stuttgart, 1900. 8vo, 72 pp. 1m. 40 pf. 62
"Des Habitations à bon marché." Robin, André. Paris, Chevalier Maresq & Co., 1900. 8vo. 63
"Legislation sur les Logements Insalubres." Jourdan, Gustave. (5th ed.) Paris, Berger-Levrault & Co., 1900. 8vo, 564 pp. Paper, 6 fr. 64

Foreign Articles: 1863-1900.

"Cité Ouvriére de 128 Logements." Nouv. Annales de la Const. p. 66, 1863.
"Die Wohnungen des Volkes, zu Ende d. 19 Jahrhunderts." Meissner, Alois. (A series of articles in the Allgemeine Bauzeitung, Vol. 54 to 59 on Housing of the People). 1889-94. 65
"Die Wohnungsnoth in grossen Städten und deren Bekämpfung." Oesterr. Monatschr. f. d. Oeffent. Baudienst March, 1897.
"Housing and Feeding of the People." Brelay, Ernest. Réforme Sociale 34:530 (Oct. 1897). 66
The Housing of the Poor and the Urgent Needs of Reform. Drucker. De Gids, March, 1898. 67
"Sur le Logement des Classes Laborieuses." Hardy, C. Ref. Soc. 37:180 (Jan. 16, 1899). 68
"Die Wohnungen des vierten Standes." May, Max. Gesellschaft, Oct. 1, 1899. 69
"Zur Wohnungsfrage." Hugo, C. Neue Zeit 17:399 (June 24, 1899). 70
Housing of the People and Sanitation. Oosterbaan, G. De Gids Dec. 1899. 71
"Les Habitations Ouvrières Municipales en Europe." Artibal, J. R. Municipale 3:1865 (Jan. 27, 1900). 72
The Housing Question. Kruseman, H. Vragen des Tijds Feb. 1900. 73
"Zur Wohnungsfrage." Hugo, C. Neue Zeit 18:87 (April 21, 1900). 74
"Le Mouvement d'Amelioration des Habitations Ouvrières." Rostand, Eugène. B. Société F. des Habitations 1:48 (1900). 75
"Les Habitations à bon marché." de Nouvion, Georges. R. Revs. 33:113 (April 15, 1900). 76
"Feuillets Detachés de l'Histoire de l'Habitation Ouvriere." Buse, Julien. R. Générale Nov. 1900. 77

REFERENCES ON SPECIAL PHASES.

"Bibliography of the Housing Question, A Select." Webb, Sidney. Fabian Tract No. 101, pp. 44-50. London, Fabian Society, 1900. 8vo, 50 pp. 1d. Same, pp. 42-8, "Houses for the Working Classes." London, P. S. King, 1900. 1s. 78
"Brussels Housing Congress." Smith, Alfred. London 6:675 (Aug. 12, 1897). 79
Children. "Housing Poor Children." Mun. J. 9:74 (Jan. 26, 1900).
"Club Homes for Unmarried Working Men." Moffat, W. Blackw. 156:701 (1894). 80
Congestion of Population in Cities. (See under **Population**).
"Co-operative Residences, The Coleman-Stuckert System of." Gardiner, Florence Mary. San. Rec. 20:313 (Sept. 17, 1897), 20:359 (Oct. 1, 1897), 20:379 (Oct. 8, 1897), 20:463 (Oct. 29, 1897). 81

Housing of Working Classes, Etc.—*Continued.*

"Co-operators and Housing." Bruce, W. Wallace. Mun. J. 9:88 (Feb. 2, 1900), 9:113 (Feb. 9, 1900).   82

Cottages or Tenements. "Villa oder Miethskaserne." Schasler, M. Gartner, J. Berlin, 1868.   83

——. "Municipal Cottages." Mun. J. & London 8:117 (Jan. 26, 1899).

"Economics of Improved Housing." Gou'd, E. R. L. Yale R. May 1896, p. 8.   84

"Factory Town, A Model." Shuey, Edwin L. Mun. Aff. 3:145 (March, 1899).   85

"Industrial Dwellings." Pp. 660-667, Vol. I. Palgrave. See 1-2.   86

Insanitary Housing Conditions. (See under Slums, Tenement Houses below).

"Land Values, The Housing Problem and." (Editorial). London 7:769 (Dec. 1, 1898).

"Lodging Houses." Chapter IX of Marcus T. Reynold's "Housing of the Poor in American Cities."   87

——. "Model Lodging Houses." Smith, Katharine Louise. Gunton's 17:125 (Aug. 1899).   88

——. "Municipal Lodging Houses." Finley, R. J. N. Y. Rec. and Guide July 18, 1891; McGuire, James K. 'City Govt. 7:7 (July 1899); Shaw, Albert. Char. R. 1:20 (1891); anon. All the Year 72:276 (1893); Mun. J. & London 8:169 (Feb. 9, 1899); The Other Side 1:98 (Sept. 2, 1899).   89

——. "Registration of Common Lodging Houses, The." San. Rec. 24:100 (Aug. 4, 1899).

——. "Das Schlafstellenwesen in den Deutschen Grossstädten und seine Reform." Cahn, E. Münchener Volkswirtschaftliche Studien, No. 28, 1898. 3m.   90

——. "Workingmen's Hotels." Thomas, John Lloyd. Mun. Aff. 3:73 (March, 1899).   91

"Management of Houses for the Poor." Hill, Octavia. Char. Or. R. 5:20 (Jan. 1, 1899).   92

Model Tenements. (See under Tenement Houses below).

"Morality, Tenement House." Huntington, J. O. S. Forum 3:513 (1887).   93

——. "Dwellings of the Poor and their Morality." McDermot, George. Catholic World Feb. 1897.   94

——. "Der Einfluss der Wohnung auf die Sittlichkeit." Laspeyres, E. Berlin, 1869.   95

Municipal or State Action Regarding Housing. "Housing Question as Affected by State Action, The." Parsons, James. Char. Or. R. 5:247 (May, 1899).   96

——. Labourers' Dwellings and their Improvement by Law. Pokrovskaya, M. J. Vyestnik Yevropu Dec. 1899.   97

——. "Legal Obligations in Respect to Dwellings of the Poor." Duff, H. London, Clowes, 1884. 1s.   98

——. "Mischief of State Aid." Shaftsbury, Earl of. 19th Cent. 14:934 (1896).   99

"Municipal Housing." de Forest, Robert W. Char. R. Vol. V, No. 15, p. 3 (Sept. 8, 1900), Char. Or. R. 8·135 (Aug. 1900).   100

——. "The State and Dwellings of the Poor." Vrooman, F. B. Arena 12:415 (1895).   1

——. "The Erection of Artisan's Dwellings by Municipal Corporations." Builder 76:79 (Jan. 28, 1899).

——. See also under Slums below.

"New Movement for Homes." Girling, G. E. Irrigation Age (Chicago) Feb. 1897.   2

"Old Age Pensions by Means of Municipal Dwellings." Thomas, E. Econ. R. 5:221 (1895)   3

"Public Opinion and Improved Housing." McDermot, George. Cath. World March, 1897.   4

Rowton Houses. "Poor Man's Hotel." London. (See Housing under **London**).

"Rural Poor, The Housing of the." Cochrane E. San. Rec. 25:338 (April 20, 1900).   5

Sanitation and Housing. "Dwellings for the Poor and Sanitary Legislation." Child, G. W. Contemp. 32:297 (1878).   6

——. "Etude sur les Conditions Hygiéniques et les Convenances Générales à Remplir dans la Construction des Maisons à bon marché et Cités Ouvrières des Faubourgs et Usines." Gossett, A. Nouv. Annales de la Const. p. 6, 1879.   7

——. "Gesunde Wohnungen, etc." Schülke, H. Berlin, 1880.   8

Housing of Working Classes, Etc.—*Continued.*

——. " Health in the Dwelling, etc. Articles written for and collected by the Mansion House Council." London, Clowes, 1884. 7s. 6d.
——. " Housing and Health." Bosanquet, Bernard. Char. Or. R. 7:193 (April, 1900). 9
——. " L'Hygiène dans la Construction des Habitations Privées." Putzeys, F., Putzeys, E. Brussels, 1882. 2d ed. Lüttich, 1885. 8vo, ill. and diagrams. 12 fr. 10
——. " Sanitary Consideration of the Housing of the Poor." Newell, Wm. H. Sanitary Monitor, Jan. 1886. 11
——. " Sanitary Oversight of Dwellings." Angell, Lewis. Van. Nos. Eng. M. 25:388 (1881); Moore, M. I. Char. R. 4:434 (1895). 12
——. " Tenement Sanitation." Wingate, C. F. Lend a H. 2:82 (1887). 13
——. (See also under **Sanitation**).
" Separate Dwellings." Sykes, John F. J. Pub. Health Feb. 1900. 14
" Shelters for the Homeless, Sanitary Supervision of." Waldo, F. J. San. Rec. Feb. 1897. 15
Slums, Insanitary Areas, etc. " The Battle with the Slum." Riis, Jacob A. Atlan. 83:626 (May, 1899). 16
——. " Bright Side of the Slums." Russel, Ernest E. Outlook 52:500 (1895). 17
——. " Cure for Slums, The Only." Gould, E. R. L. Forum 19:495 (1895). 13
——. " Crusade against Slums." San. Rec. 22:425 (Oct. 21, 1898).
——. " Dietaries of the Slums, What the Very Poor Eat." Bache, René. Sanitarian 42:105 (Feb. 1899). 19
——. " Etude sur les causes et les effets des Logements insalubres." Marjolin. Paris, Masson, 1881. 28 pp. 1 fr. 20
——. " Healthy Homes and Foods for the Working Classes." Vaughan, Victor C. American Public Health Association, 1886. 62 pp. 21
——. " Houses Unfit for Human Habitation." Stephens, J. E. R. San. Rec. 22:480 (Nov. 4, 1898). 22
——. Insanitary Houses. " Le Logement Insalubre." Strauss, Paul. R. Municipale 3:1929 (Feb. 24, 1900). 23
——. " Insanitary Property and the Responsibility of House Agents." San. Rec. 24:159 (Aug. 25, 1899).
——. " Legislation sur les Logements Insalubres. Traité pratique." Jourdan, Gustave. Paris, Berger, L. et Cie., 4th ed., 1889. 6 fr. 24
——. " Logements Insalubres, La Loi de 1850." Laurent, Emile. Paris, Piccard, 1882. 25
——. " Making a Way Out of the Slums." Riis, Jacob A. Am. R. of R. 22:689 (Dec. 1900). 26
——. " Municipality and Slums." Nation 70:333 (May 3, 1900).
——. " Problem of the Slums." Blackw. M. 149:123 (1891).
——. " Rapid Transit and the Slums." Real Estate Rec. & Guide July 30, 1892, p. 141.
——. " Removal of Insanitary Areas and the Management of Improvement Schemes under the Housing of the Working Classes Act." Addie, Peter. Sanitarian 42:19 (Jan. 1899), J. San. Inst. 20:11 (April, 1899). 27
——. " Salvation Army among the Slums." Booth, Maud B. Scrib. M. 17:102 (1895). 28
——. " Servant Class on the Farm and in the Slums, The." Hall, Bolton. Arena 20:373 (Sept. 1898). 29
——. " Seventh Special Report of the Commissioner of Labor on the Slums of Great Cities." (Baltimore, Chicago, New York and Philadelphia). Washington, Government Printing Office, 1894. 620 pp. 30
——. " Slums of Great Cities, The." Osborn, C. Econ. J. 5:474 (1895). 31
——. " Studies in the Slums." Campbell, Helen J. Lippinc. 25:568 (1880). 32
——. " Unhealthy Areas and Displacement of Town Populations." Beachcroft, R. Melville. J. San. Inst. 21:382 (Oct. 1900). 33
——. " Unhealthy Areas and Municipal Housing." Blashill, Thomas. 34
——. " Uninhabitable Dwellings." Jones, Hugh R. Sanitary Record 19:394 (April 30, 1897). 35
——. " What to do for the Slums." Gunton's 14:318 (May, 1898). 36

Housing of Working Classes, Etc.—*Continued.*

Social Significance of the Housing Question. Koch, A. Kultur Heft 2, 1900. 37
State Action Regarding Housing. (See under Municipal or State Action, Slums, above).
Tenement Houses. " Competition, Tenement House." (With analysis of plans as published in the Tribune). Engng. Rec. June 6, 1896.
———. " Better Homes for Workingmen." White, Alfred T. Paper prepared for the Twelfth National Conference of Charities, held at Washington, June, 1885. 20 pp. 38
———. " Foreign Cities, Tenement Houses in." U. S. Consular Reports, Vol. XLVIII, No. 178, July, 1895. (Berlin, Brussels, Glasgow, Liverpool, London and Paris). 39
———. Family Life in Tenement Houses. " Home in the Tenement House, The." Ames, L. T. New Eng. M. n. s. 7:594 (1893). 40
———. " How the Other Half Lives, Studies among the Tenements of New York." Riis, J. A. New York, Scribners, 1892. 304 pp. $1.25. 41
———. " Improved Dwellings for the Working Classes." White, A. T. New York, G. P. Putnam's Sons, 1879, 45 pp. "Better Homes for Workingmen." By same author. 20 pp. 1885. " Riverside Buildings." 12 pp. 1890. 42
———. " Improved Houses for Town Dwellers. Improved Means of Communication." Waterlow, Sydney H. J. San. Inst. 21:417 (Oct. 1900). 43
———. " Improved Tenements." Da Cunha, Geo. W. Am. Arch. 52:123 (1896). 44
———. " Improved Tenement Houses for American Cities." Weber, G. A. Mun. Affairs 1:745 (Dec. 1897). 45
———. " Improvement in Tenement House Construction." Real Estate Rec. & Guide Jan. 2, 1892, p. 2. 46
———. " Investment, Tenement Property as an." Real Estate Rec. & Guide July 7, 1894, p. 86; Aug. 4, 1894, p. 158.
———. " Irrational Tenement House Building." Real Estate Rec. & Guide July 7, 1894, p. 2; July 21, 1894, p. 86; Aug. 4, 1894, p. 158.
———. " Misères et Remèdes." (Tenement House Life). d'Haussonville, Comte. Paris, C. Levy, 1886. 7 fr. 50c. 47
———. Model Tenements. Tolman, William Howe. Arena Sept. 1896; Williamson, Emily E. Charities, Vol. V, No. 2, p. 1 (June 9, 1900); anon. Labor Bulletin Mass. No. 3, p. 19, July, 1897; Gunton's 17:57 (July, 1899); Engng. Rec. 41:232, 280, 304 (March, 1900). 48
———. " Model Dwellings, Blocks of." Arkell, Geo. E. and Octavia Hill. Chapter I, pp. 3-58, Vol. III, " Life and Labor of the People," by Charles Booth. 49
———. " Model Apartment Houses, Conditions of Competition for Plans of." New York Association for Improving the Condition of the Poor, 1895. 50
———. " Model Homes for the Middle Classes." Gardiner, Florence Mary. San. Rec. 20:313 (Sept. 17, 1897), 20:359 (Oct. 1, 1897). 51
———. " Modern City Dwelling, The." (Editorial). Arch. & Build. 27:109 (Sept. 25, 1897).
———. " Plans for Model Tenements and Suburban Homes." Flagg, Ernest; Ware, James E.; Griffin, Percy; Hands, Alice J.; Gannon, Mary Nevan; Huss, George Martin. Mun. Aff. 3:125-143 (March, 1899). 52
———. " Prize Designs for Model Tenements." Construction News 10:171 (March 7, 1900).
———. " Profits of Tenement Property." Real Estate Rec. & Guide Oct. 21, 1893, p. 465.
———. " Relation of Tenement Houses to the Family Life." Lend a H. 12:323 (1894).
———. " Report of the Tenement House Commission. New York Senate Doc. 36, 1885. 235 pp. 53
———. " Report of the Tenement House Committee of 1894." (Richard Watson Gilder, Chairman). New York Assembly Doc. No. 37, 1895. 649 pp. 54
———. " Side Lights on the Tenement House Evil." Flower, B. O. Arena 9:673 (1894). 55
———. " Studies among the Tenements." Riis, J. A. Scrib. M. 6:643 (1889). 56
———. " Tenement House Blight." Riis, Jacob A. Atlan. 83:760 (June, 1899). (Curing its Blight). Atlan. 84:18 (July, 1899). 57

Housing of Working Classes, Etc.—*Continued.*

———. "Tenement House Life and Recreation." Betts, Lillian W. Outlook 61:364 (Feb. 11, 1899). 58

———. "Tenement Houses and Family Dwellings." Lend a H. 12:323 (1894). 59

———. "Tenement House Problem." Bradshaw, M. Lend a H. 15:261 (1895); Rollins, A. W. Forum 5:207 (1888); Veiller, Lawrence. Public Improvements 2:198 (March 1, 1900); Wingate, C. F. Annals of Hygiene 3:41 (1888). 60

———. "Tenement Houses, an Attempt to Give Justice." Eilvart, E. Char. R. 3:343 (1894). 61

———. "Tenement Houses, the Real Problem of Civilization." Riis, J. A. Forum 19:83 (1895). 62

———. "Tenement House Reform." Veiller, Lawrence. Ann. Am. Acad. Pol. Sci. 15:138 (Jan. 1900); anon. Arch & Build. 31:17 (July 15, 1899); Char. R. 9:236 (Aug. 1899); Outlook, 62:741 (Aug. 5, 1899). 63

———. "Tenement Houses and their Tenants." Bocock, Kempner. Social Economist 6:111 (1894); Hall, L. M. Am. J. Soc. Sci. 20:91 (1885). 64

———. "Tenement Neighborhood Idea." Papers by Jean Fine Spahr, Fannie W. McLean, Helen Moore and Mary B. Damon, pp. 23 to 65. "Literature of Philanthropy," edited by Frances Goodale. 65

———. Tenements and Tenement House Reform. Pp. 1322-1328 Encyc. Soc. Ref. See 1-3.

———. "Tenant, The Tenement House. A factor that has been overlooked in the proposals for Tenement House Reform." Real Estate Rec & Guide Feb. 9, 1895, p. 204. 66

———. "The Ethical Side of Tenement House Reform." C. T. C. Open Church 2:365 (Oct. 1898). 67

———. "The Tenement House Curse." Tolman, Wm. Howe and others. (With short bibliography). Arena 9:659 (1894). 68

———. "The Tenement House Exhibit." Betts, Lillian W. Outlook 64:589 (March 10, 1900). 69

———. "The Tenement House Exhibition of 1899." Veiller, Lawrence. Char. R. 10:19 (March, 1900). 70

———. "Tuberculosis, The Tenements and." Knopf, S. A. Sanitarian 45:208 (Sept. 1900); Pryor, John H. Char. R. 10:440 (Dec. 1900). 71

———. "Twentieth Century Tenements." Davidson, Henry T. Our Day 19:255 (May, 1900). 72

Transit Facilities and Housing. "Tramways and the Housing of the Working Classes." Cuningham, Granville C. Ty. & Ry. World 8:477 (Dec. 7, 1899), Elec. R. 36:42 (Jan. 10, 1900). 73

———. "Workmen's Homes and Workmen's Trains." Welsh, Charles. New Eng. M. 20:764 (Aug. 1899). 74

"Workman's Reflections on Housing of the Poor, A." Glazier, William. 19th Cent. 14:952 (1883). 75

———. "Wage Earner's Interest in Improved Housing, A." Cent. 52:793 (1896).

Women, Housing of. "The Housing of the Educated Working Women." Reinherz, H. English Woman's R. Jan. 1900. 76

———. "A Girls' Lodging House." Leake, (Mrs.) Percy. 19th Cent. Dec. 1898. 77

———. "Cheap Lodging Houses for Women." Merry, Andrew. Humanitarian 17:413 (Dec. 1900). 78

———. "Homes for Working Women in Large Cities." Maclean, Annie Marion. Char. R. 9:215 (July, 1899). 79

———. "Housing of Single Women." Fayès, Harriet. Mun. Aff. 3:95 (March, 1899). 80

Huddersfield, Eng.

"The English Municipal Mecca." Mun. J. & London 8:1307 (Dec. 8, 1899).

Transit Facilities. "Huddersfield Tramways and the Municipalization of Tramways." Pogson, J. Elec. Rev. (London), April 23, 1897; anon. St. Ry. Rev. 7:389 (June 15, 1897). 81

———. "Huddersfield Corporation and Electric Traction." Ry. World 8:258 (July 6, 1899).

"Waterworks, Huddersfield." San. Rec. 20:123 (July 30, 1897).

"**Hudson [N. J.] County's** Experiment in Lighting." "W. B. R." Mun. Rec. & Ad. Vol. I, No. 24, p. 5 (Nov. 20, 1897).

Hull, England.
Burial, Cremation. "The First Municipal Crematorium." Mun. J. 9:361 (May 11, 1900). 82

Housing Conditions. "Hull, The Slums of." Mun. J. 9:845 (Oct. 26, 1900).

"Hull, Eng.—Through Municipal Spectacles." Mun. J. 9:417 (June 1, 1900).

Lighting. "The Municipal Electric Lighting Systems of Hull and of Folkestone, England." Elec. World 32:585 (Dec. 3, 1898).

Transit Facilities, Tramways. Armstrong, F. C. St. Ry. Jour. 14:355 (July, 1898); Elec. Rev. (London) 45:18 (July 7, 1899), Ry. World 8:279 (Aug. 10, 1899), Mun. J. 9:337 (May 4, 1900). 83

Hull House. (See Settlements under **Chicago**).

"**Hunan [China]**, Electric Lights in." Child, Jacob T. U. S. Consular Reports 56:29 (Jan. 1898). 83a

Illinois.
"Local Government in Illinois." Shaw, Albert. J. H. Univ. Studies 1:3 (1883). 84

"Local Improvement Act of Illinois." Thompson, A. D. City Govt. 6:110 (May, 1899). 85

Municipal Control, Municipal Ownership. "Private and municipal ownership of gas works, water works and electric and power plants." (Illinois). Tenth Biennial (1898) Report of the Ills. Bureau of Labor Statistics. Springfield, 1899. 271 pp. 86

"Street Railways in Illinois, and their Franchise Conditions." St. Ry. J. 13:304 (May, 1897).

"Water Supplies of Illinois." Fire & W. May 29, 1897.

———. "An Important Water Works Decision in Illinois." (Editorial). Am. Gas Light J. 67:848 (Nov. 29, 1897).

Independent Movements. (See under **Parties and Party Politics in Cities, Reform, Municipal**).

India.
"The Reconstruction of Plague Stricken Cities in India." Hughes, A. J. Eng. Nov. 11, 1898. 87

Indiana.
"Police Co-operation." Harrison, George A. City Govt. 9:124 (Nov. 1900). 88

"Sewage Disposal Law, The Indiana." Engng. Rec. 42:98 (Aug. 4, 1900).

"Street Railway Statistics, Indiana." St. Ry. Rev. 8:303 (May 15, 1898).

Indianapolis, Ind.
History, Description and Statistics of Indianapolis, Ind., in 1880. Census. See 1-7. 89

"Municipal Condition of Indianapolis." Swift, Lucius B. P. 374, Proc. Second Nat'l Conf. for Good City Govt., 1895. See 6-18b. 90

"Pavements, Notes on Indianapolis." Engng. Rec. 40:219 (Aug. 5, 1899).

———. "Creosoted Wood Block Pavements in Indianapolis." Downing, M. A. Mun. Engng. 17:288 (Nov. 1899), St. Ry. R. 10:92 (Feb. 15, 1900). 91

"Schools of Indianapolis, Public." Rice, J. M. Forum 14:429 (1892). 92

———. "Kindergarten Progress in Indianapolis." McKenzie, Anna. Cent. 54:957 (Oct. 1897). 93

"Sewerage System of Indianapolis." Brown, Charles Carroll. J. Assoc. Engng. Soc. March, 1896. 94

Transit Facilities. "Street Railways of Indianapolis." St. Ry. Jour. Aug. 1894.

———. "The Indianapolis Street Railway Franchise." Engng. Rec. 39:537 (May 13, 1899); Ann. Am. Acad. Pol. Sci. 14:145 (July, 1899).

———. Three-Cent Fare Law in Indianapolis." St. Ry. Rev. 7:269, 296, 417, 513, 580 (1897); St. Ry. J. 13:318, 418 (1897); Mun. Rec. & Adv. Aug. 7, 1897; Prog. Age 15:396 (Sept. 15, 1897).

Indianapolis, Ind.—*Continued.*

———. "Report of Commercial Club's Special Committee on Indianapolis Street Railway Franchise." Indianapolis, Commercial Club, 1899. 8vo, 29 pp.

"Women's Work in Indianapolis." McClung, Hester M. Mun. Aff. 2:523 (Sept. 1898). 95

Initiative and Referendum. (See under Direct Legislation).

Iowa.

"Brick Paving in Iowa." Engng. Rec. 41:106 (Feb. 3, 1900).

"Regulation of Public Utilities in Iowa." Siegfriedt, Thorwald A. A. Public Policy 2:372 (June 16, 1900). 96

"Special Assessments in Iowa." Campbell, C. E. City Govt. 6:4 (Jan. 1899). 97

"State Board of Control." An. Am. Acad. Pol. Sci. 16:144 (Sept. 1900).

"**Ipswich, England,** Experience with Wood Pavements at." Engng. Rec. 40:99 (July 1, 1899).

Ireland. (See Ireland under **United Kingdom**).

Irish, Influence of, in American City Politics. (See under **Foreign Element in American Cities**).

"**Issoire,** The Octroi at." Jordan, David Starr. Pop. Sci. Mo. 33:433 (1888). 98

Italy.

City Government, General References and Unclassified.

"Amministrazione dei Comuni, delle Provincii ecc. dei Pareri del Consiglio di Stato, in Materia Finanziaria e Amministrativa." Molla, Pa., e G. Grimaldi. Verona, G. Civelli, 1891. 492 pp. L. 10. 99

"Amministrazione Pubblica in Italia, L'." del Guerra, Enrico. (Contiene un compendio dell' ordinamento provinciale e comunale.) Firenze, G. Barbèra, 1893. 801 pp. L. 4. 100

"Cities of Italy and their Development." Oldrini, A. Chaut. 18:672 (1894). 1

City Leagues. "Lega di Comuni." Treves, Claudio. Critica Sociale 10:88 (March 16, 1900). 2

"Comune, Il." Coen, S., e D. Dialti. Torino, Unione Tipograficoeditrice, 1896. 3 vols. 766, 358 e 425 pp. 15 L. (Complete Legal Treatise.) 3

———. "Comune, Il, e gli altri Enti Locali Amministrativi." Presutti, E. Roma, Ermanno Loescher e C., 1892. 85 pp. In Rivista Italiana per le Scienze Giuridiche 12:191 (1892). 4

———. "Comuni, Dei, e della Provincia." Martinelli, Mass. Bologna, Composition, 1892. 111 pp. 5

———. "Comuni Italiani, I." Serra, Gius. Seconda edizione con un appendice sui debiti comunali. Chioggia, Ludovico Duse, 1889. 54 pp. 6

"Die Lokalverwaltung." Brusa, E. V Abschnitt pp. 337-379 Vol. IV, 1, 7. Marquardsen. See 2-9. 7

"Il Municipio Nuovo." Critica Sociale 10:7 (Jan. 1, 1900). 8

Law. "Il sistéma municipale inglese e la legge comunale italiana. Studii comparativi." Manfrin, Pietro. Florence, 1869-71. 8vo. 9

———. "Legge Comunale e Provinciale Annotata, La." Mazzoccolo, Enrico. Milan, Ulrico, Hoepli, 1894. 728 pp. 10

———. "Legge Comunale e Provinciale, La,—e le Discussioni Parlamentari." Mossa, Pietro. Bari, stab. tip. Gissi e Avellino, 1889. 578 pp. L. 5. 11

———. "Legge Comunale e Provinciale, La Nuova." Pierro, Luigi. Napoli, Aurelio Tocco, 1893. 174 pp. 60c. 12

———. "Legge Comunale e Provinciale, Previ Osservazioni sulla Nuova." Sipione, Corrado. Noto tip. F. Orrecchia, 1890. 19 pp. L. 1. 13

———. "Legge Comunale e Provinciale, La Vigente, Raffrontata coll' Anteriore." Calamandrei, Rod. Firenze, Luigi Niccolai, 1894. 388 pp. 3.50 L. 14

———. "Trattato di Diritto Comunale Positivo." Carnevali, Tito. Mantova, G. Mondovi, 1894. 216 pp. L. 3. 15

Italy—*Continued.*

"Libertá, La, nei Comuni: Appunti." Castiglioni, L. Gallarate, L. Checchi, 1893. 34 pp. Cent. 50.   16

Local and Municipal Government in Italy. Demombynes Vol. I, pp. 353-383. See 2-11.   17

"Modernizing of Italian Cities." Am. Arch. 52:93 (1896).

"Municipal Conditions in Italy." Dohrmann, F. W. Mchts Assoc. Rev. Vol. 2, No. 22, p. 3 (June, 1898).   18

Public Works. "La Responsabilitá del Municipio per la Construzione e Manutenzione del Demanio Comunale." Martinis, Ces de. Napoli, R. M. di Guisseppe, 1890. 78 pp.   19

"Recent Progress in Italy." Shaw, Albert. R. of Rs. 12:553 (1895). (See also Chapter IV, p. 249, "Municipal Government in Continental Europe.")   20

Art. "Municipal Art in Italy." French, Allen. New Eng. M. March, 1898.   21

Burial, Cremation, etc. "La Cremation en Italie et à l'Etranger, de 1774 jusqu' a nos jours." Pini, G. Mailand, Hoepli, 1885. 8vo. 6 fr.   22

Charity. " Assistenza Pubblica, Monografia di Scienza dell Amministrazione." Vacchelli, Giov. Cremona, Interessi Cremonesi, 1891. 239 pp.   23

———. " Abandoned Children in Italy." Salazar, Fanny Zampini. p. 19 "International Congress," vol. V, 1893. See 43-99.   24

———. " Charitable Organizations and Charitable Work in Italy." Rossi, Egisto. p. 168 "International Congress," vol. III, 1893. See 43-99.   25

———. " Le Istituzioni Pubbliche di Beneficenza nella Legislazione Italiana. Luchini, Odoardo, Carlo Rosselli e Mario Pegna." Firenze, G. Barbèra, 1894. 1307 pp. 20 L.   26

———. " Legge 17 Luglio sugli Instituti Pubblichi di Beneficenza." Guzzi, Guis. Catania, C. Galatola, 1893. 92 pp. 2.50 L.   27

Economic Transformation of the Municipality. " Il Municipio Nuovo, fattore di Transformazione Economica." Critica Sociale 10:30 (Jan. 16, 1900).

Elections. " Le Elizione Comunali; Manual per gli Elettori." Sisto, Gius. Trani, V. Vecchi, 1889. 118 pp. 1.50 L.   28

———. Municipal Electors. Pesci, Ugo. Rassegna Nazionale Oct. 1, 1899.   29

Finance. " Finanze dei Grandi Comuni in Italia: Studii." Firenze, Errera, 1882. 7m.   30

———. " I Progretti di Legge sui Manicorni e la Finanza Locale." di Verce, E. Fornasari. G. d. Economisti 21:54 (July, 1900).   31

———. " I Provvedimenti per le Finanze Comunali." Critica Sociale 10:17 (Jan. 6, 1900).   32

———. " La Finanza Locale in Italia." Lacava, P. Turin, Roux, Frassati, 1897. 252 pp. 3 L.   33

———. " Le Finanz Comunali—e i Provvedimenti Proposti dal Governo." Fazi, Fr. Foligno, tip. Co-operative, 1894. 80 pp.   34

———. " La Riforma dei Tributi Locali." Alessio, Giulio. Bologna. Garagnani, 1896. 8vo, 97 pp.   35

History. " Storia Retrospettiva dell' Amministrazione Comunale dallo 1860 al 1890." Terni, tip. dell' Industria, 1890. 56 pp.   36

———. " La Lotta di Classe nella Vita Municipale." Montemartini, Giovanni. Critica Sociale 10:299 (Oct. 1, 1900).   37

———. " Recent Insurrections in Italy." (Municipal conditions partly). de Marco, De Viti. National R. 31:902 (Aug. 1898).   38

"Housing in Italy." Mun. J. & London 8:1363 (Dec. 22, 1899).   39

Lighting. "Public Gas Works in Italy." Bachi, Riccardo. Mun. Aff. 4:595 (Sept. 1900).   40

Pawnshops in Italy. R. Municipale 3:1905 (Feb. 10, 1900); Riv. Ben. Pub. 28:166 (March, 1900).   41

———. " I Monti di Pietá in Italia." Sitta, Pietro. Roma, Union Co-operative Editrice, 1893. 28 pp.   42

Police, Organization of the, in Italy. Alongi, G. Nuova Antologia Rome, May 16, 1897.   43

Prostitution. " Prostituzione, nuove Legge e Regolamento sulla Prostituzione." Firenze, Adriano Salani, 1888. 16 pp. 10c.   44

Italy—Continued.

Reform. "Riforma Comunale e Provinciale, La." Leporini, Gius, Milano, L. Vallardi, 1890. pp. 70. — 45

Sanitary Reform. "La Riforma Sanitaria in Italia." Panizza, Mario. Roma, Alberta Piccolo, 1889. 223. pp. — 46

Schools. "Elementary Education in Italy." Lang, Evelyn M. Humanitarian 16:127 (Feb. 1900). — 47

Transit Facilities. Amoretti, P. Proc. Inst. Civil Engineers, Vol. 119, London Eng. March 22, 1895, et seq.; Lavalard, E. St. Ry. J. 13:412 (July, 1897). — 48

——. "Street and Steam Railways in Italy." Benedetti, F. Chaut. 25:176 (May, 1897). — 49

——. "The Development of Electric Tramways in Italy." Bignami, Enrico. Engng. M. 20:173 (Nov. 1900). — 50

Ithaca, N. Y.

"Street Railway System of Ithaca, N. Y., The." Cooper, H. S. St. Ry. R. 10:308 (June 15, 1900). — 51

——. "Car Tests at Ithaca, N. Y." West, E. L. St. Ry. R. 10:309 (June 15, 1900). — 52

"**Jackson, Mich.**, City Government in." Withington, W. H. Ann Arbor, Studies in Finance and History, Michigan Univ. Article in Vol. I, No. 6, Dec. 1895. 25c. — 53

Jacksonville, Fla. "Municipal Light Plant." City Govt. 7:118 (Nov. 1899). — 54

Japan.

"Law for the Organization of Cities, Towns and Villages." Yokohama Mail, 1888. Pamphlet, 27 pp. — 54

"Settlements in Japan, Social." Anon. Commons 2:1 (May, 1897); Outlook 56:511 (June 26, 1897). — 55

Transit Facilities. "Electric Railways in Japan." Eastlake, W. Delano. St. Ry. J. 15:881 (Dec. 1899). — 56

——. "Electric Railroad Building in Japan." Railroad Gaz. 30:362 (May 20, 1898).

Jersey City, N. J.

Description and Statistics of Jersey City, N. J., in 1880; History to 1880. Census. See 1-7. — 57

Electrolysis in Jersey City. Knudson, A. A. Elec. Eng. 27:228 (Feb. 23, 1899); Engng. News 41:76 (Feb. 2, 1899); Engng. Rec. 39:233 (Feb. 11, 1899). — 58

"Municipal Condition of Jersey City." Quinby, Isaac N. p. 353 Proc. Second Natl. Conf. for Good City Govt., 1895. See 6-18b. — 59

Settlements. Whittier House. Anon. Outlook Dec. 1893, May, 1895, 57:389 (Oct. 9, 1897), 59:188 (May 21, 1898); Mun. Aff. 2:458 (Sept. 1898). — 60

Water Supply. "Reply to the Expert Report on the Proposed Jersey City Water Contract." Eng. News Feb. 4, 1897.

——. "Jersey City's Water Supply." City Govt. 4:99 (March, 1898); Engng. Rec. 38:112 (July 9, 1898).

——. "Report on the Jersey City Water Question." Rafter, George W. Eng. News 37:45 (Jan. 21, 1897); Eng. Rec. Jan. 23, 1897. — 61

——. "The Jersey City Water Works." Engng. Rec. 42:56 (July 21, 1900).

——. "The Waste of Water in Jersey City." Engng. Rec. 41:145 (Feb. 17, 1900).

"**Johannesburg** of To-day." Key, A. Cooper. Cassier's 14:3 (May, 1898). 62

"**Kalamazoo, Mich.**, City Government in." Bondeman, Dallas. Ann Arbor, Studies in Finance and History, Michigan Univ. Article in Vol. I, No. 6, Dec. 1895. 25c. — 63

Kansas.

"A Typical Kansas Community." White, William A. Atlan. 80:171 (Aug. 1897). 64

"Water, Electric Light and Gas Plants." (Private or Municipal Ownership). Thirteenth Annual Report of the Kansas Bureau of Labor and Industrial Statistics, 1897. (Re-printed in pamphlet form, Topeka, 1898). — 65

Kansas City, Kans.

"**Kansas City, Kans.**, Electrolysis at." Blake, Lucien I. Engng. Rec. 40:239 (Aug. 12, 1899).   66

Kansas City, Mo.

"Municipal Condition of Kansas City." **Hopkins**, Henry. pp. 233-248 " Proc. of the Louisville Conference for Good City Government," 1897. See 6-18d.   67
" Pavements, Kansas City." Sci. Am. Sup. Feb. 14, 1885; Engng. News Dec. 13, 1885; J. Assoc. Engng. Soc. 12:180 (1893).
" Public Works in Kansas City." Engng. Rec. 40:52 (June 17, 1899).
Slums. " Kansas City's Patch." Commons July, 1897.
Transit Facilities. " System of the Metropolitan Street Railway Company in Kansas City." Anon. St. Ry. Jour. 14:2 (Feb. 1898); Elec. W. & E. 36:513 (Oct. 6, 1900).
———. " Early Street Car Days in Kansas City." Elec. Rev. 31:13 (July 14, 1897).
———. " Street Railway Franchises." Ann. Am. Acad. Pol. Sci. 13:276 (March, 1899).

Karachi, India.

" The Shone Sewerage System at Karachi." Strachan, James. Ind. Engng. April 3, 1897, Engng. Rec. 39:592 (May 27, 1899).   68

"**Keene, N. H.**" Fiske, Francis S. New Eng. M. 17:225 (Oct. 1897).   69

Kentucky.

" Primary Elections in Kentucky." McDermott, Edward J. N. Y. Conference on Practical Reform of Primary Elections, p. 40. Chicago, Hollister, 1898. 8vo, 150 pp. Paper.   70

"**Kettlewell, Eng.**, The New Water Works at." Rodwell, A. San. Rec. 23:180 (March 3, 1899).   71

"**Khandwa [India]**, Water Works." St. Clair, L. M. Ind. Engng. March 27, 1897.   72

"**Kewanee [Ill.]** Sewerage System, Construction of." Quade, J. C. Mun. Engng. 18:163 (March, 1900).

Kingston, Eng.

" Sewage Disposal, Kingston-on-the-Thames, England." Fuertes, James H. Engng. Rec. 39:424 (April 8, 1899).   73

Kitchens, Public.

" Die Volksküchen—Motive, Bedeutung, Organization, etc." Morgenstern, Lina. Berlin, Stuhrsche Buchh. 1883. 2m.   74
" Wiener Volksküchen." Kühn, Jos. Wien, Seidl u. Sohn, 1876. 2m.   75

"**Knoxville, Tenn.**, History of." Caldwell, Joshua W. See 1-4c.   76

Königsberg [Ger.] Sewerage. " Kanalisation d. Stadt Königsberg." Becker, G. Berlin, Ernst & Kron, 1890. 5m.   77

"**Kowloon** Water Works, The." Cheetham, W. Ind. Engng. Sept. 25, 1897.   78

Küchen i. W. [Germany].

Housing. " Beschreibung des Arbeiter-Quartiers und der damit zusammenhängenden Institutionen von Staub & Co. in Küchen bei Geislingen in Württemberg." Staub, A. Stuttgart, Hallberger, 1868. 26m.   79
———. " Cités Ouvrières de MM. Staub et Ce. à Küchen." Nouv. Annales de la Const. p. 100, 1869.

BIBLIOGRAPHY.

Labor and its Relation to the Municipality, Condition of Laborers in Cities, Day Labor vs. Contract System, Sweating. (See also **Housing, Unemployment**).

See also Boston, Chicago, Detroit, Germany, London, Maryland, Massachusetts, New York, Ohio, Paris, Philadelphia, Rochester, Shoreditch, United Kingdom, Washington.

"Civil Service Reform in its Bearings upon the Interests of Workingmen." Welsh, Herbert. Proc. Natl. Civil Service Reform League, Washington, 1895. P. 116. 80

——. "The Application of the Civil Service Rules to Public Laborers." Russell, Charles Theodore, Jr. P. 49 Proc. Natl. Civil Service Reform League, Buffalo, 1892. 81

"Contracts with Workingmen upon Public Works." Labor Bulletin, Mass., No. 10, p. 56 (April, 1899).

"Contract System, The." Perry, George R. Pp. 112-114 in "Proceedings of the Third Annual Convention of the League of American Municipalities, 1899." 8vo, 148 pp. Paper. 82

"Day Labor and Contract System on Municipal Works, A Comparison of." Commons, John R. American Federationist, Serial, Jan. 1897 to Feb. 1898, with letters from officials, Yale R. 5:428 (Feb. 1897); Mun. Aff. 4:294 (1900); Perry, George R. Public Improvements 1:279 (Oct. 1, 1899); City Govt. 7:56 (Sept. 1899); Snow, F. Herbert. Am. Fed. 6:124, 155 (Aug. Sept. 1899). 83

——. "Contracts given out by Public Authorities to Associations of Workmen." (Report to Labor Department, Board of Trade). R. of Rs. Art. Schloss, D. F. London, Eyre & Spottiswoode, 1897. 346 pp. 1s. 6d. 84

——. "Direct Municipal Employment." New Time 2:64 (Jan. 1898).

——. "Economics of Direct Employment, The." Fabian Tract No. 84. London, The Fabian Society, July, 1898. 15 pp. 1d. 85

Employment Bureaus, etc. "Arbeitsbureaus und arbeitsstatistische Aemter." v. Schönberg, G. Vol. I, pp. 970-978 Conrad, 2d ed., 1898. See 2-10. 86

"Labor and Municipalities." Mun. J. & London 8:439 (April 7, 1899).

Municipal Employment in Foreign Countries. "Les Conditions Municipales du Travail à l'Etranger." Veber, Adrien. R. Municipale 3:2041 (April 14, 1900). 87

"Municipal Progress and the Living Wage." Means, D. MacG. Forum 20:11 (1895). 88

Municipal Work. "L'Esecuzione ad Economia dei Lavori Municipali." Bacchi, Riccardo. Riforma Sociale 10:254 (March, 1900). 89

"Municipalities as Employers of Labor." Real Est. Rec. & Guide Nov. 5, 1892, p. 570.

"Organized Labor, The Relation of Municipalities to." Lavery, James A. Prog. Age 16:381 (Aug. 15, 1898). 90

Pensions. "City Retirement Funds." City Rec. 2:185 (March 16, 1899). (See also **Pensions**). 91

"Public Work and How to do it." Baxter, Sylvester, and George E. Hooker. R. of Rs. 15:435 (April, 1897). 92

Regulation by Municipalities. "De l'Intervention des Municipalités dans la Reglementation du Travail." Pensa, Henri. Paris, Berger-Levrault, 1891. 8vo. 2 fr. 93

Relation of the Municipality to Labor. "La Politica Municipale del Lavoro." Critica Sociale 10:72 (March 1, 1900). 94

"Sanitation, Workingmen and." Wingate, Charles F. Am. Fed. 4:6 (March, 1897). 95

Statistical offices. (See Employment Bureaus above).

Sweating. "Government Sweating in the Clothing Contracts." MacDonald, J. A. New R. 11:471 (1894). 96

——. "Legislation on Sweating." Lee, J. Am. J. Soc. Sci. 30:105, 138 (1892), 31:63 (1893). 97

——. "Report of the Committee of Manufactures on Sweating." (John DeWitt Warner, Chairman). H. R. Report No. 2309. Washington, D. C., Government Printing Office, 1893. (Sweating in New York, pp. 4, 181; Chicago, p. 66; Boston, p. 97; Philadelphia, pp. 34, 212; Rochester, N. Y. p. 57). 98

——. "Reports from the Select Committee of the House of Lords on the Sweating System." Parliamentary Reports and Documents, 1888, 1032 pp.; 1889, 3 vols., 633, 183 and 711 pp. Index to evidence taken before the House of Lords on the Sweating System, 1889. Two vols., 535 and 290 pp. 99

——. "Report of the Lords upon the Sweating System." Potter, B. 19th Cent. 27:885 (1890). 100

114   MUNICIPAL AFFAIRS.

Labor and Its Relation to the Municipality—*Continued.*

——. "Sweating: its Cause and Remedy." London, Fabian Society, 1895. Fabian Tract No. 50. 15 pp. 1d.   1

——. Sweating. Heather-Bigg, A. 19th Cent. 36:665 (1894); Lee, J. Am. J. Soc. Sci. 30:105 (1892), Char. R. 2:100 (1892); Moran, F. J. C. No. Am. 166:757 (June, 1898); Schloss, D. F. Fortn. 48:835 (1887), 55:532 (1890), Sat. R. 69:557, 723 (1890); J. Soc. Arts 36:279 (1888); White, Henry. B. Dept. Labor May, 1896, p. 360; anon. Am. J. Soc. Sci. 31:63 (1894).   2

——. "Sweating in the English Tailoring Trade." Potter, B. 19th Cent. 24:161 (1888).   3

"Wages, in the United States and Europe, 1870-1898." (Statistics given for Paris, Liege, London, Manchester, Glasgow, New York, Chicago, Philadelphia, Boston, Baltimore, Cincinnati, New Orleans, St. Louis, St. Paul, San Francisco, Richmond, Pittsburg and Allegheny). Bulletin of the Dept. of Labor, No. 18, p. 665 (Sept. 1898).   4

——. "Rates of Wages paid under Public and Private Contract." (Cities of Baltimore, Boston, New York and Philadelphia). Stewart, Ethelbert. Bulletin of the Department of Labor, No. 7, p. 721 (Nov. 1896); Labor Bulletin Mass. No. 1, p. 1 (Jan. 1897), No. 4, p. 1 (Oct. 1897); Lend a H. Jan. 1897.   5

——. "Wages and the Cost of Living in the Garment Trades." Eaton, I. Am. Statis. Asoc. 4:135 (1895).   6

"Working Population of Cities, and what the Universities owe them." Swift, Morrison I. Reprinted from Andover R. 13:589 (1890).   7

Laboratories, Municipal. (See under **Paris,** Food Inspection, and **Peoria, Ills.**)

Lafayette, Ind.
"Pavement History of Lafayette." Eldridge, W. K. Mun. Engng. 19:317 (Nov. 1900).   8

——. "Bacterial Studies of the Healthfulness of the Street Pavements of Lafayette, Ind." Luten, Daniel B. Engng. News 44:242 (Oct. 11, 1900).   9

Lancaster, Eng. "New Ideas from an Old City." Phillips, Ernest. Mun. J. & London 8:1283 (Dec. 1, 1899).   10

"**Lancaster, Pa.**, The Water Problem of." Engng. Rec. 39:474 (April 22, 1899).

Landsberg-on-the-Wartha, Prussia, Water Works of. Gesund. Ing. Nov. 30; Dec. 15, 1897.

"**Laodicea, Asia Minor,** The Water Works of." Wegmann, Edward. Engng. Rec. 40:354 (Sept. 16, 1899).   11

Latrines, Public. (See under **Public Comfort Stations**).

Lawrence, Mass.
"City of Lawrence, Mass." Young, George H. New Eng. M. 17:581 (Jan. 1898).   12

Sewage Purification. "Recent Lawrence Experiments in Sewage Disposal." Clark, H. W. Engng. Rec. 40:696 (Dec. 23, 1899).   12a

——. "Experiments on Sewage Purification at the Lawrence Experiment Station during 1898." Engng. News 42:395 (Dec. 21, 1899).

——. See also Sewage Disposal under **Massachusetts.**

Water Works. "Purification of Water at Lawrence, Mass." Engng. News Nov. 30, 1893; Engng. Rec. Feb. 10, 1894.

——. "The New High Service System, Lawrence, Mass." Engng. Rec. 39:376 (March 25, 1899).

Leamington, Eng. "Another Municipal Spa." Mun. J. 9:957 (Dec. 7, 1900).   13

Lectures, Municipal. (See also **New York City**).
"Free Municipal Lectures." Char. R. 9:272 (Sept. 1899).   14

Leeds, Eng.

"Leeds." Hepper, John. Surveyor 17:481 (May 4, 1900). 15
"Lessons from Leeds." London 6:771 (Sept. 23, 1897). 16
Sewage Disposal. Harris, Norfleet. See 56-40a; also Engng. Rec. 40:529 (Nov. 4, 1899); San. Rec. 23:91, 115 (Feb. 3, 10, 1899). 17
——. "Sewage Treatment and Experiments at Leeds." Anon. Surveyor 18:278 (Sept. 7, 1900), San. Rec. 26:206 (Sept. 7, 1900), Eng. (Lond.) 90:232 (Sept. 7, 1900), Engng. N. 44:183 (Sept. 13, 1900), Engng. Rec. 42:272 (Sept. 22, 1900). 18
"Slumdon, Leeds." Foster, D. B. Leeds, 1897. 32 pp. Ill. See also London 6:773 (Sept. 23, 1897), Mun. J. 9:300 (April 20, 1900). 19
"Street Cleaning in Leeds." Darley, George. Mun. J. & E. 9:168 (Dec. 1900). 20
Transit Facilities. Leeds Municipal Electric Tramways. Elec. R. (London) 41:275 (Aug. 27, 1897); Ry. World 6:223, 366 (Aug., Dec. 1897), 7:142, 145 (May, 1898), 8:184 (May, 1899); London 6:772 (Sept. 23, 1897); Elec. World (abstract from the London Electrician, Nov. 11, 1897) 30:640 (Nov. 27, 1897); Ty. & Ry. World 8:375 (Oct. 5, 1899); Mun. J. & London 8:757 (June 30, 1899). 21
——. "Report of the Sub-Highways (Tramways) Committee of their Investigations as to Tramway Traction, and Recommendations Thereon." (References to experience of Birmingham, Darlaston, Newcastle, Edinburgh, Glasgow, Brixton, Croydon, Isle of Man, Brussels, Paris, Havre and Roundhay). Leeds, 1895. 169 pp. 22
——. "Report on the Various Systems of Tramway Haulage by the City Engineer." Hewson, Thos. Leeds, 1895. 43 pp. 23

Legislation, Political and Municipal. (See under **United States** and **United Kingdom**).

Leicester, Eng.

"Leicester as a Municipality." Mun. J. & London 8:878 (Aug. 4, 1899).
Lighting. "Leicester's Gas and Electricity Undertaking." Mun. J. 9:764 (Sept. 28, 1900).
"Markets, Leicester's Municipal." Mun. J. 9:725 (Sept. 14, 1900).
"Municipal Enterprise at Leicester." Mun. J. & London 8:973 (Sept. 1, 1899).

Leicester, Mass.

"Historical Sketch, Leicester." Storey, John. Published by the Town, 1895. 24
"Sewage Disposal by Intermittent Filtration at Leicester, Mass." Engng. News 43:231 (April 5, 1900).

"**Leighton Buzzard, England,** The Water Works of." Nichols, H. Bertram. Engng. Rec. 42:174 (Aug. 25, 1900). 25

Leipzig, Ger.

Buildings. "Leipzig und seine Bauten." Herausgegeben von der Vereinigung Leipziger Architekten und Ingenieure. Leipzig, J. M. Gebhardt, 1892. 856 pp. 30m. 26
Charities. "Individualstatistik der öffentlichen Armenpflege in Leipzig." Lehr, A. 1886. 27
History. "Geschichte der Stadt Leipzig von der ältesten bis auf die neuesten Zeit." Grosse, Karl. Leipzig, Alvin Schmidt, 1898. 8vo, 448 pp. 5m. 28
Housing. "Die Wohnungsverhältnisse der ärmeren Volksklassen in Leipzig." Hasse, Ernst. pp. 288-378, Hft. 31, Schr. d. Ver. f. Socialpolitik. 29
——. "Overcrowding of the Leipsic Poor." Millar, S. R. U. S. Consular Report No. 74, 1887, p. 48. 30
Pawnshop and Savings Institution, Municipal. Warner, Brainard H., Jr. Cons. Rep. 64:381 (Nov. 1900). 31
Prostitution. "Die Leipziger Sittlichkeitsbewegung." Oberbreyer. Leipzig, Werther, 1892. 8vo, 43 pp. 50 pf. 32
Sanitary Condition. "Leipzig, die Stadt in Hygienischer Beziehung." Leipzig, Duncker u. Humblot. 16m. 33

"**Leith [Eng.]** Sewage Disposal." MacBride, Robert J. See 56-40a. 34

"**Lemberg [Eng.]** Electric Tramways, The." Ry. World 6:351 (Dec. 1897).

Lexington, Ky.

Water Works. "Filtration of Lexington, Ky." Fire & W. May 1, 1897.
——. "Experience with Water Meters at Lexington, Ky." Charles, S. A. Engng. Rec. 41:471 (May 19, 1900); Fire & W. 28:2 (July 7, 1900), pp. 183-186 in "Proceedings of the 25th Annual Meeting of the American Water Works Association, Richmond, Va., May 15-18, 1900." 8vo, 216 pp. Cloth, $1.   35

Leyton, Eng.

"Local Life in Leyton." London 6:835 (Oct. 21, 1897).
"Refuse Disposal at Leyton." San Rec. 21:112 (Feb. 4, 1898).

"**Liberty, N. Y.**, Septic Sewage Disposal at." Engng. Rec. 42:146 (Aug. 18, 1900).

Libraries of Cities.

See also Australia, Baltimore, Boston, Bromley (Eng.), Brooklyn, Chicago, Cleveland, Cologne, Erie, Germany, Great Britain, Hornsey, London, Massachusetts, New York, Paris, Philadelphia, Salford, Washington.

"Books for the People." Mun J. & London 8:1235 (Nov. 17, 1899).
"Do Public Libraries Foster a Love of Literature among the Masses?" Chamber's 3:134 (Feb. 1900).
"English and American Libraries." Dewey, Melvil. London 6:622 (July 22, 1897).   36
"Establishment of Free Public Libraries." Fletcher, Wm. I. Citizen 1:8 (1895). Re-printed from his "Public Libraries in America." Boston, Roberts Bros., 1894. 169 pp. $1.   37
"Free Public Libraries." Pp. 28-53. "Methods of Social Reform and other Papers." By W. Stanley Jevons. London and New York, Macmillan, 1883. 383 pp. $3. Also Barber, H. H. Am. M. Civics 6:469 (1895).   38
"Free Libraries and the Community." Putnam, Herbert. No. Am. 166:660 (June, 1898).   39
"Great Public Libraries in the United States." Holden, Edward S. Overland 30:117 (Aug. 1897).   40
"Home Libraries." Birtwell, Charles W. p. 144 "International Congress," vol. V, 1893. See 43-99.   41
"Municipal Libraries and their Development." Southern, J. W. Library Association Record Oct. 1899.   42
"Public Libraries." Randall, E. O. City Govt. 7:97 (Oct. 1899); anon. Engng. Rec. 39:455 (April 15, 1899).   43
"Public Libraries." Greenwood, T. Fourth ed. revised. London, Cassell, 1892. 8vo. 2s. 6d.   44
"Public Libraries in America." Fletcher, Wm. I. Boston, Roberts Bros., 1894. 169 pp. $1.   45
"Public Libraries and Popular Education." Adams, Herbert B. Albany, University of the State of New York, 1900. 8vo, 271 pp. Paper, 40c.   46
"Recent Progress of Public Libraries." Fletcher, Wm. I. Citizen 1:56 (1895).   47
"Relations of City Government to Libraries." Rice, W. Lib. J. 12:364 (1887).   48
"Statistics of Public Libraries in the United States and Canada." Flint, Weston. Washington, D. C. Government Printing Office, 1893. Bureau of Education, Circular of Information No. 7. Whole No. 201.   49
"Sunday Opening of Public Libraries, The." Mun. J. 9:624 (Aug. 10, 1900).
"Value of Municipal Libraries." Taggart, Frederick J. Cal. Mun. 2:52 (March, 1900).   50
"Work of Libraries." Weeks, Anna R. City Govt. 1:75 (1896).   51

Lighting. (See also under **Municipal Control, Municipal Ownership**).

See also Amsterdam, Atlantic City (N. J.), Baltimore, Belfast, Berlin, Birmingham, Bolton (Eng.), Bombay, Borsbeke (Belgium), Boston, Bradford, Buffalo, Cambridge, Carlisle Chatham (Ont.), Chicago, Colomba, Columbus, Croydon (Eng.), Des Moines, Detroit, Dolgeville, Dublin, Edinburgh, England, Erfurt, Europe, Florida, Flushing (L. I.), France, Germany, Glasgow, Gloucester, Grand Rapids, Great Britain, Guayaquil, Hackney, Halle, Hamilton, Havana, Haverhill, Hudson County (N. J.), Hull, Hunan, Italy, Jacksonville, Leicester (Eng.), Liverpool, London, Louisville, Madison,(N. J.), Manchester (Eng.), Massachu-

Lighting—*Continued.*

setts, Negaunee, Netherlands, New York, New Westminster (B. C.), Oconomowoc (Wis.), Oliva, Paris, Penig (Ger.), Peoria (Ills.), Philadelphia, Plymouth, Ponce, Providence, Richmond (Va.), Rochester, Rouen, Russia, St. Pancras, St. Paul, San Francisco, Shaffhausen (Switz.), Sheffield, Shoreditch under London, Singapore, Springfield, South Shields (Eng.), Texas, Toledo, Trieste, United Kingdom, Vienna, Warsaw, Washington, Willesden, Zurich.

GENERAL AND COMPARATIVE.

(Articles applying to more than one kind of lighting and to competition between them).

"Artificial Lighting." Lambert, Carlton. Sanitarian 42:232 (March 1899).   52

——. "Artificial Light, Modern Methods Compared." Jacobus, D. S. Mun. Rec. & Ad. Aug. 14, 1897.   53

——. "Recent Developments in Artificial Illumination." Morton, Henry. Prog. Age 17:510 (Nov. 15, 1899).   54

"Cost of Gas and Electricity, Relative." Humphreys, C. J. R. Engng. M. 4:240 (1892).   55

——. "Cost of Lighting by Gas and Electricity." Trotter, A. P. Electrician Dec. 6, 1895.   56

——. "Eclairage électrique actuel dans différents pays. Comparison de son prix avec celui de gaz à Milan, Rome, Paris, St. Etienne, Tours, Marseilles et New York." Paris, Michelet, 2 ed., 1890. 1 fr. 50c.   57

——. "Significant Comparisons as to the Cost of Light." Baxter, Sylvester. Advance Club Leaflets No. 1, Providence, 1891.   58

"Electric, Gas and Heating Plants." Adams, Alton D. Elec. R. 37:275 (Sept. 19, 1900).   59

"Gas vs. Electricity—The War of the Incandescents." Maxon, J. H: Prog. Age 16:148 (April 1, 1898).   60

——. "Gas vs. Electricity for Lighting Purposes." Cullinane, J. R. Am. Gas Light J. 72:648 (April 23, 1900); City Govt. 8:156 (June, 1900).   61

"Gas and Electric Lighting Works: Directory and Statistics." London, Hazell, Watson & Viney. Issued annually, 23d issue, 1899. 383 pp. 6s.   62

"L'Incandescence par le Gaz et le Pétrole, l'Acétyline et ses Applications." Dommer, F. Paris, Tignol, 1896. 12mo. Paper $1.40.   63

"Municipal Lighting." (Electric Lighting, Technical). Whipple, Fred H. Detroit, Mich., 1889. 8vo, 333 pp. Figs.   64

Progress in Gas and Electric Lighting and the Use of Water Gas. "Die Fortschritte der Gas und Elektrischen Beleuchtung und die Anwendung des Wasser-gases in Hygienischer Beziehung." von K. Hartmann. Wien, VI Internationaler Congress für Hygiene und Demographie zu Wien 1887. Arbeiten der Hygiensichen Sectionen. Heft VI, 1887.   65

"Why Some Lighting Plants do not Pay." Armstrong, F. C: Elec. Rev. 31:8, 32 (July 7, 21, 1897).   66

ACETYLENE.

Acetylene. Lewes, Vivian B. Prog. Age 15:600 (Dec. 15, 1897), J. Gas Lgt. 72:1408 (Dec. 20, 1898), J. Soc. Arts 47:105 (Dec. 23, 1898), 47:117 (Dec. 30, 1898), 47:129 (Jan. 6, 1899), 47:141 (Jan. 13, 1899), Prog. Age 16:581 (Dec. 15, 1898), 17:4 (Jan. 2, 1899), 17:25 (Jan. 16, 1899), 17:44 (Feb. 1, 1899); Tyler, H. L. Dom. Engng. Sept. 1899; Wilson, F. Cortez. San. Plumb. 23:18 (Dec. 1, 1899).   67

"Acetylene v. Ethylene." Eng. Dec. 16, 1898.   68

"Acetylene Gas, its Nature, Properties and Uses: also Calcium Carbide, its Composition, Properties and Method of Manufacture." Thompson, G. F. Liverpool, Spon, 1898. 8vo. 3s. 6d.   69

"Application of Acetylene to Lighting." Bullier, L. M. Prog. Age 15:514 (Nov. 1, 1897).   70

——. "L'Acétylène et ses Applications." Hubou, E. Soc. Ing. Civ. de France Feb. 1899.   71

——. "L'Eclairage a l'Acétylène." Cappelle, Ed. Paris, Retaux, 1898. 8vo. $1.25.   72

——. "L'Eclairage a l'Acétylène. Historique, Fabrication, Appareils, etc." Pellissier, Georges. Paris, Carré et Naud, 1897. 8vo. Cl. $2.   73

Lighting—*Continued.*

——. "Lighting by Acetylene." (Technical.) Gibbs, William E. New York, 2d ed., 1899. 12mo. Cl. $1.50. 74
Calcium Carbid and Acetylene Gas. Cons. Reports 55:331 (Nov. 1897), anon. Mun. Rec. & Ad. 2:606 (June 15, 1898), Prog. Age 17:33 (Jan. 16, 1899), 17:55 Feb. 1, 1899), 17:91 (March 1, 1899). 75
"Dangers of Acetylene." Jouanne, G. Prog. Age 16:76 (Feb. 15, 1898). 76
"Enrichment of Coal Gas by Acetylene." Goodwin, W. W. Prog. Age 16:256 (June 1, 1898). 77
"History, Status and Possibilities of Acetylene." Suplee, Henry Harrison. Engng. M. 13:787 (Aug. 1897). 78
Hygienic Standpoint. "Acetylene vom Hygienischen Standpunkte." Vértess, Josef. Gesund. Ing. July 31, 1898. 79
Illuminating Material. "Das Acetylene und seine Bedetung als Beleuchtungsmittel." Thomas, Karl. Zeitschr. d. Ver. Deutscher Ing. April 30, May 7, 1898. 80
Municipal Control and Ownership. (See **Municipal Control.**)
"Recent Research on Acetylene." Brown, G. E. Prog. Age 15:313 (July 15, 1897). 81
"Town Lighting with Acetylene." Prog. Age 16:551 (Dec. 1, 1898). 82

ELECTRICITY.

General References.

"A New Step in Electric Lighting." Mason, Frank H. Cons. Rep. 62:64 (Jan. 1900). 83
"Anweisung für den elektrischen Lichtbetrieb, etc." May, O. Frankfurt a. M., 1888. 84
"Das elektrische Licht in seiner neuesten Entwickelung, etc." Holthof, F. Halle, 1882. 85
Das elektrische Licht u. s. w. Uhland, W. H. Leipzig, 1883; Ditto, Behrend, G. Halle, 1883. 86
"Die Electricität und ihre Anwendungen zur Beleuchtung, etc." Graetz, L. Stuttgart, 1883. 2 Aufl., 1885. 87
Die elektrische Beleuchtung. Hagen, E. Berlin, 1885. Same title, Bernstein, A. Berlin, 1880. Ditto, Merling, A. Elektrotechnische Bibliothek, Bd. I, Braunschweig, 1882, 2 Aufl., 1884. Ditto, Urbanitsky, A. Wein, 1883, 2 Aufl., 1890. Ditto, Kruss, H. Hamburg, 1883. 88
"Die elektrischen Leitungen und ihre Anlage für alle Zwecke der Praxis." Zacharias, J. Wien, 1883. 89
"Die neuesten Fortschritte auf dem Gebiete der elektrischen Beleuchtung und der Kraftübertragung." Schellen, H. Köln, 1880. 90
"Eclairage à l'Electricité." Fontaine, H. Paris, 1877. 2d ed., 1879. 91
"Electric Lighting." Routledge, R. London, 1882. 92
"Electric Lighting and its Practical Application." Shoolbred, J. N. London, 1870. 93
"Electric Lighting Plants, their Cost and Operation." Buckley, W. J. Chicago, Wm. Johnston Printing Co., 1894. 275 pp. $2. 94
"L'Electricité et ses Applications." de Courmelles, Foveau. Paris, Schleicher Freres, 1900. 1 fr. 95
"La Lumière Electrique et ses Applications." Maissoneuve, S. Paris, 1886. 96
"La Lumière Electrique." Alglave, E., Boulard, J. Paris, 1882. 97
"Les Applications de la Lumière Electrique." van Wetter, R. Paris, 1888. 98
"Les Principales Applications de l'Electricité." Hospitalier, E. Paris, 1881. 99
"Manuel de l'Eclairage Electrique, etc." Armengaud. Paris, 1881. 100
"Notions Générales de l'Eclairage Electrique." Vivarez, H. Paris, 1884. 2 Aufl. 1886. 1
"Practical Electric Lighting." Holmes, A. B. London, 1887. 2
"The Electric Light in its Practical Application." Higgs, P. London, 1879. 3
"The Principles and Practice of Electric Lighting." Swinton, A. A. C. London, 1884. 4
"Ueber den gegenwärtigen Stand der elektrischen Beleuchtung." Schilling. München, 1888. 5

Lighting—*Continued.*

"Accounting for Electric Lighting Companies, Model Forms of." Clough, John Lyle. Mun. Engng. 19:67 (Aug. 1900). 6

——. "A Model System of Bookkeeping for Electric Lighting Companies." Clough, John Lyle. Mun. Engng. 19:251 (Oct. 1900). 7

——. "An Elaborate System of Records for a Lighting Company." Clough, John Lyle. Mun. Engng. 19:326 (Nov. 1900). 8

"American Electrical Work in Europe." Porter, Robert P. Elec. Eng. 24:498 (Nov. 25, 1897). 9

"Arc Lighting, Recent Progress in." Thompson, Elihu. Elec. Eng. 23:662, 705 (June, 16, 23, 1897). 10

——. "Arc Lamps and their Mechanism." Watts, Franklin. Elec. Eng. 24:322 (Oct. 7, 1897), 24:356 (Oct. 14, 1897). 11

——. "Arc Lighting in America and Europe." (Data from 20 large European and American Cities.) Wiler, C. Elec. Eng. 23:467 (May 5, 1897). 12

——. "Cost of Light from the Electric Arc." Adams, Alton D. Mun. Engng. 17:65 (Aug. 1899). 13

——. "Prices for City Arc Lights." (Editorial.) Elec. Eng. 26:486 (Nov. 17, 1898); Prog. Age 16:561 (Dec. 1, 1898). 14

——. "The Cost of Arc Lighting." Wait, H. M. Prog. Age 18:30 (Jan. 15, 1900). 15

"Boom in Electric Lighting." Mun. J. & London 8:1046 (Sept. 22, 1899).

"Central Station Heating in Connection with Electric Lighting Plants." Schott, W. H. Mun. Engng. 18:156 (March, 1900). 16

"Charging for Public Supply of Electricity, Methods of." Lackie, W. W. Elec'n. (Lond.) April 6, 1900. 17

"Combination of Central Stations of Electric and Water Works Plants." Fischer, Louis E. Mun. Engng. 18:240 (April, 1900). 18

"Constant Current Arc Lighting, the Development of." Biebel, H. M. Elec. R. 36:60 (Jan. 17, 1900). 19

"Construction and Maintenance of Electric Lines, Modern." Brophy, William. Am. Gas Light J. 67:609 (Oct. 18, 1897). 20

"Continental Electric Light Central Stations with notes on the methods in actual practice for distributing electricity in towns." Hedges, Killingworth. London, E. & F. N. Spön, 1892. 210 pp. $6. 21

"Economic View of Electric Lighting." Rosewater, Victor. Ind. 42:372 (1890). 22

"Elementary Principles of Electric Lighting." Swinton, A. A. C. London, 1886. 2 ed., 1889. 23

"Future of Electric Illumination." Wetmore, Jean. Am. Gas Light J. 72:91 (Jan. 15, 1900), 72:129 (Jan. 22, 1900). 24

"History and Present Position, Its Past: The Electric Light." Hepworth, T. C. London, 1879. 25

"Incandescent Lamps." Willcox, Francis W. J. Frankl. Inst. 149:282 (April, 1900), 149:353 (May, 1900), 149:419 (June, 1900). 26

——. "Poor Incandescent Electric Lighting." Monroe, H. L. Prog. Age 18:214 (May 15, 1900). 27

——. "The Present Efficiency of Incandescent Lamps." Randall, John E. Elec. Eng. 25:134 (Feb. 3, 1898). 28

"Industrial Uses, The Electric Light for." Crompton, R. E. London, 1880. 29

"Lamps, Arc and Glow: A Practical Treatise on Electric Lighting." Maier, J. London, 1886. 30

——. "Important Consideration in Lamp Tests when determining the best Available Lamp for Central Station Use." Doane, S. Everett. Elec. Eng. 25:735 (June 30, 1898). 31

"Large Districts, The Supply of Electricity to." Eng. (London) 86:251 (Sept. 9, 1898).

"Lighting and Traction, Electric." (Capital Invested, etc.) J. Frankl. Inst. 143:314 (April, 1897).

Machinery. "Electric Lighting, a Practical exposition of the art for the use of engineers, students and others." Crocker, Francis B. New York, Van Nostrand, 1896. 8vo, 444 pp. $3. 32

——. "Die Magnet und Dynamo-Elektrischen Maschinen, ihre Entwickelung, Construction und Praktische Anwendung." Schellen, H. Köln, 1879. 33

Lighting—*Continued.*

"Means of Stimulating the Demands for Electricity." Bishop, H. Collins. Mun. J. 9:571 (July 20, 1900). — 34

"Metering from the Station Standpoint, Electric." Haskins, Caryl D. Elec. Rev. 31:82 (Aug. 18, 1897). — 35

Municipal Control and Ownership. (See **Municipal Control.**)

"Population in the Cities of the World, Electricity and." Hale, R. S., and Codman, J. S. Elec. World 33:19 (Jan. 7, 1899). — 36

"Profit, Electric Lighting for." Dow, Alex. Am. Gas Light J. 68:206 (Feb. 7, 1898), Elec. Eng. 25:135 (Feb. 3, 1898), Elec. Rev. 32:108 (Feb. 16, 1898), 32:124 (Feb. 23, 1898), Elec. World 31:148 (Jan. 29, 1898). — 37

"Progress in Electric Lighting, Recent." Mun. J. & London 8:1074 (Sept. 29, 1899). — 38

"Public Electric Lighting." Engng. Rec. 40:484 (Oct. 21, 1899).

"Rates, Electric Lighting." City Govt. 4:174 (May, 1898). — 40

——. "Systems of Meter Rates." Debell, Edwin L. Elec. Eng. 27:116 (Jan. 26, 1899), Can. Elec. N. 9:31 (Feb. 1899). — 41

"Reducing the Cost of Electric Light." Perry, Nelson W. Engng. M. 9:57 (1895). — 42

"Refuse, Electric Light from City." Perry, Nelson W. Cassier's 13:99 (Dec. 1897). — 43

"Small Lighting Plants." Reeve, Fred'k C. Elec. World 30:672 (Dec. 4, 1897). — 44

——. "Electric Light Plants for Small Towns." Dow, Alex. Elec. Engng. 10:178 (Oct. 1, 1897), 10:232 (Nov. 1, 1897), Prog. Age 16:128 (March 15, 1898). — 45

——. "Electricity Supply for Lighting and Tramways, with Special Reference to Small Towns." Boot, Horace L. P. San. Rec. 26:249 (Sept. 21, 1900), Surveyor 18:364 (Sept. 28, 1900), San. Rec. 26:268 (Sept. 28, 1900), 26:292 (Oct. 5, 1900). — 46

——. "Electricity Supply for Small Towns." Brown, C. S. Vesey; Harris, G. M. Elec. Eng. (Lond.) June 22, 1900. — 47

——. "Positive and Negative Economies in the Operation of Small Electric Light Plants." Roberts, E. P. Elec. Eng. 26:233 (Sept. 8, 1898). — 48

——. "Why Some Small Electric Light Plants do not Pay." Cravath, J. R. Am. Gas Light J. 70:147 (Jan. 30, 1899), Elec. Eng. 27:59 (Jan. 12, 1899), 27:83 (Jan. 19, 1899). — 49

"Treatise on Electric Lighting, A Practical." Gordon, J. E. H. London, 1884. — 50

"Union of Electric Lighting and Traction Plants, The." Adams, Alton D. Cassier's 17:221 (Jan. 1900). — 51

"Useful Information on Practical Electric Lighting." Hedges, Killingsworth. London and New York, 1879. — 52

"Wires, Electric." Hopewell, Charles F. Prog. Age 15:463 (Oct. 15, 1897). — 53

——. "Law of Electric Wires in Streets and Highways, The." Keasby, Edward Quinton. 2d ed. Chicago, Callaghan & Co., 1900. 8vo, 358 pp. — 54

GAS.

General References.

"Both Sides of the Ledger." Humphrys, Norton H. Jour. Gas Lgt. 71:22 (Jan. 4, 1898), 71:75 (Jan. 11, 1898). — 55

"Die Gasbeleuchtung." Tieftrunk, F. Stuttgart, 1874; Ditto, Mendlik A. Budapest, 1879. — 56

"Die Gasindustrie der Gegenwart." Ilgen, F. H. W. Halle, 1873 — 57

"Gas Exhibits and Lighting." Brackenbury, C. E. Engng. Times Aug. 1900. — 58

"Gas Light." Anon. Contemp. 78:710 (Nov. 1900), Prog. Age 18:538 (Dec. 15, 1900).

"Le Gaz et ses Applications." Mont-Serrat; Brisac. Paris, 1894. 16mo. $1.20. — 59

"Handbook for Gas Engineers and Managers." Newbigging, Thomas. London & New York, 6th ed., 1898. 4to. $6. — 60

"L'Industrie du Gaz." Levy, A. Paris, 1893. 8vo. Paper $5.40. — 61

"Some Disputed Points among Gas and Water Experts." Wilkinson, John. J. Gas Light 75:1708 (June 26, 1900). — 62

"Some Plain Words about City Gas Supplies." (With special reference to bad systems of New York, Brooklyn and Boston.) Eng. News Dec. 17, 1896. — 63

"The Gas Industry." Builder June 4, 1898.

Lighting—*Continued.*

"Traité théorique et pratique de la fabrication du gaz, et de ses divers emplois à l'usage des ingenieurs, directeurs et constructeurs d'usines a gaz." Borias, Edmond. Paris, Baudry et Cie., 1890. 8vo. Cl. $7.75.   **64**

Accounts. "The Balance Sheet." Brearley, J. H. J. Gas Lgt. Nov. 29, 1898, Prog. Age 17:50 (Feb. 1, 1899).   **65**

———. "Gas Companies' Bookkeeping: A Practical Treatise on the Keeping of Gas Companies' Accounts." Brearley, John Henry; Taylor, Benjamin. London, Walter King, 1900.   **66**

———. "The Uniformity of Gas Accounts." Miller, C. O. G. Am. Gas Light J. 67:284 (Aug. 23, 1897).   **67**

"Benzol as an Illuminant, The Importance of." Kramer. Prog. Age 15:430 (Oct. 1, 1897).   **68**

Bibliography of Gas Lighting. "Litteratur des Gas- und Wasserfaches. Ein Verzeichniss von Büchern und Broschüren über Gasbeleuchtung und verwandte Beleuchtungsarten sowie für Wasserversorgung, Entwässerung und verwandte Gebiete." Steude, M. München, R. Oldenbourg. 8vo, 78 pp. 2m.   **69**

———. "Bibliography of Coal Gas." Chester, W. R. Nottingham, 1892. 8vo. Cl. $4.20.   **70**

"By-Product Coke Ovens as a Source of Gas Supply." Young, Peter. Prog. Age 18:184 (May 1, 1900).   **71**

"Candle Power: Its Present Relation to the Gas Industry." Lynn, John R. Prog. Age 18:256 (June 15, 1900).   **72**

"Chemistry of Gas Manufacture, The." Butterfield, W. J. Atkinson. Philadelphia, 1896. 8vo. Cl. $3.50.   **73**

"Coke Plant in Gasworks." Brackenbury, C. E. Engng. Times July, 1900.   **74**

Consumers. "Gas Consumers as Gas Proprietors." J. Gas Light 76:1262 (Nov. 20, 1900).   **75**

———. "Gas Works Management and Consumers' Interests." Mun. Rec. & Ad. 2:603 (June 15, 1898).

———. "The Unprofitable Consumer." Humphrys, Norton H. J. Gas Light 76:833 (Oct. 2, 1900).   **76**

"Consumption, Ways and Means of Increasing, Gas." Pooley, H. Prog. Age 15:380 (Sept. 1, 1897).   **77**

"Cost of Illuminating Gas and its Economy." Chessman, James. Van Nos. Eng. M. 30:274 (1884).   **78**

———. "Expert on the Cost of Gas." White, William Henry. City Govt. 7:23 (July, 1899).   **79**

"Dangers of Illuminating and Fuel Gas." Gerhard, William Paul. Prog. Age 18:24 (Jan. 15, 1900).   **80**

"Distributing Gas under Higher Pressure." Shelton, F. H. Engng. News 42:219 (Oct. 5, 1899).   **81**

———. "Gas Distribution in Relation to Modern Municipal Development." Canning, Thomas. (Size of mains, the precautions necessary in view of the newer condition of street paving, electrolysis of gas pipes, etc.) Gas World (London) June 19, 1897, Am. Gas Lgt. J. 67:87 (July 19, 1897).   **82**

———. "In What Manner Can the Normal Loss of Gas in Distribution be Most Largely Diminished." Gibbons, P. H. J. Gas Light 76:776 (Sept. 25, 1900).   **83**

———. "Leakage." Jenkins, E. H. Am. Gas Lgt. J. 66:950 (June 14, 1897). Prog. Age 15:270 (June 15, 1897).   **84**

———. "Locating, Determining and Laying of Street Mains and the Distribution of Gas." Gill, J. P. Am. Gas Lgt. J. 66:678 (May 3, 1897). (Continued in secceeding numbers.)   **85**

———. "Pipes and Piping." (Gas.) Russell, C. P. Am. Gas Lgt. J. 66:994 (June 21, 1897).   **86**

———. "Pumping Gas." Roberts, George. J. Prog. Age 17:491 (Nov. 1, 1899).   **87**

Engineering. "A Practical Treatise on the Manufacture and Distribution of Coal Gas." Clegg, Samuel. London, Trubner & Co., 1868. 4to, 411 pp, plates. 5th ed. 21s.   **88**

———. "King's Treatise on the Science and Practice of the Manufacture and Distribution of Coal Gas." Newbigging, Thomas; Fewtrell, W. T. London, William B. King, 1878. 4to, 3 vols. 444, 450, 417 pp.   **89**

Lighting—*Continued.*

——. "Modern Gas Engineering." Greenough, M. S. Jour. Assn. of Eng. Soc. 20:130 (Feb. 1898). 90
——. "Recent Development in Gas Engineering." Landis, Henry K. Pp. 197-213 in "Pro. Brooklyn Engineers' Club for 1899." 8vo, 233 pp. Paper $2. 91
——. "The Construction of Gas Works Practically Described." Herring, W. R. London, Hazell, 2d ed., 1893. 8vo. Cl. $2. 92
——. "The Construction of Gas Works and the Manufacture and Distribution of Coal Gas." Hughes, B. London, 1853. 6th ed., London, Richards, 1880. 93
"Enrichment of Coal Gas." Harper, George H. Prog. Age 16:252 (June 1, 1898); Livesey, George. J. Gas Light. 75:1200 (May 8, 1900). 94
"European Gas Works, Report upon." Herring, W. R. Prog. Age 17:176 (April 15, 1899), 17:192 (May 1, 1899), 17:213 (May 15, 1899), 17:238 (June 1, 1899). 95
"Foreign Countries, Gas in." Special Consular Report. Washington, Government Printing Office, 1891. 260 pp. 96
"Fuel Gas." Kitson, Arthur. Trans. of Assoc. of Civ. Engs. of Cornell Univ. June, 1897. 97
——. "A Comparison of Fuel Gas Processes." Slocum, F. L. J. Gas Lgt. 70:379 (Aug. 17, 1897). 98
——. "Chauffage et Eclairage par le Gaz." Germinet, G. Paris, 1876. 99
——. "Gas as Fuel." Foveaux, F. Am. Gas Lgt. J. 67:323 (Aug. 30, 1897). 100
——. "Gas Heating and Cooking." Levy, Auguste. Prog. Age 18:536 (Dec. 15, 1900). 1
——. "How can we make the use of Gas for Cooking more Universal." Doherty, Henry L. Prog. Age 16:506 (Nov. 1, 1898). 2
——. "Illuminating and Fuel Gas." Gerhard, Wm. Paul. Cassier's 17:224 (Jan. 1900). 3
——. "On Cooking by the Aid of Gas, and the Ventilation of Kitchens." Sugg, William. Gas World (London) June 19, 1897, Am. Gas Lgt. J. 67:1621 (Aug. 2, 1897). 4
——. "The Cost of Fuel Gas." Reichhelm, E. P. Prog. Age 16:447 (Sept. 15, 1898). 5
——. "The Present Status of Fuel Gas." Lynn, John R. Prog. Age 18:162 (April 16, 1900). 6
——. "Use of Gas for Domestic Heating and Ventilation." Beilby, George. Prog. Age 17:434 (Oct. 2, 1899). 7
"Garbage Gas Process, Mr. Smith's." Am. Gas Light J. 67:1011 (Dec. 27, 1897). 8
"Gasoline Gas Lighting Specifications." Prog. Age 18:36 (Jan. 15, 1900).
"Hygienic Effect of the Use of Gas, The." Miller, Thomas D. Prog. Age 18:263 (June 15, 1900), Am. Gas Light J. 72:966 (June 18, 1900). 9
"Incandescent Lighting, Twenty-five Years' Progress in." Swan, J. W. Elec. R. 31:267 (Dec. 1, 1897). 10
——. "Experiences with the Incandescent Gas Light." Humphrys, Norton H. Am. Gas Light J. 70:607 (April 24, 1899). 11
——. "High Pressure Gas for Incandescent Lighting." Onslow, A. W. J. Gas Light 76:1273 (Nov. 20, 1900). 12
——. "The Case for Incandescent Gas." Bellamy, R. C. London 6:740 (Sept. 9, 1897). 13
——. "The Real Meaning of Incandescent Lamp Efficiency." Willcox, Francis W. Am. Gas Light J. 68:816 (March, 1898). 14
——. "Use of Gas for Purposes other than Lighting." Blodget, C. W. Prog. Age 16:259 (June 1, 1898), Am. Gas Light J. 68:898 (June 6, 1898). 15
"Labor in Gasworks, Modern Methods of Saving; Inclined Retorts." Brackenbury, C. E. Engng. Times, May, 1900. 16
Legislation. "Some Disputed Points in Gas and Water Works." Newbigging, Thomas. J. Gas Light Nov. 28, 1899. 17
"Manufacture of Illuminating Gas." Sci. Am. 83:214 (Oct. 6, 1900).
——. "Die Steinkohlengasbereitung." Schaar, G. F. Leipzig, 1877. 2 Aufl., 1880. 18
——. "Gas Manufacture and Appliances." (Editorial.) Am. Gas Light J. 68:83 (Jan. 17, 1898). 19
——. "Handbuch der Steinkohlengas-Bereitung." Schilling, N. H. München, 1860.

Lighting—*Continued.*

3 Aufl., 1878. 20
———. "Modern Appliances in Gas Manufacture." Stevenson, F. W. Feilden's M. May, 1900. 21
———. "Modern Methods of Manufacturing Gas; With a Description of its Distribution under High Pressure." Shelton, Frederick H. Pro. Eng. C. 17:173 (July, 1900). 22
———. "Some Practical Observations on Gas Manufacture." Carpenter, S. Am. Gas Light J. 67:565 (Oct. 11, 1897). 23
———. "The Investigation of Gas Processes." Humphreys, A. C. Engng. N. 44:325 (Nov. 15, 1900). 24
"Meters, Gas." Wynkoop, Hubert S. Prog. Age 17:112 (March 15, 1899). 25
———. "Automatic Meters; With a Comparison of the Price Charged for Gas Consumed by Slot and Ordinary Consumers." Gas W. Aug. 4, 1900.
———. "Gas and Gas Meters." Wynkoop, Hubert S. Pop. Sci. M. 57:179 (June, 1900). 26
———. "Meter Testing." Doty, Paul. Prog. Age 18:91 (March 1, 1900). 27
———. "Prepayment Meters." Anon. Prog. Age 15:385 (Sept. 1, 1897); Strecker, A. H. Prog. Age 17:489 (Nov. 1, 1899), Am. Gas Light J. 71:806 (Nov. 20, 1899), McIlhenny, John D. Am. Gas Light J. 72:572 (April 9, 1900), Prog. Age 18:165 (April 16, 1900); Raynor, C. H. Prog. Age 16:262 (June 1, 1898); Ross, R. Am. Gas Light J. 69:349 (Sept. 5, 1898). 28
———. "The Prepayment Gas Meter." Am. Gas Light J. 72:771 (May 14, 1900). 29
"Monopolies, Gas." Prog. Age 18:316 (July 16, 1900). 30
Municipal Control and Ownership. (See **Municipal Control.**)
"Natural Gas." Oliphant, F. H. Prog. Age 17:104 (March 15, 1899). 31
"Nuisance Question in Gas Works, The." Shelton, Frederick H. Gas Light J. 70:333 (March 6, 1899), Prog. Age 17:109 (March 15, 1899). 32
"Pintsch Gas System To-Day." Shelton, F. H. Am. Gas Light J. 68:856 (May 30, 1898). 33
"Price of Gas." Botsford, Charles Hull. No. Am. 141:166 (1885). 34
———. "Differential versus Uniform Prices for Gas." Dean, Sedgwick. Prog. Age 18:89 (March 1, 1900), Am. Gas Light J. 72:412 (March 12, 1900). 35
———. "How to Reduce the Gas Bills." Chamber's J. Jan. 1897. 36
———. "X-Rays on the Gas Bill." Brackenridge, James. Am. Gas Light J. 67:882 (Dec. 6, 1897). 37
"Profits from Gas Undertakings in the United States and Great Britain." Mun. Rec. & Ad. 2:600 (June 15, 1898). 38
"Public Lighting by Gas and Electricity." Dibdin, W. J. San. Rec. 24:357 (Oct. 27, 1899), 24:381 (Nov. 3, 1899), 24:405 (Nov. 10, 1899), 24:429 (Nov. 17, 1899), 24:453 (Nov. 24, 1899), 24:473 (Dec. 1, 1899), 24:497 (Dec. 8, 1899), 24:521 (Dec. 15, 1899), 24:563 (Dec. 29, 1899), 25:1 (Jan. 5, 1900), 25:21 (Jan. 12, 1900), 25:44 (Jan. 19, 1900), 25:61 (Jan. 26, 1900), 25:85 (Feb. 2, 1900), 25:109 (Feb. 9, 1900), 25:173 (March 2, 1900), 25:221 (March, 16, 1900), 25:237 (March 23, 1900), 25:261 (March 30, 1900), 25:285 (April 6, 1900), 25:309 (April 13, 1900), 25:333 (April 20, 1900), 25:375 (May 4, 1900), 25:399 (May 11, 1900), 25:423 (May 18, 1900), 25:463 (June 1, 1900), 25:511 (June 15, 1900), 25:563 (June 29, 1900), 26:1 (July 6, 1900), 26:403 (Nov. 9, 1900), 26:445 (Nov. 23, 1900), 26:493 (Dec. 7, 1900), 26:535 (Dec. 21, 1900), 26:559 (Dec. 28, 1900). 39
"Review of the Gas Industry." Vautier, Theodore. Prog. Age 18:438 (Oct. 15, 1900). 40
"Sales, Gas, in the United States, Canada, England and Germany." Engng. News 39:43 (Jan. 20, 1898). 41
"Selling Gas." Copley, I. C. Prog. Age 15:228 (June 1, 1897); Am. Gas Lgt. J. 66:852 (May 31, 1897). 42
"Small Towns, The Lighting of." Harris, G. M. Am. Gas Light J. 73:131 (July 23, 1900). 43
———. "A Small Gas Works and Its Tribulations." M'Laren, J. Prog. Age 16:486 (Oct, 15, 1898). 44
———. "How to Avoid Competition in Small Towns." Schmidt, Emil G. Prog. Age 16:144 (April 1, 1898). 45
———. "The Business End of a Small Gas Works." Dole, S. Milo. Prog. Age 18:93

Lighting—*Continued.*

(March 1, 1900). 46
——. "The Lighting of Small Districts." Arch. & Cont. Rep. 58:68 (July 30, 1897). 47
——. "The Management of Lighting Plants in Small Towns." Petch, Thos. D. Am. Gas Light J. 67:249 (Aug. 16, 1897). 48
——. "Village Lighting: A Comparison." Shadbolt, R. G. Gas. Wld. (June 25, 1898); J. Gas Lgt. 72:16 (July 5, 1898). 49
"Statistics, Coal Gas." Prog. Age 17:559 (Dec. 15, 1899).
"Stoves, The Best Method of Introducing Gas." Britton, John A. Am. Gas Light J. 73:285 (Aug. 20, 1900); Prog. Age 18:523 (Dec. 1, 1900). 50
"Sunday Labor on Gas Works, The Minimizing of." J. Gas Light 76:1329 (Nov. 27, 1900). 51
"Suburban Gas Lighting." Dom. Engng. Nov. 1899. 52
"Taxation of Gas by Local Authorities, The." Carr, Isaac. Gas World (London), June 19, 1897. 53
"Text Book of Gas Manufacture for Students." Hornby, John. London, Bell, 1896. 12mo, pp. 276. Ill. Cl. $1.50. 54
"Use of Gas for Purposes other than Fuel." Douglas, Henry W. Prog. Age 17:89 (March 1, 1899). 55
"Valuation of Gas Works for Assessment, The." Newbigging, William. Gas Wld. June 25, 1898. 56
"Water Gas as an Illuminant." Strache, Hugo. Prog. Age 15:356 (Aug. 16, 1897). 57
——. "A Survey of the Position of Water Gas." Strache, Hugo. J. Gas Lighting (London) Jan. 5, 1897. 58
——. "Carburetted Water Gas." Brackenbury, C. E. Engng. Times, Sept. 1900. 59
——. "Carburetted Wates Gas as a Coal Gas Auxiliary." Glasgow, A. G. Prog. Age 17:522 (Nov. 15, 1899). 60
——. "Carburetted Water Gas and its Use in Coal Gas Works." Sospicio, Henri. J. Gas Light 76:701 (Sept. 18, 1900). 61
——. "Chemical Composition and Technical Analysis of Water Gas." Earnshaw, Edward H. J. Frankl. Inst. 146:161 (Sept. 1898). 62
——. "Der Stand der Wassergas Frage." Strache, Hugo. Weiner Bauindustrie Zeitung Jan. 14, 1897. 63
——. "Hygienic Aspect of the Use of Water Gas." M'Walter, J. C. San. Rec. 26:379 (Nov. 2, 1900). 64
——. "Notes on Carburetted Water Gas." Gas Wld. Jan. 16, 1897. 65
——. "Observations on Carburetted Water Gas." Westcott, J. T. Am. Gas Lgt. J. 66:562 (April 12, 1897). 66
——. "Prof. Lewes on Carburetted Water Gas." Gas World (London), April 17, 1897. 67
——. "Recent Advances in Lighting by Water Gas." Strache, H., and H. Dicke. Jour. Gas Lgt. Oct. 26, 1897. 68
——. "The Manufacture and Application of Water Gas." Dellwik, Carl. Prog. Age 18:311 (July 16, 1900). 69
——. "The New Gas." Webber, W. H. Y. Gas World, June 16, 1900. 70
——. "The Past, Present and Future of Water Gas." Lewes, Vivian B. Prog. Age 16:272 (June 1, 1898), 16:298 (June 15, 1898). 71
——. "Water Gas and its Recent Continental Developments." Lewes, Vivian B. Prog. Age 18:290 (July 2, 1900); Gas World, May 5, 1900. 72
——. "Water Gas as a Remedy for the Prevalent Scarcity of Coal." Dicke, H. J. Gas Light 76:522 (Aug. 28, 1900). 73

STREET LIGHTING, LIGHTING OF PUBLIC BUILDINGS AND PLACES.

"Art in Street Lighting." Foote, Allen Ripley. Elec. Eng. 24:330 (Oct. 7, 1897); Prog. Age 15:465 (Oct. 15, 1897). 74
"Cost of Street Lighting." (Editorial). Engng. Rec. 38:397 (Oct. 8, 1898).
——. "Cost of Lighting by Incandescent Street Lamps." Adams, Alton D. Mun. Engng. 17:185 (Oct. 1899). 75
——. "Cost of Street Electric Lights." City Govt. 6:139 (June, 1899). 76
——. "Cost of Street Lighting." Marechal, Henri. Elec. Rev. Aug. 10, 1894. 77
"Electric Street Lighting." Boot, H. L. P. Prog. Age 15:437 (Oct. 1, 1897); Shei-

Lighting—*Continued.*

ble, Albert. Elec. Rev. 34:238 (April 12, 1899), Am. Gas Light J. 70:570 (April 17, 1899); Wait, H. H. Prog. Age 18:378 (Sept. 1, 1900).   78

——. "A Modern Street Lighting Plant." Damon, George A. Am. Elec. Oct. 1900.   79

——. "Arc Lamps for Street Lighting." Hesketh, Thomas. Elect'n (London), April 9, 1897.   80

——. "Arrangements of Incandescent Street Lamps." Adams, Alton D. Elec. R. 36:512 (May 16, 1900).   81

——. "Electric Lighting in Streets." Boot, H. L. P. London 6:659 (Aug. 5, 1897).   82

——. "Report from the Committee on Electric Street Lighting." Cappelen, F. W. Pro. Am. Soc. Mun. Imp. (5th yr.) Pt. II, p. 101 (Oct. 1898).   83

——. "Series Inclosed Arc Light for Street Lighting Service." Robb, William Lispenard. Mun. Engng. 18:379 (June, 1900), Am. Gas Light J. 72:1019 (June 25, 1900).   84

——. "Statistics on Electric Street Lighting." Cappelen, F. W. Mun. Engng. 19:255 (Oct. 1900).   85

——. "Street Lighting by Electricity." Stevens, F. J. Warden. Architect (London), April 30, 1897.   86

——. "Street Lighting by Series Alternating Current Arc Lamps." Rice, Arthur. L. Am. Elec. 12:379 (Aug. 1900).   87

——. "Street Lighting by Electric Lamps." Minshall, F. H. Elec. W. & E. 36:836 (Dec. 1, 1900).   88

"General Street Lighting." Clark, Walton. Progressive Age July 1, 1896.   88a

"Incandescent Gas Street Lighting." Sheldrake, J. H. Gas W. April 21, 1900, Am. Gas Light J. 72:766 (May 14, 1900).   89

——. "The Return to Gas in the Street Lighting of a Municipality." Yorke, E. H. Am. Gas Light J. 71:891 (Dec. 4, 1899).   90

——. "Welsbach Incandescent Gas Light for Utility and Economy in Street Lighting, The." Wilkiemeyer, H. Am. Gas Lgt. 66:957 (June 14, 1897), Elec. Engin. 23:707 (June 23, 1897), Prog. Age 15:276 (June 15, 1897).   91

——. "Welsbach Street Lighting." Cline, J. W. R. Prog. Age 17:156 (April 15, 1899).   92

Municipal Control and Ownership. (See **Municipal Control**).

"Proper Illumination of City Streets." Hopkins, Henry. Prog. Age 15:450 (Oct. 15, 1897); Elec. Eng. 25:731 (June 30, 1898).   94

"Public Buildings, The Lighting of." Handcock, H. W. and A. H. Dykes. Electrician (London) Feb. 19, 1897.   95

"Public Places, Illumination of Streets and." Pope, Franklin L. Engng. M. 9:261 (1895).   96

"Some Notes on Street Lighting." Jolliffe, J. T. Am. Gas Light J. 68:731 (May 9, 1898).   97

"Street Lighting." Hickenlooper, Andrew. Am. Gas Light J. 72:562 (April 9, 1900), Prog. Age 18:154 (April 16, 1900); Wait, H. H. Am. Elec. 12:380 (Aug. 1900).   93

Lincoln [Eng.], The Sewage System at." McBriar, R. A. San. Rec. 24:163 (Aug. 25, 1899).   99

Lincoln, Neb.

"A City without a Park." Woodward, W. A. Public Imp. 2:147 (Feb. 1, 1900).   100

Liquor Problem in Cities.

See also England under United Kingdom, France, Germany, London, Minneapolis, New York, Norway, United Kingdom, United States.

"Centralized Administration of Liquor laws in the American Commonwealths." Sites, Clement Moore Lacey. New York, Columbia Univ., Macmillan, 1899. 164 pp. Paper, $1.   1

"Drink Evil and Its Cure, The." Herzfeld, A. G. Westm. April, 1897.   2

"Economic Aspects of the Liquor Problem." (Bibliography, p. 313). Koren, John. Boston & N. Y., Houghton M. & Co., 1899. 8vo, 322 pp. $1.50.   3

——. "Economic Aspects of the Liquor Problem." Twelfth Annual Report of the Commissioner of Labor. Washington, Government Printing Office, 1898. 275 pp.

——. "The Economics of Prohibition." Fernald, James C. New York, Funk &

Liquor Problem in Cities.—*Continued.*

Wagnalls, 1890. 8vo, 515 pp. $1.50. 4
"Excise Laws and their Enforcement." Pub. Opin. 19:486 (1895).
"Gothenburg Licensing System, The." Goadby, E. London, Chapman, 1895. 8vo, 1s. 5
———. "How the Gothenburg System Works." Bray, F. C. Chaut. 24:443 (Jan. 1897). 6
"Improved Saloons." Tekulsky, Morris and others. Municipal Program Leaflet No. 4, 1895. 12 pp. 5c. 7
"Legislation in the United States and Canada, Liquor." Fanshaw, E. L. London, Cassell, 1895. 8vo, 2s. 6d. 8
———. "Drunkenness." (Legislative Treatment of drunkenness, pp. 118 et seq.) Wilson, George R. London, Swan S. & Co., 1893. 8vo, 161 pp. 2s. 6d. 9
———. "Liquor and Law." Doane, William C. No. Am. 162:292 (1896). 10
———. "Liquor Legislation in Europe." Vidal Georges. Revue Pénitentiaire Dec. 1896. 11
———. "Sober by Act of Parliament." Mackenzie, F. G. London, Sonnenschein, 1894. 3s. 6d. 12
———. "The Liquor Problem in its Legislative Aspects." (An investigation made under the direction of C. W. Eliot, Seth Low, and J. C. Carter. Contains chapters on conditions in Maine, Iowa, South Carolina, Massachusetts, Pennsylvania, Ohio, Indiana and Missouri. Second edition, 1898, contains an account of the operation of the New York Liquor Tax Law.) Wines, F. H., and J. Koren. Boston, Houghton, Mifflin & Co., 1897. 349 pp. $1.25. 13
"Licensing at Home and Abroad, Liquor." Pease, Edward R. Fabian Tract No. 85 Oct. 1898. 14
"Municipal Drink Traffic." Fabian Tract No. 86 Nov. 1898.
"Penal Aspects of Drunkenness, The." Cummings, Edward. Char. R. 9:500 (Jan. 1900). 15
"Public Houses." Buxton, Noel. Contem. 77:556 (April, 1900). 16
Raines Law. (See Liquor Problem under New York State). 17
"Regulation of Saloons." Adams, S. A. Proc. of the Second Annual Convention of the League of American Municipalities, 1898. p. 69. Perry, Geo. R. City Govt. 5:69 (Aug. 1898). 18
"Saloon in Politics." Hall, Bolton; Crosby, Ernest H. Mun. Aff. 4:399 (June, 1900); Parsons, George Frederick. Atlan. 58:404 (Sept. 1886). 19
"Social Aspects of the Saloon in Large Cities." Ch. VIII, p. 210 "Economic Aspects of the Liquor Problem." Koren, John. Boston & N. Y., Houghton, M. & Co., 1899. 8vo, 322 pp. $1.50. 20
"Social Value of the Saloon." (With reference mainly to Chicago conditions). Moore, E. C. Am. J. Sociol. 3:1 (July, 1897). 21
"Sunday Observance Legislation." Judge, Mark H. Westm. July, 1897. 22
———. "Saloon and the Sabbath." Iuglehart, Ferdinand C. No. Am. 161:467 (1895). 23
———. (See also articles on Sunday Closing under **New York City**).
"What Shall We Do with the Excise Question?" Miller, Warner. No. Am. 162:287 (1896). 24

Lisbon, Portugal.

Project for the Improvement of Lisbon. "Memoire sur le Projet d'Aggrandissement de la Ville de Lisbonne, comprenant l'Etablissement d'un Grand Port Maritime, le Création de Quartiers Nouveaux et le Chemin de Fer de Collarès." Thomé de Gamond, A. Paris, 1870. 25

Little Falls, N. Y.

"The Slow Sand Filtration Plant for Little Falls, New York." Engng. News 41:392 (June 22, 1899).

"**Little Falls, Minn.**, Water Contract, The." Engng. Rec. 42:183 (Aug. 25, 1900).

"**Little Rock, Ark.**, History of." Rose, George B. See 1-4c. 26

Liverpool.

"A Great English Seaport." Townsend, Horace. Chaut. 29:107 (May, 1899). 27

Baths. "Free Swimming Baths, Liverpool." Mun. J. & London 8:743 (June 23, 1899). 28

Docks. "Extension of the Liverpool Docks." Boyle, James. U .S. Consular Reports 56:45 (Jan. 1898); anon. Arch. Oct .22, 1897. See also Cassier's, April, 1898. 29

History of Liverpool. (See references p. 230 Gross' Bibliography of British Municipal History). 30

"Housing of the Working Classes in Liverpool, The." San. Rec. 25:179 (March 2, 1900); Mun. J. 9:789 (Oct. 5, 1900).

——. "Artisans' Dwellings in Liverpool." Sherman, Thos. H. U. S. Consular Reports Vol. XLVIII, No. 178, p. 415-421; also No. 117, 1890, pp. 284-303. 31

——. "Pioneers in Housing." Ilbert, Lettice. Econ. R. 9:450 (Oct. 16, 1899). 32

——. "Tenement Houses in Liverpool." Neal, James E. U. S. Consular Reports Vol. XLVIII, No. 178, p. 408-414. 33

Lighting. "Revolution in Public Lighting in Liverpool." Mun. J. & London 8:855 (July 28, 1899). 34

"Liverpool Corporation's Experiment." King, F. L. Arena 3:737 (1891). 35

"Municipal Government of Liverpool." Sharpless, Isaac. Haverford College Studies No. 11. 36

"Pavements, Etc., of Liverpool." Sherman, Thomas H. U. S. Consular Reports No. 117, pp. 284 to 303, 1890. 37

Sewage Disposal. Neal, Jane E. See 56-40a; also U. S. Consular Rep. No. 117, 1890, pp. 284-303. 38

"Street Trading, The New Liverpool By-Laws Regulating." (Peddling). Dowdall, Chaloner. Econ. R. 9:503 (Oct. 16, 1899). 39

——. "Street Trading Children of Liverpool, The." Burke, Thomas. Contemp. 78:720 (Nov. 1900); anon. Mun. J. 9:904(Nov. 16, 1900). 40

Transit Facilities. Overhead Railway. Cottrell, S. B. Cassier's, 1898; anon. Elec. Rev. (London), Oct. 26, 1894, Jan. 29, 1897. 41

——. Liverpool Municipal Electric Tramways. Sherman, Thomas H. U. S. Cons. Rts. No. 117, 1890, pp. 284-303; anon. St. Ry. Rev. 7:398 (June 15, 1897); Ry. World 7:372 (Nov. 1898); London 7:715 (Nov. 10, 1898); Mun. J. & London 8:1025 (Sept. 15, 1899); Ty. & Ry. 9:117, 356 (March 8, Aug. 9, 1900). 42

——. "Rapid Transit in Liverpool." P. 36 "Rapid Transit in Foreign Cities." Parsons, W. B. New York, 1894. 43

——. "Reports of the Special Committees appointed by the Council on the 13th of March and 7th of May, 1897." Liverpool, 1897. 14 and 6 pp. 44

"Water Supply of Liverpool." Engng. News Aug. 18, 1892, p. 146.

——. "The Story of Liverpool's Water Supply." Mun. J. 9:917 (Nov. 23, 1900).

——. "The Water Works of Europe: London and Liverpool." Philadelphia, Commercial Museum, 1899. 8vo, 50 pp. Pamphlet. 45

Llandudno, Wales.

"The Municipal Works of Llandudno." San. Rec. 20:37 (July 9, 1897).

——. "The Sanitary Works of Llandudno." Little, W. San. Rec. 22:349 (Sept. 30, 1898). 46

Local Government and Institutions. (See under **Government, General References and Unclassified**).

Location of Cities. (See under **Population**).

Lodging Houses. (See under **Housing**).

"**Lombardy,** Communes of, from the VI. to the X. Century." Williams, William Klapp. J. H. U. Studies, Ninth Series, p. 233, 1891. Separate paper, 86 pp. 50c. 47

London.

Government, General References and Unclassified.

"Amalgamation of the City and County of London, Report of the Commission Appointed to Consider the." Parliamentary Reports and Documents, 1894. 2 Vols. 620 and 704 pp.   48

——. "Amalgamation of London." Harrison, F. Contemp. 66:737, Sat. Rev. 78:375, 400 (1894); anon. Hrps. Wkly. 39:15 (1895).   49

——. "Unification of London." Harrison, C. Fortn. 59:836 (1893); Knott, G. H. Am. Law R. 29:395 (1895); Whitmore, C. A. National 21:375 (1893).   50

——. "Unification of London, The Need and the Remedy." Leighton, J. London, Stock, 1895. 1s.   51

Boroughs, London. Mun. J. 8:637 (May 26, 1899), 9:217 (March 23, 1900), 9:877 (Nov. 9 1900); Spec. No. 3,776, p. 649 (Nov. 10, 1900).   52

——. "Boroughs of the Metropolis: A Handbook of Local Administration in London under Local Government Act, 1899." Hopkins, Albert Bassett. London, Bemrose & Sons, 1900. 8vo. Cloth, 7s. 6d.   53

——. "Councils London Borough." Mun. J. 9:880 (Nov. 9, 1900).   54

——. "Councils, Metropolitan Borough: Their Powers and Duties." Fabian Tract No. 100. London, Fabian Society, 1900. 8vo, 19 pp. Pamphlet, 1d.   55

——. "Elections Borough Councils." Mun. J. 9:819 (Oct. 19, 1900), 9:839 (Oct. 26, 1900).

——. "Mayors of London, The New (Borough)." Mun. J. 9:897 (Nov. 16, 1900).

——. "Metropolitan Borough Councils Elections: A Guide to the Election of the Mayor, Aldermen, and Councilors." Hunt, John. London, Stevens & Sons, 1900. 3s. 6d.   56

——. "New London Boroughs: The Electors' Guide and Handbook." London, Edward Lloyd, 1900. 12mo, 100 pp. Paper, 6d.   57

——. "Salaries, Borough Mayor's." Smith, J. E. Mun. J. & London 8:1002 (Sept. 8, 1899).   58

"City of London, The." London, Blades, East and Blades, 1884. 8vo, 171 pp.   59

——. "Analysis of the Accounts of the City of London Corporation." N. d. 2s. 3d. L. C. C. Doc. 152. (See also L. C. C. Docs. 169 and 177 (1893), on finances of city. Price 7d., 1s. 4d. respectively).   60

——. "The City: An Inquiry into the Corporation, its livery companies and the administration of their charities and endowments." (A bitter attack on the corporation and the companies). Gilbert, William. London, Daldy, Isbister & Co., 1877. 8vo, 376 pp. 7s. 6d.   61

——. "Commentaries on the History, Constitution and Chartered Franchises of the City of London." Norton, George. London, Longmans, 3d ed., 1869. 541 pp. 14s.   62

——. "Corporate and Municipal Reform of London." Hickson, W. E. Westm. 39:497 (1843); Monthly R. 115:223.   63

——. "Corporation of London: Decline and Fall of the." (Reform of London Govt.). Fraser's Magazine 49:3, 198, 318, 453, 561, 687 (1854), n. s. 13:769 (1876).   64

——. "Guilds of London." Chamb. J. 58:595 (1881); Westm. 108:1 (1878).

——. "Livery Companies of London, Bibliography of." Welsh, Charles. The Library 2:301-7 (1890). (For historical bibliography of the Livery Companies of London, see p. 303 Gross' Bibliography of British Municipal History).   65

——. "Livery Companies of the City of London, their origin, character, development and social and political importance." Hazlitt, W. Carew. New York, Macmillan, 1892. 8vo, 692 pp. $10.50.   66

——. "Report of the Commission on Livery Companies of the City of London." Parliamentary Reports and Documents, 1884. 5 Vols. 361, 819, 868, 633 and 488 pp. (For discussions of this report see Contempt. 47:1; Ed. R. 162:181; Macmil. 51:266; Nat. R. 5:268; Quar R. 159:40).   67

——. "London City, its people, buildings, traffic, history, streets. etc. Loftie, William J. New York, Scribners, 1890. $15.   68

——. "Statistical Vindication of the City of London." (An elaborate defense of the corporation). Scott, Benjamin. London, 3d ed., 1877. 8vo. (See also under History below).   69

"Counties, London and the." Ecl. M. 108:421 (1887).   70

"County Council, London." Ackworth, William M. 19th Cent. 25:418 (1889); Dick-

BIBLIOGRAPHY. 129

London—*Continued.*

inson, W. H. Mun. J. 9:813, 833 (Oct. 12, 19, 1900); Whitmore, C. A. National 12:781 (1889); anon. Quar. R. 170:226; Sat. R. 69:340 (1890). 71

———. "Annual Report of the London County Council, for year ending March 31, 1897." Quar. Rev. No. 373:259 (Jan. 1898). 72

———. "Attack on the London County Council, The." Wood, T. McKinnon. Contemp. No. 386, p. 202 (Feb. 1898). 73

———. "Commune, The London County Council towards a." Burns, John. 19th Cent. 31:496 (1892). "Towards Common Sense." Prothero, R. E. Same. 74

———. "Conservatives and the London County Council." National 21:175 (1893).

———. "Elections of London County Ciuncil." Lawson, H. L. W. Fortn. No. 374:197 (Feb. 1898); Whitmore, C. A. National 25:239 (1895). 75

———. "History of the First London County Council." Saunders, William. London, National Press Agency, 1892. 8vo, 628 pp. 10s. 76

———. "Impeachment of the London County Council." Fardell, T. G. New R. 6:257 (1892); "Defense of." Harrison, Charles. Same. 77

———. "London County Council and its Assailants." Hobhouse, Lord. Contemp. 61:332 (1892). 78

———. "London County Council: Its duties and powers according to the Local Government, Act of 1888." Gomme, George L. London, Nutt, 1888. 8vo, 5s. 79

———. "London County Council: What it is and what it does." London, Fabian Society, 1895. Fabian Tract No. 61. 15 pp. 80

———. "Lord Salisbury and the London County Council." Local Govt. J. 26:748 (Nov. 20, 1897). 81

———. "Papers prepared by the London County Council to be laid before the Royal Commission, 1893." (Government). P. S. King & Son. 1s. 11d. 82

———. "Proceedings of a Conference of Representatives of the London County Council and Local Authorities, Vestries and District Boards, to consider what Powers now possesed by the London County Council should be transferred to Local Authorities." L. C. C. Doc. 293, 1896. 4s. 83

———. "Sir John Lubbock, County Council and." Harrison, F. New R. 5:395 (1891). 84

———. "Statement as to the present powers and duties of the London County Council." L. C. C. Doc. 148, 1894. 1s. (See also L. C. C. Docs. 52 (1892, 7d.), 142 (1894, 5d.), 149 (1894, 5d.), 161 (1894, 3 1-2d.), on same general subject). 85

———. Work of London County Council. Beachcroft, R. M. National 24:828 (1895); Fox, G. L. Yale R. 4:80 (1895); Harrison, F. 19th Cent. 27:1026 (1890); Meath, Earl of. 19th Cent. 25:505 (1889); Webb, S. Contemp. 67:130 (1895). 86

———. (See also under Finance, Music Halls, Parks, Police, Sewage Disposal, Transit Facilities. London County Council abbreviated L. C. C. in listing its publications).

Elections. "Parliamentary and Local Government Franchise, 1898." L. C. C. Doc. 413. 7d. 87

Government of London. Act of 1888. Fortescue, Earl. 19th Cent. 24:481 (1888); Hobhouse, Arthur. Contemp. 53:773 (1888). 88

———. "London Government under Act of 1888." Firth, J. F. B. and Simpson. London, Knight & Co., 1888. 8vo, 20s. 89

———. Act of 1899, London Government. Ashley, Percy W. L. Mun. Aff. 4:481 (Sept. 1900); Collins, W. J. Contemp. 74:515 (April, 1899), Mun. J. 8:604 (May 12, 1899); Lambelin, Roger. Revue Municipale 2:1503 (Sept. 30, 1899); Pasquet, D. R. Paris No. 13, p. 123 (July 1, 1899); anon. Mun. J. 7:515, 8:265, 272, 333, 364, 618; 9:93 (Aug. 11, 1898, Feb. 2, 1900) (Jan. 27, 18, 25 (March 3, 31, 1899); Quarterly R. 189:492 (April, 1899). 90

———. "The Government of London under the London Government Act, 1899." Seager, J. Renwick. London, P. S. King & Son, 1899. 12mo, 102 pp. Paper, 2s.; Cl. 2s. 6d. 91

———. "The London Government Act, 1899. A Brief Explanation of its Provisions." Slater, Edward T. London, London Reform Union, 1899. 8vo, 31 pp. Pamphlet, 1d. 92

———. "Die Stadtverwaltung der City von London: Vortrag gehalten in Berliner Handwerkerverein am 17 Jan. 1867." (Brief sketch of history and government). v. Gneist, Rudolf. Berlin, 1867. 8vo, 52 pp. 93

———. "Evils of Disunity in Central and Local Government, especially with ref-

London—*Continued.*

erence to the Metropolis." Chadwick, Edwin. London, Longmans, 1885. 8vo, 125 pp. 94

——. "Future Government of London." Gomme, G. L. Contemp. 66:746 (1894). 95

——. Government of London, General Articles on. Hickson, W. E. Westm. 41:553 (1844), 43:193, 228 (1845); Hobhouse, Arthur. Contemp. 41:404 (1882); Lubbock, John. Fortn. 57:159 (1892); National 24:530 (1894); Ed. R. 175:500 (1892); Pascoe, C. E. Appletons, 10:49, 234 (1873); Pennell, E. R. Nation 48:135 (1889); Scott, B. Contemp. 41:308 (1882); Shaw, Albert, Cent. 41:132 (1890), Ch. VIII, p. 222 "Municipal Government in Great Britain," see 1-6; Torrens, W. M. 19th Cent. 8:766 (1880); anon. Ed. R. 142:549 (1875); Gentleman's M. 14:31 (1875); Westm. n. s. 49:93 (1876)); Spec. 71:168 (1893). 96

——. "Greater London, and its Government, for Electors." Whale, George. London, Unwin, 1888. 12mo. 2s. 97

——. Local Government, London. Hare, J. Macmil. 7:441 (1863); Newall, W. Contemp. 22:73 (1873). 98

——. "Local Government and Local Taxation, excluding the Metropolis." Wright, R. S., and H. Hobhouse. London, Sweet & Maxwell, 1894. 6s. Supplement, London, 1888. 34 pp. Second edition including London. 8vo. Cl. 7s. 6d. 99

——. "London Government." (Chapters on Municipal Development in London, London County Council and its committees, Local Municipal Authorities, Poor Law in London, Educational Authorities, Cost of London Government.) Whelen, Frederick. London, Grant Richards, 1898. 8vo, 291 pp. Cl. 3s. 6d. 100

——. "London Government and How to Reform it." Firth, Joseph F. B. London, Kerby, 1882. 12mo. 1s. Also in "Local Government and Taxation in the United Kingdom." Edited by J. W. Probyn. London, Cassell, 1882. 1

——. "Municipal Co-operation in the Government of London, A New Proposal for." Engng. News 41:201 (March 30, 1899). 2

——. "Municipal London or London Government as it is and London under a Municipal Council." Firth, Jos. F. B. London, Longmans, G. & Co., 1876. 775 pp. 25s. 3

——. "New Scheme of London Government." (Opinions of Mr. E. A. Cornwall and Mr. Edric Bayley). London 6:1017 (Dec. 30, 1897). 4

——. "Organisation Municipale de Paris et de Londres, présent et avenir, L'." Guyot, Yves. Paris, Marpont et Flammarion, 1883. 12mo, 100 pp. 1 fr. 50 c. 5

——. "Reform of London [Government.]" Webb, Sidney. London, Published by the Eighty Club, 1892 and 1894. 8vo, 35 pp. 6

——. "Reform of London Government and of City Guilds." Firth, Joseph F. B. London, Swan, S. & Co., 1888. 8vo, 170 pp. 1s. 7

"Life and Labor of the People in London." Booth, C. London and New York, Macmillans, 1895. 9 vols. $15. Maps of London Poverty, etc., to accompany preceding, $1.50. (Vol. I, East, Central and South London; Vol. II, Streets and Populations Classified; Vol. III, Blocks of Buildings, Schools and Immigration; Vol. IV, East London Industries; Vols. V-VIII, Population Classified by Trades; Vol. IX, Comparisons, Survey and Conclusions.) 8

——. "Life and Labor of the People in London." Booth, C. J. Statis. Soc. 56:557 (1893); Clark, W. New Eng. M. n. s. 10:572 (1894). 9

——. "Life in Darkest London, A Hint to General Booth." Jay, A. O. London, Webster & Co., 1891. 1s. 10

Livery Companies. (See under City of London above.)

"London." Blackw. 166:460 (Oct. 1899).

"London, the City of Strange Contrasts." Holmes, F. M. Quiver May, 1899. 11

London, Government, Statistics, etc. pp. 826-832 Encyc. Soc. Ref. See 1-3. 12

"London as a Jubilee City." Statham, H. Heathcote. National No. 172, p. 504 (June, 1897). 13

"London by Night." Robinson, B. Fletcher. Cassell's 28:313 (Aug. 1899). 14

"Manual for 1899-1900, The London." Donald, Robert, Editor. London, Edward Lloyd, 1899. 12mo, 368 pp. Paper 1s.; cl. 1s. 6d. 15

"Municipal London." de Montmorency, J. E. G. Law M. & R. 23:210 (May, 1898); anon. Spec. No. 3,774, p. 554 (Oct. 27, 1900). 16

"Municipal Problems of London." Tyler, G. R. No. Am. 159:448 (1894). 17

"Municipal Problems of New York and London." Shaw, Albert. Am. R. of Rs. 5:282 (April, 1892). 18

London—*Continued.*

"Municipal Work in the City." London 6:867 (Nov. 4, 1897). 19
"Municipality of London." Harkness, M. E. National 1:395; 2:96 (1883); Newall, W. Contemp. 25:437 (1875); anon. Nation 66:179 (March 10, 1898). 20
"New London, The." Mun. J. & London 8:259 (March 3, 1899). 21
"Our Great City; or London the Heart of the Empire." Arnold-Forster, H. O. London, Cassell & Co., 1900. Ill. 75 cts. 22
"Recent Municipal Progress in London." Maltbie, Milo Roy. Mun. Aff. 2:221 (June, 1898). 23
"Reform, London." (Editorial.) San. Rec. 22:579 (Dec. 2, 1898). 24
"The Transformation of London." Ch. XV, pp. 412-436 in Frederic Harrison's "The Meaning of History." New York, Macmillan, 1894. 8vo, 482 pp. $2.25. 25
"The Problem of London." [Government.] Chambers' 76:225 (April, 1899). 26
"Two Babylons, London and Chicago." Stead, W. T. New R. 10:560 (1894). 27
"Two Cities: London and Peking." Little, Archibald. Fireside June, 1899. 28
"Vestries, Scenes and Scandals on the London." National R. 33:416 (May, 1899). 29
——. "The London Vestries, what they are and what they do, with map, table of vestries, etc." London, Tabian Society Tract No. 60, 1894. 19 pp. 1d. 30
——. "Wages of the London Vestry Employees, The." Hewart, Beatrice, Economic J. 8:407 (Sept. 1898). 31
"Year in London, A." Welby, Sir Reginald Earle. Mun. J. & London 8:865 (July, 28, 1899), Mun. Aff. 3:506 (Sept. 1899). 32
"Year Book, Metropolitan." London, Cassell (Annual.) 1s. 33

Abattoirs, Municipal. (Interview with Dr. Forman, Chairman of the L. C. C. Public Health Committee.) London 6:940 (Dec. 2, 1897); anon. London 7:489 (Aug. 4, 1898). 34
Advertising. "Sky Signs Act, London, 1891." Mun. Aff. 3:718 (Dec. 1899). 35
Amusements. "Capitals at Play: London." Robinson, B. Fletcher. Cassell's May, 1898. 36
Art. "Municipal Art in London." London 7:835 (Dec. 29, 1898). 37
——. "Continental Kiosques for London." London 6:644 (July 29, 1897).
——. "London Decorated." Nation 65:45 (July 15, 1897). 38
——. "Municipal Art in Camberwell." London 7:1 (Jan. 6, 1898).
"Barnes and Mortlake: Rising Suburbs." London 6:1009 (Dec. 30, 1897).
"Baths of London, Public." Anon. Mun. J. & London 8:1389 (Dec. 29, 1899); Surveyor Sup. Dec. 21, 1900. 39
——. Baths in Bethnal Green. Mun. J. 9:540 (July 13, 1900); Deptford, same 7:249 (April 21, 1898); Lambeth, same 6:569 (July 8, 1897), 7:431 (July 7, 1898); Lewisham, same 7:439 (June 4, 1898); Newington, same 7:205 (March 31, 1898); St. Marylebone, Architect (London) March 12, 1897; St. Pancras, Mun. J. 8:1069 (Sept. 29, 1899), 9:357 (May 11, 1900). 40
——. "Public Baths and Washhouses and Public Libraries." Gomme, G. L. London, P. S. King & Son, 1899. 4to, 73 pp. Paper, 2s. (L. C. C. Doc. No. 451.) 41
——. "The Popularity of Public Baths." London 7:729 (Nov. 17, 1898).
Battersea. (See under Lighting, Public Works below.)
Bermondsey. (See under Housing below.)
"Bethnal Green Calamity, Lessons from the." London 7:5 (Jan. 6, 1898).
——. Bethnal Green. (See also under Baths, Sanitation, Settlements.)
"Bridges of the Thames. How the City Fought in Parliament for a Monopoly." London 6:579 (July 8, 1897). 42
Buildings, Building Acts, London. "London Buildings." Bremner, C. S. Fortn. 72:291 (March, 1899). 43
——. "London and its Historic Buildings." Besant, Walter. London 6:969 (Dec. 16, 1897). 44
——. "London; as arranged by Sir Christopher Wren." Builder 33:587.
——. "London Building Laws." pp. 347-389 "Fire and Building Regulations in Foreign Countries," Spl. Consular Reports of the U. S. Vol. VIII, 1892. 45
——. "Metropolitan Building Acts." Fletcher, Banister. London, Batsford, 1882. 219 pp. 6s. 6d. 46

London—*Continued.*

——. "Metropolitan Building Acts, 1855-1882, The." Glen, W. C. and R. C. London, Shaw and Sons, 1883. 287 pp. 10s. 6d. ... 47

——. "New Streets and Buildings." Part IV, p. 66, Knight's "Annotated Model By-Laws of the Local Government Board." London, Knight & Co., 1890. 242 pp. 10s. 6d. ... 48

——. "Reliques of Old London upon the Banks of the Thames and in the Suburbs south of the River." Way, T. R. London, Bell & Co., 1899. 8vo, 114 pp. Cl. 21s. ... 49

——. "Report from the Select Committee on the Building Acts and Metropolis Management." Parliamentary Reports and Documents, 1890. 97 pp. ... 50

——. "Statutes Regulating London Buildings." Griffiths, William Russell. London, Clowes, 1893. 360 pp. 12s. 6d. ... 51

——. "Tribunal of Appeal under the London Building Act." Love, Charles H. London, P. S. King & Son, 1900. 8vo, 56 pp. Cl, 2s. ... 52

"Burial Grounds, The London." Holmes, [Mrs.] Basil. New York, Macmillan, 1896. 8vo, 339 pp. ... 53

"Camberwell Reviewed." Mun. J. 9:541 (July 13, 1900). (See also under Art above.)

Census. "Results of the first quinquennial Census of the County of London, taken on 29th March, 1896, with Memorandum." 8d. L. C. C. Doc. 379. ... 54

Charities. "Beggars, How London Deals with." Norton, Lord. No. Am. 161:685 (1895). ... 55

——. "Bitter Cry of Outcast London." Mearns, A. Pamphlet, 1883. Another, same title. Preston, W. C. Cupples, Upham & Co., 1884. 10 cts. ... 56

——. "Charities of London." Bisland, E. Cosmopol. 11:259 (1891); Shaw, B. Contemp. 3:1 (1866). ... 57

——. "Charities Register and Digest." London, Longmans, G. & Co. Published annually for the Charity Organization Society, edition for 1899. 725 pp. 10s. 6d. ... 58

——. "Children under the Metropolitan Asylum Board." Acworth, W. M. Char. Or. R. 3:288 (June, 1898). ... 59

——. "London Children." Vol. III, part II of Charles Booth's "Life and Labor of the People." ... 60

——. "Free Shelters, London." Holmes, F. M. Leisure Hour Feb. 1893. ... 61

——. "Hospitals of London." Bourne, H. C. Macmil. 66:362 (1892); Gigot, A. Fortn. 39:305 (1883); anon. Mun. J. 6:594 (July 15, 1897), 9:641 (Aug. 7, 1900). ... 62

——. "Metropolitan Infirmaries for Pauper Sick." Hart, E. Fortn. 4:459 (1866). ... 63

——. "Report of Committee upon the advantages which might be expected from the establishment of a hospital with a visiting medical staff, for the study and curative treatment of Insanity." L. C. C. Doc. 47, 1890. 1s. 9½d. ... 64

——. "Reports of the Select Committee of the House of Lords on Metropolitan Hospitals." Parliamentary Reports and Documents, 1890, 692 pp.; 1892, 293 pp. ... 65

——. "Suffering London." Hake, A. E. London, Scientific Press, 1892. 3s. 6d. ... 66

——. "Jewish Poor of London, The." Leisure Hour July, 1897. ... 67

——. "Kodak Views of London Charities." Lend a H. March, 1892.

——. "London Alms and London Pauperism." Quar. R. Oct. 1876. Reprinted by the New York Association for Improving the Condition of the Poor, 1877. 16 pp. ... 68

——. "London [Charity] Methods." Loch, C. S. Lend a H. 16:436 (1896). ... 69

——. "Lunacy in London." London 6:765 (Sept. 16, 1897). ... 70

——. "Outcast London." Mearns, Andrew. Contemp. 44:924 (1883). ... 71

——. "Outcast Poor, The." (London.) Lambert, Brooke. Contemp. 44:916 (1883). ... 72

——. "Parochial Charities of London." Hadden, R. H. 19th Cent. 9:324 (1881); James, W. H. Contemp. 33:67 (1878); Wilson, A. J. Macmillan 41:469 (1880). ... 73

——. "Poor in London." Lambert, B. Contemp. 44:916 (1883); Reaney, G. S. Fortn. 46:687 (1886). ... 74

——. "Poor Law in London." Ch. VI, p. 193 Frederick Whelen's "London Government." London, Grant Richards, 1898. 8vo, 291 pp. 3s. 6d. ... 75

——. "Poor Law Administration, London." Hollond, E. W. Contemp. 8:502 (1868). ... 76

——. "Poor Law Progress and Reform, Exemplified in the Administration of East

London—*Continued.*

London Union." Vallance, William. p. 158 "International Congress," vol. I, 1893, See 43-99.. — 77
——. " Poor Law, London Bill and the." Mun. J. & London 8:661 (June 2, 1899). — 78
——. " Poor Relief of London." Lumley, W. G. J. Statis. Soc. 21:169, 308 (1858). — 79
——. " Problems of a Great City, The." (London, Overcrowding, Charity, etc.) White, Arnold. London, Remington Co., 1886. 275 pp. 2s. 6d. — 80
——. " Reforms for London Poor." Greville, Lady V. Fortn. 41:21 (1884). — 81
——. " Riverside Parish, A." Besant, Walter. Chapter VIII, p. 240, "The Poor in Great Cities." New York, Scribners, 1895. $3. — 82
——. " Salvation Army and the Poor of London." Peck, F. Contemp. 58:796 (1890). — 83
——. " Salvation Shelter in London." Vivian, H. Sat. R. 80:862 (1895). — 84
——. " Unendowed London Charities." Chignell, R. London, Cassell & Co., 1892. 1s. — 85
——. " Whitechapel Pauperism." London 6:764 (Sept. 16, 1897). — 86
——. " Year of London Poor, A." Mun. J. & London 8:1383 (Dec. 29, 1899). — 87
City of London. (See City under General References above.)
Crossness. (See under Sewerage, Sewage Disposal below.)
" Croydon: Object Lessons for London." Mun J. & London 8:198 (Feb. 16, 1899). — 88
" Defense of London." Wilkinson, Spenser. National No. 169:42 (March, 1897). — 89
Deptford. (See under Baths.)
Docks. (See under Harbor Facilities below.)
" Ealing, Enterprising." London 7:281 (May, 5, 1898).
East End. "Das Ostende von London, ein soziales Nachbild." Fischer, Paul. Berlin, 1891. 30 pf. — 90
——. " Crime, East End of London and." Jay, A. O. New R. 11:401, Ecl. M. 123:627 (1894). — 91
——. " Industries of East London." Chignell, R. London, T. V. Wood, 1892. 1s. — 92
——. East London Library. (See under Libraries below.) — 93
——. " One Square Mile in the East End of London." (Population, Conditions, etc.) Bartley, George C. T. London, Chapman & Hall, 2d ed., 1870. 74 pp. Paper, 1s. — 94
——. " Riverside of East London, The." Besant, Walter. Cent. 60:522 (Aug. 1900). — 95
——. " Social Problem in East London, The." Barnett, Canon. Humanitarian (April, 1899). — 96
——. " Twenty-five Years of East London." Barnett, Canon. Contemp. R. 74:280 (Aug. 1898). — 97
——. " Work in an East End District." Cowper, Countess. 19th Cent. 18:783 (1885). — 98
Engineering, Municipal. " Municipal London from an Engineering Standpoint." Binnie, Alexander R. London 6:611 (July 15, 1897). — 99
——. " Municipal Engineering in London." Engng. Rec. Aug. 21, 1886. — 100
Finance, Accounts. " La Comptabilité de la Cité de Londres." Heins, Maurice. R. Municipale 3:1641 (Oct. 21, 1899). — 1
——. " Enactments as to London Rating." (List of Acts of Parliament, Local and Public, which have ever been passed relating to each parish in the present County of London—Extracts from Local Acts of Parliament of Clauses relating to Rating in Parishes in the County of London.) 1896. L. C. C. Doc. 243. 11s. 2d. Supplementary Reports, L. C. C. Docs. 331, (1897, 5d.), 339, (1897, 4s. 6d.), 362, (1897, 5d.), 416, (1899, 5d.), 417, (1899, 5d.), 452, (1899, 1½d.). — 2
——. " Expenditure and Taxation, 1895-96; with explanatory memorandum." L. C. C. Doc. 382. 10½d. — 3
——. " Finances, London's." Bruce, W. W. Mun. J. & London 8:564 (May 5, 1899). — 4
——. " Local Taxation in London." Gomme, G. L. J. R. Stat. Soc. 61:442 (1898). — 5
——. " Local Taxation of Rents in London." Hobhouse, Arthur. Contemp. 54:140 (1888). — 6
——. " London County Council Finance." Chater, W. A. J. of Finance Jan. 1898. — 7

London—*Continued.*

——. " Proceedings at the Conference of the Local Government and Taxation Committee with the Assessment Authorities, March, 1893, to March, 1894." L. C. C. Doc. 165. 5s. 6d.   8

——. " Report of Committee appointed to consider the best method of ascertaining the value of land throughout the Metropolis, irrespective of the value of buildings and improvements made by the owners; with Evidence." 1889. L. C. C. Doc. 55. 1s. 10d. (L. C. C. Docs. 127, 137, 138 (1893) on same subject. Price 2½d., 1½d., 2½d. respectively.)   9

——. " Report with respect to the Incidence of Local Taxation in London." L. C. C. Doc. 17, 1891. 9½d.   10

——. " Resolutions passed at a Conference between the Local Government and Taxation Committee of L. C. C. and representatives of Metropolitan Overseers and Assessment Committees, London School Board, Metropolitan Asylums Board, and the Receiver of Police, with a view to promoting uniformity in assessment." L. C. C. Doc. 440, 1899. 3½d.   11

——. " Taxation in London, Bitter Cry of the Taxed." Costelloe, B. F. C. Contemp. 65:293 (1894).   12

——. " Demands for changes in Taxation in London." Whitmore, C. A. National 21:375 (1893).   13

——. " Debt, Repayment of the Metropolitan." Hoare, Alfred. 19th Cent. 31:403 (1892).   14

Finsbury Park. (See under Parks below.)   15

" Fire Protection." Anon. London 7:20 (Jan. 13, 1898), 7:36 (Jan. 20, 1898), 7:52 (Jan. 27, 1898), 7:82 (Feb. 10, 1898), 7:141 (March 3, 1898), 7:156 (March 10, 1898).   16

——. " Fires in London and Paris during 1891." J. Statis. Soc. 55:137 (1892).

——. " The Fire Service in London." Fire & W. 22:435 (Dec. 4, 1897).

——. " The Great City Fire." Anon. Engng. Nov. 26, 1897; London 6:921 (Nov. 25, 1897); Fire & W. 22:428 (Nov. 27, 1897).

" Fogs, Can we get rid of?" London 6:1012 (Dec. 30, 1897).   17

——. " Electric Power and Light from City Refuse. The Shoreditch Enterprise." Sanitarian 39:313 (Oct. 1897).   18

" Garbage, The Disposal of, in London." Real Estate Rec. & Guide April 4, p. 566, 1896. See also 56-40b.   19

——. " London House Refuse." Johnstone, Ralph W. Public Health Nov. 1899. 20

——. " Refuse Destruction in the Metropolis." San. Rec. 26:420 (Nov. 16, 1900). 21

" Guildhall of the City of London, Guide to, and the Municipal Work Carried on therein." Baddelley, J. J. London, Simpkin Marshall, etc., 1898. 8vo, 206 pp. 1s. 6d.   22

Hackney. (See under Lighting.)

" Hammersmith Reviewed." Mun. J. 9:457 (June 15, 1900). (See also under Lighting below.)   23

Harbor Facilities. "Information relating to the Docks, River and Port of London, with reference to the Resolution of the Council, 'that it is in the best interest of London to improve its shipping by improved and cheaper dock accommodation.'" Part I, 1s. 8½d.; Part II, 1s. 8½d.; Part III, 1s. 1½d. L. C. C. Doc. 434. n. d.   24

——. " Public Control for London Docks." (Editorial.) Mun. J. 9:145 (Feb. 23, 1900).   25

——. " The London Docks." Mun J. 8:1340 (Dec. 15, 1899), 9:140 (Feb. 23, 1900).

——. " The River, the Docks and the Port: London." Owen, Douglas. London, C. E. Ferry & Sons, 2d ed., 1900. 8vo, 80 pp. 1s.   26

——. (See also under Thames below.)

" Higher Life of London." Besant, Walter. Outlook April, 1897.   27

History. "London." Loftie, William J. London, Longmans, G. & Co. (Historic Town Series), 1892. 242 pp. $1.25.   28

——. " Ancient Customs of the City of London." Morgan, John de. Green B. 10:312 (July, 1898).   29

——. Bibliography of History of London. (See p. 286 Gross' "Bibliography of British Municipal History.")

——. Buildings, Historic. (See under Buildings above.)

BIBLIOGRAPHY.

London—*Continued.*

——. "Elizabethan London." Mun. J. & London 8:1217 (Nov. 10, 1899).

——. "Essay on the Growth of the City of London, etc." (1682.) pp. 451-478, 501-513, 515-518, Vol II, "Economic Writings of Sir William Petty." Edited by Charles H. Hull. Cambridge, University Press, 1899. 30

——. "Hanse of London." pp. 279-280. Vol. II Palgrave. See 1-2. 31

——. "History of London." (Especially pp. 222-230 on the Government of the City.) Besant, Walter. London, Longmans, 1893. 8vo, 256 pp. 75 cts. 32

——. "History of the twelve great livery companies of London." Herbert, William. London, 1836-7. 2 vols. 8vo. (See under City in general references above.) 33

"Historical Charters and Constitutional Documents of the City of London." Birch, Walter de Gray. London, 1887. 8vo, 338 pp. 34

——. "How the City of London Maintained its Charter." de Morgan, John. Green Bag 9:498 (Nov. 1897). 35

——. "London and the Kingdom: a history derived mainly from the Archives at Guildhall in the custody of the Corporation of the City of London." Sharpe, Reginald R. London, Longmans, 1894-5. 3 vols. 8vo. 10s. 6d. each. 36

——. "London in the Queen's Reign." Cook, Theo. A. Cassell's M. July, 1897. 37

——. "London in the Reign of Victoria." Gomme, G. Laurence. London, Blackie & Son, 1898. 8vo, 256 pp. Cl. 2s. 6d. 38

——. "London: A Short History with Maps and Illustrations." Meiklejon, M. J. C. London, Holden, 1898. 8vo, 262 pp. 1s. 6d. 39

——. "Modern History of the City of London: A Record of Municipal and Social Progress from 1760 to the Present Day." Welch, Charles. London, Blades, 1897. 4to, 504 pp. 42s. 40

"Hornsey, The Happy Suburb of." London 7:313 (May 19, 1898); Mun. J. 9:377 (May 18, 1900). 41

——. "Public Buildings in Hornsey." Surveyor Supp. May 18, 1900. (See also under Housing, Library.)

Hospitals. (See under Charities above.)

Housing of the Poor and of the Working Classes in London, General articles on. Brand, H. R. Fortn. 35:218 (1881); Cross, R. A. 19th Cent. 12:231 (1882); Greg, P. Macmil. 6:63 (1862); Harris, H. Percy. National R. 34:923 (Feb. 1900); Harrod, M. D. Dub. R. 94:414 (1884); Hill, Octavia. Macmil. 30:131 (1874); Hoole, E. Contemp. 45:224 (Feb. 1884); Lewis, Alice. Econ. R. 10:164 (April, 1900); Marshall, Alfred, and Mulhall, M. G. Contemp. 45:224 (Feb. 1884); Porrit, E. Pol. Sci. Q. 10:22 (1895); anon. Local Govt. Journal 27:365 (June 4, 1898); Sat. R. 88:637 (Nov. 18, 1899), Surveyor 17:270 (March 9, 1900); Mun. J. 9:946 (Nov. 30, 1900). 42

——. "Boundary Street Area. Municipal Housing." Williams, Fleming. Mun. J. 9:233 (March 23, 1900); anon. J. San. Inst. 21:451 (Oct. 1900); Mun. J. 9:193 (March 6, 1900). 43

——. "Boundary Street Area, Bethnal Green, Plans." L. C. C. Doc. 469, 1900. 7d. (See also L. C. C. Docs. 64 (1889, 2½d.), 349 (1897, 4d.), 406 (1899, 5d.), on Housing.) 44

——. "Boundary Street Estate, The Rebuilding of the." Fleming, Owen. In "Working Class Dwellings." London, P. S. King & Son, 1900. 4to, 2s. 6d. (See also County Council and Housing, Municipal Housing below.) 45

——. "Cottage Property in London." Hill, O. Fortn. 6:681 (1866). 46

——. "County Council's Housing Policy, The London." Jones, Charles S. Fortn. 68:967 (Dec. 1900); Rowe, Leo. S. The Citizen 2:268 (1896); anon. Spec. No. 3,676, p. 860 (Dec. 10, 1898); Mun. J. 9:981 (Dec. 14, 1900); 9:1002 (Dec. 21, 1900). 47

——. "County Council in Relation to Public Health and the Housing of the Working Classes, The Work of the London." Lowles, John. p. 172 "International Congress," vol. I, 1893. See 43-99. 48

——. "Existing Situation in London: Statistics of Problem." Phillimore, R. C. Fabian Tract No. 101, pp. 15-18. London, Fabian Society, 1900. 8vo, 50 pp. 1d. 49

——. Future Housing of the Working Classes of London. Blashill, Thomas. Surveyor 17:402 (April 13, 1900); J. San. Inst. 21:321 (July, 1900). 50

——. "Homes of the London Poor." Hill, Octavia. New York, State Charities Aid Association, papers republished from the Fortn. Rev. and Macmillan's Magazine, 1875. 78 pp. 25 cts. 51

London—*Continued.*

——. "Hornsey, Artisans' Estates at." Builder 44:880.
——. "House of Shelter, London's." Boulton, H. E. Fortn. 61:615 (1894). 52
——. "Housing Problem in London, The." Knowles, C. M. London, London Reform Union, 1899. 8vo, 21 pp. Pamphlet, 1d. 53
——. "How the Poor Live and Horrible London." Sims, Geo. R. London, Chatto, 1889. Pamphlet. 54
——. "Improving London." Mun. J. 9:437 (June 8, 1900). 55
——. "Land Struggle in London and the Contest in the London County Council on the Taxation of Land Values." Saunders, William. London, National Press Agency. 1s. 56
——. "Local Taxation of Rents in London." Hobhouse, Arthur. Contemp. 54:140 (1888). 57
——. "Law Affecting the Housing and Sanitary Condition of Londoners, Manual of the." Coutts, Baroness Burdett and others. London, Kegan, Paul, T. & Co., 1884. 107 pp. 1s. 58
——. "Limit of the Habitability of London." Conder F. R. Fraser 97:482 (1878). 59
——. "Lodging Houses of London, Common." Part III, p. 41, Knight's "Annotated Model Bye-laws of the Local Government Board." London, Knight & Co., 1890. 242 pp. 10s. 6d. 60
——. "Model Lodging Houses." Hollingshead, J. Good Words 2:170 (1861). 61
——. "Municipal Lodging House, The." London 6:630 (July 22, 1897). 62
——. Rowton Lodging Houses. Sommerville, W. A. 19th Cent. 46:445 (Sept. 1899); anon. London 6:817 (Oct. 14, 1897); Chamber's April, 1899; San. Rec. 24:128 (Aug. 11, 1899). 63
——. "Wanted: A Rowton House for Clerks." White, Robert. 19th Cent. No. 248:594 (Oct. 1897). 64
——. "Model Dwellings, Blocks of." Vol. III, Pt. I, "Life and Labour of the People," by Charles Booth. 65
——. "More Light and Air for Londoners: The Effect of the New Streets and Buildings Bill on the Health of the People." Williams, Robert. London, L. Reeve, 1894. 8vo, 54 pp. 1s. 66
——. Municipal Housing in London. Waterlow, David. Mun. J. & London 8:71 (Jan. 19, 1899); Mun. J. 8:1153 (Oct. 20, 1899), 9:153 (March 2, 1900). 67
——. "No Room to Live: the Plaint of Overcrowded London." (Reprinted from the Daily News.) Haw, George. London, Daily News office, 1899. 12mo, 162 pp. 68
——. "Overcrowding in London and its Remedy." Steadman, W. C. London, The Fabian Society, 1900. 8vo, 15 pp. Pamphlet, 1d. 69
——. "Overcrowding in Bermondsey, Shameful." London 7:299 (May 12, 1898). 70
——. "Overcrowding Problem in Greater London, The." San. Rec. 24:103 (Aug. 4, 1899).
——. "Peabody Buildings, The Later." Wallis, W. E. In "Working Class Dwellings." London, P. S. King & Son, 1900. 4to. 2s. 6d. 71
——. "Poor Law Scattered Homes for London." London 7:521 (Aug. 18, 1898). 72
——. "Rebuilding of London." Parker, J. Eng. Illust. Mag. 13:174 (1895); anon. Surveyor Supp. Nov. 30, 1900. 73
——. "Reconstruction of Central London." Westgarth, William (Editor.) London, Geo. Bell and Sons, 1886. 276 pp. 74
——. "Rehousing of the Poor in London." Cox, E. Westm. 134:611 (1890); Smith, Alfred. London 7:350 (June 2, 1898). 75
——. "Rehousing of the poorer classes in Central London." Corbett, J. Essay in Westgarth's "Reconstruction of Central London," p. 239. 76
——. Shoreditch. "Municipal Housing Scheme." London 6:821 (Oct. 14, 1897), 7:739 (Nov. 17, 1898); Mun. J. and London 8:827, 1241 (July 21, Nov. 17, 1899); San. Rec. 24:431 (Nov. 17, 1899). 77
——. Slums of London, The. L. A. B. Russkaya Muisl Dec. 1899. 78
——. "Back Streets and London Slums." Hastings, F. New York, Funk and Wagnalls, 1889. 20 cts. 79
——. "City Slums." Ingham, J. A. London, Swan, S. & Co., 1889. 2s. 122 pp. 80
——. "Improvement of the Slums in London." Labor Bulletin, Mass. No. 7. p. 1, (July, 1898). 81

London—*Continued.*

——. " Life in London Slums." Ecl. M. 116:511 (1891).
——. " London County Council and the Slum Problem." Rowe, Leo S. The Citizen 2:268 (1896). 82
——. " London Rookeries and Collier's Slums, a plea for breathing room." Williams, Robert. London, W. Reeves, 1893. 1s. 83
——. " Stamping out the London Slums." Marshall, Edward. Cent. 51:700 (1896). 84
——. " Suburban Municipal Cottages." London 6:1010 (Dec. 30, 1897). 85
——. " Tenants, Landlords, Agents, Houses, Rates and Taxes of London." Real Estate Rec. & Guide, Feb. 2, 1895. p. 164. 86
——. " Tenants in London, Landlords and." Hill, O. Macmil. 24:456 (1871). 87
——. " Tenements in London." Holyoake, M. O. Sanitarian 30:511 (1893). 88
——. " Tenements in London and New York, Improved." Am. Arch. 29:120 (1890).
——. " Tenement Houses in London." Collins, Patrick A. U. S. Consular Reports Vol. XLVIII, No. 178, pp. 421-454. 89
——. " Working Class Tenements in London." Porrit, E. No. Am. 160:120 (1895). 90
——. " Wanted—A new Housing Policy." London 7:720 (Nov. 10, 1898). 91
——. " West Ham, Municipal Cottages in." London 7:444 (July 14, 1898).
——. " West Ham's Slums: Corrupt Administration." London 6:804 (Oct. 7, 1897).
——. " What is being done in London and Dudley." (Housing.) R. of Rs. June 15, 1896. 92
——. " Wohnhäuser mit kleinen billigen Wohnungen in London." London, Meissner, Alois. Allgemeine Bauzeitung 59:97 (1894). 93
——. " Die Wohnungen der arbeitenden Klassen in London." Ruprecht, Wilh. Göttingen, Vandenhoech & Ruprechts Verl., 1884. 8vo. 2m. 80 pf. 94
" Ideal London." Harrison, Frederic. Eclectic M. 68:440 (Oct. 1898). 95
" Immensity of London, The." Gennings, John. Chaut. 28:219 (Dec. 1898). 96
Insanity. (See under Charities above.)
" Insurance in London, Municipal." London 7:834 (Dec. 29, 1898). 97
Islington. (See under Lighting below.)
" Italians in London." Gibbs, Phillip. Ludgate Sept. 1898; Hamer. Mun. J. 9:68 (Jan. 26, 1900). 98
Labor. "Direct Employment of Labor vs. the Contract System: The Works Department of the London County Council." Martin, J. W. Mun. Aff. 2:382 (Sept. 1898). 99
——. " A Question of Direct Labor in Shoreditch." London 6:846 (Oct. 21, 1897).
——. " Battersea Works Department." Mun. J. 9:317 (April 27, 1900).
——. " Waterside Labor in London." Booth, C. J. Statis. Soc. 55:521 (1892); Smith, H. L. Econ. J. 2:593 (1892). 100
——. Workmen's Trains. (See under Transit Facilities below.)
Lambeth. (See under Baths, Public Works.)
Lewisham. (See under Baths, Libraries.)
" Libraries, The London Boroughs and the Public." Library World Oct. 1899. 1
——. " Librarians in London. Library Movement in London." London 6:577, 599 (July 8, 15, 1897). 2
——. Libraries. East London. London 6:787 (Sept. 30, 1897); Hornsey. Mun. J. 8:1142 (Oct. 20, 1899); Surveyor Supp. June 29, 1900; Lewisham. London 6:601, 620, 658 (July 15, 22, Aug. 5, 1897). 3
——. " London Free Public Libraries." Mun. J. & London 8:1345 (Dec. 15, 1899).
——. " London Government Act and Libraries." Mason, T. Library 1:25 (Dec. 1899); anon. Library World April, 1899. 4
——. Public Baths and Washhouses and Public Libraries, 1897-98. Statistics, Finance and general information.) Gomme, G. L. London, P. S. King & Son, 1899. 4to, 73 pp. 2s. (L. C. C. Doc. 451.) 5
Lighting. "Battersea, The Light of." Mun. J. 9:639 (Aug. 17, 1900). 6
——. " City Lighting Muddle, The." Mun. J. & London 8:665 (June 2, 1899). 7
——. " Hackney, Electric Lighting in." Mun. J. & London 8:237 (Feb. 24, 1899). 8

London—*Continued.*

——. "Hackney, No Electric Lighting Monopoly in." London 7:259 (April 21, 1898).

——. "Hammersmith, Municipal Electricity in." London 7:297 (May 12, 1898).

——. "Electric Lighting in London." Mun. J. & London 8:1119 (Oct. 13, 1899).

——. "Electric Lighting. Light in the East." Mun. J. 9:621 (Aug. 10, 1900).

——. "Electric Lighting Companies, Our." London 7:369 (June 9, 1898).

——. "Electric Lighting Company's Works, The City of London." Elec. Rev. 34:163 (March 15, 1899).

——. "The Electricity Supply of London." Preece, Arthur H. Am. Gas Light J. 68:702 (May 2, 1898). 9

——. "Electric Light Stations, London." Gunton, Herbert C. Elec. World 31:297, 327, 351 (March 5, 12, 19, 1898). 10

——. "Electric Power and Light from City Refuse; The Shoreditch Enterprise." Sanitarian 39:313 (Oct. 1897). 11

——. "Electric Light Progress in London." Mun. J. & London 8:1202 (Nov. 3, 1899).

——. "Gas Supply of London." Chubb, H. J. Statis. Soc. 39:350 (1876); Liberty, W. J. J. Gas Light 75:756 (March 20, 1900); anon. Builder 74:223 (March 5, 1898); Am. Gas Light J. 68:658 (April 25, 1898); J. Gas Light 74:475 (Aug. 22, 1899); Eng. (Lond.) 90:2 (July 6, 1900). 12

——. "Accounts of the Metropolitan Gas Companies for the year 1899." J. Gas Light, 75:995 (April 17, 1900). 13

——. "City Corporation Conference on the Price of Gas in London." J. Gas Light 76:1154 (Nov. 6, 1900).

——. "Gas Works of London, The." Colburn, Zerah. New York, Van Nostrand, 1868. 12mo, 86 pp. 75 cts. 14

——. "The Lot of the Gas Worker—Coal and Coke—The London Gas Companies." Am. Gas Light J. 72:332 (Feb. 26, 1900). 15

——. "The London County Council and the Increased Price of Gas." J. Gas Light 76:230 (July 24, 1900), 76:1028 (Oct. 23, 1900). 16

——. "The 'Powers of Charge' of Metropolitan Gas Companies. A History of the Question of Price, in London from the Introduction of Gas Lighting to the Present Time." Rostron, Laurence W. S. London, Walter King, 1900. 17

——. "The Price of Gas in London." Eng. (Lond.) 90:65 (July 20, 1900).

——. "Islington's Municipal Electric Lighting." London 7:82 (Feb. 10, 1898).

——. "Light that Failed, The." Mun J. 9:73 (Jan. 26, 1900).

——. "Monopoly, The City Lighting." Hitching, Brooke. Mun. J. London 8:23 (Jan. 5, 1899). 18

——. "Fighting the Lighting Monopoly." London 7:825 (Dec. 29, 1898). 19

——. "Poplar, Electric Light for." Mun. J. 9:801 (Oct. 12, 1900).

——. "Public Lighting in Edinburgh, London and Elsewhere." J. Gas Light 73:297 (Feb. 7, 1899).

——. "Revolution in Public Lighting." Mun. J. & London 8:986 (Sept. 1, 1899).

Liquor Problem. "Drink and Drunkenness in London." No. Am. R. March, 1897. 20

"Literary London Twenty Years Ago." Higginson, Thomas Wentworth. Atlan. 80:753 (Dec. 1897). 21

Livery Companies. (See under City of London above.)

Lodging Houses. (See under Housing above.)

"Lord Mayor's Show, The." Pennell, Elizabeth Robins. Cent. 55:433 (Jan. 1898). 22

——. "Lord Mayor and the Mansion House, The." Warren, May Spencer. Cassell's p. 458 (April, 1898). 23

Margate. "London at Play." Pennell, Elizabeth R. Cent. 54:569 (Aug. 1897). 24

"Markets of London." Fletcher, J. J. Statis. Soc. 10:345 (1847); Mun. J. 9:566 (July 20, 1900). 25

——. "Clearance of Clare Market, The." Smith, Alfred. London 7:457 (July 21, 1898). 26

——. "Municipalisation of Spitalfields Market." Mun. J. & London 8:457 (April 14, 1899). 27

——. "Special Report relative to existing Markets and Market Rights, and as to the expediency of establishing New Markets in or near London." Plans. L.

BIBLIOGRAPHY. 139

London—*Continued.*

C. C. Doc. 63, 1893. 2s. 8½d.   28
"Marriage in East London." Dendy, H. Contemp. 65:427 (1894). Also see Ch. III, p. 28 Bosanquet's "Aspects of the Social Problem." London, Macmillan, 1895. 334 pp. $1.   29
"Music Halls, London County Council and." Archer W. Contemp. 67:317 (1895).   30
Newington. (See under Baths.)
"Noises, London's Many." Sanitarian 39:44 (July, 1897).
"Opera in London, Municipal." Mun. J. & London 8:614 (May 19, 1899).   31
Parks in London, General Articles on. Meath, Earl of. New R. 7:701 (1892); Thornbury, W. Belgra. 3:288, 410 (1867); 4:68, 288 (1868); Walters, Lucy. Chaut. 29:571 (Sept. 1899); anon. Blackw. 46:212 (1839), 51:380 (1842); Chamb. J. 68:337 (1891); Garden & F. 5:366, 616 (1892); Spec. 66:825 (1893); Building News 17:195. n. d.   32
——. "Bloomsbury, The Squares of." Builder 31:857.   33
——. "County Council and Open Spaces in London." Meath, Earl of. New R. 7:701 (1892).   34
——. "Finsbury Park, London, England, A Glimpse at." Meehan, Joseph. Park & Cem. 7:64, 160 (May, Sept. 1897).   35
——. "Hampstead-Heath, Public Park." Builder 2:417.
——. "Hyde Park Corner, The Proposed Improvements at." Builder 42:479.
——. "Municipal Parks, Gardens and Open Spaces of London, their History and Associations." Sexby, J. J. London, Elliot Stock, 1898. 8vo, 646 pp. Cl. $8.40.   36
——. "Note Book for 1899, giving particulars of Parks, Gardens and Open Spaces under the Control of the Council." 7d. L. C. C. Doc. 442. (See also L. C. C. Doc. 408 (1899, 5d.) on Open Spaces.)   37
——. "Peabody Square, Blackfriars-Road." Builder 30:26.
——. "Playgrounds, London." Holland, B. Macmil. 46:321 (1882); Oliver, E. Charing Cross M. May, 1900.   38
——. "Preservation of Commons in the neighborhood of the Metropolis." (London.) Hunter, Robert. Ch. V, p. 305 "Six Essays on Commons Preservation." London, Sampson, Low, Son & M., 1867. 432 pp.   39
——. "Report from the Select Committee on the Public Parks and Works Bill." Parliamentary Reports and Documents, 1887. 20 pp.   40
"Paving Trials of a New Wood in London." Surveyor 18:42 (July 13, 1900).   41
——. "Wood Pavements in London." Stayton, Geo. H. San. Eng. Aug. 20, 1887. Engng. News Nov. 22, 1884. Proceedings of the Institution of Civil Engineers Vol. 78.   42
"People's Palace, The." Besant, W. Contemp. 51:226 (1887), No. Am. 147:56 (1888), Unita. R. 34:338 (1890), Sat. R. 64:518 (1887); Bisland, Eliz. Cosmopol. 10:259 (1891); Curry, E. H. 19th Cent. 27:344 (1890); Gregory, R. A. Nature 50:144 (1894).   43
——. "A Municipal Pleasure Palace." Mun. J. 9:181 (March 9, 1900).
——. "People's Palaces and Polytechnics of London." Shaw, Albert. Cent. 40:163 (1890).   44
Police of London. Fletcher, J. J. Statis. Soc. 13:221 (1850); Meason, M. L. Macmil. 46:192 (1882); Shand, A. J. Blackw. 140:594 (1886); Warren, C. Munsey's Mag. 4:577 (1888).   45
——. "County Council and the Police of London." Evans, N. Contemp. 55:445 (1889).   46
——. "London Prisons." Argosy 55:156 (1893).
——. "Treatise on the police of the metropolis explaining the various crimes which at present are felt as a pressure upon the community and the means for their prevention." (By a magistrate.) London, 1st ed., 1796, 2d ed. enlarged and with chapter on the poor, 1801. 8vo.   47
Poor in London, Poor Law, etc. (See under Charities, Housing above.)
Poplar. (See under Lighting above.)
Population. (See under Census above.)
"Program, The London." Webb, S. London, Swan, S. & Co., 1894. 218 pp. $1. Article same subject, Whitmore, C. A. National May, 1893.   48
"Prostitution in London and other Large Cities." Acton, William. London, John

London—*Continued.*
Churchill & Sons, 1870. 302 pp. 12s. 49
———. "La Prostitution à Paris et à Londres, 1789-1877." Le Cour, C. J. Paris, Asselin et Cie., 3d edit., 1878. 416 pp. 5 fr. 50
"Public Improvements of London, How Carried Out." Statham, H. H. Fortn. 38:808 (1882). 51
———. "Public Works in London." Lefevre, G. S. 19th Cent. 12:667 (1882). 52
———. "Lambeth, Municipal Work at." Mun. J. 9:397 (May 25, 1900).
Rowton Lodging Houses. (See under Housing above.)
St. Marylebone. (See under Baths.)
St. Pancras. (See under Baths.)
Sanitation. "Annotated Model By-laws of the Local Government Board with respect to the Cleansing of Privies, Nuisances, Common Lodging Houses, New Streets and Buildings and Slaughter Houses." London, Knight & Co., 1890. 242 pp. 10s. 6d. 53
———. "By-laws as to the Drainage of Buildings, London." Builder 76:317 (April 1, 1899).
———. "Degeneration among Londoners." Cantlie, J. London, Field & T., 1885. 12mo. 1s. 54
———. "East End Sanitary Emporium, An." San. Rec. 20:8 (July 2, 1897).
———. "Etudes administratives et judiciaire sur Londres et l'Angleterre, précédé d'une étude comparative sur l'organisation sanitaire et la santé publique à Londres, Bruxelles et Paris." Bugnottet, G. et A. Noirpoudre de Sauvigney. Besancon, Pedone-Lauriel, 1889. 10 fr. 55
———. "Health of the City of London, The." Sanders, Sedgwick. San. Rec. 26:381 (Nov. 2, 1900). 56
———. "Health of London Menaced by the River Brent." London 6:677 (Aug. 12, 1897). 57
———. "Healthy London." London 7:22 (Jan. 13, 1898).
———. "Law Relating to the Public Health of London." Roberts, J. and Gollan. London, Butterworth, 1891. 14s. 58
———. "London, Ancient and Modern, from the sanitary and medical point of view." Poore, Geo. Vivian. London, Cassell & Co., 1889. 8vo, 128 pp. 5s. 59
———. "London, Health Report for 1898." San. Rec. 25:65 (Jan. 26, 1900). 60
———. "Sanitary Conveniences, New Piccadilly Circus." Builder 57:103.
———. "Sanitary Ramblings, being sketches and illustrations of Bethnal Green." (Housing Conditions in London of half a century ago.) Gavin, Hector. London, Churchill, 1848. 8vo. 4s. 6d. 61
———. "Sanitation and Reconstruction of Central London." Woodward, Wm. p. 29 Westgarth's "Reconstruction of Central London." 62
Schools. "City of London School." Allpress, R. H. Public School Magazine Oct. 1898. 63
———. "Design of the Public Schools of London." Engng. Rec. 40:178 (July 22, 1899).
———. "Educational Authorities in London." Ch. VII, p. 221 Frederick Whelen's "London Government." London, Grant Richards, 1898. 8vo, 291 pp. 3s. 6d. 64
———. "Election, The London School Board." Outlook 57:895 (Dec. 11, 1897); Educa. R. (London.) Jan. 1898. 65
———. "Feeding the Children." Mun. J. & London 8:1193 (Nov. 3, 1899).
———. "Free Evening Schools for London." London 7:569 (Sept. 8, 1898). 66
———. "Guildhall School of Music Extension." London 6:621 (July 22, 1897).
———. "Industrial Schools, L. C. C." Mun. J. 9:562 (July 20, 1900).
———. "London Progressives versus London Education." Diggle, J. R. National 24:307 (1894). 67
———. "London School Board." Diggle, Joseph R., and Headlam, Stewart D. Tomorrow Nov. 1897. 63
———. "London School Board and the Science and Art Department." School Board Gazette April, 1899.
———. "Northern Polytechnic, A New Educational Center for North London." London 6:597 (July 15, 1897).
———. "Northampton Polytechnic Institute." London 6:658 (Aug. 5, 1897).

London—*Continued.*

——. " Popular Education in London." London 7:576 (Sept. 8, 1898).

——. " Report by H. Llewellyn Smith, M. A., B. Sc., being an Inquiry into the needs of London with regard to Technical Education, the existing provision for such education, and the best means to be taken by the London County Council for improving that provision under the Technical Instruction Acts." Maps. L. C. C. Doc. 57, 1892. 5s. 4d. 69

——. " Studies in Board Schools." London 7:533 (Aug. 18, 1898). 70

——. " Technical Education in London." City Rec. 1:330 (May 26, 1898).

——. " Technical Schools, Shoreditch Municipal." London 7:203 (March 31, 1898).

——. " The Work of the London School Board." (Pt. I Historical, Pts. II and III The Foundations and Curriculum, with chapters on statistics, school buildings, school management, curriculum, teaching staff, books and apparatus, evenschools, compulsion, industrial schools, finance, day schools, training of teachers, special subjects of instruction, abnormal and defective children, evening schools.) Spalding, Thomas Alfred and others. London, Presented at the Paris Universal Exhibition, 1900. P. S. King & Son. 6 plans, 13 diagrams. 4to, 276 pp. Paper, 5s. 71

——. " Work of the School Board." Macnamara, T. J. Educa. R. June, 1896. 72

——. " Workers' School Board Program." London, Fabian Society, 1894. Fabian Tract No. 55. 19 pp. 1d.

Settlements. "Bethnal Green, Women's Settlements in." Mace, [Mrs.] Good Words 36:613 (1895). 73

——. " Bethnal Green. "The Work of a Ladies' Settlement." (St. Margaret's Women's Settlement.) Portal, Ethel M. p. 368 "Good Citizenship," edited by J. E. Hand. London, Geo. Allen, 1899. 474 pp. 74

——. " Central London, New Social Settlement for." London 6:803 (Oct. 7, 1897).

——. Educational "Settlements" of London. Davidof, L. Mir Bozhi Jan. 1900. 75

——. Mansfield House. Alden, Percy. Outlook 56:420 (June 12, 1897); Cullings, T. C. Leisure Hour 44:600, 796 (1895); King, Joseph. Andover R. Dec. 1892. 76

——. Oxford House. Anson, W. R. Econ. R. 3:10 (1893); Arnold, F. Leisure Hour 37:274 (1888); Booth, Charles. p. 122, Vol. I, "Life and Labor of the People." 77

——. " Passmore Edwards House." (Formerly University Hall, see below); Commons Vol. 2, No. 12, p. 3 (April, 1898). 78

——. " Passmore Edwards Settlement, Architecture of." Morris, G. Le. and Wood, Esther. Studio 16:11 (Feb. 1899). 79

——. " Robert Browning Hall." (Walworth.) Campbell, M. James. Commons (May, 1896); anon. London 6:589 (July 8, 1897). 80

——. " Toynbee Hall." (London.) Adams, H. B. Char. R. 1:12 Arnold, F. Leisure Hour 37:274 (April, 1888); Bailey, Cyril. Economist R. 6:88 (Jan. 1895); Barnett, S. A. 19th Cent. 38:1015 (Dec. 1895); Eclectic M. 126 183; Booth, Charles. p. 122, Vol. I, " Life and Labor of the People; Dana, M. McG. Gunton's M. 10:40 (May, 1896); Nunn, T. H. Econ. R. Oct. 1892; Potter, Henry C. Critic Sept. 17, 1887. 81

——. " Toynbee Hall." Smart, William. Glasgow, Jas. Maclehose & Sons, 6d. 82

——. " Un Settlement Anglais: Notes sur Toynbee Hall." Circulaire No. 12, Musée Social, 5 Rue des Cases, Paris. Aug. 3, 1897. 83

——. " Work for University Men in East London." Pabb & Tyler, Cambridge, Eng. 6d. 84

——. " University Hall, Opening Address at." Ward, [Mrs.] Humphrey. London, Macmillan, 1891. 45 pp. 30 cts. 85

——. " The Future of University Hall." Ward, [Mrs.] Humphrey. London, Smith, Elder & Co., 1891. 86

——. " Whitechapel, The Universities' Settlement in." Nunn, T. H. Econ. R. 2:478 (1892). 87

Sewerage and Sewage Disposal of London, General articles on. Fletcher, J. J. Statis. Soc. 7:143 (1844); Galton, Douglas. Van. Nos. Eng. M. April, 1885, San. Eng. March 26, 1885; Rawlinson, R. J. Soc. Arts 38:66, 142 (1890); Scott, H. Y. D. J. Soc. Arts 28:19 (1880); Worth, John Edward, and Crimp, William Santo. Engng. Rec. 40:17 (June 3, 1899). Also in U. S. Spl. Consular Reports, p. 129 (1897); anon. Engng. Rec. 38:275 (Aug. 27, 1898); Eng. (Lond.) 88:464 (Nov. 10, 1899); Mun. J. 8:1227 (Nov. 10, 1899). 88

London—*Continued.*

——. " Bacterial Treatment of London Sewage." Clowes, Frank. Surveyor 17:320 (March 23, 1900), City Govt. 8:102 (April, 1900), J. San. Inst. 21:308 (July, 1900), J. Soc. Arts 49:45 (Dec. 14, 1900), San. Rec. 26:542 (Dec. 21, 1900).   89

——. " Bacterial Treatment of Crude Sewage at Crossness." Eng. (London) 88:389 (Oct. 20, 1899); Engng. Rec. 40:507 (Oct. 28, 1899).

——. " Bacterial Purification of Sewage, The London County Council and." San. Rec. 22:365 (Oct. 7, 1898).

——. " Commission of Sewers, The City." The Local Government Journal 27:25 (Jan. 8, 1898); London 7:12 (Jan. 6, 1898).

——. " Filtration of Crude Sewage. Reports by the Chemist, F. Clowes, on the Bacteriological Examination of London Crude Sewage as it is delivered at the Barking and Crossness Outfall Works." Plates. 7d. and 2s. 4d. L. C. C. Docs. 388 and 436 (1897, 1900).   90

——. " Filtration of Crude Sewage through Coke at London, England, Experiments on the." Engng. News 42:299 (Nov. 9, 1899).

——. " Report of the Royal Commission on Metropolitan Sewage Discharge." Parliamentary Reports and Documents, 1884. 250 pp.   91

——. " Report of Sir B. Baker and the Chief Engineer on the Main Drainage of London." Maps. L. C. C., 3, 1891. 1s. 7d.   92

——. " Sludge Deposits on the Experimental Coke Beds, London, England, Report on Sewage." Engng. N. 43:157 (March 8, 1900).   93

Shoreditch. (See under Housing, Garbage, Labor, Lighting, Schools above.)

Slaughter Houses. (See Abattoirs above.)

Slums. (See under Housing above.)

" Social awakening in London." Woods, R. A. Scrib. M. 11:401 (1892).   94

" South London of To-day." Besant, Walter. Pall Mall 16:403 (Nov. 1898).   95

Statistics. "London Statistics." Vol. VI, 1895-96, Statistics printed by the London County Council during 1895-96, with Analysis of Statistics relating to London, printed in the Annual Reports of Vestries and Boards, for the year 1894-95, and in Parliamentary Papers of the year 1895. Diagrams and Maps. 5s. 9d. L. C. C. Doc. 325. Same for 1896-7 (L. C. C. Doc. 378) and 1897-8 (L. C. C. Doc. 432). 5s. 9d. each.   96

——. " Statistical Abstract for London, 1897." L. C. C. Vol. I. 12mo, 76 pp. 1s.   97

——. " Statistical Abstract for London." Vol. II, 1898, L. C. C. Doc. 427. 1s. 1½d. (Issued annually.)

" Streets, London." Blair, W. Nisbet. Mun. J. 9:256 (March 30, 1900).   98

——. " Characteristics of Some Great London Thoroughfares." Architect (London.) Jan. 1, 1897.

Street Cleaning. "Cleansing of London." Gordon, W. J. Leisure Hour 38:601 (1889).   99

Street Improvements. "A Comprehensive Scheme for Street Improvements in London." Cawston, Arthur. London, Stanford, 1893. 136 pp. ill. pls. maps. 4to. 21s.   100

——. " The Condition of London Streets." Surveyor 17:207 (Feb. 23, 1900).

——. " Le Développement de Londres." Pasquet, D. Annales de Géographie 8:22 (Jan. 15, 1899).   1

——. " Financial Loss Caused by Narrow Streets." Engng. Rec. 40:617 (Dec. 2, 1899).

——. " Great London Improvement, The." Mun. J. & London 8:1355 (Dec. 22, 1899).

——. " History of London Street Improvements 1855-1897." Edwards, Percy J. 8vo, 307 pp, index. Cl. 2 large Maps, 35 Plans. 18s. 1d. L. C. C. Doc. 380.   2

——. " Insanitary Conditions of London Streets." Blair, W. Nisbet. J. San. Inst. 21:289 (July, 1900).   3

——. " London Street Improvements." Lefevre, G. Shaw. Contemp. 75:203 (Feb. 1899).   4

——. " Shaping the New London." Mun. J. & London 8:1127 (Oct. 13, 1899).

——. " Special Report from the Select Committee on the Streets of London." Parliamentary Reports and Documents, 1890. 13 pp.   5

——. " The Street Makers of London." Wade, G. A. Ludgate Feb. 1900.   6

——. " Street Realignment and Reconstruction in Central London." Bridgman,

London—*Continued.*

Henry H. Essay p. 151, Westgarth's "Reconstruction of Central London." 7
——. "Street Regulations, London." Surveyor 18:541 (Nov. 9, 1900).
——. "Traffic, London Street." Barry, John Wolfe. Engng. 68:636 (Nov. 17, 1899). 8
——. "Two Big Street Improvements." London 6:675 (Aug. 12, 1897). 9
——. "Westminster Improvement Scheme." Warren, E. P. Fortn. No. 375, p. 479 (March, 1898). 10
——. "Widening the Strand." Mun. J. & London 8:1291 (Dec. 1, 1899).
Street Railways. (See under Transit Facilities below.)
"Sweating." Booth, Charles. Chapter X, Vol. IV, p. 328, "Life and Labor of the People." 11
Taxation. (See under Finance above.)
Technical Education. (See under Schools.)
"Telephones, London and." London 7:385 (June 16, 1898).
——. "Municipal Telephones." Mun. Rec. & Ad. 2:617 (June 15, 1898), 2:672 (July 15, 1898); London 7:529 (Aug. 18, 1898). 12
Tenement Houses, London. (See under Housing above.)
Thames, The. "The Conservation of the Thames." Eng. (Lond.) 89:556 (June 1, 1900).
——. "Deepening the Thames." Arch. (Lond.) Nov. 6, 1896.
——. "Report by the Chief Engineer on the flow of the Thames, with tables, etc." 1892. 3s. 8d. L. C. C. Doc. 58. 13
——. "The Thames Tunnel." English Illustrated M. Jan. 1897.
——. "The Thames from Wapping to Blackwall." Besant, Sir Walter. Cent. 60:746 (Sept. 1900). 14
"Theatre in London, The." Walkley, Arthur B. Cosmopolis 11:66 (July, 1898). 15
Transit Facilities. "Blackwall Tunnel, London, The." Sci. Am. 82:217 (April 7, 1900). 16
——. "Cable Traction in London." (Editorial.) Ry. World 7:258 (Aug. 4, 1898). (See also under Electric Traction below.) 17
——. Central London Railway. (See under Underground Railways below.)
——. "Congestion of London Street Traffic." Barry, Sir J. Wolfe. Ty. & Ry. World 8:487 (Dec. 7, 1899). 18
——. County Council Tramways, London. Ry. World 7:186, 414 (June 2, Dec. 8, 1898); Mun. J. 8:3, 881 (Jan. 5, Aug. 4, 1899); Ty. & Ry. W. 8:456 (Nov. 2, 1899), 9:566 (Nov. 8, 1900). 19
——. "County Council, The Tramway Policy of the London." Ady, Clarence E. Ty. & Ry. World 8:493 (Dec. 7, 1899); Monkswill, Lord. New R. 5:491 (1891); anon. Ty. & Ry. World 9:200, 253 (May 10, June 7, 1900). 20
——. "County Council and Tramway Traction." Baker, Allen. London 7:665 (Oct. 20, 1898). 21
——. "County Council, Mechanical Traction on Tramways of the London." Kennedy, Alexander B. W. Ty. & Ry. World 8:361 (Sept. 7, 1899). 22
——. "County Council, London Tramway Company v. The London." Ry. World 7:147 (May 5, 1898). 23
——. "Electric and Cable Railways, Report from the Joint Select Committee of the House of Lords and House of Commons on." Parliamentary Reports and Documents, 1892. 158 pp. 24
——. "Electric Tramway Service, London." Mun. J. 9:229 (March 23, 1900).
——. "Electric Tramway Schemes for London, New." Elec. R. (Lond.) 47:168 (Aug. 3, 1900). 25
——. "Electric Tramways for London, Overhead." Robinson, J. Clifton. Ty. & Ry. World 9:278 (July 5, 1900). 26
——. "Future of London Railways, The." Millin, G. F. Contemp. R. 78:103 (July, 1900); anon. Mun. J. 8:833 (July 21, 1899). 27
——. Legislation. "Tramway Legislation in London; and Tramways belonging to Local Authorities." Hopkins, A. Bassett, Chairman of the Highways Committee, 1891. 89 pp. 1s. 7½d. L. C. C. Doc. 45. 28
——. "Light Railways, London." Mun. J. & London 8:1116 (Oct. 13, 1899).

London—*Continued.*

——. " Locomotion in London." Barry, John Wolfe. London 7:750 (Nov. 24, 1898). 29

——. " Locomotion in 1837, London." Paley, W. B. Gentleman's M. 283:247 (Sept. 1897). 30

——. " London Tramways Company, The." Ry. World 8:34 (Jan. 5, 1899).

——. " Omnibuses, London." Robertson, W. B. Cassell's No. 458, p. 576 (Nov. 1900). 31

——. " Omnibus Service, Legality of Municipal." Ty. & Ry. World 9:154 (April 5, 1900). 32

——. " Public Property, Street Railways of London as." Sat. R. 72:467, 497 (1891). 33

——. " Purchase of the London Tramways." Ry. World 7:260 (Aug. 4, 1898). 34

——. " Rapid Transit in London." Quarterly Review 175:476 (1892).

——. " Rapid Transit in London." p. 7 "Rapid Transit in Foreign Cities," Parsons, W. B. New York, 1894. 35

——. " Rapid Transit in London, and Otherwise." Tilden, James A. J. Assoc. Engng. Soc. March, 1891, p. 124. 36

——. " Return of services and routes by Tramways, Omnibuses, Steamboats, Railways and Canals, in the County of London and in extra-London, together with an examination in detail of the present system of locomotive service and of the requirements to meet the needs of London." Gomme, G. L. London, Documents of the London County Council, No. 250, 1895. 199 pp. maps, diagrams. 5s. 2d. 37

——. "Steamship Service in London: Tramways." Halstead, Harshal. Cons. Rep. 64:336 (Nov. 1900). 38

——. " Traffic Problems, London." London 7:206 (March 31, 1898).

——. Tramways, General Articles on. London 6:996 (Dec. 23, 1897); Engng. (London) 66:198 (Aug. 12, 1898); Ann. Am. Acad. Pol. Sci. 13:277 (March, 1899); Mun. J. 9:226 (March 23, 1900); Ty. & Ry. World 9:141, 408, 614 (April 5, Dec. 6, 1900). 39

——. " Transit in London, Means of." Ty. & Ry. World 8:455 (Nov. 2, 1899). 40

——. Transportation. "Circulation et Locomotion a Londres." Artibal, J. R. Municipale 3:1787 (Dec. 23, 1899). 41

——. Underground Railways in London, General articles on. Bellet, D. Rev. Sci. Dec. 10, 1898; Cooper, Frederick E. Engng. M. 15:928 (Sept. 1898); Halstead, Marshal. Cons. Rept. 64:211 (Oct. 1900); Mitton, G. E. and Klickman, Wilfred. Windsor Mag. Nov. 1897; Pennell, Elizabeth Robbins. Harper 92:278 (1896); Wintle, W. J. Harmsworth Mag. 3:113 (Sept. 1899); anon. Railroad Gaz. 30:77, 134, 476, 342 (Feb. 4,-May 25, 1900); Le Génie Civil June 25, 1898; Strand M. 16:138 (Aug. 1898); Ty. & Ry. W. 9:589 (Dec. 6, 1900); Mun. J. 9:959 (Dec. 7, 1900); Ty. & Ry. World 9:80 (Feb. 8, 1900), 9:227 (June 7, 1900). 42

——. Berlin, Underground Railways in London and." Silberstein, L. Die Zeit March 26, 1898. 43

——. Central London Railway, The. Grinling, C. H. Railroad Gaz. Nov. 20, 1896; Hall, Henry W. Elec. Rev. 33:264 (Oct. 26, 1898); Knowles, A. J. Cassell's 30:131 (July, 1900); Scott, W. J. Ry. M. Oct. 1900; Twelvetrees, W. N. Feilden's M. Oct. Dec. 1900; anon. St. Ry. J. 13:423 (July, 1897), 14:141 (March, 1898), 16:667 (July 14, 1900); St. Ry. Rev. 7:478 (July 15, 1897); Elec. World 30:12 (July 3, 1897); Engng. News 38:15 (July 1, 1897), 39:367 (June 9, 1898), 44:74 (Aug. 2, 1900); Elec. Rev. 31:2 (July 7, 1897); Elec. Eng. 23:733 (June 30, 1897); Ry. World 7:67 (March, 1898); Mun. Rec. & Ad. 3:874 (Nov. 15, 1898); Mun. J. 9:101 (Feb. 9, 1900); Feilden's M. March, 1900; Engng. 69:857 (June 29, 1900); Builder 78:634 (June 30, 1900); Elec. W. & E. 36:85, 121, 164 (July 21, Aug. 4, 1900); Engng. Rec. 42:109 (Aug. 4, 1900); Railroad Gaz. 32:481 (July 13, 1900); Sci. Am. 83:40 (July 21, 1900); Ty. & Ry. W. 9:531 (Nov. 8, 1900). 44

——. City and South London Railway. Holmes, G. J. J. of Finance Dec. 1897; anon. Elec. R. (Lond.) Sept. 7, 1900. 45

——. " Comparison of the different systems of underground railways in London." Van Nos. Eng. M. 1:337 (1869). 46

——. " Construction, Methods of: Underground Electric Railway, London." Sci. Am. 83:89 (Aug. 11, 1900). 47

——. " Die Londoner Untergrundbahnen." Troske, L. Berlin, Springer, 1892. 10m. 48

London—*Continued.*

——. " Greathead Electric Underground Railway." Sterne, Simon. Forum 11:683 (1891).   49

——. " London and Southwark Subway." Greathead, J. H. Engng. News Nov. 5, 1887.   50

——. " Metropolitan Underground Railway, London." Baker, B. B. and J. W. Barry. Proceedings of the Institution of Civil Engineers, vol. 81, 1885. 74 pp.   51

——. " Ventilation for London Underground Railways, Mechanical Tunnel." Engng. News 39:237 (April 14, 1898).   52

——. " United Tramways Co., London." Ry. World 8:213 (June 8, 1899); St. Ry. R. 9:596 (Sept. 15, 1899); St. Ry. J. 15:584 (Sept. 1899).   53

——. " Underground Conduit System for London United Tramways." Ty. & Ry. World 8:379 (Oct. 5, 1899).   54

——. " Waterloo and City Railway." Ty. & Ry. World 8:485 (Dec. 7, 1899).   55

——. " Waterloo and City Railway, New Rolling Stock for the." Ty. & Ry. World 9:129 (April 5, 1900).

——. " West Ham, Tramways at." Mun. J. & London 8:1081 (Sept. 29, 1899).

——. Workmen's Trains. "Reports giving results of inquiries instituted by the Council with reference to the service of the Workmen's Trains provided by the thirteen Railway Companies having termini in the Metropolis." 1893. 6½d. L. C. C. Doc. 89. (See also L. C. C. Docs. 365 (1897, 6d.) and 366 (1897, 6d.), same subject.)   56

" Unemployed in London." Toynbee, H. V. Macmil. 69:54 (1893).   57

Unification of London. (See Amalgamation under General References above.)

Vestries. (See under General References above.)

Walworth. (See under Settlements above.)

Water Companies, Articles on, London. Costelloe, B. F. C. Contemp. 67:801 (1895); Dobbs, Archibald F. Contemp. 61:26 (1892); Lubbock, John. 19th Cent. 37:657 (1895); anon. Sat. Rev. 86:262 (Aug. 27, 1898); Mun. J. 7:565, 608, 704; 8:1190, 9:71 (Sept. 1, 1898, Jan. 26, 1900); Engng. Rec. 41:121 (Feb. 10, 1900).   58

——. " The Position of the London Water Companies considered from a Parliamentary and Legal Point of View. Report to the London County Council." Cripps, H. L. Maps, 8vo, 151 pp. L. C. C. Doc. 51, 1892. 5s. 3d.   59

——. Accounts. "London Water Supply, An Analysis of the accounts of the metropolitan water companies." Lass, Alfred. London, Walter King, Published annually, sixteenth year, 1895-96. 4to, 34 pp. 15s.   60

——. " East London Water Question." San. Rec. 22:309 (Sept. 23, 1898); Eng. (London) 86:207 (Aug. 26, 1898).   61

——. " East London Water Works Company." Nash, Vaughan. Cont. 74:474 (Oct. 1898).   62

——. " Hydrography of the Wealden: A Possible Solution of the London Water Question." Willoughby, Edward F. San. Rec. 23:203 (March 10, 1899), 23:228 (March 17, 1899).   63

——. Reservoir. "The Largest Reservoir in England." Mun. J. 9:240 (March 30, 1900).   64

——. " Sea Water to London, Supply of." Grierson, Frank W. Architect Jan. 31, 1896.   65

——. " Staines Reservoir Works." London 7:653 (Oct. 13, 1898).   66

——. " Thames, The Purification of the." Dibdin, Wm. Joseph. Jour. W. Soc. of Engs. Oct. 1897; anon. Engng. Rec. 40:53 (June 17, 1899).   67

——. " Typhoid, The London Water Supply and." Corfield, W. H. San. Rec. 24:503 (Dec. 8, 1899).   68

——. " Underground Source of Water Supply, London's." Fire & W. 26:27 (Jan. 28, 1899).

——. Water Supply of London, General articles on. Chabanne, J. B. R. Municipale 3:1612 (Oct. 7, 1899); Conder, F. R. Fraser 102:185 (1880); Dibdin, W. J. San. Rec. 20:192 (Aug. 20, 1897); Dickinson, W. H. Contemp. Feb. 1897, Engineering Feb. 19, 1897; Fletcher, J. J. Statis. Soc. 8:148 (1845); Frankland, Percy. J. Soc. of Arts (London) May 21, 1897, Jour. of Gas Lgt. (London) June 22, 1897; Hunter, Walter. J. Soc. Arts 47:475 (April 21, 1899); Lefevre, G. Shaw. 19th Cent. 44:980 (Dec. 1898); Lubbock, John. 19th Cent. 31:224 (1892); Maltbie, Milo Roy. Mun. Aff. 3:193 (June, 1899), Humanitarian 15:238 (Oct. 1899); Middleton, R. E. Public Health March, 1899, J. San. Inst. 20:201

London—*Continued.*

(July, 1899); Munro, John. Cassell's Family M. Jan. 1897; Shadwell, Arthur. 19th Cent. 45:282 (Feb. 1899); Souden, Fred T. Windsor Magazine June, 1898; anon. Sat. R. 73:356 (1892); Jour. Gas Lighting (London) Feb. 16, 1897; San. Rec. 19:504 (May 28, 1897); London 7:365 (June 9, 1898); J. Gas Light. Sept. 6, 1898; London 7:689 (Oct. 27, 1898); Spec. No. 3,671 p. 643 (Nov. 5, 1898); Eng. Jan. 6, 1899; London 7:836 (Dec. 29, 1898); Engng. 67:115 (Jan. 27, 1899); Mun. J. & London 8:1220 (Nov. 10, 1899); Builder 77:429 (Nov. 11, 1899); Eng. (London) 89:96 (Jan. 26, 1900); Spectator 84:131 (Jan. 27, 1900). 69

——. Water Supply, Reports on. L. C. C. Docs. 75 (6d.), 145 (1s. 7d.), 230 (4½d.), 254 (6d.), 256 (4s. 2d.), 263 (4½d.), 280 (2½d.), 306 (3s. 9d.), 317 (6d.), 338 (6d.), (1893-1899). 70

——. "Future Sources of London Water Supply." Conder, F. R. Fraser 94:45 (1876); Middleton, R. E. J. Gas Light. 76:1581 (Dec. 25, 1900); anon. Eng. 88:183 (Aug. 25, 1899). 71

——. "History and description of the London Waterworks." Bolton, F. London, Clowes, 1888. 14s. 72

——. "London Water Supply." Shadwell, A. London, Longmans, Green & Co., 1899. 8vo, 282 pp. Cl. 5s. 73

——. "London Water Supply: A Retrospect and a Survey." Sisley, R. 4to, 204 pl. Cl. 21s. 74

——. "London Water Supply, being a Compendium of the History, Law and Transactions relating to the Metropolitan Water Companies from the Earliest Times to the Present Day." (2d Edition.) Richards, H. C., Payne, W. H. C., and Soper, J. P. H. London, P. S. King & Son, 1899. 8vo, 310 pp. Cl. 6s. 75

——. "London Water Supply Commission." Anon. The Local Government Journal 27:192 (March 19, 1898); Builder 78:99 (Feb. 3, 1900). 76

——. "Report of the Royal Commission on the Metropolitan Water Supply." Parliamentary Reports and Documents, 1893. 555 pp. Minutes of Evidence taken before the Commission. 692 pp., maps and plans. 77

——. "Water Board for London, A." Mun. J. & London 9:69 (Jan. 26, 1900). 78

——. "Vesting the London Water Supply in a Public Trust." Engng. March, 20, 1896. 79

——. "Water Works of London." J. für Gas. u. Wasserversorgung April 20, 1895. 80

——. "Water Works of Europe: London and Liverpool." Philadelphia, Commercial Museum, 1899. 8vo, 50 pp. Pamphlet. 81

——. See also under Thames above.

"West Ham (Eng.), Its Growth and Government." London 6:573 (July 8, 1897). 82

——. "Socialism in West Ham." Billows, F. H. Econ. R. 10:52 (Jan. 1900); Legge, Hugh. Econ. R. 9:489 (Oct 16, 1899). 83

——. West Ham. (See also under Housing, Transit Facilities.)

West London. "Life in West London." Sherwell, Arthur. London, Mathuen, 2d ed., 1897. 12mo, 202 pp. Cl. 2s. 6d. 84

"Whitechapel, An Evening in." Chapin, Henry Dwight. Ind. 51:2018 (July 27, 1899). (See also under Charities, Settlements, above). 85

"Women's Club Movement in London, A." Amos, Sheldon. Am. Mo. R. of Rs. 16:440 (Oct. 1897). 86

"Women as Councillors." Fabian Tract No. 93. London, Fabian Society, 1900. 8vo, 4 pp. Pamphlet. 87

London, Ont.

"Sewerage of London, Ont." Ashbridge, W. T. Engng. Rec. 39:475 (April 22, 1899). 88

——. "The Construction of the Main Intercepting Sewers of the City of London, Ont." Tr. Can. Soc. Civ. Eng. 13:12 (1899). 89

"**Lorain, Ohio**, Bacterial Test of Mechanical Filters at." Engng. News 38:278, 281 (Oct. 28, 1897). 90

Los Angeles, Cal.

"Fire Alarm and Police Telegraph System, Los Angeles." Elec. W. & E. 35:251 (Feb. 17, 1900). 91

"Settlement in Adobe, A." Commons, May, 1897.

Los Angeles, Cal.—Continued.

"Sewer and Sewage Irrigation, Operation of the Los Angeles Outfall." Bassell, Burr. J. Assoc. Engng. Soc. 19:45 (Aug. 1897). 92

——. "Converting Portions of the Los Angeles Outfall Sewer into a Septic Tank." Engng. News 44:317 (Nov. 8, 1900). 93

Transit Facilities. "The System and Methods of the Los Angeles Railway Company." St. Ry. Jour. 14:303 (June, 1898). 95

"Water Supply Question, Los Angeles." Mun. Engng. 13:150 (Sept. 1897).

——. "Allowances for Depreciation in the Pipe System of the Los Angeles Water Works." Engng. News 41:283 (May 4, 1899).

——. "Public Purchase of the Los Angeles Water System." P. Ownership R. 2:50 (Aug.-Sept. 1898).

——. "The Los Angeles Water Works Case." Engng. Rec. 41:538 (June 9, 1900).

——. "The Water Controversy at Los Angeles." Cal. Mun. 1:99 (Nov. 1899).

"**Loughborough [Eng.]**, Corporation Water Works." Surveyor 17:292 (March 16, 1900). 96

Louisville, Ky.

"Charter in Kentucky, Louisville, The History of a Municipal." McDermott, Edw. J. Ann. Am. Acad. Pol. Sci. 7:63 (1896). 97

"History of Louisville, Ky." Rule, Lucien V. See 1-4c. 98

History, Description and Statistics of Louisville, Ky., in 1880. Census. See 1-7. 99

Lighting. "The Gas Fight in Louisville, Ky." Louisville, Kentucky, Heating Co., 1900. 8vo, 47 pp. Pamphlet. 100

"Municipal Condition of Louisville." Hartwell, Frank N. P. 391, Proc. Second Natl. Conf. for Good City Govt., 1895. See 6-18b. 1

"Park System, Louisville." Park and Cemetery 7:32 (April, 1897).

"Paving in Louisville, Ky., Cost of Asphalt Street." Engng. News 40:381 (Dec. 15, 1898). 2

Water Purification. "Lessons from the Louisville Experiments on Water Purification." (Editorial). Engng. News 11:296 (Nov. 10, 1898). 3

——. "Report on the Investigations into the Purification of the Ohio River Water at Louisville, Kentucky, made to the President and Directors of the Louisville Water Company." Fuller, George W. New York, D. Van Nostrand Co., 1898. 4to, 480 pp., ill., plates. Cloth, $10. 4

"**Low, Seth**, A Character Sketch." Cary, Edward. R. of Rs. 16:33 (July, 1897). 5

Lowell, Mass., History, Description and Statistics of, in 1880. Census. See 1-7. 6

Lübeck, Germany.

History. "Verfassungsgeschichte des Lübeckischen Freistaates, 1848-1898." Bruns, F. Lubeck, Lubcke & Hartmann, 1899. 8vo, 185 pp. Cl. 4m. 7

Lynn, Mass., History, Description and Statistics of, in 1880. Census. See 1-7. 8

Lyons, France.

Garbage Disposal. See 56-40b.

History. "L'Histoire d'une grande Ville en France." Beaune, Henri. Ref. Soc. 8:420 (Sept. 16, 1899). 9

Housing. "Les Petits Logements dans les grandes villes (et particulièrement dans la ville de Lyons.) Mangini, F. Lyons and Paris, 1891. 10

"Public Works in Lyons." Browne, Thos. N. U. S. Consular Reports 55:529 (Dec. 1897). 11

"Sewage Disposal." Hyde, Frank E. Cons. Rep. 47:220 (1895). See also 56-40b. 11a

Transit. "Electric Traction at Lyons, France." Elec. World 32:722 (Dec. 31, 1898). 12

Machine Politics. (See **Bossism, Elections, Party Politics**).

Madison, N. J.

"Electric Light and Water Plant of Madison, N. J., The Municipal." Am. Elec. June, 1899. 13

Madison, Wis.

"Sewage Disposal at Madison, Wis." Engng. Rec. 42:468 (Nov. 17, 1900). 14

———. "Chemical Precipitation and Rapid Filtration of Sewage at Madison, Wis." Engng. News 42:411 (Dec. 28, 1899). 15

———. "The Unsuccessful Sewage Purification Plant at Madison, Wis." Turneaure, F. E. Engng. News 44:253 (Oct. 11, 1900). 16

"Water Supply of the City of Madison, Wis., Artesian." Heim, John B. Pp. 41-54 "Proceedings of the Twentieth Annual Meeting of the American Water Works Association, Richmond, Va., May 15-18, 1900." 8vo, 216 pp. Cloth, $1. 17

———. "Artesian Water Supply of the City of Madison, Wis." Heim, John B. Fire & W. 28:10 (July 14, 1900), 28:18 (July 21, 1900). 18

———. "Use of Water in Madison, Wis." Engng. Rec. 37:490 (May 7, 1898). 19

Madras, India.

"Local Boards in the Madras Presidency." Vencataratnam, Ganjam. Madras Review, May, 1898. 20

"Tramways, The Madras Electric." Ty. & Ry. World 9:132 (April 5, 1900).

Madrid, Spain.

Administration. "Memoria sobre la administracion municipal de Paris y breves observaciones acerca de la de Madrid." Dicenta y Blanco, D. Jose. Madrid, 1879. 1 vol. 21

Improvement of Madrid. "Agrandissement de la Ville de Madrid." Nouv. Annales de la Const. p. 2, 1864. 22

———. "Grund-Idee des neuen Bebauungsplan für Madrid." Römer. Zeitschr. f. Bauw. p. 609, 1864. 23

Police Ordinances. "Ordenanzas de policia urbana y rural para la villa de Madrid y su término y constitucion de su Ayuntamiento del ano 1891." Barrero, E. M. Madrid, J. C. Garcia, 1891. 160 pp. 3 pes. 24

Sewerage. "Tercera memoria que contiene los trabajos hechos acerca del aprovechamiento de las aguas que discurren por las alcantarillas de Madrid." Justo y Villanueva, L. Madrid, 1877. 25

Thieves and Beggars of Madrid. "Robo o Ladrones de Madrid, Morfologia del." Lugilde y Huerta, M. 8vo. 2 pes. 26

Transit Facilities. "Electric Railways in Madrid and Barcelona." Armstrong, F. C. St. Ry. J. 15:75 (Feb. 1899). 27

———. "Madrid Electric Tramways." Ry. World 8:43 (Feb. 9, 1899).

Magdeburg, Germany.

Charity. "Armenstatistik in Magdeburg." Silbergeist, H. Magdeburg, Carl Friese, 1895. 28

"Commercial High School for Magdeburg." Moore, Thomas Ewing. Consular Reports 56:171 (Feb. 1898). 29

Water Supply. "Die Wasserversorgungsfrage der Stadt Magdeburg." Gesund. Ing. 20:193 (June 30, 1897). 30

"Maine, Town Government in." McDonald, W. Nation 60:197 (1895). 31

Mainz, Germany.

Building Laws. "Das Baurecht der Stadt Mainz." Wagner & Schafer. Mainz, H. Quasthoff, 1899. 8vo, 338 pp. 4 marks. 32

Improvement Schemes. "Stadterweiterung von Mainz." Deutsche Bauz. p. 484, 1879. 33

———. "Bemerkungen zu dem Gutachten des kgl. Baurath Hobrecht in Berlin über die Stadterweiterung von Mainz." Lippold, H. Mainz, 1873. 34

———. "Stadterweiterung von Mainz, Gutachten." Hobrecht. Mainz, Diemer, 1873. 8vo, 19 pp. 30 pf. 35

BIBLIOGRAPHY.

Manchester, Eng.
Government, General References and Unclassified.

"Manchester and Hamburg." (A Comparison). The Local Government Journal 27:46 (Jan. 15, 1898). — 36

"Manchester, A Short History." Saintsbury, George. New York, Longmans, Green & Co., 1887. 204 pp. $1.25. — 37

"Manchester's Municipal Activities." Chap. V, p. 145, "Municipal Government in Great Britain," by Albert Shaw. — 38

"Municipal Government of Birmingham, Manchester and Liverpool." Sharpless, Isaac. Haverford College Studies No. 11. — 39

"Manchester Municipality at Work." Dolman, F. New R. 11:499 (1894). (See also Chap. II in his "Municipalities at Work.") — 40

"The City of Manchester." Newland, F. W. Sunday at Home, Feb., March, April, 1900; Davies, E. A. Chaut. 28:531 (March, 1899). — 41

"Contracts Scandal, Manchester." Mun. J. 9:889 (Nov. 8, 1900). — 42

Garbage Disposal. See 56-40b.

History. "An Historical Account of Some Recent Enterprises of the Corporation of Manchester." Manchester, Blacklock, 1894. — 43

"Housing of the Poor Problem in Manchester, The." Niven, James. San. Rec. 24:444 (Nov. 17, 1899). — 44

——. "Housing Problem in the Provinces: The Manchester Experiments." Surveyor 18:88 (July 20, 1900). — 45

——. "Manchester's Record in Municipal Housing." Mun. J. & London 8:173 (Feb. 9, 1899).

Lighting. "Electric Lighting and Traction, Manchester, England." Elec. R. (London) Oct. 29, 1897. — 46

——. "Gas, Manchester Corporation's." Mun. J. & London 8:769 (June 30, 1899).

——. "Manchester Corporation Electric Works." (Technical Description). Wordingham, C. H. Practical Engineer (London) Jan. 22, 1897. — 47

——. "Manchester Corporation Gas Supply." J. Gas Light 76:1590 (Dec. 25, 1900).

——. "Profitable Municipal Lighting in Manchester." (Short statistical account.) London 6:624 (July 22, 1897). — 48

——. "Some Notes on the Comparative Cost of Supplying Light by Gas and Electricity in Manchester." Stevenson, G. E. J. Gas Lighting (London) Dec. 1, 1896; Gas Eng. M. April 10, 1897. — 49

Municipal Ownership. (See History, Housing, Lighting and Transit Facilities).

"Park System of Manchester, England, The." Park & Cem. 10:199 (Nov. 1900). — 50

Schools. "More about Manchester." (Art School.) Mun. J. 9:777 (Oct. 5, 1900). — 51

——. "Municipal Technical School, Manchester, Eng." Roscoe, H. E. Nature 47:201 (1892). — 52

Sewage Disposal at Manchester. Ansted, D. T. J. Soc. Arts 25:389 (1877); Olive, Wm. Thomas. Proceedings Institute Mechanical Engineers July, 1894; Grinnell, Wm. F. See 56-40a, 40b; anon, Eng. (London) Dec. 4, 1896, 88:511 (Nov. 24, 1899). — 53

——. "Technical Educations, Manchester." Mun. J. 9:757 (Sept. 28, 1900).

——. "Manchester, Sewage Disposal Problem." Surveyor 18:305 (Sept. 14, 1900). — 54

——. Sewage Disposal Problem at Manchester. Fuertes, James H. City Govt. 7:137 (Dec. 1899), Engng. Rec. 40:626 (Dec. 2, 1899), Engng. Rec. 41:594 (June 23, 1900), 41:613 (June 30, 1900). — 55

——. "The Disposal and Treatment of the Sewage of the City of Manchester. Report of Experts appointed by Rivers Committee of the Manchester Corporation." Dated Oct. 30, 1899. With 25 Photographs and Diagrams. London, P. S. King. Cl., 8vo. 6s. In continuation of the above. Report of the Rivers Committee, Jan. 22, 1900, with Appendices. Numerous Diagrams. London, P. S. King. 8vo. 3s. — 56

"Ship Canal, The Manchester." Dunell, George R. Engng. M. 2:204, 350 (1891); Corthell, Elmer L. J. W. Soc. of Engs., Feb. 1899. — 57

"Slums, Manchester's Insanitary." San. Rec. 19:420 (May 7, 1897). — 58

"Telephone Question, Manchester." Brocklehurst, F. Mun. J. 9:600 (Aug. 3, 1900). — 59

Manchester, Eng.—*Continued.*

Transit Facilities. "Manchester Corporation Tramways." Ty. & Ry. World 8:456 (Nov. 2, 1899).   60

——. "Manchester Tramways." London 7:716 (Nov. 10, 1898).

——. "Report of Special Committee re Tramways." Manchester Council, 1895. 31 pp. Maps.   61

——. "The Manchester Tramway System." Brocklehurst, F. Ty. & Ry. World 8:467 (Dec. 7, 1899).   62

——. "Tramways for Manchester." Mun. J. 9:465 (June 15, 1900).

"Water Power Scheme, The Manchester." Mun. J. & London 8:762 (June 30, 1899).   63

"Water Supply of Manchester, Eng., The." Fuertes, James H. Engng. Rec. 38:9 (June 4, 1898).   64

Manchester, Mass., History of the Town of." Lamson, D. F. Published by the Town, 1891.   65

Manchester, N. H., History, Description and Statistics of, in 1880. Census. See 1-7.   66

"**Manila,** Health of." (Editorial). Sanitarian 43:67 (July, 1899).   67

"**Mansfield, Ohio,** The Parks of." Park & Cem. 9:250 (Feb. 1900).   68

Marburg in Steiermark. Housing. "Die Arbeiter-Colonie bei der Werkstätte der Südbahn-Gesellschaft in Marburg in Steiermark." Flattich, W. Wein, Lehmann u. Wenzel, 1875. 24m.   69

Marion, Ia.

"Sewage Distributing Tank and Automatic dosing Apparatus for Marion, Iowa." Barbour, F. A. Engng. News 42:27 (July 13, 1899).   70

Markets.

See also Belgium, Leicester, London, New York, Paris.

"Lebensmittelversorgung von Grossstädten in Markthallen, Zeitfragen, volkswirthschaftliche." Eberty, E. Berlin, 1884. 2m.   71

"Market Play Grounds." Waring, Geo. E. Hrprs. Wkly. 39:1237 (1895).   72

"Markets of some Great Cities, Symposium on the." Boston, [Mrs.] Mary J. Lincoln; Baltimore, Agnes M. Lathe; Chicago, Antoinette Van Hoesen Wakeman and San Francisco, Mabel C. Craft. Chaut. Dec. 1896.   73

"Mitteilungen über Markthallen in Deutschland, England, Frankreich, Belgium u. Italien." Hennicke. Jul. Berlin, Ernst u. Korn, 1881. 30m.   74

Marseilles, France.

Sanitation. "Les Travaux d'Assainissement de Marseille, leur Utilité et leur Fonctionnement." Genis, M. Louis. Marseille, Borthelet et Cie., 1895. 69 pp. Plates. Pamphlet.   75

"Sewage Disposal." Thomas Claude M. Cons. Rep. 47:227 (1895).   76

——. "The Sewerage of Marseilles, France." Fuertes, James H. Engng. Rec. 36:427 (Oct. 16, 1897).   77

Martinique, W. I.

"Municipal Taxes in Martinique." Testart, A. Cons. Report 59:671 (April, 1899).   78

Maryland.

"Local Institutions of Maryland." Wilhelm, Lewis W. J. H. Univ. Studies III: 5, 6 and 7.   79

"Sweatshops in Maryland, Protection of Garment Workers in." Bulletin of the Department of Labor, July, 1896. p. 564.   80

Massachusetts.

"Caucus Laws of Massachusetts." Gay, Richard L. N. Y. Conference on Practical Reform of Primary Elections, p. 57. Chicago, Hollister, 1898. 8vo, 150 pp. Paper. 81

Charity. "The Settlement Laws of Massachusetts in their application to outside poor relief." (With judicial decisions and practical suggestions.) Shaw, Henry. Boston, Geo. H. Ellis, 1900. 8vo, 205 pp. 82

"City Government in Massachusetts." Allen, W. F. Nation 33:169 (1881); Parker, Francis J. Boston, Calkins & Co., 1881. 24 pp. 83

——. "A Massachusetts Shoe Town." Sanborn, Alvan S. Atlan. (Aug. 1897). 84

Finance, Municipal. Annual Reports of the Tax Commissioner contain considerable data.

Franchises, Taxation of. (See Taxation below.)

"Growth of Cities in Massachusetts." Wadlin, Horace G. Am. Statis. Assoc. 2:159 (1889). Separate pamphlet No. 13, $1. 85

"Highway Construction in Massachusetts." Whittle, C. L. Pop. Sci. M. May, 1897. 86

History. "Genesis of the Massachusetts Town and the Development of Town Meeting Government." Adams, Charles Francis, and others. Reprinted from proceedings of the Mass. Hist. Soc. Jan. 1892. 93 pp. 87

Home Rule. "Public Administration in Massachusetts, the relation of central to local activity." Whitten, Robert Harvey. Columbia Univ. Studies in Political Science, Vol. 8, No. 4, New York, 1898. 8vo, 167 pp. Paper $1. 88

"Library Movement in its Parent Commonwealth, The Public." Baxter, Sylvester. Am. R. of Rs. 20:324 (Sept. 1899). 89

——. "Massachusetts Library Commission." Nourse, Henry S. The Citizen 1:12 (1895). 90

Lighting. "Die Stellung der Privaten Beleuchtungs-gesellschaften zu Stadt und Staat. Die Erfahrung in Wien, Paris und Massachusetts." Gray, John Henry. Jena, Gustav Fischer, 1893. 167 pp. 91

——. "Gas Commission of Massachusetts." Gray, John H. Q. J. E. 14:509 (Aug. 1900), Prog. Age 18:546 (Dec. 15, 1900). 92

——. "Massachusetts Electric Lighting Plants." Commons, J. R. Am. Statis. Assoc. 5:87 (1896). 93

——. "Public Supervision in Massachusetts." (Gas and electric lighting.) Allen, Walter S. Mun. Aff. 4:526 (Sept. 1900). 94

——. "Report of the Board of Gas and Electric Light Commissioners of the Commonwealth of Massachusetts." (Issued annually.) 16th Report, Boston, 1900. 8vo, 186 and clxxv pp. 96

——. "The Bay State Gas Company." Prog. Age 18:467 (Nov. 1, 1900).

"Municipal Ownership in Massachusetts." Francisco, M. J. Am. Gas Light J. 70:643 (May 1, 1899), Elec. W. & E. 33:505 (April 22, 1899). 97

——. "Lighting Plants in Massachusetts, Municipal." Engng. Rec. 41:537 (June 9, 1900).

Sanitation. "Manual for the Use of Boards of Health of Massachusetts, containing the Statutes relating to the Public Health, the Medical Examiner Laws, the Laws relating to the Registration of Vital Statistics, and the Decisions of the Supreme Court of Massachusetts relating to the same." Prepared by direction of the State Board of Health, 1894. 8vo, 213 pp. 98

——. "Mortality in Twenty-three Massachusetts Cities." Burnap, Charles E. Am. Statis. Assoc. Vol. V, No. 34. 1896. 99

"Sewage Disposal in Massachusetts." Stearns, F. P. Trans. Am. Soc. Civil Engineers 18:1 (1888). 100

——. "Assessments, Sewer, in Boston," by Charles R. Cutter. J. Assoc. Engng. Soc. 18:38 (Jan. 1897); in Newton, Mass., by Henry D. Woods, same 18:47; in Malden, Mass., by George A. Wetherbee, same 18:51; in Marlboro, Mass., by James F. Bigelow, same 18:57; in Pawtucket, R. I., by George A. Carpenter, same 18:59; in Fall River, Mass., same 18:61; by Philip D. Borden. 1

——. "Massachusetts Experiments on the Purification of Fresh, Stale and Septic Sewage." Clark, H. W. Engng. News 40:75 (Aug. 4, 1898). 2

——. "Notes on Water Supply and Sewage Disposal in Massachusetts and Rhode Island." Engng. News 38:349 (Nov. 25, 1897).

——. "Purification of Sewage and Water. Experimental Investigations upon

Massachusetts—*Continued.*

Purification of Sewage, by Filtration and by Chemical Precipitation, and upon the Intermittent Filtration of Water." 10 pp.   3

——. "The Metropolitan Sewerage Systems of Massachusetts." Carson, Howard. Engng. News May 3, 1883, Jan. 25, Feb. 8, 1894. Technology Quarterly, Dec. 1893.   4

——. "The Septic Tank Experiments of the Massachusetts State Board of Health." Engng. Rec. 42:591 (Dec. 22, 1900).   5

"Sweating in Massachusetts." Wadlin, H. G. Am. J. Soc. Sci. 30:86 (1892).   6

"Taxation of Franchises in Massachusetts." Carret, James R. Mun. Aff. 4:506 (Sept. 1900).   7

Transit Facilities. "Report of Massachusetts Street Railways." St. Ry. R. 10:328 (June 15, 1900).

——. "Report to the Rapid Transit Commissioners of Massachusetts." Fitzgerald, John E. Boston, 1891. Appendix contains a detailed description of the Berlin City Railway.   8

——. Report of Special Committee on Street Railways. (See Transit Facilities under **Municipal Control.**)

——. "The Massachusetts Theory of Street Railway Rights and Privileges." (Reprinted from the New York Evening Post, Nov. 16, 1897.) Elec. Eng. 24:510 (Nov. 25, 1897).   10

"Unemployed, Massachusetts Investigation of the." Brooks, J. G. Econ. J. 4:361, 5:477 (1895), Closson, C. C. J. Pol. Econ. 3:488, 492 (1895).   11

Water Supplies. "Metropolitan Water Board." Ann. Am. Acad. Pol. Sci. 13:272 (March, 1899).   12

——. "Notes on Water Supply and Sewage Disposal in Massachusetts and Rhode Island." Engng. News 38:349 (Nov. 25, 1897).   13

——. "Purification of Sewage and Water. Experimental Investigations upon the Purification of Sewage, by Filtration and by Chemical Precipitation, and upon the Intermittent Filtration of Water." Massachusetts State Board of Health (with reports on Lawrence Experiments.) 1890. 8vo, 910 pp.   14

——. "Surface Water Supplies in Massachusetts." Haskell, John C. J. N. E. Water Works Assn. 13:79 (Dec. 1898).   15

——. "Water Supply and Sewage." Twenty-sixth Annual Report of the Massachusetts State Board of Health, 1895.   16

Mayor. (See under **United States,** and **Councils and Boards of Aldermen** for references on relative power of mayor and council in American cities.)

"Brooklyn Idea of City Government." Shepard, Edward M. Forum 16:38 (1893).   17

"City Government and Democracy." (Against concentration of power in hands of mayor.) Curley, E. A. Leslie's Wkly. 74:40, 126 (1892); Cosmopol. 14:737 (1893).   18

"Mayors of United States Municipalities." (Editorial.) M. & C. 4:12 (Sept. 1897).   19

"Municipal Cæsarism." (Concentration of power in hands of mayor.) Godkin, E. L. Nation 13:205 (1871).   20

"Office of Mayor in the United States." Greenlaw, Edwin A. Mun. Aff. 3:33 (March, 1899).   21

"Office of Mayor in the United States. A Study in Administrative Law." Bayles, G. J. Newark, M. Plum, printer, (doctor's dissertation), 1895. 8vo, 74 pp.   22

"Outgrown City Government." (Favors an autocratic mayor.) Parton, James. Forum 2:539 (1887).   23

"The Executive in the City." Bradford, Gamaliel. (Chapter XXXIII in "The Lesson of Popular Government.") New York, The Macmillan Co., 1899. 8vo, 2 vols. 520, 590 pp. Cl. $4.   24

"The Mayor and the City." Shepard, H. N. Atlan. 74:85 (1894).   25
"What a Mayor can do." Eustis, William Henry. City Govt. 1:3 (1896).   26
"What a Mayor should be." Nation 59:262 (1894).   27

"**Meat Inspection** in England, France and Germany." O'Neill, Henry. San. Rec. 26:540, 563 (Dec. 21, 28, 1900).   28

"**Medford [Mass.],** Municipal Practice in Sewer Construction." Barnes, T. Howard. Engng. Rec. 36:472 (Oct. 30, 1897).   29

BIBLIOGRAPHY.   153

"**Media [Pa.]**, The Water Works of." Ledoux, J. W. Engng. Rec.
40:618 (Dec. 2, 1899). — 30

Melbourne, Aus.
"Lessons from Municipal Melbourne." Mun. J. 9:7 (Jan. 5, 1900). — 31
"Melbourne: a City of the Empire." Dolman, Fred. Idler 15:15 (Feb. 1899). — 32
"Sewerage in the City of Melbourne, New." Sanitarian 38:232 (March, 1897). — 33
Transit Facilities. "The Great Street Railway System of Melbourne." King, F. W. N. St. Ry. R. 7:495 (Aug. 15, 1897). — 34
——. "The Melbourne Tramway Company." Ty. & Ry. World 8:457 (Nov. 2, 1899). — 35
"Water Supply, Melbourne." Engng. (London) 69:3 (Jan. 5, 1900). — 36

Memphis, Tenn.
History, description and statistics of Memphis, Tenn., in 1880. Census. See 1-7. — 37
"Municipal Condition of Memphis, Tenn." Malone, James H. p. 110 Proc. Third Natl. Conf. for Good City Govt., 1896. See 6-18c. — 38
"Sewerage of Memphis, The." Baldwin, W. C. Am. Arch. 11:245 (1882); Odell, F. S. Transactions Am. Soc. Civil Engineers 10:21 (1881); Waring, George E., Jr. London, office of the Sanitary Institute of Great Britain, 1881. 18 pp. — 39
——. "Sewers and Health—the Memphis Example." Sanitarian 43:227 (Sept. 1899). — 40

"**Mendota [Ill.]**, Sewage Disposal at." Engng. Rec. 41:493 (May 26, 1900).

Merseburg, Ger. Housing. "Aus zwei deutschen Kleinstädten, ein Beitrag zur Arbeiterwohnungsfrage." (Merseburg u. Weissenfels.) v. Mangold, Carl. Jena, Fischer, 1894. — 41

"**Merthyr Tydvil [Wales]**, The Water Works of." Engng. Rec. 41:224 (March 10, 1900). — 42

Meters. (See under **Lighting** and **Water Supply**.)
"Use of Meters for Public Utilities." Pray, W. L. City Govt. 6:1 (Jan. 1899). — 43

Mexico, City of.
"Drainage of the Valley and City of Mexico." Wright, Willis B. J. Assoc. Engng. Soc. 24:256 (April, 1900). — 44
——. "The Drainage of the City of Mexico." Engng. Rec. 4:265 (March 24, 1900). — 45
"Plaza, Alameda and Paseo in the City of Mexico." Park & Cew. 7:51, 93, 115 (May, June, July, 1897). — 46
Sanitation. "Assainissement de Mexico." R. Technique 21:397 (Sept. 10, 1900). — 47

Michigan.
"City Government of Michigan." (Principally Grand Rapids, Kalamazoo, Jackson, Saginaw and Detroit.) Ann Arbor, Studies in Finance and History, Michigan Univ., Vol. I, No. 6 (Dec. 1895). 25 cts. — 48
——. "Local Government in Michigan and the Northwest." Bemis, E. W. J. H. Univ. Studies 1:5 (1883). — 49
——. "Municipal Government in Michigan and Ohio. A Study of the Relations of City and Commonwealth." Wilcox, Delos F. New York, Macmillan, 1896. 184 pp. $1. — 50
Finance. "Valuation of Railway and Other Corporate Property in Michigan, Expert." Engng. N. 44:430 (Dec. 20, 1900). — 51
"Fire Departments of Cities and Villages, Number of Firemen, Wages and Privileges Allowed." pp. 133-153 of the "16th Annual Report of the Bureau of Labor and Industrial Statistics." Lansing, Bureau of Labor, 1899. — 52
Home Rule. "Local Self Government, so-called, as it is found in the Constitution of Michigan." Kirchner, Otto. Ann Arbor, Studies in Finance and History, Michigan Univ. Vol. I, No. 4 (April, 1899). 25 cts. — 53

Michigan—*Continued.*

"Municipal Ownership of Michigan Street Railways, The Prohibition of." Engng. Rec. 40:213 (Aug. 5, 1899). 54

"Paving in Michigan, Street." Engng. Rec. 40:625 (Dec. 2, 1899).

"Police Departments. Number employed, with Salaries and Wages Paid by Cities and Towns in the State." pp. 155-163 of the "16th Annual Report of the Bureau of Labor and Industrial Statistics." Lansing, Bureau of Labor, 1899. 55

"Public Expenditures and Permanent Improvements of 1898. Pay of City Laborers and Teams." pp. 187-200 of the "16th Annual Report of the Bureau of Labor and Industrial Statistics." Lansing, Bureau of Labor, 1899. 56

Sanitation. "Past and Present Movements for Sanitary Progress in Michigan." Baker, Henry B. Pamphlet, Reprint from Report of State Board of Health, 1893. 12 pp. 57

"Statistics of Chartered Cities and Incorporated Villages, Michigan." Published annually since 1898 in the Report of the Bureau of Labor and Industrial Statistics.

"Water and the Water Supply in Michigan." Hazlewood, Arthur. Pamphlet reprinted from the fourth annual report of the Michigan State Board of Health for 1876. 7 pp. 58

——. "Michigan Water Supplies." Williams, Gardner S. pp. 55-61 in "Proceedings of the Fourth General Conference of Health Officers in Michigan, 1899." 59

——. "Report on the Water Supply of Michigan." Kedzie, Robert C. Pamphlet reprinted from the Fourth Annual Report of the Mich. State Board of Health for 1876. 10 pp. 60

Milan, Italy.

Charity. "Sul Concentramento delle instituzióni di Beneficenza: memoria delle congregazione di carita di Milano al consiglio comunale." Milona, Tip. fr. Bietti et G. N., 1892. 35 pp. 61

City Government. "Nel Municipio di Milano." Vigoni, G. Nuova Ant. 36:722 (Oct. 16, 1899). 62

"Cremation at Milan." Edwards, H. S. Westm. 134:182 (1890). 63

Elections, Municipal. d'Arzago, A. de C. Rassegna Nazionale Nov. 1, 1899. 64

——. "Le Elezioni Amministrative a Milano." Cornaggia, C. O. Nuova Ant. 84:108 (Nov, 1, 1899). 65

Finances. "Le Finanze di Milano nel Inedio Evo: noto di conferenza." Mauri, Aug. Monza, Artigianelliorfani, 1898. 8vo, 27 pp. 66

"Municipal Ownership of Street Railways in Milan." St. Ry. Rev. 7:387 (300 w.) (June 15, 1897); St. Ry. J. 13:400 (July, 1897). 67

"Tramways in Milan." Jarvis, W. Cons. Rep. 61:135 (Sept. 1899). 68

"Working Class Settlements in Mülhouse and Milan." Hancock, C. Fortn. 62:94 (1894). 69

"**Milford, N. Y.,** A Small Water Purification Plant at." Engng. News 38:359 (Dec. 2, 1897). 70

Milk Supply, Municipal Control of the. (See under **Municipal Control, Municipal Ownership,** also under **Paris.**)

Milwaukee, Wis.

City Government, General Works, Unclassified.

"City of Milwaukee." Howard, William Willard. Hrprs. Wkly. 35:538 (1891). 71

History, description and statistics of Milwaukee, Wis., in 1880. Census. See 1-7. 72

"Milwaukee, the German City of America." Goes, Edmund. Chaut. 27:659 (Sept. 1898). 73

"Municipal Government of Milwaukee." Winkler, F. C. p. 119, Proc. Second Natl. Conf. for Good City Govt., 1895. See 6-18b. 74

Elections. "Draft of an Act to Prevent Corrupt Practices in General and Primary Elections." (With Argument.) Published by the Municipal League of Milwaukee, 1896. 16 pp. 75

"Library and Museum, Milwaukee's New." Hrprs. Wkly. 41:412 (April 24, 1897).

"Paving Report, Milwaukee." City Govt. 2:8 (Jan. 1897).

Milwaukee, Wis.—*Continued.*

"School System, The Milwaukee." Mowry, Duane. Ed. R. 20:141 (Sept. 1900). 76

——. "Duties of School Boards, School Superintendents and others in Cities of the First Class in the State of Wisconsin." Published by the Municipal League of Milwaukee, 1897. 10 pp. 77

"Sewage of Milwaukee." Benzenberg, Geo. H. Engng. Rec. Sept. 2, 1893, p. 219. (See also Engng. News Nov. 9 and 16, 1893). 78

Transit Facilities. "Decision in the Milwaukee 4-Cent Fare Case." Anon. St. Ry. Rev. 8:437 (July 15, 1898); Outlook 59:419 (June 18, 1898); St. Ry. J. 14:397 (July, 1898), 16:1122 (Nov. 10, 1900). 79

——. "Electric Railway System of Milwaukee and Eastern Wisconsin, The." St. Ry. J. 15:339 (June 1899). 80

——. "Electric Tramways, Milwaukee." Ty. & Ry. World 9:1 (Jan. 11, 1900).

——. "Street Railway Problem in Milwaukee." Butler, John A. Mun. Aff. 4:212 (March, 1900). 81

——. "Street Railway System of Milwaukee." St. Ry. Jour. Nov, 1892, p. 683. 82

"Water Rates in Milwaukee." (Editorial.) Engng. Rec. 38:177 (July 30, 1898), 39:90 (Dec. 31, 1898). 83

Minneapolis, Minn.

City Government, General References and Unclassified.

"Citizens' Law Enforcement League of Minneapolis." Speare, S. L. Our Day 9:315 (1892). 84

History, description and statistics of Minneapolis, Minn., in 1880. Census. See 1-7. 85

"Hudson's Dictionary of Minneapolis and Vicinity, a Handbook for strangers and residents." Minneapolis, Horace B. Hudson, fourth year, 1900. 124 pp. 86

"Minneapolis." In the article "Capitals in the Northwest." Ralph, Julian. Harper 84:576 (1892); Howard, William W. Hrprs. Wkly. 34:413 (1890). 87

"Municipal Government of Minneapolis." Simpson, D. F. p. 93 Proc. Second Natl. Conf. for Good City Govt., 1895. See 6-18b. 88

Liquor Problem. "Limiting Saloon Territory: The Minneapolis Plan." Cross, Judson N. Bib. Sacra. 57:405 (July, 1900). 89

——. "Minneapolis and the Saloons." Harwood, W. S. Outlook 63:206 (Sept. 23, 1899).) 90

"Park Systems of Minneapolis and St. Paul, The." Robbins, Mary C. Garden and F. 10:162 (April 28, 1897). 91

"Schools of Minneapolis, Public." Rice, J. M. Forum 15:362 (1893). 92

"Street Railway Tracks in Minneapolis and St. Paul, The Construction of." Engng. News 38:246 (Oct. 14, 1897). 93

"Water Works, New Reservoirs of the Minneapolis." Engng. Rec. 36:312 (Sept. 11, 1897).

——. "Water Waste at Minneapolis." McConnell, John H., and Moody, Frank T. City Govt. 6:116 (May, 1899). 94

Minnesota.

"Cities." pp. 64-83 in "Minnesota—State, County, Township and City." A Handbook of Information concerning the State, its Government, Officers and Resources." McVey, Frank L. Minneapolis, University Book Store, 1898. 12mo, 83 pp. 95

"Laws for Minnesota Cities, New." Ralph, Julian. Hrprs. Wkly. 39:829 (1895). 96

Minority Representation. (See **Proportional Representation.**)

Missions and Mission Philanthropy. (See **Charity.**)

"**Missouri**, Taxation in, A Treatise upon the Law and Practice of." Judson, Frederick N. Columbia, Mo., Stephens, 1900. 8vo, 258 pp. 97

"**Mobile, Ala.**, History of." Hamilton, Peter J. See 1-4c. 98

"**Moline, Ill.**, Garbage Collection and Disposal at." Kittilsen, Edward. Engng. News 43:90 (Feb. 8, 1900). 99

Monaco.

Transit Facilities. "Electric Tramways of Monaco." Ry. World 7:353 (Nov. 1898). 100
——. "Surface Contact Street Railroad at Monaco." Elec. Eng. 26:565 (Dec. 8, 1898).

Money in Politics. (See under **Elections.**)

Monopolies, Municipal. (See under **Municipal Control, Municipal Ownership.**)

"Montgomery, Ala., History of." Petrie, George. See 1-4c. 1

Montreal, Canada.

"Incomes, Wages and Rents in Montreal." Ames, Herbert Brown. Bulletin Dept. Labor No. 14, p. 39 (Jan. 1898). 2
"Municipal Reform in Montreal." Canadian M. 12:457 (March, 1899). 3
"Sewage Farm for the St. Denis Ward of Montreal, New." Engng. News 43:54 (Jan. 25, 1900).

Monts de Piete. (See under **Pawnshops.**)

Monuments, Public. (See **Art, Municipal.**)

Mortality and Vital Statistics of Cities. (See under **Statistics of Cities.**)

Moscow.

Sanitation for Fifteen Years, Moscow. Petrovsky, A. G. Russki Vyestnik Nov. 1900. 4
Transit Facilities. "Die elektrischen Linien der ersten Strassenbahn-Gesellschaft in Moskau." Krannbals, Erich. Elektrotech. Zeitschr. Feb. 8, 1900. 5
——. "Important Changes Proposed in the Tramways of Moscow." St. Ry. J. 16:470 (May 5, 1900). 6

"**Mount Vernon, N. Y.**, Sand Filtration at." Chester, John S. Fire & W. 23:2 (Jan. 1, 1898). 7

Mülhausen, Ger.

Housing. "Arbeiter-Kolonien in Mülhausen, Stuttgart u. Leinhausen." Schwering, L. Deutsche Bauz. p. 548, 1884. 8
——. "Cités Ouvrières de Mülhouse." Muller. Nouv. Annales de la Const. p. 79, 1856. 9
——. Die Arbeiterstadt zu Mülhausen im Elsass. Romberg's Zeitsch. f. pract. Bauk. p. 213, 1861; Zeitschr. d. Arch u. Ing.-Ver. zu Hannover, p. 463, 1863; Schall, M. Berlin, Kortkampf, 1876. 1m. 60 pf. 10
——. "Working Class Settlements in Mulhouse and Milan." Hancock, C. Fortn. 62:94 (1894). 11

Munich.

"Baths at Munich, The Müller Public." Engng. Rec. 39:259 (Feb. 19, 1899). 12
Burials. "Mortuary Chambers at Munich, Germany, The." Park & Cem. 8:50 (May, 1898).
Court Buildings in Munich, The New. Schweizerische Bauzeitung Jan. 22, 29, Feb. 5, 1898.
Housing. "Das Wohnungselend der Minderbemittelten in München. Nach den Ergebnissen der Statistischen Erhebungen der Katholischen organisierten Arbeiterschaft Münchens." Schirmer, Carl. 68 pp. 13
Lighting. "Experience with Street Lighting at Munich by Means of Incandescent Gas Lamps." Am. Gas Light J. 69:235 (Aug. 15, 1898). 14
——. "Die städtischen Elektricitätswerke Münchens." Elektroteknische Zeitschr. Jan. 7, 1897. 15
"Sewage Disposal." Steiner, Ralph. Cons. Rep. 47:229 (1895). 16
——. "Der gegenwärtige Standpunkt d. Städtereinigungsfrage u. die Einführung d. Schwemmkanalisations system in München." Braungart, R. Freising, Datterer, 1890. 8vo, 54 pp. 1m. 17

Munich—*Continued.*

——. "The Sewerage of Munich, Bavaria." Fuertes, James H. Engng. Rec. 37:8 (Dec. 4, 1897).   18

Streets. "Façaden für die neue Maximiliansstrasse in München." Gottgetreu, R. Zeitscher. f. Bauw. p. 313, 1855.   19

"Water Works of Munich, Germany, The." Fuertes, James H. Engng. Rec. 38:78 (June 25, 1898).   20

"**Municipal Buildings.**" Hare, H. T. Builder Jan. 18, 1896.   21

Municipal Control, Municipal Ownership.

See also under Austin (Tex.), Belgium, Birmingham (Eng.), Boston, Chicago, Columbus (O.), Concord (N. H.), Detroit, England under United Kingdom, Glasgow, Great Britain under United Kingdom, Halle, Hammersmith, Haverhill (Mass.), Illinois, Indianapolis, Iowa, Islington, Italy, Kansas, London, Massachusetts, Milwaukee, Nebraska, New York City, New York State, Omaha, Paris, Philadelphia, San Francisco (Cal.), Toledo, United Kingdom, United States, Utica, Wallingford (Conn.), Washington, West Ham.

To facilitate reference, the literature upon this subject has been arranged as follows:

General Works, pp. 157-164.
Lighting—General, pp. 164-5.
   —Electricity, pp. 165-6.
   —Gas, pp. 166-7.
Milk Supply, p. 167.
Telephones, p. 167
Transit Facilities, pp. 167-9.
Water Works, p. 169.

GENERAL WORKS.

"Accounting of Public Service Industries, The." Allen, Walter S. and Tooke, Charles W. Pp. 155-168 in "Proceedings of the Columbus Conference, 1899. See 6-18f.   22

——. "Accounting of Public Service Industries, The." Tooke, C. W. Other Side 1:307 (Dec. 30, 1899).   23

——. "Accounts of Grantees of municipal franchises." Allen, Walter S. Columbus Conference for Good City Govt.1899, p. 162. See 6-18f.   24

——. "The Bookkeeper of Public Service Industries." Tooke, C. W. Mun. Engng. 19:7 (July, 1900).   25

——. "Uniform Accounting and Municipal Ownership." Cahoon, J. B. St. Ry. R. 10:337 (June 15, 1900).   26

——. (See also under Profits below).

"Attitude of Municipal Corporations to the Public, The." Boyd, John G. Am. Gas Light J. 72:650 (April 23, 1900), St. Ry. J. 16:417 (April 28, 1900), City Govt. 8:118 (May, 1900), Prog. Age 18:212 (May 15, 1900), Public Policy 2:315 (May 19, 1900).   27

"Avarice of Municipalities, The." Raworth, John. Lightning 14:403 (Nov. 10, 1898); Discussed in Lightning 14:411 (Nov. 17, 1898), 14:435 (Nov. 24, 1898), 14:459 (Dec. 1, 1898).   28

"Business of a City, The." McGuire, James K. City Govt. 4:12 (Jan. 1898).   29

"Capitalization of Public Service Corporations, The." Ripley, William Z. Q. J. E. 15:106 (Nov. 1900).   30

"Combined Public Franchises, Practical Experience in the Operation of, by one Company." Uebelacker, C. F. St. Ry. J. 16:890 (Sept. 29, 1900).   31

Control. Control vs. Ownership. "Control of Public Service Corporations." Coler, Bird S. Mun. Ownership 1:10 (June, 1900); Foote, Allen R. Engng. M. 9:50 (1895).   32

——. "Control of Public Service Industries." Foote, Allen Ripley. Pp. 121-123 in "Pro. Third Annual Conv. League of Am. Municipalities, 1899." 8vo, 148 pp. Paper.   33

——. "Demand for the Public Regulations of Industries." Dabney, W. D. Ann. Am. Acad. Pol. Sci. 2:433 (1892).   34

——. "Fallacy of Municipal Ownership of Franchises, Control not Possession the

Municipal Control—*Continued.*

Solution of the Problem." Loomis, Frank M. Engng. M. 11:814 (1896), p. 207 Proc. Third Natl. Conf., 1896. See 6-18c. 35

———. " Municipal Control, Municipal Ownership and." Brown, Chas. Carroll. Mun. Engng. 14:1 (Jan. 1898). 36

———. " Municipal Control of Public Works." Malochee, H. J. J. Assoc. Engng. Soc. 21:149 (Oct. 1898). 37

———. " Municipal Regulation of Public Franchises." Redmond, John M. City Govt. 6:10 (Jan. 1899). 38

———. " New Plan for the Control of Quasi-Public Works." Forrest, J. D. Am. J. Sociol. 3:837 (May, 1898). 39

———. " Possibilities and Limitations of Municipal Control, The." Rowe, L. S. Ann. Am. Acad. Pol. Sci. May, 1900, Supp. p. 7. 40

———. " Public Control of Municipal Franchises." Pingree, Hazen S. P. 216, Proc. Third Natl. Conf., 1896. See 6-18c. 41

———. " Public Ownership vs. Regulated Natural Monopolies." Foote, Allen Ripley. Prog. Age 17:498 (Nov. 1, 1899), Other Side 1:271 (Dec. 9, 1899), 1:283 (Dec. 16, 1899), 1:295 (Dec. 23, 1899). 42

———. " Regulation or Ownership." Bemis, Edward W. Chapter IX, pp. 631-680, in " Municipal Monopolies," see no. 86 below. 43

———. Regulation of Rates. Barnard, Job. Public Improvements 2:269 (April 16, 1900); McLean, George. Prog. Age 18:235 (June 1, 1900); Am. Gas Light J. 72:892 (June 4, 1900), Mun. Engng. 19:41 (July, 1900). 44

———. " Relation of Modern Municipalities to Quasi-Public Works." Adams, Henry C., with George W. Knight, David R. Dewey, Chas. Moore, Frank J. Goodnow and Arthur Yager. Publications of the Am. Econ. Assoc. No. 12, 1887. 87 pp. 75c. 45

———. " Relation of a Municipality to Quasi-Public Corporations Enjoying Municipal Franchises." Salter, Wm. M. P. 219, Proc. Third Natl. Conf., 1896. See 6-18c. 46

———. " Rights of the Public over Quasi-Public Services." Clark, Walter. Arena 18:470 (Oct. 1897). 47

———. " State Control of Corporations." Cahoon, James Blake. Mun. Aff. 4:520 (Sept. 1900). 48

———. " Trials and Troubles of Instituting and Enforcing Municipal Inspection and Control." Canfield, M. G. City Govt. 9:94 (Oct. 1900). 49

" Corporations against the People, The." Flower, B. O. Arena 19:218 (Feb. 1898). 50

———. " Powers and Privileges of Corporations versus Rights of the People, The." Wright, Austin W. Elec. Engng. 10:195 (Oct. 15, 1897), 10:221 (Nov. 1, 1897), 10:249 (Nov. 15, 1897). 51

Cost of Municipal Service. (See under Municipal Ownership below).

" Economic Productivity of Municipal Enterprises, Methods of Determining the." Wilcox, Walter F. Am. J. Sociol. Nov. 1896. 52

Expropriation with or without Indemnity. " L'Expropriation avec ou sans Indemnité." Vandervelde, E. R. Soc. 31:460 (April, 1900). 53

Franchises. " Careless granting of Franchises for small Municipalities." Engng. Rec. Feb. 22, 1896. 54

———. " Construing Certain Clauses in Municipal Franchises." Hill, John W. Mun. Engng. 16:38 (June, 1899). 55

———. " Duration of Franchises." Lewis, Charlton T. Mun. Aff. 3:256 (June, 1899). 56

———. " Economic Aspects of Municipal Franchises." Foote, Allen Ripley. Elec. R. 36:210 (Feb. 28, 1900). 57

———. " Essentials of Good City Government in the Way of Granting Franchises." Bemis, E. W. P. 125, Proc. Second Natl. Conf., 1895. See 6-18b. 58

———. " Franchises." McKisson, Robert E. Prog. Age 17:71 (Feb. 15, 1899). 59

———. " Franchise Problems." (Editorial). Ind. 51:1383 (May 18, 1899). 60

———. " How Should the Franchise Question be Settled?" Foote, Allen Ripley. Prog. Age 17:234 (June 1, 1899), 17:263 (June 15, 1899), 17:298 (July 1, 1899), 17:334 (July 15, 1899), 17:353 (Aug. 1, 1899); anon. City Govt. 6:57 (March, 1899). 61

———. " Law of Incorporated Companies operating under Municipal Franchises." Foote, Allen R. and C. E. Everett. Cincinnati, Robert Clarke & Co., 1892. 2

Municipal Control—*Continued*.

vols., 2460 pp. $12. Reviewed in Yale R. 3:35 (1894), by H. C. White. **62**

——. " Mayors on Franchises." Short articles by Mayors Wurster of Brooklyn, Doran of St. Paul, McGuire of Syracuse, MacVicar of Des Moines, Taggart of Indianapolis and Ochs of Chattanooga. City Govt. 1:69 (1896). **63**

——. " Municipal Franchises." Richardson, Charles. Discussion by Jones, Samuel M. (p. 220), Swift, Lucius B. (p. 227), and Bemis, Edward W. (p. 231). Pro. Indianapolis Conf. p. 94, 1898. See 6-18e. Same subject, Richardson, Charles. Pp. 120-8 in " A Municipal Program." New York, Macmillan, 1900. 8vo, 246 pp. Cl. $1. **64**

——. " Municipal Franchises." Smith, Edwin Burritt. Other Side 1:205, 217, 234, 246, 255 (Nov. 4,-Dec. 2, 1899), Self Cult. 9:449 (June, 1899); Woodruff, Clinton Rogers. Ind. 50:538 (April 28, 1898); anon. City & State 5:250 (Oct. 20, 1898). **65**

——. " Municipal Franchise Contracts." Keeler, H. E. Engng. Rec. 38:75 (June 25, 1898) Am. Gas Light J. 69:47 (July 11, 1898) City Govt. 5:21 (July, 1898) Fire & W. 24:395 (Nov. 19, 1898), 24:404 (Nov. 26, 1898). **66**

——. " Municipal Franchises and their Abuses." McKisson, Robert E. City Govt. 6:23 (Feb. 1899). **67**

——. " Pay for City Grants." (Reprinted from Chicago Inter-Ocean). City Govt. 4:169 (May, 1898). **68**

——. " Proposed Solution of Municipal Franchise Problems." St. Ry. J. 15:537 (Aug. 1899). **69**

——. " Public Franchises." Commons, John R. Our Country 5:70 (March 1897). **70**

——. " Remuneration to cities for Franchise Rights in, over and under Public Streets and Alleys." McMurray, T. S. City Govt. 5:62 (Aug. 1898), Prog. Age 16:411 (Sept. 1, 1898). **71**

——. Taxation of Franchises. (See under **Finance.**)

——. " Valuation of Franchises, The." Marshall, Matthew. (Reprinted from the N. Y. Sun). Mun & Ry. Rec. 4:170 (May 15, 1899). **72**

——. " Municipal Franchises, What They are Worth and How They are Taxed." Meriwether, Lee. Outlook 58:920 (April 9, 1898). **73**

——. " Valuation Clauses in Municipal Franchises." Hill, John W. Engng. Rec. 39:594 (May 27, 1899) Am. Gas Light J. 70:849 (June 5, 1899). **74**

——. " What Would the Ideal Franchise Contain." St. Ry. R. 10:715 (Dec. 15, 1900). **75**

Functions, Limits of Municipal. Acworth, W. M. Economic J. 8:454 (Dec. 1898); de Mattini, G. B. Critica Sociale 10:255 (Aug. 16, 1900); Devonshire, Duke of. Mun. Rec. & Ad. 2:379 (March 5, 1898); Smart, William. Mun. J. & London 8:711 (June 16, 1899), 8:735 (June 23, 1899) Mun. World 9:154 (Sept. 1899); Wambaugh, Eugene. Atlan. 81:120 (Jan. 1898); Wattenberg, William. City Govt. 4:135 (April, 1898); (Editorial), Mun. Rec. & Ad. Vol. I, No. 23, p. 5 (Nov. 13, 1897). **76**

——. " Powers of Municipalities, A Discussion." Foote, Allen Ripley. Takoma Park, D. C., 1898. Pamphlet, 79 pp. **77**

Housing, Municipal or State Action regarding. (See under **Housing**).

——. Ideal City. " La Cité Idéale." Fournière, Eugène. Rev. Soc. 28:140 (Aug. 1898). **78**

Land in Large Cities, Municipalization of. " La Municipalization du Sol dans les Grandes Villes." Einaudi, Luigi. Paris, V. Giard & E. Brière, 1898. Pamphlet, 60 pp. **79**

" Light, Heat and Power, Municipal." Adams, Alton D. Mun. Engng. 18:293 (May, 1900). **80**

Limits of Municipal Functions. (See Functions above).

Monopolies. " City Monopolies." Pp. 194-213 of W. W. Cook's " Corporation Problem." New York, Putnam, 1891. $1.50. **81**

——. " Legal Aspects of Monopoly." Parsons, Frank. Chapter VI, pp. 425-504, in " Municipal Monopolies." See no. 86 below. **82**

——. " Monopoles Communaux. Eclairage au Gaz et à l'Electricite. Distribution D'Eau et de Force Motrice. Omnibus, Tramways (these)." Caen, impr. Valin, 1898. 8vo, 271 pp. **83**

——. " Monopolies and the People." Baker, Charles Whiting. (3d ed.) New York, G. P. Putnam's Sons, 1899. 12mo, 368 pp. Cl. $1.50. **84**

——. " Monopolies and Trusts." Ely, Richard T. New York, Macmillan Co.,

Municipal Control—*Continued.*

1900. 12mo, 278 pp. Cloth, $1.25. 85
——. " Municipal Monopolies." Bemis, Edward W. (Editor). New York, Crowell & Co., 1899. 12mo, 691 pp. Cl. $2. 86
——. " Municipal Monopolies." Commons, John R. Pp. 121-151, in his " Social Reform and the Church." New York, T. Y. Crowell & Co., 1894. 176 pp. 75c. 87
——. " Municipal Monopolies." Ogden, R. Nation 58:285 (1894). 88
——. " Municipal Monopolies and their Management." Sinclair, A. H. Toronto Univ. Studies No. 2, 1891. 89
——. " Natural Monopolies." Ely, R. T. Lend a H. 4:178 (1889); No. Am. 158:294 (1894). 90
——. Trusts in Municipal Services. "Les Trusts dans les Services Municipaux." Section 1 in " Les Services Publics et la Question des Monopolies aux Etats-Unis." Rousiers, Paul de. Rev. Pol. e Par. 18:81 (Oct. 1898). 91
" Municipal Empiricism." (Editorial). Mun. Rec. & Ad. Vol. I, No. 17, p. 3, Oct. 2, 1897. 92
Municipal Ownership, General articles on. Bemis, E. W. Other Side 1:256 (Dec. 2, 1899); Bourke, John Walton. Elec. Engng. 12:54 (Aug. 1898); Britton, John A. Am. Gas Lgt. J. Aug. 24, 1896; Foote, Allen Ripley. City Govt. 3:91 (Sept. 1897); Francisco, M. J. Engng. M. 5:725 (1893), 9:41 (1895) Elec. World, June 5, 1897; Hopkins, Henry. Elec. Eng. 23:364 (Oct. 13, 1898), 36:389 (Oct. 20, 1898), 26:407 (Oct. 27, 1898), Johnson, Henry V. City Govt. 7:59 (Sept. 1899); Public Improvements 1:234 (Oct. 1, 1899), Prog. Age 17:446 (Oct. 16, 1899) Other Side 1:235 (Nov. 18, 1899); Jones, Samuel M. City Govt. 5:59 (Aug. 1898), Arena 21:766 (June, 1899); MacVicar, John. City Govt. 7:80 (Oct. 1899), Prog. Age 17:495 (Nov. 1, 1899), Other Side 1:223 (Nov. 11, 1899); Parke, Roderick J. Can. Eng. 6:31 (June, 1898); Pingree, Hazen S. Public Improvements 2:169 (Feb. 15, 1900); Robinson, J. R. City Govt. 7:68 (Sept. 1899), Public Improvements 1:243 (Oct. 1, 1899); Other Side 1:247 (Nov. 25, 1899); Tafel, Gustav. City Govt. 7:64 (Sept. 1899), Public Improvements 1:241 (Oct. 1, 1899), Other Side 1:239 (Nov. 18, 1899); Yerkes, Charles T. Public Policy 2:101 (Feb. 17, 1900); anon. Prog. Age 15:366 (Aug. 16, 1897); Ind. 50:18 (Jan. 6, 1898); Elec. Eng. 25:578 (May 26, 1898); Ind. 51:1033 (April 13, 1899); St. Ry. J. 15:521 (Aug. 1899); Elec. Eng. 23:194 (Feb. 17, 1897); Mun. Rec. & Ad. 2:477 (April 15, 1898); P. Ownership R. 2:49 (Aug.-Sept. 1898); Am. Gas Light J. 70:533 (April 10, 1899); Mun. World 9:79 (May, 1899); Public Improvements 1:141 (Aug. 15, 1899), City and State 9:134 (Aug. 30, 1900). 93
——. " Advantages of Municipal Ownership." Shaw, Albert. Pp. 89-93 in " Report of the Street Railway Commission of the City Council of the City of Chicago." City Council, Chicago, 1900. 8vo, 136 pp. Paper. 94
——. " Business Argument against Municipal Ownership, A." Cahoon, James Blake. City Govt. 7:778 (Oct. 1899), Public Improvements 1:252 (Oct. 1, 1899), Prog. Age 17:461 (Oct. 16, 1899), Other Side 1:185 (Oct. 21, 1899). Pp. 83-88 Proceedings Third Annual Convention, League of American Municipalities, 1899. 8vo, 148 pp. Paper. 95
——. " Business Argument, A Reply to a." Gonden, Harvey James. Mun. Ownership 1:12 (June, 1900). 96
——. " City for the People, The, or the Municipalization of the City Government and of Local Franchises." Parsons, Frank. Philadelphia, C. F. Taylor, 1900. 8vo, 597 pp. Cl. $1. 97
——. " Cost of Municipal Enterprise, The." Davies, Dixon Henry. London, P. S. King & Son, 1899. 8vo, 71 pp. Paper, 2s. Reprinted in J. Soc. Arts 47:225 (Feb. 3, 1899), J. Gas Lgt. 73:301 (Feb. 7, 1899), Prog. Age 17:107 (March 15, 1899). 98
——. " Cost of Service to Users and Taxpayers." Foote, Allen R. Elec. Eng. 24:428 (Nov. 4, 1897), Prog. Age 15:539 (Nov. 1897); MacVicar, John. City Govt. 4:8 (Jan. 1898), Prog. Age 16:72 (Feb. 15, 1898). 99
——. " Essay on Public Ownership, An." Wisner, Edward. St. Ry. R. 9:845 (Dec. 15, 1899). 100
——. " Expediency and Local Conditions, Municipal Ownership; A Question of." Laughlin, J. Lawrence. Pp. 94-98 in " Report of the Street Railway Commission of the City Council of the City of Chicago." City Council, Chicago, 1900. 8vo, 136 pp. Paper. 1
——. " Experiences with Municipal Plants, Some." Shepardson, G. D. Elec. W. & E. 36:62 (July 14, 1900), Am. Gas Light J. 73:130 (July 23, 1900), City Govt. 9:35 (Aug. 1900). 2
——. " Failure of Municipal Ownership, The." Vreeland, H. H. Ind. 52:1165

Municipal Control—*Continued.*

(May 17, 1900).

——. "Fallacies of Municipal Ownership." Francisco, M. J. City Govt. 7:65 (Sept. 1899), Public Improvements 1:256 (Oct. 1, 1899), Prog. Age 17:465 (Oct. 16, 1899), Other Side 1:211 (Nov. 4, 1899). Pp. 90-99 Proc. Third Annual Convention, League of American Municipalities, 1899. 8vo, 138 pp. Paper.

——. Foreign Experience. "Shall American Cities Municipalize? Value of Foreign Experience as a Guide." Agar, John G. Mun. Aff. 4:13 (March, 1900).

——. "Franchises or Monopolies, their Public Ownership and Operation." Tremain, Henry Edwin. Ann. Am. Acad. Pol. Sci. 14:310 (Nov. 1899).

——. "Government Ownership, an account of 337 now existing National and Municipal Undertakings in the 100 principal countries of the World." Vrooman, Walter. Baltimore, Patriotic Literature Publishing Co., 1895. 219 pp. $1.

——. Jones, Mayor S. M. "Mayor Jones and Public Ownership Vivisected." Wisner, Edward. Other Side 1:199 (Oct. 28, 1899).

——. "Legal, commercial and political review of the question of municipal ownership of semi-public enterprises of profit." Quilty, C. W. Am. Gas Lgt. J. 67:286 (Aug. 23, 1897).

——. "A Matter of Municipal Ownership, and What Came of It." "F. M." Hrprs. Wkly. 41:1074 (Oct. 30, 1897).

——. "Movement to Limit Municipal Ownership." Porter, Robert P. City Govt. 7:124 (Nov. 1899).

——. "Municipal Advantages, How to Obtain them." (Against Municipal Ownership). Foote, Allen R. Progressive Age July 1, 1896. (Reviewed in Journal of Gas Lighting for Aug. 18, 1896).

——. "Municipal vs. Corporate Price." Foote, Allen Ripley. Business 19:477 (Aug. 1899).

——. "Municipal Liberty." Parsons, Frank. City Govt. 5:237 (Dec. 1898).

——. Municipal Ownership. Pp. 199. "The Social Crisis." Ostrander, Dempster. New York, F. T. Neely, 1898, 270 pp. 50c.

——. Municipal Ownership. Discussion of, in Proceedings of the Third Annual Convention of the League of American Municipalities, 1899. (8vo, 148 pp. Paper). Bemis, Edward W. pp. 123-135; Cahoon, James B. pp. 83-88; Francisco, M. J. pp. 90-99; Gemünder, M. A. pp. 71-78; Johnson, Henry V. pp. 51-55; MacVicar, John. pp. 105-110; Pierce, Frank G. pp. 58-62; Robinson, J. R. pp. 57-58; Tafel, Gustav. pp. 55-57.

——"Municipal Ownership at Home and Abroad." Porter, Robert P. New York, 1898. 12mo, 31 pp. Pamphlet.

——. "Municipal Ownership discussed by Mayors Jones of Kansas City, Wood of Seattle, Todd of Louisville, McGuinnes of Providence. Saltsman of Erie and Green of Binghamton." City Govt. 2:69 (March, 1897).

——. Municipal Ownership and Operation of Public Utilities. Baldwin, A. S., p. 2; Reed, Charles Wesley, p. 3, Mchts. Assoc. R. Vol. V, No. 49, Sept. 1900; Dohrmann, F. W., Babcock, Kendric C., Symmes, Frank J., Weinstock, Henry, Ross, Edward A. Mchts. Assn. R. Vol. V, No. 52, Dec. 1900.

——. "Municipal Ownership in Practice." Pierce, F. G. City Govt. 7:67 (Sept. 1899), Public Improvements 1:238 (Oct. 1, 1899), Prog. Age 17:447 (Oct. 16, 1899). Pp. 58-62 in Proc. Third Annual Convention, League of American Municipalities, 1899. 8vo, 148 pp. Paper.

——. "Municipal Ownership: The Proper Attitude of the Law Thereto." Lynch, William A. Public Policy 2:152 (March 10, 1900).

——. "Municipal Ownership of Quasi-Public Works." Foote, Allen R. Paper read before the Taxpayers' Assoc. of Baltimore, April 28, 1891. Pamphlet, 23 pp.

——. "Municipal Ownership of Quasi-Public Works." Foote, Allen R. Washington, D. C., Ramsey & Bisbee, 1891. Pamphlet, 14 pp.

——. "Municipal Ownership versus the Taxpayer." Lake, Edward N. Elec. Engng. 11:124 (March 1, 1898).

——. "Municipal Proprietorship." Mason, August Lynch. Arena 19:43 (Jan. 1898), Mun. Rec. & Ad. 2:160 (Jan. 15, 1898).

——. "Municipal Public Service Industries." Foote, Allen Ripley. Chicago, The Other Side Pub. Co., 1899. 12mo, 352 pp. Cl. $1.

——. Municipalization of Public Services. "La Municipalizzazione dei Servizi Publici." Portalupi, Massimo. Torino, "Germinal," 1900. 12mo, 47 pp. Paper, 50 centimes.

Municipal Control—*Continued.*

——. Municipalization of Public Services. " La Municipalisation du Services Publics." Veber, Adrien. R. Municipale 3:2073 (April 28, 1900). 28

——. " Necessity of Municipal Ownership." Grout, Edward M. City Govt. 2:42 (Feb. 1897). 29

——. " New Municipal Era, A." (Editorial). Self Cult. 9:475 (June, 1899). 30

——. " Northwestern Electrical Association, Report of a Special Committee of the, on Municipal Ownership." Doherty, H. L. and E. Coleman: Electricity (N. Y.) Jan. 27, 1897. 31

——. " Objections to Municipal Ownership of Public Works." Smith, T. Carpenter. Engng. M. 14:781 (Feb. 1898). 32

——. " Permanence in Management, Municipal Ownership and." (Editorial). Mun. Engng. 13:357 (Dec. 1897). 33

——. Pingree, Gov., on Municipal Ownership. " Gov. Pingree Replies to Mr. Yerkes." Public Improvements 2:244 (April 2, 1900). 34

——. " A Tale by Governer Pingree." Mun. Ownership 1:16 (June, 1900). 35

——. " Problem of Municipal Ownership, The." Gemünder, Martin A. City Govt. 7:61 (Sept. 1899), Other Side 1:150 (Sept. 30, 1899), Public Improvements 1:244 (Oct. 1, 1899), Am. Gas Light J. 71:573 (Oct. 9, 1899), Am. Gas Light J. 71:609 (Oct. 16, 1899), Prog. Age 17:455 (Oct. 16, 1899). Pp. 71-78 Proc. of the Third Annual Convention of the League of American Municipalities, 1899. 8vo, 138 pp. Paper. 36

——. " Public Ownership." Pp. 17-254 " The City for the People or the Municipalization of the City Government and of Local Franchises." Parsons, Frank. Philadelphia, C. F. Taylor, 1900. 8vo, 597 pp. Cloth, $1. 37

——. " Public Ownership of Telegraphs, Tramways. Gas Works." A Discussion. (With short testimonies from twenty foreign and American cities). Shaw, Albert, J. Laurence Laughlin, Edwin R. A. Seligman, E. W. Bemis, Lee Meriwether, James Paton and William Epps. Independent 49:569 (May 6, 1897). 38

——. " Public Service Companies and City Governments." Gladden, Washington. Outlook 66:502 (Oct. 27, 1900). 39

——. " Social Conscience, Public Ownership and the." Cutting, R. Fulton. Mun. Aff. 4:3 (March, 1900), Cal. Mun. 2:143 (June, 1900). 40

——. Socialism, Municipal. (See under Socialism below).

——. " Successful Substitute for Municipal Ownership, A." Potts, Alfred F. Mun. Engng. 14:181 (April, 1898), Am. R. of Rs. 20:576 (Nov. 1899). 41

——. Trading, Municipal. (See under Trading below).

——. " Trend in American Cities, The." Martin, J. W. Contemp. 76:856 (Dec. 1899). 42

——. " Weaknesses of Municipal Ownership, The." (Editorial). Elec. Eng. 24:302 (Sept. 30, 1897). 43

——. " Why Municipal Industries are not Efficient." Public Policy 2:68 (Feb. 3, 1900).

" Municipal Problems." Pingree, H. S. City Govt. 8:89 (April, 1900). 44

" Municipal Utopias." Spec. 64:364 (1890).

Our Daily Bread. " Panem Nostrum Quotidianum." Garibotti, Giuseppe. Critica Sociale 10:156 (May 16, 1900). 45

Pawnshops, Municipal. (See under **Pawnshops, Municipal**).

" Political Wrecking of Business Enterprises." Coler, Bird S. Munsey's 23:277 (May, 1900). 46

Private Ownership, Private vs. Municipal Ownership. " Corporate Ownership." Hersh, Grier. City Govt. 8:164 (June, 1900). 47

——. " Honesty in the Management of Corporations." (Comparison of Public and Private Corporations). Engng. News Nov. 12, 1896. 48

——. " The Investigation of Municipal and Private Distribution of Water, Gas and Electricity conducted by the Different Bureaus of Statistics of Labor in the United States." (Discussion before the American Economic Association, Cleveland, Ohio. Dec. 1897). Carroll D. Wright, Elroy M. Avery, and John H. Gray. Economic Studies 3:57 (Feb. 1898). 49

——. " Municipal and Business Corruption." Coler, Bird S. Ind. 52:662 (March 15, 1900). 50

——. Municipal vs. Private Ownership. Brown, Charles Carroll. Mun. Engng. 17:195 (Oct. 1899); MacVicar, John. City Govt. 3:114 (Oct. 1897), Mun. Owner-

Municipal Control—*Continued.*

ship 1:5 (June, 1900); Smith, H. T. Our Day 19:507 (Sept. 1900); Tooke, C. W. Mun. Engng. 17:126 (Sept. 1899), Other Side 1:148 (Sept. 30, 1899); anon. Ry. World 7:298 (Sept. 1898). 51

——. "Municipalities vs. Private Corporations." Francisco, M. J. Rutland, Vt., M. J. Francisco & Son, 1900. 8vo, 172 pp. Paper, 50c. 52

——. "Private Ownership of Franchises." Yerkes, Charles T. Pub. Imp. 2:193 (March 1, 1900), Arena 1:96 (June, 1900). 53

"Problems of To-day." Ely, R. T. New York, Thos. Y. Crowell & Co., 1890. 296 pp. $1.25. (Chapters XX and XXI, on Water, Gas, Electric Railways and Lighting). 54

"Profits, The Allocation of Municipal." Wilson, C. H. Mun. J. 9:847 Oct. 26, 1900). 55

——. "Methods of Determining the economic productivity of municipal enterprises." Willcox, Walter F. Am. J. Sociol. 2:378 (1896). 56

——. Municipal Enterprises and Profits. "Imprese Municipali e Profitto." Labriola, Arturo. Critica Sociale 10:349 (Nov. 16, 1900). 57

——. "Ought Municipal Enterprises to be Allowed to Yield a Profit?" Ca nan, Edwin. Econ. J. 9:1 (March, 1899). 58

——. "Ancora il Profitto nelle Imprese Municipali." Negro, Luigi. Critica Sociale 10:377 (Dec. 16, 1900). 59

——. "Il Regime Finanziario delle Imprese Municipali; Principii generali; Le Imprese Industriali Municipali debbono dare un Profitto." Critica Sociale 10:219 (July 16, 1900). 60

——. "Sul Socialismo Municipale: Le Imprese Municipali debbono dare un Profitto?" Labriola, Arturo. Critica Sociale 10:170 (June, 1900). 61

"Proposition to Abolish Municipalities in the Interests of Private Corporations." New Nation 2:274 1892). 62

"Public Prejudice against Corporations, How to Obviate." Hendricks, Geo. B. St. Ry. Rev. 7:245 (April 15, 1897). 63

"Right to Lease Public Works, The." Engng. Rec. 37:511 (May 14, 1898). 64

Socialism, Municipal. Municipal Collectivism. Bouët, H. J. Economistes 43:209 (Aug. 15, 1900); Bourdeau, J. R. d. Deux Mondes 160:180 (July, 1900); De Land, Fred. Elec. Engng. 11:53 (Feb. 1, 1898), Elec. Eng. 25:155 (Feb. 10, 1898), Prog. Age 16:128 (March 15, 1898); Saloma, G. Ricca. Nuova, Ant. (Nov. 16, 1897); Veber, Adrien. R. Municipale 3: 1881 (Feb. 3, 1900); anon. Gunton's 16:190 (March, 1899); Other Side 1:65 (Aug. 12, 1899). 65

——. Application of Collectivism. "L'Application du Systéme Collectiviste." Rev. Soc. 28:188, 341, 692 (Aug. Sept. Dec. 1898). 66

——. "Bibliographie des Socialismus und Communismus." Stammhammer, Josef. Jena, Gustav Fischer, 1893. 8vo, 303 pp. 10m. 67

——. "Europe, Municipal Socialism in." Fiamingo, G. J. Pol. Econ. 6:396 (June, 1898). 68

——. Finance, Socialism and Local. "Il Socialismo e i Bilanci Comunali." Bonomi, Ivanoe. Critica Sociale 10:365 (Dec. 1, 1900). 69

——. "I Criteri 'Socialisti' per i Bilanci Comunali." Leone, Enrico. Critica Sociale 10:314 (Oct. 16, 1900). 70

——. "Sul Socialismo Municipale: La Riforma Fiscale." Labriola, Arturo. Critica Sociale 10:154 (May 16, 1900). 71

——. Foreign Countries, Municipal Socialism in. "La Socialisme Municipale à l'Etranger." Veber, Adrien. R. Municipale 3:1996 (March 24, 1900). 72

——. "Letters from New America; or an Attempt at Practical Socialism." Persinger, Clark Edmund. Chicago, Charles H. Kerr & Co., 1900. 12mo, 89 pp. Cloth, 50c. 73

——. "Municipal Socialism." Crofts, W. C. Reprinted from "The Liberty Annual, 1892," London. Published by the Liberty and Property Defense League, 1892. 74

——. "Progress of Municipal Socialism since 1893." Ely, Richard T., and Urdahl, Thomas K. Chaut. 30:186 (Nov. 1899). 75

——. "Socialism, Democracy and Municipal Government." Real Estate Rec. & Guide Aug. 20, 1892, p. 235. 76

——. "Socialism and a Municipal Commonwealth." Barnes, L. C. Am. M. Civics 6:260 (1895). 77

Municipal Control—*Continued.*

———. "The Tendency of Municipal Socialism." Maltbie, Milo Roy. Other Side 1:61 (Aug. 12, 1899). 78

"Status of the Public Service Corporation Question, The." Garfield, Harry A. Pp. 207-215 in "Proceedings of the Columbus Conference for Good City Government." Philadelphia, National Municipal League, 1899. 8vo, 275 pp. Cloth $1. 79

Trading, Municipal. Avebury, Lord. Contemp. 78:28 (July, 1900); Bond, Wa'ter. Fortn. 66:669 (Oct. 1899); Donald, Robert. Contemp. 78:227 (Aug. 1900); Harrison, John. Econ. J. 10:251 (June, 1900); Priestman, Arthur. Mun. J. 9:760 (Sept. 28, 1900), Surveyor 18:404 (Oct. 5, 1900); anon. Ty. & Ry. W. 9:409 (Aug. 9, 1900); Char. Or. R. 8:257 (Oct. 1900); Ed. R. 192:405 (Oct. 1900). 80

———. "American View of Municipal Trading." Robinson, J. R. Mun. J. & London 8:1218 (Nov. 10, 1899). 81

———. "The 'Edinburgh Review' on Municipal Trading." J. Gas Light 76:1324 (Nov. 27, 1900). 82

———. "Municipal Trading and Profits." Donald, Robert. Mun. J. & London 8:1057 (Sept. 22, 1899). Econ. J. 9:378 (Sept. 1899). (See also under Profits). 83

"Treatment of Municipalities, The." Britton, John A. Am. Gas Light J. 71:289 (Aug. 21, 1899). 84

———. "Triumph of Municipal Trading." Mun. J. & London 8:325 (March 17, 1899). 85

Uniform Accounting. (See under Accounting above).

"Validity of Contracts held by Quasi-Municipal Corporations." Thompson, S. D. Am. Law R. 26:675 1892). 86

"Vested Wrongs." Porter, Robert P. Public Improvements 1:218 (Oct. 1, 1899), Other Side 1:174 (Oct. 1, 1899). Prog. Age 17:450 (Oct. 6, 1899), City Govt. 7:118 (Nov. 1899), St. Ry. R. 9:746 (Nov. 15, 1899). Pp. 63-71 in "Proceedings of the Third Annual Convention of the League of American Municipalities, 1899." 8vo, 148 pp. Paper. 87

"Waste in Competition in Public Service Functions, The." Bourke, John Walton. Prog. Age 15:408 (Sept. 15, 1897). 88

"What Shall the City Do?" Gunton's 16:350 (May, 1899). 89

LIGHTING—GENERAL.

"Bookkeeping for Public Lighting Companies, Best Methods of." Clough, John Lyle. Mun. Engng. 18:237 (April, 1900). 90

"Control, Difficulties of, as Illustrated in the History of Gas Companies." Gray, John H. Ann. Am. Acad. Pol. Sci. May, 1900, Supp. p. 31. 91

"Control of Private Lighting Companies." Real Estate R. & G. May 14, 1892, p. 764. 92

"Legitimate Ways of Getting Cheaper City Light." (Editorial). Elec. Eng. 26:434 (Nov. 3, 1898).

"Municipal Lighting." Parsons, Frank. Arena 15:95 (1896); Bean, W. Worth. Elec Eng 23:655 (June 16, 1897); St. Ry. R. 7:423 (July 15, 1897), Prog. Age 15:302 (July 1, 1897); Bemis, Edward W. Outlook 62:884 (Aug. 19, 1899); Francisco, M. J. City Govt. 4:131 (April, 1898). 93

———. "Problem of Municipal Lighting." Hurd, W. T. Proceedings of the Convention of the League of Wisconsin Municipalities, Bulletin No. 3, p. 34, June 26-27, 1899. 94

———. "Public Lighting in Relation to Public Ownership and Operation." Dow, Alexander. Am. Gas Light J. 68:1018 (June 27, 1898), Elec. Eng. 25:707 (June 23, 1898), Elec. Rev. 33:9 (July 6, 1898), 33:28 (July 13, 1898), Elec. World 31:738 (June 18, 1898), Prog. Age 16:328 (July 1, 1898), 16:346 (July 15, 1898). Discussed by Atkinson, H. M. Elec. Eng. 25:748 (June 30, 1898). 95

"Municipal Ownership of Gas and Electric Lighting Plants." Foote, Allen R. Columbus, O., Ohio Gas Light Assoc., 1890. Paper, 7 pp. 96

———. "A report on Municipal Lighting to the City Council of Des Moines, Ia." (Favors Municipal Lighting). MacVicar, John. City Govt. 1:146 (Dec. 1896). 97

———. "Municipal or Company Lighting." Mun. J. 9:960 (Dec. 7, 1900). 98

———. "Municipal Ownership of Water, Gas and Electric Light Plants." Discussion by Walter F. Wilcox, Edward W. Bemis, M. N. Baker, Osborn Howes, James W. Latta, John R. Commons, F. E. Barker, John S. Clark and Lee Meriwether. Proceedings of the National Association of Officials of Bureaus of Labor Statis-

Municipal Control—*Continued.*

tics in the United States. Albany, N. Y. June 23-25, 1896. pp. 75-128. 99

——. "Objections to Municipal Ownership of Lighting Plants." Mun. Engng. 16:321 (May, 1899). 100

——. "Public Ownership of Lighting Plant." Warner, George E. City Govt. 6:50 (March, 1899). 1

——. "Report on Public Lighting." Matthews, Nathan, Jr. City Rec. 1:501 (Sept. 1, 1898). 2

——. "The Municipal Ownership of Gas and Electric Plants." Persse, T. B. Prog. Age July 1, 1896. Criticised in Prog. Age July 15, 1896. 3

"Municipalities Owning Gas and Electric Works." Maltbie, Milo R. Prog. Age 17:216 (May 15, 1899). 4

"State and Lighting Corporations, The." Allen, Walter S. An. Am. Acad. Pol. Sci. 2:707 (1892). 5

"Street Lighting, Private vs. Municipal Plant for." Foster, Horatio A. Elec. Eng. March 29, 1893, p. 309. 6

——. "Street Lighting by Contract and by Municipal Ownership." MacVicar, John. Elec. Eng. 24:329 (Oct. 7, 1897), Prog. Age 15:451 (Oct. 15, 1897). 7

"The Solution of One Problem of Municipal Lighting." Hurd, W. T. Mun. Engng. 19:329 (Nov. 1900). 8

"Uniform Accounting for Gas and Electric Lighting Companies." Cahoon, James Blake. Mun. Engng. 18:383 (June, 1900). 9

LIGHTING—ELECTRICITY.

"A Co-operative City Electric Lighting Plant." Elec. Rev. 32:58 (Jan. 26, 1898). 10

"Circuits, Street Franchises for Electric." Adams, Alton D. Elec. W. & E. 36:769 (Nov. 17, 1900). 11

"Concentrating the Control of all Municipal Electric Interests under one Head, The Advisability of." Mead, Morris W. E ec. R. 35:154 (Sept. 6, 1899), 35:173 (Sept. 13, 1899), Mun. Engng. 17:368 (Dec. 1899). 12

Cost of Public Electric Lighting, Statistics of." Rosewater, Victor. Am. Stat. Assoc. 3:293 (1893); Separate Pamphlets Nos. 21, 22. $1. 13

"Electric Light Asociation, National Convention at Chicago." (Discussion of Municipal Ownership). Elec. World, March 2, 1889. 14

"Municipal Control, Ownership or Operation of Municipal Franchises, with Special References to Electric Lighting." Bowker, R. R. Mun. Affairs 1:605 (Dec. 1897). (Reprinted from Municipal Affairs) Elec. Eng. 25:27 (Jan. 6, 1898), 25:65 (Jan. 13, 1898), 25:89 (Jan. 20, 1898), 25:104 (Jan. 27, 1898), 25:130 (Feb. 3, 1898), 25:153 (Feb. 10, 1898), 25:182 (Feb. 17, 1898), Elec. Rev. 32:26 (Jan. 12, 1898); et seq. 15

——. "An Ideal Municipal Electric Plant." Adams, Alton D. Mun. Engng. 17:327 (Dec. 1899). 16

——. "Die Elektrische Beleuchtung im Verhältniss zur Stadtverwaltung." Schrader, W. Madgeburg, 1889. 17

——. "Electric Power Companies and their Relation to Municipalities." Lang, A. E. Elec. Eng. 26:645 (Dec. 29, 1898), Mun. & Ry. Rec. 5:15 (July 15, 1899). 18

——. "La Municipalizzazione dei Servizi Elettrici." L'Elettricita 18:604 (Sept. 23, 1899). 19

——. "Municipal versus Company Electricity." Mun. J. & London 8:1082 (Sept. 29, 1899).

——. "Municipal Electric Lighting." Commons, John R. Mun. Aff. 1:631 (Dec. 1897); reprinted in Elec. Eng. 25:230, 264, 296, 319, 348, 373, 426, 464 (March 3, 10, 17, 24, 31, April 7, 21, 28, 1898); also as Ch. II, pp. 55-182 in "Municipal Monopolies," see 160-86; criticism by Foster, Horatio A. Elec. Eng. 25:510 (May 12, 1898). 20

——. "Municipal Electric Light Plants." Anon. City Govt. 4:57 (Feb. 1898); Bemis, E. W. Prog. Age 16:408 (Sept. 1, 1898). 21

——. "Municipal Electricity." London 6:837 (Oct. 21, 1897). 22

——. "Municipal Ownership of Electric Light Plants." Britton, John A. Am. Gas Light J. Jan. 20, 1896; Francisco, M. J. Am. Gas Light J. 67:7 (July 5, 1897); anon. Engng. News 39:387 (June 16, 1898). 23

——. "Municipal Ownership of Electric Light Plants: its fallacy with legal and editorial opinions, tables and costs of light." Francisco, M. J. Rutland, Vt.

Municipal Control—Continued.

Carruthers & Thomas, prs., 1893. 104 pp.   24

——. "Municipal Ownership of Electric Light Stations." Elec. World 31:210 (Feb. 12, 1898).   25

——. "Objections to Municipal Ownerships of Electric Plants." Smith, T. Carpenter. Engng. M. 14:780 (Feb. 1898).   26

——. "Report to the Special Investigating Committee on Commercial Electric Lighting, South Norwalk, Conn." (Analysis of Reports from 60 cities owning Electric Lighting Plants. The same number of the Electrical Engineer contains short articles on the experience of 24 other cities in Municipal Electric Lighting.) Winchester, A. E. Elec. Eng. 23:177 (Feb. 17, 1897).   27

——. "Remonstrance to the Municipal Control of Electric Lighting before the Committee on Manufactures of the Massachusetts Legislature." Evans, Forest L. Boston, Printed by Rockwell & Churchill, 1891.   28

——. "Argument in Remonstrance to the above, before the Committee on Manufactures of the Massachusetts Legislature." Collins, Patrick A. Boston, Wright and Potter, prs., 1891. 31 pp.   29

——. "Argument in Favor of Municipal Ownership before the Committee on Manufactures of the Massachusetts Legislature." Crowley, Daniel N. Salem, Mass., The Salem Press Publishing Co., 1891. 33 pp.   30

——. "Argument in Behalf of the Town of Peabody before the Committee on Manufactures of the Massachusetts Legislature." Burdette, Everett W. Salem, Mass., The Salem Press Publishing Co., 1891.   31

——. "The Commercial and Business Aspects of Municipal Electricity Supply." Gibbings, Alfred H. Bradford, Macmillan Co., 1899. 4to, 270 pp. Cl. $4.   32

"Reports, Municipal Lighting." Thayer, George S. Elec. Eng. 23:313 (March 24, 1897).   33

——. "The Latest Electric Light Reports." Bemis, Edward W. Ch. III, pp. 183-285, in "Municipal Monopolies," see 160-86.   34

"Statistics, Municipal Electric Light." City Govt. 5:145 (Oct. 1898).   35

"Stockholder's Standard, Municipal Lighting Ownership from the." Fitzgerald, W. H. Elec. Eng. 24:601 (Dec. 23, 1897).   36

"Validity of Electric Light Comparisons." Perrine, F. A. C. Appendix to Ch. III, pp. 286-298, in "Municipal Monopolies," see 160-86.   37

"Waterworks and Electric Light Plants, Municipal Ownership of Combined." Fischer, Louis E. Public Policy 2:228 (April 14, 1900).   38

——. "A Municipal Water and Light Plant." Pierce, F. G. City Govt. 3:121 (Oct. 1897), Prog. Age 15:538 (Nov. 15, 1897).   39

"Why Some Municipal Electric Plants do not Pay Better." Shepardson, George D. Elec. R. 37:37 (July 11, 1900), 37:52 (July 18, 1900), Mun. Engng. 19:103 (Aug. 1900), St. Ry. R. 10:455 (Aug. 15, 1900).   40

LIGHTING—GAS.

"Control of Gas Works, Municipal." Keeler, Bronson C. Forum 8:286 (1889).   41

"Gas." Bemis, Edward W. Ch. VIII, pp. 587-630, in "Municipal Monopolies," see 160-86.   42

——. "Gas Supply and the Modern Municipality, The." James, E. J. Am. Econ. Assoc. Pubs. Vol. I, 1886. Separate 75 cts.   43

——. "Is the Municipalization of Gas Undertakings Advantageous?" Lees, Herbert. Gas World (London) June 19, 1897.   44

——. "Monopolies of Municipal Service, the Gas Dragon." Hildreth, Arthur. Nationalist 1:28 (1889).   45

——. "Municipal Control of Street Car, Water and Gas Plants." Canadian Eng. Feb. 1896.   46

——. "Municipal Gas not a Failure." Dodge, W. C. Elec. Engin. 23:708 (June 23, 1897).   47

——. "Municipal Gas Works." Bemis, E. W. Chaut. 16:15 (1892).   48

——. "Municipalities vs. Gas Companies." Hickenlooper, Andrew. Am. Gas Lgt. Jour. June, 1896.   49

——. "Public Gas Supply." Adams, Alton D. Mun. Engng. 19:382 (Dec. 1900).   50

——. "Recent Results in Municipal Gas Making." Bemis, E. W. R. of Rs. 7:61 (1893).   51

"Price of Gas, Governmental Control of the." Forstall, Alfred E. Am. Gas Light

Municipal Control—*Continued.*

J. 73:686 (Oct. 29, 1900), J. Gas Light. 76:1211 (Nov. 15, 1900), Prog. Age 16:520 (Dec. 1, 1900).   52

"Relation of the Gas Supply to the Public, The." Gray, John H. Mun. Aff. 2:183 (June, 1898).   53

——. "Proper Relation of the Gas Supply and the City Treasury" Armstrong, C. M. Taxpayers' Assoc. of Baltimore. Addresses 1889, p. 299.   54

"State Regulation of Corporations." (With special reference to gas companies.) Christian, Geo. H. Prog. Age 15:74 (Feb. 15, 1897).   55

MILK SUPPLY.

"Municipal Control of Milk." Mun. J. & London 8:998 (Sept. 8, 1899).   56

"Municipal Control of the Milk Supply." (Editorial.) San. Rec. 23:199 (March 10, 1899).

"Municipal Milkshops." Mun. J. & London 8:1096 (Oct. 6, 1899).

"Public Regulation of the Milk Supply." Wende, Ernest. City Govt. 8:48 (Feb. 1900).   57

"Purity of the Milk Supply." Charities, Vol. 3, No. 12, p. 2 (Aug. 19, 1899).

TELEPHONES.

"Municipal Telephones." Mun. Rec. & Ad. 3:791 (Sept. 15, 1898); Bennett, Alfred R. Mun. J. 9:45 (Jan. 19, 1900).   58

"Telephones: Monopoly or Municipality." Mun. J. & London 8:135 (Feb. 2, 1899).   59

"The Telephone." Parsons, Frank. Ch. IV, pp. 299-364, in "Municipal Monopolies," see 160-86.   60

"The Municipalization of the Telephone." Mountain, A. B. Elec. Eng. (London) June 23, 1899).   61

TRANSIT FACILITIES.

"Compensation Should Cities Receive for Street Railway Franchises, What." Phelan, James D. City Govt. 5:65 (Aug. 1898).   62

"Control, Street Railway." Pingree, Hazen S. City Govt. 2:35 (Feb. 1897).   63

"Elevated Road Franchises. Mostly Fools." Hampden, Guy. New Nation 2:712 (1892).   64

"Fares, Street Railway Franchises and." Gager, Edwin B. St. Ry. J. 15:401 (June, 1899).   65

"Foreign Cities and their Franchise Requirements, Street Railways in." Engng. News 42:359 (Nov. 30, 1899).   66

"Franchises, Street Railway." Meriwether, Lee. Part I, Eighteenth Annual Report of the Bureau of Labor Statistics, State of Missouri, 1896.   67

"Labor's Interest in Public Street Cars." Parsons, Frank. New Time 1:219 (Oct. 1897).   68

Law. "The Juridic Side of the Municipalization of Tramways." Beynon-Harris, George. Elec. Eng. (Lond.) 21:50 (Jan. 14, 1898).   69

"Length of Leases, Tramway Municipalization and." Ry. World 7:122 (April 7, 1898).   70

——. "Street Railway Franchises." Maltbie, Milo Roy. Pp. 73-76 in "Report of the Street Railway Commission of the City Council of the City of Chicago." Chicago, City Council, 1900. 8vo, 136 pp. Paper.   71

"Local Consent for Street Railways." Art. 3, Sec. 18, New York State Constitution of 1894.

"Management, Municipal Tramway." Ry. World 7:18 (Jan. 1898).

"Model Street Railway Franchise." City Govt. 7:20 (July, 1899).

Municipal Ownership of Street Railways. Parsons, Frank. Boston, Mass., Published by the Fabian Educational Co., n. d. 16 pp., Boston, Arena Pub. Co., 1896, 10 cts., New Time 1:84 (Aug. 1897); Pingree, Hazen S. Munsey's 22:220 (Nov. 1899); Richardson, Charles. p. 198, Proc. Third Natl. Conf. for Good City Govt., 1896, see 6-18c; Vreeland, H. H. Elec. World 30:332 (Sept. 18, 1897).   72

——. "More Municipal Tramways." London 7:65 (Feb. 3, 1898).   73

——. "Municipal Construction and Ownership of Works for Public Accommodation." (Rapid Transit.) Engng. Rec. Aug. 22, 1896.   74

——. "Municipal Control of Street Car, Water and Gas Plants." Canadian Eng. Feb. 1896.

MUNICIPAL AFFAIRS.

Municipal Control—*Continued.*

——. "Municipal Ownership and Operation of Street Railways." Sullivan, P. F. Elec. Eng. 24:376 (Oct. 21, 1897), 24:414 (Oct. 28, 1897), 24:439 (Nov. 4, 1897), Elec. R. 31:244 (Nov. 17, 1897), Elec. World 30:487 (Oct. 23, 1897), Railroad Gaz. 29:765 (Oct. 29, 1897), St. Ry. J. 13:751 (Nov. 1897), St. Ry. R. 7:718 (Nov. 15, 1897); Vreeland, H. H. Elec. Rev. 31:155 (Sept. 29, 1897), St. Ry. J. 13:643 (Oct. 1897); Warner, John DeWitt, and Higgins, Edward E. Mun. Aff. 1:421 (Sept. 1897). 75

——. "Municipal Street Railways." (Editorial.) Elec. Eng. 24:278 (Sept. 23, 1897). 76

——. "Municipalization of Street Railways." (Twenty-ninth Annual Joint Debate of the University of Wisconsin, December 16, 1898.) Kies, W. S., editor. Madison, Wis., Daily Cardinal Publishing Co., 1899, 8vo, 97 pp. Paper, 35 cts. See also Mun. Rec. & Ad. 3:722 (Aug. 15, 1898). 77

——. "Municipalization of Tramways." London, Fabian Society, 1897. Fabian Tract No. 77. 15 pp. 1d. 78

——. "Report of the Special Committee appointed to investigate the Relation between Cities and Towns and Street Railway Companies." (Besides the report of the Committee, it contains report of the Secretary, Walter S. Allen, "Abstracts of the Statutes of the various States relating to Franchises and Methods of Taxation." "Conditions in American Cities," "European Conditions," "Municipal Ownership and Operation of Street Railways in England" by Ropert P. Porter, "Extract from Rapid Transit and Tax Commissions' Reports in Relation to the Readjustment of the Corporation Tax," and tables showing effect of corporation and commutation taxes, etc., in Massachusetts.) Boston, February, 1898, 8vo, 296 pp. Reviewed in Engng. News 39:225 (April 7, 1898), Elec. Eng. 25:152 (Feb. 10, 1898), St. Ry. R. 8:117 (Feb. 15, 1898), Railroad Gaz. 30:122 (Feb. 18, 1898). 79

——. "Sollen Kommunen Strassenbahnen Bauen und Betreiben." Deutsche Zeitschr. f. Elektrotechnik July 15, 1897. 80

——. "Street Railroads and Municipal Corporations." Railroad Gaz. 29:868 (Dec. 10, 1897). 81

——. "Street Railways." Parsons, Frank. New Time 1:138, 1:281 (Nov. 1897); Bemis, Edward W. Ch. VII, pp. 505-586 in "Municipal Monopolies," see 160-86. 82

——. "Street Railways vs. Municipalities." (Editorial.) St. Ry. Jour. 13:299 (May, 1897). 83

——. "The Case for Municipal Operation of Street Railways." (Editorial.) St. Ry. J. 13:852 (Dec. 1897).

——. "The Street Railway Problem." (Editorial.) Ind. 50:13 (May 19, 1898).

Paving, Street Railways and. (See Street Railways under **Pavements.**)

"Power Companies and their Relation to Municipalities, Electric." Lang, Albion E. St. Ry. Rev. 8:336 (May 15, 1898). 84

"Pingreeism, Reflections Concerning." (Editorial.) St. Ry. J. 13:104 (Feb. 1897).

"Public Ways, Use of, by Private Corporations." Powers, Samuel L. Arena 5:681 (1892); Schindler, Solomon. Arena 5:687 (1892). 85

——. "Conflicting Rights of Street Railways and Municipalities in the Highways." Hodge, J. Aspinwall. St. Ry. Jour. 13:296 (May, 1897). 86

"Regulation of Cost and Quality of Service as Illustrated by Street Railway Companies." Speirs, F. W. Ann. Am. Acad. Pol. Sci. May, 1900, Supp. p. 61. 87

Relation of the Public to the Street Railways. Boyle, John W. St. Ry. R. 9:266 (April 15, 1899); Curtis, C. E. Yale R. 6:17 (May, 1897); Lardner, James F. St. Ry. R. 9:39 (Jan. 15, 1899); Little, J. T., Jr. St. Ry. R. 8:716 (Oct. 15, 1898), Elec, Rev. 33:266 (Oct. 26, 1898); Moore, Clarence S. Outlook 62:665 (July 22, 1899); Parsons, Frank. New Time 2:319 (May, 1898); Mun. Rec. & Ad. 3:724 (Aug. 15, 1898). 88

——. "Relations of Railways to Municipalities." Jones, Dwight A. Engng. M. 8:813 (1895). 89

——. "Relations of Street Railways and Municipal Corporations." Argument before the Special Committee Appointed by the Governor (Mass) to investigate this subject. Reprinted in St. Ry. Rev. 8:5 (Jan. 15, 1898.) Burdett, Everett W. Boston, 1897. Pamphlet, 119 pp. 90

"Revenue from Street Railroads, Municipal." Dewey, Davis R. Am. Econ. Assoc. 2:551 (1888). 91

"Service Required by the Municipality, Street Railway." St. Ry. R. 7:567 (Sept. 15, 1897). 92

"Subways, The Municipal Ownership of Electric." (Practice of Baltimore and St.

Municipal Control—*Continued.*

Louis, with general considerations.) Engng. News 37:57 (Jan. 28, 1897).   93
"Urban Transit, Public Control of." Baxter, Sylvester. Cosmopol. 18:54 (1894).   94
"Value of Street Railway Franchises, Financial." Stevens, E. R. Outlook 51:600 (1895).   95

WATER WORKS.

"A Form of Municipal Control of Water Works." Mun. Engng. 14:275 (May, 1898).   96
"Combined Water Works and Electric Light Plants, Municipal Ownership of." Fischer, Louis E. Public Policy 2:228 (April 14, 1900), Mun. Engng. 18:147 (March, 1900).   97
——. "A Municipal Water and Light Plant." Pierce, F. G. City Govt. 3:121 (Oct. 1897), Prog. Age 15:538 (Nov. 15, 1897).   98
"Experiences of Cities with Municipal Water Works." Sweet, J. S. Cal. Mun. 1:211 (Feb. 1900).   99
"Financial Statement of Municipal Water Works, Examination of." Davis, F. A. W. Mun. Engng. 15:10 (July, 1898).   100
"Franchises, Water Works." (Statistics of one-third of the companies in the United States, with discussion.) Engng. News Jan. 9, 1892, p. 37.   1
——. "Value of Water Works Franchises, The." Wallace, J. M. Mun. Engng. 17:146 (Sept. 1899).   2
"Municipal Ownership of Water Works." Heim, John B. Mun. Engng. 17:87 (Aug. 1899).   3
——. "About a Municipal Water Plant." Caulfield, John. City Govt. 3:131 (Oct. 1897).   4
——. "A Few Considerations of Municipal Water Supply." Kuichling, E. Trans. of Assn. of Civ. Engs. of Cornell Univ., 1898.   5
——. "Municipal Ownership of Water, Gas and Electric Light Plants," see 160-86.   6
——. "Municipal Control of Street Car, Water and Gas Plants." Canadian Engineer Feb. 1896.
——. "Municipal vs. Private Water Plants." City Govt. 4:90 (March, 1898).   7
——. "Municipal Water." Fabian Tract No. 81 (Feb. 1898). London, Fabian Society, 1898.   8
——. "Water Supplies, Municipal." Hill, William R. Pp. 110-111 in "Pro. of the 3d Annual Conv. of the League of Am. Municipalities, 1899." 8vo, 143 pp. Paper.   9
——. "Municipal Water Supply." Heim, John B. Proc. of the Conv. of the League of Wisconsin Municipalities, Bulletin No. 3, p. 25, June 26-27, 1899, Pub. Imp. 1:6 (May 1, 1899).   10
——. "Municipal Water Works." McGuire, James K. City Govt. 5:57 (Aug. 1898).   11
——. "Nation's Water Supply and Its Effective Control." Jones, C. E. J. Gas Light 75:541 (Feb. 27, 1900).   12
——. "Public Control of the Water Works." City & State 6:211 (March 30, 1899).   13
——. "Public and Private Ownership of Water Works." Baker, M. N. Outlook 59:76 (May 7, 1898).   14
——. "Water Works." Baker, M. N. Ch. I, pp. 3-54, in "Municipal Monopolies," see 160-86.   15
"Ownership of Water Works in the United States and Canada." Engng. News Jan. 23, 1892, p. 83.   16
"Particulars in which Municipal Officers should protect the Municipal Corporation in granting Water Works Franchises to Private Companies." Tubbs, J. Nelson. Engng. News May 19, 1892, p. 518; Proc. Am. Water Works Assoc., 1892, p. 36.   17
"Politics, Taking Water Works out of." Mun. Engng. 13:307 (Nov. 1897).   13
"Private Water Companies, their Relation to Municipal Authorities and the Public." Dunham, H. F. San. Eng. July 30, 1887.   19

Municipal Control, State Boards for. (See under **Home Rule for Cities.**)

"**Municipal Democracy.**" Baxter, Sylvester. Address before Advance Club, Providence, May 9, 1891. Printed by the Club. 20

Municipal Improvements. (See **Engineering.**)

Municipal Insurance. "Assurances Municipales." Veber, Adrien. Rev. Soc. 28:516 (May, 1898). 21

"**Municipal Officials,** National Societies of." (Editorial.) Engng. News 40:113 (Aug. 25, 1898). 22

"**Municipal Patriotism.**" Barrows, John H. A sermon preached at Plymouth Church, Chicago, Nov. 27, 1890. 22 pp. 23

"**Municipal Salaries**" Ardagh, Judge. Mun. World 9:148 (Sept. 1899). 24

Municipal Socialism. (See under **Municipal Control, Municipal Ownership.**)

Municipal Statistics. (See under **Statistics.**)

Municipal Trading. (See under **Municipal Control, Municipal Ownership.**)

"**Museums.**" pp. 53-82, "Methods of Social Reform," by W. Stanley Jevons. London and New York, Macmillan, 1883. 383 pp. $3. 25

Naples.

Finance. "La Finanza del Municipio di Napoli, osservazioni e proposte." Amore, Nic. Napoli, Giannini, 1891. 5 pp. 26
Municipality, The Naples. Turiello, P. Nuova Ant. Feb. 1, 1898. 27
Sanitation. "Die Neubauten des Sanitäts-Vereines in Neapel in den Jahren 1888 und 1889." Meissner, Alois. Allgemeine Bauzeitung 52:86 (1892). 28

Nashville, Tenn.

City Government, General References.
"Appointment of a Receiver for Nashville in 1869." Merriam, Lucius S. Am. Law R. 25:393 (1891). 29
"Experiments in Municipal Government." Colyar, A. S. Southern Bivouac 2:306 30
History, description and statistics of Nashville, Tenn., in 1880. Census. See 1-7. 31
"Municipal Condition of Nashville, Tenn." Lindsley, A. V. S. p. 102, Proc. Third Natl. Conf. for Good City Govt., 1896. See 6-18c. 32
"Municipal Government of Nashville." Kennedy, John L. City Govt. 1:108 (1896). 33
"History of Nashville, Tenn." Thurston, Gates P. See 1-4c. 34
"Water Works of Nashville." Engng. Rec. Oct. 6, 1894. 35

Nebraska.

"Private and Municipal Ownership of Water Works, Electric Light and Power Plants, and Gas Works." (Relates almost exclusively to Nebraska.) Sixth Biennial Report of the Bureau of Labor and Industrial Statistics of Nebraska, 1897-8. pp. 494-572. Lincoln, Neb., 1898. 36

Negaunee, Mich.

"Municipal Electric Lighting Plant at Negaunee, Mich." Anon. Elec. R. 35:187 (Sept. 20, 1899); Other Side 1:245 (Nov. 25, 1900). 37

"**Negro,** Conditions of the, in various cities." (Atlanta, Ga., Nashville, Tenn., Cambridge, Mass. and other cities.) Bulletin of the Department of Labor, No. 10, p. 257 (May, 1897). 38

Neuchâtel, Switz. "Agrandissement de la Ville de Neuchâtel." Eisenb. 10:45. 39

Newark, N. J.

"Consolidation at Newark, N. J. Prog. Age 16:580 (Dec. 15, 1898).
History, description and statistics of Newark, N. J., in 1880. Census. See 1-7. 40
——. "Records of the Town of Newark, New Jersey, from its settlement in 1666, to its incorporation as a city in 1836." Newark, New Jersey, Historical Society, 1864. 8vo, 294 pp. 41
"Police Department of Newark, History of." Newark, Relief Publication Co., 1893. 419 pp.
"Water Supply of Newark, N. J." Herschel, Clemens. J. N. E. Water Works Assoc. 8:18 (1893). 42
——. "Preventing Water Waste in Newark, N. J." Engng. Rec. 40:148 (July 15, 1899). 43

"**New Bedford** [**Mass.**], The Further Water Supply of the City of, now being Constructed." Wood, Edmund. Jour. N. E. Water Works Assoc. March, 1897. 44

"**New Brighton, N. Y.**, Garbage Disposal System of." Engng. Rec. March 13, 1897. 45

"**Newburgh, N. Y.**, History of." Skeel, Adalaide. See 1-4b. 46

"**Newburyport** [**Mass.**] Water Works Litigation, The." Engng. Rec. 42:362 (Oct. 20, 1900). 47

Newcastle, Eng.

City Government. "Some Impressions of Municipal Newcastle." Watson, Aaron. Mun. J. 9:679 (Aug. 31, 1900). 48
History. (See references p. 343 Gross "Bibliography of British Municipal History.") 49
"Slums of Newcastle, The." Wallace, Johnstone. Mun. J. 9:204 (March 16, 1900), 9:224 (March 23, 1900). 50
Transit Facilities. "A Chance for Newcastle." Mun. J. & London 8:105 (Jan. 26, 1899). 51
——. "Cable versus Electric Traction in Newcastle." Ry. World 7:378 (Nov. 1898). 52
——. "Mechanical Power for Newcastle Tramways." Colam, W. N. Ry. World 7:380 (Nov. 1898). 53
——. "Newcastle Tramways." Laws, W. George. Ry. World 8:189 (May 11, 1899). 54
——. "Tramway Question in Newcastle." Ry. World 7:58 (Feb. 1898). 55

New England.

"Direct Legislation in New England." (Town Meetings.) Janes, L. G. (Abstract in Senate Document on Direct Legislation p. 192. See above.) 56
"Germanic Origin of New England Towns." Adams, Herbert B. J. H. Univ. Studies 1:2 (1883). 57
"Origin and Development of Local Self-Government in New England and the United States." Bugbee, J. M. Address before the American Social Science Association, Boston, Jan. 14, 1880. Boston, A. Williams & Co., 1880. 39 pp. 58
"Parks, New England." Garden & F. 4:482, 566, 602 (1891). 59
"Town and County Government as a factor of New England Government." Adams, Herbert B. J. H. Univ. Studies II:10 (1884). 60
Transit Facilities. "Electricity as a Motive Power for the Suburban Railway Service of New England." Short, Sidney H. St. Ry. J. 13:673 (Oct. 1897). 61
"Vital Statistics of the New England States. A Summary for the year 1892; being a Concise Statement of the Marriages, Divorces, Births and Deaths in the six New England States." Compiled under the direction of the Secretaries of the State Boards of Health. 8vo, 2s. 6 d. 62

New Haven, Conn.

"Charities, A Day's Work in New Haven Organized." Preston, S. O. Char. R. 3:159 (1894). 63

"History of New Haven, Conn." Cogswell, Fredrick Hull. See 1-4a. 64

———. "The Republic of New Haven: A History of Municipal Evolution." Levermore, Charles H. Balitmore, J. H. Univ. Press, 1886. $2. 65

———. "Town and City Government of New Haven." Levermore. Charles H. J. H. Univ. Studies IV:10 (1886). 66

History, description and statistics of New Haven, Conn., in 1880. Census. See 1-7. 67

"Law and Order League of Connecticut." Prince, Walter A. Reprinted from the Connecticut Citizen, 1895. 22 pp. 68

"Municipal Condition of New Haven." Fox, George L. pp. 164-174, Proc. of the Louisville Conference for Good City Government, 1897. See 6-18d. 69

"Parks of New Haven, The Public." Blake, Henry T. Park & Cem. 9:159 (Oct. 1899). 70

New Jersey.

Charities. "The State Charities Aid Association of New Jersey." Williamson, Emily E. P. 72 "International Congress," vol. III, 1893, see 43-99. 71

City Government. "An Act Relating to Boroughs (Revision of 1897) in the State of New Jersey; with Notes." Skinner, A. F. Newark, Loney & Sage, 1898. 8vo, 94 pp. $1.50. 72

"Financial Condition of the Several Counties, Cities, Townships, Towns, Boroughs and Villages of the State of New Jersey." 2d part of the Annual Report of the Comptroller of the Treasury of the State of New Jersey. Trenton, Comptroller, issued annually. 73

———. "Franchise Tax Law, Expected Effect of the New Jersey." Black, Charles C. Public Policy 2:338 (June 2, 1900); anon. St. Ry. J. 16:584 (June 16, 1900). 74

Parks. "Saving the Palisades." Parsons, Samuel, Jr. Hrprs. Wkly. 44:176 (Feb. 24, 1900). 75

"Sewage Disposal in New Jersey." Engng. Rec. 41:289 (March 31, 1900). 76

———. "An Important Decision on River Pollution by Sewage in New Jersey." Engng. News 41:158 (March 9, 1899). 77

———. "Commissioners' Report on the Passaic River Pollution." Trenton, N. J., 1899. 8vo, 54 pp. Reviewed in Engng. News 41:157 (March 9, 1899). 78

———. "Sewage Consumption in New Jersey." Phillips, Samuel. Sanitarian 11:300 (April, 1898). 79

———. "Sewage Disposal in the Passaic Valley." Engng. News 42:8 (July 6, 1899). 80

———. "Sewerage Disposal and Stream Pollution in the Lower Passaic Valley, New Jersey." Engng. News 39:129 (Feb. 24, 1898). 81

———. "The New Jersey Sewage Disposal Law." Engng. Rec. 42:102 (Aug. 4, 1900). 82

———. "The Prevention of Water Pollution in New Jersey." Engng. News 43:224 (April 5, 1900). 83

Transit Facilities. "Reports of Cable, Electric and Horse Railroad Companies." Trenton, N. J., State Board of Assessors, issued annually since 1890. 8vo, 68 pp. Pamphlet. 84

"Water Supply, New Jersey Forests and their Relation to." Vermeule, C. C. Engng. Rec. 42:8 (July 7, 1900), Engng. N. 44:58 (July 26, 1900). 85

New Orleans, La.

City Government, General References.

"Municipal Affairs in New Orleans." Janvier, Charles. Pp. 199-217 "Pro. of the Louisville Conference, 1897." See 6-18d. 86

"Municipal Condition of New Orleans." Spencer, Walter B. p. 407, Proc. Second Natl. Conf., 1895. See 6-18b. 87

"Municipal Reform in New Orleans." Walker, Norman. City & State 7:278 (Nov. 2, 1899). 88

"New Orleans, Our Southern Capital." Ralph, Julian. Harpers 86:364 (1893). 89

New Orleans, La.—*Continued.*

"Notes on Municipal Progress in New Oreans." p. 266 Pro. Indianapolis Conf., 1898. See 6-18e. 90

Bridges. "The Proposed Mississippi River Bridge at New Orleans." Eng. News 37:208 (April 1, 1897). 91
Direct Legislation. "Referendum in New Orleans, A Unique." Pomeroy, Eltweed. Dir. Leg. Rec. 6:65 (Sept. 1899). 92
"Garbage Utilization at Cincinnati and New Orleans." Engin. News Oct. 8, 1896. 93
"Higher Life of New Orleans." King, Grace. Outlook 53:754 (1896). 94
"History of New Orleans, La." King, Grace. See 1-4c. 95
——. History, description and statistics of New Orleans, La., in 1880. Census. See 1-7. 96
——. "Municipal History of New Orleans." Howe, W. W. J. H. Univ. Studies VII:4 (1889). 25 cts. 97
Municipal Ownership. "Ownership of Public Utilities." Woodruff, Clinton Rogers. Ann. Am. Acad. Pol. Sci. 15:126 (Jan. 1900). 98
"Park Development in the City of New Orleans." Johnson, Lewis. Park and Outdoor Art Association, p. 76, 1897. 99
Paving. "History and Selection of Street Paving in the City of New Orleans." Bell, A. C. J. Assoc. Engng. Soc. 22:45 (Feb. 1899). 100
"Public Improvements at New Orleans." Flower, Walter C. pp. 111-145 in "Proc. of the 3d Annual Conv. of the League of Am. Municipalities, 1899." 8vo, 148 pp. Paper. 1
Sanitation in New Orleans. Bell, A. N. Sanitarian 43:314 (Oct. 1899), Engng. Rec. 40:45 (June 17, 1899), Sanitarian 43:64 (July, 1899). 2
Schools. "Kindergarten Outlook in New Orleans, The." Waldo, Eveline A. Kindergarten M. 10:229 (Dec. 1897). 3
Sewerage, Drainage. Sewage Disposal in New Orleans. Brown, L. W. Engng. News 43:180 (March 15, 1900), 44:86 (Aug. 9, 1900); Flower, William C. City Govt. 7:57 (Sept. 1899), Public Improvements 1:270 (Oct. 1, 1899); Harrod, B. M. Engng. Rec. 40:360 (Sept. 16, 1899); Harrod, B. M. Eng. News Dec. 15, 1888; Theard, Alfred F. Engng. Rec. 40:550 (Nov. 11, 1899), J. Assoc. Engng. Soc. 24:62 (Jan. 1900); Waring, G. E. Am. Arch. 7:145 (1879); anon. Engng. Rec. 37:511 (May 14, 1898); Engng. Rec. 40:146 (July 15, 1899); Sanitarian 43:299 (Oct. 1899). 4
——. "Electric Drainage of New Orleans, The." Reed, Lyman C. Elec. W. & E. 34:771 (Nov. 18, 1899). 5
"Telephone Service." Ficklen, John R. Ann. Am. Acad. Pol. Sci. 15:474 (May, 1900). 6
Transit Facilities. "Canal and Claiborne (Street) Railway Company. St. Ry. Jour. 13:265 (May, 1897). 7
"Water Supply of New Orleans, The." Ordway, John M. J. Assoc. Engng. Soc. 24:311 (May, 1900). 8
——. "Water Works, Mayor Flower on New Orleans." City Govt. 7:86 (Oct. 1899). 9
"Women's Work for the Public in New Orleans." Mount, May Wilkinson. Mun. Aff. 2:509 (Sept. 1898). 10

Newport, R. I.

"History of Newport, R. I." Coolidge, Susan. See 1-4a. 11
——. History, description and statistics of Newport, R. I., in 1880. Census. See 1-7. 12

Newton, Mass.

"Crossings on the Main Line of the Boston and Albany Railroad in Newton, Mass., Abolition of the Grade." Farnham, Irving T., Parker, William, and Chamberlain, W. G. S. J. Assoc. Engng. Soc. 21:37 (Aug. 1898). 13
"Sewers at Newton, Mass., Maintenance of the System of Separate." Childs, Stephen. J. Assoc. Engng. Soc. 22:94 (March, 1899). 14

"**New Westminster, B. C.,** Municipal Electric Light Plant at." Can. Elec. N. 8:47 (March, 1898).

New York City.

Government, General References and Unclassified.

"American Metropolis, The—New York City Life." Moss, Frank. New York, Collier, 1897. 3 Vols. 8vo, 1194 pp. ill. $4. 15

Brooklyn. (For references on government and general conditions in the former city of Brooklyn, see under Brooklyn below.)

"Charter of the City of New York with notes thereon, The: also a treatise on the powers and duties of the mayor, aldermen and assistant aldermen." (Contains Dongan Charter, 1686, Montgomerie Charter, 1708, Charter of 1730 and amended charters of 1830 and 1849.) Kent, Chancellor. New York, Published for the Common Council, 1854. 336 pp. (See also Charter under Greater New York.) 16

"Citizens and Officials of New York City, their rights and duties according to law, together with a popular description of all departments of the City Government." Compiled by the Brooklyn Leader, Brooklyn Leader Pub. House, 1895. 109 pp. 25 cts. 17

"Consolidation Act, The New York City."Ash, Mark. Albany, Weed, Parsons and Co., 1890. $6. 18

"Future Metropolis, The." Coler, Bird S. Pub. Imp. 2:145 (Feb. 1, 1900). 19

——. "Twelve Letters on the Future of New York." (Growth and Commercial Development, Taxation, etc., in New York.) Andrews, Geo. H. New York, M. B. Brown, 1877. 8vo, 45 pp. 20

Government of New York. Bishop, J. B. Nation 50:216 (1890); Buel, C. C. Cent. 49:769 (1895); Flower, R. P., and Pavey, Frank D. Forum 23:531 (July, 1897); Jameson, J. F. Mag. Am. His. 8:315, 598 (1882); Kelly, Edmond. Forum 27:61 (March, 1899); Nadal, E. S. Forum 2:49 (1886); Parkhurst, Charles H. Our Day 9:451 (1892); Parton, James, No. Am. 103:413 (1866); Sears, E. I. Nat. Q. 27:114 (1874); New York Quarterly 3:80 (1854); Hrprs. Wkly. 38:966 (1894); Ann. Am. Acad. Pol. Sci. 12:129 (Sept. 1898). 21

——. "Alleged Frauds in Departments of the City Government of New York." Butler, Geo. B. Report of Committee of the Union League Club, 1884. 14 pp. 22

——. "Borough System in Municipal Government, The." Kelly, Edmond. Forum 27:61 (March, 1899). 23

——. Greater New York, Government of. (See under Greater New York below.)

——. "Misgovernment of New York, A Remedy suggested." Nordhoff, Charles. No. Am. 113:321 (1871). 24

——. "Municipal Code of New York, General." Silvernail, W. H. New York, Banks & Bros., 1895. 95 cts. 25

——. "Municipal Government of New York." Kelly, Edmond. p. 103, Proc. (First) Natl. Conf., 1894. See 6-18a. 26

——. "Municipal Government as Illustrated by the Charter, Finances and Public Charities of New York." Coler, Bird S. New York, D. Appleton & Co., 1900. 12mo, 200 pp. Cl. $1. 27

——. "Property and Good Municipal Government." Real Estate Rec. & Guide Feb. 24, 1894, p. 292.

Greater New York. De Witt, W. C. Munsey's 17:923 (Sept. 1897); Fanton, Mary A. Demorest's Sept. 1897; Matthews, Franklin. Leslie's Wkly. 78:340 (1894), Hrprs. Wkly. 41:385 (April 17, 1897); Palmer, Emerson. No. Am. Rev. 153:250 (1891); Poindexter, Philip. Leslie's Wkly. 78:87 (1894); Thorne, W. H. Globe 7:369 (Dec. 1897); Waldron, Geo. B. McClure's 9:1097 (Oct. 1897); anon. R. of Rs. 10:476 (1894); Gunton's M. May, 1896; Public Life p. 35, (Nov. 1896); N. Y. Educa. 1:296 (Jan. 1898); Ind. 50:19 (Jan. 6, 1898); Outlook 58:107 (Jan. 8, 1898). 28

——. Charter of Greater New York. Pryor, James W. Ann. Am. Acad. Pol. Sci. 10:20 (July, 1897); Rowe, Leo S. Ann. Am. Acad. Pol. Sci. 11:148 (March, 1898); Shaw, Albert. Independent 49:303, 335 (March 11, 18, 1897); Sterne, Simon. Public Improvements 2:150 (Feb. 1, 1900); anon. City Govt. 2:137 (May, 1897), 3:191 (Dec. 1897), 4:22, 52 (Jan., Feb., 1898); Nation 66:103 (Feb. 10, 1898); Ann. Am. Acad. Pol. Sci. 14:136 (July, 1899). 29

——. "Report accompanying the Proposed Greater New York Charter." (With text of Charter.) N. Y. Assembly Doc. No. 53, Feb. 22, 1897, Albany, State Printers. 892 pp. 30

——. "Charter for the Greater New York as submitted in the first report of the committee on draft." Published by the Brooklyn Eagle, Jan. 1897. 56 pp. 5 cts. 31

——. "Charter, Calendar of the New York City." New York, City Club, 1900.

BIBLIOGRAPHY. 175

New York City—*Continued.*

12mo, 54 pp. Free.   32

——. " Charter with Table of Amendments, General Index of the New York City." New York, City Club, 1900. 12mo, 36 pp. Free.   33

——. Charter. " Matter of the Hearing in Relation to the Greater New York held before the Sub-Committee of the Joint Committee on the Affairs of Cities." Senate Doc. No. 44, 1896. (Clarence Lexow, Chairman.) 667 pp.   34

——. Charter. " Proceedings of the Association of the Bar of the City of New York regarding the proposed charter of the Greater New York and report of the special committee appointed to examine the said proposed charter." Peckham, Wheeler H. (chairman.) New York, Published by the Bar Association. Pamphlet, 28 pp.   35

——. " Charter for Greater New York, A New." Mun. Aff. 4:449 (Sept. 1900).   36

——. " Charter Revision, New York." (Editorial). Outlook 65:198 (May 26, 1900).

——. " Charter Revision Commission's Report." Baldwin, Henry De Forest. Mun. Aff. 4:768 (Dec. 1900).   37

——. " Consolidation." Real Estate Rec. & Guide Dec. 21, 1895, p. 887; Jan. 18, 1896, p. 84; Jan. 25, 1896, p. 131; Feb. 22, 1896, p. 294; April 4, 1896, p. 564.   38

——. " Against Consolidation; Letters Worth Reading." Storrs, Richard Salter and others. 23 pp. Published by the League of Loyal Citizens, Brooklyn. (No. 4).   39

——. " Against Consolidation; taxes and tenements, a study of municipal conditions." Redfield, William C. Brooklyn, League of Loyal Citizens. 56 pp. 1894, (No. 3).   40

——. " Consolidation, A Brooklyn Boomer on." Real Estate Rec. & Guide Jan. 6, 1894, p. 30.

——. Consolidation. " Greater New York. For re-submission: addresses before the legislative joint sub-committee on consolidation." Storrs, Richard Salter and others. 34 pp. Published by the League of Loyal Citizens, Brooklyn. (No. 7.)   41

——. Election of 1897 in Greater New York. (See under Elections below).

——. " Financial Effects of Consolidation, The." Coler, Bird S. Engng. Rec. 40:608 (Nov. 25, 1899).   42

——. " Government of Greater New York " Coler, Bird S. No. Am. 169:90 (July, 1899); Greene, Francis V. Scrib. M. Oct. 1896; anon. Hrprs. Wkly. 42:20 (Jan. 1, 1898).   43

——. " Greater New York: A Century Hence." Waring, George E., Jr. Mun. Aff. 1:713 (Dec. 1897).   44

——. " Greater New York. Writings and Addresses." Green, Andrew H. New York, 1893. 64 pp. Maps. Paper.   45

——. " Gross New York, eine Studie zur Einverleibungsfrage." Herzfeld, Gustav. Berlin, Dietrich Reimer, 1898. 12mo, 66 pp. Map. 1.50m.   46

——. " Historical Sketch of the Municipal Consolidation." Henschel, Albert E. New York, American News Co., 1895. 72 pages. 25c.   47

——. " History of Greater New York, Leslie's." (Vol. I, To the Consolidation; Vol. II, Brooklyn and other Boroughs; Vol. III, Biography and Geneology). Van Pelt, Daniel. New York, Arkell Pub. Co., 1899. 4to, 554, 539, 649 pp. Cl. $25.   48

——. " Manhattan: The Mother City of Greater New York." van Rensselaer, (Mrs.) Schuyler. Cent. 56:138 (May, 1898).   49

——. " Municipal Problem and Greater New York, The." Shaw, Albert. Atlan. 79:733 (June, 1897).   50

——. " Political Inauguration of the Greater New York." Shepard, Edward M. Atlan. 81:104 (Jan. 1898).   51

——. " Politics of Greater New York." Gunton's 10:166, 341 (1896).   52

" Handbook of New York." King, Moses. Boston, King, 2d. ed., 1893, 928 pp. $1. (Pp. 245-66, "Rule of City.")   53

" Laws, Special and Local, affecting Public Interests in the City of New York." New York Asembly Doc. 148, 1880. 2196 pp.   54

" New York." Chap. II, in " The Land of the Dollar," by G. W. Steevens. New York, Dodd, Mead & Co., 1897. 12mo, 316 pp. $1.50.   55

" New York City." Godkin, E. L. Encyclopaedia Britannica, Vol. 17, pp. 457-66. (With list of books on New York City).   56

New York City—*Continued.*

"New York To-Day." Crosby, Howard. Lend a H. 4:788 (1889). 57

"Political Primer of New York State and City, A." Fielde, Adele M. New York, Macmillan, 1897. 12mo, 100 pp. 58

"Reform in New York, Municipal." Godkin, E. L. Nation 13:84 (1871), 28:331 1879); Leavitt, John B. Forum 17:659 (1894); Nott, C. C. Nation 13:157 (1871); Porrit, E. National 26:237 (1895); Riis, Jacob A. Outlook 64:911 (April, 21, 1900); anon. Nation 70:14 (Feb. 22, 1900). 59

"Reform Organizations in New York City." Tolman, Wm. Howe. Part V, p. 185, "Municipal Reform Movements in the United States." New York, Fleming H. Revell Co., 1895. 219 pp. $1. 60

———. Citizens' Union. Schurz, Carl. Hrprs. Wkly. 41:1215 (Dec. 11, 1897); anon. City and State 4:86 (Nov. 11, 1897); Ind. 49:1536 (Nov. 25, 1897); Nation 66:143 (Feb. 24, 1898). 61

———. "Citizens' Union, Campaign Book of the." First and second edition, 1897. 45 and 151 pp. 62

———. "City Vigilance League." Lawton, Charles E. Outlook 51:54 (1895); Parkhurst, Charles H. No. Am. 156:98 (1893). 63

———. "Committee of Seventy." Hrprs. Wkly. 38:966 (1894).

———. Good Government Clubs. Hale, E. E. Cosmopol. 16:735 (1894); Kelly, Edmond. Christian Union, June 17, 1893, Outlook 50:1124 (1894); Mellen, Chase. Pamphlet Published by Good Government Club F, 1895, 10 pp.; Tucker, Preble. Leslie's Wkly. 79:328 (1894); Tucker, R. S. No. Am. 150:389 (1894); anon. Good Govt. 13:92, 112, 125 (1894). 64

———. "The Independent Movement in New York." Eaton, Dorman B. New York, Putnam, 1880. 65

———. "The Woman's Municipal League." Lowell, Josephine Shaw. Mun. Aff. 2:465 (Sept. 1898). 66

———. (See also under Bossism, Parties, Tammany, etc. below).

"Relations of New York City and State." Bernheim, A. C. Pol. Sci. Q. 9:377 (1894). 67

"Unpaid Boards of Paid Commissioners." Cutting, R. Fulton. New York, The Author, 1900. 8vo, 9 pp. Free. 68

"Walk Uptown, The." Williams, Jesse Lynch. Scribner's 27:44 (Jan. 1900). 69

"Aldermen, New York." Nadal, E. S. Forum 2:49 (1886). 70

Almanac. "New York Press Quarterly." New York, Published quarterly by the New York Press. Edition for the first quarter, 1899, 448 pp. 35c. per year. 71

———. "The World Almanac and Encyclopedia." New York, Published by the New York World. Edition for Jan. 1900, 608 pp. 25c. 72

———. (See also under Brooklyn below).

"Amusements in New York, Popular." Coates, Foster. Chaut. 24:706 (Feb. 1897). 73

Architecture. "Appellate Court House, New York City, The New." Lord, James Brown. Arch. Rec. 9:429 (April, 1900). 74

Art in New York, Public. "Battery, The." Spencer, Nelson S. Public Imp. 2:122 (Jan. 15, 1900). 75

———. "Battery to Harlem, From." (Suggestions of the National Sculpture Society with regard to Municipal Art in New York). Mun. Aff. 3:616 (Dec. 1899). 76

———. "Beautifying New York City." Lopez, Charles A. Public Imp. 2:127 (Jan. 15, 1900). 77

———. "City Beautiful, The." Caffin, Charles H. Hrprs. Wkly. 43:241 (March 11, 1899). 78

———. "Dedication of the Grant Monument." Hrprs. Wkly. May 1, 8, 1897; Park and Cem. 7:54 (May, 1897).

———. "Monuments, New York City." Bush-Brown, H. K. Mun. Aff. 3:602 (Dec. 1899). 79

———. "Temple to Liberty, A." Bush-Brown, H. K. Public Imp. 2:125 (Jan. 15, 1900). 80

"Assemblymen and Senators from the City of New York, Annual Records of the. What are you going to do about it?" New York. Published annually by the City Reform Club, 1886-1893. 8 pamphlets. 72, 65, 106, 93, 88, 127, 132 and 115 pp. 81

BIBLIOGRAPHY. 177

New York City—*Continued.*

Bakeshops and Bakers in New York. (See under Labor below).

Baths and Lavatories. Brown, Goodwin. Sanitarian 45:36 (July, 1900); Faure, John P. Municipal Program Leaflet No. 5, New York, 1894, 7 pp. 5c.; Scudamore, Amy L. Lend a H. 17:43 (1896); Tolman, Wm. Howe. Mun. Program Leaflet No. 6, New York, 1894, 10 pp. 5c.; Engng. Rec. Feb. 13, 1892, p. 183; Committee of 70. New York, 1895, 15 pp.; Citizens' Union Pamphlet No. 1, 1897, New York, 12 pp.; Engng. Rec. 40:227 (Aug. 5, 1899), 42:446 (Nov. 10, 1900). 82

——. "Baths and Public Comfort Stations, Report of Mayor's Committee on." Tolman, William Howe, Moreau Morris and William Gaston Hamilton. New York, Published by the Mayor's Committee on Public Baths and Public Comfort Stations, 1897. 195 pp. Ill. Cloth, $1; paper, 50c. 83

Boss Rule in New York City. Leavitt, John B. Forum 17:659 (1894); Editorial. Hrprs. Wkly. 42:1051 (Oct. 29, 1898); Editorial. Ind. 51:1444 (May 25, 1899); Hrprs. Wkly. 43:832 (Aug. 26, 1899); Gunton's 17:161 (Sept. 1899). 84

"Botanical Garden, New York's New." Hrprs. Wkly. 41:718 (July 17, 1897). 85

Bridges. "Aesthetics of Bridge Design as exemplified by two Recent New York Bridges." Boller, Alfred P. Engng. News 38:226 (Oct. 7, 1897). 86

——. "Brooklyn Bridge, The Management of the." Engng. Rec. 38:552 (Nov. 26, 1898).

——. "Bridge Transportation System between New York and Brooklyn." (Illustrated description, engineering features, traffic conditions, terminal facilities, financial results, etc.) St. Ry. Jour. 13:69 (Feb. 1897). 87

——. "Terminals of the Brooklyn Bridge Railway." Emery, Charles E. Engng. News 37:43 (Jan. 21, 1897). 88

——. "Through Train Service across the Brooklyn Bridge, Report on." Engng. News 37:107 (Feb. 18, 1897); Electricity (N. Y.) Feb. 10, 1897. 89

——. "New Electric Power Plant." (Description, statistics on construction and operation of the bridge). Elec. Wld. Jan. 23, 1897. 90

——. "City of Bridges." Warner, John DeWitt. Mun. Aff. 3:651 (Dec. 1899). 91

—— East River Bridge, New. Real Estate Rec. & Guide Oct. 24, 1896, p. 590; Sci. Am. May 8, 1897. 92

——. "East River Bridge, Brooklyn Anchorage of the New." Engng. Rec. 37:514 (May 14, 1898).

——. "East River Bridge Foundation, The New." Engng. News 37:331 (May 27, 1897); Engng. Rec. Nov. 6, 1897; 37:207 (Feb. 5, 1898), 37:228 (Feb. 12, 1898), 37:251 (Feb. 19, 1898).

——. "East River Bridge, Towers and End Spans for the New." Engng. News 39:112 (Feb. 17, 1898).

——. Hudson River, Bridge across the. Lindenthal, Gustav. Engng. M. 6:213 (1893), 10:261 (1895). 93

——. "Long Span Bridges for Great Cities." (With especial references to projects for crossing the East River). Engng. Rec. March 13, 1897. 94

——. "Third Avenue Bridge, The." Real Estate Rec. & Guide Oct. 31, 1896, p. 630.

——. "Washington Bridge Over the Harlem River. Description of its Construction." Hutton, Wm. R. New York, Engineering News Pub. Co., 1889. 8vo, 96 pp. pl. il. cl. $4 95

"Bronx's Past and Future, The Borough of the" Haffen, Louis F. The Christian City 11:192 (Nov. 1899). 96

——. "The Great North Side or Borough of the Bronx." (History, Street Improvements, Educational Advantages, Public Works, Parks and Parkways, Map, etc.) New York, Issued by the North Side Board of Trade, 1897. 8vo, 248 pp. 97

Brooklyn. Godkin, E. L. Nation 42:140 (1886); Halstead, Murat. Cosmopol. 15:131 (1893); Ralph, Julian. Harper's 86:651 (1893). 98

——. Almanac. "Brooklyn Daily Eagle Almanac." Brooklyn, Published annually by the Brooklyn Daily Eagle. Edition for 1899, 600 pp. 25c. 99

——. "Government of Brooklyn City." City Govt. 1:77 (1896).

——. "Government of Brooklyn, Municipal." Low, William G. P. 72, Proc. First Natl. Conf., 1894. See 6-18a. 100

——. "Law Enforcement Society of Brooklyn." Tully, T. DeQuincy. P. 272, Pro. Indianapolis Conf., 1898. See 6-18e. 1

New York City—*Continued.*

——. " Organized Misgovernment." Reid, Sidney. Hrprs. Wkly. 38:326 (1894). 2

——. " Report on the Affairs of the City of Brooklyn and the County of Kings, Preliminary." New York Assembly Doc. 82, 1887. 10 pp. 3

——. " Report of the Commission to Revise all Laws affecting the City of Brooklyn." New York Assembly Doc. 77, 1887. 206 pp. 4

——. " Report in the Matter of the Brooklyn Investigation." New York Assembly Doc. 110, 1887. 80 pp. Minority Report, Doc. 111, 1887. 20 pp. 5

——. (Articles dealing with Brooklyn will also be found under the following subject heads of the present list on New York City: Building Law, Charities, Electrolysis, Garbage Disposal, History, Libraries, Parks, Police, Sanitation, Sewage Disposal, Statistics, Transit Facilities, Water Supply). 6

" Buildings, Tall Office, of New York." Robinson, John B. Engng. M. 1:185 (1891); Real Estate Rec. and Guide, p. 703, April 7, 1894; p. 405, March 17, 1894; p. 1009, June 23, 1894. 7

——. " Brooklyn's New Building Law." Real Estate Rec. & Guide, May 5, 1894.

——. " Building Department, Investigating the New York." Engng. News 41:285 (May 4, 1899).

——. " Building Department, Work of the." Mayer, Julius M. Mun. Aff. 4:760 (Dec. 1900). 8

——. Building Laws, New York. Veiller, Lawrence. Char. R. 9:388 (Nov. 1899); Sci. Am. Sup. March 7, 1896; Arch. and Buil. 27:195 (Dec. 4, 1897); Engng. News 39:39 (Jan. 20, 1898); Engng. Rec. 40:333, 367 (Sept. 9, 16, 1899). 9

——. " Building Laws, Revision of New York's." Real Estate Rec & Guide, July 27, 1895, p. 111; Nov. 23, 1895, p. 714; Jan. 11, 1896, p. 39; Feb. 1, 1896, p. 173; Feb. 8, 1896, p. 217; Feb. 15, 1896, p. 260; March 14, 1896, p. 428; March 28, 1896, p. 519; Aug. 22, 1896, p. 261. 10

——. " Building Laws of New York and Boston, Abstract and Discussion of." Am. Arch. Nov. 21, 1892, p. 97; Engng. Rec. Aug. 6, 1892, p. 159.

——. " Building Law in re High Buildings, The New York." Strachan, Robert C. Pp. 183-196 in " Pro. Brooklyn Engineers' Club for 1889." 8vo, 233 pp. Paper $2. 11

——. " Building Laws and Code, and Health Department Regulations, New York City." Morgan, R. M. New York, N. Y. Banks Laws Pub. Co., 1900. 16mo, 364 pp. Cloth, $1.50. 12

——. " Laws Relating to Buildings in the City of New York." Fryer, William J. Published by the New York Real Estate Rec. & Guide, 1895. 251 pp. $5. (Part I, The Building Law; Part II, Regulations of the Building Department; Part III, Tenement and Lodging House Laws; Part IV, Law Limiting the Height of Dwelling Houses; Part V, Law Relating to Extinction and Prevention of Fires; Part VI, Regulations of Department of Public Works; Part VII, State Factory Inspection Law; Part VIII, Mechanics' Lien Law). 13

——. " Laws Relating to Building in the City of New York." Fryer, William J. New York, D. Van Nostrand Co., 1898. 8vo, Cl. $2.50. 14

——. " Rebuilding of New York." Soc. Econ. 5:327 (1893).

——. " Registration of Plumbers under the New York Building Law." Engng. Rec. 40:392 (Sept. 23, 1899). 15

——. " Paris and New York Contrasted." (Height and Character of Buildings). Real Estate Rec. & Guide April 7, p. 703, 1894. 16

——. " Sky Line of New York, The." 1881-1897. Schuyler, Montgomery. Hrprs. Wkly. March 20, 1897. 17

——. " Statistics of Building Operations. New York City." B. Labor Stat. New York 1:167 (Dec. 1899). 18

Burial. " Graveyards as a Menace to the Commonweal." Windmüller, L. No. Am. 167:211 (Aug. 1898). 19

——. " Thrown in with the City's (Pauper) Dead." Gardner, Helen H. Arena 3:61 (1890). 20

" Catholics, Municipal Donations to, in New York." Hassard, J. R. G. Cath. World 30:846 (1880). 21

Central Park. (See under Parks below).

" Charities of New York." Ritter, John P. Social Econ. 7:152 (1894). 22

——. " Brooklyn, N. Y., Charity in." Lend a H. 3:445 (1888).

——. " Charities of New York, Brooklyn and Staten Island." Cammann, Henry

BIBLIOGRAPHY.

New York City—*Continued.*

J. and Camp, and Hugh N. New York, Hurd & Houghton, 1868. 8vo, 596 pp. Cl. $5.25.   23

———. " Charities Directory, New York; a classified and descriptive directory to the charitable societies, institutions and churches of the City of New York." New York, Charity Organization Society, issued annually. Edition for 1900. 773 pp. $1.   24

———. " Charity Organization Society of New York City." Lend a Hand. 1:196 (1887).   25

———. " Child Labor, The Evil of." Kelly, Florence. Leslie's Wkly. 70:84 (1890).   26

———. " Children, Placing Out of New York City, in the West." White, F. H. Char. R. 2:215 (1893).   27

———. " Children, Support of, in private institutions at public expense in New York." Lend a H. 12:421, 13:339 (1894). (See also under Public Charities below).   28

———. " Dangerous Classes of New York, The." Brace, Charles Loring. New York, Wynkoop & Hollenbeck, 1880. 448 pp. $1.25.   29

———. " Fresh Air Charities in New York." Browne, Junius Henri. Hrprs. Wkly. 38:803 (1894); Tolman, Wm. Howe. Chaut. 21:713 (1895).   30

———. " Hospitals, Public." Folks, Homer. Mun. Aff. 2:271 (June, 1898).   31

———. " Need of Food, Fuel and Shelter in New York." Phillips, Barnet. Hrprs. Wkly. 38:255 (1894).   32

———. " Penny Provident Fund in New York." McBride, M. M. Char. R. 1:280 (1892).   33

———. " Poor, The City's." New York, Citizens' Union, Pamphlet No. 5, 1897. 16 pp.   34

———. " Poor in New York, Special Needs of the." Riis, J. A. Forum 14:492 (1892).   35

———. Poor in New York. " The Shoe that Pinches." Ralph, Julian. **Hrprs.** Wkly. 38:33 (1894).   36

———. Poor in New York. " Sketches of Lowly Life in a Great City." Woolf, M. A. New York, G. P. Putnam's Sons, 1899. 4to, 185 pp. Cloth, $2.   37

———. Public Charities. Subsidies to Private Charities in New York. Coler, Bird S. Charities, Vol. III, No. 16. (See also his " Municipal Government," New York, Appleton, 1900, 12mo, 200 pp., cl. $1.); Devine, Edward T. Char. R. 9:338 (Oct. 1899); Folks, Homer. Char. R. 7:869 (Dec. 1897), Char. Vol. III, No. 19, p. 2 Oct. 7, 1899; Hinton, R. J. Old and New 11:477 (1875); Keller, John W. Arena Q. 1:62 (June, 1900); Kinkead, T. L. Char. Vol. III, No. 17, p. 6, Sept. 23, 1899; Rowe, Leo S. Ann. Am. Acad. Pol. Sci. 11:155 (March, 1898); Williams, Henry S. Hrprs. Wkly. 39:148 (1895); anon. Lend a H. 2:574, 633 (1888).   38

———. " Salvation Army Shelter Brigade." Booth, Ballington. Hrprs. Wkly. 37:1257 (1893).   39

———. " Sociological Canvass of the Fifteenth Assembly District of New York City." Laidlaw, Walter. New York, Federation of Churches and Christian Workers. 112 pp.   40

———. " Sociological Information, Handbook of, with especial reference to New York City." Tolman, Wm. Howe. New York, G. P. Putnam's Sons, 1894. 257 pp. $1.   41

———. " Sociological Laboratory, A Year's Work in a City." New York, Published by the Association for Improving the Condition of the Poor, 1896. 139 pp. 10c.   42

———. " Street Begging in New York." Charities Vol. III, No. 24, p. 2, Nov. 11, 1899.

———. " West Side, New York, Charitable Work in the." Thaw, A. B. Lend a H. 10:309 (1893).   43

———. " Woman's Work in the Slums." Booth, Maud B. Hrprs. Wkly. 37:1257 (1893).   44

———. " Women in Philanthropic Work." Mount, May Wilkinson. Mun. Aff. 2:447 (Sept. 1898).   45

Charters of New York, Greater New York. (See under Government, General References, etc. above).

Chinatown. Chinese in New York. (See under Foreign Element below).

Church and Religious Condition. " The Religious Condition of New York City."

New York City—*Continued.*

Addresses at a Christian Conference in Chickering Hall, Dec. 3, 4 and 5, 1888. New York, Baker & Taylor Co., 1888. 12mo, 196 pp. 50 cts.   46

——. "Famous Night Mission in New York." Hereward, L. A. Ecl. M. 121:507 (1894).   47

Citizens' Union. (See Reform Organizations under General References above, also under Elections.)

"City Hall, Preservation of the Historic." Green, Andrew H. New York State Society, Sons of the American Revolution, 1894. 15 pp.   48

——. "A Municipal Opportunity." (New City Hall.) Hrprs. Wkly. 38:198 (1894).

City History Club. (See under History below.)

Civil Service. McAneny, George. Mun. Aff. 4:708 (Dec. 1900); Ralph, Julian. Hrprs. Wkly. 40:131 (1896); Citizens' Union Pamphlet, New York, 1897, 10 pp; Rowe, Leo. S. Ann. Am. Acad. Pol. Sci. 11:113 (Jan. 1898); anon. Nation 66:419 (June 2, 1898); Ann. Am. Acad. Pol. Sci. 13:407 (May, 1899).   49

——. Brooklyn Civil Service. "Address on the Subject of Public Affairs." Carter, Luther C. Brooklyn, Bunce & Co., 1873. 12 pp.   50

——. "Merit System in the Civil Service." New York, Citizens' Union Pamphlet, 1897. 10 pp.   51

——. Police Appointments. (See under Police below.)

"Commercial Growth and Greatness of New York." Kettell, T. P. DeBow's Commercial Review 5:30 (1848).   52

Comptroller of New York City. (See under Finances below.)

Conduits. "The Success of the Open Conduit in New York City." Elec. World 32:254 (Sept. 10, 1898).   53

Courts. "The Law and Practice of the Municipal Court under the Greater New York Charter, with the Boundaries of Boroughs, Districts and Wards; with Forms and Exhaustive Index." Langbein, G. F. and J. C. L. (4th ed.) New York, Banks & Bros., 1898. 8vo, 609 pp. Cloth $5.   54

——. "Bench within New York City." Green Bag July, 1897.   55

——. "Boss and the Bench, The." (Editorial.) Hrprs. Wkly. 42:1051 (Oct. 29, 1898).

——. "City Magistrates' Courts, The." Cornell, Robert E. Scrib. M. 21:221 (Feb. 1897).   56

——. Police Courts. (See under Police below.)

Crime. (See under Police below.)

Croker, Richard. (See under **Croker, Richard.** Also under Tammany below.)

"Department Store in the East, The: General Storekeeping in New York." Steele, John S. Arena 22:174 (Aug. 1899).   57

Driveways. "Gotham's Greater Rotten Row, Peter B. Sweeny's Project for a Grand Terrace on the West Side." New York, Municipal Improvement Association, 1890. 80 pp.   58

"East Side Considerations, New York City." Martin, E. S. Harper's M. 96:853 (May, 1898).   59

——. "East Side Living Conditions." Gunton's 15:194 (Sept. 1898).   60

——. "Spectator on the East Side." Outlook 54:365 (1896).

——. (See also under Streets below.)

Elections. "Ballot in New York." Bernheim, A. C. Pol. Sci. Q. 4:130 (1889).   61

——. "Ballot Bill Proposed by the City Club of New York." New York, Published by the City Club, 1896. 57 pp.   62

——. "Ballot, Party Column, and the Massachusetts Ballot. A Statement of objections to the present (New York) Ballot Law and of Proposed Amendments." New York, Published by the City Club, 1896. 20 pp.   63

——. "Ballot Reform." Ann. Am. Acad. Pol. Sci. 14:137 (July, 1899).

——. "Ballot Reform Law, The New York City and Rural Registry Law." Murlin, Edgar L. Albany, Jas. B. Lyon, 1890. 5th edition, 142 pp. 15 cts.   64

——. "Cumulative Vote, Municipal Reform in New York and the." Law Magazine and Review n. s. 1:206 (1872).   65

——. "Election Day in New York." Ingersoll, Ernest. Cent. 53:3 (Nov. 1896).   66

BIBLIOGRAPHY. 181

New York City—*Continued.*

———. " Election Day in Poorer New York." Banks, E. L. English Illustrated M. Jan. 1897. 67

———. " Election Frauds of New York City and their Prevention." New York, American News Co., 1881. $1.50. 68

———. " Election Frauds in New York, 1869." Sedgwick, A. G. Nation 8:165 (1869). 69

———. " Election Law in New York City, Plain Statement of the." Pryor, James W., Arthur H. Ely and Geo. W. Mil er. New York, City Club, 1894. 62 pp. 10 cts. 70

———. " The Election Law so far as it relates to the conduct of elections in the city and county of New York." New York, Published by authority, 1897. Pamphlet 121 pp. 71

———. " Election Officers and Voters, Manual for General Election Law and Additional Laws regulating the Conduct of Elections in the Cities of New York and Brooklyn." Jewett, F. G. Albany, Bender, 1895. $1.50. 72

———. Election of 1897. (First municipal election in Greater New York.) Bacon, L. W. Ind. 49:1425 (Nov. 4, 1897); Bryce, James. Contemp. No. 383, p. 750 (Nov. 1897); Moireau, Auguste. Rev. Bleue 8:617 (Nov. 13, 1897); Reynolds, James B. Ind. 49:1225 (Sept. 23, 1897); Schurz, Carl. Hrprs. Wkly. 41:555, 967, 1023, 1047, 1071, 1119, 1191 (June 5, Dec. 4, 1897); Sterne, Simon. Forum 24:553 (Jan. 1898); Stevans, C. M. Our Day 17:515 (Dec. 1897); Wilcox, Delos F. Mun. Aff. 2:207 (June, 1898); anon. City and State 4:6, 22, 38, 39 (Oct. 7-21, 1897); Commons 2:5 (Sept. 1897); Gunton's M. 13:169, 333 (Sept.-Nov. 1897); Hrprs. Wkly. 41:998, 999, 1166, (Oct. 9, Nov. 27, 1897); Ind. 49:1204, 1269, 1302, 1336, 1366, 1398, 1432 (Sept. 16, Nov. 11, 1897); Lit. Dig. 15:603, 636, 787 (Sept. 18, Oct. 30, 1897); Mun. Rec. & Ad. p. 12 (June 19, 1897); Vol. I, No. 19, p. 5 (Oct. 16, 1897), Vol. I, No. 19, p. 3 (Oct. 16, 1897); Nation 65: 123, 216, 292, 332, 350, 368, 430 (Aug 12, Dec. 2, 1897); Outlook 57:214, 263 (Sept. 25, Oct. 2, 1897); Spectator Oct. 9, 1897. 73

———. " Election in Greater New York, The First Municipal." Blair, James L. St. Louis, Nixon-Jones Printing Co., 1898. Pamphlet, 28 pp. 74

———. " Elector's Handbook for the City of New York." Levy, J. M. New York, W. P. Mitchell, 1895, 76 pp. 20 cts. 75

———. " Party Organizations and their Nominations to Office in New York." Bernheim, A. C. Pol. Sci. Q. 3:99 (1888). 76

———. " Police Control of a Great Election, The." Andrews, Avery D. Scribner's 23:131 (Feb. 1898). 77

———. Separate Elections. " An American Utopia." (Separation of municipal from state politics in New York City.) Porritt, Edward. Ecl. M. 123:669 (Nov. 1894). 78

———. " Suffrage in New York, Universal." Mills, C. Internat. R. 8:199 (1879). 79

———. " Suffrage in New York, The Lodging House Vote." Gumbleton, H. A. No. Am. 144:631 (1887). 80

———. See Parties below, also Elections under **New York State**.) 81

Electrolysis. " Conditions of Electrolytic Corrosion in Brooklyn." Sheldon, Samuel. Elec. W. & E. 35:868 (June 9, 1900), Prog. Age 18:297 (July 2, 1900). 82

" Finances of New York City, The." Durand, Edward Dana. New York, Macmillan Co., 1898. 12mo, 397 pp. $2. (See also under History below.) 83

———. " The City's Purse." Baldwin, Henry DeF. Municipal Affairs 1:329 (June, 1897). 84

———. " Comparison as to Cost of Administration in Berlin and New York." Real Estate Rec. & Guide Nov. 10, 1894, p. 673. 85

———. " Comptroller, The New York." Ind. 51:2472 (Sept. 14, 1899).

———. " Confession of Judgment Act." Ann. Am. Acad. Pol. Sci. 16:148 (July, 1900). 86

———. " Cost of Government in City and State." Maltbie, Milo Roy. Mun Aff. 4:685 (Dec. 1900). 87

———. " Debt of New York City, Detailed Statement of the." Mun. Rec. & Ad. July 3, 1897. 88

———. " Estate and Rights of the Corporation of the City of New York as Proprietors, Treatise upon the." Hoffman, Murray. New York, Edmund Jones, Corporation Printer, 1862. 2 vols. 415 and 260 pp. 89

———. Finances of New York with especial reference to charter changes and char-

New York City—*Continued.*

ities. See "Municipal Government," Coler, Bird S. New York, Appleton, 1900. 12mo, 200 pp. Cl. $1.   90

——. "Financial Resources of New York." Martin, William R. No. Am. 127:427 (1878),   91

——. Ford Franchise Tax Law. (See Finances under **New York State.**)

——. "Most Expensive City in the World, The." Coler, Bird S. Pop. Sci. Mo. 57:16 (May, 1900), Public Policy 2:350 (June 2, 1900).   92

——. "Municipal Ownership of Land, History of, on Manhattan Island to the beginning of sales by the Commissioners of the Sinking Fund in 1844." Black, G. Ashton. New York, Columbia College Studies I:3 (1892). 83 pp. 50 cts.   93

——. "Plundering the City." Nation 70:141 (Feb. 22, 1900).

——. "Report relative to the Finances." New York Assembly Doc. 100 (1878). 90 pp.   94

——. "Sinking Funds of New York City." Levey, Edgar J. Mun. Aff. 4:651 (Dec. 1900).   95

——. "Special Assessments in the City of New York." Jasper, William H. Public Policy 3:365 (Dec. 8, 1900).   96

——. Assessment of Taxes. "State Laws relative to the making and perfecting Assessments applicable to the city and county of New York." Stephens, Thomas. compiler. New York, Edmund Jones & Co., 1863. 8vo, 442 pp.   97

——. "Tax Rate of New York, The Future." Arch. & Buil. 29:73 (Sept. 3, 1898).   98

——. Taxation. "Compilation of the Laws of the State relative to the Assessment and Collection of the Taxes in the City and County of New York." Lawrence, A. R., compiler. New York, C. S. Westcott & Co., 1863. 8vo, 253 pp.   99

——. "Taxation in New York City, Some Problems of." Hawley, Walter L. Public Improvements 2:1 (Nov. 1, 1899), Other Side 1:289 (Dec. 23, 1899); Editorial, Arch & Build. 29:73 (Sept. 3, 1898).   100

——. "Taxation of Elevated Railways in the City of New York." Foster, Roger. New York, Putnams. 25 cts.   1

——. Taxation. "History of the New York Property Tax." Schwab, John C. Am. Econ. Assoc. Pubs. Vol. V, No. 5, 1890. Paper, 103 pp. $1.   2

"Fire Brigade, The New York." Bonner, Hugh. Mun. J. & London 8:1357 (Dec. 22, 1899).   3

——. "Fire Department, New York." Croker, E. F. Home M. Oct. 1900; Fire & W. 22:373 (Oct. 9, 1897).   4

——. "Fire Department Electrical Rules, The New York." (Editorial.) Elec. Eng. 24:327 (Oct. 7, 1897).   5

——. "Fire Department Hospital and Training Stables." City Govt. 2:177 (June, 1897).   6

——. "Fire Fighting in New York during 1898." Fire & W. 26:212 (July 1, 1899).   7

——. "Firemen, The New York." Sheffield, James R. Outlook 58:579 (March 5, 1898).   7

——. "La Nouvelle Brigade des Pompiers de New York." Artibal, J. R. Municipale 3:1851 (Jan. 20, 1900).   8

——. "Law Relating to the Extinction and Prevention of Fires, New York." Fryer, William J. Published by the Real Estate Rec. and Guide, New York, 1895. 251 pp. $5.   9

——. "Organization of the Fire Department of Greater New York." Docharty, Augustus T. Mun. & Ry. Rec. 3:895 (Dec. 15, 1898).   10

——. "Our Firemen, a History of the New York Fire Department, volunteer and paid." Costello, Augustine E. New York, Costello, 1887. 8vo.   11

——. "Our Flimsy Fire Traps." (New York Tenement Houses, see also under Housing below.) Marshall, Edward. Hrprs. Wkly. 39:1157 (1895).   12

Foreign Element. "Character Studies in New York's Foreign Quarters." Earle, E. Lyell. Catholic W. 68:782 (Mar. 1899).   13

——. "Chinatown, New York's. An historical presentation of its people and places." Beck, Louis J. New York, Bohemia Pub. Co., 1899. 8vo, 350 pp. $1.50.   14

——. Chinese of New York, The. Clark, Helen F. Cent. 53:104 (Nov. 1896); Forman, A. Arena 17:620 (1893); Hall, Charlott C. Missionary R. March,

New York City—*Continued.*

1897; Welch, J. H. Demorest's Family M. Jan. 1897. 15

——. "Foreign Element in New York City, The Germans." Manson, George I. Hrprs. Wkly. 32:581 (1888); "Norwegians, Swedes and Danes," 32:661 (1888); "The French," 33:77 (1889); "The Italians," 34:817 (1890); "The Scotch," Wilson, John L. Same 34:513 (1890); "Mulberry Bend Italian Colony." Bengough, W. Same 39:607 (1895); "Russo-Polish Jew Colony." Bengough, W. Same 39:725 (1895); "Syrian Colony." Same 39:746 (1895); "Chinese Colony." Same 40:214 (1896). 16

——. Irish "Home Rule" in New York. Russell, T. W. Fortn. 59:341 (1893); Quar. 171:260 (1890). 17

——. Statistics on foreign population of New York and other cities. Eleventh census, 1890, Report on Population, Pt. I, pp. 90-92, table 50, pp. 704-706. 18

Franchises of New York. (See under Municipal Control, Municipal Ownership below).

Free Lectures. (See under Lectures below).

"French in New York." (See under Foreign Element above).

Gambling, etc. "The Campaign against Vice." Outlook 66:874 (Dec. 8, 1900). 19

Garbage Disposal. Baker, E. Burgoyne,. Munsey's 23:81 (April, 1900); Welles, Henry J. American M. 2:39 (Nov. 1898); anon. Sci. Am. 77:136 (Aug. 28, 1897); Engng. Rec. 40:30 (June 10, 1899), San. Rec. 26:125 (Aug. 10, 1900). 20

——. "Barren Island Garbage Reduction Works, Greater New York." Engng. Rec. 38:275 (Aug. 27, 1898), 39:208 (Feb. 4, 1899); Engng. News 43:66, 76 (Feb. 1, 1900). 21

——. "Brooklyn Solves the Garbage Problem." Williams, Henry Smith. Hrprs. Wkly. 38:844 (1894). 22

——. "Cremating New York's Garbage, About." City Govt. 8:1 (Jan. 1900). 23

——. "Paris and New York Contrasted." (Garbage Removal, etc.) Real Estate Rec. & Guide, p. 703, April 7, 1894.

——. "Report on the Final Disposition of the Wastes of New York." Waring, Geo. E., Jr. New York, 1896, 159 pp. (Article same subject Engng. News, Feb. 20, 1896). 24

——. "Report of Sub-Committee of the Committee of Seventy on Garbage Disposal." 1894. Pamphlet, 16 pp. 25

——. "The Utilization of New York Garbage." Sci. Am. 77:102 (Aug. 14, 1897). 26

Gas. (See under Lighting below).

Germans in New York. (See under Foreign Element above).

Harbor Facilities. "Department of Docks." Cram, J. Sergeant. Public Improvements 1:77 (July 1, 1899). 27

——. "Commercial Blight, New York's." Black, William Nelson. Engng. M. 3:291, 463 (1892). 28

——. "The Crippled Commerce of New York." Black, William Nelson. New York, W. K. Farrington Co., prs., 1891. 41 pp. 29

——. "Docks, Bulkheads and Matter Relating thereto in the City of New York, Report Relative to the Building and Leasing of." New York State Assembly Doc. 132, 1882. 1501 pp.; New York Senate Doc. 64, 1886, 73 pp. 30

——. "Harbor of New York." (Features, amount of trade, number of vessels). Seaboard (N. Y.) Feb. 18, 1897.

——. "Harbor and Trade, New York." Transport (London) Nov. 18, 1893.

——. Harbor Police. (See under Police below).

——. "Municipal Ownership of Docks in New York City." Coler, Bird S. Mun. Aff. 4:207 (March, 1900), Municipal Ownership 1:21 (June, 1900). 31

——. "Storage and Transportation in the Port of New York." Black, William Nelson. New York, G. P. Putnam's Sons, 1884. 37 pp. 32

——. "The Water Front of New York." Sommer, Berthold. Arena Q. 1:89 (June, 1900); Williams, Jesse Lynch. Scribner's 26:385 (Oct. 1899). 33

——. "Value of Our Municipal Water Front Property." Real Estate Rec. & Guide June 17, 1893, p. 944.

Harlem. "The City to the North of Town." Barnes, James. Harper 95:866 (Nov. 1897). (See also under History below). 34

Health Department. (See under Sanitation below).

"Higher Life of New York City." Shaw, Albert. Outlook 53:132 (1896). 35

New York City—*Continued.*

History. "The American Metropolis from Knickerbocker Days to the Present Time. New York City Life in all its various phases." Moss, Frank. New York, P. F. Collier, 1897. 3 vols. 8vo, 425, 429, 340 pp. $4.   36

———. "Annals and Occurrences of New York City and State in the olden time, being a collection of memoirs, anecdotes and incidents concerning the city, county and inhabitants from the days of the founders." Watson, John F. Philadelphia, H. F. Anners, 1846. 8vo, 390 pp.   37

———. "Annetje Jans' Farm." Putnam, Ruth. New York, Vol. I, No. 3, City History Club Publications, 1897. 5c.   38

———. "Bibliography of the Dutch Period." New York, City History Club, pamphlet, 3 pp., 1896.   39

———. "Bowery, The." Hewitt, Edward Ringwood, and Hewitt, Mary Ashley. New York Half Moon Series. Published by G. P. Putnam's Sons, 1897. 25 pp. 10c.   40

———. "Bowery under Dutch Rule, The." Stephenson, John. Ind. 50:208 (Feb. 17, 1898).   41

———. "Bowling Green." Trask, Spencer. Half Moon Series 2:165 (May, 1898). New York, G. P. Putnam's Sons, 1898. 10c.   42

———. "Brief History of the City of New York." Todd, Charles B. New York, American Book Co., 1899. 12mo, 299 pp. $1.   43

———. Brooklyn. "The Civil, Political, Professional and Ecclesiastical History and Commercial and Industrial Record of the County of Kings and City of Brooklyn, 1683-1884." Stiles, Henry R. 3 vols. Albany, Munsell. $15.   44

———. Brooklyn. "Historical Sketch of the City of Brooklyn, and the surrounding neighborhood, including the village of Williamsburg, and the towns of Bushwick, Flatbush, Flatlands, New Utrecht and Gravesend, etc." Brooklyn, 1840. 12mo, $5.   45

———. Brooklyn. "History of Brooklyn, N. Y." Putnam, Harrington. See 1-4b.   46

———. Brooklyn. "A History of the City of Brooklyn and Kings County." Ostrander, S. M. Brooklyn, 1894. 8vo, 2 vols. Ill. $10.   47

———. Brooklyn. "Origin of Breuckelen." Putnam, Harrington. Half Moon Series 2:387 (Nov. 1898).   48

———. City History Club of New York, The. Kelley, Frank Bergen. Mun. Aff. 3:61 (March, 1899); Todd, Charles Burr. Gunton's 18:444 (May, 1900).   49

———. City History Club. "Women's Work on City Problems." Winsor, Anna Ware. Mun. Aff. 2:463 (Sept. 1898).   50

———. "Colonial New York, Golden Age of." Lamb, Martha J. Mag. of Am. History 24:1 (July, 1900).   51

———. Colonial Period in New York. Ch. XVII, "English Colonies in America." Lodge, Henry Cabot. New York, Harper, 1882. 8vo, 560 pp. $3.   52

———. "Description of the Province and City of New York with plans of the city and several forts as they existed in the year 1695." Miller, John. Edited by John Gilmary Shea. New York, William Gowans, 1862. 8vo, 127 pp.   53

———. "Dongan Charter to the City of New York." Gerard, James W. Mag. of Am. History 16:30 (July, 1886).   54

———. "Dutch on Manhattan." Lossing, Benson J. Harper's M. 9:433 (1854).   55

———. "Earlier New York, The." Stephenson, John. Ind. 49:1424 (Nov. 4, 1897), Ind. 50:208 (Feb. 17, 1898).   56

———. "English in New York." Vol. III, p. 385 and Vol. V, pp. 189-207; 231-58 of Winsor's "Narrative and Critical History of America." Boston, Houghton M. & Co., 1884-9. 8vo.   57

———. "English and Dutch Towns of New Netherland." McKinley, A. E. Am. Hist. R. Oct. 1900.   58

———. "Evolution of New York, The." Janvier, Thos. A. Harper 86:813, 87:15 (1893).   59

———. Finances. "The City Chest of New Amsterdam." Durand, Edward Dana. New York, Half Moon Series, Published by G. P. Putnam's Sons, 1897. 29 pp. 10c.   60

———. "Fort Amsterdam in the Days of the Dutch." Goodwin, Maud Wilder. New York, Half Moon Series, Published by G. P. Putnam's Sons, 1897. 36 pp. 10c.   61

———. "Governor's Island." Bellamy, Blanche Wilder. New York, Vol. I, No. 5, City History Club Publications, 1897. 10c.   62

New York City—*Continued.*

——. " Greenwich, Old." Bisland, Elizabeth. New York, Half Moon Series. Published by G. P. Putnam's Sons, 1897. 26 pp. 10c. 63

——. Harlem. " Deduction of the title of Harlaem Commons, with abstract of the title of Dudley Seldon (Commencing with a grant from Gov. Nicholls, 1666)." New York, 1872. 8vo. 64

——. " Historians, New York and its." van Rensselaer, (Mrs.) Schuyler. No. Am. 171:724 (Nov. 1900), 171:872 (Dec. 1900). 65

——. " Historic Town Series: New York." Roosevelt, Theodore. New York. Longmans, G. & Co., 2d ed., 1895. 232 pp. $1.25. 66

——. " Historical Sketch of New York City." Kelley, Frank Bergen. Our Country 6:69 (Oct. 1897). 67

——. " History of the City of New York." Booth, Mary L. New York, W. R. C. Clark, 1867. 2 vols. 8vo, 892 pp. 68

——. " History of the City of New York; its origin, rise and progress." Lamb, Martha J. and Harrison, (Mrs.) Burton New York, Barnes, 1877-80. 3 vols. $20. 69

——. " History of New Amsterdam, or New York, as it was in the Days of the Dutch Governors." Davis, A. New York, 1854. 16mo, 240 pp. 70

——. " History of New York City." (1609-1884). Lossing, Benson J. N. Y., Perine, 1884. 8vo, 2 vols., 881 pp. $15. 71

——. " History of New York City, with supplement." Stone, William L. New York, Cooke, 1876. 8vo, 252 pp. 72

——. " History of New York from the beginning of the World to the End of the Dutch Dynasty." Humorous. (Knickerbocker, Diedrich). Irving, Washington. Knickerbocker Edition, New York, Putnam, 1864. 73

——. " History of New York, N. Y." Gilder, J. B. See 1-4b. 74

——. History, Description and Statistics of New York City in 1880. Census. See 1-7. 75

——. " Kings College, now Columbia University." Pine, John B. New York, Vol. I, No. 2, City History Club Publications, 1897. 5c. 76

——. " Liberty in New York, The Beginnings of." van Rensselaer, (Mrs.) M. G. Lippincotts M. May, 1897. 77

——. " Local History and the Civic Renaissance in New York." Am. Mo. R. of Rs. 16:446 (Oct. 1897). 78

——. " Mayor of New York, First." (Thomas Willett). Mag. of Am. History 17:233 (March, 1897). 79

——. " Memorial History of the City of New York." Wilson, James Grant (Editor). New York History Co., 1892. 4 vols. $7.50 each. 80

——. " Municipal Government of New York City, Origin and Development of the." Jameson, J. F. Mag. Am. His. 8:315, 598 (1882). 81

——. " Nationalities, Impress of, on New York City." Gerard, James W. Mag. of Am. History 23:40 (Jan. 1890). 82

——. " New York, Past, Present and Future, and the American Advertiser." Belden, E. Porter. N. Y., 1850. 3d ed. 83

——. " Nooks and Corners of Old New York." Hemstreet, Charles. New York, Charles Scribner's Sons, 1899. 12mo, 228 pp. Cloth, $2. 84

——. " Old New York." Munsey's 19:43 (April, 1898). 85

——. " Our Great Metropolis: Its Growth, Misgovernment and Needs." Butler, William Allen. New York, 1880. 48 pp. $1. 86

——. " Prisons and Punishments, Old." Lewis, Elizabeth Dike. Half Moon Series 2:83 (March, 1898). 87

——. " Recollections of Persons and Events, 1810-1865." Matthews, J. M. New York, 1865. 8vo. 88

——. " Records of New Amsterdam from 1653 to 1674 Anno Domini." Edited by Berthold Fernow. New York, Published under the authority of the City of New York (Knickerbocker Press), 1897. 7 vols. with index. 89

——. " Reminiscences of an Octogenarian of the City of New York, 1816-1860." Haswell, C. H. New York, Harper, 1896. 12mo, 581 pp. $3. 90

——. " Schools and Schoolmasters of New Amsterdam, Early." Van Vechten, Emma. Half Moon Series 2:321 (Sept. 1898). 91

——. " Slavery in New York." Morgan, Edwin V. Half Moon Series 2:1 (Jan. 1898). New York, G. P. Putnam's Sons. 12mo, 30 pp. 10c. 92

New York City—*Continued.*

——. "Stadt Huys of New Amsterdam, The." Earle, Alice Morse. New York, City History Club, (Putnams and Brentanos) 1897. Vol. I, No. 1, Half Moon Series on Historic New York. 5c. 93

——. "Story of the City of New York." Todd, Charles Burr. New York, Putnams, 1888. 478 pp. $1.75. 94

——. "Syllabus of a Course on: I, The English Period; II, The Revolutionary Period." New York, City History Club, pamphlet, 17 pp., 1896. 95

——. "Syllabus of a Course of Study in the History of the City of New York." Hoy, William Alexander. New York, City History Club, pamphlet, 15 pp., 1897. 96

——. Tammany, History of. (See under Tammany, Tweed Ring below).

——. "Teacher's Handbook of the City History Club." New York, City History Club, 1899. Pamphlet, 24 pp. 97

——. "Two Years' Journal in New York and Part of its Territories in America." 1679. Wooley, Charles. Edited by E. B. O'Callaghan. New York, William Gowans, 1860. 8vo, 97 pp. 98

——. "Valentine's Manuals of the Corporation of the City of New York." (Historical matter, reminiscences, maps, views, etc.) New York, 1841-1870. 28 vols. 18mo, 8vos, over 4,000 pages. (Historical Index to the above by O. H. New York, Francis P. Harper, 1900. 8vo, 95 pp.) 99

——. "Wall Street, 1653-1789, Early History of." Villard, Oswald Garrison. New York, Vol. I, No. 4, City History Club Publications, 1897. 5c. 100

——. "Washington's Inauguration, The City of New York in the Year of 1789." Smith, Thomas E. V. New York, A. D. F. Randolph & Co., 1889. 8vo, 244 pp. 1

——. "Wells and Water Courses of the Island of Manhattan, Old." Hill, Geo. Everett and Waring, Geo. E., Jr. New York, Half Moon Series, Published by G. P. Putnam's Sons, 1897. 66 pp. 20c. 2

——. (See also History under **New York State**).

Hospitals. (See under Charities above).

Housing. "Apartment Houses, Model." (New York City and Suburban Homes Company Designs). Arch. and Buil. 26:7 (Jan. 2, 1897). 3

——. "A City Block in 1896." White, Gaylord I. Char. R., vol. V, No. 20, p. 2 (Oct. 13, 1900). 4

——. "Cat Alley, The Passing of." Riis, Jacob A. Cent. 58:166 (Dec. 1898). 5

——. East Side, Housing. "Living Conditions, The City's Health." Daniel, A. S. Mun. Aff. 2:247 (June, 1898). 6

——. "Homewood." Gould, E. R. L. Am. R. of Rs. 16:43 (July, 1897). 7

——. "Improved Dwellings for the Poor." (City and Suburban Homes Co). Independent 49:96 (Jan. 21, 1897). 8

——. "Improved Housing Effort, Half a Century of, by the New York Society for Improving the Condition of the Poor." Tolman, W. H. Yale R. 5:288, 389 (Nov. 1896, Feb. 1897). 9

——. "Inferno Explored, New York's." Booth, (Mr. and Mrs.) Ballington. New York, Published at Salvation Army Headquarters, 1891. 96 pp. 10

——. "Letting in the Light in New York City." Riis, Jacob A. Atlan. 84:495 (Oct. 1899). 11

——. "Lodging House Laws, New York City." Part III, "Laws Relating to Buildings in the City of New York." Fryer, William J. Published by the Real Estate Rec. and Guide, New York, 1895. 251 pp. $5. 12

——. Lodging Houses, New York City. Barry, Richard. Hrprs. Wkly. 33:429 (1894); Byrnes, T. No. Am. 149:355 (1889); Johnson, W. P. Lend a H. 8:304 (1892); Moss, Isaac. Leslie's Wkly. 80:87 (1895); anon. Hrprs. Wkly. 34:450 (1890); Leslie's Wkly. 82:296 (1896); R. of Rs. 15:59 (1897). 13

——. "Mills Hotel, New York, The." Macdonald, J. R. Puritan, July, 1899. 14

——. "Mulberry Street Barons, The Last of the." Riis, Jacob A. Cent. 53:119 (May, 1899). 15

——. "Out of Mulberry Street." (Tenement Stories). Riis, Jacob A. New York, Cent. Co., 1898. 12mo, 269 pp. Cl. $1.25. 16

——. "Sanitary Condition of the Laboring Population of New York with suggestions for its Improvement." Griscom, John H. New York, Harper Bros., 1845. 58 pp. 17

——. "Slums of New York." Forman, A. Am. M. 9:46 (1889). 18

BIBLIOGRAPHY.

New York City—*Continued.*

——. "Slums in New York, An Account of the Battle with the: A Ten Years' War." Riis, J. A. New York, Houghton, Mifflin & Co., 1900. 12mo, 267 pp. Cloth, $1.50.   19

——. Slums of New York. See the Seventh Special Report of the Commissioner of Labor on "The Slums of Great Cities." 1894.   20

——. Tenement Houses in New York. Tenement House Reform. Cadman, S. Parkes. Chaut. 25:587 (Sept. 1897); Elsing, W. T. Scrib. M. 11:697 (1892); Flagg, E. Scrib. M. 16:108 (1894); George, Henry. Leslie's Wkly. 80:200 (1895); Marshall, Edward. No. Am. 157:753 (1893); Potter, E. T. Char. R. 1:129 (1892); Riis, Jacob A. Hrprs. Wkly. 39:42 (1895), Cent. 53:246 (1896); Rollins, A. W. Forum 4:221, 5:207 (1888); Tricoche, George Nestler. Jour. des Economistes 23:3, 182 (1895); Valesh, Eva McD. Arena 7:580 (1893); Wingate, C. F. A series of six articles beginning in the New York Tribune, Nov. 23, 1884; anon. Real Estate Rec. & Guide Feb. 9, 1895, p. 204; Charities, Vol. V, No. 4, p. 1, June 23, 1900.   21

——. "Christmas in the Tenements." Riis, Jacob A. Cent. 55:163 (Dec. 1897).   22

——. Commissions. "Report of Tenement House Commission." N. Y. Senate Doc. No. 36, 1885. (Mr. Joseph W. Drexel, Chairman). 232 pp.   23

——. Commissions. "Tenement House Problem in New York, For the Information of the Commission on Legislation Affecting Tenement and Lodging Houses." Bayles, James C. New York, W. P. Mitchell, prs., 1887. 45 pp.   24

——. Commissions. "Tenement House Problem in New York." N. Y. Sen. Doc. No. 16. Transmitted to the Legislature, 1888. (History with Diagrams).   25

——. Commissions. "Tenement House Committee of 1894, Report of." N. Y. Assembly Doc. No. 37, 1894. (Richard W. Gilder, Chairman). 649 pp.   26

——. Commissions. "Tenement House Committee Maps." Pierce, Frederick E. Hrprs. Wkly. 39:62 (1895).   27

——. Commissions. "The New York Tenement House Commission." Riis, Jacob A. Am. R. of Rs. 21:689 (June, 1900).   28

——. "Evictions from Tenement Houses in New York." McLoughlin, W. P. Arena 7:48 (1892).   29

——. "Fire Traps, Our Flimsy." (Tenement Houses in New York). Marshall, Edward. Hrprs. Wkly. 39:1157 (1895).   30

——. "Improved Tenements in London and New York." Am. Arch. 29:120 (1890).   31

——. Laws. "Laws and Ordinances relating to Tenement and Lodging Houses in New York." Published by the Health Department, 1891.   32

——. Laws. "Tenement House Laws of New York." Part III of "Laws relating to Buildings in the City of New York." Fryer, William J. New York, Published by the Real Estate Rec. & Guide, 1895. 251 pp. $5.00.   33

——. Laws. "The New Tenement House Law of New York." Real Estate Rec. & Guide June 1, 1895, p. 912; Nov. 23, 1895, p. 715.   34

——. Laws. "Proposed Amendments to the Tenement House Law." New York, Real Estate Rec. & Guide April 4, 1896, p. 566.

——. Laws. "Tenement House Legislation in New York, 1852-1900." Veiller, Lawrence. New York, Tenement House Com., 1900. 8vo, 197 pp. Paper.   35

——. Laws. "Tenement House Requirements of the New York Building Law." (Editorial.) Engng. Rec. 40:377 (Sept. 23, 1889).   36

——. "Life in a New Tenement House." Daley, Agnes. Charities, p. 1, Dec. 8, 1900.   37

——. Model Tenement Houses. "A Contribution to the Study of the Tenement Houses of New York City by the Tenement House Building Co." 1891. 33 pp., diagrams.   38

——. "Model Tenements in New York." Real Estate Rec. & Guide Feb. 16, 1895, p. 247.

——. "New York's Tenement Houses." New York, Citizens' Union Pamphlet No. 4, 1897. 8 pp.   39

——. "Rear Tenements, Passing of the." Leslie's Wkly. 83:75 (1896).

——. Reform. "Tenement House Reform in the City of New York." Gallatin, James. Transactions American Public Health Association, Vol. VI, 1881. Reprinted in pamphlet form. 11 pp.   40

——. "Tenement House Reform in New York, 1834-1900." Veiller, Lawrence. New York, 1900. 8vo, 48 pp. Pamphlet.   41

New York City—*Continued.*

——. " Studies among the Tenements. How the Other Half Lives." Riis, Jacob A. New York, Scribners, 1892. 304 pp. $1.25. 42

——. " Where New York Lives." Chap. III in " The Land of the Dollar," by G. W. Steevens. New York, Dodd, Mead & Co., 1897. 12mo, 316 pp. $1.50. 43

Industrial Education. (See under Schools.)

Irish in New York. (See under Foreign Element above.)

Italians in New York. (See under Foreign Element above.)

Jews in New York, Russo-Polish. (See under Foreign Element above.)

Labor in New York. " Bakeshops and Operative Bakers in New York, Brooklyn and vicinity, Conditions of." Weissman, Henry. New York, 1895. Pamphlet, 29 pp. 5 cts. 44

——. Sweating. Sweat Shops in New York. Curley, E. A. Leslie's Wkly. 79:124 (1894); Mayer, Julius M. Gunton's M. August, 1896. Warner, John De Witt. Hrprs. Wkly. 39:135 (1895); anon. Sanitarian, 38:413 (May, 1897). 45

——. " Effects of New York Sweat Shop Law." White, Henry. Gunton's 18:345 (April, 1900). 46

——. " Report of the Committee of Manufactures on Sweating." p. 4, 181 et seq. H. R. Reports No. 2309, 1893. John De Witt Warner, Chairman. 47

——. " Sweaters of New York, The." Righter, G. Emil. New Time 2:383 (June, 1898). 48

——. " My Experience as a Sweater." Tompkins, Elizabeth A. Leslie's Wkly. 70:529 (1890). 49

——. Working Women in New York. Brown, E. S. Am. J. Soc. Sci. 25:78 (1887); Daniel, Annie S. Am. J. Soc. Sci. 30:73 (1892); Fawcett, E. Arena 5:26 (1891). 50

" Lecture Course of New York, The Free." Leipziger, Henry M. Mun. Aff. 3:462 (Sept. 1899). (See also under Schools below). McCormick, S. D. Outlook 64:121 (Jan. 13, 1900). 51

Legislation. " Notes on Bills introduced in the New York State Legislature, 1899." New York City Club, 1899. 118 pp. 52

——. " Special and Local Laws affecting Public Interests in the City of New York." New York Assembly Doc. 148, 1880. 2196 pp. 53

Lexow Investigation. (See under Police below.)

Library, New York Public. Billings, John S. Outlook 58:55 (Jan. 1, 1898); Emerson, Edwin J., Jr. Hrprs. Wkly. 41:1223 (Dec. 11, 1897); Hutton, Lawrence. Hrprs. Wkly. 39:273 (1895); anon. Lib. J. 20:84 (1895); Arch. Rec. 7:385 (Jan.-Mar. 1898). 54

——. " Brooklyn, Libraries of." Ford, P. L. Lib. J. 13:286 (1888); White, W. A. Lib. J. 11:111 (1886). 55

——. Library Building, New York Public. Arch. & Buil. 27:52, 207 (June 5, Dec. 11, 1897). 56

——. " Library Consolidation in New York City, For." Lib. J. Oct. 1900.

Lighting in New York, Electric. Knudson, A. A. Elec. Eng. 26:440 (Nov. 3, 1898); anon. Elec. World 31:4, 70 (Jan. 1, 18, 1898); Elec. Engng. 25:161 (Feb. 10, 1898); Elec. W. & E. 33:331 (March 18, 1899). 57

——. " Gas Combination, The New." Mun. & Ry. Rec. 6:168 (April 15, 1900). 58

——. Gas Commission, Gas Statistics. (See also under **New York State.)**

——. " Gas Consolidation in New York." Prog. Age 15:333 (Aug. 2, 1897).

——. Gas. " History of the Gas Supply of New York, A Sketch of the." J. Gas. Light. 76:828 (Oct. 2, 1900), 76:892 (Oct. 9, 1900). 59

——. " Gas Inquiry for New York City." Prog. Age 15:24 (Jan. 15, 1897).

——. Gas. " Report of the Special Committee to Investigate the Consolidated Gas Company." N. Y. Senate Doc. No. 47, 1886. 60

——. Municipal Ownership of Lighting Facilities. (See under Municipal Control, Municipal Ownership below.)

——. " Waste a Million Yearly." (Lighting.) Municipal Ownership 1:2 (June, 1900). 61

Liquor Problem in New York. Crosby, Howard. Forum 2:420 (1886); Gribayédoff, V. Leslie's Wkly. 82:292 (1896); Raines, J. No. Am. 162:481 (1896); anon. R. of Rs. 12:143 (1895); Hrprs. Wkly. 40:290 (1896). 62

New York City—*Continued.*

———. "Liquor Traffic in New York, The." Rowe, Leo S. Ann. Am. Acad. Pol. Sci. 11:157 (March, 1898). 63
———. "New York City and its Masters." (Liquor Problem in New York City.) Graham, Robert. New York, Church Temperance Society, 1887. 47 pp. 64
———. "Operation of the New York Liquor Tax Law." p. 338 "The Liquor Problem in its Legislative Aspects." Wines, Frederick H. and John Koren. Boston and New York, Houghton, M. & Co., 1898. 65
———. Saloon in New York City Politics. Dorman, Lester M. Church R. 42:158 (1883); Waring, Geo. E. Outlook 60:436 (Oct. 15, 1898). 66
———. Sunday Closing of Saloons in New York. Iglehardt, F. C. No. Am. 161:467 (1895); Roosevelt, Theodore. Forum 20:1 (1895), McClure's 5:475 (1895); Windmüller, L. Forum 20:211 (1895); Pub. Opin. 19:38, 134, 167 (1895); Chaut. 21:760, 22:97 (1895); R. of Rs. 12:389, 464, 648 (1895); Outlook 52:420 (1895). 67
Lodging Houses. (See under Housing above.)
"Market Play Grounds." (New York.) Waring, Geo. E. Hrprs. Wkly. 39:1237 (1895). (See also under Parks below.) 68
Markets. "How New York is Fed." Riding, William H. Scrib. M. 14:729 (1877). 69
"Mayor, Power of Appointment of the." Ann. Am. Acad. Pol. Sci. 12:129 (Sept. 1898). 70
Mazet Investigation. (See under Police below.)
Mills Hotels. (See under Housing above.)
"Mulberry Bend, Clearing of a New York Slum." Riis, J. A. R. of Rs. 12:172 (1895). (See also under Housing above.) 71
Municipal Control, Municipal Ownership. Franchises of New York. Bernheim, A. C. Cent. 50:149 (1895); West, Max. Chapter V, pp. 365-424 in "Municipal Monopolies," by Edward W. Bemis, also same Yale R. 6:387 (Feb. 1898). 72
———. "Gas Franchises, New York City." Myers, Gustavus. Prog. Age 18:420 (Oct. 1, 1900). 73
———. Gas Supply, Municipal Ownership of, in New York City. Pro. Grout, Edward M. Contra. Foote, Allen R. Mun. Aff. 1:245 (June, 1897). Commented on in Prog. Age 15:314, 334 (July 15, Aug. 2, 1897). 74
———. "History of Public Franchises in New York City." Myers, Gustavus. Mun. Aff. 4:71 (March, 1900). 75
———. "Street Railroad and Lighting Franchises, Municipal Ownership of." Public Hearings before the Greater New York Charter Commission on. (Memorandum on behalf Kings County Democratic League favoring.) Cruikshank, Alfred B. New York, 1897. 9 pp. 76
———. "Municipal Street Railways of New York, Ownership and Operation of." A discussion. Warner, John De Witt, Aff.; Higgins, Edward E., Neg. Mun. Aff. 1:421 (Sept. 1897). 77
———. (See also under **New York State.**)
Municipal Ownership of Land in New York. (See under Finances above.)
Nominations. (See under Elections above.)
Norwegians, Swedes and Danes in New York. (See under Foreign Element in New York.)
Parks, New York. Matthews, A. F. Leslie's Wkly. 81:74 (1895); Nadal, E. S. Scrib. M. 11:439 (1892); anon. Soc. Econ. 2:65 (1891); Garden & F. 5:132, 144, 420 (1892); Hrprs. Wkly. 38:44 (1894); Real Estate Rec. & Guide June 1, 1895, p. 913. 78
———. Bronx Park. Vail, Anna Murray. Garden & F. 4:314 (1891). 79
———. "Bronx Park Horticultural Buildings, New York Botanical Garden." Park & Cem. 8:4 (March, 1898). 80
———. Brooklyn. "Prospect Park." DeWolf, John. Engng. M. 3:16 (1892); anon. Garden & F. 1:217, 262, 335 (1888); Park & Cem. 7:162 (Sept. 1897). 81
———. "Brooklyn's New Parks." City Govt. 2:83 (March, 1897).
———. "Central Park." Cook, Clarence. Scrib. M. 6:523, 673 (1873). 82
———. "Central Park's Approaches." Guggenheimer, Randolph. Public Improvements 1:37 (June 1, 1899). 83
———. "Central Park under Ring Leader Rule." Nat. Quarterly Rev. 22:294 (Mar. 1871). Published also in pamphlet form by Edward I. Sears, New York, 1871. 24 pp. 84

New York City—*Continued.*

——. "Spoils of the Park." Olmsted, Frederick Law. 1882. 57 pp. 85
——. "City Hall Park." Stephenson, John. Ind. 49:1607 (Dec. 9, 1897), 49:1646 (Dec. 16, 1897). 86
——. "Coney Island Park." Coler, Bird S. Pub. Imp. 1:57 (June 15, 1899). 87
——. "Establishment of Public Parks in the City of New York." Davis, Gherardi. Paper read before the New York Historical Society, April 6, 1897. Pamphlet, 47 pp. 88
——. "History of the Parks of New York City, Some Early." Park & Cem. 7:81, 130 (June, Aug. 1897).
——. "Jeanette Park." Garden & F. 3:498 (1890). 89
——. "Our Parks." Seguin, E. Papers read before the New York Academy of Science, April 30, 1877, Feb. 1, 1878. New York, Public Parks Protective Association, 1878. 8vo. 90
——. "Playgrounds for Children." Vrooman, Walter. Hrprs. Wkly. 35:350 (1891). 91
——. "Playgrounds, Market." Waring, Geo. E., Jr. Hrprs. Wkly. 39:1237 (1895). 92
——. "Playgrounds, New York's Summer." Brackett, Mary Morrell. Kindergarten M. 11:621 (June, 1899). 93
——. "Riverside Park." Stiles, W. A. Cent. n. s. 8:911 (1885). 94
——. "Riverside Park, New York's." Cady, Thomas. Munsey's 20:73 (Oct. 1898). 95
——. "Society for Parks and Playgrounds, New York." Garden & F. 3:594 (1890). 96
——. "Zoological Park, New York," Hornaday, William T. Hrprs. Wkly. April 3, 1897. 97
——. (See also Recreation Piers below.)

Parties, Partisan Politics in New York. "The Issues of Next City Campaign." Coler, Bird S. Ind. 52:3079 (Dec. 27, 1900). 98
——. "Criminal Politics." (Especially in New York City.) Godkin, E. L. No. Am. 150:706 (1890). 99
——. "Jobs in Cities." (Corruption in New York City Politics.) Seeger, Ferdinand. No. Am. 143:87 (1886). 100
——. "Machine Politics in New York City." Roosevelt, Theodore. Cent. 33:74 (1886). Same essay, p. 46, in his "Practical Politics," and Ch. VI, p. 102 in his "American Ideals and Other Essays." 1
——. "Non-partisanship in Municipal Government." Flower, R. P., Pavey, Frank D. Forum 23:531 (July, 1897). 2
——. "Republican Reorganization of New York City." Hrprs. Wkly. 38:76 (1894). 3
——. (See Reform Organizations under General References above, also Boss Rule, History, Tammany Hall, Tweed Ring, etc.)

Paving, New York. Newberry, J. S. School of Mines Quarterly, Columbia College 10:289 (1889). 4
——. "Alcatraz Streets in New York." City Govt. 2:104 (April, 1897).
——. "Asphalt in New York." Palmer, O. M. Pub. Imp. 1:22 (May 15, 1899). 5
——. "Municipal Engineering in New York." (A sample "job"—repaving of 5th Ave.) Engng. News Oct. 2, 1886. 6
——. "Street Railway Tracks and the Pavements in New York City." Waring, Geo. E., Jr. Hrprs. Wkly. Feb. 13, 1897. 7

Playgrounds. (See under Parks above.)

Police Force, New York's. Ingersoll, Ernest. Scrib. M. 16:342 (1878); Matthews, Franklin. Hrprs. Wkly. 40:231 (1896); Riis, Jacob A. Outlook 60:581 (Nov. 5, 1898); Roosevelt, Theodore. Atlan. 80:289 (Sept. 1897); Wheatley, Richard. Harper 74:495 (1887); Chaut. 16:689 (1893); Williams, C. Contemp. 53:214 (1888); anon. Hrprs. Wkly. 38:39 (1894). 8
——. "Administering the New York Police Force." Roosevelt, Theodore. Ch. VIII, p. 160 "American Ideals and Other Essays," New York, Putnams, 1897. 12mo, 354 pp. $1.50. 9
——. "Appointment and promotion in the New York City Department of Police, Report of a Special Committee on the system of." Schurz, Carl, and others. Good Govt., May 15, 1896. 10
——. "Broadway's Grenadiers." Harrington, John W. Munsey's 22:43 (Oct. 1899). 11

BIBLIOGRAPHY. 191

New York City—*Continued.*

——. "Brooklyn's Guardians: a Record of the faithful and heroic men who preserve the peace in the City of Brooklyn." Fales, W. E. S. Brooklyn, Caxton, 1887. 8vo. $6. 12

——. Courts. "Reform in New York's Police Courts." Matthews, Franklin. Hrprs. Wkly. 39:1036 (1895). 13

——. Courts. "Social Aspects of New York Police Courts." Smith, Mary Roberts. Am. J. Sociol. 5:145 (Sept. 1899). 14

——. "Crime and Punishment in New York." Crosby, Howard. No. Am. 133:-167 (1881). 15

——. "Dangerous Classes of New York City." Brace, C. L. New York, Wynkoop & Hallenbeck, 1872. 448 pp. 16

——. "Harbor Police, New York's." Stoddard, W. O. Harper 45:672 (1872). 17

——. History. "New York Police Force." (History during Strong administration.) Roosevelt, Theodore. Atlan. 80:289 (Sept. 1897). 18

——. "Our Police Protectors; History of the New York Police, from the earliest period to the present time." Costello, Augustine E. New York, Costello, 1885. 8vo. $5. 19

——. "Recollections of a New York Chief of Police." Walling, Geo. New York, Caxton, 1887. 8vo. 20

——. Legislation. "Problem of Police Legislation. A consideration of the best means of dealing with it in New York City." Eaton, Dorman B. New York, Putnam, 1895. Questions of the Day Series No. 81. 21

——. Lexow Investigation. "Report of the Committee appointed by the Senate to investigate the Police Department of the City of New York." Transmitted to the Legislature, Jan. 18, 1895. 61 pp. (Clarence Lexow, Chairman.) 22

——. Lexow Investigation. "Report and Proceedings of the Senate Investigating Committee on the Police Department of the City of New York." 5 vols. Albany, 1895. (Known as the Lexow Committee.) 23

——. Lexow Investigation. Gribayédoff, V. Leslie's Wkly. 81:7 (1895); Leavitt, John B. Forum 17:659 (1894); Matthews, Franklin. Leslie's Wkly. 79:167 (1894); Parkhurst, Chas. H. Chap. XX, p. 240, "Our Fight with Tammany"; Reid, Sidney. Hrprs. Wkly. 38:663 (1894); anon. Hrprs. Wkly. 38:607 (1894); Soc. Econ. 7:9 (1894); Sat. R. 80:199 (1895). 24

——. "Satan's Invisible World Displayed or Despairing Democracy." (Mainly Lexow evidence.) Stead, W. T. New York, R. T. Fenno & Co., 1897. 12mo, 300 pp. $1.25. 25

——. "Mazet Investigation, The." Moss, Frank. Ind. 52:299 (Feb. 1, 1900). 26

——. "Parkhurst, Dr., and the New York Police." Homiletic R. May, 1892. 27

——. "Police Station, A New York City." Engng. Rec. 37:499 (May 7, 1898).

——. Politics. "Taking the Police out of Politics." Roosevelt, Theodore. Cosmopol. 20:40 (1895). 28

——. "Roll of Honor of the New York Police." Roosevelt, Theodore. Cent. 54:803 (Oct. 1897). 29

——. (See also Police under **New York State**.)

Primaries. (See also under Elections above.)

Prostitution. "How to Solve the Problem of the Social Evil." Flagg, J., Jr. New York, 1895. 23 pp. 10 cts. 30

——. "Prostitution in New York." Ch. XXXII-XXXVI, pp. 450-676 of W. W. Sanger's "History of Prostitution," 1876. (See History under **Prostitution**.) 31

——. The Campaign against Vice. Outlook 66:874 (Dec. 8, 1900); Mun. Aff. 4:698 (Dec. 1900). 32

"Public Conveniences in New York City." Engng. Rec. (London) 37:341 (Sept. 18, 1897). (See also under Baths above.) 33

"Public Works, Investigation of the Department of. Report of Committee." Roosevelt, Theodore. New York Assembly Docs. 125, 153 and 172 of the session of 1884. 34

——. "Management of Public Works in Greater New York." Engng. Rec. 36:470 (Oct. 30, 1897).

——. "Recent Administration of the Department of Public Works of the City of New York." The City Club of New York, 1897. 16mo, 133 pp.

Ramapo Water Project. (See under Water Supply below.)

New York City—*Continued.*

Rapid Transit in New York. (See under Transit Facilities below.)

Recreation Piers. Kendall, Edward H. Public Imp. 1:78 (July 1, 1899); O'Brien, Edward C. Mun. Aff. 1:509 (Sept. 1897); Rogers, W. H. Hrprs. Wkly. 41:706 (July 17, 1897).   35

Reform. Reform Organizations in New York. (See under General References above.)

Religious Condition. (See under Church above.)

Russo-Polish Jew Colony. (See under Foreign Element in New York.)

Saloons in New York. (See under Liquor Problem above.)

Salvation Army Work. (See under Charities above.)

Sanitation, Sanitary Condition, New York. Biggs, Herman M. Sanitarian 39:385 (Nov. 1897); Billings, John S. Forum 16:346 (1893); Waring, Geo. E. Scrib. M. 22:64, 179 (1881); Wheatley, Richard. Hrprs. Feb. 1897; Wingate, C. F. Engng. M. 3:316 (1892).   36

——. "Brooklyn, Sanitation in." Billings, J. S. Forum 16:346 (1893).   37

——. "Brooklyn, Unwholesome Environs of." Williams, Henry Smith. Hrprs. Wkly. 38:726 (1894).   38

——. "Health Board, Report of The New York." Tolman, W. H. Altruist Vol. 5, No. 4, p. 15 (Oct. 1897).   39

——. "Health Department of the Greater New York." Smith, Stephen. Sanitarian 38:293 (April, 1897).   40

——. "Improvement in New York during the last quarter of a Century, Sanitary." Clarke, Emmons. Pop. Sci. Mo. 39:319 (1891).   41

——. "Plumbing and Ventilation Inspection in New York." Eng. and Buil. Rec. 21:315 (1890).   42

——. "The Women's Health Protective Association." Trautmann, Mary E. Mun. Aff. 2:439 (Sept. 1898).   43

Schools. School System of New York. Maxwell, William H. Mun. Aff. 4:742 (Dec. 1900); Olin, Stephen H. Educa. R. 8:1 (1894); Reprinted by Good Govt. Club E, 1894, 6 pp., Harper 90:584 (1895); Rice, J. M. Forum 14:616 (1893); Van Rensselaer, (Mrs.) Schuyler. Hrprs. Wkly. 40:463 (1896); anon. Hrprs. Wkly. 40:99, 219 (1896); Dial 24:101 (Feb. 16, 1898).   44

——. "Attendance upon the Public Schools." Draper, A. S. Leslie's Wkly. 73:428 (1892).   45

——. "Buildings of New York, School." Robinson, John Beverley. Arch. Rec. 7:359 (Jan., March, 1898); Snyder, C. B. J. Educa. R. 15:17 (Jan. 1898).   46

——. "Public School Buildings in New York City, their condition as shown in official reports." Publications of Good Government Club E, No. 7, 1895. 23 pp.   47

——. "Education in the Greater New York Charter." Fitzpatrick, F. A. Educa. R. May, 1897.   48

——. "Free Lectures in New York Schools." Willis, S. T. Forum 29:332 (May, 1900).   49

——. "Greater New York, Educational System of." Butler, Nicholas Murray. Independent 49:305 (May 11, 1897).   50

——. "Schools of Greater New York—How the New System is to be Administered." N. Y. Educa. 1:275 (Jan. 1898).   51

——. "Industrial Education in New York." Science 9:553 (1887).

——. "Kindergartens of New York City, Public." Kindergarten M. 10:110 (Oct. 1897).

——. "More and Better Public Schools." New York, Citizens' Union Pamphlet No. 3, 1897. 16 pp.   52

——. "Public Education in the City of New York; its History, Condition and Statistics, official report to the Board of Education." New York, 1869. 8vo.   53

——. "Sanitary defects in Primary Schools." Chapin, Henry D. Leslie's Wkly. 72:40 (1891).   54

——. "Vacation Schools in New York." Tolman, William Howe. R. of Rs. 16:191 (Aug. 1897), Mun. Aff. 2:433 (Sept. 1898).   55

Scotch in New York, The. (See Foreign Element in New York.)

Settlements, College, Social, University, in New York. Betts, Lillian W. Outlook 51:684 (1895); Taylor, Graham. Commons, Vol. 2, No. 5, p. 12 (Sept.

New York City—*Continued.*

1897); Todd, Charles Burr. Gunton's 19:166 (Aug. 1900); anon. Lend a H. July, 1893. 56

———. "The Church Settlement." (329 E. 84th St.) Atterbury, Anson P. Open Ch. 1:161 (Oct. 1897); Sanford, Mary B. Churchman March 23, 1895; anon. Harper's Bazar 29:300 (April 11, 1896). 57

———. College Settlement. (95 Rivington St., New York.) Dyer, Francis J. Harper's Bazar May 31, 1890, Churchman June 11, 1892; Freeman, H. F. Lend a H. 5:154 (March, 1890); Halstead, Carolyn. Delineator July, 1895; Richardson, Hester D. Lippincott's June, 1891; Scudder, Vida D. Christian Union May, 10 and 17, 1888; anon. Nation Feb. 9, 1893; Ann. Am. Acad. Pol. Sci. 9:164 (Jan. 1897). 58

———. "East Side House." Wheeler, Everett P. Churchman Aug. 12, 1893, Outlook Feb. 10, 1894. 59

———. "Gospel Settlement." Outlook 57:732 (Nov. 1897).

———. "Grace Church Settlement Work." Winslow, F. E. Char. R. 8:418 (Nov. 1898). 60

———. "Hartley House." Char. R. 6:380 (June, 1897). 61

———. "Neighboring Guild." (Now University Settlement). Stover, Charles B. J. H. Univ. Studies VII, p. 65, appendix to F. C. Montague's "Arnold Toynbee." 62

———. "Union East Side Settlements." Brown, Wm. Adams. Ind. 49:1691 (Dec. 23, 1897). 63

———. The University Settlement. (26 Delancey St.) Gilder, Joseph B. Hrprs. Wkly. May 4, 1895; Char. R. Dec. 1891; Hrprs. Wkly. 35:615 (1891), 37:647 (1893), 39:423 (1895); The Critic June 20, 1891; Lend a H. 12:204 (March, 1894); Leslie's Wkly. 78:178 (1894). 64

———. "Women in New York Settlements." Kingsbury, Mary M. Mun. Aff. 2:458 (Sept. 1898). 65

"Sewage of the Metropolis, Disposal of." Denton, J. B. New York, E. & F. N. Spon, 1887. 21 pp. $1.60. 66

———. "Sewage Disposal in New York, Damages Due to." Engng. Rec. 41:561 (June 16, 1900). 67

———. "Sewerage System, Care and Maintenance of the New York." Potter, F. D. City Govt. 4:167 (May, 1898). 68

———. "Sewage Treatment, Brooklyn, N. Y., Chemical." Engng. Rec. 39:378 (Mar. 25, 1899).

"Singing Classes in New York, The People's." Stevenson, E. Irenaeus. Ind. 49:1041 (Aug. 13, 1897). 69

Sinking Funds, New York's. (See under Finances above.)

Slums of New York. (See under Charities, Housing, above.)

"Sociological Laboratory, A Year's Work in a." New York, Published by the Association for Improving the Condition of the Poor, 1896. 139 pp. 10 cts. (See also under Charities, Housing, above.) 70

Special Assessments. (See under Finances above.)

Statistics. "Vital Statistics of New York City and Brooklyn covering a period of six years ending May 31, 1890." Billings, John S. Washington, Government Printing Office, 1894. 529 pp. Eleventh Census of the United States. 71

Street Cleaning in New York. Agnew, S. H. City Govt. 1:1 (1896); Gibson, F. M. Public Improvements 1:4 (May 1, 1899); Hewes, F. W. Hrprs. Wkly. 39:233 (1895); Waring, George E. Hrprs. Wkly. 39:1022 (1895), Independent 49:105 (Jan. 28, 1897), McClure's 9:911 (Sept. 1897); Williams, Henry Smith. Hrprs. Wkly. 38:971 (1894); anon. Engng. News p. 173, Aug. 22, 1891; Engng. Rec. Dec. 21, 1895; Sanitarian Sept. 1896: Engng. Rec. 37:121 (Jan. 8, 1898). 72

———. "City Cleansing in New York City." Meade, Charles A. Mun. Aff. 4:721 (Dec. 1900). 73

———. "Clean Streets." New York, Citizens' Union Pamphlet No. 2, 1897. 16 pp. 74

———. "Clear Streets." Pumpelly, J. C. Municipal Program Leaflet No. 2, 1894. 7 pp. 5 cts. 75

———. "Cost of Street Cleaning in New York City." Andrews, William S., and George E. Waring. Mun. Rec. & Ad. p. 15, June 26, 1897. 76

———. "The Labor Question in the Department of Street Cleaning of New York." Waring, Geo. E., Jr. Mun. Aff. 1:515 (Sept. 1897). Reprinted in the New Zealand Journal of Department of Labour 6:175 (Feb. 12, 1898). 77

New York City—*Continued.*

——. "Report of the Commissioner of Street Cleaning to the Mayor." Andrews, William S. New York Sept. 15, 1893. 13 pp. 78

——. "Street Cleaning Clause in the Proposed Charter for Greater New York." Sanitarian Sept. 1896. 79

——. "Street Cleaning of New York, for 1895-6-7, Report of the Department of." Mun. Aff. Supplement to June, 1898. 8vo, 234 pp. 50 cts. 80

Street Railways. (See under Transit Facilities below.)

"Streets of New York, The Cross." Williams, Jesse Lynch. Scribner's 28:571 (Nov. 1900). 81

"Streets, Plan for the Widening of New York East Side." Van der Weyde, N. J. Sci. Am. Supp. 47:19642 (June 24, 1899), 48:19714 (July 29, 1899). 82

"Strong, Mayor." Chaut. June, 1897; Ind. 49:1526 (Dec. 30, 1897). 83

——. "New York's Civic Assets, a Summing up of the progress made during Mayor Strong's administration." Tolman, Wm. Howe. Am. Mo. R. of Rs. 17:55 (Jan. 1898). 84

Sunday Closing of Saloons in New York. (See under Liquor Problem above.)

Sweating. (See under Labor above.)

Syrian Colony in New York. (See under Foreign Element in New York.)

Tammany Hall. Bishop, J. B. Nation 50:236 (1890); Cary, Edward. Forum 26:200 (Oct. 1898); Croker, Richard. No. Am. 154:225 (1892); Davis, Hartley. Munsey's 24:55 (Oct. 1900); Denslow, Van Buren. Internat. R. 8:428 (1880); Eaton, Dorman B. No. Am. 154:297 (1892); Edwards, E. J. McClure's 4:445, 569, 5:325, 542 (1895); Godkin, E. L. Nation 50:235, 290 (1890), 53:385 (1891), 56:60 (1893), 59:356 (1894); Howe, Rufus. Harper's M. 44:685, 835 (April, May, 1872); Matthews, Franklin. Hrprs. Wkly. 40:494 (1896), 44:957 (Oct. 13, 1900); Merwin, Henry C. Atlan. 73:240, 74:680 (1894); Mowry, Arthur M. Am. Hist. R. 3:292 (Jan. 1898); Phelps, E. J. Lakeside 7:330 (1871); Taylor, Warren. Munsey's M. May, 1893; de Varigny, C. Rev. d. Deux Mondes 124:878 (1894); Viallate, A. Correspondant April 25, 1898; Wheeler, D. H. Lakeside 5:402 (1871); Williams, Talcott. Lalor's Cyclopedia, Vol. III, pp.850-6, Half-Moon Series 2:33 (Feb. 1898); anon. Am. Hist. Rev. 3:415 (1874); Hrprs. Wkly. 38:39 (1894); Leslie's Wkly. 79:17 (1894); Hrprs. Wkly. 40:99 (1896); Gunton's 14:325 (May, 1898); Outlook 66:99 (Sept. 8, 1900). 85

——. "Richard Croker, as 'Boss' of Tammany." Edwards, E. J. McClure 5:542 (1895). 86

——. "Kelly, John, Tammany under." Edwards, E. J. McClure 5:325 (1895). 87

——."Life and Times of John Kelly, Tribune of the People." McLaughlin, J. Fairfax. New York, American News Co., 1885. 12mo, 309 pp. $1.50. 88

——. "Our Fight with Tammany." Parkhurst, Charles H. New York, Scribner's, 1895. 296 pp. $1.25. 89

——. "Political Mission of Tammany Hall." King, A. B. New York, 1892. 30 pp. 10 cts. 90

——. "Politics in a Democracy." Thompson, Daniel Greenleaf. New York, Longmans, Green & Co., 1893. 176 pp. (Chapters X, XI and XII present a philosophical justification of Tammany Hall.) 91

——. "Tammany Ring in New York City, The." Chap. LXXXVIII, p. 377, Vol. II, Bryce's "American Commonwealth." 92

——. "Tammany from within." Tyng, T. Mitchell. New York, Tammany Hall Souvenir, 1893. 93

——. Unemployed, Tammany and the. (See under Unemployed below.)

——. (See also under Bossism in New York, Police, Tweed Ring, etc., above.)

Taxation in New York. (See under Finances above.)

Telephone Rates and Services, New York. Elec. Rev. April 14, 1897, 31:180 (Oct. 13, 1897), 33:327 (Nov. 23, 1898); Elec. W. & E. 33:572 (May 6, 1899). 94

——. "Reconstruction of the Telephone Lines in Westchester County, N. Y." Elec. Eng. April 21, 1897.

Tenement Houses of New York. (See under Housing above.)

"Topography of Greater New York." Real Estate Rec. & G. 60:161 (Nov. 20, 1897).

Transit Facilities of New York, General articles on. Barry, Richard. Hrprs. Wkly. 42:204 (Feb. 26, 1898); Ingersoll, Ernest. Outlook 58:829 (Apr. 2, 1898); Rowe, Leo S. Ann. Am. Acad. Pol. Sci. 11:115 (Jan. 1898); anon. St. Ry. J.

New York City—*Continued.*

Aug. 1892, p. 469; Mun. Rec. & Ad. Aug. 14, 1897; Ry. World 6:332 (Nov. 1897). 95
——. Broadway Cable Road, New York. Iles, Geo. Engin. M. 4:351 (1892); anon. Engng. Rec. July 25, 1891. 96
——. Brooklyn Bridge, Use of, by Transportation Companies. Engng. News 38:323 (Nov. 18, 1897); St. Ry. J. 14:39 (Jan. 1898); Elec. World 31:179 (Feb. 5, 1898); Railroad Gaz. 30:460, 476 (June 24, July 1, 1898). 97
——. "Brooklyn—Electrical Equipment of the Suburban Service of the Long Island Railroad System." Elec. World 30:607 (Nov. 20, 1887).
——. "Brooklyn Electrical Subways, Report of the Bureau of Commissioners of." Barrett, John A. St. Ry. Jour. 13:46 (Jan. 1897). 98
——. "Brooklyn Elevated, The Long Island Railroad and the." Railroad Gaz. 30:256 (April 8, 1898). 99
——. "Brooklyn Elevated, Report of the." Railroad Gaz. Jan. 15, 1897.
——. "Brooklyn Heights Railroad Company, The General Passenger Department of the." Kennedy, H. Milton. St. Ry. Jour 13:341 (June, 1897). 100
——. "Brooklyn Rapid Transit System, Financial Characteristics and Operating Organization of the." St. Ry. J. 13:842 (Dec. 1897); St. Ry. J. 15:370 (June, 1899).
——. "Brooklyn Rapid Transit System, The Traffic Difficulties of the." St. Ry. J. 16:31 (Jan. 6, 1900).
——. "Cars and Car Service in Metropolitan New York." Vreeland, H. H. St. Ry. J. 16:958 (Oct. 13, 1900). 1
——. "Compressed Air Surface Cars in New York." Safety V. (New York) Nov. 1895.
——. "Consolidation of Street Railway Companies." Real Estate Rec. & Guide April 30, 1892, p. 682 Dec. 17, 1892, p. 799.
——. "Dead Man's Curve." (Recommending change of motive power to electricity to overcome danger at corner 14th Street and Broadway.) Elec. World March 6, 1897.
——. "Earnings and Profits on Manhattan Island, Transportation." St. Ry. J. 15:876 (Dec. 1899). (See also under Traction below.)
——. "Eighth Avenue Railroad, The City and the." New York, pamphlet, dated May 25, 1897. 72 pp.
——. "Elevated Railway Contracts, The." Elec. Rev. 32:40 (Jan. 19, 1898).
——. "Elevated Railways, Electricity on the." Fransioli, W. J. and Sidney H. Short. Elec. World March 6, 1897; anon. Elec. World Feb. 27, 1897; Elec. Eng. 25:61 (Jan. 13, 1898); St. Ry. J. 15:165 (March, 1899); Railroad Gaz. 32:793 (Nov. 30, 1900). 2
——. Elevated Railway, The Manhattan. Densmore, George C. Mun. & Ry. Rec. 4:203 (June 15, 1899); Nichols, O. F. Railroad Gaz. 30:469 (July 1, 1898); Towner, Hiram. Ind. 49:1126 (Aug. 26, 1897); anon. Mun. Rec. & Ad. 2:219, 602 (Jan. 29, June 15, 1898); Elec. Eng. 26:178 (Aug. 25, 1898). 3
——. Elevated Railroads in the City of New York, Taxation of. (See under Finance above.)
——. "The Elm Street Subway in New York." Engng. Rec. 42:463 (Nov. 17, 1900). 4
——. "Harlem River Bridge and Street Railway Service, The New." Mun. Rec. & Ad. 2:583 (June 15, 1898).
——. "Horse Railways, Communication from the Comptroller of New York City regarding the Income from." Senate Doc., 1885, no. 35. 5
——. Manhattan Elevated Railway. (See under Elevated Railways above.)
——. "Metropolitan Street Railway of New York." Railroad Gaz. 32:359 (June 1, 1900).
——. Metropolitan Street Railway Conduit Lines. (Underground Trolley.) Railroad Gaz. March 5, 1897; St. Ry. R. 7:248 (April 15, 1897); Elec. Eng. 24:149 (Aug. 19, 1897); Elec. World 30:239, 328, 615 (Aug. 28, Sept. 18, Nov. 13, 1897); Mun. Rec. & Ad. Vol. I, No. 25, p. 8 (Nov. 27, 1897); St. Ry. J. 13:825 (Dec. 1897), 14:719 (Nov. 1898). 6
——. "Metropolitan Street Railway System, Earnings of the." Mun. Rec. & Ad. 3:870 (Nov. 15, 1898); Elec. W. & E. 34:336 (Sept. 2, 1899). 7
——. "The Metropolitan System: Horse Car, Cable, Compressed Air and Electric." Densmore, George C. Mun. & Ry. Rec. 7:39 (Aug. 15, 1900). 8

New York City—*Continued.*

——. Metropolitan Street Railway Company of New York. Main Power Station and Transmission System. Ty. & Ry. W. 9:57 (Feb. 8, 1900); St. Ry. J. 16:213 (Mar. 3, 1900). 9

——. "Metropolitan Street Railway Company and Rapid Transit." Mun. & Ry. Rec. 4:141 (April 15, 1899).

——. "Metropolitan Street Railway Company, The Track Construction of the." Reed, W. B. Mun. & Ry. Rec. 6:157 (April 15, 1900). 10

——. Municipal Control, Municipal Ownership. (See under Municipal Control, etc., above, also Municipal Control under **New York State**.)

——. "Operating Expenses of Street Railways in New York and Brooklyn." St. Ry. J. July, 1891, p. 406.

——. Rapid Transit Problem, New York. Chittenden, L. E. Hrprs. Wkly. 35:134 (1891); Gribble, T. Graham. Engng. M. 1:165, 338 (1891); Heilprin, Louis. Engng. M. 3:447 (1882); Sprague, Frank J. St. Ry. J. March, 1891, St. Ry. Gaz. March, 1891; White, W. Howard. Railroad Gaz. April 24, 1891, p. 279; anon. Engng. News Jan. 2, 1886; Railroad Gaz. Jan. 11, 1886; Elec. World Jan. 9, 1886; Railroad Gaz. Oct. 9, 1891, p. 700, Oct. 16, 1891, p. 720, Oct. 23, 1891, p. 745; Engng. News Oct. 10, 1891, p. 342, Oct. 17, p. 352, Oct. 24, p. 389; Engng. Rec. Oct. 24, 1891, p. 334; Real Estate Rec. & Guide Nov. 19, 1892, p. 649, Nov. 26, 1892, p. 683, Dec. 3, 1892, p. 715, Dec. 10, 1892, p. 759, Dec. 24, 1892, p. 835, Dec. 31, 1892, p. 873, Jan. 14, 1893, p. 41, June 10, 1893, p. 903, Oct. 13, 1894, p. 501, March 9, 1895, p. 368, March 23, 1895, p. 455, May 30, 1896, p. 926; Am. Arch. 44:90 (1895); Outlook 61:398 (Feb. 18, 1899); Mun. & Ry. Rec. 5:305 (Dec. 15, 1899). 11

——. "Rapid Transit Act Constitutional, New York State." Engng. Rec. Aug. 22, 1896. 12

——. "Rapid Transit, City Officials of New York on." Real Estate Rec & Guide Sept. 30, 1893, p. 369, Oct. 7, 1893, p. 398.

——. "Rapid Transit for New York City, Financial Discussion of." Cooper, Theodore. Railroad Gazette March 20, 1891, p. 191. 13

——. "Rapid Transit, Inter-Metropolitan." (New York, Brooklyn.) Nichols, O. T. Rensselaer Soc. Engrs. Vol. I, p. 163. 14

——. "Rapid Transit Lines, New York." Parsons, Wm. Barclay. Engng. Rec. Dec. 29, 1894. 15

——. "Rapid Transit, Some Lessons in." Heilprin, Louis. Engng. M. 3:447 (1892). 16

——. Rapid Transit. "The Making of a Model New York City." Foote, Allen R. 1891. Pamphlet, 22 pp. 17

——. Rapid Transit. "Report of the Board of Rapid Transit Railroad Commissioners in and for the City of New York on Rapid Transit in Foreign Cities." (London, Glasgow, Liverpool, Berlin, Paris, American practice, Baltimore and Chicago.) Parsons, Wm. Barclay. New York, 1894. Ill. plates, 66 pp. 18

——. Rapid Transit. (See also under Underground Railway below.)

——. "Rapid Transit Plan for Broadway, New York." Reno, J. W. Sci. Am. Supp. April 24, 1897. 19

——. "Sixth and Eighth Avenue Surface Railroad in the City of New York. The City's Interest. Facts." (Proposes that New York should reclaim and sell franchises of these roads.) N. Y., April, 1897. Pamphlet. 55 pp. 20

——. "Statistics, New York Street Railway." St. Ry. R. 8:795 (Nov. 15, 1898); St. Ry. J. 16:95 (Jan. 27, 1900). 21

——. Street Railroads. "City Railroads." p. 45 "The Growth of New York." New York, Geo. W. Wood, 1865. Pamphlet. 49 p. 22

——. "Street Railways of Greater New York." Pamphlet 72 pp. Redmond, Kerr & Co., 1898. 23

——. "Suburban New York in comparison with like service afforded in London, Railroad Facilities of." Crowell, Foster. Engng. M. 10:1029 (1896). 24

——. "Suburban Rapid Transit Railroad." Railroad Gaz. July 24, 1891, p. 509. 25

——. Suburban Transit Facilities. "The 'Trolley' near New York." Ingersoll, Ernest. Hrprs. Wkly. 40:755 (1896). 26

——. "Third Avenue Lease, Statement by Mr. Vreeland on." St. Ry. J. 16:510 (May 26, 1900).

——. Traction,—Cable, Electric and Horse. Costs and Profits. Vreeland, H. H.

New York City—*Continued*.

St. Ry. J. 14:721 (Nov. 1898); anon. Eng. News Jan. 14, 1897; Sci. Am. Jan. 16, 1897; Ry. World 7:402 (Dec. 8, 1898); St. Ry. J. 15:579, 16:999 (Sept. 1899, Oct. 13, 1900).

———. "The Transfer System." R. R. Gaz. Dec. 21, 1894.

———. Tunnels under East River. Engng. News March 14, 1891, p. 249, 37:22 (Jan. 14, 1897), 38:329, 344 (Nov. 18, Nov. 25, 1897), 41:319 (May 18, 1899), 42:416, 420 (Dec. 28, 1899); Pub. Imp. 1:169 (Sept. 1, 1899); Sci. Am. 81:10 (Ju.y 1, 1899).

———. "Tunnel Plans for New York, New Jersey and Long Island, Electric." Elec. W. & E. 34:76 (July 15, 1899).

———. Underground Railway, New York Rapid Transit. Armstrong, Albert H. St. Ry. R. 8:478 (July 15, 1898), Elec. Eng. 26:77 (July 28, 1898); Lewis, Alfred Henry. Arena Q. 1:35 (June, 1900); Lindenthal, G. Railroad Gaz. 29:207, 215 (March, 1897); Mayo, Earl W. Outlook 65:21 (May 5, 1900); Orr, Alexander E. Mun. & Ry. Rec. 3:911 (Dec. 15, 1898); Parsons, William Barclay. Scribner's 27:545 (May, 1900); Pryor, James W. Ann. Am. Acad. Pol. Sci. 11:421 (May, 1898); Rowe, Leo S. Ann. Am. Acad. Pol. Sci. 11:138 (March, 1898); Standiford, Charles W. Arena Q. 1:50 (June, 1900); v. d. Werra, F. M. Zeitschr. d. Ver. Deutscher Ing. May 26, June 2, 1900; Whalen, John. Arena Q. 1:38 (June, 1900); anon. Arch & Buil. 27:145, 189 (Oct. 23, Nov. 27, 1897), 28:13, 97 (Jan. 8, March 19, 1898), 30:105 (April 8, 1899), 31:33 (July 29, 1899); Mun. Rec. & Ad. Vol. I, No. 24, p. 10 (Nov. 20, 1897); Railroad Gaz. 29:870 (Dec. 10, 1897), 30:214 (March 25, 1898), 31:223 (March 31, 1899); Engng. News 38:409 (Dec. 23, 1897), 40:416 (Dec. 29, 1898); St. Ry. J. 15:225, 873 (April, Dec., 1899), 16:30, 93 (Jan. 6, 27, 1900); Engng. Rec. 39:399, 562 (April 1, May 20, 1899), 40:497 (Oct. 28, 1899); Outlook 61:809 (April 8, 1899); Ann. Am. Acad. Pol. Sci. 13:409 (May, 1899); Public Improvements 2:7, 123 (Nov. 1, 1899, Jan. 15, 1900), 3:361 (July, 1900); Ty. & Ry. World 9:14 (Jan. 11, 1900); Sci. Am. 82:69 (Feb. 3, 1900); Eng. (Lond.) 89:424 (April 27, 1900).

———. Underground Railway. "Brief for Rapid Transit Board." (Case of Sun Publishing Co. v. Rapid Transit Board.) Boardman, Albert B. and Edward M. Shepard. New York, Jan. 1897. 120 pp.

———. Underground Railway. "The Contract for the New York Rapid Transit Railway." Engng. News 42:336 (Nov. 23, 1899).

———. Underground Railway. "Contracts and Quantities in the New York Rapid Transit Railway Work." Engng. N. 43:344 (May 24, 1900).

———. Underground Railway. Courts and Rapid Transit in New York. Arch. & Buil. 27:215 (Dec. 18, 1897); St. Ry. J. 14:44 (Jan. 1898).

———. Underground Railway. "Expert Opinion of the New Rapid Transit Proposition in New York." Fish, Stuyvesant. St. Ry. J. Supp. April, 1899.

———. Underground Railway. "The New York City Rapid Transit Proposition of the Metropolitan Street Railway Company." St. Ry. J. 15:230 (April, 1899).

———. Underground Railway. "Progress of Work on the Rapid Transit Tunnel, New York." Sci. Am. 83:326 (Nov. 24, 1900).

———. Underground Railway. "Rapid Transit and Politics." Outlook 58:212 (Jan. 22, 1898).

———. Underground Railway. "Rapid Transit in New York; Its Aid to Commerce and Finance." Clews, Henry. Arena Q. 1:33 (June, 1900).

———. Underground Railway. "The Real Dangerous Classes (Illustrated by the Rapid Transit Contract)." Hennessy, Charles O'Connor. Brooklyn Single Tax League, 1900. 12mo, 31 pp.

———. Underground Railway. "Specifications and Plans for the Building of." Bogart, John, and Parsons, W. B. Engng. Rec. Dec. 3, 10 and 17, 1892; Engng. News Dec. 1, 1892, p. 516; anon. Same Nov. 24, 1891, p. 499, Engng. Rec. Nov. 26, 1892, p. 411.

———. Underground Railway. "Structural Details of the New York Rapid Transit Tunnel Railway, General." Engng. News 42:380 (Dec. 14, 1899).

———. "Underground Electric Railway for New York City." Sprague, Frank J. Elec. Eng. March 4, 1891.

———. Underground Trolley Lines. (See under Metropolitan Street Railway above.)

"Trees, Shade, in the Streets of New York." Real Estate Rec. and Guide Feb. 24, 1894, p. 293.

Tunnels under East River and to New Jersey. (See Tunnels under Transit Facilities above.)

New York City—*Continued.*

Tweed Ring. Edwards, E. J. McClure's 5:132 (1895); Godkin, E. L. Nation 13:300 (1871), 17:349 (1873), 21:67 (1875); Nadal, E. S. Nation 14:284 (1872); Sears, E. I. Nat. Q. 31:116 (1875); Sterne, Simon. Nation 13:125 (1871), Law M. & Rev. n. s. 2:525 (1873); Wingate, Charles F. No. Am. 119:359 (1874), 120:-119 (1875), 121:113 (1875); anon. No. Am. 123:362 (1876). 42

———. Citizens' Association of New York. "Address to the Public: History of its work, the Department of Docks, of Health, the Fire Department." New York, Published by the Association, 1871. 34 pp. "Reform in New York City." 19 pp. 1870. "Correspondence showing a portion of its work," 1871. 47 pp. 43

———. "Dishonesty in New York Government." Parton, James. No. Am. 103:413 (1866). 44

———. "Financial Operations of the Tweed Ring." Ch. V, p. 119 E. D. Durand's "Finances of New York City." (See under Finance above.) 45

———. "Municipal Abuses." Tilden, Samuel J. Argument in the trial of W. M. Tweed and others. See his Writings and Speeches, 1885, Vol. I, pp. 516-551. 46

———. "The New York City 'Ring:' Its Origin, Maturity and Fall discussed." Tilden, Samuel J. Pamphlet n. d. 31 pp. 47

———. "Peculation Triumphant, being the record of four years' campaign against official malversation in the City of New York, 1871 to 1875." O'Conor, Charles. New York, Polhemus, 1875. 329 pp. 48

———. "Three Years' Struggle with Municipal Misrule in New York." Green, Andrew H. Comptroller's Report, Feb. 18, 1875, in response to certain resolutions of the Board of Aldermen. 31 pp. 49

Underground Railway, New York. (See under Transit Facilities above.)

"Unemployed in New York City, Five Months Work for." Lowell, C. R. Char. R. 3:323 (1894). 50

———. "Tammany's Million Dollar Fraud on the Workingmen." (Account of appropriation for park improvements designed to furnish work to unemployed in the winter of 1893-4.) New York, leaflet published by Citizens' Union, 1897. 24 pp. 51

Vacation Schools in New York. (See under Schools above.) 52

Valentine's Manuals. (See under History above.)

Vigilance League, City. (See Reform Organizations under General References above.)

Vital Statistics. (See under Statistics above.)

Water Supply of New York. Baker, M. N. Mun. Aff. 4:486 (Sept. 1900); Croes, James R. City Govt. 7:146 (Dec. 1899); Dalton, William. Mun. Engng. 17:167 (Sept. 1899); Freeman, J. R. J. Gaslight 76:108 (July 10, 1900); Milne, Peter. Fire & W. (Nov. 18, 1899); Phillips, Barnet. Hrprs. Wkly. 40:55 (1896); Thurber, F. B. No. Am. 167:90 (July, 1898); anon. Sci. 13:208 (1890); Fire & Water Nov. 14, 1896; Sci. Am. May 15, 1897; Fire & Water April 24, Nov. 6, Dec. 18, 1897; Engng. Rec. 40:285 (Aug. 26, 1899); Eng. (London) 88:264 (Sept. 15, 1899); Fire & W. 26:376 (Nov. 11, 1899); Engng. Rec. 40:335 (Sept. 16, 1899), 40:570 (Nov. 18, 1899), 41:338 (April 14, 1900), 41:373 (April 21, 1900), 41:609 (June 30, 1900); Railroad Gaz. 32:561 (Aug. 24, 1900). 53

———. "Water Supply, An Inquiry into the Conditions Relating to the Water Supply of the City of New York." Merchants' Association of New York. New York, Merchants' Association, 1900. 8vo, 627 pp. Maps and Charts. Cl. $3. Reviewed in Eng. Rec. 42:169 (Aug. 25, 1900). 54

———. "Outline of Plans with illustrations for furnishing an abundant supply of water to the City of New York." Maps and plans. (Source, Great Notch Reservoir in New Jersey.) New York, Published by John R. Bartlett and associates, 1888. 4to, 99 pp. 55

———. "Report upon New York's Water Supply with particular reference to the Need of Procuring Additional sources and their Probable Cost with Works Constructed under Municipal Ownership, made to Bird S. Coler, Comptroller." Freeman, John R. New York, City Comptroller, 1900. 8vo, 587 pp. Maps and Charts. 56

———. "Aqueduct, Report of the Committee appointed to investigate certain abuses on the new." (Fassett, J. S., Chairman.) N. Y. Senate Documents 1889, no. 57. 2094 and 1394 pp. 57

———. Brooklyn Water Supply, Scarcity of Water in Brooklyn. Milne, Peter. Fire & W. 26:225 (July 15, 1899); Waring, Geo. E. Hrprs Wkly. Feb. 6, 1897; White, Alfred T. Engng. News Feb. 13, 1896; anon. Fire & W. 23:90 (March 19, 1898);

BIBLIOGRAPHY.

New York City—*Continued.*

Sanitarian 43:63 (July, 1899); Engng. Rec. 41:25 (Jan. 13, 1900).   58

——. Brooklyn. "History and description of the Water Supply." Brooklyn, 1896. 4to, 324 pp. Plates, tables. $10.   59

——. Brooklyn Water Supply, How Polluted.. Sanitarian 38:453 (May, 1897).

——. "Brooklyn Water Supply, Impure Source of." Hrprs. Wkly. 39:828 (1895).

——. Brooklyn. "The Mt. Prospect Laboratory." Whipple, George C. Engng. N. 43:381 (June 7, 1900).   60

——. Brooklyn. "Report on Future Extension of Water Supply." White, Alfred T. Brooklyn, 1896. 4to, 76 pp. Plates, diagrams. $5.   61

——. Brooklyn. "Report of the Manufacturers' Association of Kings and Queens Counties on the Water Supply of Brooklyn." Eng. Rec. March 27, 1897.   62

——. "Brooklyn Water Works." Tuttle, Arthur S. Brooklyn, 1899. 8vo, 136 pp.   63

——. "Consumption of Water in Greater New York." Pruyn, Francis L. Engng. Rec. 39:322 (March 11, 1899). (See also under Waste below.)   64

——. "Croton Aqueduct Embankment." Landis, H. K. Engng. News 38:164 (Sept. 9, 1897).   65

——. "Croton Aqueduct, Preliminary Alinement of the New." Gould, E. Sherman. Engng. N. 43:357 (May 31, 1900).   66

——. "Construction and Capacity of the Croton Aqueduct, Memoir of the Cost, together with an account of the civic celebration of the fourteenth of October, 1842, on occasion of the completion of the great work, preceded by a preliminary essay on ancient and modern aqueducts." King, Charles. New York, 1843. 4to, 308 pp.   67

——. Croton Dam, New. Gowen, Charles S. Trans. M. Soc. Civ. Eng. 26:2 (Jan. 1900); anon. Sci. Am. 78:88 (Feb. 5, 1898); Engng. Rec. 38:27 (June 11, 1898), 39:113 (Jan. 7, 1899).   68

——. "Department of Water Supply." King, William F. Mun. Aff. 4:751 (Dec. 1900).   69

——. "Electricity, Purifying the Water Supply of New York by." Wetzler, Joseph. Hrprs. Wkly. 37:771 (1893).   70

——. "Future Water Supply of New York." Duane, Gen. Fire and Water Mar. 20, 1897; anon. Engng. News Feb. 13, 1896, 42:121 (Aug. 24, 1899), 44:120 (Aug. 23, 1900).   71

——. History. "The Water Supply of the City of New.York from 1658 to 1895." Wegmann, Edward, Jr. New York, Wiley & Sons, March 5, 1896. 1st ed. 4to, 328 pp. 148 plates. Cloth, $10.   72

——. "Jerome Park Reservoir, Construction of the." Engng. Rec. 37:9 (Dec. 4, 1897), 41:148 (Feb. 17, 1900).   73

——. Ramapo Water Project. King, William F. Public Improvements 2:175 (Feb. 15, 1900); Rice, George S. Engng. Rec. 40:325 (Sept. 2, 1899); anon. Engng. Rec. 38:68 (June 25, 1898); Fire & W. 26:296 (Sept. 9, 1899); Nation 69:347 (Nov. 9, 1899).   74

——. "The Ramapo Water Contract, Report of a Preliminary Inquiry, and action taken and proposed, for a radical investigation." New York, Merchants' Assoc. Nov. 16, 1899. 50 pp.   75

——. "Underground Water in New York, The Ownership of." Engng. Rec. 39:447 (April 15, 1899).   76

——. "Underground Water Supplies, Borough of Brooklyn, New York City, The Latest Decision Affecting." Engng. N. 44:385 (Dec. 6, 1900).

——. Waste of Water, New York. Croes, J. James R. Mun. Engng. 17:366 (Dec. 1899); Freeman, John R. Mun. Engng. 18:324 (May, 1900), Engng. N. 43:260 (April 19, 1900); anon. Public Improvements 1:80 (July 1, 1899); Engng. N. 44:120 (Aug. 23, 1900); Mun. Engng. 13:344 (Dec. 1897).   77

Water Front, New York's. (See under Harbor Facilities above.)

"Wealth of New York." Gilroy, Thomas F. No. Am. 157:307, 403, 541 (1893).   78

"West Side of New York, Growth of the Upper." Hill, C. T. Hrprs. Wkly. 40:730 (1896).   79

Women's Work in New York City. (See under Charities, Sanitation, Settlements, also City History Club under History and Reform Organizations under General References.)

Working Women in New York. (See under Labor above.)

New York State.

Government, General References.

"Centralization of Administration in New York State." Fairlie, John Archibald. Columbia Univ. Studies in Political Science. Vol. 9, No. 3, New York, 1898. 8vo, 207 pp. Paper, $1. **80**

Constitution of 1894, Articles of, on Municipal Administration: Art. 3, § 18, Local consent for street railways; Art. 5, § 9, Requiring civil service examinations; Art. 8, § 1, Legislature may create by special acts; Art. 8, § 10, Municipal indebtedness; Art. 10, § 2, Election of municipal officers; Art. 12, Government of cities and villages.

Documents of the New York Constitutional Convention of 1867. Nos. 109, 112, 114, 138, 173. Proceedings and Debates of the New York Constitutional Convention of 1867. 2926-3180 pp. **81**

"The Municipal Code (New York State). As presented by the revision Commissioners and passed by the Legislature of the State." New York, Banks, 1894. 1700 pp. $3.50. **82**

Preliminary report of the Senate Committee on cities pursuant to resolution of the Senate adopted January 20, 1890. (Fassett Committee.) N. Y. Senate Documents, 1891, No. 72. 135 pp. **83**

——. Testimony taken before the Senate Committee on cities pursuant to resolution of the Senate adopted January 20, 1890. N. Y. Senate Documents, 1891. No. 80. 4 vols, 3650 and 967 pp. **84**

Record of the New York Constitutional Convention of 1894. (This doubtless contains interesting debates on the subject but as there is no index to the six volumes the matter is practically buried.) **85**

Report of the commission to devise a plan for the government of cities in the State of New York. (Tilden commission, Wm. M. Evarts, chairman.) N. Y. Assembly Documents, 1877, No. 68. 48 pp. **86**

Report of the Commissioners appointed to propose legislation for cities of the second class. (Robert Earl, Chairman.) N. Y. Assembly Documents, 1896, No. 44. 8 pp. (This was accompanied by Assembly Bill No. 595, an act for the government of cities of the second class. Introduced by Mr. Speaker. (Not passed.) **87**

"Second Class Cities, New Charter for." City Govt. 7:123 (Nov. 1899).

"State of New York: embracing historical, descriptive and statistical notices of cities, towns, villages, etc., with a complete list of the post offices, counties and county towns, etc." Kollock, Henry. New York, 1882. 304 pp. **88**

State and Local Government of New York, with the text of its Constitution. Appendix to "Our Republic." Leach, Orlando. Boston, Leach, 1895. 139 pp. 35 cts. **89**

Third Class Cities. Report of the Commissioners appointed to propose legislation for cities of the third class. (Robert F. Wilkinson, Chairman.) N. Y. Assembly Documents, 1896, No. 45. 8 pp. (This was accompanied by Assembly Bills No. 602, 832, an act for the government of cities of the third class. Introduced by Mr. Sanger. (Not passed.) **90**

Charities. "State Charities Aid Association of the State of New York." Schuyler, Louisa Lee. p. 57 "International Congress," vol. III, 1893. See 43-99. **91**

——. "Annual report of the State Board of Charities." XXXII Annual Report for 1898, Senate Doc. No. 19, Jan. 16, 1899. Albany, State Printers, 2 vols. 1262, 1151 pp. **92**

Civil Service. "The New System in New York." Burt, Silas W. p. 47, Proc. Natl. Civil Service Reform League, Philadelphia, 1896. **93**

——. "Civil Service Law." Pryor, James W. Ann. Am. Acad. Pol. Sci. 14:268 (Sept. 1899). **94**

——. "Report of the New York Civil Service Commission." Published annually. XVI annual report for 1898, Assembly Doc. No. 55, March 3, 1899. Albany, State Printer, 912 pp. **95**

Crime. (See under Police below.)

"Election Law of the State of New York, with notes and instructions." McDonough, John T. N. Y. and Albany, Wyncoop, H. C., & Co., 1899. 175 pp. **96**

——. "Code of Election Laws of the State of New York with annotations, forms, instructions, etc." Silvernail, William H. New York, Banks & Bros., 1896. 8vo, 252 pp. **97**

——. "Primary Elections." Ann. Am. Acad. Pol. Sci. 11:420 (May, 1898).

New York State—*Continued.*

——. " Primary Election Legislation in the State of New York." Stürcke, Louis. New York, Wynkoop, Hallenbeck, Crawford Co., 1898. Pamphlet, 116 pp. **98**

——. " Primary Legislation in the State of New York." Lauterbach, Edward. N. Y. Conference on Practical Reform of Primary Elections, p. 109. Chicago, Hollister, 1898. 8vo, 150 pp. Paper. **99**

——. " The New York Primary Election Law." Branson, Walter J. Ann. Am. Acad. Pol. Sci. 11:381 (May, 1898). **100**

——. " Proposed Primary Laws in New York." Ford, John. N. Y. Conference on Practical Reform of Primary Elections, p. 116. Chicago, Hollister, 1898. 8vo, 150 pp. Paper. **1**

——. " Report of the State Superintendent of Elections." Issued annually. First annual report for 1898, Assembly Doc. 20, Jan. 12, 1899. Albany, State Printer, 172 pp. **2**

Elmira Reformatory. (See under Police below.)

Excise. (See under Liquor Problem below.)

Factory Inspection. (See under Labor below.)

Finances. Ford Franchise Tax Law. Hodge, J. Aspinwall, Jr. St. Ry. J. 15:532 (Aug. 1899); Seligman, Edwin R. A. Q. J. E. 13:445 (July, 1899); Warner, John De Witt. Mun. Aff. 3:269 (June, 1899); anon. Arch. & Buil. 30:137 (May 6, 1899); City Govt. 6:141 (June. 1899); Prog. Age 17:240 (June 1, 1899); Ann. Am. Acad. Pol. Sci. 14:136 (July, 1899); Other Side 1:127 (Sept. 16, 1899). **3**

——. Ford Bill. "Taxation of Corporate Franchises, argument against the Ford Bill in behalf of the Rapid Transit and Electric Light Companies of Brooklyn." Collin, Charles A. Before Senate Comm. on Taxation and Retrenchment, March 2, 1899. Pamphlet 31 pp. **4**

——. " Laws of the State of New York relating to the assessment and collection of taxes, including the statutes of 1880." New York, S. A. Wilder & Co., 1880. 8vo, 325 pp. **5**

——. " Local Taxation, (Report of the) New York State Commission to revise the Laws for Assessment and Collection of Taxes." New York, Harper & Bro., 1871. 8vo, 74 pp. **6**

——. " Phases of Taxation in New York State." Roberts, James A. Ind. 50:141 (Feb. 3, 1898). **7**

——. " Report of the committee on banks on the financial condition of the cities of the State." 8 pp. N. Y. Senate Documents, 1857, No. 54. **8**

——. " Report of the Commissioners appointed to revise the laws for the assessment and collection of taxes in New York in 1871." (D. A. Wells.) (This report was reprinted by the Cobden Club at Manchester, Eng. in 1871, paper, 142 pp. 2s. 6d.) **9**

——. " Special message from the Governor [Tilden] in relation to city debts and taxes, leading to the appointment of the Tilden Commission." N. Y. Senate Documents, 1875, No. 90, 20 pp. **10**

——. " Report of the clerk of the senate in answer to a resolution of the senate passed March 16, 1882, in relation to separate valuations of real and personal property for local taxation in cities of this State since 1860." N. Y. Senate Documents, 1882, No. 95, 25 pp. **11**

——. " Reports of the Comptroller of the State of New York." Albany, State Printer. Published annually. Report for 1899, 710 pp. **12**

——. " Reports of the State Board of Tax Commissioners." Annual Report for 1898, Senate Doc. No. 9, Feb. 7, 1899. Albany, State Printers, 330 pp. **13**

——. " Reports of the State Treasurer." Annual Report for 1898, Senate Doc. 3, Jan. 4, 1899, Albany, State Printer, 322 pp. **14**

"History of the State of New York, 1609-1691." Brodhead, John Romeyn. New York, Harper, 1871-4. 8vo, 2 vols, $6. **15**

——. " History of New Netherlands or New York under the Dutch." O'Callaghan, Edw. B. New York, Appleton, 1848. 2 vols. 8vo. $6. **16**

——. " The History of Political Parties in the State of New York, 1789-1847." Hammond, Jabez D. Cooperstown, H. & E. Phinney, 4th ed., 1846. 3 vols. 594, 749, 553 pp. **17**

——. " Thirty Years of New York Politics up to date." Breen, Matthew P. New York, Matthew P. Breen, 1899. 8vo, 843 pp. Cloth, $3. **18**

——. " Documentary History of the State of New York." O'Callaghan, E. B. Arranged under direction of Christopher Morgan, Secretary of State. Albany,

New York State—*Continued.*

Weed, Parsons & Co., Public Printers, 1849. 4 vols, 8vo, 786, 1211, 1215, 1144 pp.

Labor. "Report of the Bureau of Labor Statistics." Published annually. XVIth Annual Report for 1898, Assembly Doc. No. 70, 1899. Albany, State Printer. 1179 pp.

——. "Report of the Factory Inspector of the State of New York." Published annually. XIIIth Annual Report for 1898, Assembly Doc. No. 51, Jan. 23, 1899. Albany, State Printer. 857 pp.

Lighting. "New York's Need of a Gas Commission." Mun. & Ry. Rec. 4:13 (Jan. 15, 1899).

——. "Gas Statistics, New York State." Prog. Age 16:468 (Oct. 1, 1898).

Liquor Problem. "The Operation of the New York Liquor Tax Law." p. 338 "Liquor Problem in its Legislative Aspects." Wines, F. H. and J. Koren. Boston, Houghton, M. & Co., 1897. 349 pp. $1.25.

——. "Report of the State Commissioner of Excise." Published annually. Third Annual Report for 1898, Senate Doc. No. 18, Jan. 16, 1899. Albany, State Printers. 599 pp.

——. "Report of the Special Committee of the Senate appointed to investigate the working of the Liquor Tax Law." N. Y. Senate Doc. 41, March 12, 1897. Albany, State Printers. 1146 pp.

Municipal Control, Municipal Ownership. "The Ownership and Operation of Electric Light and Power, Gas and Water Plants." Part II, pp. 497-601 of the Fifteenth Annual Report of the Bureau of Labor Statistics of the State of New York for the year 1897. 497 pp. Albany, Wynkoop, H. C. Co., 1898.

——. "Report of the Committee appointed by the Assembly to investigate the question of municipal ownership of the street and elevated railroads of the various cities of the State." (S. Frederick Nixon, Chairman.) N. Y. Assembly Documents, 1896, No. 53. 24 pp.

"Party Government in the Cities of New York State." Wilcox, D. F. Pol. Sci. Q. 14:681 (Dec. 1899).

Police, Crime, etc. "The State Constabulary Bill." Outlook 66:872 (Dec. 8, 1900).

——. "Report of the Secretary of State on statistics of crime in the State of New York." Issued annually. Report for 1896, Assembly Doc. 82, April 21, 1897. Albany, State Printers. 458 pp.

——. "New York State Reformatory in Elmira." Winter, Alexander. London, Swan, S. & Co., 1891. 8vo, 172 pp. 2s. 6d.

——. "Year Book of the New York State Reformatory." Published annually. XXIII issue for 1898. Albany, State Printers, 1899. 187 pp.

Primary Elections. (See under Elections above.)

Sanitation. "Report of the State Board of Health." Published annually. XIXth Annual Report for 1898, N. Y. Assembly Doc. No. 73. Albany, State Printer. 771 pp.

Savings Banks, etc. "Report of the Superintendent of Banks relative to Building and Loan and co-operative savings and loan associations." Published annually. IXth Annual Report for 1898, Assembly Doc. 52, March 1, 1899. Albany, State Printer. 440 pp.

Schools. "Report of the State Superintendent of Public Instruction." Published annually. XLVth Annual Report for 1898, Assembly Doc. 56, March 6, 1899. 1174 pp.

Taxation. (See under Finances above.)

Transit Facilities. "The Railroad Laws of the State of New York analytically arranged with judicial decisions, a table of railroad charters and local enactments." McMaster, R. Bach. New York, Baker, Voorhis & Co., 1872. 12mo, 341 pp. 50 cts.

——. "Reports of the Board of Railroad Commissioners of the State of New York." Published annually. XVIIth Annual Report for 1899, Senate Doc. No. 10, Jan. 10, 1900. Albany, State Printers. 2 vols, 441, 1532 pp. (These reports contain much important matter on street railroads in cities.)

Water Supply. "Purchase of Private Water Plants in New York, The." Engng. Rec. 38:340 (Sept. 17, 1898).

New Zealand.

"Cities and Government, New Zealand." Krout, Mary H. Chaut. 29:480 (Aug. 1899); Stout, Robert. Open Court 11:577 (Oct. 1897).   36

——. Local and Municipal Government in New Zealand. Chs. II, X, XVIII, XXXVII, XXXIX, XLIII, "The Government of Victoria, Australia." Jenks, Edward. London, Macmillan, 1891. 8vo, 403 pp. 14s.   37

"Referendum in Australia and New Zealand." Tomn, Lillian. Contemp. 72:242 (Aug. 1897).   38

Street Railways. "Possibilities for Electric Traction in New Zealand." Cicott, Frank X. St. Ry. Rev. 8:782 (Nov. 15, 1898).   39

"Taxation in the Australian Colonies and New Zealand, Local Government and." Dilke, C.; Ware, Thomas Webb; Archer, W. H. p. 233 "Local Government and Taxation," J. W. Probyn, editor. New York, Cassell, 1875. 5s.   40

Niagara, N. Y.

History. "Early History of the Falls and City." St. Ry. R. 7:634 (Oct. 15, 1897).

"Street Railways of Niagara." St. Ry. R. 7:650 (Oct. 15, 1897).

——. "The Electric Railway of the Niagara River Region." St. Ry. J. 13:585 (Oct. 1897); Ry. World 7:35 (Feb. 1898).   41

Nice, France.

Garbage Disposal. See 56-40b.

Sewage Disposal. See 56-40a, 40b.

Transit Facilities. "Electric Tramways of Nice and of the Littoral." Ty. & Ry. W. 9:184 (May 10, 1900).

Noises, City.

"Suppression of City Noises." Hubert, P. C. No. Am. 159:633 (1894).   42

"The Plague of City Noises." Girdner, J. H. No. Am. 163:296 (1896).   43

"To Abate the Plague of City Noises." Girdner, John H. No. Am. 165:460 (Oct. 1897).   44

Nominating Systems. (See under **Elections.**)

Non-Partisanship in Municipal Elections. (See **Parties and Party Politics in Cities, etc.**)

Norfolk, Va.

History, description and statistics of Norfolk, Va., in 1880. Census. See 1-7.

Water Works. "The Norfolk, Va., Filter Plant." Weston, Edmund B. Fire & W. 27:170 (May 19, 1900), 27:178 (May 26, 1900), City Govt. 9:14 (July, 1900); Engng. Rec. 41:470 (May 19, 1900); Engng. N. 43:346 (May 24, 1900); pp. 108-120 in Proc. of the 20th Annual Meeting of the American Water Works Assoc., Richmond, Va., May 15-18, 1900. 8vo, 216 pp. Cl. $1.   45

Northampton, Eng.

"Architecture of our Large Provincial Towns." Builder April 24, 1897.   46

"The Development of Northampton." Mun. J. & London 8:1139 (Oct. 20, 1899).

North Carolina.

"Water Supplies in North Carolina, Legislation for the Protection of Public." Engng. News 42:5 (July 6, 1899).   47

"**North Tonawanda, N. Y.**, Water Works, The." Barrally, T. W. Engng. Rec. 38:515 (Nov. 12, 1898).   48

Norway.

Liquor Problem. "Local Option in Norway." Wilson, T. M. London, Cassell, 1891. 8vo. 1s.   49

Local and Municipal Government in Norway. Demombynes. Vol. I, pp. 162-185. See 2-11.   50

"**Norwich [Eng.]**, Electric Tramways." Ty. & Ry. W. 9:577 (Dec. 6, 1900). 51

Nottingham, Eng.
Garbage Disposal. See 56-40b.
"Housing, Nottingham and Municipal." Mun. J. & London 8:1265 (Nov. 24, 1899). 52
"Sewerage of Nottingham, England, The." Fuertes, James H. Engng. Rec. 38:142 (July 16, 1898); Mun. J. and London 8:107 (Jan. 26, 1899). See also 56-40b. 53
Transit Facilities. "Nottingham Municipal Tramways." London 6:667 (Aug. 5, 1897); Ry. World 7:155 (May 5, 1898); Brown, H. Ty. and Ry. World 8:408 (Oct. 5, 1899); McFarland, S. C. Cons. Rep. 43:183 (June, 1900). 54

Nuremburg, Germany.
Garbage Disposal. See 56-40b.
History. "Mediæval Towns: the Story of Nuremberg." Headlam, Cecil. New York, Macmillan Co., 1899. 16mo, 303 pp. Cloth, $1.50. 55
Sewage Disposal. See 56-40b.
Streets. "Noch einmal die Projektirte Ringstrasse Nürnbergs." Deutsche Bauz. p. 500, 1879. 56
———. "Ein Entwurf zur Anlage einer Ringstrasse an Stelle der alten Vertheidigungswerke Nürnbergs." Deutsche Bauz. pp. 453, 481, 1879. 57

"**Nyack, N. Y.**, Slow Sand Filtration." Engng. Rec. 41:397 (April 28, 1900). 58

"**Oberlin, O.**, Sewerage System of." Engng. News March 8, 1894.

"**Oconomowoc [Wis.]**, Municipal Lighting for." Meissner, Gustav. Municipality vol. I, no. 4, p. 15 (Oct. 1900). 59

Octrois. (See under **Finance.**)

Ohio.
"Charities in Ohio Cities, Plea for Associated." Gunkle, L. B. City Govt. 8:68 (March, 1900). 60
City Government. "Municipal Corporations in the State of Ohio." Peck, Hiram D. Cincinnati, Robert Clark & Co., 3d edition, 1892. 983 pp. $4. 61
———. "Municipal Government in Michigan and Ohio." Wilcox, Delos F. New York, Macmillan, 1896. 8vo, 184 pp. Paper $1. 62
———. Municipalities, Ohio. Blandin, E. J. p. 454 Proc. Second Natl. Conf. for Good City Govt., 1895, see 6-18b; Cassat, Alfred C. pp. 192-198 Proc. of the Louisville Conference for Good City Govt., 1897. Reprinted in City Govt. 2:147 (May, 1897); Ghent, W. J. Ind. 51:3427 (Dec. 21, 1899); Smith, Rufus B. p. 138 Proc. Natl. Civil Service Reform League, Philadelphia, 1897. 63
———. "Municipal Code of Ohio, The Revised." Pugh, David F.; Kibler, Edward. Columbus, O., Herr, 1899. 8vo, 280 pp. 64
———. "Municipal Government, articles in connection with the report of the Ohio municipal code commission." Foote, Allen R. Chicago, Public Policy Publishing Co., 1900. Pamphlet, 111 pp. 65
———. Report of the Ohio Code Commission. Kibler, Edward. 8vo, 17 pp. City Govt. 6:47 (March, 1899), Other Side 1:68 (Aug. 12, 1899), Mun. Aff. 3:528 (Sept. 1899), pp. 188-198 in Proc. of the Columbus Conf. for Good City Govt., 1899, see 6-18f; Blandin, E. J. pp. 199-206, Proc. of the Columbus Conf., see 6-18f; anon. Other Side 1:66, 221 (Aug. 12, Nov. 11, 1899); Stewart, Gilbert M. Public Policy 2:139 (March 3, 1900). 66
"Commerce, The Work of the Ohio State Board of." Johnson, Thomas L. p. 192, Proc. Third Natl. Conf. for Good City Govt., 1896. See 6-18c. 67
"Employment Offices in Ohio, Free Public." Ayres, P. W. p. 124 International Congress, Vol. I, 1893. See 43-99. 68
"Indebtedness in Ohio, Municipal." Mann, Wilbur E. Public Policy 2:108 (Feb. 17, 1900). 69
Water Supply. "Water Department Statistics, Ohio." Brennan, John P. City Govt. 6:55 (March, 1899). 70
———. "Preliminary Report of an Investigation of Rivers and Deep Ground Waters of Ohio as Sources of Public Water Supplies." Cleveland, Ohio State Board of Health, 1898. 8vo, 259 pp. 71

"**Old Dover, N. H.**" Garland, Caroline H. New Eng. M. 17:97 (Sept. 1897). 72

Oldenburg, Street Cleaning. " Wasserleitung zur Spülung von Strassengossen in Oldenburg." Noack, Fr. Gesund. Ing. 20:210 (July 15, 1897). 73

"**Oldham [Eng.]**, Sewage System of." Wilkinson, James B. San. Rec. 23:392 (May 5, 1899). 74

Oliva, Germany.
Municipal Acetylene Plant. " Die Acetylen Stadtanlagen in Oliva." Wolff, Paul. Zeitschr. f. Klein. u. Strassenbahnen Jan 16, 1899. 75

Omaha, Neb.
History, description and statistics of Omaha, Neb., in 1880. Census. See 1-7.
" Municipal Condition of Omaha, Neb." Powell, Rev. Gregory J. p. 418, Proc. Second Natl. Conf. for Good City Govt. Published by the National Municipal League, Philadelphia, 1895. 76
" Paving Specifications of Omaha, The New." Rosewater, Andrew. Mun. Engng. 13:136 (Sept. 1897). 77
" Police Board, State vs. Local." Ann. Am. Acad. Pol. Sci. 12:448 (Nov. 1898). 78
" Tax Commissioner." Rosewater, Victor. Ann. Am. Acad. Pol. Sci. 11:429 (May, 1898). 79
" Water Works of Omaha. Veto Message of the Mayor." Broatch, W. J. City Govt. 2:20 (Jan. 1897); Eng. Rec. (Jan. 9, 1897); Mansfield, Howard. Eng. Rec. (Feb. 6, 1897). 80
———. " Municipalization of Water Works." Lobingier, Charles S. Ann. Am. Acad. Pol. Sci. 14:384 (Nov. 1899). 81

Ontario.
" Growth of Municipal Institutions in Ontario, The." Biggar, C. R. W. Canada Law J. Jan. 2, 1897. 82
Municipal Institutions. " First Report of the Commission on Municipal Institutions appointed by the Government of the Province of Ontario." Toronto, 1888. 233 pp. 83
———. " Municipal System of Ontario." Bourinot, J. G. J. H. Univ. Studies No. 1; James, C. C. Appendix to the Rep. of the Ontario Bureau of Industries, p. 16, 1898. 84

Opera Houses, Municipal. (See under **Theatres and Opera Houses, Municipal.**)

"**Orange [N. J.]** Water Works Extension, The." Engng. Rec. 42:394 (Oct. 27, 1900). 85

"**Orchestras, Municipal.**" Mun. J. & London 8:1099 (Oct. 6, 1899). 86

Origin of Cities and Towns. (See under **Population.**)

"**Osnabruck [Ger.]** Die Wohnungsverhältnisse der ärmeren Volksklassen in der Stadt." Brünning. Pp. 129-151 Hft. 31 Schr. d. Ver. f. Socialpolitik. 87

Ostend, Belgium, Housing. " Stadterweiterung von Ostend." Stübben, J. Zeitschr. f. Bauw. p. 229, 1879. 88

Oswestry, Eng.
" Sewage at Oswestry, The Bacterial Treatment of." Lewis, W. A. Aylmer. Surveyor 17:20 (Jan. 12, 1900); Engng. Rec. 41:226 (March 10, 1900). 89

"**Ottawa [Canada]**, The Main Drainage." Engng. Rec. 40:600 (Nov. 25, 1899).

"**Overbrook, N. J.**, Septic Tank at." Owen, James. Engng. Rec. 40:669 (Dec. 16, 1899). 90

Oxford, Eng.

"Charities, Municipal, of Oxford, England." Spooner, W. A. Econ. R. April, 1897.   91

History. "Oxford." Boase, C. W. London, Longmans, 1887. Historic Towns Series. 8vo, 3s. 6d. (For other references see p. 358 Gross' "Bibliography of British Municipal History.")   92

Padua, Italy.

"Architecture and Arts of Padua." Mereu, H. Am. Arch. Feb. 27, 1897.   93

Municipal Government. "La Gouvernement Municipal de Padoue (Italie.)" Einaudi, Luigi. R. Municipale 2:1585 (Sept. 23, 1899), Mun. Aff. 3:215 (June, 1899).   94

Palermo, Italy.

City Government. "Sulle condizioni demographiche, economiche et amministrative della città di Palermo nel 1891." Maggiore-Perin. Palermo, Virzi, 1895. 140 pp.   95

"Theatre, The New Municipal, at Palermo." Builder Jan. 4, 1896.   96

"**Panama,** Water Works in." Gudger. Cons. Rep. 62:50 (Jan. 1900).   97

"**Paraguay,** Cities of." Ruffin, John N. Cons. Rep. 62:35 (Jan. 1900).   98

Paris.

Government, General References, Unclassified.

"Administration de la ville de Paris et du Département de la Seine." (Principal topics discussed: History of Paris pp. 1-30, Ch. I-III; Population pp. 37-39, Ch. V; Administrative Organization of the City and Department pp. 41-96, Ch. VI-VII; Finances pp. 97-250, Ch. VIII-XI; Streets and Highways pp. 251-329, Ch. XII-XXI; Street Cleaning and Watering pp. 351-362, Ch. XXII; Parks, Gardens, Promenades pp. 363-377, Ch. XXIII; Street Franchises, pp. 377-384, Ch. XXIV; Street Cars, Omnibuses, Seine River Boats, etc. pp. 390-428, Ch. XXVI-XXVII; Lighting pp. 429-455, Ch. XXVIII; Water Supply pp. 459-484, Ch. XXX; Sewage Disposal pp. 485-509, Ch. XXXI-XXXII; Markets pp. 557-581, Ch. XXXVII; Slaughter Houses, Abattoirs, Cattle Markets pp. 583-598, Ch. XXXVIII; Food Inspection pp. 618-626, Ch. XLII; Burial pp. 630-655, Ch. XLIII-XLIV; Public Schools and Education pp. 671-759, Ch. XLVI-LIV; Police pp. 761-792, Ch. LV; Prisons pp. 793-799, Ch. LVI; Fire Protection pp. 801-819, Ch. LVII; Public Health pp. 823-849, Ch. LVIII-LX; Charity pp. 881-951, Ch. LXIII-LXV; Pawn Shops (Monts de Piété) pp. 953-963, Ch. LXVI-LXVIII). Block, Maurice. Paris, Guillaumin et Cie., 1884. 8vo, 1032 pp.   99

"Administration de Paris." Part III of Fernand Bournon's "Paris, Histoire, Monuments, Administration." Paris, Armand Colin et Cie., 1888. 384 pp. 7 fr.   100

"Administration de la ville de Paris et du département de la Seine." de Pontich, H. (Publiée sous la direction de Maurice Block.) Paris, Guillaumin et Cie., 1884. 1032 pp.   1

Government of Paris. Burnell, G. R. J. Soc. Arts 13:240 (1865); Charnay, Maurice. Mouvement Soc. 2:482 (April 15, 1900), 2:533 (May 1, 1900); Dilke, C. W. J. Statis. Soc. 39:299 (1876); Gigot, A. Fortn. 39:305 (1883); Guyot, Yves. Contemp. 43:439 (1883); Laugel, A. Nation 28:147, 178, 214, 263 (1879); Lavallée, Albert. R. Gén d'Administration 69:385 (Dec. 1900); Shaw, Albert. Cent. 42:449 (1891); anon. Surveyor 17:649 (June 15, 1900), 17:672 (June 22, 1900), 17:704 (June 29, 1900), 18:36 (July 13, 1900).   2

——. "Du Régime Municipal de Paris." Artigues, George. Paris, Arthur Rousseau, 1898, 8vo, 193 pp.   3

History of Paris City Government. (See under History below.)

Life in Paris. "La Vie à Paris." Clareti, J. Paris, Fasquelle, 1898. 18mo, 500 pp. 3.50 fr.   4

"Municipal Trip to Paris." San. Rec. Supp. June 15, 1900.   5

"New York and Paris Contrasted. Height and Character of Buildings, Garbage Removal, etc." Real Estate Rec. & Guide April 7, 1894, p. 529.   6

"L'Organisation Municipal de Paris et de Londres, présent et avenir." Guyot, Yves. Paris, Marpont et Flammarion, 1883. 100 pp. 1 fr. 50c.   7

"Paris the Magnificent." Ragan, H. H. Chaut. June, 1897.   8

"Paris: Notable Municipal Features." Dohrmann, F. W. Mchts. Assoc. Rev. Vol.

Paris—*Continued.*

2, No. 24, p. 1 (Aug. 1898).
"Paris, Organisation Municipale, Institutions Administratives." (Entretiens Familiers sur l'Administration de Notre Pays.) Block, Maurice. Paris, Hetzel et Cie., 1881. 2 vols. 128 and 128 pp. (Topics same as in his Administration de la Ville de Paris, treatment briefer and colloquial.) 128 pp. 3 fr.
"Paris, ses Organes, ses Fonctions et sa Vie dans le seconde moitié du XIX siècle." du Camp, Maxime. Paris, Hachette, 1875. 5 vols. 37 fr. 50c. (Chap. XIII, La Police; XV, Les Prisons; XVII La Prostitution; XVIII to XXIII (Vol. IV), L'Assistance Publique; Chap. XXIV, Le Mont de Piété; XXVIII, Le Service des Eaux; XXIX, L'Eclairage; XXX, Les Egouts; XXXIII, Les Cimetières; XXXIV, Les Bibliotheques.)
"Paris of To-day." Whiteing, Richard. New York, Century Co., 1900. 4to, 249 pp. Cl. $5.
"Paris, the Typical Modern City." Shaw, Albert. pp. 1-146 "Municipal Government in Continental Europe." See 1-6.
"Parisian Pastimes." Whiteing, Richard. Cent. 40:87 (May, 1900).
"Recueil annoté des lois et décrets sur l'administration communale et départementale, comprenant les textes speciaux a l'administration de la ville de Paris et du département de la Seine." Souviron, Alfred et Pontich, Henri de. Paris, Muzard et fils, 1889. 8vo. 10 fr.

Abattoir, The New Paris. "Das neue Schlachthaus der Stadt Paris." Oesterr. Monatschr. f. d. Oeffent. Baudienst June, 1897.
"Artistic Paris." Whiteing, Richard. Cent. 60:400 (July, 1900).
——. "Monuments Elevés par la ville, 1850-1880, Paris." Narjoux, Félix. Paris, Morel, 1882. 5 vols.
Baths at Rouen and Paris, Public. "Les Bains-Douches à bon marché à Rouen et à Paris." Sarrey, Paul. Génie Civil May 6, 1899.
Building and Street Regulations. "Dictionnaire des Usages et Réglements de Paris et du département de la Seine en matière de location, constructions, voirie, etc." Emion V. et Ch. Bardies. Paris, Larose et Forcel, 1893. 4 fr.
Burial, Cremation, etc. "Cremation at Père la Chaise." de Lautreppe, Lecoq. Nation 49:190 (1889); anon. Am. Arch. 23:41 (1887).
——. "De la création des maisons ou dépots mortuaries de Paris." du Mesnil, O. Ann. d'Hyg. 2:515 (1879); 11:331 (1884.)
Charity. "Assistance Publique à Paris." D'Echérac et Nielly. p. 210, Vol. I, Say's "Dictionnaire des Finances." See 2-12.
——. "L'Assistance Publique à Paris." Feillet, Paul. Paris, Berger, Levrault et Cie., 1888. 132 pp. 3 fr.
——. "L'Assistance Publique en 1900." Paris, Administration Générale de L'Assistance Publique à Paris, 1900. 4to, 834 pp. Paper.
——. "Paris et L'Assistance Publique." Lefevre, A. R. Paris, No. 13, p. 71 (July 1, 1899).
——. Beggars. "Paris qui mendie, mal et remède." Paullian, Louis. Paris, Ollendorf, 1893. 3 fr. 50c. (Translated into English by Lady Herschell. London, Edw. Arnold, 1897. 8vo, 192 pp. 60 cts. Reviewed by Alexander Johnson. Char. R. 6:257 (May, 1897).
——. "Blind, Paris and the." Price, E. C. Gentlemen's Magazine Aug. 1898.
——. "Le Bureau de Bienfaisance central de Paris." Bompard, Raoul. R. Pol. e. Par. 24:360 (May 10, 1900).
——. "Charities of Paris." Lincoln, G. W. Church R. 44:82 (1884).
——. "La Charité à Paris, des diverses formes d'assistance dans le département de la Seine." Lecour, C. J. Paris, Asselin et Cie., 1876. 3 fr. 50c.
——. Children, Dependent. "Enfants assistés of Paris." Cooper, Edward H. New R. May, 1897.
——. "Les Enfants assistés dans le Départment de la Seine." Napias, Henri. Revue Municipale 3:1659 (Oct. 28, 1899).
——. "Christian Work in Paris Slums." Tooley, S. A. Quiver May, 1900.
——. Insane, Care of. "Les Aliénés dans le Départment de la Seine." Rebeillard, E. R. Municipale 3:1743 (Dec. 2, 1899), 6:1755 (Dec. 9, 1899), 3:1772 (Dec. 16, 1899).

Paris—*Continued.*

———. Insane. "L'Assistance des Aliénés devant la Conseil Général de la Seine." Marie. A. R. Municipale 3:1963 (March 10, 1900). 36

———. "Outdoor Relief of Paris, The Department of Public." Carstens, C. C. Ann. Am. Acad. Pol. Sci. 16:167 (July, 1900). 37

———. "Poverty in Paris." Hooper, L. H. Appletons 11:716 (1873). 38

Conduits. "Underground Paris." Mun. J. & London 9:47 (Jan. 19, 1900). 39

———. "Electric Conduit Construction in Paris." Connett, A. N. St. Ry. J. 15:845 (Dec. 1899). 40

Council, Municipal. "Quatre années au Conseil Municipal de Paris." Cochin, Denys. Paris, C. Levy, 1883. 3 fr. 50c. 41

———. "Dix-neuf ans du Conseil Municipal élu de la ville de Paris, 23 Juillet, 1871, Mai, 1890. Des faits." Chassagne. Paris, Dentu, 1890. 92 pp. 2 fr. 42

———. "L'Oeuvre du conseil municipal de Paris." Strauss, P. Le Grande Revue, April 1, 1900. 43

Courts. "La Cour d'Assises de la Seine." Cruppi, J. Revue d. Deux Mondes June 15, 1897. 44

Elections. "Le Vote de Paris: Les Elections Municipales et le Socialisme." La Semaine (Paris), May 10, 1900. 45

———. "Les Elections de Paris et le Parti Socialiste." Rouanet, Gustave. R. Soc. 31:716 (June, 1900). 46

"Finances of Paris, 1879." Laugel, A. Nation 28:281, 315 (1879). 47

———. Berlin and Paris. "Die Gemeindefinanzen von Berlin und Paris." Rowe, Leo S. Jena, Gustav Fischer, Pubs. Economic Seminary at Halle, 1893. 236 pp. 48

———. "Financial Condition." (Berlin and Paris). Ann. Am. Acad. Pol. Sci. 12:311 (Sept. 1898). 49

———. Budget. "Le Budget de Paris." Veber, Adrien. R. Soc. 31:432 (April 1900). 50

———. Financial Claims of Paris and the Department of the Seine. "Les Revendications Financières de Paris et de la Seine." Strauss, P. Revue Municipale 3:1721 (Nov. 25, 1899). 51

———. "Les Finances de la Ville de Paris de 1798 à 1900, suivies d'un essai de statistique comparative des charges communales des principales villes françaises et étrangères de 1878 à 1898." Cadoux, Gaston. Paris, Berger, 1900, 8vo, 831 pp., 6 tables, 15 fr. 52

———. Management of Communal Property. "La Regie des Propriétés Communales de la Ville de Paris." R. Municipale 3:1891 (Feb. 3, 1900). 53

———. "Municipal Taxation." Ann. Am. Acad. Pol. Sci. 13:132 (Jan. 1899).

———. "Octroi Taxes in Paris." Beaulieu, Paul Leroy. Bank M. (N. Y.) 35:105 (1881). 54

———. "La Question de l'Octroi à Paris." Veber, Adrien. Rev. Soc. 28:544 (Nov. 1898). 55

———. "La Suppression des Octrois et le Conseil municipal de Paris." Guyot, Yves, 1880. 18mo. Pamphlet. (See also Octrois under **Finance, France**). 56

"Fires in London and Paris during 1891." J. Statis. Soc. 55:137 (1892).

———. Fire at the Paris Bazaar. Statham, H. H. Engng. M. 13:504 (July 1897); anon. Builder (London) May 8, 1897; Engineering (London) May 14, 1897. 57

———. "The Sapeurs-Pompiers of Paris." Fire & W. 28:26 (July 28, 1900).

Food Supplies of Paris. "L' Alimentation de Paris." Funck-Brentano, Th. Revue de Paris, 15 Mai, 1895, p. 381. 58

Garbage Disposal. "Notice Monographique sur les Ordures Ménagéres de Paris." Vincey, Paul. Bull. Soc. d'Encour. Aug. 1900. 59

Gas Supply of Paris. (See under Lighting).

Harbor Facilities. "Les Quais de Paris." Escudier, Paul. R. Municipale 3:1737 (Dec. 2, 1899). 61

"Haussmann, Memoires du Baron." (Contains an account of the transformation of Paris). Haussmann, Georges Eugène. Paris, Victor Havard, 1890. 3 vols. 587, 576 and 567 pp. 22 fr. 50c. 62

"Higher Life of Paris, The." Wagner, Charles. Outlook, May 1, 1897. 63

History. "Paris as an Historic City" and "The Transformation of Paris." Chs. XIII. and XIV., pp. 368-411, in Frederic Harrison's "The Meaning of History." New York, Macmillan, 1894. 8vo, 482 pp. $2.25. 64

Paris—Continued.

——. "Etudes sur l'administration de la Ville de Paris et du departement de la Seine." Say, Horace. Paris, Guillaumin, 1846. 8vo, 8 fr.   65

——. "De l'organisation municipale de Paris sous l'ancien régime." Robiquet, Paul. Paris, Berger-Levrault, 1881. 8vo, 1 fr. 50c.   66

——. "Paris municipal au tableau de l'administration de la Ville de Paris depuis les temps les plus reculés jusqu'à nos jours." de Laborde, Alexandre Louis Joseph. Paris, F. Didot. 1833. 8vo, 120 pp.   67

——. "Paris, son administration ancienne et moderne, étude historique et administrative." Lazare, Louis. Paris, Ledoyen, 1856. 12mo. 2 fr. 50c.   68

"Hotel de Ville, Paris, The." Gevaert, Fierens. R. de l'Art 6:475 (Dec. 10, 1899).   69

Housing. "L'Hygiène à Paris, l'Habitation du Pauvre." du Mesnil, O. Paris, Baillière et Fils, 1890. 223 pp. 3 fr. 50c.   70

——. "A Citizen's Household in Paris." Jagow, Eugen von. Chaut. 26:428 (Jan. 1898).   71

——. Lodging Houses. "Au Pays de Misère: Les Bouges de Paris." Loliée, F. R. Revs. 29:129 (April 15, 1899).   72

——. Lodgings for Workmen. "Les Garnis d'Ouvriers à Paris." Picot, Georges. Ref. Soc. 9:823 (June 1, 1900).   73

——. "L'Habitation ouvrière à Paris: Le Logement en Garni." Picot, Georges. Soc. Fran. Hab. à bon marché. No. 2, p. 171 (1900).   74

——. "Les Logements à bon marché. Recueil annoté des discussions délibérations et rapports du Conseil municipal de Paris." (Monographie municipale). Paris, Imprimerie Municipale, 1897. 8vo, 1343 pp.   75

——. The Mechanism of Modern Life; the Parisian House. d'Avenel, G. Revue d. Deux Mondes April 15, 1897.   76

——. Pointe-d'Ivry. "Une Enquête sur les Logements, Professions, Salaries et Budgets dans le Quartier de la Pointe d'Ivry." Mangenot. Ref. Soc. 37:768 (May 16, 1899); 37:832 (June 1, 1899).   77

——. "Tenement Houses in Paris." Morss, Samuel E. U. S. Consular Reports, Vol. XLVIII, No. 178, p. 454-473.   78

Improvement of Paris. "Paris Demolished and Paris Embellished." Bristed, C. A. Fraser 51:73 (1855). (See also under Haussmann above).   79

Labor in Paris, The Condition of. Veber, A. Revue Socialiste (Paris) April, 1897.   80

——. "Les Conditions du Travail dans les Chantiers communaux." (Monographie municipale, Recueil annotée des discussions délibérations et rapports du conseil municipale de Paris.) Paris. Imprimerie municipale, 1896. 2012 pp.   81

——. "Municipal Refuge for Workingmen." Zimmern, Helen. Char. R. 2:226 (1893).   82

——. "Workingmen's Cafés, Paris." Sanborn, A. F. No. Am. 158:251 (1894).   83

——. (See also Point d'Ivry under Housing above, Transit Facilities, Unemployment below).

"Laboratory, The Paris Municipal." Tarbell, Ida M. McClure's 3:177 (1894).   84

——. "Le Laboratoire Municipal de Chimie de la Ville de Paris." P. C. R. Municipale 3:1884 (Feb. 3, 1900).   85

"Libraries of Paris." James, H., Jr. Nation 20:131 (1875), Lib. J. 12:135 (1887).   86

——. "Les Bibliothèques municipales de la ville de Paris." Saint-Albin, Emm. de. Paris, Berger-Levrault, 1896. 8vo, 7 fr. 50c.   87

"Lighting of Paris." (Historical and statistical review). Annales des Ponts et Chaussées, Sept. 1894.   88

——. Gas. "La Compagnie du Gaz et la ville de Paris." Cochin, Denys. Paris, Doin, 1883. 2 fr.   89

——. "Gas Supply of Paris, The." Connor, Edward. Plumb. & Dec. April 1, 1898.   90

——. "Les Services Publics: L'Eclairage au Gaz à Paris." Charnay, Maurice. R. Soc. 29:703 (June 1899).   91

——. "Paris Gas Accounts." Gas Wld. July 3, 1897.   92

——. "Paris Gas Question." Allen, Walter. Mun. Aff. 2:134 (March 1898).   93

——. "Public Lighting in Paris." Levy, Auguste. Gas W. Oct. 6, 1900.   94

——. "Welsbach System, Public Lighting by the." Maréchal, M. J. of Gas Light. Feb. 16, 1897.   95

Paris—*Continued.*

———. " Questions departementales. Du gaz, d'éclairage chauffage et force motrice dans le département de la Seine." Moïse, Charles. Paris, Dentu, 1883. 1 fr. 50c. ... 96

———. " Die Stellung der Privaten Beleuchtungsgesellschaften zu Stadt und Staat. Die Erfahrung in Wien, Paris und Massachusetts." Gray, John Henry. Jena, Gustav Fischer, 1893. 167 pp. ... 97

Lodging Houses. (See under Housing above).

" Markets in Paris." Gowdy, John K. Cons. Rep. 60:121 (May 1899). ... 98

Mayoralty of Paris. " Paris et la Marie Centrale, Etude de la décentralisation administrative." Villain, Georges. Paris, Ghio, 1884. 1 fr. ... 99

———. " Paris, son Maire et sa Police." Depasse, H. Paris, Marpont et Flammarion, 1881. 1 fr. 25c. ... 100

———. The Central Mayoralty of Paris. Combarieu, A. R. Pol. et Par. July 10, 1897. ... 1

———. " The Mairies of Paris." Arch. Rec. 7:401 (June 30, 1898).

Milk Supply. " Municipal System of Sterilizing Milk in Paris, The." Conner, Edward. San. Rec. Supp. Oct. 21, 1898. Mun. World 9:155 (Sept. 1899). ... 2

Municipal Control, Etc. " Municipal Franchises in Paris." Lespinasse, Geo. S. Real Estate Rec. & Guide Dec. 3, 1892, p. 719. ... 3

Octrois. (See under Finance above).

Omnibuses. (See under Transit Facilities below).

" Parks of Paris, The." Building News 16:498.

———. Designing. " Die Anlage und Umwandlung der neuen öffentlichen Gärten und Squares in Paris." Allg. Bauz. p. 96, 1862. ... 4

———. " Nurseries of the City of Paris, The New." Park & Cem. 8:32 (April, 1898).

———. " Parks and Gardens of Paris, The." Raper, G. A. Ludgate May 1900. ... 5

———. " Parks, Promenades and Gardens of Paris described in relation to the wants of our own cities." Robinson, Wm. London, 3d ed., 1883. 644 pp. ... 6

———. " Promenades et Plantations, Parcs, Jardins Publics, Squares et Boulevards de Paris." R. Gen. de l'Arch. pp. 128, 173, 245, 1863. ... 7

———. " Les Promenades de Paris, Bois de Boulogne et de Vincennes, Parcs, Squares, Boulevards de la Ville de Paris." Alphand, A. Paris, 1867-73. ... 8

———. Trees. " Les nouvelles Plantations d'Arbres à Paris." Nouv. Annales de la Const. p. 181, 1876. ... 9

" Pavements of Paris, The." Gowdy, John K. Cons. Rep. 60:123 (May 1899). ... 10

———. Wood Pavements in Paris. Laurent, M. A. Eng. & Buil. Rec. April 7, 1887, June 9, 1888; anon. San. Rec. 19:559 (June 11, 1897). ... 11

" Pawnbroking in Paris." Ralston, W. R. S. Good Words 9:230 (1868). ... 12

———. " Pawnbrokers of Paris." About, E. Bank M. (N. Y.) 16:193 (1862). ... 13

———. " Public Pawnshop." Patterson, W. R. Ann. Am. Acad. Pol. Sci. 15:483 (May 1900). ... 14

Police of Paris. " Paris, son maire et sa police." Depasse, H. Paris, Marpont et Flammarion, 1881. 1 fr. 25c. ... 15

———. " La Police Parisienne, le service de la sureté." Macé, G. Paris, Charpentier et Cie., 1884. 3 fr. 50c. ... 16

———. " Police of Paris." Griffiths, A. Cassell's, July 1897. ... 17

Population. " Resultats Statistiques du Dénombrement de 1891 pour la ville de Paris et le département de la Seine et renseignments relatifs aux dénombrements anterieurs." Masson, Préfecture de la Seine, Service de la statistique municipale, 1894. 6 fr. ... 18

———. " Le Sol et la Croissance de Paris." Dupuy, Paul. Ann. de Géographie 9:340 (July 15, 1900). ... 19

"Prostitution à Paris, La." Richard, Emile. Paris, Baillière et Fils., 1890. ... 20

———. " Prostitution considérée sous le rapport de l'hygiène publique, de la morale et de l'administration." Parent-Duchatelet, A. J. B. Paris, Baillière et Fils., 3e édit., 1857. 2 vols. 731, 892 pp. ... 21

———. " La Prostitution à Paris et à Londres, 1789-1877." Le Cour, C. J. Paris, Asselin & Cie., 3e édit., 1878. 416 pp. 5 fr. ... 22

Public Comfort Stations in Paris. Baugwks.-Ztg. p. 304, 1875; La Semaine des Const. pp. 304, 341 (1876-7), p. 246 (1877-8). ... 23

Paris—*Continued.*

"Public Works and Improvements of Paris, 1856." Quar. 99:200 (1856). 24

———. "Government of Paris, with especial reference to Public Works." Woods, Henry D. J. Assoc. Engin. Soc. March 1892. 25

"Sanitary Administration in Paris." Ecl. Engin. M. 13:547 (1875), 19:124 (1878), 24:296 (1881). 26

———. "L'Assainissement de Paris." Jourdan, Gustav. Paris, Berger-Levrault, 1885. 8vo, 2 fr. 50c. 27

———. "L'Assainssement de la Seine." Bechmann, G. Bulletin de la Société d'Encour. Feb. 1898. 28

———. "Assainissement de Paris, Suppression complète de la Vidange." Miotat, Eug. Paris, Ducher et Cie., 1883. 2 fr. 50c. 29

———. "Etat Actuel de l'Assainissement de Paris." Génie Civil July 22, 1899. 30

———. "Les Services Sanitaires de la ville de Paris." Joltrain, A. Paris, Berger, 1893. 300 pp. 3 fr. 31

———. "Die Stadt Paris vom Gesundheitstechnischen Standpunkte." Beraneck, Hermann. Zeitschr. d. Oest. Ing. u. Arch. Verein, April 27, 1900. 32

———. "Tuberculosis, How the Paris Municipality Fights." Conner, Edward. Mun. World 8:136 (Sept. 1898). 33

Savings Banks. "La Caisse d'Epargne et de Prévoyance de Paris." Bayard, E. Paris, Hachette, 1892. 7 fr. 50c. 34

———. "Les Caisses d'Epargne et de Prévoyance de Paris depuis leur origine jusqu'à nos jours." Laurent, M. H. Pithiviers, imprimeries des caisses d'épargne, 1892. 35

Schools. "A Municipal School of Physics and Chemistry." Lauth, Charles. R. Sci. 13:781 (June 23, 1900). 36

Sewerage, Sewage Disposal of Paris. Adams, S. H. Engng. Times, Aug. 1900, San. Rec. 26:495, 517, 538, 561 (Dec. 7, 14, 21, 28, 1900); Chancellor, C. W. U. S. Cons. Reports, Vol. XLVII, No. 173, p. 149 (Feb. 1895); Flagg, J. F. Eng. Rec. Dec. 5, 1896; Fourrey, E.R.Technique, Sept. 25, 1899, Oct. 10, 1899; Fuertes, James H. Engng. Rec. 38:33 (June 11, 1898); Hooper, L. H. Lippinc. 19:256 (1876); Rabot, M. E. Ann. D'Hyg. Pub. 40:397 (Nov. 1, 1898); Thoinot, L. Ann. D'Hyg. Pub. 42:560 (Dec. 1899); anon. Van Nos. Engin. M. 19:124 (1878); Engin. News Nov. 6, 1886; Engin. News June 20, 1885; Oesterr, Monatschr. f. d. Oeffent. Baudienst, May 1897; Glaser's Annalen May 15, 1897; Engng. News 42:107 (Aug. 17, 1899); Eng. (Lond.) 88:510 (Nov. 24, 1899); Mun. J. & London 9:47 (Jan. 19, 1900). 37

———. "Les Egouts de Paris." Liger, François. Paris, Guillaumin, 1883. 3 fr. 38

———. Farms, Paris Sewage. Use of Sewage in Irrigation. Bechmann & Launay, Engng. News p. 121, Aug. 22, 1895; Conner, E. Land M., Jan. 1900; anon. Engng. News 39:170 (March 17, 1898); Engng. Rec. 40:213 (Aug. 5, 1899). 39

———. Incineration of the Sewage of Paris. "L'Incineration des Gadoues de Paris." La Revue Technique Feb. 25, 1897. 40

———. "Utilization of the Sewage of Paris" Am. Arch. 13:145 (1883).

"Smoke Prevention in Paris." San. Rec. 22:483 (Nov. 4, 1898).

Socialism, Municipal. "L'Oeuvre des Municipalités Socialistes, Paris." Charnay, M. Le Mouvement Socialiste, April 15, 1900. (See also under Elections above). 41

Street Cleaning in Paris. Grimshaw, Robert. Engng. M. 13:99 (April, 1897); Rockwell, Alfred P. Pav. & Mun. Engineer, March 1896; Vaissière, M. Ecl. M. 19:103, 24:431 (1881); Williams, Henry Smith. Hrprs. Wkly. 38:947 (1894); anon. Engng. News Aug. 22, 1891, p. 173; Sanitary Record 19:391 (April 30, 1897); Public Improvements 1:58 (June 15, 1899). 42

"Street Improvement of Paris." Tite, W. J. Statis. Soc. 27:378 (1864). 43

"Street Scenes in Paris." (Eight Ills.) Chaut. 25:153 (May 1897). 44

Streets, Etc. "Paris in Bezug auf Strassenbau und Stadterweiterung." Stübben, J. Zeitschr. f. Bauw p. 377, 1879. Auch in Buchhandel Erschienen, Berlin, 1879. 45

———. "L'Avenue de l'Opera." Nouv. Annales de la Const. p. 176, 1876.

———. "Les Démolitions de l'Avenue de l'Opera." Gaz. des Arch. et du Bat. p. 187, 1876.

———. "Des dépôts de voire de la ville de Paris, considérés au point de vue de la salubrite." du Mesnil, O. Ann. d'Hyg. 7:155 (1882). 46

"Suburbs of Paris, The." Warren, Frederick M. Chaut. 30:510 (Feb. 1900). 47

Taxation. (See under Finance above.)

Paris—*Continued.*

Tenement Houses. (See under Housing above.)
Theatre. "Le Théâtre Paris." Sarcey, Francisque. Cosmopolis 11:169 (July 1898). 48
Transit Facilities. Electric Traction. Dieudonné, Emil. La Revue Technique March 10, 1898; anon. same, Dec. 25, 1896; Oesterr. Monatschr. f. d. "offentl. Baudienst, June, 1897; Ry. World 7:290 (Sept. 1893), 8:13 (Jan. 5, 1899); Zeitschr. f. Klein-u. Strassenbahnen, March 16, 1900. 49
——. "Elevated Roads for Paris." Lespinasse, Geo. S. Real Estate Rec. & Guide Feb. 4 1893, p. 168, April 29, 1893, p. 660. 50
——. Heavy Underground Electric Railroading. anon. Railroad Gaz. 30:390 (June 3, 1898); Elec. Eng. 25:680 (June 16, 1998). 51
——. Mechanically Operated Tramways in Paris. "Die Bahnen mit Mechanischem Betrieb in Paris." Zeitschr. f. Klein- u. Strassenbahnen June 1, 16, July 1, 1900.
——. Metropolitan Underground Railway, Paris. de Néronde, C. Monde Moderne 10:225 (Aug. 1899); Dumas, A. Génie Civil 37:197 (July 21, 1900); Haag, M. Mem. Soc. des Ing. Civ. Paris, Dec. 1884, Feb. 1885; James, Edmund J. pp. 124-136 in Report of the Street Railway Commission of the City Council of the City of Chicago, City Council, Chicago, 1900, 8vo, 136 pp.; Leugny, Georges. La Revue Tecnique Dec. 10, 1898; anon. Engin. News 38:132 (Aug. 26, 1897); Le Génie Civil Oct. 22, 1898; Eng. (London) 89:84 (Jan. 26, 1900); Moniteur Industriel July 28, 1900, Aug. 4, 1900; Elec. W. & E. 36:203 (Aug. 11, 1900); Sci. Am. 83:120 (Aug. 25, 1900); Engng. Rec. 42:122 (Aug. 11, 1900); St. Ry. J. 16.797 (Sept. 1, 1900); Ty. & Ry. World 9:486 (Oct. 11, 1900); Engng. N. 44:392 (Dec. 6, 1900). 52
——. "Omnibus et Tramways de Paris." (Recueil annoté de documents legislatifs et administratifs.) Paris, Imprimerie municipale, 1894. 147 pp. 53
——. "Rapid Transit in Paris." anon. Engng. News 39:271 (April 28, 1898); Parsons, W. B. p. 44 in his "Rapid Transit in Foreign Cities," New York, 1894. 54
——. "Street Railway Employees in Paris." James, Edmund J. Am. J. Sociol. 5:826 (May 1900). 55
——. Tramways, Paris. Jean, Charles. Génie Civil Jan. 13, 1900; Lavalard, M. St. Ry. Jour. 13:16 (Jan. 1897); anon. Ty. & Ry. World 9:135 (April 5, 1900); Mun. J. 9:298 (April 20, 1900); Mun. J. 9:690 (Aug. 31, 1900). 56
"Trees of Paris." Lespinasse, Geo. S. Real Estate Rec. & Guide Jan. 14, 1893, p. 42. (See also under Parks above.) 57
Tuberculosis. (See under Sanitation above). 58
Unemployed in Paris, Aid to. Brelay, Ernest. L'Economiste Française 1:239, 549 (1897); Conner, Edward. Mun. World 10:4, 20 (Jan., Feb. 1900); Dawson, W. H. Econ. J. 8:138 (March 1898); Honoré, F. Réf. Soc. 32:265-275 (1896). 59
——. "Bourse du Travail of Paris, The." Carstens, C. C. Ann. Am. Acad. Pol. Sci. 16:168 (July 1900). (See also Housing, Labor above.) 60
Water Supply of Paris. Arago, Ch. Ann. d'Hyg. Pub. 43:254 (Mar. 1900); Meunier, Stanislas. R. Sci. Apr. 22, 1899; anon. J. Gas Light. Jan. 12, 1897; Eng. Dec. 16, 1898; Revue Technique Feb. 25, 1899; Ann. Am. Acad. Pol. Sci. 14:144 (July 1899); Engng. News 44:281 (Oct. 25, 1900). 61
——. Consumption of Water. "La Consommation de l'Eau à Paris." Revue Municipale 2:1509 (Aug. 19, 1899). 62
——. "The Recent Water Famine in Paris; Water Waste and Purification." Hazen, Allen. Engng. News 44:274 (Oct. 25, 1900). 63
——. "Report on the Paris Water Supply." (Presented to Water Committee of London County Council, April 13, 1894). Binnie, A. R. London, Edward Stanford, 1894. 26 pp., plates. 1 s. 64
——. Suburbs. "Die Wasserleitung für die Umgebung von Paris." Hofer, Thomas. Oesterr. Monatschr. Oeffent. Baudienst Oct. 1900. 65

"**Paris, Tex.**, Sewage Filter Beds at." Engng. News 38:98 (Aug. 12, 1897).

Parks, Playgrounds, Squares, Etc. (See also **Streets**).

See also Baltimore, Barcelona, Boston, Brooklyn, Brussels, Cambridge, Chicago, Cleveland, Detroit, Hague, Italy, Lincoln (Neb.), London, Louisville, Manchester (Eng.), Mansfield, Minneapolis, New England, New Haven, New Orleans, New York, Paris, Philadelphia, Providence, Rochester, St. Louis, Vienna, Washington, Wilmington.

General References.

Parks, Playgrounds, Etc.—*Continued.*

"L'Art des Jardins. Traité général de la composition des parcs et jardins." (avec fig. et 11 pl.) André, E. Paris, G. Masson, 1879. 4to. 35 fr. 66
"City Parks." Jones, Beatrix. Mun. Aff. 3:687 (Dec. 1899); anon. City & State 8:391 (June 21, 1900). 67
"Construction et décorations pour jardins: kiosques—orangeries—volières—abris divers." (avec 50 planches.) Boussard, J. Paris, Ve Morel et Cie., 1881. 60 fr. 68
"Europe, Parks and Gardens of." Thayer, R. Philadelphia, Report to Commissioners of Fairmount Park, 1880. 4to. 68a
"Lehrbuch d. schönen Gartenkunst, m. bes. Rücksicht auf. d. praktische Ausführung v. Gärten u. Parkanlagen." Meyer, G. Berlin, Ernst u. Korn, 2 Aufl., 1873. 4to, 251 pp., tables, diagrams, etc. 26m. 69
"Les Parcs et Jardins." Lefèvre, A. Paris, Hachette et Cie., 1867. 12mo. 2 fr. 70
Metropolitan Parks. Meath, Earl of. New R. 11:201 (1894), 2:432 (1890). 71
"Parks and Gardens." Fraser 47:686 (1853). 72
"Parks, Gardens and Public Squares in Cities." pp. 141-206, 439-514, J. Stübben's "Städtebau." Darmstadt, Bergsträsser, 1890. 561 pp. 32m. 73
"Parks for Growing Cities." Garden & F. 5:61 (1892). 74
"Parks, Parkways and Pleasure Grounds." Olmsted, Frederick Law. Engng. M. 9:253 (1895). 75
"Praktische und Aesthetische Anforderungen an neue landschaftliche Anlagen." Jürgens, R. Leipzig, 1886. 76
"Public Spaces, Parks and Gardens." Blomfield, Reginald. Ch. IV, p. 167 of "Art and Life and the Building and Decoration of Cities." London, Rivington, Percival & Co., 1897. 260 pp. $2.40. 78
"School Grounds, Home Grounds, Play Grounds, Parks and Forests." Dock, Mira Lloyd. Pa. Dept. of Agriculture, Bulletin No. 62, 1900. 8vo, 33 pp. Free. 79
"Social Arrows." Brabazon, Lord. London, Longmans G. & Co., 1887. 414 pp. 5s. (Parks, Play Grounds, Public Baths, etc.) 80
"Standard of Taste for Parks, The." Soc Econ. 8:321 (1895).
"The Coming of Garden Cities." Mun. J. & London 8:928 (Aug. 18, 1899).
"The Parks and Gardens of the World described and illustrated." London, T. Nelson & Sons, 1880.

"Abuse of Public Parks." Garden & F. 7:412 (1894). 81
"Accounts, Park Nomenclature and." Parker, G. A. Park & Cem. 9:141 (Sept. 1899). 82
"Administration of Public Parks." Garden & F. 2:61 (1889).
——. "Care of Urban Parks." Garden & F. 8:82 (1895).
Amusements, Park. Pincus, Henry. St. Ry. J. 15:163 (March, 1899); Davis, E. H. St. Ry. R. 8:786 (Nov. 15, 1898), St. Ry. J. 14:741 (Nov. 1898). 83
Art and Ornamentation. "Art Societies and City Parks." Garden & F. 6:290 (1893). 84
——. "Garten-Architektur." Abel, L. Wien, 1876. 85
——. "Outdoor Art and Workingmen's Homes." Shuey, Edwin L. Park and Outdoor Art Association p. 112, 1897-8. 86
——. "Park Ornamentation." (Editorial.) Mun. World 7:221 (Nov. 1897).
——. "Parks and Municipal Art." Jones, Harry W. Park and Outdoor Art Association, p. 29, 1897. 87
——. "Statue in the Park, The." Partridge, William Ordway. City Govt. 9:52 (Aug. 1900). 88
Bibliography. "Check List of Works on Landscape Gardening and Parks in the New York Public Library." Nov. 1, 1899. (Exclusive of magazine articles.) Bulletin of the New York Public Library, Vol. III, No. 12 (Dec. 1899), pp. 506-517. 89
——. "Bibliography on the Art of Landscape Gardening." (Containing many references to material on parks.) Codman, Henry Sargent. Garden & F. 3:131, 135 (1890). 90
Boulevards, Parks and. Cleveland, H. W. S. Lakeside 7:412 (1872); Sargent, C. S. Garden & F. 7:11 (1894); Schrader, A. C. J. W. Soc. Eng. 5:157 (June, 1900). 91

Parks, Playgrounds, Etc.—*Continued.*

——. "Note sur les Plantations d'Alignement pour Routes, Canaux, Allées, Avenues, Promenades, Parcs et Quinconces." Nouv. Annales de la Const. p. 37, 1856. 92

——. "Parks and Tree Lined Avenues." Jones, Augustine. Pubs. of Advance Club, No. 7, Providence, R. I., 1891. 93

"Breathing Spaces, How to Ensure." Lewes, C. L. 19th Cent. 21:677 (1887). 94

Bridges, Park. Sanne, Oscar. Mun. Engng. 15:228 (Oct. 1898); anon. Engng. Rec. 39:160 (Jan. 21, 1899). 95

Cemeteries. (See under **Burial in Cities.**)

"Commissioners, The Duties of Park." Wahl, Christian. Park and Outdoor Art Assn., p. 132, 1897-8; anon. Park & Cem. 8:143 (Oct. 1898). 96

——. "Park Boards and their Professional Advisers." Garden & F. 7:461 (1894).

"Common Land, Our." (Preservation of Commons and Public Parks.) Hill, Octavia. London, Macmillan, 1877. 206 pp. 3s. 6d. 97

——. "Commons, Parks and Open Spaces." Hunter, Robert. Contemp. 50:387 (1886). 98

"Confiscation of Public Parks." Garden & F. 2:229. (1889).

"Construction of Parks." Cleveland, H. W. S. Garden & F. 3:129 (1890). 99

——. "Behelfe zur Anlage und Bepflanzung von Gärten." Czullik, A. Wien, 1882 and 1885. 100

——. "Common Errors in Park Construction." Pincus, Henry. St. Ry. J. 16:460 (May 5, 1900). 1

——. "Design and Park Planting, Park." Manning, Warren H. Park and Outdoor Art Association p. 50, 1897, Park & Cem. 7:75 (June, 1897). 2

——. "Gärten Architektur. Gärten Pläne und Park-Anlagen." Hiersemann, K. W. Leipzig, 1897. 8vo. 3

——. "Park Making." (Editorial.) Garden & F. 10:489 (Dec. 15, 1897). 4

——. "Park Making as a National Art." Robbins, Mary Caroline. Atlan. 79:86 (Jan. 1897). Reviewed in Garden and F. 10:11 (Jan. 13, 1897). 5

"Cost of Park Maintenance, One Way to reduce the." (Editorial.) Garden & F. 10:271 (July 14, 1897).

"Defacement of City Parks." Garden & F. 8:231 (1895). 6

"Essential Features of a Park System." Pav. and Mun. Engng. March, 1896.

"Function of City Parks, The True." Anon. Garden & F. 4:97 (1891), 10:261 (July 7, 1897).

"Garden and Park Improvement." Park and Cemetery 7:27 (April, 1897).

History. "L'Art des jardins. Parcs—jardins—promenades. Etude historique—principes de la composition des jardins—plantations." Ernouf, A. A. Paris, Rothschild, 3d. ed., 1886. 4to, 500 vignettes. 20 fr. 7

——. "Gartenkunst und Gärten Sonst und Jetzt." Jager, H. Berlin, 1887-88. 8

"Influence of Parks." Hall, W. H. Overland 11:527 (1889). 9

——. "Influence of Parks on the Character of Children." Cleveland, H. W. S. Park and Outdoor Art Association, p. 105, 1897-8. 10

——. "The City as a Child-Saver." City & State 4:386 (March 10, 1898). 11

"Investments and Educators, Parks as." Holden, L. E. Park and Outdoor Art Association, p. 42, 1897. 12

"Landscape Engineering." Eldridge, W. K. Mun. Engng. 16:293 (May, 1899). 13

——. "Appreciation of Natural Beauty." Simonds, O. C. Park and Outdoor Art Association, p. 73, 1897-8. 14

——. "Art and Nature in Landscape Gardening." Garden & F. 10:191 (1897)

——. "Der Gärten: Seine Kunst und Kunstgeschichte." Falke, J. V. Stuttgart, 1884. 15

——. "Die moderne Teppichgärtnerei." Hampel, W. Berlin, 1887. 16

——. "Italian Renaissance Landscape Gardening. "Die Gartenkunst der Italienischen Renaissance-Zeit." Tuckermann, W. P. Berlin, 1884. 17

——. "Landscape Gardens." McCormick, Cyrus H. Park & Cem. 10:141 (Aug. 1900). 18

——. "Lehrbuch der schönen Gartenkunst." Meyer, G. Berlin, 1873. 19

——. "Natural Beauty in Urban Parks." (Editorial.) Garden & F. 10:251 (June 30, 1897). 20

——. "Ornamental Planting for Public Parks and Grounds." Egerton, William

BIBLIOGRAPHY. 215

Parks, Playgrounds, Etc.—*Continued.*

S. Park and Outdoor Art Association, p. 56, 1897. 21
——. " Park Landscapes." King, George R. Pp. 40-45 in " Proceedings of American Park and Outdoor Art Association," Vol. 3, Pt. 3, 8vo. 56 pp. Pamphlet. 22
——. " Park Woodlands and Plantations." Pettigrew, J. A. Park and Outdoor Art Association, p. 147, 1897-8. 23
" Land for Parks, Danger of Delay in Acquiring." Cleveland, H. W. S. Garden & F. 5:131 (1892). 24
" Large Public Park, The True Purpose of a." Olmsted, John C. Park and Outdoor Art Association, p. 11, 1897. 25
" Lighting Plant, Park." (Chicago plant which supplies current for the chain of parks and boulevards on the west side.) Heldt, P. M. American Electrician (New York) April, 1897. 26
" Milk Distribution in the Public Parks." Straus, Nathan. Sanitarian 43:60 (July, 1899). 27
" Municipal Parks and Open Spaces." Pp. 18-25 in " Municipal Extension and Other Essays." Ellery, T. George. Adelaide, Thomas & Co., 1899. 12mo, 51 pp. 28
——. " Municipalities and Pleasure." Mun. J. & London 8:755 (June 30, 1899). 29
——. " Service municipal. Plantations d'alignement, promenades, parcs et jardins publics." Lefebre, G. Paris, 1897. 12mo. 30
——. " The Relation of Parks to the Municipality." Robertson, R. F. Cal. Mun. 1:79 (Oct. 1899). 31
" Need of Parks, The." Eliot, Charles. Address before the Advance Club, Providence, R. I., 1891. 32
——. " Need of More Public Pleasure Grounds, The." Garden & F. 10:30 (Jan. 27, 1897). 33
" Next Stage in the Development of Public Parks." Hyatt, A. Atlan. 67:215 (1891). 34
" People, The Parks and the." Parsons, Samuel, Jr. Outlook 59:23 (May 7, 1898); Coryell, J. R. Park & Cem. 9:100 (July, 1899), pp. 3-9 in Proc. of the Amer. Park and Outdoor Art Assn., 1899. Vol. 3, pt. 3. 35
Playgrounds, Public. American, Sadie. Mchts. Assn. R. Vol. 5, No. 49, p. 1 (Sept. 1900); Betts, Lillian W. Outlook 54:327 (1896); Loring, Florence Barton. Park & Cem. 10:31 (April, 1900); Folwell, Wm. W. Park & Outdoor Art Assn., p. 65, 1897-8; Mackenzie, Constance. Kindergarten M. 9:688 (May, 1897); anon. Garden & F. 9:501 (Dec. 16, 1896), 10:479 (Dec. 8, 1897); Outlook 59:464 (June 25, 1898). 36
Playgrounds and Parks. White, H. L. Arena 10:279 (1894); Will, T. E. (with a brief bibliography of the subject), Arena 10:274 (1894); anon. Garden & F. 7:221 (1894), Dec. 10, 1898; Parks and Playgrounds. p. 972-975, Encyc. Soc. Ref. See 1-3. 37
——. " Educational and Civic Necessity, Public Playgrounds as an." Tsanoff, Stoyan Vasil. City Govt. 4:187 (May, 1898). 38
——. " Educational Value of the Children's Playgrounds." Tsanoff, Stoyan Vasil. Philadelphia, Published for the author, 1897. 203 pp. 39
——. " Market Playgrounds." Waring, Geo. E. Hrprs. Wkly. 39:1237 (1895). 40
——. " Playgrounds, Baths and Gymnasia." Quincy, Josiah. City Rec. 1:517 (Sept. 3, 1898), Sanitarian 41:303 (Oct. 1898), Ann. Am. Acad. Pol. Sci. 12:444 (Nov. 1898), N. Y. Educa. 2:135 (Nov. 1898). 41
——. " Playgrounds for Children." Vrooman, Walter. Hrprs. Wkly. 35:350 (1891), Cent. 43:317 (1891), Arena 10:284 (1894); Tsanoff, Stoyan Vasil. Mun. Aff. 7:293 (June, 1898). 42
——. " Playgrounds Movement, Stoyan Tsanoff and the." Truslow, Arthur. Outlook 58:772 (March 26, 1898). 43
——. " Playgrounds for Poor Children." Garden & Forest Dec. 10, 1898. 44
——. " The Movement for Small Playgrounds." American, Sadie. Am. J. Sociol. 4:159 (Sept. 1898). 45
" Pleasure Grounds." Westm. 35:418 (1841).
——. " A City's Small Pleasure Grounds." Baxter, Sylvester. Cent. 55:315 (Dec. 1897). 46
" Public Health, The Relation of Public Parks to." Douglas, Orlando B. Park and Outdoor Art Association, p. 123, 1897-8. 47
" Reservoirs to Public Parks, The Re'ation of." Olmsted, Frederick Law, Jr.

Parks, Playgrounds, Etc.—*Continued.*

Park & Cem. 9:99 (July, 1899), Mun. Engng. 18:71 (Feb. 1900), Engng. Rec. 41:173 (Feb. 24, 1900), Am. Park and Outdoor Art Association, Vol. III, pt. II, pp. 3-32, Detroit, Mich., 1899. 48

Roads, Park. Alexander, H. C. J. of Western Soc. of Engineers Oct. 1896; Foster, J. F. Ibid., Park & Cem. 10:109 (July, 1900), City Govt. 9:132 (Nov. 1900). 49

"School Yard Playgrounds." Commons No. 28. p. 1 (Aug. 1898). 50

——. "Playgrounds for City Schools." Riis, Jacob A. Cent. 48:657 (1894). 51

"Seaside Pleasure Grounds for Cities." Baxter, Sylvester. Scribner's 23:676 (June, 1898). 52

"Small Parks and Public School Playgrounds." Riis, Jacob A. Hrprs. Wkly. 41:903 (Sept. 11, 1897). 53

Squares, Public. Newton, T. M. Am. Arch. 43:52, 135 (1894); anon. Gaz. d'Arch. et du Bât. pp. 5, 46, 59 (1863). 54

——. "Evolution of the City Square." Parsons, Samuel, Jr. Scrib. M. 12:107 (1892). 55

Street Railway Parks. Anon. St. Ry. J. 13:93, 149, 289 (Feb., March and April, 1897), 14:275 (May, 1898). 56

——. "Practical Hints on the Design and Improvement of Street Railway Parks." Pincus, Henry. St. Ry. Jour. 14:211 (April, 1898). 57

"Suburban Home Grounds." Lowrie, Charles N. Park and Outdoor Art Association, p. 83, 1897-8. 58

"Superintendent, The Ideal Park." Simonds. O. C. Park & Cem. 7:116 (July, 1897). 59

"Trees and Parks in Cities, A Plea for." Windmüller, Louis. Forum 29:337 (May, 1900). 60

——. "Behandlung von Alleebäumen." Lehmann, O. Deutsche Bauz. p. 233, 1881. 61

——. "Care of Park Trees." Garden and F. 10:151 (April 21, 1897). 62

——. "Die Baumpflanzungen in der Stadt und auf dem Lande." Abel, L. Wien, 1882. 63

——. "Städtische Baumpflanzungen." Dietrich, E. Baugwks.-Ztg. pp. 517, 532, 548, 1890. 64

——. Trees and Gardens in Cities. pp. 439-515 J. Stübben's "Städtebau." Darmstadt, Bergsträsser, 1890. 561 pp. 32 m. 65

——. "Ueber Anpflanzung von Bäumen im Innern der Städte vom Gesichtspunkte der öffentlichen Hygiene." Jeannel. Rec. de Mém. de Med. etc. Milit. p. 596, 1872. 66

——. "Ueber Baumpflanzungen auf Strassen in grösseren Städten." Riedel, J. Wochschr. d. Oest. Ing.-u. Arch.-Ver. p. 238, 1883. 67

——. "Welches ist der Zweck der Strassenbäumen im Innern der Grossstadt und wie erfüllen sie denselben?" Schulze, G. A. Sammlung gemeinnütziger Original-Vorträge und Abhandlungen auf dem Gebiete des Gartenbaues, Heft 16, Berlin, 1881. 68

"Use of City Parks." Garden & F. 4:349 (1891). 69

——. "Nutzen von freien Plätzen und Bäumen in den Städten." Heath, F. G. Sanitary Rec. 4:36, 101, 121, 173, 210; 5:308. 70

——. "The Proper Use of Public Parks." Garden & F. 2:457 (1889).

——. "Use and Management of Public Parks." Cowan, Andrew. Park and Outdoor Art Association, p. 19, 1897. 71

"Village Parks and Gardens." Riordan, R. Chaut. 8:545 (1890). 72

"Walks and Drives." Park & Cem. 9:210 (Dec. 1899). 73

"Water Front of Public Parks." Garden & F. 6:421 (1893). 74

Parties and Party Politics in Cities, Non-Partisanship. (See also **Elections**).

See also Chicago, Germany, New York City, New York State, United States.

"A New Type in City Politics." Cleveland, E. C. Our Day 19:361 (July, 1900). 75

"A Study in Municipal Politics." Nation 15:260 (1872), 19:21 (1874); Sedgwick, A. G. Nation 28:365 (1879). 76

"Assessments, Political." Roosevelt, Theodore. Atlan. 70:103 (1892); Whitredge, Frederick W. Lalor's Encyclopedia, Vol. I, pp. 153-5. 77

BIBLIOGRAPHY.

Parties and Party Politics in Cities—*Continued.*

"Between Elections." Chapman, John Jay. Atlan. 85:26 (Jan. 1900). 78
"Business Man in Municipal Politics, The." MacVeagh, Franklin. Pp. 133-144, Pro. of the Louisville Conf. for Good City Govt., 1897. See 6-18d. 79
"Great Cities, Party Politics in." Garrett, Philip C. 1882. 12 pp. 80
"Independence in Municipal Elections, Progress of." Schurz, Carl. Hrprs. Wkly. 41:1023 (Oct. 16, 1897). 81
"Limits of Party Obligation." Budd, Henry. Municipal League of Philadelphia Pubs, 1893. 20 pp. 82
"Municipal Parties." Eyre, Lincoln L. To-Day March, 1894. 83
——. "Independent Politics." Haight, A. S. Mun. Aff. 4:338 (June, 1900). 84
——. "Is a Third Party Necessary in Municipal Reform Work?" Chapman, John Jay. Mun. Aff. 4:329 (June, 1900), Cal. Mun. 3:7 (Aug. 1900). 85
——. "Municipal Parties." p. 129, "The Cosmopolis City Club." Gladden, Washington. New York, Century Co., 1893. 135 pp. $1. 86
——. "Need of Municipal Parties." McKelway, St. Clair. Good Govt. 15:121 (1896). 87
——. "Permanent Municipal Parties." Richardson, Charles. p. 204, Proc. First Natl. Conf. for Good City Govt., 1894. See 6-18a. 88
"National Parties, Municipal Government by." Richardson, Charles. p. 464, Proc. Second Natl. Conf. for Good City Govt., 1895. See 6-18b. 89
——. "Evils of Drawing Party Lines in Local Affairs." Speakman, Thomas H. Pamphlet. 10 pp. 1873. 90
——. "Municipal Threat in National Politics." Adams, J. C. New Eng. M. 4:570 (1891). 91
——. "Non-Partisanship in Municipal Government." Flower, R. P. Forum July, 1897. 92
——. "Non-Partisanship, a Municipal Necessity." Bolles, D. H. Gunton's M. 10:367 (1896). 93
——. "Non-Partisanship in Local Affairs." Ivins, Wm. M. (Reprinted from the Sun.) Mun. Rec. & Ad. Vol. 1, No. 22, p. 7 (Nov. 6. 1897). 94
—— "Partisan Municipal Government." Schurz, Carl. Hrprs. Wkly. 41:751 (July 30, 1897). 95
——. "The Exclusion of Partisan Politics from Municipal Affairs—The Democratic-European Method." Loomis, Frank M. Pp. 103-117, Proc. of the Louisville Conf. for Good City Govt., 1897. See 6-18d; M. & C. 4:35 (May, 1897). 96
——. "The Theory and Practice of Non-Partisanship." Gunton's M. 13:259 (Oct. 1897). 97
"Party Government." Richardson, Charles. Ann. Am. Acad. Pol. Sci. 2:518, 653 (1892). 98
——. "Government by Party." Waring, Geo. E. No. Am. 163:587 (1896). 99
——. "Party Organization in the United States and Belgium." Réforme Sociale June 16, 1897.
——. "Political Parties and City Government." Goodnow, Frank J. Intern. M. 1:618 (June, 1900). 100
——. "Political Parties and City Government under the Proposed Municipal Program." Goodnow, Frank J. Pp. 63-76 in Proc. of the Columbus Conf. for Good City Govt., 1899. See 6-18f. 1
——. "The Party System." Pt. III, Chs. LVII-LXXIII, pp. 55-227, Vol. II, of James Bryce's "American Commonwealth." New York, Macmillan, 3d ed., 1895. 2
"People vs. the Politicians, The." Speakman, Thomas H. Pamphlet, 16 pp. 1878. 3
"Politics as a Duty and a Career." Storey, Moorfield. New York, G. P. Putnam's Sons, 1889. 33 pp. 25 cts. 4
"Reformers in Party Politics, Municipal." Keller, John W. Mun. Aff. 4:343 (June, 1900). 5
"Rich Men in City Politics." Nation 13:316 (1871).
"State Control of Political Parties." Pavey, F. D. Forum 25:99 (March, 1898). 6
"The Political Wrecking of Business Enterprises." Coler, Bird S. Public Policy 2:398 (June 23, 1900). 7
"The Power of Public Plunder." Parton, James. No. Am. 133:41 (1881). 8
"Wage-Earner in Politics, The." Chance, George. Pp. 129-132, Proc. of the Louis-

Parties and Party Politics in Cities—*Continued.*

ville Conf. for Good City Govt., 1897. See 6-18d.   9

"What is a Party." Morse, A. D. Pol. Sci. Q. 11:68 (March, 1896).   10

Pasadena, Cal. "Sewage Farming at a Profit." Mun. J. & Eng. 9:156 (Dec. 1900).   11

Paterson, N. J.

"City Government of Paterson, N. J." Agnew, S. H. City Govt. 1:47 (1896).   12

History, description and statistics of Paterson, N. J., in 1880. Census. See 1-7.   13

Pauperism in Cities. (See under **Charities.**)

Pavements, Paving, etc. (See also **Streets.**)

See also Boston, Buffalo, Chicago, Cincinnati, Cleveland, Germany, Indianapolis, Iowa, Kansas City, Lafayette (Ind.), London, Louisville, Michigan, New Orleans, New York, Omaha, Paris, Peoria, Philadelphia, St. Louis, Switzerland, Sydney (N. S. W.), Trenton, Vancouver, United States, Washington.

General References.

"Asphalt and Brick Pavements." City Govt. 4:171 (May, 1898).   14

"City Streets and Country Roads." Mun. World 9:176 (Nov. 1899).

"City Roads and Pavements." (With special reference to small towns.) Judson, William Pierson. New York, Engineering News Pub. Co., 1894. 8vo, 60 pp. Paper, 75 cts. Cl., $1.   15

"Construction of Pavements and City Growth." Towle, Stevenson. Engng. M. 12:59 (1896).   16

——. "A Treatise on Highway Construction." Byrne, Austin T. New York, John Wiley & Sons, 3d ed., 1896. 8vo, 771 pp. Cl. $5.   17

——. "Construction and Care of Streets." Greene, F. V. Paper read before the Commonwealth Club of New York City. Eng. & Build. Rec. March 1, 1890, p. 106.   18

"Development of Roads and Street Pavements, The." Blackford, Francis W. J. Assoc. Engng. Soc. 22:156 (April, 1899).   19

"Economics of Street Paving." Whinery, S. Engng. Rec. 42:127 (Aug. 11, 1900), 42:148 (Aug. 18, 1900), Trans. Assn. Civ. Engs, Cornell Univ. 1900.   20

"Evolution of Public Roads." Hulbert, Archer Buller. Public Policy 2:119 (Feb. 24, 1900).   21

"Importance and Economy of Pavement Construction, The." Whinery, S. Engng. M. 12:245 (1896).   22

"Maintenance of Highways." Bond, Edward A. Engng. Rec. 40:576 (Nov. 18, 1899).   23

"Notes on Road Construction and Maintenance." Mills, Charles. Engng. Rec. 41:369 (April 21, 1900).   24

"On Pavements in General." Madden, M. B. City Govt. 1:9 (1896).   25

"Pavements, Confined Rivers and the Water Supply of Ancient Rome." Blackford, Francis W. J. Assoc. Engng. Soc. Dec. 1896.   26

"Pavements, Sidewalks, Roads and Bridges." Howard, J. W. Engng. M. 8:1014 (1895).   27

"Pavements for Street and Roads." Whinery, S. Engng. Rec. 42:170 (Aug. 25, 1900).   28

"Paving Town Streets." Mun. World 9:60 (April, 1899).   29

"Prices and Conditions, Paving." City Govt. 1:42 (1896).

"Repairing, Systematic Street." Mchts. Assoc. R. Vol. 3, No. 33, p. 4 (May, 1899).

"Report of the Committee on Street Paving." Pro. Am. Soc. Mun. Imp. (5th yr.) Pt. II, p. 115, Oct. 1898.   30

"Road Making and Maintenance." Herschel, Clemens, and E. P. North. New York, Engng. News Pub. Co., 1894. 8vo, 156 pp. 50c.   31

——. "Prize Essays on Road Making." New York, articles reprinted from Engng. Rec., 12mo, 100 pp. Engineering Record Press, 1892. $1.   32

"Street Pavements and Paving Materials. A Manual of City Pavements: The Methods and Materials of their Construction." Tillson, George W. New York, John Wiley & Sons, 1900. 8vo, 532 pp. Cloth, $4.   33

Pavements, Paving, Etc.—*Continued.*

"Street Paving." Mun. World 10:173 (Nov. 1900).
Text Book on Roads and Pavements, A." Spalding, Fred P. New York, Wiley & Sons, 1894. 12mo, 213 pp. Cl. $2.   34
"The Paving Question." Nicholl, T. J. St.Ry. R. 9:577 (Sept. 15, 1899); anon. Mun. & Ry. Rec. 5:127 (Sept. 15, 1899).   35
"Why Good Paving Is Essential to the Success of a City." Howard, J. W. Pav. and Mun. Eng. April, 1896, p. 227.   36
"What Pavements Do for a City." Howard, J. W. Mun. Engng. 18:356 (June, 1900).   37

"Asphalt and Asphalt Pavements." Tillson, Geo. W. Pro. Am. Soc. Civ. Engrs., April, 1897, Engng. News 38:157 (Sept. 2, 1897).   38
——. "Better Work and Better Prices for Asphalt and Other Pavements." Howard, J. W. Mun. Engng. 15:368 (Dec. 1898).   39
——. "Construction of Asphalt Pavements." Tillson, George W. City Govt. 9:74 (Sept. 1900); Mun. Engng. 19:179 (Sept. 1900), Engng. Rec. 42:198 (Sept. 1, 1900).   40
——. "Examination, Asphalt." Endeman, H. Mun. Engng. 13:6 (July, 1897), Am. Gas Lgt. J. 67:130 (July 26, 1897).   41
——. Failures in Asphalt Pavements. Dow, A. W. Mun. Engng. 18:18 (Jan, 1900); Engng. News 43:222 (April 5, 1900); anon. Engng. Rec. 41:6 (Jan. 6, 1900).   42
——. "Guaranties, Asphalt Paving." Engng. Rec. 38:155 (July 23, 1898).   43
——. "How to Obtain a Good Asphalt Street for the Least Money." Peckham, S. F. City Govt. 3:151 (Nov. 1897).   44
——. "Laboratory, Advantages of Asphalt Testing." Lewis, N. P. City Govt. 1:99 (1896).   45
——. "Manufacture of Asphalt Pavements, The." Engng. Rec. 38:529 (Nov. 19, 1898).   46
——. "Municipal Asphalt Plants." City Govt. 4:49 (Feb. 1898).   47
——. "Origin and History of Asphalt." Bienenfeld, Bernard. Mun. Eng. 12:271 (May, 1897).   48
——. "Physical Properties of Asphalts and Asphaltic Cements, The." Broadhurst, W. H. Mun. Engng. 17:282 (Nov. 1899).   49
——. "Repairs, Asphalt Pavements." Guthrie, E. B. City Govt. 1:106 (1896); anon. Mun. Engng. 17:14 (July, 1899).   50
——. "Residuum as a Flux for Asphalt." Richardson, Clifford. Mun. Engng. 16:354 (June, 1899).   51
——. "Specifications for Asphalt, Faulty." Peckham, F. S. City Govt. 2:163 (June, 1897).   52
——. "Street Grades and Cross Sections in Asphalt and Cement." Woods, Robert P. Mun. Engng. 17:190 (Oct. 1899).   53
——. "Testing Asphalts, One Year's Work with a Chemical Laboratory for." Tillson, Geo. W. Mun. Engng. 13:271 (Nov. 1897).   54
——. "Tests, Asphalt Paving." Puffer, F. E. Mun. Engng. 18:291 (May, 1900).   55
——. "The Relative Viscosity of Asphalts and Allied Bodies." Dow, A. W. Mun. Engng. 16:160 (March, 1899).   56
——. "Theory and Practice of Asphalt Mixtures." Dow, A. W. Mun. Engng. 15:364 (Dec. 1898), Pro. Am. Soc. Mun. Imp. (5th yr.) Pt. II, p. 144 (Oct. 1898).   57
——. "Water on Asphalt Pavements, The Action of." Luten, Daniel B. Engng. N. 44:113 (Aug. 16, 1900).   58
Assessment of Cost of Paving. (See Special Assessments under **Finance**).
"Bingham Paving, The." San. Rec. 26:382 (Nov. 2, 1900).   59
Brick Paving. Brown, Charles C. City Govt. 4:95 (March, 1898); Hastings, L. M. Engng. Rec. 40:454 (Oct. 14, 1899), Mun. Engng. 17:279 (Nov. 1899); Hathaway, S. J. City Govt. 1:104 (1896); Howe, Irving E. J. Assoc. Engng. Soc. 20:235 (March, 1898); Kemmler, E. A. Engng. Rec. 40:701 (Dec. 23, 1899); Luten, Daniel B. Engng. Rec. 41:196 (March 3, 1900); March, H. J. J. Assoc. Engng. Soc. 23:91 (Aug. 1899); Thompson, A. D. Brick, Feb. 1899; anon. Engng. Rec. 41:281 (March 24, 1900).   60
——. "Construction of Brick Pavements." Grimes, George R. Brick, March 1, 1900, Mun. Engng. 18:180 (March, 1900).   61
——. "Construction and Maintenance of Brick Pavements." Kemmler, E. A.

Pavements, Paving, Etc.—*Continued.*

Engng. Rec. 42:275 (Sept. 22, 1900), Brick, Nov. 1, 1900, Mun. Engng. 14:80 (Feb. 1898), Mun. Engng. 18:187 (Sept. 1900).   62

——. "Development of the Paving Brick Industry." Thompson, A. D. Mun. Engng. 16:157 (March, 1899).   63

——. "Noise on Brick Pavements." Mun. Engng. 14:198 (April, 1898).   64

——. "Secrets of Success in Making Good Paving Brick." Plumb, F. Mun. Engng. 16:226 (April, 1899).   65

——. "Small Towns, Brick Paving in." Smith, A. W. Mun. Engng. 12:83 (Feb. 1897).   66

——. Tests for Paving Brick. Brown, Charles Carroll. Mun. Engng. 15:1 (July, 1898); Elliott, A. C. Surveyor 18:142 (Aug. 3, 1900); Luten, Daniel B. Mun. Engng. 18:223 (April, 1900); Thompson, A. D. City Govt. 1:101 (1896), Mun. Engng. 12:211 (April, 1897), Mun. Engng. 18:8 (Jan. 1900); anon. Engin. News 37:285 (May 6, 1897), Engng. Rec. 41:244 (March 17, 1900).   67

——. Standard Specifications for Paving Brick Tests. Anon. Mun. Engng. 12:154 (March, 1897); Mun. Engin. 12:215 (April, 1897); Orton, Edward, Jr., Clay Rec., April 29, 1897.   68

——. "The Market Side of the Paving Brick Industry." Stevens, F. B. Mun. Engng. 18:152 (March, 1900).   69

——. "Vitrified Brick for Street Paving." Hatcher, E. N. City Govt. 6:30 (Feb. 1899).   70

——. "Wearing Power of Paving Brick, The." Orton, Edward. Mun. Engng. 12:161 (March, 1897).   71

"Cement Paving in Europe." Grimshaw, Robert. Mun. Engng. 13:76 (Aug. 1897).   72

——. "Cost of Concrete Mixtures, Relative." Mun. Engng. 14:4 (Jan. 1898).   73

——. "Development of the Cement Industry in America." Percy, G. W. Mun. Engng. 18:360 (June, 1900).   74

——. "Testing, Methods of Cement." Mun. Engng. 12:222 (April, 1897), 12:284 (May, 1897), 12:348 (June, 1897), 13:16 (July, 1897).   75

"Crowning Paved Streets, Mr. Rosewater's Rules for." Mun. Engng. 14:247 (May, 1898).

"Health, Influence of Pavements on Public." Campbell, A. W. Sanitarian 42:131 (Feb. 1899).   76

"Iron Slag Paving, American." Hayes, George W. Mun. Engng. 12:346 (June, 1897).   77

——. "German Iron Slag Paving." Grimshaw, Robert. Mun. Engng. 12:284 (May, 1897).   78

"Legislation for Better Roads, Practical." Beatty, William T. Mun. Engng. 15:217 (Oct. 1898).   79

"Life of Pavements, The." Tillson, George W. City Govt. 7:104 (Nov. 1899), Mun. Engng. 17:272 (Nov. 1899); anon. Eng. Rec. 40:477 (Oct. 21, 1899).   80

"Macadam for Streets." Mun. Engng. 17:80 (Aug. 1899).   81

Materials, Relative Value of. Bell, J. J. Can Eng. 6:61 (July, 1898); Lewis, Nelson P. pp. 51-82 in Pro. of Brooklyn Engrs. Club, 1899, 8vo, 233 pp. Paper, $2; Tillson, George W. Pro. Am. Soc. Mun. Imp., Pt. 2, p. 149, 1898, City Govt. 5:187 (Nov. 1898), Mun. Engng. 15:353 (Dec. 1898); anon. St. Ry. J. July, 1890, p. 334, Pub. Imp. 1:40 (June 1, 1899).   82

"Modern City Roadways." Lewis, Nelson P. Pop. Sci. Mo. 56:524 (March, 1900), Pub. Imp. 3:454 (Aug. 1900).   83

——. "Modern Street Pavements." Gunn, O. B. J. Assoc. Eng. Soc., Oct. 1893.   84

"Motor Carriages and Street Paving." Conyngton, Thomas. Mun. Engng. 16:220 (April, 1899).   85

"Oiled Roads, A Report on." Brundage, Ben L. Cal. Mun. 2:112 (May, 1900).   86

"Promoter, The Paving." Engng. Rec. 40:45 (June 17, 1899).   87

"Smoothness of Pavements." Luten, Daniel B. Engng. Rec. 41:292 (March 31, 1900).   88

Stone Block Pavements, Construction of. Briggs, Josiah A. Mun. Engng. 19:184 (Sept. 1900); Fisher, E. A. Mun. Engng. 19:285 (Oct. 1900).   89

——. "Artificial Stone Pavements." Grimshaw, Robert. Mun. Engng. 13:193 (Oct. 1897).   90

"Street Railways and Street Pavements." Fisher, Edwin A. Engng. Rec. 40:457

Pavements, Paving, Etc.—*Continued.*
(Oct. 14, 1899). 91
——. " Compensation for Street Railway Franchises, Street Paving an Improper Basis of." Engin. News 37:376 (June 17, 1897).
——. " The Modern Street Rail and its Relation to Pavement." Howard, J. W. Mun. Engng. 12:81 (Feb. 1897). 92
——. " Rails, Influence of, on Street Pavements." North, Edward P. Am. Soc. Civil Engrs. Nov. 1896. 93
——. " Street Railway Tracks, Pavements Between." Rust, Charles H. City Govt. 7:138 (Dec. 1899), Engng. Rec. 40:455 (Oct. 14, 1899), Mun. Engng. 17:291 (Nov. 1899), St. Ry. R. 9:848 (Dec. 15, 1899). 94
——. " Tracks and Pavements, Car." Owen, James. City Govt. 2:17 (Jan. 1897). 95
" Waste Coal Ashes, Pavement from." City Govt. 3:86 (Sept. 1897).
" Wooden Block Pavements." Downing. M. A. City Govt. 1:139 (Dec. 1896). 96
——. " California Redwood for Street Pavements." McCullough, Ernest. Mun. Eng. 12:362 (June, 1897). 97
——. Creosoted Wood Block Pavement. Hetherington, F. A. Mun. Engng. 15:137 (Sept. 1898); Kenyon, Clarence A. Mun. Engng. 15:141 (Sept. 1898). 98
——. " Hygienic View of Wood Paving." Petsch, A. Sci. Am. Sup., March 20, 1897. 99
——. " Maintenance of Wood Pavement in European Cities." Grimshaw, Robert. Mun. Engng. 12:205 (April, 1897). 100

Pawnshops, Monts de Piété.

See also Austria, France, Germany, Leipsic, Italy, Paris, Spain.

" Benevolent Loan Asociation." Smith, Katherine Louise. Arena 24:86 (July, 1900). 1
Interest at Two Per Cent., Pawnshops and. Rodriguez, Pedro. Ciudad de Dios Nov. 5, 1899. 2
" Leihhäuser." Würzburger, Eugen. Handw. d. Staatswissenschaften 5:601 (1900). 3
" Meccanismo di un monte di pietà." Tavernari, C. Modena, Bassi e Debri, 1891. 67 pp. 4
" Monti di Pietà e Beneficenza." Fanelli, Aug. Roma, Union Co-operativa editrice, 1895. 38 pp. 5
" Mont de Piété System of Pawnbroking." Porter, H. J. J. Statis, Soc. 3:293, 4:348 (1840-1). 6
" Mont de Piété." Campagnole, Edouard. Pp. 617-624, Vol. II, Say's " Dictionnaire des Finances"; Hooper, L. H. Lippinc. 21:117 (1878); Renouard, Alfred. Pp. 333-4, Vol. II, " Dict. d. Economie Politique." 7
" Municipal Pawnshops." London, The Fabian Society, 1900. 4 pp. Pamphlet, 1d. 8
——. " How to Municipalize the Pawnshops." Donald, R. New R. 11:581 (1894). 9
——. " Why not Municipalize the Pawnshops." Donald, R. Contemp. 66:177 (1894). 10
" Pawnbroking." Giles, William A. Civic Federation Papers, No. 16, 27 pp. Chicago, Civic Federation, 1899. Pamphlet. 11
" Pawnbroking in Various Countries." Baldwn, Elbert F. Outlook 52:173 (1895). 12
" Pawnbroking in Europe and United States." Patterson, W. R. Bulletin Dept. Labor No. 21, p. 173, March, 1899. 13

Pekin, China.
" Streets of Peking, The." Scidmore, Eliza Ruhamah. Cent. 58:859 (Oct. 1899). 14
" Two Cities: London and Peking." Little, Archibald. Fireside, June, 1899. 15

Penig, Germany, Electrical Works. " Das städtische Elektrizitätswerk in Penig." Rühlmann, Richard. Zeitschr. d. Ver. Deutscher Ing. 43:1313 (Oct. 28, 1899). 16

Pennsylvania.
" Ballot Reform." Woodruff, Clinton Rogers. An. Am. Acad. Pol. Sci. 14:385 (Nov. 1899). 17
" Boroughs, Pennsylvania." Holcomb, William P. J. H. Univ. Studies IV:4 (1886). 50c. 18
——. " The Law of Boroughs, including the Rights and Duties of Borough Officers."

Pennsylvania—Continued.

Trickett, W. (2nd vol.) Philadelphia, T. & J. W. Johnson Co., 1893-8. 8vo, 381 pp. Cloth, $4. ... 19
" Corporations in Pennsylvania." Murphy, Walter. Philadelphia, Rees, Welsh & Co. 1891. 2 vols., 510-513 pp. $10. (The first volume deals with Municipal Corporations). ... 20
" Elections in Pennsylvania, Primary." Woodruff, Clinton Rogers. N. Y. Conference on Practical Reform of Primary Elections, p. 51. Chicago, Hollister, 1898. 8vo, 150 pp. Paper. ... 21
——. " Pennsylvania Election Laws." Bird, Albert A. The Citizen 1:14, 35, 61, 114, 132, 160 (1895), 2:54 (1896). ... 22
" Government in Pennsylvania, Local." Gould, E. R. L. J. H. Univ. Studies I:3. 25c. ... 23
——. " Government of Cities, Report of the Commissioners to devise a plan for the." Pennsylvania Legislature, Doc. No. 4, 1878. 216 pp. ... 24
" Legislation, Local and Special." Ann. Am. Acad. Pol. Sci. 14:269 (Sept. 1899).
" Poor Laws of Pennsylvania, A Treatise on the." Beitel, Calvin G. Philadelphia, T. & J. W. Johnson, 1899. 8vo, 607 pp. $6. ... 25
" Street Railways in Pennsylvania." Brown, I. B. St. Ry. Rev. 8:100 (Feb. 15, 1898); Sanders, Dallas. St. Ry. Rev. 7:591 (Sept. 15, 1897); anon. 16:1223 (Dec. 29, 1900). ... 26
" Tax Laws of Pennsylvania, Synopsis of the." Eastman, T. W. Harrisburg, 1892. ... 27

Pension Funds. (See also Labor and its Relation to the Municipality and Schools).

See also Belgium.
" City Retirement Funds." City Rec. 2:185 (March 16, 1899). ... 28
" Municipal and Other Pension Schemes." City Rec. 3:265 (April 26, 1900). ... 29
" Old Age Pension by Means of Municipal Dwellings." Thomas, E. Econ. R. 5:221 (1895). ... 30

Peoria, Ills.

" Electrolysis in Peoria." Maury, Dabney H. Engng. Rec. 41:467 (May 19, 1900). ... 31
" Laboratory, A Municipal Testing." Thompson, A. D. Pav. and Mun. Eng., Jan. 1896. ... 32
Lighting. " The People vs. Peoria Gas Light & Coke Company." Public Policy 3:414 (Dec. 29, 1900). ... 33
" Paving in Peoria." City Govt. 2:100 (April, 1897).
" Sewer System, Peoria, Ill., West Bluff." Thompson, A. D. Engng. News 37:50 (Jan. 28, 1897). ... 34

" **Perth [Aus.]**, The Electric Tramway System of." St. Ry. J. 16:336 (April 7, 1900). ... 35

" **Petrolea [Ont.]**, Water Works, The." Can. Eng. Nov. 1897.

Philadelphia.

City Government, General References.

Almanacs. " Philadelphia Record Almanac." Philadelphia, Published annually by the Philadelphia Record. Edition for 1899, 122 pp. ... 36
——. " Philadelphia Times Almanac." Philadelphia, Published annually by the Philadelphia Times. Edition for 1899, 70 pp. ... 37
——. " Public Ledger Almanac." Philadelphia, Published annually by the Philadelphia Public Ledger. Edition for 1899, 118 pp. ... 38
" Brooklyn and Philadelphia." Godkin, E. L. Nation 42:140 (1886). ... 39
" Bullit Bill, Reorganizing the Municipal Government of Philadelphia." Philadelphia, 1887. 36 pp. 25c. ... 40
" Charter Amendments, Philadelphia." City Govt. 1:154 (Dec. 1896).
" Citizen and the City, The." Bird, Albert A. The Citizen 2:100, 130, 167 (1896). ... 41
" Commercial Success; How it has been Gained in Glasgow, Liverpool, and How it May be Secured for Philadelphia." Philadelphia, Union Committee on Transportation, Manufacturing and Commercial Interests, 1894. 56 pp. ... 42

Philadelphia—*Continued.*

"Handbook for Philadelphia Voters." Brinley, Chas. A. (With an Introduction by E. J. James). Printed for the author, 1894. 210 pp. 50c. ... 43
History, Description and Statistics of Philadelphia, Penn., in 1880. Census. See 1-7.
"Letter to the People of Philadelphia." Lea, Henry C. Forum 2:532 (1887). ... 44
"Manual for Philadelphia Voters." Alcorn, W. B. Philadelphia, Town Ptg. Co. ... 45
"Municipal Affairs of Philadelphia." Welsh, Herbert (Editor). A regular department in City and State. ... 46
"New Philadelphia." Morris, Charles. Lippinc. 51:221 (1893). ... 47
"Officials of Philadelphia: Their Powers and Duties, The Public." Woodruff, Clinton Rogers. City & State Vol. 3, No. 17, p. 4 (Aug. 26, 1897), No. 18, p. 4 (Sept. 2, 1897), No. 19, p. 4 (Sept. 9, 1897), No. 21, p. 4 (Sept. 23, 1897), No. 22, p. 4 (Sept. 30, 1897). ... 48
"Philadelphia." Chap. XIV. in "The Land of the Dollar," by G. W. Steevens. New York, Dodd, Mead & Co., 1897. 12mo, 316 pp. $1.50. ... 49
"Philadelphia: What are its Needs?" Osborn, H. V. B. Pro. Eng. Club 17:24 (Feb. 1900). ... 50
"Reform in Philadelphia, Progress of Municipal." Woodruff, Clinton R. Hrprs. Wkly. 38:1019 (1894); Nation 70:159 (March 1, 1900). ... 51
Reform Organizations. "Civic Club of Philadelphia, The." Stevenson, (Mrs.) Cornelius. Address before the Club, March 3, 1894. Published by the Club, Good Govt. 14:5 (1894); Wetherill, Edith. Mun. Aff. 2:467 (Sept. 1898). ... 52
——. "Municipal League of Philadelphia." Ann. Am. Acad. Pol. Sci. 2:141 (1892); Woodford, Arthur Burnham. Social Economist 2:366 (1892); Woodruff, C. R. Am. J. Pol. 5:287 (1894). ... 53
"The City Government." Allinson, E. P., and Boies Penrose. J. H. Univ. Studies V:1 and 2, 1887; Members of Senior Class, Wharton School of Finance and Economy, 1893, 8vo, 300 pp. $1.50; Bullit, John C. Address before the Philadelphia Social Science Assoc. and C. S. R. A., Jan. 18, 1882, Philadelphia, Allen, Lane & Scott, 42 pp., 1882; Burnham, George, Jr. Pp. 185-187 Pro. of the Louisville Conf. for Good City Govt., 1897, see 6-18d.; Mercer, George Gluyas, p. 94. Proc. First Nat'l Conf. for Good City Govt., Philadelphia, 1894, see 6-18a; Hrprs. Wkly. 39:134 (1895). ... 54
"The City of Philadelphia: Its Stockholders and Directors." Richardson, Charles. Tract No. 1, Municipal League of Philadelphia Publications, 1883. 15 pp. ... 55

"Baths, Philadelphia Public." Kirkbride, Franklin B. Ann. Am. Acad. Pol. Sci. 11:127 (Jan. 1898); Lowrie, Sarah D. The Citizen 1:249 (1896). ... 56
"Bossism in Philadelphia, Fall of. History of the Committee of One Hundred." Vickers, George. Philadelphia, N. C. Boysen. 1883. 232 pp. 12mo. $1.15. See also Smalley, E. V. Cent. 4:395 (1883); Report of Committee. Pub. by Dands, 1884, 41 pp. ... 57
"Charity Problem in Philadelphia, The." Lindsay, Samuel McCune. The Citizen 2:263 (1896). ... 58
"Charitable and Educational Institutions and Societies in Philadelphia, Civic Club Digest of." With an introduction on the "Social Aspects of Philadelphia Relief Work" by Samuel McCune Lindsay. Philadelphia, Civic Club, 1895. 201 pp. $1.00. ... 59
"Councils of Philadelphia, City." Bird, Albert A. The Citizen 1:186 (1886); Sanitarian 11:305 (April, 1898). ... 60
"Department Store in the East, The: Large Stores in Philadelphia." Kirkpatrick, Samuel R. Arena 22:181 (Aug. 1899). ... 61
Elections. "The Philadelphia Nominating System." Branson, W. J. Ann. Am. Acad. Pol. Sci. 14:18 (July, 1899). ... 62
——. "Philadelphia Election Frauds." Woodruff, Clinton Rogers. Arena 24:397 (Oct. 1900), Ind. 52:3106 (Dec. 27, 1900). ... 63
Finance. "Ground Rents in Philadelphia." Allinson, E. P., and Boies Penrose. Philadelphia, Wharton School of Finance and Economy, 1889. 19 pp. 25 cts. ... 64
——. "Municipal Taxes of Philadelphia." Cochran, T. Penn. Mo. 2:221 (1871); Commons, John R. J. Pol. Econ. 3:434 (1895). ... 65
——. "Philadelphia's New Loan." Hoster, Wm. Johnson. Hrprs. Wkly. 41:1182 (Nov. 27, 1897). ... 66

Philadelphia—*Continued.*

"Harbor of Philadelphia, Improvement of the." Birkinbine, John. Eng. M. 9:839 (1895). 67

History. "Philadelphia, 1681-1887." Allinson, E. P., and Boies Penrose. J. H. Univ. Publications, Extra Volume III, 1887. $3.00. 68

——. "A Glimpse of Old Philadelphia." Weaver, Emily P. Lippinc. 59:557 (April 1897). 69

——. "Annals of Philadelphia and Pennsylvania in the Olden Time." Watson, John. Phila., Lippinc., 1845. 2 vols. 8vo. $7.50. 70

——. "History of Philadelphia, Pa." Williams, Talcott. See 1-4b. 71

——. "History of Philadelphia, 1609-1884." Scharf, J. T., and Wescott, Thompson. Phila., Everts, 1884. 3 vols. 8vo. $25.00. 72

Housing. "Homes for the People in Philadelphia." Bank, A. B. Am. J. Soc. Sci. 15:135 (1882). 73

——. "Tenement Houses in Philadelphia." Van Gasken, Frances. Philadelphia, Publications of the Civic Club, 1895. 8 pp. 74

"Laboratory, Cement, of the City of Philadelphia. Its Equipment and Methods." Humphrey, Richard L. Proc. Engrs. Club (Phila.) Nov. 1896. 75

Libraries. "Library of Philadelphia, The Free." The Citizen 1:227 (1895), 2:266 (1896). 76

Lighting. "Electric Lighting in Philadelphia." City and State Vol. I, (July 11, 1895); Swoope, C. Walton. Elec. W. & E. 35:279 (Feb. 24, 1900). 77

——. "Gas Works, Philadelphia." (A series of addresses in the 12th Annual Report of the Citizens' Municipal Ass'n of Phila., by William Potter, Wayne McVeagh, Edwin S. Stuart and Peter Boyd.) Phila., Citizens' Municipal Ass'n, 1898. Pamphlet. 78

——. Some Recent Municipal Gas History. Bemis, Edward W. Forum 25:72 (March 1898); Dodge, W. E. Elec. Eng. 25:207 (Feb. 24, 1898); Lewis, Wm. Draper. Q. J. Econ. 12:209 (Jan. 1898); Rogers, John I. Mun. Aff. 1:730 (Dec. 1897); Rowe, L. S., City and State 4:57 (Oct. 28, 1897); Ann. Am. Acad. Pol. Sci. 11:116, 301 (Jan., May, 1898); Speirs, Frederick W. Citizen 3:201 (Nov. 1897); Mun. Aff. 1:718 (Dec. 1897); Stallard, J. H. Star. Vol. 28, No. 3, p. 6 (Jan. 15, 1898), Overland 33:175 (Feb. 1899); Woodruff, Clinton Rogers. Hrprs. Wkly. 41:1038 (Oct. 16, 1897), Am. J. Sociol. 3:601 (March, 1898); anon. City Govt. 1:67 (1896); Prog. Age 15:414 (Sept. 15, 1897); Elec. R. 31:152 (Sept. 29, 1897); Mun. Rec. and Ad. Vol I, no. 17, p. 6 (Oct. 2, 1897); City and State (Editorials) (Oct. 7, 1897), City and State 4:23, 38 (Oct. 14, Oct. 21, 1897); Lit. Dig. 15:751 (Oct. 23, 1897); Prog. Age 15:521 (Nov. 15, 1897); City and State 4:104 (Nov. 18, 1897); Am. Gas Light J. 68:212 (Feb. 7, 1898); Prog. Age, 16:91 (March 1, 1898); City and State 4:591, 600 (May 26, 1898). 80

——. "The Philadelphia Gas Ring." Chapter 89, p. 404, Bryce's American Commonwealth. 81

"Mayor of Philadelphia, The." Bird, Albert A. The Citizen 1:233 (1895). 82

Parks. "Park Association of Philadelphia." Garden & F. 3:268 (1890), 6:248 (1893); Hrprs. Wkly. 40:107 (1896); St. Ry. J. 13:459 (Aug. 1897). 83

Party Politics. "Solid for Mulhooley." Shapely, Rufus E. Spofford and Shapely's Library of Wit and Humor. Philadelphia, 1884. 84

Paving. "Repaving the Streets of Philadelphia, Report of Experts on." J. Frankl. Inst. 118:210 (1884). 85

"Public Works, The Philadelphia Department of." Bird, Albert A. The Citizen 2:14 (1896). 86

Sanitation. "Health of Philadelphia." Billings, J. S. Forum 17:595 (1894); Bird, Albert A. The Citizen 2:206 (1896); Ford, W. H. Sanitarian 30:515 (1893). 87

Schools, Public. "Public School System of Philadelphia." Mumford, Mrs. Mary E. Published by the Civic Club, Philadelphia, 1894; Rice, J. M. Forum 15:31 (1893); Turner, W. L. Penn. Mo. 5:750 (1874). 88

——. "Story of a Woman's Campaign by the Civic Club for School Reform in the Seventh Ward of the City of Philadelphia." Williams, (Mrs.) Talcott. Pubs. of the American Academy, 1895. 89 pp. 50 cts. 89

——. "Suggestions of Reform in the Public School System of Philadelphia." Welch, Herbert, and others. Philadelphia, Civic Club Pamphlets, 1894. 31 pp. 90

Settlements. "University Settlements in Philadelphia." Fox, H. Lend a H. 11:43 (1893). 91

——. College Settlement. "Tenement House Work in St. Mary St." Fox, Han-

Philadelphia—Continued.

nah, and other pamphlets published by the College Settlement; anon. Ann. Am. Acad. Pol. Sci. 9:137 (March 1900).

Sewage. "Sewerage Reconstruction Necessitated by the Philadelphia & Reading Railroad Subway and Tunnel in Philadelphia." Atlee, Walter. Railroad Gaz. Dec. 18, 1896; Webster, George S., and Wagner, Samuel Tobias. Trans. Am. Soc. Civ. Eng. 84:129 (Feb. 1900).

——. "Drainage System of Philadelphia." Hering, R. Ecl. Engng. M. 18:429 (1878).

Slums of Philadelphia. See the Seventh Special Report of the Commissioner of Labor on "The Slums of Great Cities." 1894.

"Smoke Nuisance and Its Regulation. With Special Reference to the Conditions Prevailing in Philadelphia—Improved Furnaces and Mechanical Stokers, The." J. Frankl. Inst. 143:393 (June 1897), 144:17 (July 1897); Reviewed in Engng. News 38:111 (Aug. 12, 1897); J. Frankl. Inst. 144:401 (Dec. 1897), 145:1 (Jan. 1898), 145:107 (Feb. 1898), 147:244 (March, 1899).

"Statistics of Births, Deaths and Marriages, etc., 1861-72." Hough, J. S. Penn. Mo. 4:599 (1873).

——. "Vital Statistics of Boston and Philadelphia Covering a Period of Six Years ending May 31, 1890." Billings, John S. Washington Government Printing Office, 1895. 269 pp. Eleventh Census of the United States.

"Sweating System in Philadelphia." Goodchild, F. M. Arena 11:261 (1895).

——. "Report of the Committee of Manufactures on Sweating." H. R. Report 2309, 1893. pp. 34, 212 et seq. John De Witt Warner, Chairman.

Taxation. (See Finance above.)

Transit Facilities. "Philadelphia Street Railway and the Municipality." Bird, Albert A. The Citizen 1:256, 286 (1896); Haupt, Lewis M. Proc. of the Eng. Club, Phila. vol. 4, No. 3; Mawson, Harry P. Leslie's Wkly. 74:230 (1892); St. Ry. J. 14:691 (Nov. 1898).

——. "Street Railway System of Philadelphia; Its History and Present Condition." Speirs, Frederic W. Baltimore, J. H. Univ. Studies, Fifteenth Series, Nos. III-IV-V. March, April, May, 1897. 123 pp. Cloth, $1. Paper, 75 cts.

Water Supply of Philadelphia. Bird, Albert A. The Citizen 2:270, 299 (1896); Branson, W. J. City Govt. 7:11 (July 1899); Carr, William Wilkins. Phila., Buchanan, 46 pp., 1886; Haines, R. J. Frankl. Inst. 111:275 (1880); Hazen, Allen. Pamphlet reprinted from J. Frankl. Inst. for Nov. 1896, 19 pp.; Hooker, S. C. J. Frankl. Inst. 127:390, 129:411 (1890); Leffman, Henry. Proc. Engineers' Club of Phila. 10:24 (1893); Maignen P. J. A. Proc. Eng. C. 16:83 (March 1899); Maltbie, Milo Roy. Mun. Aff. 3:193 (June, 1899), San Rec. 24:363 (Oct. 27, 1899); Marburg, Edgar. Engng. Rec. 39:430 (April 8, 1899), Pro. Eng. Club 16:209 (May 1899); Smith, Edwin F. J. Frankl. Inst. (May, 1896), Pro. Eng. Club, Nov. 1896; Trautwine, John C., Jr. Engng. Rec. 38:428 (Oct. 15, 1898), Pro. Eng. Club 16:199 (May, 1899); Woodruff, Clinton Rogers. Forum 28:305 (Nov. 1899); anon. Engng. News, Feb. 27, 1896; Sanitarian, Nov. 1896; Mun. Engng. 11:353 (Dec. 1896); Engng. News 37:322 (May 27, 1897); City and State 4:223 (Jan. 6, 1898); Engng. Rec. 37:247 (Feb. 19, 1898); Engng. News 39:145 (March 3, 1898); Engng. Rec. 39:111 (Jan. 7, 1899); Fire & W. 26:58 (Feb. 25, 1899); Report Com. Manuf. Club. pamphlet, 16 pp. March 1899; Engng. Rec. 39:417 (April 8, 1899); Fire & W. 26:234 (July 22, 1899); Engng. Rec. 40:404, 433 (Sept. 30, Oct. 7, 1899); Engng. News 42:230 (Oct. 5, 1899); Engng. Rec. 40:449 (Oct. 14, 1899); Fire & W. 26:346, 352, 360 (Oct. 14, Oct. 21, Oct. 28, 1899); Engng. News 43:203 March 29, 1900).

——. "Report to Samuel H. Ashbridge, Mayor of the City of Philadelphia; on the Extension and Improvement of the Water Supply." Hering, Rudolph; Wilson, Joseph M.; Gray, Samuel M. Philadelphia, City of Philadelphia, 1899. 8vo, 123 pp. and maps. Free. Report summarized in J. Frankl. Inst. 148:390 (Nov. 1899).

——. "Water Works Management—Professional and Councilmanic." Trautwine, John C., Jr. Pp. 136-143 in "Proceedings of the 20th Annual Meeting of the American Water Works Association, Richmond, Va., May 15-18, 1900." 8vo, 216 pp. Cloth, $1.

Philippine Islands.

"El regimen municipal en las Islas Filipinas." Paterno, P. A. Madrid, Sucesores de Cuesta, 1893. 280 pp. 7 pes.

Pirna on the Elbe, Ger. "Volksbad in Pirna an dem Elbe." Deutsche Bauzeitung March 23, 1898.

Pittsburgh, Pa.

City Government, General References.

Almanac. "Pittsburg Press Almanac and Cyclopedia." Pittsburg, published quarterly by the Pittsburg Press. Edition for first quarter, 1899. 576 pp. Yearly, 50 cts.

History, description and statistics of Pittsburgh, Penn., in 1880. Census. See 1-7.

"Municipal Condition of Pittsburgh." Guthrie, Geo. W. p. 146, Proc. Third Natl. Conf. for Good City Govt. See 6-18c; also p. 336, Proc. of the Second Natl. Conf. 1895, see 6-18b; McClintock, Oliver. Proc. Indianapolis Conf. p. 257, 1898, see 6-18e; Woodruff, Clinton Rogers. Ann. Am. Acad. Pol. Sci. 13.415 (May 1899).

"The Rise of Pittsburgh." Logan, Charles T. Leslie's Pop. Mthly., Sept. 1897.

"Amalgamation." Ann. Am. Acad. Pol. Sci. 16:483 (Nov. 1900).

"Bath-House, A Pittsburg." Engng. Rec. 37:414 (April 9, 1898); City Rec. 1:235 (April 14, 1898).

"Fire, The Pittsburgh." Engng. Rec. May 22, 1897. Engng. News 37:313 (May 20, 1897); Arch. & Buil. 26:279 (June 12, 1897).

——. "An Instructive Fire in Pittsburg, Pa." Engng. Rec. May 22, 1897.

——. "Fireproof Building Construction in the Pittsburg, Pa., Fire." Engng. News. 37:313 (May 20, 1897); Arch. & Buil. 26:279 (June 12, 1897).

"History of Pittsburgh, Pa." Church, S. H. See 1-4b.

Settlements. Kingsley House. Char. R. 7:784 (Nov. 1897); Arena 24:193 (Aug. 1900).

"Street Railways of Pittsburgh and Allegheny, Pa." St. Ry. J. May 1890, p. 254; Oct. 1891, p. 1; Fairchild, C. B. Elec. Eng. 26:54 (July 21, 1898).

"Water Supply of Pittsburgh and Allegheny City, Pa." Harlow, James H. Proc. of the Eng. Soc. of Western Penn. March, 1893; Engng. Rec. June 19, 1897.

——. "Report of the Filtration Commission of the City of Pittsburg, Pa." City of Pittsburgh, Jan. 1899. 8vo, 393 pp. With maps and plans. Report discussed Engng. News 41:123 (Feb. 23, 1899); Engng. Rec. 39:230 (Feb. 11, 1899).

——. "The Experimental Filter Plant at Pittsburgh." Knowles, Morris. J. Assoc. Engng. Soc. 25:217 (Nov. 1900).

Plainfield, N. J.

"Sewerage and Sewage Disposal Systems of Plainfield, N. J." Gavett, A. J. New York, Engineering News Co. 1896. Pamphlet, 32 pp. 25 cts. (Reprinted from Engng. News of Sept. 10, 1896.)

——. "Notes on the Operation of the Sewage Filter Beds of Plainfield, N. J." Engng. News 41:162 (March 16, 1899).

Plymouth, Eng.

"Lighting and Tramways System, Plymouth, Eng." Elec. R. 35:129 (Aug. 30, 1899); St. Ry. J. 15:589 (Sept. 1899); Elec. W. and E. 34:847 (Dec. 2, 1899).

"Municipality of Plymouth." Mun. J. & London 8:1211 (Nov. 10, 1899).

"Water Works, Plymouth." Engng. (London) 66:394 (Sept. 23, 1898); Engng. Rec. 39:181 (Jan. 28, 1899).

"**Plymouth, Mass.**, History of." Watson, Ellen. See 1-4a.

Police.

See also Baltimore, Berlin, France, Germany, Indiana, Italy, London, Los Angeles, Michigan, Newark (N. J.), New York City, New York State, Paris, Prussia, Scotland under United Kingdom, United States.

"Abuse of the Police Power, The." Kudlich, Herman C. Forum 24:487 (Dec. 1897).

"Charity, The Department of Police as a Means of Distributing." Campbell, A. F. Open Court 11:333 (June 1897).

"Classes for Policemen, Municipal." Mun. J. & London 8:998 (Sept. 8, 1899).

"Crime, How to Protect a City from." Byrnes, T. No. Am. 159:100 (1894).

Police—*Continued.*

"Criminal, The." Ellis, Havelock. London, Scott, 1890. 337 pp. 3s. 6d.   31
Criminals. (See also International Congress under **Charities.**)
"Ethnology of the Police." Roosevelt, Theodore. Munsey's June 1897.   32
"Etudes de physiologie social, La Police." Guyot, Yves. Paris, G. Charpentier, 1882. 3 fr. 50c.   33
"Juvenile Offenders, The Value of Discrimination in Dealing with." Putnam, Elizabeth C. P. 100 "International Congress," see 43-99.   34
"Mysteries of Police and Crime." Griffiths, Arthur. New York, G. P. Putnam's Sons, 1899. 8vo, 2 vols., 495 & 483 pp. Cl., $5.00.   35
"Nature and Sphere of Police Power." Woolsey, T. D. J. Soc. Sci. 97:114 (1871).   36
"Notes of an Itinerant Policeman." Flynt, Josiah. Boston, L. C. Page & Co., 1900. 8vo, 252 pp.   37
"Ordinances, Municipal Police, Treatise on the Power to Enact, the Passage, Validity and Enforcement of." Bemis, Alton A., and Nelson T. Horr. Cincinnati, R. Clark, 1887. 312 pp. $4.00.   38
"Pauperism and Crime." Weber, John B. P. 131 "International Congress," see 43-99.   39
"Police." Loening, Edgar. Lalor's Cyclopedia, Vol. III, pp. 206-12, see 1-1.   40
"Police Control of Dangerous Classes Other Than by Criminal Prosecutions." Tiedeman, Christopher G. Am. Law R. 19:547 (1885); (Chap. V, "Limitations of Police Power.")   41
"Police and Prison Cyclopedia." Hale, Geo. W. Boston, The W. L. Richardson Co., 2d edition, 1894. 792 pp. $4.00 net.   42
"Police Problem, The." Balch, William R. Internat. R. 13:507 (1882); anon. Hrprs. Wkly. 43:1202 (Dec. 2, 1899).   43
"Problem of Police Administration, The." Moss, Frank. Forum 27:278 (May 1899).   44
"Public Health, Police Power and." Black, H. C. Am. Law R. 25:170 (1891).   45
"Punishment and Reformation, an Historical Sketch of the Rise of the Penitentiary System." Wines, Frederick Howard. New York, T. Y. Crowell, 1895. 8vo, 339 pp. $1.75   46
"Reform, Police." Lend a H. 8:43 (1892).   47
"State Oversight of Police." Moss, Frank. Mun. Aff. 3:264 (June, 1899).   48
"State of Prisons and of Child-Saving Institutions in the Civilized World." Wines, E. C. Cambridge University Press, 1880. 8vo, 719 pp. 25s.   49
"Telegraph System, Model Police." City Govt. 4:11 (Jan. 1898).   50

Political Assessments, Politics, Party Politics, Exclusion of Politics from Municipal Affairs. (See under **Parties,** also under **Elections, Bossism.**)

"**Pompeii**—A City of the First Century." Adams. Can. Arch. March, 1898.   51
"**Ponce, Puerto Rico,** The Gas Works at." Hough, D. L. Am. Gas Light J. 71:769 (Nov. 13, 1899).   52

Poor in Cities. (See under **Charities**).

Population, Growth of Cities, Decrease of Rural Population. (See also **Housing** and **History**).

See also Austria, Belgium, Boston, Chicago, England under U. K., France, Frankfurt a. M., Germany, London, Massachusetts, New York, Paris, United Kingdom, United States.

Abnormal Growth of Great Cities. Farrar, F. W., in article "Some Problems of the Age." No. Am. 161:412 (1895).   53
"Advantages and Disadvantages, Town Life." Pp. 142-169 of Chas. H. Pearson's "National Life and Character." London, Macmillan, 1893. 8vo, 357 pp. 10s.   54
Ancient Cities. "Die Uebervölkerung der antiken Grossstädte." Pöhlmann, R. Leipzig. Jablonowikischen Ges., 1884.   55
"Congestion of Population in Cities." New York, Publications of the Assoc. for Improving the Condition of the Poor, No. 3, 1896. 61 pp. 10c.   56
——. "Congestion of Cities." Hale, E. E. Forum 4:256 (1888).   57
——. "Felix qui causam rerum cognovit." Lowell, Josephine Shaw. Char. R. 2:420 (1893).   58

Population, Growth of Cities—*Continued*.

——. " Overcrowding in Cities." Potter, E. T. Am. Arch. 26:156, 266 (1889).   59

——. " Pauperism and Overcrowding." Crooks, W. Mun. J. 9:305 (April 20, 1900).   60

——. " Remedies for Overcrowding of Population." Nation 46:379 (1888).   61

——. " To-morrow: A Peaceful Path to Reform." (Plan to draw population from overcrowded cities). Howard, Ebeneezer. London, Swan, S. & Co., 1900. Book reviewed, Humanitarian 16:117 (Feb. 1900).   62

——. (See also under **Housing**).   63

" Decadent Tendencies of City Life, Some." Ferguson, F. L. Presbyterian Quarterly (Richmond, Va.), April, 1897.   64

" Decrease of Rural Population." Rose, John C. Nation 52:333 (1891). Pop. Sci. Mo. 42:621 (1893).   65

——. " Agricultural Conditions and Needs." New York, Publications of the Association for Improving the Condition of the Poor, 1896. 61 pp. 10c.   66

——. " Analysis of Agricultural Discontent in the United States." (Statistics of urban and rural wealth and population in the U. S.) Emerick, C. F. Pol. Sci. Q. 11:435 (Sept. 1896).   67

——. " Back to the Land: An Inquiry into the Cure for Rural Depopulation." Moore, H. E. London, Methuen & Co., 1893, 216 pp. 2s. 6d.   68

——. " Crowding of Cities: The Flight from the Fields." Gaye, A. Macmil. 65:293 (1891).   69

——. " Depopulation." Pp. 551-560, Vol. I. Palgrave. See 1-2.   70

——. " Doom of the Small Town." Fletcher, Henry J. Forum 19:214 (1895).   71

——. "Du Progrès des Agglomérations Urbaines et de l'Emigration Rurale." Legoyt, Alfred. Paris, L'auteur, 60, rue Saint-Dominique, 1870. 8vo, 280 pp. 5 fr.   72

——. " Emigration de la Population des Campagnes dans les Villes." Gower, F. Leveson. Jour. des Economistes 27:388 (1896).   73

——. " Farm Villages." Waring, Geo. E. Scrib. M. 13:756 (1877).   74

——. " Rural Exodus, The." Graham, P. Anderson. London, Methuen & Co., 1893. 216 pp. 2s. 6d.   75

——. " Wohnungsnot oder Uebervö̈kerung d. Städte und Entvölkerung des Landes." Weinstein. Berlin, Bibliogr. Bur., 1893.   76

" Democratic Institutions, Great Cities and." Pickard, C. E. Am. J. Pol. 4:378 (1894).   77

" Distribution of Population of Cities." Hammond, M. B. Am. Statis. Assoc. 4:113 (1895).   78

——. " What are the Principles which regulate the Distribution of Inhabitants into Farms, Villages, Hamlets, Towns and Cities." Steuart, Sir James. " Inquiry into the Principles of Political Economy." Ch. IX, Vol. I, " Works of Steuart," edited by J. Steuart, London, 1805. 6 vols. 8vo.   79

Duration of Life. " Die Lebensfähigkeit d. städtischen und ländlichen Bevölkerung." Ballod, Paul. Leipzig, Duncker u. Humblot, 1807, 03 pp. 2.20m   80

——. " Städtesorgen, Gespräche über die das Leben der Städtbewohner verkürzende Faktoren." Volkmer, Volkher. Strassburg, Strassburger Druckerei u. Verlagsanstalt, Schultz & Co., 1897. 8vo, 54 pp. 1m. 50 pf.   81

——. " Ueber den Einfluss des städtischen Lebens auf die Volksgesundheit." (Aus Centralblatt f. allg. Gesundheitspfl.) Kruse, W. Bonn, E. Strauss. 8vo, 79 pp. M. 1.60.   82

" Farm and the City, The." Besant, Walter. Eclectic M. 67:151 (Feb. 1898).   83

" Geography and Sociology." (With Bibliography). Ripley, W. Z. Pol. Sci. Q. 10:636 (1895).   84

" Great Cities." Hibbard, George S. Lend a H. 7:155 (1891).   85

Growth of Cities. Haupt, Lewis M. Cosmopol. 14:83 (1892), Pro. Eng. Club, Philadelphia, Vol. IV, No. 3; Fletcher, H. J. Forum 19:737 (1895); James, Edmund J. Ann. Am. Acad. Pol. Sci. 13:1 (Jan. 1899); Means, D. MacG. Nation 61:92 (1895); Tracy, Roger S. Cent. 55:79 (Nov. 1897); Viele, Egbert L. Pub. Imp. 1:1 (May 1, 1899); Walker, J. B. Cosmopol. 9:62 (1891); anon. Eng. Ill. M., No. 190, p. 361 (July, 1899), Pub. Opin. 15:501 (1893).   86

——. " Des Agglomérations urbaines dans l'Europe contemperaine. Essai sur les Causes, les Conditiones, les Conséquences de leur Développement (thése)." Meuriot, Paul. Paris, 1897. 8vo, 475 pp. 20 fr.   87

Population, Growth of Cities—*Continued.*

——. "Des Développements Urbains dans les Grandes Villes Européennes." Artibal, J. R. Municipale 3:1709 (Nov. 18, 1899). 88

——. "Growth of Cities in the Nineteenth Century, The: A Study in Statistics." Weber, Adna Ferrin. New York, Columbia University, 1899. 8vo, 495 pp. Cloth, $3.50. 89

——. "Growth of Cities in Germany and America." Hamilton, James H. Our Country 5:193 (June, 1897), 6:177 (Dec. 1897). 90

——. "Party Politics, City Growth and." Springer, Wm. N. Forum 10:472 (1890). 91

——. "Political Consequences of City Growth, The." Rowe, L. S. Yale R. 9:20 (May, 1900). 92

——. "Tendency of Men to Live in Cities, The." Kingsbury, F. J. J. Soc. Sci. 33:1 (Nov. 1895). 93

——. "Stadt und Land unter dem Einfluss der Binnenwanderung." Wirminghaus, A. Jr. Nat. Stat. 64:1-34, 161-182 (1895). 94

——. "Der Zug nach der Stadt." Rauchberg, Heinrich. Statistische Monatschrift (Vienna) 19:127 (1893). 95

——. "Der Zug nach der Stadt. Statistische Studien über Vorgänge der Bevölkerungsbewegung im Deutschen Reiche." Kuczynski, R. Stuttgart, Verlag der J. G. Cotta'schen Buchhandlung, 1897. 8vo, 284 pp. 96

"Immigration to Cities, Decline of." Cannon, E. National 22:624 (1894). 97

"Land Depression, City Slums." Ingham, J. A. London, Swan S. & Co., 1889. 122 pp. 98

Location of Cities. Cooley, C. H. Ch. X in "Theory of Transportation." Am. Econ. Assoc., Publications 9:233-370 (May, 1894). 99

——. "Der Verkehr und die Ansiedelungen der Menschen in ihrer Abhängikeit von der Gestaltung der Erdoberfläche." Kohl, J. C. Dresden u. Leipzig, Arnold'sche Buchh., 1843. 100

——. "Ueber die geographische Lage der grossen Städte." Roscher, Wilhelm. Ch. VIII, p. 317, Vol. I, "Ansichten der Volkswirtschaft." Leipzig, C. F. Winter, 3d. ed., 1878. 8vo, 386 and 493 pp. 1

"Machinery and the Modern Town." (Population of Cities as Affected by Modern Industrial Development). Ch. XIII. pp. 324-50 of John A. Hobson's "Evolution of Modern Capitalism." New York, Scribners, 1894. 8vo, 388 pp. $1.25. 2

"Proportion between Urban and Rural Population." de Molenari, G. Lalor's Cyclopedia, Vol. I, pp. 468-73, see 1-1. 3

"Racial Geography of Europe, The. Urban Problems." Ripley, William Z. Pop. Sci. Mo. 52:591 (March, 1898). 4

"Shall the City Grow Haphazard or be Shaped by Intelligence?" Hamilton, James H. Our Country 5:161 (May, 1897). 5

Statistics. "Die Bevölkerung der Erde. Periodische Übersicht üb. neue Arealberechnungen, Gebietsveränderungen, Zählgn. u. Schätzgn. der Bevölkerung auf d. gesammten Erdoberfläche." Wagner, Herm. u. Supan, Alex. Gotha, 1893. 130 pp. 7m. (Earlier volumes edited by E. Behm and H. Wagner). 6

Transportation, Effect of, on Population. "De la Transformation des Moyens de Transport et ses Conséquences économiques et sociales." de Foville, A. Paris, Guillaumin et Cie., 1880. 8vo, 7 fr. 50c. 7

——. "Die Lage der Städte und der Verkehr: Die Städte als geschichtliche Mittelpunkte." Vol. II, pp. 464-509 of Fredrich Ratzels' "Anthropo-Geographie." Stuttgart, J. Engelhorn, 2d. vol., 1891. 8vo, 781 pp. Vols. 1 & 2. 28m. 8

——. "Die Verkehrsmittel in Volks- und Staatswirtschaft." Sax, E. Vienna, 1878, 2 vols. 8vo. 23m. 9

Urban Populations. Billings, R. C. Fortn. 59:388 (1893); Wright, Carroll D. Pop. Sci. Mo. 40:459 (1892); anon. Leslie's Wkly. Supp., Aug. 3, 1890. 10

——. "Die drei Bevölkerungsstufen, ein Versuch die Ursachen für das Blühen und Altern der Völker nachzuweisen." Hansen, Georg. München, Lindauer, 1889, 8vo, 407 pp. 7m. 11

——. "France, Populations urbaines en—comparées à celles de l'étranger." Levasseur, E. Paris, Picard, 1877. 12

——. "Om Byerne og Landt, i deres indbyrdes forhold med hensyn til Befolkring og Produktion." Gamborg, J. Christiana, 1877. 13

——. "Staat und Land." Vol. I, p. 333. "Reden und Aufsatze." Rümelin, Gustav. Freiburg, Mohr, 1875. 8vo, 454 pp. 14

Population, Growth of Cities—*Continued.*

"Statistics and Economics, Urban and Rural Population." Mayo-Smith, Richmond. Am. Econ. Assoc. Pubs. 3:264-7 (1888), pp. 365-72 "Statistics and Sociology." New York, Macmillan, 1895. 8vo, 399 pp. $3.   15

"**Portland, Eng.**, The Water Works of." Engng. Rec. 41:32 (Jan. 13, 1900).   16

Portland, Me.

"History of Portland, Me." Pickard, Samuel T. See 1-4a.   17

——. History, Description and Statistics of Portland, Me., in 1880. Census. See 1-7.   18

"Street Railways of Portland, Me., and Vicinity, The." Fairchild, C. B. St. Ry. R. 10:483 (Sept. 15, 1900).   19

Portland, Ore.

"Municipal Condition of Portland." Strong, Thomas N. P. 432, Proc. Second Nat'l Conf. for Good City Govt., 1895. See 6-18b.   20

"Street Railway System of Portland." St. Ry. Jour. May, 1893, p. 297.   21

Portugal.

Local and Municipal Government in Portugal. Demombynes. Vol. I, pp. 505-533. See 2-11.   22

——. Gemeinde- und Districtsverwaltung. de Medeiros, J. J. Tavares. V. Abschnitt pp. 61-80, Vol. IV, 1, 8 Marquardsen. See 2-9.   23

"**Potato Patch, The.**" (See under **Vacant City Lots, Cultivation of in Cities**).   24

"**Potsdam [Ger.]**, Electric Locomotives at." Ry. World 7:9 (Jan. 1898).   25

"**Poughkeepsie, N. Y.**, Slow Sand Filtration at." Engng. News 39:179 (March 17, 1898).   26

Prenzlau, Ger., Water Works. "Das Wasserwerk der Stadt Prenzlau." Scheven, H. Zeitschr. d. Ver. Deutschr. Ing. 44:33 (Jan. 13, 1900).   27

"**Preston [Eng.]**, The Progress of." Toulmin, George. Mun. J. 9:323 (April 27, 1900).   28

Primary Elections. (See under **Elections**).

"**Princeton, N. J.**, History of." Sloane, W. M. See 1-4b.   29

Prisons, Municipal. (See under **Police**).

Proportional Representation, Minority Representation, etc.

See also Belgium.

"Bibliography of Proportional Representation." Commons, John R. Pro. Rep. Rev. 1:58 (1893); also p. 92 of his "Proportional Representation."   30

——. "Reference List on Proportional Representation." Monthly Bulletin of the Providence (R. I.) Public Library, Vol. 2, No. 12, Dec. 1896. Pp. 275-279.   31

"Cumulative Vote, Municipal Reform in New York and the." Law Magazine and Review n. s. 1:206 (1872).   32

"Election of Representatives, Parliamentary and Municipal, Treatise on the." Hare, Thomas. London, Longmans, 1st ed. 1859. 8vo, 380 pp. 7s.   33

"Legal Disfranchisement." Cooley, Stoughton. Atlan. 69:542 (1892).   34

"Machinery of Representation." Hare, Thomas. London, 2d. ed., 1857. 8vo, 55 pp.   35

"Minorities, Representation of." Laffitte, J. P. Revue Bleue Jan. 23, 1897.   36

——. "Political Reform by the Representation of Minorities." With bibliography, pp. 180-188. Forney, Matthias Nace. New York. Published by the author. 1894. 199 pp.   37

Municipal Councils. "La Représentation Proportionnelle dans les Conseils Municipaux." Rendu, Ambroise. R. Municipale 3:1945 (March 3, 1900).   38

Proportional Representation, Etc.—*Continued*.

"Municipal Election at Large, and Proportional Representation." Adams, Charles Francis. Pro. Rep. Rev. 2:48 (1894). — 39

Municipal Reform by Proportional Representation. Adams, Charles Francis. Prop. Rep. R. 1:69 (1894); Forney, M. N. The Citizen 1:278 (1896); Foulke, William Dudley. Pro. Indianapolis Conf. Good City Govt., 1898, see 6-18e, Prop. Rep. R. 1:37 (1893); Jenks, Jeremiah W. Pro. Minn. Conf. for Good City Govt., 1894, see 6-18a, Pro. Phila. Conf., 1895, see 6-18b; Spence, C. H. Arena 10:767 (1894); Whitney, J. Eugene. Am. M. Civics 8:127 (1896). — 40

"Objection to Proportional Representation." Naville, E. R. Pol. et Par. April 10, 1897. — 41

"Preferential Voting." Pp. 484-487 in "The City for the People or the Municipalization of the City Government and of Local Franchises." Parsons, Frank. Philadelphia, C. F. Taylor, 1900. 8vo, 597 pp. Cloth, $1. — 42

Proportional Representation, General Articles on. Commons, John R. Twentieth Cent. serial, beginning June 29, 1893, So:. Econ. 7:28 (1894); Cooley, Stoughton. New Eng. M. 8:116 (1893); Horton, S. D. Am. Law R. n. s. 6:255 (1885); McCracken, W. D. N. Eng. M. 9:698 (1894), Arena 7:290 (1893); pp. 1123-1127 Encyc. Soc. Ref., see 1-3. — 43

———. "Proportional Representation." Commons, John R. New York, Thomas Y. Crowell & Co., 1896. 298 pp. $1.75. (Chapter VIII, p. 197, on "City Government." Bibliography of Proportional Representation, p. 292). — 44

———. "Proportional Representation." Forney, Matthias N. New York, E. W. Johnson, 1900. 12mo, 61 pp. Paper, 25c. — 45

———. "Proportional Representation." Pp. 474-483 in "The City for the People or the Municipalization of the City Government and of Local Franchises." Parsons, Frank. Philadelphia, C. F. Taylor, 1900. 8vo, 597 pp. Cloth, $1. — 46

———. "Proportional Representation." Moffett, S. E. Ch. XIII, p. 167, "Suggestions on Government." Chicago, Rand, McN. & Co., 1894. 12mo, 200 pp. $1. — 47

"Representation of Interests." Commons, John R. Ind. 52:1479 (June 21, 1900). — 48

Prostitution.

See also Berlin, Chateau Gontier, France, Geneva, Hamburg, Italy, Liepsic, London, New York, Paris, Rio de Janeiro, Vienna, Zürich.

History, Statistics and Regulation of Prostitution. "Zur Geschichte, Statistik und Regelung der Prostitution." Hügel. Wien, Typo. Lit. Art. Anstalt, 1865. 1 m. 10 pf. — 49

———. "Histoire de la Prostitution chez tous les peuples du monde depuis l'antiquité le plus reculée jusqu'à nos jours." Dufour, Pierre. Paris, Seré, editeur, 1851-1853. 6 vols. 8vo. — 50

———. "History of Prostitution. Its Extent, Causes and Effects throughout the World." Numerous notes and appendix relative to New York Prostitution. Sanger, W. W. New York, The Medical Pub. Co., 1898. 8vo, 709 pp. — 51

———. "Die Prostitution in neunzehnten Jahrhundert v. sanitätspolizeil. Standpunkt u. d. Vorbeugung d. syphilis." Kühn, Julius, neu bearbeitet von Eduard Reich. Leipzig, Barsdorf, 1888. 8vo, 243 pp. — 52

———. "State Iniquity, History of the System of State Regulated and Licensed Vice." Scott, Benjamin. London, Kegan, Paul, Trench, T. & Co., 1890. 401 pp. 3s. 6d. — 53

"Laws Favoring Immorality." Flower, B. O. Arena 11:56, 167, 399 (1894-5). — 54

Legal Regulation of Prostitution. "Frage der staatl. Regulirung der Prostitution." Forel, Aug. Bremerhaven, 1892. 50 pf. — 55

———. "A Comparative Survey of Laws in Force for the Prohibition, Regulation and Licensing of Vice in England and other Countries." (Contains texts of many laws and an historical account of English laws on the subject.) Amos, Sheldon. London, Stevens and Sons, 1877. 542 pp. 18s. — 56

———. "Der Staat in d. Prostitutionsfrage." Eckstein, Ant. Leipzig, Centralverbandes der Haus u. städtischen Grundbesitzer Vereine, 1891. 75 pf. — 57

———. "Gefahren der Prostitution und ihre gesetzliche Bekämpfung mit bes. Berücksichtigung d. zürcherischen Verhältnisse." Zehnder, C. Zürich, Albert Müller, 1891. 247 pp. 8vo. — 58

———. "Réglementation der Prostitution." Moeller. Bulletin d. l'Acad. Roy. de Medicine de Belgique, 1886. — 59

Prostitution—*Continued.*

———. " Zu dem Kampfe gegen die Reglementirung der Prostitution." Schlesinger-Eckstein, Therese. Neue Zeit 17:365 (June 17, 1899). 60
" Municipalities and Vice." Mun. Aff. 4:698 (Dec. 1900). 61
Prostitution. Pp. 1127-1134 Encyc. Soc. Ref., see 1-3; Renck, Vol. V, pp. 295-306 Conrad, see 2-10. 62
———. " Die Prostitution und ihre Bekämpfung." Stursberg. Düsseldorf, 1892. 63
———. " La Prostitution." Guyot, Yves. Paris, G. Charpentier, 1883. 598 pp. 3 fr. 50c. 64
———. " La Prostitution, saggio di statistica morale." Tammeo, G. Torino, L. Roux e C., 1890. 324 pp. (Appendici: Regolamento sulla prostituzione). L. 4. 65
Reform of Police Measures against Prostitution. " Zur Austilgung der Syphilis, abolitionistische Betrachtungen über Prostitution, Geschlechtskrankheiten und Volksgesundheit nebst Vorschlägen zu einem Syphilisgesetz." (M. 7 Curventafeln.) Kromayer, Ernst. Berlin, Bomtraeger, 1898. 8vo, 105 pp. 3m. 50 pf. 66
———. " Die Bestrafung und polizeiliche Behandlung der Gewerbmässigen Unzucht." Schmölder. Düsseldorf, Voss & Co., 1892. 8vo, 84 pp. 1m. 60 pf. 67
———. " Die Prostitution: Ansichten und Vorschläge auf dem Gebiete des Prostitutionswesens." Mueller, Eugen. München, Münchner Medizinische Abhandlungen. 1892. 68
———. " Prostitution und Abolitionismus." Tarnowsky. Hamburg u. Leipzig, Voss, 1890. 8vo, 222 pp. 5m. 69

Providence, R. I.

City Government, General References.

" Advance Club of Providence, R. I., Aims and Objects of the." Thompson, David M. Publications of the Club No. 6, 1891. 70
" Almanac, Providence Journal." Providence, Published annually by the Providence Journal. Edition for 1899, 96 pp. 10c. 71
" Charter, City." Wilson, George G. Ann. Am. Acad. Pol. Sci. 13:128 (Jan. 1899). 72
" Commercial Advantages of Providence, The." Miller, Joseph A. Advance Club Pubs. No. 4, 1891. 73
History, Description and Statistics of Providence, R. I., in 1880. Census, See 1-7. 74
" Municipal Condition of Providence, R. I." McGuinness, Edwin D. Pages 154-163 " Pro. of the Louisville Conference for Good City Government, etc." 1897. See 6-18d. Reprinted City Govt. 2:173 (June, 1897). 75

" Electrolysis in Providence, R. I." Engng. Rec. 42:106 (Aug. 4, 1900). 76
" Fire Service System at Providence, R. I., New High Pressure." Mun. Engng. 14:195 (April, 1898); City Govt. 4:133 (April, 1898). 77
" History of Providence, R. I." Weeden, William B. See 1-4a. 78
———. " Government of Providence, Town and City, 1636-1889." Wilson, George C. Providence, Preston and Rounds, 1889. 77 pp. Paper, $1. 79
" Lighting of Providence, R. I." Snow, J. Lippit. Advance Club Leaflets Nos. 2 and 3, 1881. 80
" Park System of Providence, R. I." Robbins, M. C. Garden & F. 5:590 (1892). 81
" School System, The Investigation of the Public." Wilson, George W. Ann. Am. Acad. Pol. Sci. 14:386 (Nov. 1898). 82
Sewers, Maintenance of. Aldrich, Allen. Engng. News 41:194 (March 30, 1899), Engng. Rec. 39:372 (March 25, 1899); Waring, G. E. Am. Arch. 17:43, 53 (1885). 83
Water Supply. " Test of a Mechanical Filter, East Providence, R. I." Engng. Rec. 40:96 (July 1, 1899). 84

Prussia. (See under **Germany**).

Public Comfort Stations, Latrines. (See also under **Baths**).

See also Berlin, Boston, Düsseldorf, London, Paris.

Latrines. " Latrines Publiques et Privées avec Ecoulement direct à l'Egout à Paris." Barré, L. A. La Semaine des Const. p. 486, 1884-5. 85
———. General Articles. Anon. La Semaine des Const. p. 376, 413, 438, 510, 1876-77, p. 29, 1881-2. 86

Public Comfort Stations—*Continued.*

——. " Nouveaux Types de Latrines Publiques et Privées avec Ecoulement direct à l'Egout, Système Durand-Claye." Nouv. Annales de la Const. p. 86, 1885. 87
——. " Oeffentliche Abortanlage." Baugwbe. Jahrg. 1, p. 29. 88
——. " Ueber öffentliche Urinalanstalten." Dietrich, E. Wochbl. f. Baukde. p. 411, 1886. 89
Public Comfort Stations. " Oeffentliche Bedürfnissanstalten." Herzberg, E. Baugwks.-Ztg. pp. 522, 637, 1888; anon. Deutsches Baugwks.-Bl. p. 439, 1889. 90
——. " Ueber Closet-Häuschen." Wiener Bauind.-Ztg., Jahrg. 3, p. 454. 91

Public Health. (See **Sanitation**).

Public Works. (See **Engineering**).

"**Pullman, Ills.**, Sewage Farm at." Williams, Benezette. J. Assoc. Engng. Soc. 1:311 (1881). 92

"**Purleigh [Eng.]**, Water Works, Inauguration of the." Surveyor 17:677 (June 22, 1900).

Quasi-Public Works. (See under **Municipal Control, Municipal Ownership**).

Quebec.
" Quebec: The Gibraltar of America." Stewart, George. Self-Cult. 9:601 (Aug. 1899). 93
" Railway System of Quebec, The Electric." St. Ry. J. 15:495 (Aug. 1899).
——. " Conditions of Operation of Street Cars in the City of Quebec." Blair, D. E. St. Ry. R. 10:590 (Oct. 15, 1900). 94

"**Quincy, Ill.**, Settling Reservoir, The." Gwinn, Dow R. Engng. Rec. 38:8 (June 4, 1898). 95

Quincy, Mass.
" A New Departure." Godkin, E. L. Nation 55:197 (1892). 96
" Centennial Milestone of Quincy, Mass., The." Adams, Charles Francis. Cambridge, Mass., John Wilson and Sons, 1892. 97
" Lessons in Municipal Government from the Experience of Quincy, Mass." Adams, Charles Francis. Forum 14:282 (1892). 98

Railways. (See **Transit Facilities** and **Population**).

"**Ramsgate [Eng.]**, Reviewed." Mun. J. 9:657 (Aug. 24, 1900). 99

Rapid Transit. (See under **Transit Facilities**).

Reading, Pa.
" Electrolysis in Reading, Pa." Knudson, A. A. Engng. Rec. 42:443 (Nov. 10, 1900). 100
Sewage. " Improved Methods for the Purification of Sewage and Water, as Shown in the Operation of the Municipal Plant at Reading, Pa." Deery, John Jerome. Frankl. Inst., 148:227, 279 (Sept., Oct. 1899). 1
" Water Filtration at Reading, Pa." Engng. Rec. 37:534 (May 21, 1898). 2

Recreation. (See **Amusements, Public; Parks**).

Referendum. (See under **Direct Legislation**).

Reform, Municipal; Reform Organizations. (See **General Works, City Government, Unclassified; Church and Municipal Conditions**).

Refuse Disposal. (See under **Garbage Disposal**).

"**Reigate [Eng.],** Bacteriological Sewage Purification at." Surveyor 18:46 (July 13, 1900). 3

Religious Condition of Cities. (See under **Churches and Religious Conditions**).

"**Restaurants for the Laboring Classes.**" Mallock, M. M. National 21:62 (1893). (See also under **Grenoble, France**). 4

Rhode Island.
"Tammany Societies of Rhode Island, The." Jernegan, Marcus W. (Papers from the Historical Seminary of Brown University). Providence, R. I. 50c. 5
"Town Government in Rhode Island." Foster, Wm. E. J. H. Univ. Studies IV:2. 50c. 6
"Water Supply and Sewage Disposal in Rhode Island." (Editorial). Engng. News 38:349 (Nov. 25, 1897). 7
——. "Notes on Water Supply and Sewage Disposal in Massachusetts and Rhode Island." Eng. News 38:349 (Nov. 25, 1897). 8

"**Rhondda [Wales],** Water Works." Thomas, Octavius. Surveyor 18:303 (Sept. 14, 1900). 9

"**Rhyl [Wales],** Sewage of." Fuertes, James H. Engng. Rec. 36:400 (Oct. 6, 1897). 10

Richmond, Eng.
"Housing of the Working Classes, with a Description of the Richmond Municipal Cottages." Thompson, W. London, P. S. King & Son, 1899. 4to, 52 pp. Paper, 2s. 6d. 11
——. "Municipal Cottages." Mun. J. & London 8:117 (Jan. 26, 1899).
——. "Municipal Workmen's Dwellings, Richmond, Surrey." J. San. Inst. 21:452 (Oct. 1900). 12

"**Richmond, Ind.,** Garbage Cremation at." Whelan, D. P. City Govt. 7:149 (Dec. 1899). 13

Richmond, Va.
"History of Richmond, Va." Henry, William Wirt. See 1-4c. 14
——. History, Description and Statistics of Richmond and Manchester, Va., in 1880. Census. See 1-7. 15
"Lighting and Power Stations of the Richmond Railway and Electric Co." Elec. World 30:662 (Dec. 4, 1897). 16
"Municipal Condition of Richmond, Va." Newton, Virginius. p. 88, Proc. Third Natl. Conf. for Good City Govt., 1896. See 6-18c. 17
Water Works. "Physical and Bacteriological Characteristics of James River Water at Richmond, Va. with Special Reference to Clarification Methods." Levy, E. C. pp. 81-93 in "Proceedings of the 20th Annual Meeting of the American Water Works Association, Richmand, Va., May 15-18, 1900." 8vo, 216 pp. Cl. $1. 18
——. "The Results of the Meter System in Richmond, Va." Bolling, Charles E. Engng. Rec. 40:12 (June 3, 1899). 19

Riga, Russia, City Plan of. "Der neue Bebauungsplan der Stadt Riga." Stegman, R. Rigasche Ind.-Ztg. p. 135, 1881. 20

Rio de Janeiro.
Prostitution. "A Prostituição na Cidade do Rio de Janeiro, necessidade de medias e regeilamentos contra a propagação da syphilis." de Gáes e Siqueira Filha, José. Rio de Janeiro, Typ. da Riforma, 1875. Pamphlet, 108 pp. 21
"Street Railways of Rio Janeiro." St. Ry. J. 16:975 (Oct. 13, 1900). 22

"**Ripley, N. Y.,** The Water Works and Filter Plant of." Wilder, E. A. Engng. News 39:363 (June 9, 1898). 23

Rochester, N. Y.
Almanac. "Rochester Union and Advertiser Year Book." Rochester, Published annually by the Rochester Union and Advertiser. Edition for 1898, 112 pp. 25 cts. 24

BIBLIOGRAPHY. 235

Rochester, N. Y.—*Continued.*
"Building Operations, Buffalo, Rochester and Syracuse, Statistics of." B. Labor
  Stat. New York 1:170 (Dec. 1899). 25
"Electric Lighting System of Rochester, N. Y., The." Muldaur, George B. Elec:
  Eng. 24:293 (Sept. 30, 1897). 26
History, description and statistics of Rochester, N. Y., in 1880. Census. See 1-7. 27
"Municipal Milk Stations, Rochester." City Govt. 9:127 (Nov. 1900).
"Municipal Reforms in Rochester, N. Y." Alling, Joseph T. Pp. 175-184, "Proc.
  of the Louisville Conference for Good City Government 1897." See 6-18d. 28
"Parks, The Rochester, N. Y." Park & Cem. 9:190 (Nov. 1899). 29
Sweating in Rochester, N. Y. p. 57 et seq. "Report of the Committee of Manufactures on Sweating." H. R. Report No. 2309, 1893. John De Witt Warner, Chairman. 30
"Water Works of Rochester, N. Y." Kuichling, Emil. Engng. Rec. April 13, 1895, et seq. 31

Rockford, Ill.
Water Supply. "Difficult Engineering Problem Solved in Rockford's New Water
  Works." Mun. Engng. 16:215 (April, 1899); Engng. News 42:18 (July 13, 1899). 32
——. "A Brief History of the Water Supply of Rockford, Ill." Kimball, W. M.
  pp. 30-40 in "Proc. of the 20th Annual Meeting of the Am. W. W. Assoc.,
  Richmond, Va., May 15-18, 1900." 8vo, 216 pp. Paper, $1. 33

Roman Cities. "City State of the Greeks and Romans, a Survey introductory to the Study of Ancient History." Fowler, W. Warde. London,
  Macmillan, 1895. 12mo, 332 pp. $1. 34

Rome.
"Comune, Il, ed il governo a Roma; Studio economico, finanzario." Fiordispini,
  Biagio. Roma, Ermanno Loescher e C., 1889. 195 pp. L. 3.50. 35
Finance. "Bilancio, Il, del comune di Roma spiegato al popolo, illustrato da
  alcune considerazioni sull' amministrazione comunale." Canti, S. Roma, Pallota, 1888. 36
——. "Imposta sui fabbricati in Roma, Dell'. Relazione della commissione eletta
  nell' assemblea dell' 8 luglio, 1892." Marrucci, C. Roma, Forzani e C., 1892.
  24 pp. 37
——. "Per Roma; appunti e rilievi sulla finanza municipale." Guastalla, Mich.
  Roma, Stab. tip. dell' Opinione, 1890. 20 pp. 38
——. "Sempre per Roma, il problema finanziario municipale." Guastalla, Mich.
  Stab, tip. dell' Opinione, 1890. 20 pp. 39
——. "Situazione finanzaria di Roma, Sulla." Simonetti, Lu. Roma, tip Innocenzo Artero, 1890. 39 pp. 40
"Fire Department of the City of Rome, The." Sci. Am. Sup. 46:19035 (Oct. 1, 1898).
History. Rome and Roman Life in Antiquity. "Rom und römisches Leben im
  Altertum." Bender, Herm. Tübingen, H. Laupp, 1898. 8vo, 594 pp. 7m. 41
——. City Government under the Roman Empire. "Städteverwaltung im römischen Kaiserreiche." Liebenam, W. Leipzig, Duncker & Humblot, 1900. 8vo,
  577 pp. 14m. 42
——. "History of the City of Rome in the Middle Ages." Gregorovius, Ferdinand. (Translated by Annie Hamilton.) New York, Macmillan Co., 1898.
  12mo, 5 vols. Cloth, $2 each. 43
——. "Ruins and Excavations of Ancient Rome, The." Lanciani, Rodolfo. Boston, Houghton, Mifflin & Co., 1897. 12mo, 619 pp. Cl. $4. 44
Improvement. "Die Stadterweiterung Roms." Mühlke, C. Wochbl. f. Arch. u.
  Ing. p. 206, 1882. 45
Markets. "Mercati di Roma, I, ed il bagarinaggio, riforma progettata al municipio." Faina, Annibale. Roma, Domenico Vaselli, 1891. 16 pp. 46
"Pavements, Confined Rivers and the Water Supply of Ancient Rome." Blackford,
  Francis W. J. Assoc. Engng. Soc. Dec. 1896. 47
Sewerage System. "Il colletore basso delle fogne di Roma a sinistra del Tevere."
  Giornale del Genio Civile, Anno 28, p. 49 (1890); Jones, Wallace S. See 56-40a. 48

Rome—*Continued.*

"Water Supply of the City of Rome of Sextus Julius Frontinus, Water Commissioner of the City of Rome A. D. 97, The Two Books on the." Herschel, Clemens, Translator. Boston, Estes & Co., 1899. 4to, 296 pp. Cl. $6.50. 49
——. "The Water Supply of Rome." Fuertes, James H. Engng. Rec. 38:337 (Sept. 17, 1898). 50

Rotterdam, Holland.
Garbage Disposal. See 56-40b.
"Sewage Disposal." Reque, Lars S. See 56-40a, 40b. 51

Roubaix, France.
Municipality. "La Municipalité de Roubaix." Chabrouillaud, F. Mouvement Soc. 2:545 (May 1, 1900). 52
Socialism, Municipal. "L'Oeuvre des Municipalités Socialistes, Roubaix." Chabrouillard, F. Le Mouvement Socialiste May 1, 1900. 53

Rouen, France.
Baths, Public, at Rouen and Paris. "Les Bains-Douches à bon marché à Rouen et à Paris." Sarrey, Paul. Génie Civil May 6, 1899. 54
History. "Mediæval Towns: The Story of Rouen." Cook, F. A. New York, Macmillan Co., 1899. 16mo, 409 pp. Cl. $2. 55
Lighting. "The Cost of Various Illuminants at Rouen in France." Piequet, O. Prog. Age 15:497 (Nov. 1, 1897). 56

Roumania, Local and Municipal Government in. Demombynes Vol. I, pp. 678-695. See 2-11. 57

Rural Population, Decrease of. (See under **Population**).

Russia.
Government, General References.
Local and Municipal Government in Finland. Demombynes Vol. I, pp. 651-657. See 2-11. 58
——. "Die Selbstverwaltung d. Kommunen." Mechelin, L. IV. Abs. pp. 335-339, Vol, IV, Marquardsen. See 2-9. 59
Local and Municipal Government in Russia. Demombynes Vol. I, pp. 547-617. See 2-11. 60
——. "Die russische Städteordnung vom 16 Juni, 1870." Schwanebach, P. St. Petersburg, Kaiserliche Hofbuchhandlung H. Schmitzdorff, 1874. 8vo, 35 pp. 1 m. 60 pf. 61
——. "Die Selbstverwaltung." Engelmann, J. VI. Abschnitt, pp. 102-201 Vol. IV, Marquardsen. See 2-9. 62
——. "L'Empire des Tsars et les Russes; le self-government en Russie." Leroy-Beaulieu, Paul. R. Mondes. Nov. 15, 1876, July 15, 1878. 63
——. "Local Government and Taxation in Russia." Dilke, Ashton Wentworth. p. 309 "Local Government and Taxation," J. W. Probyn, editor. London & New York, Cassell, 1875. 5s. 64
"Municipal Reform in Russia." Schuyler, E. Nation 11:364 (1870); Mun. J. 9:146 (Feb. 23, 1900). 65

"Charity in Russia, The Organization of." Georgievsky, H. p. 244 "International Congress." vol. III, 1893. See 43-99. 66
Finance Statistics. "Zur Finanzstatistik der Städte Russlands." Sodoffsky, G. Zeit. f. d. Ges. Staats. 55:510 (Heft 3, 1899). 67
——. "Die Besteuerung der Städtischen Liegenschaften Russlands zu Communalen Zwecken I.") Sodoffsky, Gustav. Zeit. f. Volks. Soc. u. Verwaltung 8:602 (Heft. 6, 1899). 68
"Lighting Systems in Russia." Luloslawski, M. Elec. World 30:36 (July 10, 1897); Am. Gas. Lgt. J. 67:90 (July 19, 1897). 69
"Sanitation in Russia." Wilke, D. Am. Arch. 64:59 (May 20, 1899), 64:67 (May 27, 1899). 70
Street Railways. "Possibilities for Electric Tramway Construction in Russia." Ry. World 7:15 (Jan. 1898). 71

"**Rutland, Vermont.**" Dorr, Julia C. R. New Eng. M. 18:201 (April, 1898). 72

"History of Rutland, Vt." Mead, Edwin D. See 1-4a. 73

Sacramento, Cal. "A Municipal Employment Bureau." Cal. Mun. 2:150 (June, 1900). 74

"**Saginaw, Mich.**, City Government in." Webber, Wm. L. Ann Arbor, Studies in Finance and History, Michigan Univ. Article in Vol. I, No. 6, (Dec. 1895). 25 cts. 75

"**St. Augustine, Fla.**, History of." Fairbanks, George R. See 1-4c. 76

St. Gall, Switzerland.
Sewage and Garbage Disposal. See 56-40b.
"Unemployment, Insurance against, in St. Gall and Berne." L'Avenir Social (Bruxelles) 1:189-194 (1896); Curti, Theodor. Ar. Soz. Gesetz. Stat. 10:157 (1897); Garrelts, Fr. Goettingen, L. Horstmann, pub. (1896), two pages with one table, one mark; Hofmann, E. Ar. Soz. Gesetz. Stat. 13:85 (1 Heft, 1898); Jay, Raoula. R. Pol. e. Par. 1:267, 6:140, 8:397, 11:397 (1894), (1895), (1896), (1897); Stolz, Ferd. Schweiz. Bl. 2:12 (1894); Zuppinger, C. Pub. at Berne, 1895. 77

——. "Die Auflösung der Arbeitslosen-Kasse in St. Gallen." Soziale Praxis Nov. 19, 1896, pp. 169-172; Zeit. Staatswissen 53:692-696 (1897). 78

"**St. Helens [Eng.]**, Subway." Surveyor 17:67 (Jan. 26, 1900).

St. Louis.
Government, General References.
"City Government of St. Louis." Snow, Marshall. J. H. Univ. Studies V:4 (1887); Dewart, Frederick W. Pp. 218-232, Proc. of the Louisville Conference for Good City Govt., 1897, see 6-18d; Shaw, Albert. Cent. 52:253 (1896); Verdier, A. R. Proc. Indianapolis Conf. p. 270, 1898, see 6-18e. 79
"Growth of St. Louis." Ralph Julian. Harper 85:917 (1892). 80
"Higher Life of St. Louis." Snyder, John. Outlook 54:372 (1896). 81
History, description and statistics of St. Louis, Mo., in 1880. Census. See 1-7. 82
"The Central Continental Metropolis." Logan, C. T. Frank Leslie's March, 1897. 83

"Art, Public, in St. Louis." Mauran, John Lawrence. Mun. Aff. 3:702 (Dec. 1899). 84
"Conduit Construction in St. Louis." Cosby, Frank Clark. Elec. World 30:242 (Aug. 28, 1897), 30:267 (Sept. 4, 1897). 85
"Municipal Engineering in St. Louis." Moore, Robert. Engng. News Jan. 23, 1892, p. 76, Engng. Rec. Jan. 23, 1892, p. 127. 86
Parks. "Notes from Tower Grove Park." Seavey, Fanny Capley. Park and Cem. 7:58 (May, 1897). 87
"Pavements of St. Louis." Engng. Rec. Feb. 7, 1891, p. 159. 88
"Plumbing Inspection in St. Louis." Engng. Rec. April 4, 1891, p. 298.
"Sanitary Survey of St. Louis." Homan, George (Editor.) Concord, N. H. Reprinted from transactions of the American Public Health Assoc., 1885. 77 pp. 89
"Schools of St. Louis, Public." Rice, J. M. Forum 14:429 (1892). 90
"Sewerage System of St. Louis." Moore, Robert. J. Assoc. Engng. Soc. 4:139 (1885). 91
"Street Railways of St. Louis." Anon. St. Ry. Jour. Feb. 1890, p. 56; Engng. M. 8:449 (1894). 92
"Water Works, The St. Louis." Discussed in the following papers: I, Historical Review, by M. L. Holman; II, Points of Interest in the Design and Construction, by S. Bent Russell; III, New Machinery, by John A. Laird; IV, Quality of the Supply, by Robert E. McMath; and V, Filtration, by Robert Moore. J. Assoc. Engin. Soc. Jan. 1895; Fire and W. 23:50 (Feb. 12, 1898); 23:58 (Feb. 19, 1898); Engng. Rec. 38:111 (July 9, 1898); Mun. Engin. 13:78 (Aug. 1897). 93

Saint Nazaire, France. Improvement. "Agrandissement de la Ville de Saint Nazaire." Nouv. Annales de la Const. p, 1, 1865. 94

St. Pancras. (See under London).
St. Paul.
Government, General References.

"Government of St. Paul." Gonden, H. J. and Irwin Beaumont. City Govt. 1:13 (1896); Lightner, W. H. p. 105, Proc. Second Natl. Conf. for Good City Govt., 1895, see 6-18b. Wheelock, Webster. Mun. Aff..3:491 (Sept. 1899). 95

History, description and statistics of St. Paul, Minn., in 1880. Census. See 1-7. 96

"St. Paul." Howard, William W. Hrprs. Wkly. 34:149 (1890); in article, "Capitals of the Northwest." Ralph, Julian. Hrprs. 84:576 (1892). 97

"Assuring Real Estate, The St. Paul Method of." Clow, F. R. J. Pol. Econ. Dec. 1896. 98

"Baths, The St. Paul Public." Pomeroy, Eltweed. Outlook 66:126 (Sept. 8, 1900). 99

——. "Municipal Lighting for St. Paul." Mun. J. & E. 9:158 (Dec. 1900).

"Park Systems of Minneapolis and St. Paul, The." Robbins, Mary C. Garden & F. 10:162 (April 28, 1897); Park & Cem. 10:106 (July, 1900). 100

"Schools of St. Paul, Public." Rice, J. M. Forum 15:200 (1893). 1

"Water Works, St. Paul." Caulfield, John. Fire & W. May 29, 1897. 2

St. Petersburg, Russia.

"Electric Railway in St. Petersburg." (Editorial.) St. Ry. R. 7:587 (Sept. 15, 1897). 3

History. A Critical Review of Three Periods of Municipal Government in St. Petersburg. Viestnik Europy p. 852, Aug. 1898. 4

"Sewage Disposal, St. Petersburg." Jonas, Charles. See 56-40a. 5

Salem, Mass.

"History of Salem." Latimer, George D. See 1-4a. 6

"Salem: Historic and Picturesque." Benjamin, Anna N. Outlook 57:591 (Nov. 6, 1897). 7

Salford, Eng.

"Housing of the Working Classes at Salford, The." Tattersall, C. H. San. Rec. 26:88 (Aug. 3, 1900). 8

"Libraries Movement, Salford and the Inauguration of the Public Free." Mullen, Ben H. Salford, Borough Council, 1900. 8vo, 52 pp. 9

Street Railways. "Corporation Electric Tramways, Salford, Eng." Ty. & Ry. W. 9:77 (Feb. 8, 1900). 10

Saloon Problem in Cities. (See under Liquor Problem in Cities).

Salt Lake City, Utah.

History, description and statistics of Salt Lake City, Utah, in 1880. Census. See 1-7. 11

"Municipal Engineering Work at Salt Lake City, Notes on." Engng. News 37:284 (May 6, 1897). 12

Sewerage. "Outfall Sewer and Sewage Farms at Salt Lake City, Utah." Engng. News 37:166 (March 18, 1897).

Salvation Army Work in Cities. (See under Church and Municipal Conditions, also under London, New York).

San Antonio, Texas.

"The Founding of the First Texas Municipality." Cox, I. J. Texas Hist. Ass'n Quar. Jan. 1899. 13

San Francisco.

Government, General References.

"City by the Golden Gate, The." Fitch, Geo. Hamlin. Chaut. Sept. 1896. 14

History, Description and Statistics of San Francisco, Cal., in 1880. Census. See 1-7. 15

"Ideas of City Government at San Francisco." A. Z. Engng. News 38:314 (Nov. 11, 1897). 16

San Francisco—*Continued.*

"Municipal Affairs in San Francisco." Freud, J. Richard. Pp. 249-255, Proc. of the Louisville Conf. for Good City Govt., 1897, see 6-18d; Kerr, James W. Mchts. Assoc. Rev. p. 3 (July, 1897); Knapp, A. Arena 12:241 (1895); Law, Herbert E. Mchts. Assoc. Rev. p. 2 (Aug. 1897); Milliken, Isaac T. p. 449, Proc. Second. Natl. Conf. for Good City Govt., 1895, see 6-18b; Shinn, Charles H. Outlook 54:53 (1896); Stallard, J. H. Overland 29:44, 135, 278, 386 (Jan., Feb., March and April, 1897), Reprinted by Overland Monthly Pub. Co., San Francisco. Paper, 40 pp. 50 cts.   **17**

"Needed Enlightenment as to Public Affairs in San Francisco." Mun. Engng. 13:197 (Oct. 1897).

"San Francisco." Ralph, Julian. Hrprs. Wkly. 36:130, 39:231 (1892, 1895).   **18**

"San Francisco and New York Governments." Mun. Engng. 17:28 (July, 1899).   **19**

"San Francisco's Struggle for Good Government." Blackmar, Frank W. Forum 26:567 (Jan. 1899).   **20**

"Saving the Cities." City & State 8:342 (May 31, 1900).

Art. "Market Street, A Plan to Beautify." Cahill, B. J. S. Cal. Arch. Oct. 1899.   **21**

"Charities of San Francisco." Weitzel, S. W. Lend a H. 3:617 (1888).   **22**

——. "Almshouses at San Francisco." Weaver, [Mrs.] E. A. Lend a H. 9:28 (1892).   **23**

——. "Directory and Digest of Laws relating to Almshouses." Jenness, C. K. San Francisco, Methodist Book Depository Pub., 1895. 93 pp. 50 cts.   **24**

Charter. "A New Charter Wanted." Kelly, Daniel V. Mchts. Assoc. Rev. p. 3 (June, 1897).   **25**

——. "A Charter for the People." Stallard, J. H. Star Vol. 27, No. 16, p. 6, No. 17, p. 6 (Oct. 16, 23, 1897), Vol. 28, No. 18, p. 6 (Oct. 30, 1897), Star, Supplement Nov. 6, 1897.   **26**

——. "An Iron-Clad Charter and the Beneficial Effects Thereof." McCardy, J. J. City Govt. 3:130 (Oct. 1897).   **27**

——. "Making a City Charter: Charter Convention of One Hundred." Mchts. Assoc. R., Vol. 2, No. 3, p. 3 (Nov. 1897).   **28**

——. "Municipal Conditions and the New Charter." Phelan, J. D. Overland 28:104 (1896), Star Vol. 27, No. 25, p. 9 (Dec. 18, 1897).   **29**

——. "Referendum in San Francisco's New Charter." Lit. Dig. 16:726 (June 18, 1898).   **30**

——. "San Francisco's New Charter." Lewis, Austin. Arena 22:368 (Sept. 1899); Shaw, Albert. Am. M. R. of Rs. 19:56) (May, 1899); Woodruff, Clinton Rogers. Ann. Am. Acad. Pol. Sci. 13:413 (May, 1899).   **31**

——. "Synopsis of the New Charter." Freud, J. Richard. Mchts. Assoc. R. Vol. 2, No. 21, p. 1 (May, 1898).   **32**

——. "The Contest for Charter Freeholders." Center, Geo. L. Mchts. Assoc. Rev. Vol. 2, No. 16, p. 4 (Dec. 1897); Vol. 2, No. 17, p. 2 (Jan. 1898).   **33**

——. "The New City Charter." Mchts. Assoc. Rev. Vol. 2, No. 20, p. 1 (April, 1898); Engng. News 39:335 (May 26, 1898), (Editorial) p. 337.   **34**

"Civil Service." Star Vol. 27, No. 23, p. 6 (Dec. 4, 1897); Good Govt. 15:119 (1896); Stallard, J. H. Star. Vol. 27, No. 24, p. 7 (Dec. 11, 1897); Proc. Natl. Civil Service Reform League, 1899, p. 69; Mchts. Assoc. Rev. Vol. 4, No. 48, p. 3 (Aug. 1900).   **35**

"Election Machinery of San Francisco." Beatty, W. A. Overland n. s. 21:27 (1893).   **36**

Finance. "Merchants' Association Memorial upon the Tax Levy." Mchts. Assoc. Rev. p. 1 (Aug. 1897).   **37**

"Garbage, How San Francisco Disposes of its." Sci. Am. 79:260 (Oct. 22, 1898); Ellert, L. R. Mchts. Assoc. Rev. p. 3 (Aug. 1897), City Govt. 7:17 (July, 1899); Mills, F. J. Engng. News 43:318 (May 17, 1900; anon. Engng. News 43:325.   **38**

History. "Vigilance Committee, San Francisco." Cary, Thomas G. Atlan. 40:702 (1877), Internat. R. 11:78 (1881).   **39**

——. "Early Days in San Francisco: A Near View of Vigilante Times." Knight, Maria. Overland 30:252 (Sept. 1897), 30:313 (Oct. 1897).   **40**

——. "Establishment of City Government in San Francisco." Moses, B. J. H. Univ. Studies VII:2 and 3 (1889).   **41**

——. "Fort Gunnybags." Overland 31:73 (Jan, 1898).   **42**

San Francisco—*Continued.*

"Lighting of San Francisco." Hasson, W. F. C. Overland 23:385 (1894); Mchts. Assoc. Rev. Vol. 2, No. 20, p. 4 (April, 1898); Engng. News 41:331 (May 25, 1899). 43

"Markets of San Francisco." Craft, Mabel C. Chaut. Dec. 1896. 44

"Municipal Ownership and Management of Public Utilities in San Francisco." Doyle, John T. Mchts. Assoc. R. Vol. 5, No. 51, p. 3 (Nov. 1900). 45

——. "Public Utilities in San Francisco." Phelan, James D. Mchts. Assoc. Rev. p. 1 (July, 1897). 46

——. "Public Utilities in San Francisco under the New Charter." Reed, Charles Wesley. Cal. Mun. 3:43 (Sept. 1900). 47

——. "San Francisco Follies." Symmes, Frank E. Public Policy 3:312 (Nov. 17, 1900). 48

Reform Organizations. "Civic Service of the Merchants' Association of San Francisco." Freud, J. Richard. Mun. Affairs 1:706 (Dec. 1897); Bibo, Nathan. Mchts. Assoc. Rev. p. 2, July, 1897, p. 4, Aug. 1897. 49

Sanitation. "Municipal Boards of Health and Quarantine Regulations." Lewis, Austin. Am. Law R. 34:722 (Sept., Oct. 1900). 50

"Settlement, South Park." McLean, Fannie. Commons June, 1897; anon. Mchts. Assoc. Rev. Feb. 1900. 51

"Sewage of San Francisco." Stallard, J. H. San Francisco Polyclinic, Pamphlet, 30 pp. 1892. 52

"Streets, How San Francisco's are Cleaned." King, L. M. Mchts. Assoc. Rev. Vol. 2, No. 16, p. 5 (Dec. 1897); Engng. Rec. 39:522 (May 6, 1899) 53

Street Railways. "Four-Cent Fare Struggle in San Francisco." St. Ry. J. 16:82, 492 (Jan. 20, May 12, 1900). 54

"Water Supply of San Francisco." O'Connell, Daniel. Hrprs. Wkly. 38:990 (1894); Fire & W. 23:83 (March 12, 1898); Baldwin, A. S. Mchts. Assoc. Rev. 4:2 (April, 1900), Public Policy 2:301 (May 12, 1900), City Govt. 8:146 (June, 1900), Mun. Aff. 4:317 (June, 1900). 55

Sanitation, Public Health, etc. (See also **Garbage Disposal, Housing, Population, Sewage Diposal, Water Supplies.**)

See also Amsterdam, Baltimore, Berlin, Birmingham, Bordeaux, Boston, Brussels, Cape Town, Chicago, Cleveland, Dundee, England, France, Geneva, Glasgow, Great Britain under U. K., Hamburg, Hammersmith (Eng.), Havana, Hong Kong, India, Italy, London, Los Angeles (Cal.), Manila, Marseilles, Massachusetts, Mexico, Michigan, Moscow, New Orleans, New York, Paris, Philadelphia, Russia, St. Louis, San Francisco, Santiago, Spain, Switzerland, Topeka, Toronto, United Kingdom, United States, Washington.

"Air, Water and Food from a Sanitary Standpoint." Richards, Ellen H., and Woodman, Alpheus G. New York, Wiley & Sons, 1st ed., 1900. 8vo, 230 pp. Cl. $2. 56

Bacteriology in its Relation to Public Health. Novy, F. G. Pp. 17-24 in Proc. of the 4th General Conf. of Health Officers in Michigan, 1899; McClintock, Charles T. Pp. 24-28 same; Abbott, A. C. Prog. Eng. Club 17:47 (May, 1900). 57

——. Boards of Health. Bryce, P. H. Mun. World 8:6, 22 (Jan., Feb. 1898), 8:36 (March, 1898); Probst, C. O. City Govt. 6:31 (Feb. 1899); anon. Sanitarian 39:509 (Dec. 1897). 58

"Building Cities for Health." Swift, Morrison I. Unitarian Review 34:270 (1890). 59

"Building Construction and Public Health." Fyfe, Peter. Arch. Nov. 5, 1897, San. Rec. 20:640 (Dec. 10, 1897); anon. San. Rec. 20:629 (Dec. 10, 1897) 60

City Government and Sanitation. "Good City Government from the Physician's and Sanitarian's Standpoint." Billings, John S. p. 492, Proc. Second. Natl. Conf. for Good City Govt., 1896, See 6-18c. 61

——. "Municipal Government and Public Health." Billings, John S. Ann. Am. Acad. Pol. Sci. Vol. I, Supplement. 23 pp. 25 cts. 62

"Civic Helps for Civic Life." Dana, M. M. G. Soc. Econ. 8:226 (1895). 63

"Cleansing of Cities and Public Health." Waring, G. E. Engng. M. 8:805 (1895). 64

"Contagious Diseases." White, James H. Mun. Aff. 2:286 (June, 1898). 65

"Cost of Living as Modified by Sanitary Science, The." Richards, Ellen H. New York, Wiley & Sons, 1899. 12mo, 125 pp. Cl. $1. 66

Sanitation, Public Health—*Continued.*

"Curative and Preventive Sanitation." Sykes, John F. J. Mun. J. 9:609 (Aug. 3, 1900). — **67**

Engineering, Sanitary. "The Elements of Sanitary Engineering." Merriman, Mansfield. New York, John Wiley & Sons, 2d ed., 1899. 8vo, 222 pp. $2. — **68**

——. "Progress of Sanitary Engineering." Noble, Andrew. Sanitarian Dec. 1896. — **69**

——. "Sanitary Engineering." Gerhard, Wm. Paul. New York, The Author, 1899. 8vo. 132 pp. Cl. $1.25. — **70**

——. "Sanitary Engineering." Latham, Baldwin. London, Spon, 1878. 8vo, 559 pp., il. pl. 30s. — **71**

——. "Sanitary Engineering. A Practical Treatise on the Collection, Removal and Final Disposal of Sewage, etc." Moore, E. C. S. New York, Longmans, G. & Co., 1899. 8vo, 648 pp. Ill. Cl. $10. — **72**

——. "Sanitary Engineering." Twenty-third Annual Report of the State Board of Health of Massachusetts. (Water Supply. Sewage Disposal. Pollution of Streams, Sewage Purification, etc.) Abbott, Samuel. (Secretary.) Boston, 1895. — **73**

——. "The Municipal and Sanitary Engineer's Handbook." Boulnois, H. P. (3d ed.) New York. Spon & Chamberlain, 1898. 8vo, 474 pp. Cl. $6. — **74**

"European Sanitation." Ellery, T. George. Mun. J. & London 8:1359 (Dec. 22, 1899). — **75**

——. "Public Health Matters in Continental Europe." Pp. 34-37 in "Municipal Extension and Other Essays." Ellery, T. George. Adelaide, W. K. Thomas & Co., 1899. 12mo, 51 pp. Pamphlet. — **76**

"Expropriation for Sanitary Purposes." Chap. III, pp. 53-68, Eighth Special Report of the Commissioner of Labor on "The Housing of the Working People," by E. R. L. Gould. — **77**

Garbage and Sanitation. "Sanitary Care and Utilization of Refuse of Cities." Storer, J. J. J. Frankl. Inst. 97:48 (1874). — **78**

"Graveyards as a Menace to the Commonweal." Windmüller, Louis. No. Am. 167:211 (Aug. 1898). (See also under **Burial**.) — **79**

"Health of Nations, The." Richardson, Benjamin W. London, Longmans, 1887. 2 vols. 8vo. 28s. — **80**

"House-Drainage and Sanitary Plumbing." Gerhard, William Paul. New York, D. Van Nostrand Co., 7th ed., 1898. 16mo, 231 pp. 50 cts. — **81**

——. "House Drainage and Sanitary Fitments." Jensen, Gerard J. E. London, Sanitary Publishing Co., Ltd., 1900. 8vo, 257 pp. 5s. — **82**

——. "Principes d'Assainissement des Habitations des villes et de la banlieu." Pignant, P. Dijon, Darantière, 1889. 30 fr. — **83**

"Housing of the Poor, The Sanitary Consideration of the." Newell, Wm. H. Sanitary Monitor Jan. 1886. (See also under **Housing of the Poor**.) — **84**

——. "Dwellings for the Poor and Sanitary Legislation." Child, G. W. Contemp. 32:297 (1878). — **85**

——. "Sanitary Supervision of Dwellings." Angell, Lewis. Van Nos. Eng. M. 25:388 (1881); Moore, M. I. Char. R. 4:434 (1895). — **86**

——. "Tenement Sanitation." Wingate, C. F. Lend a H. 2:82 (1887). — **87**

Hygiene. (See under Public Health below.)

"Hygeia, A City of Health." Richardson, B. W. London and New York, Macmillan, 1876. 47 pp. 25 cts. — **88**

"Inspection, Revelations of Sanitary." Robins, E. C. Van Nos. Eng. M. 25:505 (1881). — **89**

——. "The Importance of the Sanitary Inspector." Pp. 26-30 in "Municipal Extension and Other Essays." Ellery, T. George. Adelaide, W. K. Thomas & Co., 1899. 12mo, 51 pp. Pamphlet. — **90**

"International Sanitary Conferences." Smith, S. Am. J. Soc. Sci. 32:92 (1894). — **91**

——. Transactions of VI Congress upon Hygiene und Demographie at Vienna, 1887. "Verhandlungen des VI Congresses für Hygiene und Demographie zu Wien 1887." Deutsche Viert. f. Oeff. Gesundheitspfl. p. 114, 1887. — **92**

"Laboratory in Municipal Public Health Work, The Practical Place of the." Mackenzie, J. J. p. 58 Assoc. Ex. Hlth. Officers of Ont. XIth Meeting, 1896. — **93**

"Law, Sanitary." Chap. II, pp. 21-52, Eighth Special Report of the Commissioner of Labor on "The Housing of the Working People," by E. R. L. Gould. — **94**

——. "Lectures on Sanitary Law." Blyth, A. W. New York, Macmillan, 1893. 287 pp. $2.50. — **95**

Sanitation, Public Health—*Continued*.

———. " Legislation sur les logements insalubres, traité pratique." Jourdan, Gustav. Paris, Berger, L. et Cie., 4th ed., 1889. 6 fr. 96
———. " Model Sanitary Ordinances." Gerhard, William Paul. Engng. News Sept. 26, 1885. 97
———. " Sanitary Legislation." Lee, B. Penn. Mo. 9:417 (1878). 98
" Lectures, Reports, Letters and Papers on Sanitary Questions." Rawlinson, R. London, P. S. King, 1880. 8vo. 3s. 6d. 99
" Life Insurance and Public Health Problems." Hoffman, Frederick L. Sanitarian 39:38 (July, 1897). 100
" Mayors and City Councilmen to Sanitary Problems, The Relation of." Potter, Alexander. City Govt. 3:125 (Oct. 1897). 1
" Modern Sanitary Science, A City of Health." Richardson, B. W. Van Nos. Eng. M. 14:31 (1876). 2
" Nationalization of Health." Ellis, Havelock. London, Unwin, 1892. 244 pp. 3s. 6d. 3
" Nuisances, Problem of Municipal." Tracy, R. S. Pop. Sci. Mo. 18:585 (1881). 4
———. " Summary Condemnation of Nuisances by Municipal Corporations." Uhle, John B. Am. Law R. n. s. 30:157 (1891). 5
" Parks to Public Health, The Relation of Public." Meehan's Monthly 9:112 (July, 1899). 6
" Pavements on Public Health, What Influence have." Campbell, A. W. Proc. p. 78 Assoc. Ex. Hlth. Officers of Ont., XIIIth Meeting, 1898. 7
Plumbing. " Evolution of Sanitation in Relation to the Plumber." Glaister, John. Plumber and Decorator (London). March 1, 1897. 8
" Police Power and Public Health." Black, H. C. Am. Law R. 25:170 (1891). 9
Poor, Sanitation and the. Marryat, R. 19th Cent. 15:840 (1884); Welch, William H. Char. R. 2:203 (1893). 10
Powers as to Public Health. " De la Détermination des Pouvoirs Publics en Matière d'Hygiène." R. Municipale 3:2028 (April 7, 1900). 11
———. " Des Pouvoirs de L'Autorité municipale en Matière d'Hygiène et de salubrité." Jonary, Léon. Paris, Giard et Brière, 1899. 12
" Profitable Sanitation." Poore, G. V. San. Rec. 26:119 (Aug. 10, 1900), Mun. J. 9:661 (Aug. 24, 1900). 13
Public Health, Hygiene. " Etudes d'Hygiene Publique." Jourdan, Gustav. Paris, Berger-Levrault, 1894. 4th ed. 8vo. 4 fr. 14
———. " Etude sur l'assainissement urbaine, hygiène et salubrité publique." Tackels, C. J. Bruxelles, Office de Publicité, 1890. 4 fr. 15
———. " Hygiène Générale des Villes." Lanck, L. Gaz. des Arch. et du Bât. pp. 165; 172, 209, 221, 229, 237, 1878. 16
———. " Hygiene and Public Health." Whitelegge, B. Arthur. London, Cassell & Co., 1890. 12mo, 531 pp. 7s. 6d. 17
———. " Manual of Public Health." Blyth, A. W. London, Macmillan, 1890. 8vo. 17s. 18
———. Municipal Hygiene. " L'Hygiène Municipale." Strauss, Paul. R. Municipale 3:1833 (Jan. 13, 1900). 19
———. " Public Health, The." Harris, Elisha. No. Am. 127:444 (1878); anon. Mun. W. 7:105 (May, 1897). 20
———. " Public Health and Demography, Handbook of." Willoughby, Edward F. London, Macmillan, 1893. 509 pp. 4s. 6d. 21
———. " Public Health Problems." Sykes, J. F. J. New York, Scribner, 1892. 370 pp. $1.25. (Contemporary Science Series No. 22). 22
———. " Social Problems, Public Health and." Russell, James B. San. J. No. 49, p. 1 (March, 1898). 23
———. " Treatise on Hygiene and Public Health." Buck, Albert H. New York, W. Wood & Co., 1890. 2 vols., 792 and 657 pp. $10. 24
———. " Treatise on Hygiene and Public Health." Stevenson, Thomas, and Shirley Murphy. Churchill, London, 1892-94. 3 vols., 8vo. 80s. 25
———. " Treatise on Public Health and its application in different European countries." (England, France, Belgium, Germany, Austria, Sweden and Finland). Palmberg, Albert, and Albert Newsholme. New York, Macmillan & Co., 1893 8vo, 539 pp. $5. 26

Sanitation, Public Health—*Continued.*

"Quarantine and Port Sanitation." Bell, A. N. Sanitation 38:481 (June, 1897). 27
"Rural Districts, Sanitary Defects in." Smith, G. H. Sanitarian 42:36 (Jan. 1899). 28
Sanitary Care of Cities. Gordon, J. Sci. Am. Supp. Nov. 19, 1887; Leas, C. A. J. Frankl. Inst 97:206 (1873). 29
"Sanitary Conditions of Cities." Young, S. G. Am. Arch. 22:218 (1887). 30
"Sanitary Science, Notes on Practical." Maxwell, William H. San. Rec. 19:364, 475, 530, 587; 20:6, 61, 117, 116 (1897). 31
———. "A Year's Progress in Sanitary Science." Priestly, Joseph. San. Rec. 21:394 (April 15, 1898), 21:450 (April 29, 1898). 32
"Sanitation, A Half Century of." Gerhard, William Paul. Am. Arch. 63:61, 67, 75 (Feb. March, 1899). Pp. 83-118 in "Pro. Brooklyn Engineers' Club for 1899." 8vo, 233 pp. Paper, $2. 33
———. "Some Phases of Public Sanitation." Gardner, E. C. Am. Arch 69:27 (July 28, 1900). 34
School Houses, Sanitation of. (See under **Schools**).
"Sewage and Water Supply to Public Health, The Relation of." Riggs, H. F. Pp. 36-49 in "Pro. of the 4th Gen. Conf. of Health Officers in Michigan, 1899." 35
"Shelters and Sanitation." Waldo, F. J. London 6:589 (July 8, 1897). 36
———. "Shelters for the Homeless, Sanitary Supervision of." Waldo, F. J. San. Rec. Feb. 1897. 37
Small Towns. "Abfuhr der Abfallstoffe, u. s. w. in mittler und kleineren Städten." Gesund. Ing. 20:231 (July 31, 1897). 38
———. "Village Sanitation." Bashore, Harvey B. Sanitarian 39:315 (Oct. 1897). 39
"Soil Conditions: Their Practical Relations to Infectious Diseases." San. Rec. 21:395 (April 15, 1898). 40
———. "Superficial Soils of Cities are Unsanitary, Why the." San. Rec. 21:141 (Feb. 11, 1898). 41
"Teaching of Sanitary Science, A Plea for the." Fall, Delos. Education, Jan. 1897. 42
"Theory of Sanitation, The." San. Rec. 21:399 (April 15, 1898). 43
"Town Dweller, The: His Needs and His Wants." Fothergill, John M. New York, Appleton, 1889. 118 pp. $1. 44
Tuberculosis. "The Duty of Municipal Health Officers and Boards of Health in dealing with Tuberculosis." Mitchell, F. H. p. 12 Assoc. Ex. Hlth. Officers of Ont., XIVth Meeting, 1899. 45
"Typhoid Fever. The Monetary Loss to Cities from." Turnbull, Thomas. "Thirteenth Annual Report of the State Board of Health * * * of Pennsylvania." P. 305. Harrisburg, 1898. 46
"Unhealthfulness of Cities, its Cause and Cure." Peek, Francis, and Edwin T. Hall. Contemp. 61:221 (1892). 47
"Vagaries of Sanitary Science." Dibble, F. L. Philadelphia, Lippincotts, 1893. 462 pp. $2. 48
"Waste of Power in Sanitary Improvement." Conder, F. R. Fraser 93:506 (1876). 49
"Water Analysis, The Interpretation of Sanitary." Davis, Floyd. Engng. M. 15:68 (April, 1898), Mun. Engng. 14:336 (June, 1898). 50
Women. "What Women have done for the Public Health." Thomson, Edith Parker. Forum 24:46 (Sept. 1897). 51
"Workingmen and Sanitation." Wingate, Charles F. Am. Fed. 4:6 (March, 1897). 52
———. "Working Conditions." White, Henry. Mun. Aff. 2:237 (June, 1898). 53

Santa Cruz, Cal.

"What a City has Done and is Doing." Lamb, W. H. Cal. Mun. 1:131 (Dec. 1899). 54

Santiago, Cuba.

"Government of Santiago, The." Kennan, George. Outlook 62:109 (May 13, 1899). 55
Sanitation. Cleaning of Santiago. Barbour, George M. Sanitarian 43:8 (July, 1899); Kennan, George. Outlook 61:871 (April 15, 1899); Engng. Rec. 40:689 (Dec. 23, 1899); Wood, Leonard. Scribners 25:515 (May, 1899). 56

"**Saratoga, N. Y.,** History of." Walworth, Ellen H. See 1-4b. 57

Savannah, Ga.
"History of Savannah, Ga." Stoval; Pleasant A. See 1-4c. 58
History, Description and Statistics of Savannah, Ga., in 1880. Census. See 1-7. 59

Savings Banks, Municipal. (Caisses d'Epargne, Sparkassen.)
See also France, Leipsic, Switzerland.
"Administration des Caisses d'Epargne." (Historique, Organisation, Legislation). Wallet, Paul. Paris, P. Dupont, 1886. 6 fr. 60
Communal Finances and Savings Banks. "Sparkassen u. Gemeindefinanzen, deren Gestaltung u. Einrichtung." Kuntze, Osc. Berlin, Heymann, 1882. 8vo, 176 pp. 2m. 50 pf. 61
"Das Sparkassenwesen in seiner Bedeutung für die Arbeiterwohlfahrt." (Schriften d. Zentralstellen für Arbeiterwohlfahrtseinrichtung, No. 6.) Berlin, 1895. 62
"Die Kontrole u. die sonstigen Hilfseinrichtung bei Sparkassen und Vorschussvereinen." Bahrt, A. F. Leipzig, Gloeckner, 1882. 8vo, 225 pp. 5m. 63
"Fortschritte in Sparkassenwesen." Böhmert, Vict. Berlin, Simion, 1882. 8vo, 55 pp. 1m. 64
"Guides des caisses d'épargne et de leur déposants." Armand, Léopold. Paris, Lahme, 2e édit., 1894. 3 fr. 65
"Les Caisses d'Epargne et de Prévoyance depuis leur origine jusqu'à nos jours." (Première partie; Histoire, Régime actuel, Projets de réforme, Opinion publique, Appréciations de différentes caisses d'épargne françaises, Aperçu de l'organisation des caisses etrangères. Deuxième partie: Legislations française et étrangères). Laurent, H. Pithiviers, Imprimerie des Caisses d'Epargnes, 1892. 2 vols. 8vo, 429 and 551 pp. 66
"Mécanisme, statuts et réglements des Institutions de Prévoyance, l'Economiste pratique." Cacheux, Emile. Paris, Baudry, 1884. 40 fr. 67
Postal Savings Banks. "Postsparkassen, 1. Tl. Geschichte u. Hauptresultate d. besteh. Postsparkassen." Grimm, Karl. Stuttgart, Strecker u. Moser, 1896. 8vo, 47 pp. 50 pf. 68
School Savings Banks. (See under **Schools**).

Schaffhausen, Switzerland, Electric Plant. "Das Elektrizitätswerk der Stadt Schaffhausen." Täuber, K. P. Schweiz. Bauz. June 4, 11, 18, 1898. 69

"**Schenectady, N. Y.,** History of." Landon, Judson S. See 1-4b. 70

School Systems of Cities.
See also Baltimore, Berlin, Boston, Buffalo, Chicago, Cincinnati, England under United Kingdom, France, Germany, Glasgow, Great Britain under United Kingdom, Indianapolis, Italy, London, Magdeburg, Manchester (Eng.), Milwaukee, Minneapolis, New York, Paris, Philadelphia, Providence, Prussia, St. Louis, St. Paul, United Kingdom, United States.

"Administration of City Schools." Marble, A. P. Educa. R. 8:154 (1894); Young, James T. Ann. Am. Acad. Pol. Sci. 15:171 (March, 1900). 71
"Architecture, Schools and School House." Gardner, E. C. Engin. M. 10:478 (1895). 72
"Art in the Public Schools." Whitman, Sarah W. Atlan. 79:617 (May, 1897). 73
——. "Decoration of Schools and School-Rooms." Haney, James P. Mun. Aff. 3:674 (Dec. 1899). 74
——. "Pictures for Our Public Schools." Van Rensselaer, M. G. Hrprs. Wkly. 41:1295 (Dec. 25, 1897); anon. Phila., Pub. Civic Club, 1895, 17 pp. 75
——. "School Sanitation and Decoration." Burrage, Severance, and Bailey, Henry Turner. Boston, D. C. Heath & Co., 1899. 12mo, 191 pp. Cloth, $1.50. 76
——. "Traveling Pictures and School-Room Decoration." Avery, Myrtilla. Bul. Univ. State of N. Y., Dec. 1900. 8vo, 430 pp. Paper, 50c. (A Bibliography.) 77
"Better City School Administration." De Weese, Truman A. Educa. R. 20:61 (June, 1900). 78
"Board, Destruction of the School." Clifford, J. Contemp. 66:626 (1894). 79
——. "Organization of City School Boards." Boykin, James C. Educa. R. March, 1897. 80
City School Systems. Draper, Andrew S. Forum 27:385 (June, 1899); Harris, Wm. T. Educa. R. 3:167 (1892); Hinsdale, B. A. Dial 25:251 (Oct. 16, 1898); anon. Dial 16:290 (1894); Gunton's 16:430 (June, 1899). 81

School Systems of Cities—*Continued.*

"Civic Instruction in Schools." Giles, Wm. A. City Govt. 2:74 (March, 1897).   82
——. "Public Schools and Good Citizenship." Skinner, Chas. R. Am. Mag. Civics 7:87 (1895).   83
——. "Gill School-City, The." Altruist, Vol. V, No. 4, p. 7 (Oct. 1897).   84
"Compulsory Education." Schaeffer, Nathan C., Miss Clare de Graffenreid and Mrs. Mary E. Mumford. Addresses delivered before the Civic Club of Philadelphia, March 21, 1896. Published by the Club. 15 pp.   85
"Continuous Sessions of Schools." Kirkpatrick, E. A. R. of Rs. 16:190 (Aug. 1897).   86
"Crowding of Public Schools, Criminal." Penniman, Jas. H. Forum 19:289, 20:547 (1896).   87
——. "Crowded Schools as Promoters of Disease." Chapin, H. D. Forum 19:296 (1895).   88
"Educational Conditions and Problems." White, A. D.; Higginson, T. W.; Hart, A. B. Educa. R. May, 1897.   89
——. "L'Enseignment primaire dans les pays civilizés." Levasseur, E. Paris, Berger-Levrault, 1897. 8vo, 638 pp. 15 fr.   90
——. "School Supervision." Pickard, J. L. New York, Appleton, 1890. 175 pp. $1.   91
——. "Unterrichtswesen." (Germany, Austria, Switzerland, France, England). Jolly, L. Pp. 937-1015 in Gustav Schönberg's "Handbuch d. Pol. Oekonomie," 3 Bd. Finanzwissenschaft. Tübingen, H. Laupp, 1885.   92
——. "Volkschulwesen." Silbergleit.. Pp. 955-976 2d supplement to 1st ed. of Conrad. See 2-10.   93
"Extension of the Public School System." Soc. Econ. 3:27, 159 (1892).   94
"Financial Relation of the Department of Education to the City Government, The." Rowe, L. S. Ann. Am. Acad. Pol. Sci. 15:186 (March, 1900).   95
"Gardens, School." Clapp, Henry Lincoln. Pop. Sci. Mo. 52:445-456 (Feb. 1898).   96
——. "School Gardens in Europe." Special Con. Rep., Vol. XX, part 2, 1900. 8vo, 221 pp.   97
——. "School Gardens and School Grounds." (Editorial). Garden and F. 10:171 (May 5, 1897).   98
"Higher Education, The Duties of the State and City to." Thomas, (Miss) M. Carey. Publications of the Civic Club, Philadelphia, 1895. 7 pp.   99
——. Municipal Public Universities. "Universités Populaires Municipales." Strauss, Paul. Revue Municipale 3:1657 (Oct. 28, 1899).   100
——. "Secondary School and College." Eliot, Charles W. Educa. R. May, 1897.   1
"Industrial Education." Eighth Annual Report of the Commissioner of Labor. Washington, Government Printing Office, 1893. 707 pp.   2
——. "Industrial Education." Dickie, George W. J. Assoc. Engng. Soc. 18:150 (March, 1897), Arch. & Buil. 26:251 (May 22, 1897); Thurston, R. H. Western Elec. April 24, 1897.   3
——. "Juvenile Crime, Industrial Schools and." Drew, A. A. W. Contemp. 63:732 (1893).   4
"Kindergartens, Why Municipalize." Kindergarten M. March, 1897.   5
——. "The Kindergarten." Cooper, Sarah B. p. 155 "International Congress," vol. V, 1893. See 43-99.   6
"Lock Step of the Public Schools, The." Shearer, William J. Atlan. 79:749 (June, 1897).   7
"Manual Training, Educational Value of." Chapin, T. F. Char. R. 6:335 (June, 1897).   8
"Meals, Provision of, at Public Schools." Chapter III, p. 194, "Some Poor Relief Questions," by Miss Gertrude Lubbock.   9
"Organization of School Systems of Cities." Draper, A. S., and others. Educa. R. 6:1 (1893), 9:304 (1895).   10
"Pensions for Teachers." Report of Commissioner of U. S. Bureau of Education, Vol. 1, p. 1079, 1894-5.   11
——. "Teachers' Pensions: The Story of a Women's Campaign." Allen, Elizabeth A. R. of Rs. 15:700 (June, 1897).   12
"Play Grounds for City Schools." Riis, J. A. Cent. 48:657 (1894). (See also under **Parks.**)   13
"Politics, How to Free Public Schools from." Rice, J. M. Forum 16:500 (1893).   14

School Systems of Cities—*Continued.*

——. "The Politician and the Public School." Jones, L. H. Atlan. June, 1896. 15

Progress. "Improvement in City Life, II." Robinson, Charles Mulford. Atlan. 83:654 (May, 1899). 16

"Public Health, Relation of the Public Schools to." Caverly, C. S. Sanitarian 41:289 (Oct. 1898). 17

"Ragged School Union." Besant, W. Contemp. 65:688 (1894). 18

Sanitation, School. Beitzell, A. J. Public Health 5:2 (Nov. 1900); Dearness, J., and McKeough, G. T. p. 96 and 113 Assn. Ex. Hlth. Officers of Ont., IXth Meeting, 1894; Gerhard, Wm. Paul. Arch. & Buil. 26:67 (Feb. 6, 1897); Stewart, D. H. Forum. 20:103 (1895); anon. Engng. Rec. April 25, May 2, 1891; Dom. Engng. June, 1896; Sanitarian 38:505 (June, 1897), 11:432 (May, 1898). 19

——. "Heating School Buildings by Gas." Progressive Age 15:34 (Jan. 15, 1897). 20

——. "Hygienic Demands for School Buildings." Sloan, A. M. Sanitarian 38:297 (April, 1897). 21

——. "Infectious Disease in Schools, Hints to Teachers Regarding." Macdonald, C. R. San. Rec. 19:625 (June 25, 1897). 22

——. School Ventilation. Dearness. John. p. 63, Proc. Assoc. Ex. Hlth Officers of Ont., XIVth Meeting, 1899; Woodbridge, S. H. San. Plumb. April 15, 1897; anon. San. 38:507 (June, 1897). 23

"Savings Banks, School." Oberholtzer, Sara Louisa. Ann. Am. Acad. Pol. Sci. 3:14 (1893). Separate, paper, 15 cts. Note on same subject. Ann. Am. Acad. Pol. Sci. 4:972 (1894); City Govt. 2:76 (March, 1897). 24

——. "Jugend u. Schulsparkassen." Senckel, Ernst. Frankfurt a/O., Harnecker u. C. 2m. 25 pf. 25

——. "Savings Bank, The, as a Public School of Primary Economic Instruction." Trenholm, William L. Bank. M. 54:860 (June, 1897). 26

——. "School Savings Banks—Their Growth in France." de Malarce, A. Bank. M. (N. Y.) 55:211 (Aug. 1897). 27

"Science in the Schools." Davis, W. M. Educa. R. (N. Y.) May, 1897. 28

"State Education at Home and Abroad." Martin, J. W. London, Fabian Soc., 1894. Fabian Tract, No. 52. 15 pp. 1d. 29

Vacation Schools. American, Sadie. Ind. 51:1499 (June 1, 1899), Commons March 1898, Am. J. Sociol. 4:309 (Nov. 1898); Robinson, Charles M. Educa. R. (N. Y.) 17:250 (March, 1899); Stewart, Seth T. Outlook 62:798 (Aug. 5, 1899); Tolman, Wm. H. Park & Outdoor Art Assn. p. 108, 1897-8; anon. Ann. Am. Acad. Pol. Sci. 13:419 (May, 1894). 30

Schwerin, Ger., Improvement.
"Der Erweiterungs- und Verschönerungsplan der Residenzstadt Schwerin in seiner Entstehung und geschichtlich actenmässigen Entwickelung von 1862 bis Ende August des Jahres 1866 mitgetheilt." Demmier, G. A. Schwerin, 1867. 31

Scotland.
(See under **United Kingdom**.)

Scutari.
Water Supply. "Die Wasserversorgung von Skutari und Kadikoi." Friedrich, Adolf. Oesterr. Monatschr. f. d. Oeffent. Baudienst July, 1899. 32

Seattle, Wash.
"Municipal Condition of Seattle." Graves, E. O. p. 439, Proc. Second Natl. Conf. for Good City Govt. 1895. See 6-18b. 33

——. "Seattle." Brainard, Erastus. Hrprs. Wkly. 41:1127 (Nov. 18, 1897); Colver, Henry Clay. Frank Leslie's June, 1898; Howard, William Willard, Hrprs. Wkly. 35:426 (1891); Praft, J. W. New Eng. M. n. s. 8:292 (1893). 34

"Street Railways of Seattle, Wash." St. Ry. Jour. May, 1893, p. 311. 35

"Waterways, The New, and Land Reclamation at Seattle, Wash." Engng. News 37:333 (May 27, 1897).

Seoul,
Electric Railroads in." Allen, Horace N. Cons. Rep. 57:63 (May, 1898). 36

Separation of Municipal from National and State Elections.
(See under **Elections**.)

Servia, Local and Municipal Government in. Demombynes. Vol. I, pp. 727-735. See 2-11.   37

Settlement Movement; College, Social and University Settlements.

See also Baltimore, Boston, Buffalo, Cambridge (Mass.), Chicago, Cleveland, Des Moines, England under United Kingdom, Glasgow, Japan, Jersey City, London, Los Angeles, New York, San Francisco, Philadelphia, Pittsburg, Toronto, United Kingdom, United States, Walworth.

Andover House. (See Settlements under **Boston.**)

"Bibliography of College, Social and University Settlements." Jones, M. Katharine. 54 pp. 10 cts. For sale at 95 Rivington St., New York City. 1st edition, 1893; 2d, 1895.   38

———. "Bibliography of College, Social and University Settlements." Gavit, John Palmer. (3d Edition of above.) Cambridge Co-operative Press, 1897. Pamphlet, 74 pp. Gratis.   39

———. "Bibliography of College, Social, University and Church Settlements." Montgomery, Caroline Williamson. (4th edition of above). Compiled for the College Settlements Association. Printed in New York, 1900. Pamphlet, 68 pp. 10 cts.   40

"Church to the Settlement, The Relation of the." Gordon, Clarence. Commons Vol. 2, No. 7, p. 1 (Nov. 1897).   41

———. "The Church and the Settlement." Gavit, John P. Commons Vol. 3, No. 1, p. 3 (May, 1898).   42

"College Settlements Association." Outlook Dec. 29, 1894.

———. "Les 'College Settlements.'" Cremnitz, M. Revue Philanthropique Oct. 10, 1897.   43

Commons, Chicago. (See Settlements under **Chicago**).

"Denison, Edward." Green, John Richard. Macmillan's M. Sept. 1871.   44

———. "Letters and other Writings of Edward Denison." Leighton, Baldwin (Editor). London, Bentley, 1875. 16mo, 3s. 6d.   45

"Experiment in Altruism, An." (Social Settlement Movement). Hastings, Elizabeth. New York, Macmillan, 1895. 215 pp. 75c.   46

"Function of the Social Settlement, A." Addams, Jane. Ann. Am. Acad. Pol. Sci. 13:323-345 (May, 1899).   47

"Future of the Social Settlement." Elliott, J. L. Ethical Record Dec. 1899.   48

Hull House. (See Settlements under **Chicago**).

"Idea of University Settlements." Woods, Robert A. Andover R. 18:317 (1892). (See also Chap. III, p. 57, "Philanthropy and Social Progress," same subject).   49

"Labor Question, Social Settlements and the." Addresses by leading American Settlement Workers at 23d Nat'l Conf. of Charities and Corrections, Grand Rapids, June, 1896. Published separately by The Commons, Chicago. 25c. (See also **Labor and the Municipality**).   50

"Misrepresentations of Settlement Work." Outlook 57:389 (Oct. 9, 1897).

"Missions and Settlements." Gavit, John P. Commons Vol. II, No. 10, p. 3, Feb. 1898).   51

———. "The Ways of Settlements and Missions." Barnett, S. A. 19th Cent. 42:978 (Dec. 1897), Ecl. M. 130:189 (Feb. 1898).   52

"Municipal Reform, Social and College Settlements of America and their Relation to." Alden, Percy. Outlook 51:1090 (1895).   53

"Necessity for Social Settlements, Objective." Addams, Jane. Chap. II, p. 27, "Philanthropy and Social Progress." "Subjective Necessity," Chap. I. See also Forum 14:345 (1892), by same author.   54

"Neighboring Guilds." Coit, Stanton. London, Swan S. & Co., 1891. 150 pp. 2s. 6d. Reviewed by Edward King in Char. R. 1:77 (1891).   55

"Philanthropy and Social Progress." Adams, Henry C., editor. New York, T. Y. Crowell & Co., 1893. 268 pp. $1.50. Essays by Jane Addams and R. A. Woods on Social Settlements.   56

"Place of University Settlements." Scudder, V. D. Andover R. 18:339 (1892).   57

"Plan of Social University." Swift, Morrison I. Ashtabula, O., Chas. H. Golluth, printer, 20c.   58

"Politics, Settlement Houses and City." Woods, Robert A. Mun. Aff. 4:395 (June, 1900).   59

Settlement Movement—*Continued.*

"Report on the Questions drawn up by Present Residents in our College Settlements and Submitted to Past Residents." Reprinted for the College Settlements Association, 1897. Pamphlet, 24 pp. 60

"Scientific Aspect of University Settlements." Perrine, F. A. C. Science 21:91 (1893). 61

Settlement Work, Discussion of. Char. R. 4:462 (June, 1895).

"Social Amelioration and the University Settlement." McLean, S. J. Can. M. April, 1897. 62

"Socialism, The Settlement and." Foster, Maud B. Commons Vol. IV, No. 1, p. 3, May, 1899. 63

"Social Settlements." Henderson, C. R. New York, Lentilhon & Co., 1899. 16mo, 196 pp. Cl. 50c. Also see Hanson, J. M. The Kingdom (St. Paul), Sept. 27, 1895. 64

——. "Social Settlements and the Civic Sense." Campbell, Helen. Arena 20:589 (Nov.-Dec. 1898). 65

"Tenement Neighborhood Idea, University Settlement." Moore, Helen. P. 35, "The Literature of Philanthropy." edited by Francis A. Goodale. 66

"Toynbee, Arnold." Addams, Herbert. Char. R. 1:12 (Nov. 1891); Gilman, (Mrs.) M. R. F. Lend a H. 4:330 (1889); Montague, F. C. J. H. Univ. Studies VII:1. 70 pp. (1889). (The appendix contains a paper on the New York Neighborhood Guild by Chas. B. Stover). 67

——. "Arnold Toynbee, a Reminiscence." Milner, Alfred. London, Edw. Arnold & Co., 1895. 8vo. Cl. 2s. 6d. 68

Toynbee Hall. (See Settlements under **London**).

"Trained Workers for the Poor." Hill, Octavia. 19th Cent. Jan. 1893. 69

"Universities and the Poor." Barnett, S. A. 19th Cent. 15:255 (1884). 70

"Universities and the Social Problem, University Settlements in East London." Knapp, J. M. London, Rivington, 1895. 235 pp. 71

University Settlements. Barnett, S. A. 19th Cent. 38:1015 (1895), Chaut. 18:393 (Jan. 1894); Cummings, E. Q. J. Econ. 6:257 (1892); Ecl. M. 63:183 (Feb. 1896); Freeman, H. F. Lend a H. 5:154 (1890); Gulick, Sydney L. Chap. III, in "The Growth of the Kingdom of God." N. Y., Revell, 1897. 12mo, cloth, $1.50; Woods, R. A. Chap. III, p. 79 "English Social Movements"; anon. Gunton's M. 10:429 (1896). 72

——. "University Settlements, their Point and Drift." Woods, Robert A. Q. J. Econ. 14:167 (Nov. 1899). 73

——. "University Settlements and the Social Question." Davies, Henry. Self-Cult. 10:21 (Sept. 1899). 74

——. "University and Social Settlements." Reason, W. London, Methuen & Co., 1898. 12mo, 195 pp. Cloth, $1. 75

"Value of the Social Settlements, Scientific." Hegner, Herman F. Am. J. Sociol. 3:171 (Sept. 1897), R. of Rs. 16:469 (Oct. 1897). 76

"Women's University Settlements." Talbot, M. Econ. R. 5:489 (1895). 77

"Working Population of Cities and what the Universities Owe them." Swift, M. I. Andover R. 13:589 (1890). 78

Sewage Disposal, Sewerage Systems. (See also **Sanitation** and **Water Supplies**).

See also Acton, Aldershot, Alliance, Altoona, Amsterdam, Antwerp, Atlanta, Austin, Baltimore, Berlin, Birmingham, Bolton, Bordeaux, Boston, Brocton, Bradford (Eng.), Bremen, Brookfield (Mo.), Brussels, Budapest, Bury (Eng.), Calcutta, Cambridge (Eng.), Canada, Canton, Cardiff (Wales), Central Falls, Charlottenburg, Chautauqua, Chicago, Chichester, Cincinnati, Cleveland, Clinton, Cohoes, Cologne, Concord, Connecticut, Constantinople, Copenhagen, Depew (N. Y.), Dresden, Dublin, Edinburgh, England under United Kingdom, Exeter, Florence, Frankfort a. M., Germany, Ghent, Glasgow, Gothenberg, Great Britain under U. K., Hale (Eng.), Hamburg, Hamilton (Ont.), Hampton (Eng.), Hanley, Havana, Havre, Indiana, Indianapolis, Karachi, Kewanee (Ill.), Kingston, Königsberg, Lawrence (Mass.), Leeds, Leicester, Leith, Liberty, Liverpool, Lincoln, London, London (Ont.), Lyons, Madison (Wis.), Madrid, Manchester (Eng.), Marion, Marseilles, Massachusetts, Medford, Melbourne, Memphis, Mendota, Mexico, Milwaukee, Montreal, Munich, New Jersey, New Orleans, Newton, New York, Nice, Nottingham, Nuremberg, Oberlin, Oldham, Oswestry,

Sewage Disposal—*Continued.*

Ottawa, Overbrook (N. Y.), Paris, Paris (Texas). Pasadena (Cal.), Passaic Valley (N. J.), Peoria, Philadelphia, Plainfield, Providence, Pullman, **Reading,** Reigate, Rhode Island, Rhyl (Wales), Rome, Rotterdam, St. Gall, St. Louis, St. Petersburg, Salt Lake City, San Francisco, Sheffield, Shipley, Southampton, Sutton, Spandau, Staines (Eng.), Stettin, Stockholm, Tampico, Toronto, Trieste, United Kingdom, United States, Victoria, Vienna, Walsall, **Washington,** Wilmington, Wimbledon, Wolverhampton, Woonsocket (R. I.), Worcester, Zurich.

"Analysis, Sewage; A Practical Treatise on the Examination of Sewage and Effluents from Sewage; including a Chapter on Utilization and Purification." Wanklyn, Alfred J.; Cooper, W. J. London, Paul, 1899. 8vo, 232 pp. Cl. $2. **79**

——. "Practical Hints on the Analysis of Water and Sewage." Barwise, S. Public Health July, 1899. **80**

"Assessments, Sewer." Snow, F. Herbert. J. Assn. Engng. Soc. 18:1 (Jan. 1897), 18:189 (March, 1897); anon. Mun. Engng. 14:38 (Jan. 1898). **82**

——. "Municipal Sewage Systems and Assessments." Bouton, George T. Mun. Engng. 19:203 (Sept. 1900). **83**

Bacterial Treatment of Sewage. Adams, S. H. Surveyor 18:560 (Nov. 16, 1900); Clowes, Frank, Nature 62:128 (June 7, 1900), San. Rec. 24:371 (Oct. 27, 1899); Dibdin, W. J. and Thudichum, George. Engng. Rec. 38:404 (Oct. 8, 1898); Dibdin, W. J. Sanitary Rec. (London) Dec. 11, 1896; Fletcher, Robert. San. Rec. 25:440 (May 25, 1900); Hering, Rudolph. Engng. M. 15:960 (Sept. 1898); Martin, Arthur J. San. Rec. 23:122, 138, 163, 179, 206 (Feb. 10 to March 10, 1899); Owen, James. Engng. Rec. 40:669 (Dec. 16, 1899); Rideal, Samuel. San. Rec. 23:48, 67, 117 (Jan. 20-Feb. 10, 1899), J. Soc. of Arts 46:81 (Dec. 17, 1897), 47:683, 695, 707, 719 (July 7-28, 1899); Scoble, H. T. Sanitarian 44:298 (April, 1900); Talbot, Arthur N. Mun. Engng. 16:158 (March, 1899); anon. Engng. Dec. 9, 1898, 68:462 (Oct. 13, 1899); Eng. Rec. 38:33, 185, 561 (June 11, July 30, Nov. 26, 1898), 39:97 (Dec. 31, 1898), 39:229 (Feb. 11, 1899), 40:167, 195, 476 (July 22, 29, Oct. 21, 1899), 41:319 (April 7, 1900); Mun. J. & London 8:1146 (Oct. 20, 1899); Eng. (London) 89:530 (May 25, 1900); San. Rec. 25:466 (June 1, 1900). **84**

"Bibliography of House Drainage, Plumbing Work and Sewage Disposal for Houses." Gerhard, Wm. Paul. New York, 1897. Leaflet, 3 pp. **85**

"Cesspool, The." Kinnicutt, Leonard P. Mun. Engng. 19:99 (Aug. 1900). **86**

"Chemical Treatment of Sewage, Analysis and the." Kinnicutt, Leonard P. Engng. News 41:294 (May 11, 1899). **87**

——. "Treatment of Sewage by Chemicals in perfect solution." (Proposed treatment at Oldham). Law, Herbert Henry. Sanitary Plumber (N. Y.) Dec. 1, 1897. **88**

"Civilization, Sewage and." Railroad Gaz. 31:504 (July 14, 1899).

"Cleaning and Sewerage of Cities." Baumeister, R. Adopted from the German with the permission of the author by J. M. Goodell. New York, Engineering News Pub. Co., 1891. 291 pp. $2.50. **89**

"Cleaning Sewers." Fletcher, Elmer D. Engng. Rec. 41:328 (April 7, 1900). **90**

——. "Cleaning, Catch-Basins and Sewers." Folwell, Prescott A. Engng. Rec. 41:563 (June 16, 1900), **91**

——. "Systems of Sewer Flushing and Suggestions on Flush-Tank Design and Construction." Rosewater, Andrew. Engin. News 37:275 (May 6, 1897). **92**

"Coal, Filtration of Sewage through." Allen, Kenneth. Mun. Engng. 14:333 (June, 1898); Hill, A. Bostwick. Mun. Eng. 14:29 (Jan. 1898); Hill, A. Bostwick, and Garfield, Joseph. Engng. Rec. 41:101 (Feb. 3, 1900); anon. Mun. Engng. 14:248 (May, 1898). **93**

Coke in Sewage Purification. Alvard, John W. Prog. Age 16:394 (August 15, 1898); Clowes, Frank. Am. Gas Light J. 71:812 (Nov. 20, 1899); anon. J. Gas Lgt. 74:998 (Oct. 24, 1899). **94**

"Combined Drainage: Its Pros and Cons." Priestley, Joseph. Sanitarian 42:32 (Jan. 1899). **95**

——. "Combined and Separate Systems of Sewerage, A Comparison of the." Collins, C. P. Mun. Engng. 15:222 (Oct. 1898). (See also Separate Systems below). **96**

"Construction and Maintenance, Sewer." Engng. Rec. 40:74 (June 24, 1899).

——. "Cost and Construction of Thirty-five Sewerage Systems." Engng. Rec. Oct. 24, 1891, p. 331; Engng. News Oct. 24, 1891, p. 397. **97**

——. "Experience in Sewer Construction." Hastings, L. M. J. Assoc. Engng. 22:84 (March, 1899). **98**

"Damages for Inadequate Sewerage Works." Engng. Rec. 38:287 (Sept. 3, 1898).

Sewage Disposal—*Continued.*

"Death Rate in Cities, Influence of Sewerage and Water Supply on the." Smith, Erwin F. Supplement Michigan Board of Health Report for 1885. 168 pp. — 99

"Designing, Construction and Maintenance of Sewerage Systems." Folwell, A. Prescott. London, Chapman & Hall, 1898. 8vo, 372 pp. Cl. $3. New York, Wiley & Sons, 1900. 3d ed., 8vo, 445 pp. Cl. $3. — 100

"Designs of Town Sewerage Schemes, Some Consideration on the." Wood, Frank. Eng. (London) Nov. 12, 1897. — 1

——. "New Units in the Design of Sewers." Engng. Rec. 39:369 (March 25, 1899). — 2

"Dilution Process of Sewage Disposal, The." Hering, Rudolph. Engng. M. 15:575 (July 1898); anon. San Rec. 22:187 (Aug. 19, 1898), 22:215 (Aug. 26, 1898). — 3

"Drainage." Park & Cem. 9:30 (April 1899).

——. "Sewerage and Drainage of Cities." Waring, G. E. Am. Arch. 6:197 (1879). — 4

——. "The Sanitary Drainage of Houses and Towns." Waring, Geo. E., Jr. New York, Hurd & Houghton, 1876. 12mo, 336 pp. $2. — 5

"Effluent from Sewage Precipitation Works, Treatment of the." Allen, Kenneth. Mun. Engng. 13:125 (Sept. 1897). — 6

"Estuaries, The Disposal of Sewage in." Woodhead, G. Sims. J. San. Inst. 19:2 (Apr. 1898). — 7

Europe, Sewage Disposal in. Billings, J. S. Engng. Rec. Nov. 10, 1894; Hazen, Allen. J. Assoc. Engng. Soc. 15:216 (1895); Engng. News Mar. 27, 1886, Trans. Am. Soc. Civ. Eng. Dec. 1886. See also 56-40a, 40b. — 8

"Evolution of a Sewage System, The." Martin, Arthur J. San Rec. 25:492 (June 8, 1900). — 9

"Excavation, Sewer." Crowell, Foster. Pub. Imp. 1:38 (June 1, 1899). — 10

"Excreta, The Removal of." Maxwell, William H. San Rec. 20:492 (Nov. 5, 1897). — 11

"Experiments, Important Sewage Disposal." Reid, George. San. Rec. 25:267 (Mar. 30, 1900), 25:292 (April 6, 1900), 25:314 (April 13, 1900). — 12

Farming, Sewage. Disposal of Sewage by Irrigation. Campbell, A. W. Mun. World 7:201 (Oct. 1897); Carpenter, A. J. Soc. Arts. Feb. 4, 1887; Dibdin, W. J. San Rec. 21:335 (April 1, 1898); Garrett, J. H. San. Rec. Aug. 28, 1896; Janin, George. San. 45:193 (Sept. 1900); Waring, Geo. E. Engng. News Feb. 15, 1894; Watson, W. M. Can. Eng. 6:151 (Oct. 1898); anon. Am. Arch. 18:297 (1885); Engng. News Feb. 23, 1893, pp. 180, 183. — 13

——. "Die Förderung d. Hygiene u. d. Beseitigung städtischer Kanalwasser durch Berieselung." Degener, P. Frankfurt a. M., Jaeger, 1894. 8vo. 26 pp. 1m. — 14

——. "Sewage Irrigation in Europe and America." Roechling, H. Alfred. Sanitary Record (London), Dec. 4, 1896. — 15

Filtration of Sewage. Crane, Albert S. Mun. Engng. 14:126 (Mar. 1898); Law, Henry. San. Rec. Nov. 20, 1896; Reid, G. Builder 73:7 (July 3, 1897); Van Buskirk, W. F. Mun. World 9:114 (July 1899). (See also Coal and Coke above.) — 16

Flushing Devices, Flushing of Sewers. Phillips, Asa E. Pro. Am. Soc. Mun. Imp. (5th yr.) Pt. II, p. 70 (Oct. 1898), City Govt. 5:184 (Nov. 1898), Engng. Rec. 38:516 (Nov. 12, 1898), Mun. Engng. 16:24 (Jan. 1899); Rosewater, Andrew. Engng. News 37:275 (May 6, 1897); anon. Engng. Rec. 38:551 (Nov. 26, 1898). — 17

Foreign Countries, Sewage Disposal in. See 56-40a, 40b.

"Future of the Sewage Question, The." Willoughby, Edward F. San. Rec. 20:305 (Sept. 17, 1897). — 18

——. "Future Methods of Sewage Disposal." Hedenberg, W. L. Engng. M. 10:76 (1895). — 19

"Gases in Sewers, The Effective Prevention and Dissemination of Noxious." Latham, Frank. San. Rec. 22:105 (July 29, 1898). — 20

"House Drainage and Sewerage." Sanitarian 42:26 (Jan. 1899). — 21

——. "Construction and Ventilation of House Drains." Hill, A. Bostock. Sanitarian 42:28 (Jan. 1899). — 22

"Inland Sewage Disposal." Bassett, C. Ph. Trans. Am. Soc. Civ. Engrs. 25:125 (1891). — 23

Irrigation, Disposal of Sewage by. (See under Farming, Sewage, above.)

"Lectures on Water Supply, Sewerage and Sewage Utilization." Corfield, W. H. London, Spon, 1874. Paper, $1.00. — 24

"Liernur System of Sewerage and SewageTreatment, The." City Govt. 7:90 (Oct. 1899). — 25

Sewage Disposal—*Continued*.

"Maintenance, Sewer." Parmley, W. C. J. Assoc. Engng. Soc. 24:370 (June, 1900), Mun. Engng. 19:109 (Aug. 1900).   **26**

"Manufacturing Wastes, The Relation of, to the Sewerage Problem." Engng. News 41:334 (May 25, 1899).   **27**

Pipe. "Dimensions of Sewer Pipe." Thompson, A. D. Mun. Engng. 14:123 (Mar. 1898).   **28**

——. "A Steel Street Sewer." Engng. Rec. 37:388 (April 2, 1898).

——. "The Strength of Sewer Pipe and the Actual Earth Pressure in Trenches." Barbour, Frank A. J. Assoc. Engng. Soc. 19:193 (Dec. 1897).   **29**

Poudrette. "Die Verwandlung der Faeces in Poudrette." Vogel. Gesund. Ing. March 15, 1897.   **30**

"Principles of Drainage and Sewerage." Dom. Engng. Aug. 15, 1900.   **31**

Purification of Sewage, General Articles on. Barrow, E. G. Can. Eng. 6:121 (Sept. 1898), City Govt. 5:192 (Nov. 1898); Brix. Gesund. Ing. Jan. 15, 1898; Dibdin, W. J. San. Rec. (serial) 19:334 et seq. to 20:164 (1897); Herman, E. A. Mun. Engng. 19:195 (Sept. 1900), Cal. Mun. 3:49 (Sept. 1900); Janin, George. Can. Soc. Civ. Eng. April 12, 1900; Lowcock, Sidney R. Surveyor 18:300 (Sept. 14, 1900); Parry, W. Kaye. Builder Sept. 3, 1898, City Govt. 8:7 (Jan. 1900); Rideal, S. San. Rec. (serial) 24:414 (Nov. 10, 1899), et seq to 25:154 (Feb. 23, 1900); Thomson, Gilbert. Arch. & Cont. Rep. 58:25 (Sept. 3, 1897), San. Rec. 20:284 (Sept. 10, 1897), San J. 4:350 (Sept. 1897); Thudichum, George. San. Rec. Dec. 18, 1896; anon. Gesund. Ing. Jan. 15, 1897; Oesterr, Monatschr. f. d. öffent. Baudienst May 1897; Ed. R. No. 385, p. 151 (July 1898).   **32**

——. "Natural Purification of Sewage." Mills, Hiram F. Lend a H. Sept. 1890.   **33**

——. "The Purification of Sewage and Wated." Dibdin, W. J. London, Sanitary Pub. Co., 1898, 2d ed. pp. 292. 8vo. Cl., $8.40.   **34**

——. "The Purification of Sewage: Being a Brief Account of the Scientific Principles of Sewage Purification, and their Practical Application." Barwise, Sidney. London, 1899. 12mo. Cl., $2.00.   **35**

——. "Sewerage and Sewage Purification." Baker, M. N. New York, D. Van Nostrand Co., 1896. 16mo, 144 pp. 50 cts.   **36**

——. "Standard of Purity for Sewage Effluents." Rideal, S. San. Rec. 22:320 (Sept. 23, 1898).   **37**

——. "Still Another Purifying Box." Butterworth, Irvin. Prog. Age 16:151 (Apr. 1, 1898).   **38**

"Rainfall and Run-Off in Relation to Sewerage Problems." Parmley, Walter C. J. Assoc. Eng. Soc. 20:204 (March 1898).   **39**

"Recently Improved Methods of Sewage Disposal." Johnson, John Butler. Bull. Univ. Wis., June 1900, Municipality vol. 1, no. 4, p. 1 (Oct. 1900), vol. 1, no. 5, p. 1 (Dec. 1900).   **40**

"Regulations as to Sewers and Drains." Stephens, J. E. R. San. Rec. 23:535 (June 23, 1899).   **41**

"Reports, Proposed Form for Sewer." Pro. Am. Soc. Mun. Imp. (5th yr.) Pt. II, p. 205 (Oct. 1898).   **42**

"River Pollution." Flower, Lamorock. J. San. Inst. 18:317 (Oct. 1897).   **43**

——. "Pollution of Running Streams by Sewage." Tooke, C. W. Mun. Engng. 19:87 (Aug. 1900).   **44**

——. "Sewage Disposal Works. Guide to the Construction of Works for the Prevention of the Pollution by Sewage of Rivers and Estuaries." Crimp, W. Santo. London, 1894. $7.50.   **45**

——. "Stream Contamination and Sewage Purification." McMath, R. E., and others. Pro. Am. Soc. Civil Engineers 25:405 (Aug. 1899).   **46**

——. "Streams and Sewage." Mun. & Ry. Rec. 5:317 (Dec. 15, 1899).   **47**

"Roots, Injuries to Sewers by." Engng. Rec. 38:251 (Aug. 20, 1898).

"Rural Districts, The Disposal of Sewage in." Stott, H. Public Health, Sept. 1899.   **48**

——. "Sewerage Purification in Rural Districts." Davenport, J. Aldersey. San. Rec. 20:553 (Nov. 1900).   **49**

"Sand Filters, The Somersworth, N. H." Engng. Rec. 38:271 (Aug. 27, 1898).

"Sanitary Sewerage." Griggs, Julian. City Govt. 6:28 (Feb. 1899).   **50**

——. "Perfect Sewerage and Perfect Health." Morrison, W. R.; Sinclair, Graham M. San. Plumb. May 1, 1899; Meyer, Louis F. San. Plumb. April 15, 1899; Wade, James J. Dom. Engng. April, 1899.   **51**

Sewage Disposal—*Continued.*

———. "Report of the Committee on Sewerage and Sanitation." Eldridge, W. K. Mun. Engng. 19:192 (Sept. 1900). 52

Sceptic Tanks. (See Bacteriological Treatment above.)

"Scott-Moncrieff System of Sewage Disposal, The." Eng. (London) 89:90 (Jan. 26, 1900).

"Sedimentation Process in Sewage Disposal, The." Talbot, Arthur N. San. Rec. 20:172 (Aug. 13, 1897). 53

"Separate System of Sewerage." Staly, Cady, and G. S. Pierson. New York, Van Nostrand, 1891. 281 pp. 54

———. "Advantages of the Separate Sewage System." Watson, W. M. Can. Eng. 5:188 (Nov. 1897). 55

———. "Ueber Trennungssysteme." Gesundheits Ingenieur 20:241 (Aug. 15, 1897). 56

———. "Sewerage and Health." Mailler-Kendall, Theo. San. Rec. 25:111, 152, 176, 201 (Feb. 9, Feb. 23, March 2, March 9, 1900). 57

Sewage Disposal, General articles on. Andrews, Elmer L. Mun. Engng. 16:73 (Feb. 1899); Bazalgette, C. M. Eng. M. 17:106, 213 (1877); Billings, John S. Hrprs. 71:577 (1885); Blyth, A. W. Engng. Times, May, June, July, 1900; Cannell, C. S. San. Rec. March 20, 1896; Flagg, J. Foster. Pav. & Mun. Engng. 5:1 (1893); Francis, Charles. Fire & W. 22:258 (July 31, 1897), Mun. Engng. 13:340 (Dec. 1897); Fuertes, James H. Pro. 24th An. Meeting N. J. Sanitary Assn., 1898, p. 69; Garstang. Sanitarian 44:487 (June, 1900); Grunsky, C. E. Sanitarian 11:289 (April, 1898); Hering, Rudolph. Engng. M. 8:1007 (1895); Hill, G. Everett. Pp. 138-141 Pro. 3rd An. Conv. of the League of Am. Mun., 1899. 8vo, 148 pp., Public Imp. 1:268 (Oct. 1, 1899), City Govt. 7:89 (Oct. 1899), Cal. Mun. 1:139 (Dec. 1899); Horetska, Charles. Can. Eng. 5:157 (Oct. 1898); Hosmer, G. W. Hrprs. Wkly 34:565 (1890); La Ruse, Benj. F. Sci. Am. Sup. June 11, 1898; McClintock, John N. Pub. Imp. 3:319 (May 15, 1900); McKellar, P. D. p. 70, Assoc. Ex. Health Officers of Ont. 1894; Mansergh, James. Surveyor 18:538 (Nov. 9, 1900); Marston, A. Engng. Rec. 41:177 (Feb. 24, 1900); Mitchell, S. A. J. Assn. Engng. Soc. 12:463 (1893); Waring, George E. 47:939 (1894); Watson, W. M. Can. Eng. March, 1897; anon. Engng. Rec. 38:1 (June 4, 1898); San. Rec. 22:139 (Aug. 5, 1898); Engng. Rec. 38:310 (Sept. 10, 1898). 58

———. "A Digest of Facts Relating to the Treatment and Utilization of Sewage." Corfield, W. H. London, Macmillan, 2d ed., 1871. 8vo, 343 pp. 10s. 6d. 59

———. "Menschliche Exkremente in national-ökonomischer, hygienischer, finanzieller u. landwirtschaftlicher Beziehung." Heiden, E. Hannover, Cohen, 1882. 8vo, 96 pp. 1m. 50pf. 60

———. "Modern Methods of Sewage Disposal for Towns, Public Institutions and Isolated Houses." Waring, G. E. New York, D. Van Nostrand & Co. 253 pp. $2.00. 61

———. "On Sewage Treatment and Disposal for Cities, Towns, Villages, Private Dwellings." Wardle, Thomas. Manchester, 1893. 8vo, ill. Cl. $6. 62

———. "Sewage Disposal." Kiersted, Wynkoop. New York, Wiley & Sons, 1894. 106 pp. 12mo, cl. $1.25. 63

———. "Sewage and Sewage Disposal." Robinson, H. New York, Spon & Chamberlain, 1896. 8vo, 192 pp. Cl. $4.50. 64

———. "Sewage Question." Fergus, Andrew. Glasgow, Porteous Bros., 1872. 34 pp., 1s. 65

———. "Sewage Treatment, Purification and Utilization." Slater, J. W. London, 1897. 12mo, cl. $2.25. 66

Sewer Systems. "Kanalisation und Abfuhr." Vogel, J. H. Pp. 522-532, 1st supplement to 1st ed. Conrad. See 2-10. 67

———. "De l'Application du tout-a-l'Egout." Le Génie Civil Oct. 9, 1897. 68

———. "L'Epandage des Eaux d'Egout." Rendu, Ambroise. Revue Municipale 3:1689 (Nov. 11, 1899). 69

———. "Untersuchungen zur Kanalisation." Soyka, I. München, Oldenbourg, 1885. 4m. 70

"Sludge Disposal, The Problem of Sewage." Hedenberg, W. L. Mun. Engng. 18:10 (Jan. 1900). 71

———. "Illuminating Gas from Sewage Sludge." J. Gas Light 76:1140 (Nov. 6, 1900), Am. Gas Light J. 73:851 (Nov. 26, 1900). 72

———. "Sewage Sludges." Engng. Rec. 39:209 (Feb. 4, 1899).

———. "The Conversion of Sludge into Fuel." San. Rec. 20:474 (Oct. 29, 1897).

Sewage Disposal—*Continued.*

"Small Cities, Sewers for." Phillips, Alfred E. Wisconsin Eng. (Madison, Wis.) Jan, 1897. ... 73

——. "Economical Sewage Purification for Small Communities." Fletcher, Robert. Public Improvements 2:172 (Feb. 15, 1900). ... 74

——. "Sewerage and Sewage Disposal of a Small Town." Savage, E. B. London, Biggs, 1895. 8vo, cl. $2.00. ... 75

——. "Village Sewerage Schemes." Cox. J. San. Inst. 20:33 (April, 1899). ... 76

"Storm-Water Sewers, Notes on." Engng. Rec. 38:379 (Oct. 1, 1898). ... 77

——. "A Graphical Method for Determining the Capacity of Storm-Water Sewers." Burns, Clinton S. Engineering Journal (Stanford Univ.) May, 1897. ... 78

——. "The Provision for Storm Water in Sewage Purification Work." Martin, A. J. Engng. News 42:327 (Nov. 16, 1899). ... 79

"Supervision of Sewerage Work, The." Engng. Rec. 37:269 (Feb. 26, 1898).

"Tables and Diagrams for facilitating the making of estimates for sewerage Work." Swaab, S. M. New York, Engineering News Pub. Co., 1896. Pamphlet, 4to, 20 pp. 16 pl. 50 cts. ... 80

"Treatment of Sewage." Horetzky, C. P. 65 Assoc. Ex. Hlth. Officers of Ont., XIIIth Meeting, 1899; Tidy, C. M. J. Soc. Arts Oct. 8, 1886. ... 81

——. "Die Behandlung städtischer Spüljauche mit besonderer Berücksichtigung neuerer Verfahren." Dunbar. Gesund. Ing. Dec. 15, 1898. ... 82

"Typhoid, Sewage and." Sat. Rev. 84:414 (Oct. 16, 1897). (See also **Water Supply**.)

"Utilization of Town Sewage." Burn, Robert Scott. London, 1865. ... 83

——. "Sewage Utilization." Burke, Ulick Ralph. London, Spon, 1873. 2nd ed., 12mo. 3s. 6d. ... 84

——. "Sewerage and Sewage Utilization." Corfield, W. H. New York, Van Nostrand, 1875. 75 cts. ... 85

——. "Utilization of Town Sewage." Maskery, Alderman. San. Rec. March 19, 1897. ... 86

——. "Verwertung d. städtischen Fäkalien." Heiden, Ed.; Müller, Alex; v. Langsdorff, Karl. Hannover, Cohen, 1885. 8vo, 467 pp. 9m. 50 pf. ... 87

Ventilation of Sewers. Edwards, H. C. J. San. Rec. 24:167 (Aug. 25, 1899); Folwell, A. Prescott. Engng. Rec. 41:201 (March 3, 1900); Morgan, J. City Govt. 7:38 (Aug. 1899); Read, R. City Govt. 7:14 (July, 1899), San. Rec. 24:51 (July 21, 1899); Stewart, Alex. San. Rec. 22:217 (Aug. 26, 1898); Walford, Edward. San. Rec. 20:93, 119 (July 23, 30, 1897); anon. San. Rec. 24:81 (July 28, 1899); Plumber Dec. April 1, 1897. ... 88

"Water Purification, Sewage Disposal and." McClintock, John N. Mun .Engng. 19:199 (Sept. 1900), City Govt. 9:77 (Sept. 1900). ... 89

Shanghai, China.

"Telephone and Street Railway Systems in Shanghai." Goodnow, John. Elec. World 33:86 (Jan. 21, 1899), Cons. Reports 59:552 (April, 1899). ... 90

Sheffield, Eng.

"Architecture of our large Provincial Towns, Sheffield, England." Builder, 73:273 (Oct. 9, 1897). ... 91

"Civic Center, Sheffield as a." Mun. J. & London 8:1019 (Sept. 15, 1899).

Lighting. "Wages and Conditions of Labour at the Sheffield Gas-Works." J. Gas Light 76:1529 (Dec. 18, 1900).

"Sewage Disposal at Sheffield, England." Anon. Engng. Rec. 41:543 (June 9, 1900); Surveyor 17:346, 372, 400 (March 30, April 6, 13, 1900). ... 92

"Snow Problem is Dealt with in Sheffield, How the." San. Rec. 26:298 (Oct. 5, 1900).

Street Railways. "The Sheffield Corporation Tramways." Anon. Ry. World 8:309 (Aug. 10, 1899); Mun. J. and London 8:951 (Aug. 25, 1899); Elec'n (London) Sept. 1, 1899; Ty. and Ry. World 8:340, 423, 483 (Sept. 7, Nov. 2, Dec. 7, 1899); St. Ry. R. 10:17 (Jan. 15, 1900); Mun. J. 9:543 (July 13, 1900). ... 93

"**Shipley [Eng.]** Sewerage Works." San. Rec. 24:281 (Sept. 29, 1899).

Shoreditch, Eng. (See under **London**.)

254   *MUNICIPAL AFFAIRS.*

"**Siam**, Railroads and Street-Car Lines in." King, Hamilton. Cons. Rep.
62:232 (Feb. 1900).   94

"**Simla [India]** Water-Works." Anon. Engng. Rec. 38:321 (Sept. 10,
1898); Goument, C. E. V. Ind. and East. Eng. Jan. 21, 1899.   95

"**Singapore** Municipality and the Gas-Works." J. Gas Light 76:1591 (Dec.
25, 1900).

Single Tax in Cities. (See Taxation under **Finance.**)

Sinking Funds. (See under **Finance.**)

"**Sioux City** Traction Company, Recent Track Construction of the." Wilson, Chester P. St. Ry. J. 14:439 (Aug. 1898).   96

"**Skaneateles [N. Y.]** Water Works Company v. Village of Skaneateles."
Mun. Aff. 4:222 (March, 1900).

Slaughter Houses, Municipal. (See **Abattoirs.**)

Slums. (See under **Housing.**)

Smoke Nuisance.
See also Glasgow, Paris, Philadelphia.
"Abatement, Smoke." Bryan, Wm. H. Cassier's 19:17 (Nov. 1900).   97
———. "A Century's Smoke Abatement." Mun. J. & London 8:1068 (Sept. 20, 1899).
———. "Fortschritte auf dem Wege zur Rufsbeseitung." Gesund. Ing. Aug. 31, 1897. 98
"Coal Combustion and Smoke Prevention." Am. Gas Light J. 69:298 (Aug. 29, 1898).
"Economy of Fuel, Smoke Consumption and." Mason, Frank H. Cons. Rep. 60:49
(July, 1899).   99
"Furnace, A New Smoke-Consuming." Engng. Rec. 40:344 (Sept. 9, 1899).
"Health, Effects of Smoke and Fog upon." Littlejohn, Harvey. San. Rec. 19:592
(June 18, 1897).   100
"Nuisance, The Smoke." (Editorial.) Elec. Eng. 24:134 (Aug. 12, 1897).   1
"Practical Smoke Prevention." Nicholson, W. (Serial.) San. Rec. 21:391 (April
15, 1898), 24:67, 115, 179, 226, 292, 340, 382, 430, 475, 523, 565 (July 28 to Dec. 29,
1899), 25:63, 110, 151, 199, 239, 287, 334 (Jan. 26 to April 20, 1900).   2
"Prevention of Smoke, The." Dee, Thomas G. San. Rec. 24:155 (Aug. 25, 1899);
Anon. Engng. Rec. 40:365 (Sept. 16, 1899).   3
"Purification, Smoke and its." Rideal S. San. Rec. 25:89 (Feb. 2, 1900).   4

Social Statistics of Cities. (See under **Statistics).**

Socialism, Municipal. (See under **Municipal Control, Municipal Ownership).**

"**South America,** The Electric Railway Field in." St. Ry. Rev. 8:571
(Aug. 1898).   5

Southampton, Eng.
"Lodging House at Southampton, Muncipal." Mun. J. & London 8:1191 (Nov. 3, 1899). 6
"Rise of Southampton, The Rapid." Mun. J. & London 8:166 (Feb. 9, 1899).
"Sewage Precipitation Works and Refuse Destructor, Southampton." Bradley, J. P.
Cons. Rep. 1893, No. 154, pp. 300-5. See also Engng. News Sept. 1, 1892, p. 198. 7
Street Railways. "Southampton Corporation Tramways." Anon. Ty. & Ry. World
8:437 (Nov. 2, 1899), 9:171 (May 10, 1900); Mun. J. 9:85,464 (Feb. 2, June 15,
1900); Elec. R. (Lond.) 47:103 (July 20, 1900); Elec. Eng. (Lond.) June 8, 1900. 8
"Water Softening at Southampton, England." Fuertes, James H. Engng. Rec. 39:203
(Feb. 4, 1899).   9

"**South Australia,** Water Supply in." Engineering (London) April 23,
1897.   10

"**South Carolina,** Local Government in." Ramage, B. J. J. H. Univ. Studies 1:12 (1883).   11

"**South Framingham, Mass.,** Sewage Disposal Works at." Engng. News 22:497 (1889).

"**Southport [Eng.],** The Tramways of." Mun. J. 9:557 (July 20, 1900).

South Shields, Eng.
"Civic South Shields." Mun. J. & London 8:106 (Jan. 26, 1899).
"Electricity Works, South Shields Corporation." Elec. R. 45:719 (Nov. 3, 1899).

"**Southwark [Eng.],** Problems of." Mun. J. 9:921 (Nov. 23, 1900).

Spain.
Contracts. "Contratos administrativos municipales." Gonzales de Junguitu, L. Madrid, Miguel Romero, 1891. 253 pp. 2 pes.   12
Courts. "Jueces municipal, El sumario y el juez de instrucción con un apéndice qui contiene algunas ideas sobre organizición de los Tribunales para los." Sainz y Gomez, Miguel. 4to. 4 pes.   13
——. "Manuel enciclopedico teorico-practico de los juzgados municipales." Abella, D. F. Madrid, 1883. 1 vol.   14
——. "Pratica de los juzgados municipales." Navarro y Reig, V. Valencia, Union Tipografica, 1894. 802 pp. 7 pes.   15
Elections. "Leyes electoral, municipal y provincial de 20 de agosto de 1870." Blas, D. Andrès. Madrid, 1877.   16
"Electric Tramways in Northern Spain." Lay, Julius G. Cons. Rep. 61:532 (Dec. 1899), Ty. & Ry. World 9:38 (Jan. 11, 1900).   17
Finance. "Local Government and Taxation in Spain." Prendergast, Moret Y. P. 337 "Local Government and Taxation," J. W. Probyn, editor. London & New York, Cassell, 1875. 5s.   18
Laws. "Constitucion y Leyes Municipal." Blas y Melendo, Andrés. 4 pes.   19
——. "Ley para la mejora, saneamiento y reforma o ensanche interior de las grandes poblaciones, sancionada por Su Majestad la Reina Regent el 18 de Marzo de 1895." Madrid, Jos. Perales. 1895. 34 pp. 50 pes.   20
Local and Municipal Government in Spain. Demombynes. Vol. I, pp. 426-466. See 2-11.   21
——. "Agenda de Administración municipal y general." Torrents y Monner, A. Barcelona, Bayer Hermanos. 1895. 184 pp. 2 pes.   22
——. "Die lokale Organisation." Torres Campos, Manuel, in II Theil, pp. 49-163, Vol. IV, 18 pp. Marquardsen. See 2-9.   23
——. "Direcho Municipal y Provincial." Blas y Melendo, Andrés. 1 vol. 2 pes.   24
——. "Manuel del Secretario de Ayuntamientos ó tratado teórico prático de administración municipal." Abella, F. Madrid, Riva, sexta edicion, 1892. 9 pes.   25
——. "Presupuestos municipales, manuel que contiene: Sección doctrinal, sección legislativa y sección prática." Madrid, Álvarez, 1891. 194 pp. 2 pes.   26
Pawnshops. "Montes de piedad y Cajas de ahorros." Ramirez, D. B. Anton. Madrid, 1876.   27
Sanitation. "Folleto sanitario profesional." Mesa, E., Medico Municipal de Villada. Salamanca, Fran. Nunez Izquierdo. 1891. 52 pp. 2 pes.   28

Spandau, Plans for the Sewage Purification Plant at. "Entwurf zur Kanalwasser-Reinigungs-Anlage für Spandau." Pfeffer, Walter. Gesund. Ing. Sept. 15, 1897.   29

Special Assessments. (See Assessments, Special, under **Finance**).

"**Spencer, Mass.,** Sewerage Purification by Intermittent Filtration at." Engng. News 39:190 (March 24, 1898).   31

Spitalfields, Eng. (See under **London**).

Springfield, Mass.

Lighting. "The Municipal Plant in Springfield." Bourke, John Walton. Elec. Eng. 11:129 (March 1, 1898); anon. City Gov't 6:2 (Jan. 1899); Prog. Age 17:261 (June 15, 1899). 32

"Municipal Condition of Springfield, Mass." Denison, Geo. A. p. 128, Pro. Third Natl. Conf. for Good City Gov't. 1896. See 6-18c. 33

——. "Springfield, Mass." Bryan, Clark W. Hrprs. Wkly. 35:73 (1891). 34

"**Staines [Eng.]**, Sewage Disposal at." Surveyor 17:504 (May 11, 1900).

State Administrative or Supervisory Boards, Relation of State and Municipality. (See under Home Rule for Cities.)

Statistics, Municipal. (See also under each topic.)

See also Austria, Birmingham, Boston, Dublin, Frankfort a M., Germany, Glasgow, Massachusetts, United Kingdom, United States, Wisconsin.

"Europe, Report on Municipal Statistical Offices in." Hartwell, Edward M. Boston City Document No. 94, 1897, 32 pp.; see also Mun. Aff. 1:525 (Sept. 1897). 35

"Municipal Statistics." James, C. C. Mun. World 9:20 (Feb. 1899); anon. Prog. Age 16:119 (March 15, 1898). 36

"Report of the Committee on Municipal Data." Pro. Am. Soc. Mun. Imp. (5th yr.) Pt II, p. 188 (Oct. 1898); Mun. Engng. 15:291 (Nov. 1898). 37

"Statistics of Eighty-five of the Largest Cities of the World." Population, number of houses and ratable value, length of streets and sewers, water supply, rainfall, amount of refuse and method of removing it, number of police, length of street railways, number of slaughter houses and management, street lighting, death rate, etc. Pro. of the Institution of Civil Eng. Vol. 76, 1884. 38

"Statistique Internationale des grandes Villes, Mouvement de la Population." (Vital statistics of 38 cities in Europe and America.) Körösi, Joseph. Budapest, M. Rath, 1876. 4to, 283 pp. 39

"Tabulation of Municipal Statistics, The." Engng. Rec. 40:460 (Oct. 14, 1899).

"Value and Use of Municipal Statistics." James, C. C. Mun. World 9:3 (Jan. 1899). 40

Stettin, Germany.

"Sewage Disposal, Stettin." Kickbusch, F. W. Cons. Rep. 47:237 (1895). 41

Street Railways. "Elektrische Strassenbahn Stettins." Ill. Zeitschr. für Klein- und Strassenbahnen, June 16, 1898. 42

"**Steubenville, Ohio,** Water System of." Fire & W. 23:74, 82 (Mar. 5, 12, 1898).

"**Stockholm** Sewage Disposal." O'Neil, Thos. B. Cons. Rep. 47:238 (1895). 43

Strassburg, Germany.

City Government. "Verwaltungsbericht der Stadt Strassburg i. E. für die Zeit von 1870 bis 1888-89." Buechel, Carl. Strassburg, 1895. 4to, 551 pp. "Von 1889-90 bis 1893-94." Strassburg, 1898. 4to, 354 pp. 44

History of Strassburg to 1681. "Verfassungs, Verwaltungs, und Wirthschaftsgeschichte der Stadt Strassburg bis 1681." Eheberg, Th. Strassburg, J. H. E. Heitz, 1899. 8vo, 771 pp. Cl., 1st vol., 15m. 45

Housing. "Die Arbeiterwohnungsfrage in Strassburg i. E." Weill, Friedrich, pp. 147-160, Hft. 30, Schr. d. Ver. f. Socialpolitik. 46

Improvement of Strassburg. "Die Stadterweiterung von Strassburg." Deutsche Bauz. pp. 343, 356, 411, 428, 516, 1878. 47

——. Proposed City Plan. "Entwurf zu einem Bebauungsplan für Strassburg." Orth, A. Leipzig, 1878. 48

Street Lighting. (See under Lighting.)

Streets, Street Building, Street Cleaning, Trees in City Streets.
(See also **Garbage Disposal, Parks, Paving**.)

See also Aachen, Amsterdam, Baltimore, Berlin, Boston, Breslau, Brussels, Buffalo, Chicago, Cleveland, Cologne, Dresden, Frankfort, Geneva, Glasgow, Great Britain under United Kingdom, Hamburg, Hanover, Leeds, Lisbon, Liverpool, London, Madrid, Mainz, Manchester, Milwaukee, Munich, New York, Nottingham, Nuremburg, Oldenburg, Ostend, Paris, Pekin, Riga, Rome, St. Nazaire, San Francisco, Schwerin, Springfield, Strassburg, Szegedin, United Kingdom, United States, Vienna, Washington.

Assessment of Cost of Street Improvements. (See. Special Assessments under **Finance**.)

"Beautiful Streets, The Commercial Value of." Howard, J. W. Engng. M. Dec. 1896.   49

——. "Influences of Beautiful Streets Upon Public Health." San Rec. April 16, 1897.

——. "The Positive Value of Quiet and Beautiful Streets." Howard, J. W. Engng. M. 12:924 (March 1897).   50

Cleaning, Street. Clarke, E. Pop. Sci. Mo. 38:748 (1891); Howard, J. W. Mun. Engng. 13:287 (Nov. 1897); Lovegrove, James. San. Rec. 23:476 (June 2, 1899); Waring, George E., Jr. City Govt. 3:117 (Oct. 1897).   51

——. "A New Street Cleaning and Disinfecting Method." Pub. Imp. 1:85 (July 1, 1899).   52

——. "Cleaning and Sewerage of Cities." Baumeister, R. Adapted from the German by J. M. Goodell. New York, Engng. News Pub. Co., 1891. 291 pp. $2.50.   53

——. "Cleansing of Great Cities." Ferris, G. T. Hrprs. Wkly. 35:33 (1891).   54

——. "Cost of Street Cleaning, The." Stutler, Warner. Pub. Imp. 2:200 (Mar. 1, 1900).   55

——. "Cost of Street Cleaning and Methods of Paying for Municipal Improvements, Street Cleaning and Sprinkling." Engng. News Sept. 29, 1892.

——. "Europe, Street Cleaning in." Leslie's Wkly. 80:54 (1895).   56

——. "European Cities, Observations on Street Cleaning Methods, in." Waring, George E., Jr. Mun. Aff. Supplement to June, 1898.   57

——. "Mechanical Cleansing of Cities." Mun. J. 9:760 (Sept. 28, 1900).

——. "Mechanical Power to Street Cleansing, The Application of." Smith, E. Shapnell. Pp. 56-63 in "Pro. of the Assn. of Cleansing Superintendents of Great Britain, Sept. 6-9, 1899." Rochdale, James Clegg, 1900. 8vo, 63 pp.   58

——. "Paving and Street Cleaning." Waring, Geo. E. Engng. M. Jan. 1897.   59

——. "Paving to Street Cleaning, Relations of Good." Waring, Geo. E. Engng. M. 12:781 (Feb. 1897).   60

——. "Städtisches Strassenwesen und Städtereinigung." Baumeister, R. In "Handbuch der Baukunde." Berlin, Tceche, 1890. 356 pp. 372 diagrams. 8m.   61

——. "Street Cleaning and the Disposal of a City's Wastes: Methods and Results and the Effect Upon Public Health, Public Morals and Municipal Prosperity." Waring, Geo. E., Jr. New York, Doubleday & McClure Co., 1898. 12mo, 230 pp. $1.25.   62

——. "Street Cleaning and Disposal of Refuse." Eng. & Buil. Rec. Nov. 29, 1890. p. 410.   63

——. "Street Cleaning and Its Effects." Waring, George E., Jr. New York, Doubleday & McClure Co., 1898. 8vo, 500 pp. $1.25.   64

——. "Street Cleaning and Watering." Jackson, J. Pp. 31-40 in "Pro. of the Assn. of Cleansing Superintendents of Great Britain, Sept. 6-9, 1899." Rochdale, James Clegg, 1900. 8vo, 63 pp.   65

——. "Studie zur Städte Reinigungs-Frage" Schultz, A. Berlin, Decker, 1881. 2m. 50 pf.   66

——. "Die Torfstree in ihrer Bedeutung für die Landwirtschaft u. d. Städtereinigung." Junger, O. Berlin, Parey, 1890. 8vo, 44 pp. 1m.   67

——. "Ueber Strassenwaschmaschinen." Wayl, Th. Gesund. Ing. Aug. 31, 1899.   68

"Clear Streets." Pumpelly, J. C. Municipal Program Leaflet No. 2, 1894. 7 pp. 5 cts.   69

"Cost of City Streets." Leslie's Wkly. 74:49 (1892).   70

"Curbing of Streets, The Proper." Andrews, Horace. Engng. Rec. 38:473 (Oct. 29, 1898), Mun. Engng. 15:278 (Nov. 1898), City Govt. 5:225 (Dec. 1898), Pro.

Streets, Etc.—*Continued.*

Am. Soc. Mun. Imp. pt. II, p. 130 (Oct. 1898). 71
"European Streets, Cross Sections of." Grimshaw, Robert. Mun. Engng. 12:139 (March 1897). 72
——. "Streets and Highways in Foreign Countries." Special Cons. Rep. 1891, 592 pp.
"Excavations in City Streets." Snyder, Geo. D. City Govt. 1:103 (1896). 73
"Grades, Street." Chase, Charles B. Mun. Engng. 16:357 (June, 1899); anon. Engng. Rec. 40:497 (Oct. 28, 1899). 74
History. "The Evolution of City Streets." Fish, Williston. St. Ry. R. 10:445 (Aug. 15, 1900). 75
Hygiene, Street. "Strassenhygiene in europaischen Städte." Sammelbericht der aus Anlass des 9 internationalen Knogresses f. Hygiene u. Demographie in Madrid, 1898. Hirschwald, A. 83 pp. 8vo. 2.40m. 76
"Inlets, Street." Wilcox, J. W. Mun. Engng. 13:195 (Oct. 1897). 77
"Names, Our Street." Crane, William H. Lippincott's, August, 1897. 78
"New Streets and Buildings." Pickering, J. S. Sanitarian 42:7 (Jan. 1899). 79
"Paving for Street Improvements, Method of." Brown, Charles Carroll. Mun. Engng. 12:67 (Feb. 1897); anon. Mun. Engng. 17:12 (July 1899). (See also Assessments under **Finance.**) 80
Planning of Cities. Harder, Julius F. Pub. Imp. 1:297 (Oct. 15, 1899); North, Edward P. Same 2:5 (Nov. 1, 1899); Post, George B. Same 2:26 (Nov. 15, 1899); anon. Builder 31:279. 81
——. "Anlage der Städtebebauungspläne." Wieck, B. Deutsche Bauz. p. 579, 1883; Wochbl. f. Arch. u. Ing. p. 490, 1883. 82
——. "Der Städtebau." Stübben, J. Handbuch der Ark. 4 Pt. 9 Vol. Darmstadt, Bergsträsser, 1890. 8vo. 561 pp. Cloth, $12.00. 83
——. "Der Städte-Bau nach seinen künstlerischen Grundsätzen." Sitte, C. Wien, 1889. 84
——. "Grundriss einer schönen Stadt in Absicht ihrer Anlage und Einrichtung." Willebrand, J. P. Hamburg and Leipzig, 1775. 85
——. "Projet d'une Capitale Modèle." Mathieu, A. Paris, 1881. 86
——. "Stadterweiterungen in Technischer, Baupolizeilicher und Wirthschaftlicher Beziehung." Baumeister, R. Berlin, 1876. 87
——. "Ueber Städteanlagen und Stadtbauten." Eitelberger, R. Wien, 1858. 88
——. "Ueber Stadterweiterungen." Hecht, E. Wochbl. f. Baukunde, pp. 32, 42, 1887. 89
——. "Ueber Strassenverhältnisse und Bebauungsart grösserer Städte." Turner, M. A. Romberg's Zeitschr. f. Pract. Bauk. pp. 305, 428, 451, 1880. 90
"Reports, Proposed Forms of Street Construction." Pro. Am. Soc. Mun. Imp. (5th yr.) Pt. II, p. 201 (Oct. 1898).
"Residence Streets." Simonds, O. C. Park & Cem. 7:179, 244, 264 (Oct. 1897, Jan., Feb., 1898), anon. Park & Cem. 8:10, 25, 42, 64, 103 (March, April, May, June, Aug., 1898). 91
"Scavenging, Street." Weaver, William. London 6:644 (July 29, 1897). 92
"Streets and Bridges." Caröe, D. Builder 78:615 (June 23, 1900). 93
Streets, City. "Voies Publics: Principes de Distribution des Voies de Circulation dans les Grandes Villes." Revue Gén. de l'Arch. p. 165, 1862. 94
Trees in City Streets. Lewis, John C. Pub. Imp. 1:167 (Sept. 1, 1899), Park & Cem. 9:137 (Sept. 1899); Loring, Charles M. Park & Outdoor Art Assn. p. 139, 1897-8; Mitchell, Cornelius B. Mun. Aff. 3:691 (Dec. 1899); anon. Park & Cem. 8:176 (Nov. 1898), 9:32 (April 1899). 95
——. Trees on City Streets. pp. 439-467, J. Stübben's "Städtebau." Darmstadt, Bergsträsser, 1890. 32m. 96
"Underground Construction in Streets." (Editorial.) Mun. Engng. 13:359 (Dec. 1897).
"Walks, Specifications for Cement." Mun. Engng. 13:140 (Sept. 1897). 97
"Watering, Street." Maxwell, William H. San. Rec. 20:222 (Aug. 27, 1897), 20:277 (Sept. 10, 1897). 98
——. "Salt Water for Sprinkling Streets and Flushing Sewers." Grant, Joseph D. Mchts. Assoc. Rev. Vol. 2, No. 23, p. 1 (July, 1898). 99
——. (See also Cleaning, Street, above.)

Stuttgart Housing. " Arbeiter-Kolonien in Mülhausen, Stuttgart u. Leinhausen." Schwering, L. Deutsche Bauz. p. 548, 1884. 100

Suburbs.
" Annexations, Suburban." Weber, A. F. No. Am. 166:612 (May, 1898). 1
" Evils of Our Wooden Suburbs, The." Sturgis, R. Clipston. New Eng. M. 18:739 (Aug. 1898). 2
" The Surburbs and the Cities." Bradford, Amory H. Open Church 2:351 (Oct. 1898). 3

Subways for Pipes and Wires. (See **Conduits.**)

Suffrage. (See under **Elections.**)

Sunderland, Eng. "Tramways, Sunderland Corporation." Ty. & Ry. World 8:392 (Oct. 5, 1899, 9:433 Sept. 6, 1900); Mun. J. 9:637 (Aug. 17, 1900). 4

" **Superior [Wis.].**" In article " Capitals of the Northwest." Harper's Mo. 84:576 (1892).

Supervisory Boards for Cities, State. (See under **Home Rule for Cities.**)

Suresnes, Municipal Buildings of. "Les Nouveaux Edifices Communaux de la Ville de Suresnes." La Revue Technique Oct. 25, 1897. 5

" **Sutton, England,** The Bacterial Treatment of Sewage at." Engng. Rec. 41:79 (Jan. 27, 1900).

Swansea, Wales. "Tramway, Swansea Constitution Hill." Ty. & Ry. World 8:433 (Nov. 2, 1899); Elec. Eng. (Lond.) 32:6 (July 6, 1900). 6

Sweating. (See under **Labor and its Relation to the Municipality**).

Sweden.
Local and Municipal Government in Sweden. Demombynes, Vol. I, pp. 114-36. See 2-11. 7
Telephones in Sweden. " Das Telephonwesen in Schweden." Hemming, A. Jr. Nat. Stat. 17:245 (2 Heft, 1899); Engng. 68:830 (Dec. 29, 1899); Elec. R. 36:62 (Jan. 17, 1900); Elec. W. and E. 35:137 (Jan. 27, 1900). 8

Switzerland.
Housing. " Die Ergebnisse der Schweizerischen Wohnungsenquêten." Hofmann, Emil. Ar. Soz. Gesetz. u. Stat. 15:684 (1900). 9
———. " Die Arbeiterverhältnisse und Fabrikeinrichtungen in der Schweiz." Böhmert, Victor. Zurich, Schmidt, 1873. 2 vol. 8vo, 16m. 10
" Legislation in Switzerland, Direct." Sullivan, J. W. Dir. Leg. Rec., Sept. 1894. Reprinted and brought down to date, p. 203, Senate Document, No. 340, 55th Congress, 2d session, 1898; Waurin, Louis. Progressive Review (English), July, 1897; abstracted, p. 250, Senate Document, No. 340. 11
Lighting. " Die Entwickelung der Schweizerischen Gaswerke in den letzten zwanzig Jahren." Schweiz. Bau., Dec. 29, 1900. 12
" Pavements in Switzerland." Gifford, George. Cons. Rep. 64:59 (Sept. 1900). 13
" Referendum in Switzerland." Deploige, Simon. Translated by C. P. Trevelyan. London, Longmans, 1898. 8vo, 334 pp. 7s. 6d. 14
———. " Government and Parties in Continental Europe." P. 238, Ch. 12. Lowell, A. L. Boston, Houghton, M. & Co., 1897. 2 vol. 8vo. $5. 15
———. " The Rerefendum in Switzerland." Curti, Th. Revue Pol. et Parl. Aug. 1897; Droz, Numa. Contemp. 67:328 (March, 1895). 16
Sanitation. " Systematische Uebersicht der Gesetze betreffend das öffentliche Gesundheitswesen in der Schweiz." Schmid, F. Bern, Department d'Innern, 1892. 2m. 17
Savings Banks. " Les Caisses d'Epargne de la Suisse: Histoire d' un Siècle, 1795-1895." Fatio, Guillaume. Bern, Staempfli & Co., 1896. 4to, 62 pp. 18
Taxation. " Progressive Taxation as levied in Switzerland, cantons Basel-Stadt,

Switzerland—Continued.

de Vaud and Uri." Palgrave, R. H. T. Journal of the London Statistical Society 51:225 (1888). 19

"Unemployment in Switzerland, Insurance Against." Bellour, Maurice. Bulletin du Congrès International des accidents du travail, etc. Pp. 507-510 (1895); Hofmann, Emil. Ar. Soz. Gesetz. Stat. 8:226-239 (1895); Lange, E. Schweiz, Bl. 1:383 (1894); Micheli, Horace. Bulletin du Congrès, etc. 7:552-607 (1896); Musée Social, Serie B., Circulaires No. 2 and 5, Aug. 31 and Nov. 29, 1896. 20

——. "The Problem of the Unemployed." Ch. III, p. 131. "Social Switzerland." Dawson, William Harbutt. London, Chapman & Hall, 1897. 8vo, 301 pp. 6s. (Poor Law Agencies, Ch. IV, p. 201; Control of Drink Traffic, Ch. VI, p. 277). 21

Sydney, N. S. W.

"City of the Empire, A: Sydney." Dolman, Fred. Idler Jan. 1899. 22

"Greater Sydney Conference, Minutes of the Proceedings of the." Sydney, Turner & Henderson, 1900. 4to, 37 pp. 23

"Pavements, Hardwòod, in Sydney, N. S. W." Richards, R. W. Engng. News March 18, 1897, Indian and Eastern Engineer (Calcutta), April 17, 1897. 24

Street Railways. "Railway System of Sydney, N. S. W." St. Ry. J. 13:661, 14:193 (Oct. 1897, April, 1898); Elwell P. B. St. Ry. J. 14:134 (March, 1898). 25

Syracuse, N. Y.

"Building Operations, Statistics of: Buffalo, Rochester and Syracuse." B. Labor Stat. New York 1:170 (Dec. 1899).

"City Hall Ring, Syracuse." City Govt. 8:9 (Jan. 1897).

"Garbage Disposal Works." Engng. News 44:247 (Oct. 11, 1900). 26

History, Description and Statistics of Syracuse, N. Y. in 1880. Census. See 1-7. 27

"Street Railway System of Syracuse." St. Ry. J. 13:129 (March, 1897). 28

Water Supply. Hamilton, James H. Mun. Aff. 4:60 (March, 1900); Hill, William R. Fire & W. 22:363 (Oct. 2, 1897), 26:301 (Sept. 9, 1899), City Govt. 6:103 (May, 1899), 7:56 (Sept. 1899), Pub. Imp. 1:23, 277 (May 15, Oct. 1, 1899); Engng. Rec. Dec. 1, 1894, 39:566 (May 20, 1899); Engng. News Dec. 13, 1894; Trans. Am. Soc. Civil Eng. 34:23 (1895). 29

Szegedin, Hungary, Reconstruction of.

"Der Wiederaufbau der Stadt Szegedin." Stübben, J. Deutsche Bauz. P. 3, 1889. 30

Tacoma, Wash.

"City of Tacoma." Howard, William Willard. Hrprs. Wkly. 35:469 (1891). 31

——. "Tacoma—Past, Present and Future." Rothery, S. E. Overland 31:244 (March, 1898). 32

"Lighting Litigation, Tacoma." Prog. Age 17:113 (March 15, 1899).

Tammany Hall. (See under New York).

"**Tampico [Fla.]**, Water Works and Sewerage in." Pressly, Neill E. Cons. Rep. 61:563 (Dec. 1899). 33

Tananarivo, Madagascar, and its Municipal Services. "Tananarivo et ses Services Municipaux." Pérès, H. Revue Municipale 3:1630 (Oct. 14, 1899). 34

"**Tarrytown, N. Y.**, History of." Mabie, H. W. See 1-4b. 35

Taxation, Municipal, Taxation of Franchises, etc. (See under **Finance**.)

Teachers' Pensions. (See under **Schools).**

Telephone Systems. (See also **Municipal Control**).

See also Amsterdam, Canada, Cleveland, Detroit, Glasgow, Manchester, New York City, Shanghai, Sweden, United Kingdom, United States.

"Cost of Constructing, Operating and Maintaining a Telephone Plant for 2,600 Subscribers." Elec. Engineering (Chicago), May 15, 1897. 36

"Improvements in Telephone Systems." Miller, Kempster B. Elec. W. & E. 33:502 (April 22, 1899). 37

Telephone Systems—*Continued.*

"Independent and Industrial Telephone Systems, The Merits of." Miller, Kempster B. Engng. M. 18:550 (Jan. 1900). — 38
Municipal Control, Ownership, Regulation of Telephones. (See under **Municipal Control, Municipal Ownership**).
"Popular Telephones." Mountain, A. B. Mun. J. 9:37 (Jan. 12, 1900). — 39
"Rates in Cities, Telephones." City Govt. 6:81 (April, 1899). — 40
"Telephones." Gavey, John. J. Soc. Arts 47:463 (April 14, 1899). — 41

Tenement Houses. (See **Housing of the Working Classes.**)

Terre Haute, Ind. "Street Railways. High-handed Treatment of a Local Company." Elec. Eng., 24:411 (Oct. 28, 1897). — 42

Texas, Lighting in. "Recent Developments in Texas." Miller, Thomas D. Prog. Age 16:266 (June 1, 1898); Am. Gas Light J. 68:934 (June 13, 1898). — 43

Theatres and Opera Houses, Municipal.
See also Berlin, Germany, London, Paris.
"A Neglected Principle in Civic Reform." (Municipal Theatres). Hamilton, James H. Am. J. Sociol. 5:746 (May, 1900). — 44
"Municipal Opera." Mun. Rec. & Ad. 3:670 (July 15, 1898).
——. "A Municipal Opera House." London 7:441 (July 14, 1898). — 45
"Municipal Theatres." Mun. Rec. & Ad. 3:669 (July 15, 1898).
——. "Spese facoltative Municipali, Sovvenzione al Teatro d'Opera e Scuola di Ballo." Arnaudon, G. G. Segonda Ediz. Torino, Camilla e Bertolero, 1889. 54 pp. — 46

"**Thebes;** Her Ruins and Her Memories." Hunter, Dunlany. Cosmopol. 30:3 (Nov. 1900). — 47

"**Tientsin,** The City of." Ragsdale, James W. Cons. Rep. 58:550 (Dec. 1898). — 48

Toledo, O.
"City of Toledo." Howard, William Willard. Hrprs. Wkly. 35:230 (1891). — 49
"Election, The Toledo." Ghent, W. J. Ind. 51:1022 (April 13, 1899). — 50
Gas Supply, Municipal. "Traveler." Am. Gas Light J. 69:458 (Sept. 26, 1898); Prog. Age 16:477 (Oct. 15, 1898); Jones, Samuel M. City Govt. 8:63 (March, 1900), City Govt. 9:34 (Aug. 1900). — 51
History, Description and Statistics of Toledo, O., in 1880. Census. See 1-7. — 52
Street Railways. St. Ry. J. 13:9 (Jan. 1897); Harding, Burcham. St. Ry. J. 16:109 (Feb. 3, 1900); Smith, W. S. Elec. World 31:491 (April 23, 1898). — 53
"Water Works of Toledo, O." Fire & W. April 11, 1896.

"**Toledo,** The Imperial City of Spain." Bonsal, Stephen. Cent. 56:163 (June, 1898). — 54

Topeka, Kansas.
History, Description and Statistics of Topeka, Kas., in 1880. Census. See 1-7. — 55
"Sanitation of Topeka." Barnes, William H. Pub. Imp. 1:117 (Aug. 1, 1899). — 56

Toronto, Canada.
Government and General References.
"Municipal Toronto." Gregory, W. D. Outlook 58:351 (Feb. 5, 1898). — 57
"The Municipal Act, Consolidated, Condensed, Classified." (Toronto, Can.) Willson, Arthur L. Toronto, Carswell Co., 1896. 8vo, 131 pp. — 58
"Toronto." Hughes, J. L. New Eng. M. 23:305 (Nov. 1900). — 59
"Toronto as a Municipal Object Lesson." Shaw, Albert. R. of Rs. 10:165 (1894). — 60

"Buildings, the New Toronto Municipal." Can. Arch. Dec. 1897.
"Garbage Disposal at Toronto, Ontario." Eng. Rec. 40:479 (Oct. 21, 1899). — 61

Toronto, Canada—Continued.

——. "An Outline of the System of Garbage Collection in the City of Toronto." Jones, John. Mun. Engng. 19:392 (Dec. 1900).   62

"Sanitary Appliances." (Objections to sanitary rules in force in Toronto, with reasons). Watson, W. M. Can. Eng. (Montreal), April, 1897.   63

Sewage Disposal in Toronto. Anon. Mun. World 8:185 (Dec. 1898); Horetsky, C. G. Can. Eng. 6:249 (Jan. 1899).   64

Street Railways, Toronto's. Parsons, Frank. New Time 2:113 (Feb. 1898); Sinclair, A. H. Q. J. Econ. 6:98 (1891); City Govt. 1:37 (1896); Boston, Leaflet issued by the Citizens' Committee, 1897, 2 pp; Ty. & Ry. World 8:386 (Oct. 5, 1899).   65

——. "Sunday Cars in Toronto." Withrow, W. H. Ind. 49:678 (May 27, 1897).   66

"Water Supply of Toronto." Fire & W. March 27, 1897.

Torquay, Eng.

"Refuse Destructor Trials, Torquay, Eng." Garrett, Henry A. Engng. Rec. 40:318 (Sept. 2, 1899).   67

"Water Works, The Torquay." Ingham, W. J. Gas Lgt. 70:324 (Aug. 10, 1897).   68

Tours, France.

Housing. "Cité Ouvrière de la Maison Mame de Tours." Racine. Moniteur des Arch., p. 114, 1876.   69

Street Railways. "Les Tramways de Tours." Montpelier, J. A. L'Electricien April 29, 1899.   70

Track Elevation. (See under **Grade Crossings**).

Trading, Municipal. (See under **Municipal Control, Municipal Ownership**).

Toynbee, Arnold; Toynbee Hall. (See Settlements, under **London**).

Tramps in Cities. (See under **Unemployed**, also Vagrancy under **Charities**).

Transit Facilities, Street Railways, Transportation Problem in Cities. (See also **Municipal Control**).

See also Aberdeen, Africa, Alexandria, Algiers, Amiens, Argentine, Austria, Baltimore, Basle, Batavia (Java), Belfast, Belgium, Bergen, Berlin, Binghamton (N. Y.), Birmingham, Bolton, Bombay, Boston, Bradford, Breslau, Brighton, Bristol, Brooklyn under New York, Brussels, Budapest, Buenos Ayres, Buffalo, Cairo, Cardiff (Wales), Carlisle (Eng.), Chicago, Cincinnati, Cleveland, Columbus, Connecticut, Cork, Coventry, Dayton, Detroit, Dover (Eng.), Dublin, Edinburgh, England under United Kingdom, Europe, Fall River, Florence, France, Geneva, Georgetown (Demarara), Georgia, Germany, Glasgow, Gothenburg, Great Britain under United Kingdom, Greece, Halifax, Hamburg, Hanover, Hartford, Havana, Holland, Huddersfield, Hull, Indiana, Indianapolis, Ithaca, Italy, Japan, Leeds, Lemberg, Liverpool, London, Los Angeles, Lyons, Madras, Madrid, Manchester Massachusetts, Melbourne, Michigan, Milan, Milwaukee, Minneapolis, Monaco, Moscow, Neuchâtel, Newcastle, New England, New Orleans, New York, Niagara, Nice (Italy), Norwich (Eng.), Nottingham (Eng.), Paris, Pennsylvania, Perth, Philadelphia, Pittsburg, Plymouth, Portland (Me.), Portland (Ore.), Quebec, Rio de Janeiro, Russia, St. Louis, St. Paul, St. Petersburg, Salford, San Francisco, Seattle, Seoul, Shanghai, Sheffield, Siam, South America, Southampton, Southport, Spain, Stettin, Sunderland, Swansea, Sydney, Syracuse, Terre Haute, Toledo, Toronto, Tours, United Kingdom, United States, Vera Cruz, Versailles, Vienna, Washington, West Ham, Willesden, Zurich.

"Accidents, Street Railway." Robinson, Henry A. St. Ry. J. 14:86 (Feb. 1898); Mun. Rec. & Ad. 2:609 (June 15, 1898).   71

——. "A Chapter of Accidents." Clark, Wm. J. St. Ry. J. 13:667 (Oct. 1897).   72

——. "The Best Method of Settling Damage Cases, and the Prevention of Accidents by the Use of Fenders or Otherwise." Hield, Willard J. St. Ry. J. 13:770 (Nov. 1897), St. Ry. R. 7:750 (Nov. 15, 1897).   73

——. "The Organization of a Claim Department." Uppercu, J. W. St. Ry. J. 16:124 (Feb. 3, 1900).   74

Transit Facilities—*Continued.*

"Accounts, An Ideal System of Street Railway." Kittredge, A. O. St. Ry. Jour. 15:30 (Jan. 1899). 75

——. " Blanks and Forms, Street Railway." St. Ry. J. 15:32 (Jan. 1899).

——. " Bookkeeping, Central Station, and suggested forms with an appendix for street railways." Foster, Horatio A. New York, W. J. Johnston & Co., 1896. 139 pp. $2.50. 76

——. " Departmental Accounts." Wilson, H. L. St. Ry. J. 16:1086 (Nov. 3, 1900), St. Ry. R. 10:676 (Nov. 15, 1900). 77

——. " Notes on Street Railway Accounting." St. Ry. J. 14:101 (Feb. 1898).

——. Standard System of Accounts. Calderwood, J. F. St. Ry. R. 9:243 (April 15, 1899); Duffy, C. N. St. Ry. J. 16:1083 (Nov. 3, 1900); Kittredge, A. O. St. Ry. J. 14:99, 796 (Feb. Dec. 1898); anon. St. Ry. J. 13:771 (Nov. 1897), 16:1085 (Nov. 3, 1900). 78

——. " Time-Keeping, Pay Roll and Method of Paying." Henry, Frank R. St. Ry. R. 7:763 (Nov. 15, 1897). 79

——. " Voucher System of Book-keeping." Kittredge, A. O. St. Ry. J. 14:731 (Nov. 1898). 80

——. " What Does the General Manager Want to Know from the Accounting Department?" Beggs, John I. St. Ry. J. 16:1081 (Nov. 3, 1900). 81

" Advertising in Street Cars." Kissam, George. St. Ry. R. 10:615 (Oct. 15, 1900). 82

——. " Is Advertising as Profitable to Street Railways as to Steam Railways?" Derrah, Robert H. St. Ry. R. 10:33 (Jan. 15, 1900). 83

" Amusement Business, To What Extent Should Street Railways Engage in the." Holmes, Walton H. St. Ry. Rev. 8:622 (Sept. 15, 1898), Mun. Rec. & Ad. 3:767 (Sept. 1898), St. Ry. J. 14:641 (Oct. 1898). 84

Bookkeeping. (See Accounting above).

" Cable Railways of the World." (General data of 55 lines). Engng. News Oct. 11, 1895. 85

——. " Cable Motors and the Underground Trolley." Vreeland, Herbert H. Mun. Rec. & Ad. 2:592 (June 15, 1898). 86

——. " Electric and Cable Railways, Working Expenses of." Ty. & Ry. World 9:138 (April 5, 1900). 87

——. " Working Expenses of Electric and Cable Railways." Ry. World 8:132 (April 13, 1899).

Cars. " Building, Street Car." Davis, Charles Henry. St. Ry. J. 16:250 (March 3, 1900). 88

——. " Car Service and its Practical Application." McCormack, Ira A. Ty. & Ry. World 9:31 (Jan. 11, 1900). 89

——. " Car Trucks." Heulings, W. H., Jr. St. Ry. R. 9:742 (Nov. 15, 1899). 91

——. " Cleaning of Street Cars, The Systematic." McAdoo, M. R. St. Ry. Jour. 14:363 (July, 1898.) 92

——. " Comparative Earnings and Economy of Operation between Single and Double Truck Cars for City Use." McCullough, Richard. Elec. Eng. 26:251 (Sept. 15, 1898), Engng. News 40:170 (Sept. 15, 1898), St. Ry. J. 14:627 (Oct. 1898). 93

——. " Electric Cars, Construction of." (Serial.) Mun. Rec. & Ad. 2:95 to 343 (Jan. 1 to Feb. 26, 1898). 94

——. " Inspection and Testing of Motors and Car Equipments by Street Railway Companies." Perkins, F. B. St. Ry. J. 14:630 (Oct. 1898). 95

——. Receipts and Car Efficiency, "Beziehungen zwischen Einnahmen und Wagen-Kilometerleistung bei Strassenbahnbetrieb." Mattersdorff, W. Elek. Zeit. Dec. 21, 1899. 96

——. " Tramway and Light Railway Car Trucks." Ty. & Ry. W. 9:78 (Feb. 8, 1900).

" Charter Route, The Right of a Street Railway to Deviate from its." Mun. Rec. & Ad. Vol. 1, No. 25, p. 11 (Nov. 27, 1897). 97

" Compensation for Special Use of Public Rights-of-Way, Property Owners' Rights to." Public Policy 3:339 (Dec. 1, 1900).

" Competition and Combination." Mun. Rec. & Ad. Vol. 1, No. 22, p. 6 (Nov. 6, 1897).

" Compressed Air for Street Railway Service." Elec. Rev. (Landon) April 7, 1897. 98

Transit Facilities—*Continued.*

———. "Compressed Air for City and Suburban Traction." Haupt, Hermann. J. Frankl. Inst. 143:13, 119 (Jan. and Feb.1897). 99

———. "Motors, Compressed Air." St. Ry. J. 13:487 (Aug. 1897).

———. "Reports of Experience with Compressed Air Motors on Elevated and Street Railways." Haupt, Hermann; Emack, Edward G.; Black, W. M.; and McFarland, W. A. Engng. News 38:228 (Oct. 7, 1897). 100

———. "The Comparative Economy of Compressed Air and Electric Traction." Engng. News 38:233 (Oct. 7, 1897). 1

"Congress, International Tramways." Ty. & Ry. World 9:505 (Oct. 11, 1900).

———. "Die Strassen- und Kleinbahnen auf der Pariser Weltaustellung." Zeitschr. f. Klein u. Strassenbahnen Aug. 1, 1900. 2

"Consolidation, Street Railway." Anon. Outlook 64:712 (March 31, 1900); St. Ry. J. 16:823 (Sept. 1, 1900).

———. "Consolidation of Street Railways and its Effect upon the Public." Holmes, Daniel B. St. Ry. J. 16:1073 (Nov. 3, 1900), Mun. & Ry. Rec. 7:156 (Nov. 15, 1900), St. Ry. R. 10:644 (Nov. 15, 1900). 3

"Contagion in Street Cars, Danger of." Borland, E. B. Sanitarian Dec. 1896. 4

"Cost of Construction and Operation of Street Railways." Statistics from Berlin, Brussels, Budapest, Blackpool, Dresden and Milan. St. Ry. R. 7:395 (June, 15, 1897). 5

———. "Building, Cost of Street Railway." Harris, T. William. Engng. M. 5:206 (1893). 6

———. "Cost per Care-mile vs. Cost per Passenger. A Symposium." St. Ry. R. 7:287 (May 15, 1897). 7

———. "Running Street Railways, The Cost of." Parsons, Frank. New Time 2:44 (Jan. 1898). 8

———. (See under Electric Railways below.)

"Courts and Street Railways, The." St. Ry. Jour. 14:102 (Feb. 1898).

"Crowded Street Cars." Public Policy 2:346 (June 2, 1900).

———. "The Question of Standing Room in Tramcars." Ty. & Ry. World 9:195 (May 10, 1900).

"Depreciation of Plant, and its Relation to General Expense, The." Norris, H. M. Engng. M. 17:76 (April, 1899). 9

"Earning Power of Street Railway Properties, How to Determine the True Net." Higgins, Edward E. St. Ry. J. 16:246 (March 3, 1900), Public Policy 2:284 (May 5, 1900). 10

Electric Street Railways, General Articles on. Bancroft, C. F. Elec. R. 37:436 (Oct. 24, 1900), St. Ry. J. 16:1075 (Nov. 3, 1900), St. Ry. R. 10:645 (Nov. 15, 1900); Carr, C. E. A. St. Ry. R. 7:396 (June 15, 1897); Conaty, G. Ry. W. 8:110 (March, 1899); Davis, C. H. Eng. M. 12:942 (March, 1897); Dawson, Philip. J. Soc. Arts 47:399 (March 24, 1899), Ry. World 8:152 (April 13, 1800), St. Ry. J. 15:316 (May, 1899), St. Ry. R. 9:345 (May 15, 1899); Garton, W. R. St. Ry. R. 8:224 (April 15, 1898); Gerry, M. H. Elec. W. 30:124 (July 31, 1891), St. Ry. R. 7:518 (Aug. 15, 1897); Marshall, Cloyd. Elec W. 30:760 (Dec. 25, 1987), Elec. R. 31:314 (Dec. 29, 1897); Parshall, H. F. St. Ry. J. 15:178 (March, 1899), Ry. W. 8:71 (Feb. 9, 1899); Perry, Nelson W. Cassiers' (April, 1897); Prindle, H. B. Engng. M. 1:671 (1891); Sprague, Frank J. Forum, 12:120 (1891), Engng. M. 14:553 (Jan. 1898); Thompson, Silvanus P. St. Ry. R. 10:20 (Jan. 15, 1900); Walsh, Gertrude Ethelbert. Chaut. 24:580 (Feb. 1897); anon. Eng. 87:216 (March 3, 1899); Local Govt. J. 27:44, 46 (Jan. 15, 1898); London 7:681 (Oct. 27, 1898); Mun. Rec. & Ad. 3:649 (July 15, 1898); St. Ry. R. 8:484, 732, 878 (July 15, Oct. 15, Dec. 15, 1898); Sur. 17:4, 146, 264, 344, 428, 536, 620 (Jan. 5, Feb. 9, March 9, 30, April 20, May 18, June 8, 1900), same 18:168, 276, 508 (Aug. 10, Sept. 7, Nov. 2, 1900); Ty. & Ry. W. 8:459 (Nov. 2, 1899), same 9:20 (Jan. 11, 1900). 11

———. "Accumulator Traction on the Continent, Electric." Ry. World 7:78 (Mar. 1898). 12

———. "Aldridge Electric Tramway System, The." Ry. World 6:342 (Nov. 1897).

———. "Anderson's Surface Contact Tramway System." Ty. & Ry. World 8:440 Nov. 2, 1899).

———. "Builders, Advice to, of Electric Railways." Chance, G. Whitefield. Western Electrician, Chicago, June 5, 1897. 13

BIBLIOGRAPHY. 265

Transit Facilities—*Continued.*

——. " Building an Electric Railway." Serrell, Lemuel W. Cassiers' 16:303 (Aug. 1899). — 14

——. " Claim and Operating Departments of Electric Railways, Relationship between." Day, Richard W. Mun. Rec. & Ad. Vol. 1, No. 13, p. 18 (Sept. 4, 1897), St. Ry. R. 7:589 (Sept. 15, 1897). — 15

——. " Conduits and Cables, Electrical." Dow, Alex. Engng. News 38:419 (Dec. 30, 1897). — 16

——. Conduit Roads, Electric. Adams, Alton D. Mun. Engng. 18:102 (Feb. 1900); Cudworth, F. G. St. Ry. J. 16:1130 (Nov. 17, 1900); Pearson, F. S. Cassiers' 16:257 (Aug. 1899). — 17

——. " Conduit vs. Trolley." Robinson, J. Clifton. Elec. Eng. (Lond.) 32:195 (Aug. 10, 1900); anon. Ry. World 7:415 (Dec. 8, 1898). — 18

——. " Construction and Maintenance of Electric Lines, Modern." Brophy, William. Elec. Eng. 24:328 (Oct. 7, 1897), Elec. R. 31:190 (Oct. 20, 1897). — 19

——. " Construction and Operation of Electric Street Railways, Some of the Difficulties Existing in the." Knox, George W. Elec. World 30:488 (Oct. 23, 1897), Elec. Eng. 24:418 (Oct. 28, 1897), Elec. R. 31:212, 226 (Nov. 3, 10, 1897); St. Ry. J. 13:755 (Nov. 1897), St. Ry. R. 7:723 (Nov. 15, 1897). — 20

——. " Cost and Advantage of Electrical Equipment for Railways." Henry, John C. Elec. Eng. 23:586 (June 2, 1897). — 21

——. " Cost of Electric Power for Street Railways at the Switchboard—Steam and Water Power." Conant, R. W. Elec. Eng. 26:307 (Sept. 29, 1898), Elec. Rev. 33:202, 218, 236 (Sept. 28, Oct. 5, 12, 1898); Elec. World 32:313 (Sept. 24, 1898), Eng. News 40:181 (Sept. 22, 1898), Engng. Rec. 38:386 (Oct. 1, 1898), Mun. Rec. & Ad. 3:772 (Sept. 1898), Railroad Gaz. 30:704, 722 (Sept. 30, Oct. 7, 1898), St. Ry. J. 14:621 (Oct. 1898), St. Ry. R. 8:631 (Sept. 15, 1898). — 22

——. "Cost of Operating Electric Tramways." Surveyor 18:624 (Nov. 30, 1900).

——. " Current Distribution, Systems of." van Vloten. Ty. & Ry. World 9:516 (Oct. 11, 1900). — 23

——. " Early Electric Railway Installations, Some." St. Ry. R. 10:322 (June 15, 1900).

——. " Electric Railways and Tramways." Dawson, Phillip. New York, Wiley & Sons, 1897. 8vo, 705 pp. $12.50. — 24

——. Europe, Electric Street Railways in. Anon. St. Ry. Jour. 13:189 (April, 1897); J. Frank. Inst. 144:156 (Aug. 1897); Elec. W. 30:736 (Dec. 18, 1897); Elec. R. 33:164 (Sept. 14, 1898). — 25

——. " Electric Railway Practice in Europe." (Descriptions of Street Railway Systems of Budapesth, Belgrade, Vienna, Munich, Paris, Odessa, Bristol and light railways of Belgium. Also describes street railway systems of Buenos Ayres, Dunedin, Sydney and Siam.) St. Ry. J. 13:383 (July, 1897). — 26

——. "Statistik der elektrischen Bahnen in Europa." Die Elektrizitat, May 22, 1897. — 27

——. " Finance, Electric Railway." Lawson, W. R. Bank. M. (London) 65:577 (May, 1898). — 28

——. "Franchises, Electric Railway." Mun. World 9:195 (Dec. 1899).

——. " Freight and Express Matter on Electric Railways, Hauling." St. Ry. R. 10:199 (April 15, 1900). — 29

——. " Ground Current of Electric Railways." Herrick, Albert B. Engng. M. 15:451 (June, 1898). — 30

——. " Grounds on Underground Trolley Systems." St. Ry. J. 16:344 (April 7, 1900).

——. " Inspection of Street Car Eqiupments, The Electrical." Herrick, Albert B. St. Ry. J. 15:179 (March, 1899). — 31

——. " Insurance Companies, Electric Traction and." Ty. & Ry. World 9:44 (Jan. 11, 1900).

——. " Land Values in Cities, The Influence of Electric Railroads on the Distribution of Population and." Knight, Frank E. Mun. Rec. & Ad. 2:474 (April 15, 1898). — 32

——. Modern Electric Tramways. "Neuere Systeme elektrischer Bahnen." Elektrotechnische Zeitschr. (Berlin), March 25, 1897. — 33

——. " Power and Equipment of Electric Railways." Hunt, H. H., and Stearns, C. K. J. Assoc. Engng. Soc. 22:11 (Jan. 1899). — 34

Transit Facilities—*Continued.*

——. "Power Transmission, Practical Limitations of Electric." Bell, Louis. Cassier's 17:113 (Dec. 1899). 35

——. "Power Schemes on Electric Railways, The Influence of the." Ty. & Ry. World 9:140 (April 5, 1900). 36

——. Progress of Electric Traction. Anon. Ry. World 7:113 (April 7, 1898); Houston, Edwin J. Cassier's 17:145 (Dec. 1899). 37

——. "Development, A Decade of Electric Railway." Clark, W. J. Elec. World 30:335 (Sept. 18, 1897), Elec. Eng. 24:271 (Sept. 23, 1897), Railroad Gaz. 29:688 (Oct. 1, 1897), St. Ry. J. 13:636 (Oct. 1897). 38

——. "Recent Progress in Electric Railways." (A summary of current periodical literature relating to electric railway construction, operation, systems, machinery, appliances, etc.) Hering, Carl. New York, W. J. Johnston Co., 1892. 389 pp. 39

——. "Repair Shops, Electric Street Railway." Dunning, R. Elec. Eng. 24:304 (Sept. 30, 1897), Elec. R. 31:166 (Oct. 6, 1897). 40

——. "Small Electric Railways be Operated at a Profit, Can?" Cahoon, James Blake. St. Ry. J. 17:708 (Aug. 4, 1900), 16:812 (Sept. 1, 1900). 41

——. "Stations, The Development of Electric." Adams, Alton D. Cassier's 17:91 (Dec. 1899). 42

——. Statistics. "Some Electric Street Railway Data." Ryan, Harris J. St. Ry. R. 9:580 (Sept. 15, 1899). 43

——. Steam Railway Conditions, Electric Traction under. Boynton, Edward C. Elec. R. 36:298 (March 21, 1900); Davis, Charles H. Engng. M. 13:172, 367 (May, June, 1897). 44

——. Storage Batteries, Application of, to Electric Railways. Appleton, Joseph. St. Ry. J. 15:110 (Feb. 1899); Hewett, Charles. Elec. W. 30:483 (Oct. 23, 1897), Elec. Eng. 24:413 (Oct. 28, 1897), R. R. Gaz. 29:782 (Nov. 5, 1897), St. Ry. R. 7:726 (Nov. 15, 1897); Lloyd Robert McA. St. Ry. J. 15:175 (March, 1899). 45

——. "Supply of Electric Energy for Traction Purposes." Dawson, Philip. Elec. R. (Lond.) 45:827 (Nov. 24, 1899). 46

——. Surface Contact Electric Railways. Johnson, Edward H. Elec. R. 33:339, 388 (Nov. 30, Dec. 21, 1898), Elec. Eng. 26:530 (Dec. 1, 1898); anon. St. Ry. R. 7:832 (Dec. 15, 1897). 47

——. "The Engineering and Electric Traction Pocket-Book." Dawson, Philip. New York, Wiley & Sons, 1899. 16mo, 1096 pp. $5.00. 48

——. Third-Rail Electric Traction. Andrews, Horace. Mun. Engng. 19:386 (Dec. 1900); Daft, Leo. Cassier's 17:235 (Jan. 1900); Davis, Charles Henry, and Howell, W. G. Mun. Rec. & Ad. 3:701 (Aug. 15, 1898). 49

——. "Tracks and Roadbed, Electric Street Railway." Mun. Rec. & Ad. Vol. 1, No. 25, p. 6 (Nov. 27, 1897). 50

——. "Trolley, The Overhead." Potter, W. B. Mun. Rec. & Ad. 2:594 (June 15, 1898). 51

——. "Trolley in Rural Parts, The." Mun. Rec. & Ad. 2:596 (June 15, 1898).

Elevated Railways, Franchises of. "Mostly Fools." Hampden, Guy. New Nation 2.712 (1892). 52

——. "Electricity as a Motive Power on Elevated Railroads." Short, S. H. Elec. Eng. 24:114, 140, 151, 184 (Aug. 5, 12, 19, 26, 1897), St. Ry. J. 13:494 (Aug. 1897), Elec. W. 30:159 (Aug. 7, 1897), Railroad Gaz. 29:552 (Aug. 6, 1897). 53

——. "La Traction Eléctrique sur les Chemins de Fer Elevés." La Revue Technique, Feb. 25, 1898.

——. "Future of Elevated Roads." Klapp, Eugene. Engng. M. 11:34 (1896). 54

——. "New Street and Electric Elevated Roads in Europe." (Vienna, Edinburgh, Budapest, Liverpool and Lyons.) Railroad Gaz. 29:164 (March 5, 1897). 55

——. "Some Elevated Railway Problems and Results." St. Ry. J. 14:755 (Dec. 1898). 56

——. "The Passing of the Elevated Railway." (Editorial.) Engng. News 40:168 (Sept. 15, 1898). 57

"Employees, Discipline of." Davis, Geo. H. St. Ry. J. 13:767 (Nov. 1897), Elec. R. 31:233 (Nov. 15, 1897), St. Ry. R. 7:740 (Nov. 15, 1897). 58

——. "How Can We Increase the Efficiency of Employes?" Rounds, F. D. St. Ry. R. 9:573 (Sept. 15, 1899). 59

"European Street Railway Practice." Howes, Osborne. Engng. News, Nov. 21, 1891, p. 428; Dec. 5, 1891, pp. 532, 549; Engng. Rec. Nov. 21, 28 and Dec. 5, 1891;

Transit Facilities—Continued.

St. Ry. J. Dec. 1891, p. 678.   60
——. "Les Chemins de Fer d'Intérêt Local en Europe." de Freund, E. Ann. l'Ec. Lib. 13:581 (Sept. 15, 1898), 13:730 (Nov. 15, 1898).   61
——. (See under Electric Railways above.)
Fares. "Advantages of Up-to-Date Street Railway Service: Why the Rate of Fare Should Not Be Reduced." Rossiter, C. L. St. Ry. R. 7:617 (Sept. 15, 1897), Elec. R. 31:181 (Oct. 13, 1897).   62
——. "A system of Collection of Fares and Checking Employees." Walter, A. E. St. Ry. J. 14:741 (Nov. 1898), St. Ry. Rev. 8:787 (Nov. 15, 1898).   63
——. "Depreciation as a Factor in Four-Cent Fare Litigation." St. Ry. J. 14:381 (July, 1898).
——. "Fares in 136 Cities, Street Car." Poppleton, William S. City Govt. 9:63 (Sept. 1900).   64
——. "Ownership and Railway Fares." Slater, T. Month April, 1899.   65
——. "Reduction in Street Car Fares." (Claims a reduction of price greater than that of any other article in common use. Service has increased without increase of charges.) St. Ry. R. 7:75 (Feb. 1897).
——. "The Care and Handling of Fares from Receipt to Bank." Wight, Chas. L. St. Ry. J. 13:786 (Nov. 1897), St. Ry. R. 7:755 (Nov. 15, 1897).   66
——. "Two-Cent Fares." New York, American Fabian Society, n. d. 15 pp. 5 cts.   67
"Ferries and Steam Boats, Municipal." London 6:643 (July 29, 1897).
"Finance, Modern Methods of Tramway." Clark, William J. St. Ry. J. 16:966 (Oct. 13, 1900).   68
——. "Financial Characteristics of the Large City Transportation Systems of the World." Higgins, Edward E. St. Ry. J. 15:680 (Oct. 1899).   69
——. (See also Accounting above.)
"Fire Protection for Street Railways." St. Ry. R. 7:305 (May 15, 1897).
"Foreign Cities, Local Transportation in." Con. Rep. No. 139, 1892, pp. 597-738.   70
——. "American and British City Transportation Methods, Some Differences between." Higgins, Edward E. St. Ry. J. 16:357 (April 7, 1900), Public Policy 2:334 (May 26, 1900).   71
——. "Comparison of Street Railway Conditions and Methods in Europe and in the United States." Sullivan, F. P. St. Ry. Rev. 7:253 (April 15, 1897).   72
——. "Stadtbahnen in Europa, Amerika und Wien." Czepelka, A. Die Zeit, 21:99 (Nov. 18, 1899).   73
——. "Street Railways in Foreign Cities." St. Ry. J. 15:605 (Sept. 1899).
Franchises, Street Railway. (See under **Municipal Control, Municipal Ownership.**)
"Freight, The Right of a Street Railway to Carry." Hodge, J. Aspinwall, Jr. St. Ry. J. 15:459 (July, 1899).   74
——. "Systematic Organization of the Transportation of Goods in Towns and Cities." Engng. News May 14, 1896.   75
——. "Street Railways as Freight Carriers." Beattie, H. S. Mun. & Ry. Rec. 5:178 (Oct. 15, 1899).   76
"Gas Tramways." Lavezzari, A. Prog. Age 15:29 (Jan. 15, 1897).   77
——. "Gasbahnen." Nachtsheim, Hubert. Mitt. d. Ver. f. d. Förd. d. Local-u Strassenbahnwesens, May, 1898.   78
——. "The Gas (Street) Railroad." Egner, Frederick. Am. Gas Lgt. J. 67:47 July 12, 1897).   79
Grade Crossings. (See under **Grade Crossings.**)
"Gravity System of Rapid Transit." Henning, B. S. Engng. M. 5:167 (1893).   80
"Horse Traction and Electric Power: Some Comparisons." Challenger, Charles. Ry. World 8:107 (March 9, 1899).   81
"Investments in Street Railways: How Can they be Made Secure and Remunerative?" Yerkes, Charles T. Mun. & Ry. Rec. 5:185 (Oct. 15, 1899), St. Ry. R. 9:22 (Oct. 18, 1899), St. Ry. R. 9:755 (Nov. 15, 1899), St. Ry. J. 15:781, 789 (Nov. 1899), Other Side, 1:310 (Dec. 30, 1899), Public Policy, 2:85 (Feb. 10, 1900), City Govt. 7:109 (Nov. 1899).   82
——. "The Intrinsic Value of Investments in Street Railways." (Statistics of Capitalization, etc.) Higgins, Edward E. St. Ry. Jour. Jan, 1894, et seq.   83

Transit Facilities—*Continued.*

"Law, Street Railway." Clark, Frank Humboldt. St. Ry. Rev. 7:303, 385, 455, 527 (May 15, June 15, July 15, Aug. 15, 1897), 8:31, 167, 245 (Jan. March, April, 1898). 84

——. "Law of Street Railways." Booth, Henry J. Philadelphia, T. and J. W. Johnson, 1892. 749 pp. $6.00. 85

——. "Legal Notes and Comments. Street Railways." St. Ry. J. 13:296, 352, 415, 482 (May to Aug. 1896). 86

——. "Recent Street Railway Decisions." Rosenberger, J. L. St. Ry. Rev. 8:311 (May 15, 1898). 86

——. "Street Railway Law." Clark, Frank H. St. Ry. R. 7:585 (Sept. 15, 1897). 87

——. "Street Railway Legislation." Sanders, Dallas. Mun. Rec. & Ad. Vol. 1, No. 13, p. 21 (Sept. 4, 1897). 88

"Licenses, Legality of City Street Car." St. Ry. Rev. 7:445 (July 15, 1897). 89

"Lighting of Railway Cars, The." Gordes, H. Prog. Age 15:412 (Sept. 15, 1897), 15:432 (Oct. 1, 1897). 90

——. "Car Lighting with Acetylene." (Editorial.) Prog. Age 15:425 (Oct. 1, 1897).

"Location, Handbook of Street Railroad." Brooks, John P. New York, Wiley & Sons, 1898. 16mo, 146 pp. $1.50. 91

"Management, Street Railway." Sergeant, Charles S. Public Policy 2:84 (Feb. 10, 1900). 92

"Mechanical Power for Tramway Cars." Chamber's Journal Jan. 1897.

——. "Comparative Utility of Mechanical Tramway Systems." Ziffer, E. A. Railway World Dec. 1896. 93

——. "Mechanical Traction in Europe." Ziffer, E. A. St. Ry. Jour. 13:24 (Jan. 1897). 94

——. "Recent Improvements in Mechanical Traction for Railways." Ziffer, E. A. St. Ry. J. 14:710 (Nov. 1898). 95

——. "Report on some forms of Mechanical Tramway Traction that have been tried and more or less successfully worked in various towns and cities in England, on the Continent, and in America." Baker, J. Allen. Photographs. L. C. C. Doc. 396, 1899. 1s. 2d. 96

"Mileage, Car." Mackay, H. C. St. Ry. R. 9:47 (Oct. 19, 1899), St. Ry. J. 15:797 (Nov. 1899). 97

——. "Car Mileage—How Arrived at and Its Use." Ford, A. H. St. Ry. R. 8:645 (Sept. 15, 1898). 98

——. "Railway Mileage in Foreign and American Cities." St. Ry. R. 8:858 (Dec. 15, 1898).

——. "Unnecessary Track and Car Mileage." St. Ry. J. 14:438 (Aug. 1898). 99

"Money Centers and Tramway Opportunities of the World, The." St. Ry. J. 15:98 (Feb. 1899).

"Motive Powers, The Battle of the." (Editorial.) St. Ry. J. 13:650 (Oct. 1897).

Municipal Control, Municipal Ownership of Street Railways, etc. (See under **Municipal Control, Municipal Ownership.**)

"Parks, Street Railway." St. Ry. Jour. 13:93, 149, 289, 346 (Feb. March, April, June, 1897).

"Pavements, Street Railways and Street." Boyle, John W. Mun. & Ry. Rec. 4:175 (May 15, 1899). 100

"Paving an Improper Basis of Compensation for Street Railway Franchises, Street." Engng. News 37:376 (June 17, 1897). 1

"Power Distribution and the Use of Multiphase Current Transmission for Ordinary Street Railways." Hoopes, Maurice. Elec. World 30:479 (Oct. 23, 1897), Engng. News 38:275 (Oct. 28, 1897), Elec. Eng. 24:440 (Nov. 4, 1897), Railroad Gaz. 29:796 (Nov. 12, 1897), St. Ry. J. 13:763 (Nov. 1897), St. Ry. R. 7:733 (Nov. 15, 1897). 2

——. "The Supply of Power to Private Persons by Street Railways." Mun. Rec. & Ad. 3:872 (Nov. 15, 1898). 3

——. "Tramway Power from Lighting Stations." Ry. World 7:21 (Jan. 1898).

"Profits on Tramway Undertakings." Gadsby, C. H. Elec. R. (Lond.) 47:75 (July 13, 1900), St. Ry. J. 16:684 (July 28, 1900). 4

"Public Policy Concerning Rapid Transit." Hooker, George E. (Pp. 77-88 in Report of the Street Railway Commission of the City Council of the City of Chi-

Transit Facilities—*Continued.*

cago." Chicago City Council, 1900. 8vo, 136 pp. Paper.)

Rapid Transit in Large Cities. Clarke, Thomas C. Scrib. M. 11:567, 743 (1892); Gribble, T. G. St. Ry. J. March, 1891, p. 147, Railroad Gaz. April 3, 1891, p. 227; Haupt, Lewis M. Cosmop. 12:175 (1891), J. Frankl. Inst. 125:1 (1888); Johnson, G. H. Frank Leslie's July, 1900; Lundie, John. St. R. J. 15:229 (April, 1899); Sprague, Frank J. Elec. Eng. Aug. 1888; Walker, John Brisben. Cosmop. 20:26 (1895).

———. "Electricity or Steam in Rapid Transit—Which?" Moffat, George. Am. Engineer & Railroad Jour. (New York) June, 1897.

———. "Passenger Traffic, Rapid Transit—in Large Cities." Croes, James. R. R. Gaz. Dec. 16 and 30, 1892.

———. "Slums, Effect of Rapid Transit on." Real Estate Rec. & Guide July 30, 1892, p. 141.

———. "Subways in Metropolitan Cities, Rapid Transit." Mun. Aff. 4:458 (Sept. 1900).

"Receipts, Conscience a Factor in Street Railway." Other Side 1:311 (Dec. 30, 1899).

"Roadbed, Street Railway." Pratt, Mason D. New York, Wiley & Sons, 1898. 8vo, 139 pp. Cl. $2.

Sidewalks, Traveling. "Stufenbahn und ihre Bedeutung für den Massenverkehr in Grossstädten." Glaser's Annalen (Berlin) Feb. 1, 1897.

"Small Cities, Operation of Street Railways in." Leseure, E. K. St. Ry. R. 8:359 (June 15, 1898), St. Ry. J. 14:375 (July, 1898).

———. "How to make Profitable Small Street Railways." St. Ry. J. 14:140 (Mar. 1898).

———. Tramway Extension in Smaller Towns and City Suburbs. Ry. World 6:201 (July, 1897).

"Speeds, Tramway." Geron, M. H. Ry. World 7:265 (Aug. 4, 1898), St. Ry. R. 8:712 (Oct. 15, 1898).

"Statistics—Their Use and Abuse." Hibbs, E. D. St. Ry. J. 14:638 (Oct. 1898).

"Street Railways." Elec. R. 31:156 (Sept. 29, 1897).

———. "Construction, Operation and Maintenance of Street Railways. A Practical Handbook for Street Railway Men." Fairchild, C. B. New York, Street Ry. Pub. Co., 1892. $4.

———. "Construction, Some Details of Street Railway." Rosencrans, W. H. Mun. Engng. 16:139 (March, 1899).

———. "Facts and Fancies Concerning Street Railroads." Cole, W. W. St. Ry. R. 7:615 (Sept. 15, 1897).

———. "Operation and Maintenance of Street Railways." MacGregor, H. P. St. Ry. J. 16:416 (April 28, 1900).

———. "Public Service, Street Cars and." (Editorial.) Railroad Gaz. 31:316 (May, 5, 1899).

———. Report of Massachusetts Special Committee on Street Railways. (See Transit Facilities under **Municipal Control.**)

———. "Street and Elevated Railway Mileage, Cars and Capitalization in the United States and Canada." St. Ry. J. 16:558 (June 2, 1900).

———. "Street Railways in Public Highways." St. Ry. R. 8:262 (April 15, 1898).

———. Street Railways in their relation to the plan of the city. pp. 213-224 J. Stübben's "Städtebau." Damstadt, Bergsträsser, 1890. 561 pp. 32m.

———. "The Present Status of the Street Railway." Rogers, G. Tracy. Elec. R. 35:178 (Sept. 20, 1899).

"Tracks, Construction and Maintenance of Street Railway." Butts, Edward. St. Ry. J. 15:795 (Nov. 1899), St. Ry. R. 7:766 (Nov. 15, 1899).

———. "Car Tracks and Pavements." Owen, James. Am. Soc. Civil. Engrs. Nov. 1896.

———. Track Construction on Paved Streets. Beeler, John A. Mun. Engng. 13:214 (Oct. 1897); Burke, M. D. J. Assoc. Engng. Soc. (April, 1899); Lewis, N. P. Guthrie, Edw. B., and Ames, Geo. N. St. Ry. R. 8:881 (Dec. 15, 1898); anon. City Govt. 5:190 (Nov. 1898); Mun. Engng. 15:346 (Dec. 1898).

———. "Tramway Foundations." Surveyor 18:724 (Dec. 28, 1900).

"Traction, Tramway." (Review and criticism of the report of committee of the

Transit Facilities—*Continued.*

Corporation Tramways of Sheffield, Eng., after a trip including the principal towns of England and the Continent where different systems of tramway traction were in operation.) Engineer (London) May 14, 1897.   28

———. "Tramway Traction. Report on some forms of Mechanical Tramway Traction that have been tried and more or less successfully worked in various towns and cities in England, and on the Continent and in America." Baker, J. Allen. London, P. S. King & Son, 1898. 1s.   29

"Traffic, Methods of Increasing." Banks, W. St. Ry. J. 14:795 (Dec. 1898).   30

"Train Resistance." Blood, John Balch. St. Ry. J. 15:142 (March, 1899).   31

———. "A New General Formula for Train Resistance." St. Ry. J. 15:96 (Feb. 1899).

"Train Service and Its Practical Application." McCormack, Ira A. St. Ry. J. 15:790 (Nov. 1899), St. Ry. R. 9:770 (Nov. 15, 1899).   32

"Transfers from the Printer to the Furnace, The Handling of." Calderwood, John F. St. Ry. J. 13:783 (Nov. 1897), St. Ry. R. 7:759 (Nov. 15, 1897).   33

"Transportation of a Busy People, The." Hammer, William J. Ind. 51:1288 (May 11, 1899), Mun. & Ry. Rec. 4:214 (June 15, 1899).   34

"Transportation Problems in Cities, Some of the Larger." Higgins, Edward E. J. Frankl. Inst. 147:315 (April, 1899), 147:344 (May, 1899), St. Ry. J. 15:311 (May, 1899), Mun. Aff. 3:234 (June, 1899).   35

"Underground Railroads in Cities." San. Eng. May 20, 27, 1896, et seq.

———. Operating System for City Subways. "Die Wahl des Betriebs-Systemes für Städtische Tiefbahnen." Schimpff, Gustav; Kübler, William. Deut. Bau. May 5, 1900.   36

———. "The Future of the 'Underground' Railway." Bird, George Frederick. Eng. 87:105 (Feb. 3, 1899).   37

Trees in Cities. (See under **Parks, Streets.**)

Trenton, N. J.

"Paving in Trenton, Brick." Haven, C. C. City Govt. 3:193 (Dec. 1897).   38

"Police Force of Trenton, N. J." City Govt. 2:46 (Feb. 1897).   39

Trieste, Austria.

Lighting, Electric. Herzog, Josey. Elec. W. & E. 35:21 (Jan. 6, 1900); Szuk, G. Elektrotech. Zeitschr. 21:94 (Feb. 1, 1900).   40

Sewage and Garbage Disposal. See 56-40a, 40b.

Troy, N. Y., History, description and statistics of, in 1880. Census. See 1-7.   41

"**Tunbridge Wells [Eng.],** The Growth of." Mun. J. & London 8:923 (Aug. 18, 1899).   42

Turin, Italy. "I Monopolii dannósi in materia di Acquedótti cittadíni e l'Ordine del giórno del Circolo centrale di Torino, dell'ing." Corradini, F. Ingegneria Sanitaria June, 1896.   43

Turkey.

"Charity in Turkey." Flakky, T. p. 284 "International Congress," Vol. I, 1893. See 43-99.   44

Local and Municipal Government in Turkey. Demombynes, Vol. I, pp. 752-756. See 2-11.   45

Tweed Ring. (See under New York.)

Typhoid Fever and Water Supply. (See under **Water Supplies of Cities.**)

"**Ulm [Ger.],** Workingmen's Homes in the City of." Crowell, John F. Outlook 63:160 (Sept. 16, 1899).   46

Unemployed, The.

See also Baltimore, Basle, Berne, Boston, Chicago, England under United Kingdom, Germany, Hartford, Massachusetts, New York, Paris, Sacramento, Switzerland, United Kingdom, United States, Zürich.

"Agencies for Dealing with the Unemployed." Econ. J. p. 181, 1894.

Causes and Remedies. "Die allgemeine Arbeitslosigkeit, ihre Ursachen und Beseitigung." Schmidt, C. D. Berlin, Buchh. Vorwärts, 1895. 8vo, 48 pp. 20 pf. 47

——. "Economic Cause of Unemployment." Hobson, J. A. Contemp. 67:744 (1895).

——. "Le Chômage Moderne: Causes et Remèdes." Thury, M. Geneva, Eggimann, 1895. 12mo, 2fr. 50c. 48

Employment Agencies. "Bureaux Municipaux de placement gratuit, leur situation actuelle." Le Bailly, A. J. Paris, Le Bailly, 1890. 7fr. 50c. 49

——. "Cooper Union Labor Bureau." (New York.) Publications New York Association for Improving the Condition of the Poor, 1896. 23 pp. 50

——. "Free Public Employment Offices." Labor Bulletin, Mass. No. 14, p. 45 (May, 1900). 51

——. "Public Employment Offices in the United States and Germany." Bogart, E. L. Q. J. E. 14:341 (May, 1900). 52

——. "Municipal Labor Bureaux." Mun. J. & London 8:393 (March 31, 1899). 53

"Experiments in behalf of Unemployed." Speirs, F. W. Char. R. 1:304 (1892); Warner, Amos G. Q. J. E. 5:1 (1890).

"Future Problem of Charity and of the Unemployed." Brooks, J. G. Ann. Am. Acad. Pol. Sci. 5:1 (1894). Separate, pamphlet, 27 pp. 25 cts. 54

"Insurance against Unemployment." Appendix I, p. 361 "Workingmen's Insurance." Willoughby, William Franklin. New York, Crowell, 1898. 8vo, 386 pp. $1.75. 55

——. "Die Arbeitslosigkeit und ihre Abwehr oder Linderung." Böhmert, Victor. Arbeit. 33:1 (1895). 56

——. "L'Assurance contre le Chômage." Denjean, G. Paris, Guillaumin, 1899. 8vo. 57

——. "L'Assurance contre le Chômage Involontaire." Rostand, Eugèn. Ref. Soc. p. 721 (Nov. 16, 1894). 58

——. "L'Assurance contre le Chômage et la Société Moderne." Egger. Neuchâtel, 1894. 59

——. "Insurance against non-employment." Monroe, Paul. Am. J. Sociol. 2:771 (May, 1897). 60

——. "Insurance against Unemployment." Willoughby, William Franklin. Pol. Sci. Q. 12:476 (1897). 61

——. Municipal Insurance. "L'Assurance Municipal contre le Chômage Involuntaire." Cornil, Georges. (Contains a bibliography, p. III-XI, mainly of French and German works on the subject.) Brussels, Imprimerie Universitaire, 1898. 12mo, 202 pp. Paper, 5f. 62

——. "Die Gemeinden und die Arbeiterversicherung." v. Frankenberg, H. Jr. Gesetz. Ver. Volks. 21:105 (1897). 63

——. "Gemeinde-Versicherung gegen Arbeitslosigkeit." Berghoff, Ising. Soziale Praxis, 1895; I semestre, p. 133; 2 semestre, p. 72. 64

——. "Vorschläge sur kommunalen Arbeitslosen-Versicherung." Soziale Praxis, No. 34, p. 917, 1895. 65

——. "Neue Beiträge zur Frage der Arbeitslosen-Versicherung." Schanz, Georg. Berlin, C. Heymanns Verl. 1897. 8vo, 216 pp. 4m. 66

——. Versicherung gegen Arbeitslosigkeit. v. Boenigk, Otto. Zeit. Staatswissen 51:689 (1895); Faisst, Rudolf. Evangelisch-sociale Zeitf. 2nd. series, Heft 9, 1894; Herkner, H. Sociale Praxis, No. 39, p. 1037 (1895); v. Lenz, Richard. Schweiz. Bl. 1:278 (1894); Schartlin, G. Schweiz. Bl. No. 2 (1893). 67

——. "Die Versicherung gegen die Folgen der Arbeitslosigkeit." Schorrer, A. Schweiz. Bl. 2:289 (1894). Reviewed by Schanz, George, same 1:136 (1895). 68

——. "Die Versicherung gegen Stellenlosigkeit im Handelsgewerbe." Hall, Hans. Munich, Handels Zeitg., 1894. 8vo, 20 pp. 20 pf. 69

——. "Zur Frage der Arbeitslosen-Versicherung." Schanz, George. Bamberg, C. Buchners Verl., 1895. 8vo, 384 pp. 6m. 50 pf. 70

——. "Zur Frage der Arbeitslosen-Versicherung." Schindler, Huber. Zurich, 1895. 71

72

Unemployed—*Continued.*

——. " Workingmen's Insurance." Willoughby, William Franklin. New York, Crowell, 1898. 8vo, 386 pp. $1.75. ... 73

——. " Workmen's Insurance and The Unemployed." Ferraris, C. F. Nuova Antologia, Jan. 1, 16, 1897. ... 74

Involuntary Unemployment. " La Question du Chômage Involontaire." Fonsalme. R. Pol. e. Par. 8:416 (1896). ... 75

" Labor Colonies. and the Unemployed." Mayor, L. J. Pol. Econ. 2:26 (1893). ... 76

——. " Colonies for the Unemployed." Moore, H. E. Contemp. 63:423 (1893). ... 77

——. " Europe, Labor Colonies in." Stevenson, D. M. New R. 7:493 (1892). ... 78

——. " German Labor Colonies." Warner, Amos G. Q. J. Econ. 6:462 (1892). ... 79

" Manufacturing a new Pauperism." Loch, C. S. 19th Cent. 37:697-708 (1895). ... 80

" Meaning and Measure of Unemployment." Hobson, J. A. Contemp. 67:415 (1895). ... 81

Municipalities and Unemployment. " Le Chômage et les Municipalités." Heins, Maurice. R. Municipale 3:2076 (April, 28, 1900). (See also under Insurance above.) ... 82

Mutual Aid Associations. "L'Assurance contre le Chômage et les Sociétés de Secours Mutuels." Jay, Raoul. R. Pol. e. Par. 7:348 (1896). ... 83

——. " Les Assurances Ouvrières: Mutualités contre la Maladie, l'Incendie et le Chômage." Rochetin, Eugène. Paris, Guillaumin et Cie., 1896. 12mo. 3 fr. 50c. ... 84

" Problem of the Unemployed." Hobson, J. A. London, Methuen & Co., 1895, 163 pp. $1; MacDonald, J. A. New R. 9:561 (1893); Salter, W. M. New Eng. M. 4:108 (1886); anon. Soc. Econ. 6:11 (1894). ... 85

Remedies. " Le Chômage Professionel: les Moyens de le Combattre et de l'Atténuer." Leroy-Beaulieu, Paul. L'Economiste Française 1:417, 449 (1894). ... 86

——. " Le Chômage et les Moyens de l'Atténuer et d'y Remèdier." Michel, Georges. L'Economiste Française 2:782 (1894), 2:380, 799, 835 (1895). ... 87

——. " How to Help the Unemployed." George, H. No. Am. 158:175 (1894). ... 88

——. " Methods of Relief for the Unemployed." Lowell, J. S. Forum 16:655 (1894). Same subject Westergaard, Nationock Tids. Nos. 1 and 2 (1894). ... 89

——. " Relief for the Unemployed." Shaw, Albert. Am. R. of Rs. 9:29 (1894). ... 90

——. " Relief for the Unemployed by extra Public Service." Char. R. 3:132 (1894). ... 91

——. " Succor for the Unemployed." Browne, Junius Henri. Hrprs. Wkly. 38:10 (1894). ... 92

——. " Treatment of Unemployed." Preston, S. O. Char. R. 3:218 (1894). ... 93

——. " What to do with the Unemployed." Godkin, E. L. Nation 57:481 (1893). ... 94

——. " Workless Man, What to do with the." Gladden, Washington. Ohio Bulletin of Charities and Correction, vol. 5, No. 2, p. 10 (June 30, 1899). ... 95

" Report of an Enquiry into the Condition of the Unemployed, conducted under the Toynbee Trust." Woodworth, A. V. London, J. M. Dent & Co. 1897. 60 pp. 6d. ... 96

Right to Work. " Die Arbeitslosigkeit und das Recht auf Arbeit." Delbrück, Hans. Preuss. Jahrbücher, 85:80 (1896). ... 97

——. " Das Recht auf Arbeit und die Arbeitslosenversicherung." Drexler, A. Bale. 1894. ... 98

——. " Das Recht auf Arbeit und der Kampf gegen die Arbeitslosigkeit." Schäppi, J. Zurich, 1894. 2d ed. 8vo, 39 pp. 50 pf. ... 99

——. " Recht auf Arbeit." Adler, J. Vol. v, pp. 363-369, Conrad. 1st ed. 1893. See 2-10. ... 100

Socialism. " Le Socialisme municipal." Mataja, Victor. R. Econ. Pol. Dec. 1894. ... 1

" State Aid, Necessity of." Coit, Stanton. Forum 17:276 (1894). Reply by Means, MacG. Forum 17:287 (1894). ... 2

——. " Duty of the State toward the Unemployed." Cowell, H. C. B. Pub. Opin. 16:121 (1893). ... 3

——. " Ueber die Aufgaben des Staats angesichts der Arbeitslosigkeit." Adler, Georg. Tübingen, Laupp, 1894. 54 pp. 1 m. 20 pf. ... 4

Statistics. " Zur methode der Arbeitslosenstatistik." Schikowski, John. Leipzig, W. Friedrich, 1895. 8vo, 66 pp. 1 m. ... 5

——. "Die neuen statistischen Erhebungen über Arbeitslosigkeit in Deutschland." Schanz, Georg. Ar. Soc. Gesetz. Stat. 10:325-378, 1897. ... 6

Unemployed—Continued.

——. " Ein Beitrag zur Arbeitslosenstatistik." Oldenberg. Sozialpol. Centralbl. Nov. 14, 1892, May 8, 1893; Jr. Gesetz. Ver. Volks. 1:631, 655 (1895). 7

——. " Methoden der deutschen Arbeitslosenstatistik." Thiess, Karl. Deutsche Worte, pp. 673-706 (Nov. 1893). 8

——. " Ueber Arbeitslosigkeit und Arbeitslosenstatistik." Schikowski, John. Leipzig, W. Friedrich, 1894. 8vo, 88 pp. 1m. 20 pf. 9

——. " Zur Methode der Arbeitslosenstatistik." Braun, Adolf. Sozialpol. Centralbl. Oct. 10, 1892, Nov. 7. 1892. 10

" Training Farms for the Unemployed." Barnet, A. A. 19th Cent. 24:753 (1888). 11

Tramps, Articles on. McCook, J. J. Char. R. 1:355 (1892), 3:57 (1893), p. 97 International Congress, vol. I, 1893, see 43-99, Forum 15:753 (1893); Flynt, Josiah. Cent. 47:706 (1895), June, 1899, Critic 36:564 (June, 1900). 12

——. " Das Bettelwesen in Grossstädten." Münsterberg, E. Deut. Rund. 26:221 (May, 1900). 13

——. "Club Life among Outcasts." Flynt, Josiah. Harpers 90:712 (1895). 14

——. " Le Problème du Vagabondage." Fourquet, Emile. R. Pol. e. Par. 22:595 (Dec. 10, 1899). 15

——. " The Tramp Problem in Cities." City Govt. 4:87 (March, 1898). 16

——. " Tramping with Tramps: studies and sketches of vagabond life." (Prefatory note by Andrew D. White.) Flynt, Josiah. New York, Century Co., 1899. 398 pp. $1.50. 17

——. " Foreign Countries, Vagrancy and Public Charities in." U. S. Sp. Cons. Rep., 1893. 350 pp. 18

Unemployment, General. (The Bulletin de l'office du Travail, France; the Revue du Travail Belge; and the Labour Gazette, London, continuously devote considerable attention to the question of unemployment.)

——. " Arbeitslose, Heimatslose, Hoffnungslose." v. Bodelschwingh. Arbeit (Berlin) 35 Jahrg., pp. 214-220, 1897. 19

——. " Arbeitslosigkeit." Adler, Georg. pp. 920-951, Vol. I, Conrad, 2d ed. See 2-10. 20

——. " Die Arbeitslosigkeit und ihre Bekämpfung." Jutzi, W. Darmstadt, H. L. Schlapp, 1895. 8vo, 144 pp. 1m. 50 pf. 21

——. " Die Arbeitslosigkeit und ihre Bekämpfung." Wolf, J. Dresden, Zahn & Janesch, 1896. 8vo, 40 pp. 1 m. 22

——. " Die Arbeitslosigkeit und ein neuer Vorschlag zu ihrer Bekämpfung." Kotzmann, A. Frankfurt a. M., 1895. 23

——. " Die Arbeitslosigkeit und die moderne Wirthschaftsentwicklung. Eine Mahnung zur Vorsicht gegenüber der obligatorischen Arbeitslosen-Versicherung und dem kommunalen Arbeitsnachweis." Forster. Berlin, 1898. 24

——. " Ein Beitrag zur Lösung der Arbeitslosenfrage." Buschmann, Nikolaus. Berlin, Putthammer & Mühlbrecht, 1897. 8vo, 129 pp. 2 m. 25

——. " The Conservative Programme of Social Reform; the Unemployed." Gorst, John E. 19th Cent. 38:5 (1895). 26

——. " I Disoccupati." Rabbeno, Ugo. Riforma Soc. 2:137 (1894). 27

——. " German Cities, The Unemployed in." Brooks, J. G. Q. J. E. 7:353 (1893). 28

——. " Der Kampf gegen die Arbeitslosigkeit." v. Wattenwyl, J. Berne, 1893. 29

——. " Die Massnahmen gegenüber der Arbeitslosigkeit." Hirschberg. Volksw. Zeit., Berlin, 1894. 30

——. " Le Soluzioni del Problema dei Disoccupati." Fiamingo, Guiseppe. G. degli Econ. pp. 607-637, 1895; Annales de l'Institut International de Sociologie pp. 111-139, 1895. 31

——. " Städtische Socialpolitik." Mataja, Victor. Zeit. Volks. Soc. u. Ver. 3:519 (1894). 32

——. " Unemployed Labor." Bourne, H. C. Macmil. 67:81 (1892); Burns, J. 19th Cent. 32:845 (1892). 33

——. " The Unemployed." Barnet, S. A. Fortn. 60:741 (1893); Bonsfield, W. R. Contemp. Dec. 1896; Burns, John. London, Fabian Soc. 1893, Tract No. 47, 18 pp., 1d.; Ely, Richard T. Hrprs. Wkly. 37:845 (1893); Lee, G. W. Lend a H. 14:185 (1895); Mackay, Char. Or. R. p. 3, 1894; White, A. Fortn. 64:454 (1893); Will, T. E. Arena 10:701 (1894); Wright, Carrol D. Soc. Econ. 2:71 (1891); anon. Encyc. Soc. Ref. pp. 1340-1357. See 1-3. 34

Unemployed—*Continued.*

——. "The Unemployed." Drage, Geoffrey. London and New York, Macmillan, 1895. 277 pp. 3s. 6d.   35

Vagrancy. (See Tramps above.)

United Kingdom.

Government, General References, Unclassified.

"Activity of the English Municipalities, The Present." Porritt, Edward. Ind. 51:816 (March 23, 1899).   36

"Centralization." Ed. R. 85:221 (1847), 115:323 (1862).   37

——. "Il decentramento in Inghilterra et le sue possibli applicazioni in Italia." Baer. Nuova Antologia Vol. XI, XII, XIII.   38

"City and Borough." (Past and present application of these terms.) Freeman, E. A. Macmil. 60:29 (1889).   39

Commissions. "Government by Commissions Illegal and Pernicious." Smith, J. Toulmin. London, Sweet, 1849. 8vo, 10s. 6d.   40

"Conservative Municipal Policy, The." London 7:103 (Feb. 17, 1898); Elec. Eng. 26:642 (Dec. 29, 1898).   41

"County Boards." Acland, C. T. D. p. 89 "Local Government and Taxation in the United Kingdom." J. W. Probyn, editor. London & New York, Cassell, 1882.   42

"County Borough, The Youngest." Mun. J. & London 8:1331 (Dec. 15, 1899).   43

——. "A Statement of the County Boroughs, other boroughs, urban districts other than Boroughs and Rural Districts in England and Wales (excluding the metropolis) on the 1st of September, 1895, with notes and appendix showing changes of areas, etc., to the 1st of April, 1897." London, Eyre & Spottiswoode, 1897. 2s.   44

"Curiosities, Some Municipal." Knight, Herbert. Harmsworth M. 4:568 (July, 1900).   45

Decentralization. (See under Centralization above.)   46

"Disunity in Central and Local Administration, Evils of, especially with relation to the Metropolis." Chadwick, Edwin. London, Longmans, 1885. 8vo, 125 pp.   47

"Englishman at Home, The." (Local Government discussed.) Porritt, Edward. New York, Crowell, 1893. $1.75.   48

Government of Cities. (See under Local Government, Municipal Government below.)

Ireland, Local Government in. Clancey, John J. No. Am. 167:287 (Sept. 1898); Morris, William O'Connor. Scottish R. 32:133 (July, 1898); McDermot, George. Catholic W. 68:361 (Dec. 1898); anon. Mun. J. 9:120 (Feb. 16, 1900).   49

——. "Law Relating to Local Government in Ireland." Ponsonby, E. 8vo, 704 pp. 21s.   50

——. "Local Government in Ireland." London, The Fabian Society, 1900. 15 pp. Pamphlet, 1d.   51

——. "Local Government and Taxation in Ireland." Hancock, W. Neilson. p. 173 "Local Government and Taxation." J. W. Probyn, editor. London & New York, Cassell, 1875. 5s.   52

——. "Local Government and Taxation in Ireland." O'Shaughnessy, Richard. p. 319 "Local Government and Taxation in the United Kingdom." J. W. Probyn, editor. London & New York, Cassell, 1882. 5s.   53

——. "Municipal Government, Irish." Westm. 48:82 (1848).

——. "Rural Administration in Ireland." Bagwell, Richard. National R. No. 178, p. 535 (Dec. 1897).   54

Local Government, etc. "English Municipal Code, Municipal Corporations Act, 1882." Williams, J. H. W. and Vine, J. B. London, Waterlow, 1888. 373 pp. 7s. 6d.   55

——. "Evolution of Local Government." Webb, Sidney. Mun. J. & London 8:1199 (Nov. 3, 1899), 8:1227 (Nov. 10, 1899), 8:1247 (Nov. 17, 1899), 8:1271 (Nov. 24, 1899), 8:1295 (Dec. 1, 1899), 8:1313 (Dec. 8, 1899), 9:111 (Feb. 9, 1900).   56

——. "Lectures on the Principles of Local Government." (Great Britain.) Gomme, George Laurence. Westminster, Archibald Constable & Co., 1897. 8vo, 267 pp. Cl. $4.80   57

——. "L'Administration locale de l'Angleterre." Arminjon, Pierre. Paris, Che-

BIBLIOGRAPHY. 275
United Kingdom—*Continued.*

valier Marescq, 1895. 8vo, 6 fr. — 58

——. "L'Administration locale en France et en Angleterre." Leroy-Beaulieu, Paul. Paris, Guillaumin, 1872. 8vo. — 59

——. "Le Gouvernement local de l'Angleterre." Vauthier, Maurice. Brussels, Mayolez, 1895. 8vo. 8 fr. — 60

——. "Le Gouvernement local et la Tutelle de l'Etat en Angleterre." Boutmy, Emile. Annales de l'Ecole Libre des Sciences Politiques, April, 1886. — 61

——. "Local Administrative Government." Ch. IX, Bk. III, p. 725 "Institutions of the English Government." Cox, Homersham. London, H. Sweet, 1863. 757 pp. 24s. — 62

——. "Local Government." Chalmers, M. D. London, Macmillan & Co., 1883. 160 pp. 3s. 6d. — 63

——. "Local Government." Odgers, William Blake. London, Macmillan & Co., 1899. 12mo, 284 pp. Cl. 3s. 6d. — 64

——. "Local Government Annual, The: An Official Directory, 1899." Edgecumbe-Rogers, S. London, The Local Government Journal Office, 1899. 12mo, 320 pp. Cl. 2s. 6d. — 65

——. "Local Government Act, 1888,—Main Roads." Minett, R. Report of the Proceedings of the Eighth Annual Meeting of the Corporate Treasurer's and Accountants' Institute, Hull, June 22-23, 1893, p. 51. — 66

——. Local Government Bill, 1888. Goodnow, Frank J. Pol. Sci. Q. 3:311 (1888); Manning, H. E. C. Fortn. 49:790 (1888); Thring, Lord. 19th Cent. 23:423, 641 (1888). — 67

——. "Local Government, Bill for, in England in 1892." Spec. 68:257 (1892). — 68

——. "Local Government Act, 1894." MacMorran, A., and Dill. London, Shaw and S., 1894. 15s. — 69

——. "Local Government Act, Handbook on the, 1894." Hadden. London, Hadden, Best & Co., 2d ed., 1895. 8vo. 9s. — 70

——. "Local Government Board, The." Maltbie, Milo Roy. Pol. Sci. Q. 13:232 (June, 1898). — 71

——. "Local Government Considered in its Historical Development in Germany and England, with special reference to Recent Legislation on the Subject in Prussia." Morier, R. B. D. p. 357 "Local Government and Taxation." J. W. Probyn, editor. London & New York, Cassell, 1875. 5s. — 72

——. "Local Government in England." Goodnow, F. J. Pol. Sci. Q. 2:638 (1887). — 73

——. "Local Government in England." Brodrick, George C. p. 1 "Local Government and Taxation." J. W. Probyn, Editor. London & New York, Cassell, 1875. 5s. — 74

——. "Local Government in England." Brodrick, George C. p. 5 "Local Government and Taxation in the United Kingdom." J. W. Probyn, editor. London & New York, Cassell, 1882. 5s. — 75

——. "Local Government in England and Wales." Rathbone, William, Jr. 19th Cent. 13:297, 509 (1883). — 76

——. "Local Government, Outlines of English." Jenks, E. London, Methuen & Co., 1894. 236 pp. 2s. 6d. — 77

——. "Local Government and Taxation." Rathbone, William; Pell, Albert; Montague, F. C. London, Sonnenschein, 1885. 8vo. 1s. — 78

——. "Local Government and Taxation in the United Kingdom: a series of essays published under the sanction of the Cobden Club." Probyn, J. W. editor. London, Paris & New York, Cassell, 1882. 520 pp. 5s. — 79

——. "Local Government and Taxation, excluding London." Wright, R. S. and Hobhouse, Henry. London, Sweet and Maxwell, 1884. 6s. Supplement, London, 1888. 34 pp. — 80

——. "Local Government of To-day, English: A Study of the Relations of Central and Local Government." Maltbie, Milo Roy. Columbia University Studies, Vol. IX, No. 1, 1897. 8vo, 296 pp. Cl. $2.50. — 81

——. Local Institutions. "Institutions locales de l'Angleterre." Ch. IV, pp. 331-421 H. de Ferron's "Institutions Municipales et Provinciales comparées." Paris, Alcan, 1884. 8vo, 570 pp. — 82

——. "La Commune en Angleterre, Régime Municipal et Institutions Locales de l'Angleterre, de l'Ecosse et de l'Irlande." Valframbert, Charles. Paris, Larose et Forcel, 1882. 6 fr. — 83

——. Local and Municipal Government in Great Britain. Demombynes, Vol. I, pp. 24-54. See 2-11. — 84

MUNICIPAL AFFAIRS.

United Kingdom—*Continued.*

——. "Municipal Boroughs and Urban Districts." Bunce, J. Thackeray. p. 271 "Local Government and Taxation in the United Kingdom." J. W. Probyn, editor. London & New York, Cassell, 1882. 5s. — 85

——. "Powers of Local Authorities." Thompson, W. Fabian Tract No. 101, pp. 19-26. London, Fabian Society, 1900. 8vo, 50 pp. 1d. — 86

——. "Self-Government, Communalverfassung und Verwaltungsgerichte in England." von Gneist, Rudolph. Berlin, Julius Springer, 3d ed., 1871. 1018 pp. 13m. 20 pf. — 87

——. "The Value of Local Government." Chamberlain, Joseph. Local Govt. J. 26:734 (Nov. 13, 1897). — 88

Municipal Functions, Recent Development of. "Le nouve Forme della Funzione Municipale in Inghilterra." Bachi, Riccardo. Turin, Roux Frassati & Co., 1897. 8vo, 67 pp. Pamphlet, 50c. — 89

"Municipal Government in England." Shaw, Albert. J. H. Univ. Studies. Notes No. 1, 1884; Porritt, E. Chaut. 21:168 (1895). — 90

——. "Municipal Government in England and the United States." (Refers mainly to Boston and Birmingham.) Chamberlain, Joseph. Forum 14:267 (1892). See also Our Day 11:123 (1893). — 91

——. "Municipal Government in Great Britain." Shaw, Albert. New York, Century Co., 1895. 8vo, 500 pp. $2. — 92

——. "Municipal Government in Great Britain." Shaw, Albert. Pol. Sci. Q. 4:2 (1889). — 93

"Municipal Institutions in their past and future, Our." Picton, J. A. Liverpool, 1882. 8vo. — 94

"Municipal Officer, The." Gomme, G. L. Mun. J. & London 9:9 (Jan. 5, 1900). — 95

——. "Municipal Reform." Hickson, W. E. Westm. 25:71 (1836), 39:263 (1843); Roebuck, J. A. Westm. 30:48 (1838); anon. Quar. 54:231 (1835). — 96

——. "Basis of Municipal Reform." Emmet, J. T. London, Simpkins, 1895. 6d. — 97

"Municipal Representatives." (Eng.) Wormsley, B. J. San. Inst. 18:327 (Oct. 1897). — 98

"Municipal Spirit in England." Porter, Robert P. No. Am. 161:590 (1895). — 99

Municipalities, English. "Les Municipalités Anglaises. Loi Organique du 18 août. notice, traduction et notes." Dehaye, A. Paris, Cotillon, 1883. 4 fr. — 100

"Municipalities on their Trial, English." Leighton, S. National 9:418 (1887). — 1

"Of the Municipality." Gomme, G. Laurence. p. 52 "Good Citizenship," edited by J. E. Hand. London, Geo. Allen, 1899. 474 pp. — 2

"Parish, The." Smith, J. Toulmin. London, Sweet, 1857. 18s. — 3

——. "Handy Book of Parish Law." Holdsworth, W. A. London, Routledge, 1891. 12mo. 2s. 6d. — 4

——. "Parish and District Councils: What they are and what they can do." London, Fabian Society, 1895. Fabian Tract No. 62, 15 pp. 1d. — 5

——. "Parochial Self-Government in Rural Districts." Stephens, Henry C. London, Longmans, G. & Co., 1893. 4to, 270 pp. 12s. 6d. — 6

——. "Practical Guide to the Parish Councils Act." Graham. A. H.; S. Brodhurst. London, Ward, Lock, 1894. 8vo. 1s. — 7

——. "Ready Reference Guide to Parish Councils and Parish Meetings." Stone, J. H.; Pease, J. G. London, Philip, 7th ed., 1895. 8vo. 2s. 6d. — 8

——. "Separate Parishes contrasted with Municipal Boroughs." Adams, Ernst A. R. Report of the Proceedings of the Eighth Annual Meeting of the Corporate Treasurers' and Accountants' Institute, Hull, June, 22-23, 1893. p. 66. — 9

Scotland. "Byelaws and Standing Orders for Burghs in Scotland." Muirhead, J. Glasgow, 1895. 8vo. — 10

——. "The County Council Guide for Scotland. Handbook to Local Govt. Act (Scotland), 1889." Nicolson, J. B. and Mure, W. J. Edinburgh, Blackwoods, 1889. 8vo. 5s. — 11

——. "Local Government [in Scotland.]" Goudy, H., and Smith, W. C. Edinburgh and London, 1880. — 12

——. "Local Government in Scotland." Shaw, C. G. Scottish Review 13:1 (1889). — 13

——. "Local Government and Taxation in Scotland." M'Neel-Caird, Alexander, p. 97 "Local Government and Taxation." J. W. Probyn, editor. London & New York, Cassell, 1875. 5s. — 14

United Kingdom—*Continued.*

——. " Local Government and Taxation in Scotland." Macdonald, William. p. 385 " Local Government and Taxation in the United Kingdom." J. W. Probyn, editor. London & New York, Cassell, 1882. 5s. — 15

——. " Municipal and Corporate Revolution [in Scotland.]" Blackw. 37:964 (1835.) See also Westm. 24:156 (1836). — 16

——. " Municipal Home Rule for Scotland." Mun. J. 9:688 (Aug. 31, 1900). — 17

" Township and Borough." Maitland, Frederic William. (With special reference to Cambridge, Eng.) Cambridge University Press, 1898. 8vo, 220 pp. Cl. 10s. — 18

" Year Book of the United Kingdom for 1900, The Municipal." Donald, Robert. London, Edward Lloyd, 1900. (Issued annually.) 12mo, 526 pp. Cl. 2s. 6d. — 19

" Allotments in England, Land." Lloyd, Caro. Outlook 59:428 (June 18, 1898). — 20

——. " Garden Allotments." Crespi, Alfred J. H. Land M. Aug. 1899. — 21

Baths, Washhouses, etc. " Have Our Public Baths Failed?" Mun. J. & London 8:1129 (Oct. 13, 1899). — 22

——. " Public Washhouses in Great Britain." City Rec. 1:609 (Oct. 27, 1898). — 23

Bibliography. " Literature of Local Institutions, The." Gomme, G. L. London, Elliot Stock, 1886. 248 pp. — 24

——. Useful list of parliamentary papers in Fabian Bibliography, Fabian Tract 29, 1896.

——. (See also under History below.)

" Building, Building Leases, and Building Contracts, The Law of." London, Stevens & Haynes, 1885. 947 pp. 25s. — 25

" Burial Grounds. Report from Select Committee. With proceedings, evidence, appendix and index." London, Eyre & Spottiswoode, 1898. 3s. 6d. — 26

Charities. " Infant Life Protection Bill, Reports from the Select Committee on the." Parliamentary Reports and Documents, 1890. 104 pp. — 27

——. " History of the English Poor Law." Vols. I and II, 924-1853 A. D. Nichols, George. Vol. III (Independent as well as supplementary to preceding) 1834-1898. Mackay, Thomas. London, King. 8vo, Vol. I and II, 30s., Vol. III, 21s. — 28

——. " Modern Criticisms of the Poor Law." Phelps, L. R. Econ. R. 7:374 (July, 1897). — 29

——. Organization of Charities. " Papers on Charity Organization in Great Britain." Loch, C. S., and others. pp. 250-391 " International Congress," vol. III, 1893. See 43-99. — 30

——. " Our Treatment of the Poor." (England.) Chance, W. London, P. S. King, 1899. 8vo, 240 pp. 2s. 6d. — 31

——. " Poor Law, The." (History, administration, statistics, etc., of English Poor Law.) Fowle, T. W. London, Macmillan, English Citizen Series, 1893. 8vo, 175 pp. 2s. 6d. — 32

——. " Poor Law Conferences Central and District." Papers published by P. S. King and Son, London. Annual bound volume containing papers read at all the Central and District Poor Law Conferences, 12s. Vol. for 1897-8, 8vo, 742 pp. Contained papers on assessment, agricultural labourers, barrack schools, boarding out, causes of pauperism, education, industrial training, infectious diseases, local taxation, lunatics, medical economics, nursing, orphans, out relief, overseers, rating schools, vagrants, workhouses. — 33

——. " Poor Law Labour Homes." Buxton, Noel. Mun. J. & London 8:1343 (Dec. 15, 1899). — 34

——. " Report from the Commissioners for Inquiry into the Administration and Practical Operation of the Poor Laws." (Evidence separate.) Parliamentary Papers and Documents, 1834. 8vo. cl. 3s. — 34a

——. " Sixty Years of Poor Law." Vallance, William. London 6:574 (July 8, 1897). — 35

——. " The English Poor Law: Its Intention and Results." McCallum, [Mrs.] May. p. 151 " International Congress." Vol. I, 1893. See 43-99. — 36

——. " The English Poor Laws: Their History, Principles and Administration." (Three Lectures given at the University Settlement for Women, Southwark.) Lonsdale, Sophia. London, King. 8vo, paper, 1s. — 37

——. " The English Poor Law System, Past and Present." (Translated by H. Preston-Thomas.) Aschrott, P. F. London, Knight, 1888. 8vo. 10s. 6d. — 38

United Kingdom—*Continued*.

——. "The Parish Net, How it's dragged and what it catches." Bartley, George C. T. London, Chapman & Hall, 1875, 8vo, 260 pp. 6s. 6d.   39

——. "The Poor Law." Dodd, J. Theodore. p. 156 "Good Citizenship," edited by J. E. Hand. London, Geo. Allen, 1899. 474 pp.   40

——. "The Poor Law and Aged Poor." Nicholson, C. N. Mun. J. & London 8:1361 (Dec. 22, 1899).   41

"Civil Service in Great Britain, a History of Abuses and Reforms." Eaton, Dorman B. New York, Harper, 1880. 8vo, 469 pp. $2.50.   42

"Concerts, Municipal." City Rec. 1:118 (Feb. 24, 1898).   43

"Contracts, Town Councillors and." Mun. J. 9:963 (Dec. 7, 1900).   44

"Corporation Cases, American and English, a collection of corporation cases, private and municipal, decided in the courts of last resort in the United States, England and Canada." New York, Thompson, 1895. 3 vols., each $6.50.   45

Corruption, Corrupt Practices Acts. (See under Elections below.)

"Economics of Local Government, The." Cannan, Edwin. Mun. J. & London 9:53, 67 (Jan. 19, 26, 1900).   46

Elections, Corrupt Practices Acts, etc. "Caucus, The." anon. Sat. R. 61:210 (Feb. 13, 1886); Chamberlain, Joseph. Forum 30:721 (Nov. 1878).   47

——. "Caucus and Camorra." Trollope, T. A. National R. 4:842 (Feb. 1885).   48

——. "Caucus and Caucus." Sat. R. 59:810 (June 20, 1885).   49

——. "Caucus and its Consequences, The." Wilson, E. D. J. 19th Cent. 4:695 (Oct. 1878).   50

——. "Caucus and its Critics, The." Schnadhorst, F. 19th Cent. 12:8 (July, 1882).   51

——. "Caucus in England." Godkin, E. L. Nation 27:141 (Sept. 5, 1878).   52

——. "Caucus, A Defense of the." Sat. R. 54:7 (July 1, 1882).

——. "Caucus, Government by." Sat. R. 53:653 (May 27, 1882).

——. "Caucus a Necessity, Is the?" Macdonnell, J. Fortn. o. s. 44:780 (Dec. 1885).   53

——. "Corrupt Practices Act." Seager, J. R. London, P. S. King & Son, 1883. 8vo, 1s.   54

——. "Corrupt Practices Acts." Hutchinson, Joseph. Am. Law R. 27:345 (1893).   55

——. Corrupt Practices Bill. Buxton, S. C. Contemp. 39:758 (1881); James, H. Forum 15:129 (1893); anon. Blackw. 134:728 (1883); Sat. R. 56:489 (1883); Spec. 56:731, 1405 (1883), 57:1294 (1884).   56

——. "Corruption, Spread of, in England." Spec. 61:811 (1888).   57

——. "Electioneering Methods in England." No. Am. 155:338 (Sept. 1892).

——. "Law of Elections as Viewed in the Election Petitions of 1892." London, Hayman & Co., 2d ed., 1893. 2s.

——. "Rogers Law of Elections." (Vol. I, Registration; Vol. II, Elections and Petitions; Vol. III, Municipal Elections and Petitions. Day, H. S., Editor.) London, Stevens, 17th ed., 1894-5. 8vo. 21s.   58

——. "Notes on Registration." London, London Liberal and Radical Union, 1896. 1s.   59

——. "Powers, Duties and Liabilities of Election Agent and Returning Officer." Parker, F. R. London Knight, 2d ed., 1891. 8vo, 31s. 6d.   60

——. "Rogers on Elections." (See under Law above.)   61

——. "Suppression of Bribery in England." Jenks, J. W. Cent. n. s. 25:781 (March, 1894).   62

"Electrical Engineering and the Municipalities." Swinton, A. A. Campbell. 19th Cent. 47:297 (Feb. 1900).   63

——. Electric Lighting. (See under Lighting below.)

——. "Electric Power Distribution in Great Britain." Booth, W. H. Engng. M. 20:41 (Oct. 1900).   64

——. "Electrical Power Monopolies." Mun. J. 9:382 (May 18, 1900).

——. "Electric Power Bill, Lancashire." St. Ry. J. 16:192 (Feb. 17, 1900).   65

Engineering, Municipal. "The Legal Precedents of 1899 in Relation to Municipal Engineering." Conder, J. B. Reignier. Surveyor 17:60 (Jan. 26, 1900).   66

——. "A Survey of the Legislation of 1899 in connection with Municipal Engineer-

United Kingdom—*Continued.*

ing." Surveyor 17:71 (Jan. 26, 1900). 67

——. "Works Projected by Local Authorities for 1900." Surveyor 17:87 (Jan. 26, 1900).

Finance. "Audit of Public Accounts, On the." Rees, William. Transactions of the Manchester Statistical Society, May 9, 1866. 68

——. "Cost of Local Government in England." Craigie, F. G. J. Statis. Soc. 40:262 (1877). 69

——. "Dialogues on Taxation, Local and Imperial." Urquhart, W. P. Aberdeen, Longmans, G. & Co., 1867. 12mo, 168 pp. 3s. 6d. 70

——. "Distribution of Revenue between the Central Government and Local Authorities." Bastable, C. F. Econ. J. 9:541 (Dec. 1899). 71

——. "Ground Rents, Taxation of." Bastable, C. F. Econ. J. 3:255 (June, 1893); Williams, I. P. 19th Cent. 33:293 (Feb. 1893); anon. Mun. J. & London 8:1169 (Oct. 27, 1899), 9:1001 (Dec. 21, 1900.) 72

——. "Ground Rents and Building Leases." Sargant, C. H. London, Sonnenschein, 1886. 8vo. 2s. 73

——. "The Taxation of Ground Values." Moulton, J. Fletcher. London, United Committee for the Taxation of Ground Rents and Values, 1889. Pamphlet. 16 pp. 74

——. "Town Holdings." (Taxation of Ground Rents and Building Land in England.) London, Cassell & Co., 1881. 331 pp. 2s. 75

——. "Growth and Incidence of Local Taxation in England." Murray, G. H. Econ. J. 3:698 (1893). 76

——. "History of Local Rates in England." Cannan, Edwin. London, Longmans, Green & Co., 1896. 12mo, 140 pp. 75 cts. 77

——. "Incidence of Urban Rates." Blunden, G. H. Econ. R. 1:486 (Oct. 1891). 78

——. "Urban Rating, being an Inquiry into the Incidence of Local Taxation in Towns, with special reference to current proposals for change." Sargant, Charles Henry. London, Longmans, G. & Co., 1890. 8vo, 162 pp. 79

——. "Inequality of Local Rates in England." Cannan, E. Econ. J. 5:22 (1895). 80

——. Loans. "Emprunts Municipaux en France et en Angleterre." Puibarand, L. Paris, Berger, L. et Cie., 1879. 1 fr. 50c. 81

——. "Local Administration and Taxation." J. Gas Light. 76:1389 (Dec. 4, 1900). 82

——. "Local Authorities and Income Tax." Mun. J. 8:1360 (Dec. 22, 1899). 83

——. "Local Debts and Government Loans." Ed. R. 153:548 (April, 1881), Sanitary Progress vol. 173 (Jan. 1891). 84

——. Local Finance in England. Pp.622-624, Vol. II, Palgrave. See 1-2. 85

——. "Local Finances of Great Britain." Blunden, G. H. Pol. Sci. Q. 9:78 (1894). 86

——. "Betrachtungen über das communal Finanzsystem in England." Artom, Ern. Turin, Vincenza Bona, 1894. 11 pp. 87

——. "Local Government and State Aid: an essay on the effect on local administration and finance of the payment to local authorities of the proceeds of certain imperial taxes." (England.) Chapman, Sydney J. London, Swan, S. & Co., 1899. 142 pp. 2s. 6d. 88

——. "Local Government and Taxation." Rathbone, William, Jr., and others. London, Sonnenschein, 1885. 12mo, 139 pp. 1s. 89

——. "Local Government and Taxation, and Goschen's Report." Baxter, R. Dudley. London, Buch, 1874. 3s. 6d. 90

——. "Local Taxation." Noble, John. London, P. S. King, 1876. 8vo, 162 pp. 91

——. "Local Taxation and Finance." Blunden, G. H. London, Swan & Co., 1895. 8vo, 136 pp. 2s. 6d. 92

——. "Local Taxation in England and Wales." Phillips, J. Roland. p. 465 "Local Government and Taxation in the United Kingdom." J. W. Probyn, editor. London & New York, Cassell, 1882. 5s. 93

——. "Local Taxation in Great Britain and Ireland." Palgrave, R. H. I. London, Murray, 1871. 8vo, 124 pp. 5s. 94

——. "Local Taxation, Scotland. Evidence before the Royal Commission 37th to 42d days, appendix and index." London, P. S. King & Son. 2s. 11d. 95

——. "Local Taxation: Some Recent Modifications of Our Rating System." Williams, W. M. J. London, P. S. King & Son, 1899. 8vo, 22 pp. Paper, 6d. 96

United Kingdom—*Continued.*

——. "Die Localbesteuerung." (England.) pp. 39-48 Ergänzungsheft to Adolph Wagner's Finanzwissenschaft. Leipzig, Winter, 1896. 8vo, 168 pp. Also pp. 345-365 of his Finanzwissenschaft. 3 Theil. Leipzig, Winter, 1889. 8vo, 916 pp. **97**

——. "Rating of Public Companies, The." Wilkins, H. J. Gas Light. 76:106 (July 10, 1900). **98**

——. "Report of Poor Law Commission on Local Taxation." London, W. Clowes & Sons, 1844. 8vo, 360 pp. **99**

——. "Reports and Speeches on Local Taxation." Goschen, G. J. London, Macmillan, 1872. 8vo, 218 pp. 5s. **100**

——. "Taxation, Local and Imperial, and Local Government." Graham, J. C. (Third edition by Marmington, M. D.) London, P. S. King & Son, 1899. 12mo, 122 pp. Cl. 2s. **1**

——. Water Undertaxings, Taxation of. (See under Water below.)

"Fire Brigades." Fire & W. 23:60 (Feb. 19, 1898).

Fire Insurance in England, Municipal. "Creation d'Assurances Municipal contre l'Incendie en Angleterre." Artibal, J. R. Municipale 3:1903 (Feb. 10, 1900). **2**

"Garbage Disposal in England." Fuertes, James H. Engng. N. July 2, 1896. **3**

——. "Garbage as Fuel for Electric Light Stations, English Experience with." Campbell, A. H. Engng. News 42:21 (July 13, 1899). **4**

Gas Lighting. (See under Lighting below.)

History. "Bibliography of British Municipal History, Including Gilds and Parliamentary Representation." Gross, Charles. New York, Longmans, Green & Co., 1897. 8vo. 461 pp. $2.50. **5**

——. "An Essay on English Municipal History." Thompson, James. London, Longmans, 1867. 8vo. 5s. **6**

——. "An historical treatise of cities and burghs or boroughs. Showing their original, and whence and from whom they received their liberties, privileges and immunities, etc., etc." (A partisan work attempting to justify the measures of Charles II. and James II. against municipal corporations.) London, 1st ed., 1690, 2d. ed., 1704. Account and criticism of this work in Merewether and Stephens, Vol. III, pp. 1900-1938. **7**

——. "An Introduction to English Economic History and Theory." (In Pt. I, Merchant and Craft Guilds.) Ashley, W. J. New York, Putnam, 1889. 8vo, $1.50. **8**

——. "Boroughs, Origin of the." Maitland, F. W. Eng. Hist. R. 11:13 (1896). **9**

——. "Boroughs in the Reign of John, The English." Ballard, A. English Historical R. 14:93 (Jan. 1899). **10**

——. "Cinque Ports." (Hastings, Sandwich, Dover, Romney and Hythe, History of.) Burrows, Montagu. Historic Towns Series. London, Longmans, 1888. 8vo. 3s. 6d. (For historical bibliography of the Cinque Ports see p. 110 of Gross' Bibliography of British Municipal History.) (See No. 5 above.) **11**

——. "Constitutional History of England in its Origin and Development." Stubbs, William. (For general sketch of municipal history to end of 15th Century see §§ 44, 131, 165, 211-14, 218, 219, 422, 484.) Oxford, Clarendon Press, 5th ed. 1896. 8vo, 3 Vols. 12s. each. **12**

——. Decay of Mediæval Towns in England. p. 552, Vol. III, Palgrave. See 1-2. **13**

——. "Domesday Book and beyond." (Account of the boroughs just after the Norman Conquest, pp. 172-219.) Maitland, F. W. Cambridge University Press, 1897. 8vo, 542 pp. 15s. **14**

——. "English Municipal Institutions; their growth and development from 1835-79, statistically illustrated." Vine, John, and Somers, Richard. London, Waterloo, 1879. 8vo, 272 pp. 10s. 6d. **15**

——. "L'Evolution des Institutions communaux en Prusse et en Angleterre." Paul-Dubois, L. Rev. Pol. et Par. Aug. 1897. **16**

——. "Firma burgi, or an historical essay concerning the cities, towns and boroughs of England, taken from records." Madox, Thomas. London, 1726. **17**

——. "Gild Merchant, a contribution to British municipal history." Gross, Charles. New York, Macmillan, 1890, 2vols, 8 vo, 332, 447 pp. $6. (The same writer gives a sketch of the general history of gilds in Palgrave, Vol. II, p. 209. See 1-2.) **18**

——. "History of Boroughs and municipal corporations of the United Kingdom." Merewether, H. A., and Stephen, Archibald. London, Stevens, 1835. 3 vols. 8vo. **19**

BIBLIOGRAPHY. 281

United Kingdom—*Continued.*

——. Ireland. " Law of Election in the ancient cities and towns of Ireland traced from original records." Lynch, William. London, E. Wilson, 1831. 8vo. 6s.   20

——. Ireland. " An Inquiry into the ancient corporate system of Ireland, and suggestions for its immediate restoration and extension." Gale, Peter. London and Dublin, Bentley, 1834. 8vo. 12s.   21

——. Irish Municipal History, Bibliography of. pp. 114-123 of Gross, British Municipal History.   22

——. " Scottish Municipal Heraldry." Scottish R. 31:1 (Jan. 1898).

——. Scottish Municipal History, Bibliography of. pp. 123-146 of Gross' British Municipal History.   23

——. " Select Charters and other illustrations of English constitutional history from the earliest times to the reign of Edward the First." Stubbs, William. (Contains extracts from a number of early English borough charters.) Oxford, 8th ed., 1895. 8vo. 8s. 6d.   24

——. " Self-government in towns." (Condition of English boroughs since 1835.) Picton, J. A. Contemp. 34:678 (1879).   25

——. " Town Life in the Fifteenth Century." Green, Mrs. J. R. London, Macmillan, 1895. 2 vols. 8vo, 441, 476 pp. 32s.   26

——. " Towns and Roads in the Thirteenth Century, English." Law, Alice. Econ. R. 7:289 (July, 1897).   27

——. Wales. References on the Municipal History of Wales. p. 146 of Gross' British Municipal History.   28

Housing. " Block Buildings; The Associated and Self-Contained Systems." Spalding, Henry. In " Working Class Dwellings." London, P. S. King & Son, 1900. 4to. 2s. 6d.   29

——. " Church Congress, The Housing Question at the." San. Rec. 26:293 (Oct. 5, 1900).

——. " Consideration of Practical Difficulties as regards Building." Lander, H. C. Fabian Tract No. 101, pp. 27-31. London, Fabian Society, 1900. 8vo, 50 pp. 1d.   30

——. " Effects of Injudicious Legislation." Honeyman, John. In " Working Class Dwellings." London, P. S. King & Son, 1900. 4to. 2s. 6d.   31

——. " Fen Districts, The Housing Question in the." Cochrane, Constance. San. Rec. 26:567 (Dec. 28, 1900).   32

——. " Free Homes for the People." Boulter, Stanley. (A scheme by which English municipalities shall be empowered to advance to the working classes the necessary money to purchase their houses, the advances to be repaid by installments, instead of rent.) Ill. Carpenter & Builder (London) June 11, 1897.   33

——. " House Famine and How to Relieve it, The." (Seven papers and a Bibliography.) Fabian Tract No. 101. London, Fabian Society, 1900. 8vo, 50 pp. 1d.   34

——. " Houses for the People: A Summary of the Powers of Local Authorities under the Housing of the Working Classes Act, 1890, and the use which has been and can be made of them." London, The Fabian Society, May, 1897. Fabian Tract No. 76, 16 pp. 1d.   35

——. " Housing of the Poor in England, Existing Law on." Arnold-Forster, H. O. 19th Cent. 14:940 (1883).   36

——. " Housing of the Working Classes Act 1890, and Amending Acts, annotated and explained together with the statutory forms and instructions." Allan, Charles E. London, Butterworth & Co., 1898. 8vo, 186 pp. Cl.   37

——. " Housing of the Working Classes Act 1890." (English. Notes, introduction, forms prescribed under the act, all existing enactments on the subject, tables of cases and index.) Bernard, W. C. and H. Morgan-Brown. London, Butterworth, 1891. 8vo, 188 pp.   38

——. " Housing of the Working Classes Act." Allan, C. E. London, Butterworth, 1899. 8vo, 215 pp. Cl. 7s. 6d.   39

——. Housing of the Working Classes Act. " Suggestions for Improving Part II of the Act." Holder, W. Mun. J. 9:611 (Aug. 3, 1900).   40

——. " Housing of the English Poor." Monkswell, Lord. No. Am. 165:52 (July, 1897).   41

——. " A New Housing Policy." Blashill, Thomas. Mun. J. & London 8:1177 (Oct. 27, 1899).   42

United Kingdom—*Continued.*

———. "Arbeiterwohnungsfrage in England." Aschrott, P. F. pp. 93-147 Hft. 30, Schr. d. Ver. f. Socialpolitik. 43

———. "Der Gegenwärtige Stand der Wohnungsfrage in England." Bernstein, Eduard. Ar. Soc. Gesetz. u. Stat. 15:616 (Nos. 5-6.) 44

———. "Die Wohnungsnot und Wohnungsreform in England mit besonderer Berücksichtigung der neueren Wohnungsgesetzgebung." v. Oppenheimer, Fel. Leipzig, 1900. 8vo, 167 pp. 4m. 45

———. "Ireland, Congested Districts Board of." Russel, T. W. Fortn. 62:61 (1894). 46

———. "Lodging Houses, Municipal." Mun. J. 9:800, 852 (Oct. 12, 26, 1900).

———. "Lodging Houses and their Bye-Laws, Common." Maconnachie, George. San. Rec. 20:224, 253 (Aug. 27, Sept. 3, 1897). 47

———. "Overcrowding in the North Country." Mun. J. & London 8:769 (June 30, 1899).

———. "Overcrowding, The Facts as to Urban." Bowmaker, Edward. Fabian Tract No. 101, pp. 10-14. London, Fabian Society, 1900. 8vo, 50 pp. 1d. 48

———. "Removal of Insanitary Areas and the Management of Improvement Schemes under the Housing of the Working Classes Act." Addie, Peter. Sanitarian 42:19 (Jan. 1899), J. San. Inst. 20:11 (April, 1899). 49

———. "Report of Her Majesty's Commission on the Housing of the Working Classes in England and Wales." Parliamentary Reports and Documents, 1885. 728 pp. 49a

———. "Rise of the Suburbs." (English.) Low, Sidney J. Contemp. 60:544-558 (Oct. 1891). 50

———. "Rural Districts, Bad Housing in." Edwards, Clement. Fabian Tract No. 101, pp. 3-6. London, Fabian Society, 1900. 8vo, 50 pp. 1d. 51

———. "Sanitary Inspectors and the Houses of the Poor." Fyfe, Peter. San. Rec. 26:204 (Sept. 7, 1900). 52

———. "Sanitation of Dwellings in England, The." Fletcher, Banister F. Arch. Rec. 8:407 (June, 1899). 53

———. "Scotland and Ireland, Report of her Majesty's Commission on the Housing of the Working Classes in." Parliamentary Reports and Documents, 1885. 2 vols, 171 and 110 pp. 54

———. "Workmen's Dwellings as they are." Fireside Nov. 1900.

Ireland. (See under General References, History, Housing, Lighting, Police.)

Labor. "Sweating in the United Kingdom." Schloss, D. F. Am. J. Soc. Sci. 30:65 (1892). 55

"Libraries of Greater Britain, The." Boosé, J. R. Library 1:123 (Dec. 1899). 56

Lighting, Directory. "Gas and Electric Lighting Works: Directory and Statistics." London, Hazell, Watson and Viney. Issued annually, 23d issue, 1899. 383 pp. 6s. 57

———. "Electric Lighting." (Latest Rules of English Board of Trade in regard to the procedure for obtaining a provisional order or licenses.) London, Butterworth, 1898. 15s. 58

———. "Electric Lighting in Great Britain, The Commercial Aspects of." Hammond, Robert. Engng. M. 16:624 (Jan. 1899). 59

———. "Electric Light in Ireland." Mun. J. 9:721 (Sept. 14, 1900).

———. "Electric Lighting Plants, Statistics on English." D'Oyly, Claud P. Elec. Eng. 25:157 (Feb. 10, 1898), 25:393 (April 14, 1898), 25:425 (April 21, 1898), 25:482 (May 5, 1898). 60

———. "Electric Lighting and Energy, Law relating to." Will, J. S. London, Butterworth, 2d ed., 1900. 8vo. 17s. 6d. 61

———. "Electrical Undertakings, The Common Law Liabilities of." Engng. 70:20 (July 6, 1900).

———. "Electricity in Small Towns." Boot, Horace. Mun. J. 9:783 (Oct. 5, 1900); anon. Mun. J. & London 8:640 (May 26, 1899). 62

———. Garbage as Fuel for Lighting Plants. (See under Garbage above.)

———. "Gas Affairs, English." Child, W. D. Prog. Age 16:480 (Oct. 15, 1898); Ritson, T. N. Prog. Age 18:142 (April 2, 1900). 63

———. Gas. "Authorized Gas Undertakings in the United Kingdom." Board of Trade J. 26:48 (Jan. 1899). 64

BIBLIOGRAPHY.

United Kingdom—*Continued.*

— —. Gas. "The Cost of Coal Gas in England." Humphreys, Norton H. Am. Gas Light J. 73:3 (July 2, 1900). 65

——. "Gas Engineer's Annual and Directory of Gas Undertakings." (20th year.) Hastings, Charles W. Birmingham, J. G. Hammond & Co., 1899. 8vo, 120 pp. Cl. 4s. 66

——. Gas. "Illuminating Power as Exhibited in the Parliamentary Returns." Newbigging, Thomas. J. Gas Lighting Dec. 1, 1896, discussion Dec. 8, 1896. 67

——. "Gas Lighting in Great Britain." Maltbie, Milo Roy. Mun. Aff. 4:538 (Sept. 1900). 68

——. "Gas, Price of, in England." Schoenhof, J. U. S. Consular Reports No. 75, 1887, p. 535. 69

——. "Gas Statistics, English." Prog. Age 16:312 (July 1, 1898).

——. "Gas Statistics, Illuminating." Still, A. J. of Finance 5:207 (March, 1899). 70

——. "Gas Supplies, Municipal." Mun. J. & London 8:1141 (Oct. 20, 1899).

——. "Gas Undertakings Returns, The." J. Gas Light. 72:1470 (Dec. 27, 1898). 71

——. "Gas Undertakings in England, Scotland and Ireland, for the year 1897, an analysis of the accounts of the principal." Field, John W. London, Eden Fisher & Co., 1898. 34 pp. Pamphlet, 15s. 72

——. "Gas Undertakings, The Purchase of." Browne, Frank Balfour. J. Gas Light. 73:1028 (Nov. 8, 1898). 73

——. "Gas World Year Book, The." Douglas, John. London, John Allen & Co., 1899. 8vo, 213 pp. Cl. 7s. 7d. 74

——. "Gas Works in Ireland, Impressions of Small." Griffith, Percy. Am. Gas Light. J. 73:402 (Sept. 10, 1900). 75

——. "Law of Gas, Water and Electric Lighting." Will, J. Shirless. London, Butterworth, 1894. 8vo. 32s. 76

"Liquor Interests in English Politics, The." Porritt, Edward. Chaut. 28:554 (Mch. 1899). 77

——. "Liquor Problem in England." Hrprs. Wkly. 41:424 (April 24, 1897). 78

——. "Municipal Public Houses." Mun. J. 9:984 (Dec. 14, 1900).

——. "Temperance Problem and Social Reform." Rowntree, Joseph; Sherwell, Arthur. (7th ed.) New York, Truslove Hansom and Comba, 1900. 8vo, 784 pp. Cl. $4. 79

"Literary and Municipal Problems in England." Harrison, Frederic. Forum 14:644 (1893). 80

Lodging Houses. (See under Housing above.)

Municipal Control, Municipal Ownership, General. "Municipal Finance and Municipal Enterprise." Fowler, H. H. London, P. S. King & Son, 1900. 8vo, 25 pp. Paper, 1s.; same, J. Royal Stat. Soc. 63:383 (Sept. 1900). 81

——. "Municipal Ownership in England, Private and." Raworth, J. S. Prog. Age 16:562 (Dec. 1, 1898). 82

——. "Municipal Plants in Great Britain." City Govt. 6:143 (June, 1899).

——. "Municipal Socialism in England." Ann. Am. Acad. Pol. Sci. 16:147 (Sept. 1900). 83

——. "Municipal Trading." Anon. Mun. J. 9:314 (April 20, 1900); Ty. & Ry. World 9:196 (May 20, 1900); Surveyor 17:617 (June 8, 1900), 18:17 (July 6, 1900), 18:44 (July 13, 1900), 18:76 (July 20, 1900), 18:116 (July 27, 1900). 84

——. "Municipal Trading, The Attack on." Rollitt, Albert. Mun. J. 9:269 (April 6, 1900). 85

——. "Municipal Trading, Board of Trade and." Mun. J. 9:406 (May 25, 1900). 86

——. "Municipal Trading, The Cost of." (Against municipal ownership in England.) Davies, Dixon H. London, P S. King & Son. 71 pp. 5 explanatory diagrams. 2s. 87

——. "Municipal Trading, Mr. Joseph Chamberlain on." Mun. J. 9:643 (Aug. 17, 1900).

——. "Municipal Trading, Parliament and." Mun. J. 9:409 (May 25, 1900), 9:429 (June 1, 1900), 9:489 (June 22, 1900), 9:503 (June 29, 1900), 9:523 (July 6, 1900), 9:549 (July 13, 1900), 9:572 (July 20, 1900), 9:591 (July 27, 1900), 9:604 (Aug. 3, 1900), 9:632 (Aug. 10, 1900). 88

——. "Municipal Trading, The Parliamentary Committee on." J. Gas. Light. 75:1503 (June 5, 1900), 76:33 (July 3, 1900), 76:94 (July 10, 1900), 76:166 (July

United Kingdom—*Continued.*

17, 1900), 76:226 (July 24, 1900). 89
——. "Municipalities at Work." Dolman, F. London, Methuen & Co., 1895. 143 pp. $1. (Chapters on Birmingham, Manchester, Liverpool, Glasgow, Bradford and Leeds.) 90
——. "Municipalism, The British Association and." J. Gas. Light. 76:692 (Sept. 18, 1900). 91
——. "Le Socialisme Municipal en Angleterre." François, M. G. Jour. des Economistes 36:382 (1896). 92
——. "Städteverwaltung und Municipalsozialismus in England." Hugo, C. Stuttgart, J. H. W. Dietz, 1897. 8vo, 312 pp. 2m. 50 pf. 93
Municipal Control, etc. Lighting. "Attacks on Municipal Electricity." Hammond, Robert. Mun. J. & London 8:40 (Jan. 12, 1899); anon. Mun. J. & London 8:11 (Jan. 5, 1899), 9:5 (Jan. 5, 1900), 9:52 (Jan. 19, 1900), 9:141 (Feb. 23, 1900). 94
——. "Municipal Electricity." Mountain, A. B. Mun. J. 9:484 (June 22, 1900). 95
——. "Municipal Electrical Untertakings in 1899." Surveyor 17:76 (Jan. 26, 1900).
——. Municipal Gas Plants in Great Britain. Maltbie, Milo Roy. Mun. Aff. 4:538 (Sept. 1900). 96
——. "Municipal Gas Profits." Mun. J. & London 8:20 (Jan. 5, 1899).
——. "Municipal Gas Works in Great Britain." City Govt. 7:7 (July, 1899). 97
——. "The Purchase of Gas and Water Works with the latest statistics of Municipal Gas and Water Supply." Silverthorne, Arthur. London, Crosby, Lockwood & Co., 1881. 8vo, 131 pp. 5s. 6d. 98
Municipal Control, etc. Telephones. Hunter, Thomas. Mun. J. & London 8:1289 (Dec. 1, 1899); anon. Elec. Eng. 26:106 (Aug. 4, 1898); Mun. J. & London 8:765, 1292 (June 30, Dec. 1, 1899). 99
——. "Report from the Select Committee on Telephones." (Parliamentary Committee, England.) 4to, 659 pp. Paper, $1.50. 100
Municipal Control, etc. Transit Facilities. "Control of Tramways in England." City Government 1:38 (1896). 1
——. "Corporation Tramways and the Rates." Ry. World 7:270 (Aug. 4, 1898). 2
——. "Cost of Operating Municipal Electric Tramways." Surveyor 18:273 (Sept. 7, 1900).
——. "Municipal Electric Tramways." Mun. J. 9:891 (Nov. 8, 1900).
——. "Municipal Ownership of Tramways in the United Kingdom, The." Ackworth, W. M. Railroad Gaz. 29:400 (June 4, 1897); Taylor, Benjamin. Cassiers' 16:381 (Aug. 1899). 3
——. "Municipal Ownership and Operation of Street Railways in England, Statement in Relation to." Porter, Robert P. Appendix E in Report of the Special Committee on Street Railways (Mass.) Boston (1898). 4
——. "Municipal Tramways and Foreign Contracts." Mun. J. 9:444 (June 8, 1900).
——. "Street Railways in British Towns: Municipal Systems compared with Company Enterprises." Donald, Robert. Mun. Aff. 4:31 (March, 1900). 5
——. "The New Development in Municipal Trams." Mun. J. & London 8:103 (Jan. 26, 1899).
——. "Tranvie Municipali in Inghilterra." Critica Sociale 10:302 (Oct. 1, 1900). 6
Municipal Control, etc. Waterworks. Ann. Am. Acad. Pol. Sci. 14:143 (July, 1899). 7
——. "Municipal Ownership of Water Works in England and Wales." Engng. News 42:63 (July 27, 1899). 8
——. "The Terms of Purchase of Municipal Water Undertakings." (List of county boroughs in which water works have been purchased, dates, terms, conditions, etc. Prepared by order of the London County Council.) Jour. Gas Lighting (London) Feb. 16, 1897. 9
"Parliament, Municipal Men in." Mun. J. 9:851 (Oct. 26, 1900). 10
——. "The Municipality in Parliament: New Powers Demanded by Corporations." Mun. J. 9:1003, 1023 (Dec. 21, 28, 1900).
Police. "Executive Powers in relation to crimes and disorder; or Powers of Police in England." Haycraft, Thomas Wagstaff. London, Butterworth, 1897. 8vo, 144 pp. 6s. 11
——. "A Problem of Municipal Police." Mun. J. & London 8:101 (Jan. 26, 1899).

United Kingdom—*Continued.*

——. Ireland. "The Policeman's Manual." Reed, Andrew. Dublin, Alex, Thom & Co., 1898. 265 pp. ... 12

——. "Report of the Commissioners appointed to inquire as to the best means of establishing an efficient Constabulary Force in the Counties of England and Wales." Parliamentary Papers and Documents, 1839, vol. 19. ... 12a

——. Scotland. "The Burgh Police Act, 1892." Muirhead, James. Scottish Law Review 8:317, 9:234 (1892, 1893). ... 13

"Population of Cities of England." Humphries, N. A. J. Statis. Soc. 54:311 (1891). ... 14

——. "Alleged Depopulation of the Rural Districts." Ogle, W. J. Statis. Soc. 52:205 (1889). ... 15

——. "Decrease of Rural Population in England." Longstaff, G. B. J. Statis. Soc. 56:380 (1893). ... 16

——. "Distribution of Towns and Villages in England." Chisholm, Geo. C. Geographical J. 10:511 (Nov. 1897). ... 17

——. "Growth of Our Great Cities, The." Leisure Hour Feb. 1900.

"Private Bill Legislation." Ed. R. 189:76 (Jan. 1899); Ty. & Ry. World 9:311 (July 5, 1900). ... 18

——. "Guide to the Procedure upon Private Bills together with forms, standing orders of the House of Commons, etc." Dodd, Cyril, and Wilberforce, H. W. W. London, Eyre and Spottiswoode, 1898. 8vo, 360 pp. 7s. 6d. ... 19

——. "History of Private Bill Legislation." Clifford, Frederick. London, Butterworth, vol. I, 1885; vol. II, 1887. 2 vols, 8vo. Vol. I, 20s; vol. II, 35s. ... 20

"Rifle Ranges, Municipal." Bradley, J. W. Mun. J. & London 9:65, 283 (Jan. 26, April 13, 1900). ... 21

Sanitation. "English Sanitary Institutions, in their development and political and social relations." Simon, John. London, Smith & E., 2d ed., 1897. 8vo, 536 pp. 18s. ... 22

——. "Law Relating to Public Health, Local Government and Urban and Rural Sanitary Authorities." Glen, W. C. and A. London, Knight, 10th ed., 1888. 45s. ... 23

——. "Lectures on Sanitary Law." Blyth, A. Wynter. London, Macmillan, 1893. 8vo, 279 pp. 8s. 6d. ... 24

——. "Public Health Progress in the Queen's Reign." (1837-1897.) Bailey, T. Ridley. San. Rec. 21:39 (Jan. 14, 1898), 21:65 (Jan. 21, 1898), 21:118 (Feb. 4, 1898). ... 25

——. "Report of the Commissioners for inquiring into the State of Large Towns and Populous Districts." Parliamentary Papers and Documents, 1844, vol. 17; 1845, vol. 18.

——. "Reports of the Royal Sanitary Commission." Parliamentary Papers and Documents, 1870, vol. 32; 1871, vol. 35.

——. "Report on the Sanitary Condition of the Labouring Population of Great Britain." Parliamentary Papers and Documents, 1843, vol. 12.

——. "Sanitary Advances in Municipal Engineering in England." Boulnois, H. Percy. Mun. Engng. 14:21 (Jan. 1898). ... 26

——. "Sanitary Inspector's Handbook." Taylor, A. London, Lewis, 1897. 8vo, 348 pp. 5s. ... 27

——. "Sanitary Legislation in England since 1875." Calkins, G. N. Am. Statis. Assoc. 2:297 (1891). ... 28

——. "Les Mesures Sanitaires en Angleterre depuis 1875 et leurs Resultats." Monod, Henri. Revue d'Hygiène Vol. 13, 1891. ... 29

——. "Twenty Years Sanitation in an Urban District." Young, James. San. Rec. 20:576 (Nov. 26, 1897). ... 30

Schools. "English National Education: A Sketch of the Rise of Public Elementary Schools." Holman, H. London, Blackie & Son, 1898. 12mo, 256 pp. Cl. 2s. 6d. ... 31

——. "Education Authority and Municipal Boroughs." Porritt, E. Westm. Rev. 148:558 (Nov. 1897). ... 32

——. "History of the Elementary School Contest in England." Adams, F. London, Chapman, 1882. 8vo. 6s. ... 33

——. "Report of the Commissioners appointed to inquire into the State of Popular Education in England." Parliamentary Papers and Documents, 1861, vol. 21, six parts.

United Kingdom—*Continued.*

——. "Report of the Royal Commission appointed to inquire into the working of the Elementary Education Acts." Parliamentary Papers and Documents, 1886, vol. 25; 1887, vols. 29, 30; 1888, vols. 35-7.

——. "Reports on Elementary Schools (1852-1882.)" Arnold, Matthew. London, Macmillan, 1893. 3s. 6d.   34

——. "Studies in Secondary Education." Acland, A. H. D., and Smith, H. London, Percival, 1892. 7s. 6d.   35

——. "The State in Relation to Education." Craik, H. London, Macmillan (English Citizen Series), 1893. 2s. 6d.   36

Scotland. (See under General References, Finance, History, Lighting, Police.)

Settlements. "University Settlements in England." King, Joseph. Zeit. Staatswissen. 53 Jahrg. 3 Hft. p. 559 (July, 1897), Schweiz. Zeitschrift f. Gemeinnützigkeit, 34 Jahrg. 2 Hft., 1895.   37

Sewerage, Sewage Disposal. Bacterial Treatment of Sewage in England. Easby, William, Jr. Pro. Eng. C. 17:133 (July, 1900), Surveyor 18:84 (July 20, 1900), Engng. Rec. 42:78 (July 28, 1900), 42:103 (Aug. 4, 1900); Kinnicutt, Leonard P. J. Assoc. Engng. Soc. 24:107 (Feb. 1900); Thudichum, George. Surveyor 18:110 (July 27, 1900), Engng. Rec. 42:124 (Aug. 11, 1900).   38

——. "Duties of Sanitary Authorities in Relation to Sewerage." Stephens, J. E. R. San. Rec. 25:288 (April 6, 1900).   39

——. "Joint Sewerage Scheme, Stalybridge and Dukinfield." Surveyor 18:492 (Oct. 26, 1900).   40

——. "Local Government Board and Sewage Disposal Schemes." San. Rec. 23:559 (June 30, 1899).

——. "Purification of Sewage in England." Alvord, John W. Mun. Engng. 14:262 (May, 1898); Fowler, Gilbert J. Mun. Engng. 19:262 (Oct. 1900).   41

——. "River Pollution in England." (Pollution of the Irwell and Mersey by manufacturer's and sewage discharges. Action taken in the matter.) Fire and W. Jan. 23, 1897.   42

——. Sewage Disposal in England. Maxwell, Wm. H. San. Rec. 20:632 (Dec. 10, 1897); Shenton, Henry C. H. San. Rec. 26:519 (Dec. 14, 1900); Thompson, T. Kennard. Engng. M. 1:831 (1891); anon. San. Rec. 21:368 (April 8, 1898), 22:558 (Nov. 25, 1898), 25:352 (April 27, 1900), 26:565 (Dec. 28, 1900); Engng. Rec. 38:429, 560 (Oct., Nov. 1898); Surveyor 18:512 (Nov. 2, 1900).   43

Special Legislation. (See under Private Bill Legislation above.)

Street Cleaning. "Municipal Cleansing in Great Britain." Engng. News 43:272 (April 26, 1900).   44

Street Railways. (See under Transit Facilities below.)

"Street Works Act, 1892, Private." San Rec. 23:45 (Jan. 20, 1899).

Sweating. (See under Labor above.)

Taxation. (See under Finance above.)

Telephones, Municipal Ownership of, in England. (See under Municipal Control, Municipal Ownership above.)

Transit Facilities. "Accounts, Forms of Tramway." Ty. & Ry. W. 9:602 (Dec. 6, 1900).   45

——. "Accounts Electric Tramway." Ty. & Ry. World 9:501 (Oct. 11, 1900).

——. "British Street Cars." Curtis, William E. St. Ry. R. 7:582 (Sept. 15, 1897).   46

——. "British Tramway Development." Robinson, J. Clifton. Cassier's 17:279 (Feb. 1900).   47

——. Electric Tramways and Electric Traction in Great Britain. Blackwell, Robert W. Cassier's 16:283 (Aug. 1899); Boyle, James. St. Ry. R. 9:53 (Jan. 15, 1899), Sci. Am. 47:19372 (Feb. 25, 1899), U. S. Cons. Rep. 59:268 (Feb. 1899); Robinson, J. C. Engng. Times Nov. 1900; Short, Sidney H. St. Ry. J. 15:663 (Oct. 1899); anon. St. Ry. R. 8:304 (May 15, 1898), 9:257, 599 (April 15, Sept. 15, 1899); Railroad Gaz. 30:321, 847 (May 6, Nov. 25, 1898), 31:281 (April 21, 1899); St. Ry. J. 16:191 (Feb. 17, 1900).   48

——. "Electric Tramways and British Industry." Hill, Hawthorne. Ir. Age Nov. 23, 1899.   49

——. "Electric Traction under British Conditions, The Calculation of Distributing Systems of." Sayers, H. M. Brit. Inst. of Elec. Engs. May 3, 1900; St. Ry. J. 16:599 (June 30, 1900).   50

——. "Electric Traction in Great Britain, Commercial Aspects of." Garcke,

United Kingdom—*Continued.*

Emile. Engng. M. 17:45 (April, 1899). 51
——. "Electrical Energy on English Street Railways, Cost of." St. Ry. J. 16:505 (May 19, 1900). 52
——. "Electrical Tramway Construction in England, Recent." Lomas, Harold. Elec. World 31:143 (Jan. 29, 1898), 31:180 (Feb. 5, 1898). 53
——. "Electric Street Traction in England, Legal Aspects of." Knox, E. F. Vesey. Engng. M. 16:25 (Oct. 1898). 54
——. "Electric Tramways, The Principal Features of." Surveyor 17:40 (Jan. 19, 1900). 55
——. "Electric Traction in the United Kingdom, The Prospects of." Ty. & Ry. World 9:312 (July 5, 1900). 56
——. "Electric Railways, Working Expenses of English." Ry. World 6:269 (Sept. 1897).
——. "Fares, Tramway." Geron, H. Ty. & Ry. World 9:520 (Oct. 11, 1900). 57
——. Finance. "Municipal Tramways Finance." Mun. J. 9:589 (July 27, 1900).
——. "First English Tramway, The." Mun. J. 9:477 (June 22, 1900).
——. "Legislation, Tramway and Electric Railway." Ry. World 7:123 (April 7, 1898), 7:197 (June 2, 1898), 8:69 (Feb. 9, 1899), 8:345 (Sept. 7, 1899), 9:72 (Feb. 8, 1900). 58
——. "The Tramways Act of 1870." Ry. World 6:340 (Nov. 1897).
——. "The Tramways Act 1870 with introduction, notes, Board of Trade Rules, forms of By-laws and Provisional Order, List of Tramways." Phillips, Geo. I. London, Reeves and Turner, 1890. 8vo, 152 pp. 5s. 59
——. "Tramway and the Light Railways Act." Ry. World 7:221 (July 7, 1898).
——. "Light Railways." Bryce, James. Ty. & Ry. World 9:30 (Jan. 11, 1900). 60
——. "Light Railways as Tramways." London 7:329 (May 26, 1898).
——. "Light Railway Commission, The Work of the." Scotter, R. H. Ty. & Ry. W. 9:458 (Sept. 6, 1900). 61
——. "Manual of Electrical Undertakings." (Telegraph, Telephone, Electricity Supply, Electric Traction, Electrical Manufacturing and miscellaneous electrical undertakings in Great Britain.) Garcke, Emile. London, Donington House, Norfolk St. Published annually. Fourth ed. for 1899-1900, 1036 pp. 12s. 6d. 62
——. "Manual of Tramways, Omnibuses and Electric Railways containing abstracts of accounts, directory of directors, officials, firms and individuals connected therewith, and extract of tramways act and bye-laws." Duncan. London, Whiting and Sons, 22d ed., 1899. 12mo, 428 pp. Cl. 3s. 6d. 63
——. "Monopoly, A New Tramway." Donald, Robert. Contemp. 76:174 (Aug. 1899). 64
——. Municipal Control, Municipal Ownership of Street Railways. (See under Municipal Control, Municipal Ownership above.)
——. "Profits on Railway Undertakings." Gadsby, Charles H. Ty. & Ry. W. 9:462 (Sept. 6, 1900). 65
——. "Street Railways of Great Britain." Martin, Rufus. St. Ry. Jour. Nov. 1889. 66
——. Tramways Act. (See under Legislation above.)
——. "Tramways in England." Smith, William R. U. S. Consular Report No. 135, 1891. pp. 453-60. 67
——. "Tramway Companies' Reports." Ry. World 7:312 (Sept. 1898). 68
——. "Tramway Schemes, New." Mun. J. 9:284 (April 13, 1900). 69
——. "Wages of Tramway Employees." Ty. & Ry. W. 9:570 (Nov. 8, 1900). 70
Unemployment. "Die Arbeitslosenfrage im Licht der englischen Erfahrungen." v. Nostitz, Hans. Jr. Gesetz. Ver. Volks. 2:1279-1323 (1896). 71
——. "Die Arbeitslosen-Versicherung der Englischen Gewerkvereine." Schweiz. Bl. June, Aug. 1894. 72
——. "English Cities and the Unemployed." Porritt, E. Char. R. 3:373 (1894). 73
——. "Die Fürsorge für die Arbeitslosen in England." v. Heckel, Max. Jr. Natl. Stat. 63:265-282 (1894). 74
——. "Das Problem der Arbeitslosigkeit in England." Loew, Emil. Ar. Soc. Gesetz Stat. 9:79 (1896). 75
——. "Die Statistik über Arbeitslose in England." Barnreither. Ar. Soc. Gesetz. Stat. 1:43 (1888). 76

United Kingdom—*Continued.*

——. " Unemployed in England, The." Murray's Mag. 2:596, 749 (1887). 77

Vacant City Lots, Cultivation of. (See under Allotments above.)

Wales. (See under General References, Finance and History above.)

Washhouses. (See under Baths, etc., above.)

" Water Works in England." Smyth, William R. U. S. Consular Report No. 135, 1891, pp. 453-60. 78

——. " Charges, Water and Gas." Carter, James. Mun. J. & London 8:1360 (Dec. 22, 1899). 79

——. " Consumption and Waste of Water in Great Britain." Engng. Rec. 40:148 (July 15, 1899). 80

——. " Control of Water Undertakings and Sources of Water Supply." J. Gas Light. 76:1519 (Dec. 18, 1900). 81

——. " Corporation Water Works." Penn-Lewis, W. Report of the Proceedings of the Eighth Annual Meeting of the Corporate Treasurers' & Accountants' Institute, Hull, June 22-23, 1893, p. 33. 82

——. " Directory and Statistics, Water Works." London, Hazell, Watson and Viney. Published annually, 23d issue, 1899. 8vo, 128 pp. 83

——. " Filtration of Water, The English System of." Davis, Floyd. Mun. Engng. 19:394 (Dec. 1900). 84

——. " Law of Gas, Water and Electric Lighting." Will, J. Shirless. London, Butterworth, 1894. 8vo. 32s. 85

——. " Local Government and its Relation to Parish Water Supply and Sewerage." Meade-King, W. O. F. J. Soc. Arts Jan. 26, 1900, Surveyor 17:128 (Feb. 2, 1900), San. Rec. 25:90 (Feb. 2, 1900). 86

——. " Local Government Board and the Protection of Water Supplies from Pollution." Griffith, Percy. J. of Gas Light. Aug. 9, 1898. 87

——. Municipal Control, Municipal Ownership of Water Works. (See under Municipal Control, Municipal Ownership above.)

——. Taxation. " The Rating of Water Undertakings." Bancroft, F. J. J. Gas Light. 76:24. (July 3, 1900), Surveyor 18:4 (July 6, 1900). 88

——. " Underground Water." Mansergh, James. Engng. Rec. 42:596 (Dec. 22, 1900). 89

——. " British Law in regard to Underground Water." Will, J. Shirless. Engng. N. 44:383 (Dec. 6, 1900). 90

——. " Underground Water Supplies, The Protection of." Matthews, William. Surveyor 18:679 (Dec. 14, 1900), J. Gas. Light. 76:1579 (Dec. 25, 1900). 91

——. " Water Acts for 1900." J. Gas Light. 76:1078 (Oct. 30, 1900). 92

——. " Water Supply of English Cities." Fire and W. May 22, 1897. 93

" Women's Work on Vestries and Councils." (England.) Busk, Alice E. p. 379 " Good Citizenship," edited by J. E. Hand. London, Geo. Allan, 1899. 474 pp. 94

United States.

City Government, General References.

" A Continuing City." Jordan, David Starr. Cal. Mun. 1:229 (Feb. 1900). 96

" A Municipal Program: Report of a Committee of the National Municipal League, adopted by the League, November 17, 1899, together with Explanatory and other Papers." New York, Macmillan Co., 1900. 8vo, 246 pp. Cl. $1. 97

——. " An Examination of the Proposed Municipal Program." Wilcox, Delos F. Pp. 51-62 in Proc. of the Columbus Conf. for Good City Govt., 1899. See 6-18f. Anon. pp. 225-239 in "A Municipal Program." New York, Macmillan Co., 1900. 8vo, 246 pp. Cl. $1. 98

——. " A General View of the New Municipal Program." Butler, John A. Pp. 87-95 in "Proc. of the Columbus Conf., 1899, see 6-18f. 99

——. " A Summary of the Program." Rowe, Leo S. Pp. 157-173 in "A Municipal Program." New York, The Macmillan Co., 1900. 8vo, 246 pp. Cl. $1.) 100

——. " Public Opinion and City Government under the Proposed Municipal Program." Deming, Horace E. Pp. 77-86 in " Proc. of the Columbus Conf., 1899, see 6-18f; also pp. 146-156 in "A Municipal Program." New York, Macmillan, 1900. 8vo, 246 pp. Cl. $1. 1

" American Citizen, The." Dole, Chas. F. Boston, D. C. Heath & Co., 1891, 294 pp. 90 cts. (Chapter XIII on City Government.) 2

United States—*Continued.*

"American Citizen's Manual, The." Ford, Worthington C. New York, Putnams, 1883, 184 pp. $1.25. (Chap. II, p. 53, on Local and Municipal Government.)   3

"American Commonwealth, The." Bryce, James. London and New York, Macmillan, 3d ed., 1895. 2 vols. $5. (Part III, Vol. II on "The Party System," Chapter LXXXVIII, p. 377, on "The Tammany Ring in New York," and Chapter LXXXIX on "The Philadelphia Gas Ring.")   4

"American Ideals and Other Essays, Social and Political." Roosevelt, Theodore. New York, G. P. Putnam's Sons, 1897. 12mo, 354 pp. Cl. $1.50. (Chap. VI, "Machine Politics in New York City." Chap. VIII, "Administering the New York Police Force.")   5

"Charter Needs of Great Cities." Coler, Bird S. No. Am. 170:850 (June, 1900).   6

"City Government in the United States." Conkling, A. R. New York, Appletons, 1894, 227 pp. $1.   7

——. "City Government." Bradford, Gamaliel. Ch. 24 and 25 in "The Lesson of Popular Government." New York, Macmillan, 1899. 8vo, 2 vols., 520, 590 pp. Cl. $4.   8

——. "City Government." Part IV, Ch. 5 in "An Outline of American Government." Wilcox, Delos F., and Gill, Wilson L. Our Country 10:55 (Oct. 1899).   9

"City Problems." Wilcox, Delos F. Our Country 7:61 (March, 1898).   10

——. "The City Problem." Hoskin, A. A. New York, J. B. Alden, 1900. 12mo, 153 pp. 50 cts.   11

——. "The Problems of City Life." Byles, W. P. Mun. J. 9:186 (March 9, 1900).   12

"Civil Government in the United States." Fiske, John. Boston, Houghton, M. & Co., 1890. 12mo, 360 pp. $1. (Chap. V on "The City.")   13

——. "Civil Government in the United States, General Outline of the States, Counties, Townships, Cities and Towns." Higby, Clinton D. Boston, Lee, 1895. 133 pp. 30 cts.   14

"Constitutional Municipal Government." Foote, Allen Ripley. Public Policy 2:171 (March 17, 1900), 2:187 (March 24, 1900), 2:202 (March 31, 1900).   15

"Decay of State and Municipal Government in America." Patten, Simon N. Ann. Am. Acad. Pol. Sci. 1:26 (1892). Separate, 25 cts.   16

"Development of American Cities." Quincy, Josiah. Arena 17:529 (March, 1897).   17

"Failure of the Government of Cities in America." Porritt, E. National 24:245, Ecl. M. 123:669 (1895).   18

"Government of American Cities." White, A. D. Forum 10:357 (1890).   19

——. "Government of Cities in the United States." Low, Seth. Cent. 42:730 (1891).   20

"Higher Life of American Cities." Roosevelt, Theodore. Outlook 52:1082 (1895).   21

"Local Administration in the United States and in the United Kingdom." Montagu, F. C. London and New York, Cassell & Co., 1888. 32 pp.   22

"Local Government in America." Shaw, Albert. Fortn. 38:485 (1882).   23

"Local Government in the South and Southwest." Bemis, E. W. J. H. Univ. Press. 115 pp. $1.00.   24

"Local Government and City Government." Willoughby, W. W., and W. F. (in "Government and Administration in the United States." J. H. U. Study on Government and Administration in the United States, Ninth Series, p. 88, Jan. Feb. 1891. Separate, paper. 75 cts.   25

Municipal Government in the United States. Pp. 837-840, Vol. II, Palgrave. See 1-2.   26

——. "La République Americaine, Etats-Unis, Institutions d'Etat, Régime Municipale, etc." Carlier, A. Paris, Guillaumin et Cie., 1890. 4 vols. 36 fr.   27

——. "Le Régime Municipal aux Etats-Unis." Lambelin, Roger. R. Municipale 3:2025 (April 7, 1900).   28

"Municipal Institutions in America and England." (Comparison of Birmingham and Boston mainly.) Chamberlain, Joseph. Forum 14:267 (1892). See also Our Day 11:123 (1893).   29

"Municipal Organization in the United States." Chap. III, p. 193, Vol. I, "Comparative Administrative Law." Goodnow, Frank J.   30

"Municipal Problem in the United States, The." Deming, Horace E. p. 53 Pro. Indianapolis Conf, 1898, see 6-18e. Same, pp. 36-58 in "A Municipal Program." New York, Macmillan, 1900. 8vo, 246 pp. $1.00.   31

United States—*Continued.*

"Municipal Problems in America." Janes, Louis G. Social Economist 2:395 (1892). 32

"Our Cities." Waring, Geo. E. Pp. 214-93, Vol. II, Nathaniel S. Shaler's "United States of America." New York, Appleton, 1894. 2 vols. 670 and 641 pp. $10.00. 33

"Peculiarities of American Municipal Government." Ch. V, p. 145, "Unforeseen Tendencies of Democracy." Godkin, E. L. New York, Houghton, M. & Co., 1898. 12mo, 265 pp. Cl. $2.00. Also in Atlan. 80:620 (Nov. 1897). 34

"Political Ideas and Institutions in their Relations to the Conditions of City Life, American." Rowe, Leo S. Pages 75-88, Pro. of the Louisville Conf., 1897. See 6-18d. 35

"Politics and Administration." Goodnow, Frank J. New York, Macmillan Co., 1900. 12mo, 270 pp. Cloth, $1.50. 36

"Practical Agitation." Chapman, John J. New York, Charles Scribner's Sons. 1900. 12mo, 157 pp. Cloth, $1.25. 37

"Problem of City Government in the United States." Low, Seth. Outlook 53:624 (1896). 38

"Reform in the United States, Municipal." Culham, J. A. Mun. World 9:166 (Oct. 1899). 39

——. "American Municipal Reform." Bonney, C. Carroll. Our Day 7:418 (1891). 40

——. Municipal Reform during the Past Year. Woodruff, Clinton Rogers. pp. 45-62 Louisville Conference, 1897, see 6-18d; 1898, p. 101, see 6-18e; 1899, pp. 169-187, see 6-18f; Engng. N. 44:194 (Sept. 20, 1900). 41

"Social Atheism, A Picture of. The Rottenness of American Municipalities." R. of Rs. 3:56 (1891). 42

"The Coming Democracy." Smith, Orlando J. New York, The Brander Co., 1900. 12mo, 162 pp. Cloth, $1.00. 43

"The Higher Municipality." Snow, R. W. Cal. Mun. 2:111 (May, 1900). 44

"Town Government, American." Hale, Edward Everett. p. 1, New Series No. 1, American Institute of Civics, New York, 1895. 21 pp. 20 cts. 45

——. "Decay of Town Government, The." (Editorial.) Nation 65:180 (Sept. 2, 1897). 46

——. "Democratic Government a Study of Politics." Stickney, Albert. New York, Harper, 1885. 166 pp. $1. (Revival of Town Meeting Government.) See also "The Political Problem," by the same author. New York, Harper, 1890. 189 pp. $1.00. 47

——. "Legislation of Town Meetings." Connor, R. Nation 20:186, 203 (1875). 48

——. "Town Meeting, The." Fiske, John. Harper 70:265 (1885). 49

——. "Town Meeting Idea applied to the Government of Cities." Thomas, J. F. Am. J. Pol. 2:503 (1893). 50

——. "Town Meetings for Great Cities." Allen, W. F. Nation 2:684 (1865). 51

"Towns and Cities." Deady, Matthew P. Address before the students of the University of Oregon. Published by the Board of Regents of the U. of O. 1886. 52

"Town and Village Government." Nelson, Henry Loomis. Harper 83:111 (1891). 53

"Young Men's Municipal Clubs, Municipal Government and." Shaw, Albert. p. 5, New Series No. 1, American Institute of Civics, New York, 1895. 21 pp. 29 cts. 54

"Charity Organization in the United States, History of." Kellogg, Charles D. p. 43, "International Congress," vol. III, 1893, see 43-99. 55

——. "National Conferences of Charities and Corrections, Proceedings of the." Published annually 1874-1899. 56

"Civil Service in the United States." (Pt. iv, pp. 425-475, on the State and Municipal Service.) Comstock, John M. New York, Holt, 1885. 8vo, 602 pp. $2.00. 57

"Contracts with Cities, Legal Status of." Prog. Age 18:446 (Oct. 15, 1900).
Court Decisions. "American and English Corporation Cases, a collection of corporation cases, private and municipal, decided in the courts of last resort in the United States, England and Canada." New York, Thompson, 1895. 3 vols. Each $6.50. 58

"Damage Suits against Municipalities." Aylward, John A. Muncipality vol. 1, No. 4, p. 32 (Oct. 1900), No. 5, p. 9 (Dec. 1900). 59

Depopulation. "Urban Populations in the South, the country being deserted, etc." U. S. Department of Agriculture, Report of the Statistician, Sept. 1894, p. 572. 60

United States—*Continued.*

Direct Legislation. "The Referendum in America, a discussion of law making by popular vote." (Especially Ch. IV, pp. 86-104, on "The People and their City Charters.") Oberholtzer, Ellis Paxon. Pubs. of the U. of Pa., Vol. IV, No. 12, 1893. 225 pp. $1.50. 61

Engineering, Municipal. "A Review of Important Municipal Work in America." Mun. Engng. 16:7 (Jan. 1899).

——. "Laws Governing Public Works, An Outline of Municipal." Mun. Engng. 14:10 (Jan. 1898). 62

——. "Laws Governing them, Municipal Public Improvements and the." Molitor, David. Mun. Engng. 13:331 (Dec. 1897). 63

——. "Municipal Work in America." Mun. Engng. 17:249 (Nov. 1899).

——. "Public Works of Last Year." City Engineers' Reports on extent, character and cost of Public Improvements made under their direction. (Newark, N. J., Allegheny, Pa., Albany, N. Y., Kansas City, Mo., Providence, R. I., Kansas City, Kas., Peoria, Ill., Richmond, Va., Troy, N. Y., Springfield, Mass., Milwaukee, Wis.) City Govt. 2:2 (Jan. 1897). 64

"Finance." pp. 88, 92, "American Statute Law," by F. J. Stimson. Boston, Soule, 1886. 2 vols. 8vo, 779, 622 pp. 65

——. "American Tax Methods." Taussig, F. W. Ind. 50:137 (Feb. 3, 1898). 66

——. "Corporation Finance: A Study of the Finances of Corporations in the United States, with special reference to the valuation of corporation securities." Greene, Thomas L. New York, G. P. Putnam's Sons, 1897. 185 pp. $1.25 67

——. "Das Finanzwesen der Staaten und Städte d. nordamerikanischen Union." Patten, Simon Nelson. Jena, Fischer, 1878. 61 pp. 68

——. "Municipal Revenues and Expenses." Herrmann, August. City Govt. 5:219 (Dec. 1898). 69

——. "Staats- u. Lokalfinanzen d. Verein. Staaten v. Nord Amerika." Kaufman, R. v. 1891. 8vo. 70

——. Statistics. "Suggestions in regard to the Statistics of Municipal Finance in the Census of 1900." Critical essays on the Federal Census. Am. Econ. Assoc. Publications, March 1899, pp. 415-65. N. Y., Macmillan, 1899. 8vo, 525 pp. Paper $2; cl. $2.50. 71

——. "Taxation in American States and Cities." Ely, R. T., and John H. Finley. New York, Thos. Y. Crowell & Sons, 1838. 544 pp. $1.75. 72

——. Taxation. "Relief of Local and State Taxation through distribution of the national surplus." Thompson, R. E. Philadelphia, E. Stern & Co., 1888. 8vo, 28 pp. 25 cts. 73

——. "Taxation, Some Possible Reforms in State and Local." Howe, Frederic C. Am. Law. R. 33:685 (Sept.-Oct. 1899). 74

——. "Taxation, State and Municipal." Shearman, T. G. Nation 4:455 (1867). 75

——. "Taxation in the Larger Cities of the United States, Rates of." Herrmann, August. Pro. Am. Soc. Mun. Imp. (5th yr.) Pt. II, p. 3 (Oct. 1898). 76

——. "Uniform Accounting." Cahoon, James Blake. Prog. Age 18:333 (Aug. 1, 1900). (See also under Statistics below.) 77

——. "Valuation, Taxation and Indebtedness." Porter, Robert P. Washington, Government Printing Office, 1884. 909 pp. Tenth Census of the United States. 78

Foreign Element in American Cities, Statistics of. Report on Population, Pt. I, pp. xc-xcii; Table 50, pp. 704-6. 79

"Growth of Cities of the United States." Lossing, Benson J. Harper's M. 7:171 (1853); Magie, B. C. Scribner's 15:418 (1878). 80

——. "Growth of Cities in the United States during the decade 1880-90." Boyd, Carl. Am. Stat. Assoc. 3:416, No. 23 (1893). 75 cts. 81

——. "Rise of American Cities." Hart, A. B. Q. J. E. 4:129 (1890). For same article see also his "Practical Essays on American Government," VIIIth Essay. New York, Longmans, G. & Co., 1893. 311 pp. 82

History. American Historic Towns. Series edited by Lyman P. Powell. Three vols. "Historic Towns of New England," with sketches of Portland, Rutland, Salem, Boston, Cambridge, Concord, Plymouth, Cape Cod Towns, Deerfield, Newport, Providence, Hartford, New Haven; "Historic Towns of the Middle States," with sketches of Albany, Saratoga, Schenectady, Newburg, Tarrytown, Brooklyn, New York, Buffalo, Pittsburgh, Philadelphia, Princeton and Wilmington. "Historic Towns of the Southern States," with sketches of Baltimore, Annapolis, Frederick, Washington, Richmond, Williamsburg, Wilmington, N. C.,

United States—*Continued.*

Charleston, Savannah, St. Augustine, Mobile, Montgomery, New Orleans, Vicksburg, Knoxville, Nashville, Louisville and Little Rock. New York, Putnams, 1898, 1899, 1900. 8vo, 597, 439, 528 pp. Cl. $3.50 per vol. 83

——. "A Century of Social Betterment." McMaster, John Bach. Atlan. 79:20 (Jan. 1897). 84

——. "Germanic Origins of New England Towns." Adams, Herbert B. J. H. Univ. Studies I:2 (1883). 85

——. "Introduction to the Local Constitutional History of the U. S." Howard, Geo. Elliot. J. H. U. Series extra vol. 8vo, 542 pp. Cl. $3.00. 86

——. "Municipal Corporations in the Colonies." Fairlie, John Archibald. Mun. Aff. 2:341 (Sept. 1898). 87

——. "Municipal Development in the United States." Fairlie, John A. Pp. 1-35 in "A Municipal Program." New York, Macmillan, 1900. 8vo. 246 pp. Cloth, $1. 88

——. "Municipal Government now and a Hundred Years Ago." Woodruff, Clinton Rogers. Pop. Sci. Mo. 58:60 (Nov. 1900). 89

Housing. "Maisons pour Ouvrières des Grandes Cités aux Etats-Unis d'Amérique." Escard, Paul. Ref. Soc. 9:927 (June 16, 1900). 90

——. "Municipal Lodging Houses." Mun. J. & Eng. 9:148 (Dec. 1900).

Legislation. "Recent Economic and Social Legislation in the United States." Stimson, F. J. Yale R. 6:148 (Aug. 1897). 91

——. "American Statute Law." Stimson, Frederic J. Boston, Soule, 1886. 2 vols. 8vo, 779, 622 pp. 92

——. "Legislation in 1895, 1896, 1897, 1898, Political and Municipal." Durand, E. Dana. Ann. Am. Acad. Pol. Sci. 7:411; 9:231; 11:174; 13:212 (May, 1896, March, 1897, 1898, 1899). 93

——. "Legislation in 1899, Political and Municipal." (Continuation of above series.) Whitten, Robert H. Ann. Am. Acad. Pol. Sci. 15:160 (March, 1900). 94

——. "Legislation by States in 1900." Whitten, Robert H. Bull. N. Y. State Library Dec. 1900. 95

——. "Recent Municipal Experiments." (Legislation in various States.) Gunton's 15:116 (August, 1898).

"Licenses, Municipal." Kirkbride, C. N. Cal. Mun. 2:43 (March, 1900). 96

Lighting. "A Great Gas Business." (Methods of the United Gas Improvement Co., controlling the gas supply of Philadelphia and thirty-two other cities.) City & State 4:624 (June 2, 1898). 97

——. "American Gas Affairs." Chandler, C. F. Prog. Age 18:359 (Aug. 15, 1900). 98

——. "Directory of American Gas Companies." Brown, E. C. New York, Progressive Age, 1899. (Eighth year.) 8vo, 156 pp. Cl. $5. 99

——. "Directory of Gas Light Companies in the United States and Canada." Goodwin, William W. Philadelphia. Published by the Goodwin Gas Stove and Meter Co., fifth edition, 1886. 263 pp. 100

——. "Directory, Johnston's Electrical and Street Railway." New York, W. J. Johnston Co. Published annually, edition for 1897, 748 pp. $5. 1

——. "Fuel Gas in the United States, The Failure of the Commercial Attempts to Supply." Shelton, F. H. Prog. Age 15:259 (June 15, 1897), Am. Gas Lgt. J. 66:903 (June 7, 1897), Engng. News 38:108 (Aug. 12, 1897). 2

——. "Incandescent Gas Lighting in the United States, Development of." Brown, D. Walter. Prog. Age 16:78, 129, 164, 185, 231, 304 (Feb. 15, March 15, April 1, April 15, May 15, June 15, 1898). 3

——. "Law of Electric Wires in Streets and Highways, The." Keasbey, Edward Quinton. (2nd Ed.) Chicago, Callaghan & Co., 1900. 8vo, 358 pp. 4

——. Municipal Ownership, etc. (See under Municipal Control.)

——. "Photometrical Standards in the United States." J. Gas Light. 76:1338 (Nov. 27, 1900).

——. "Price of Gas in seventy-nine Cities of the United States, 1873-1887." Progressive Age, April, 1887. 5

——. "Price of Gas in 100 Cities in the United States from 1878-1887." Progressive Age and Water Gas Journal, March, 1887. 6

——. "Some Notes upon Typical American Gas Works." Am. Gas Light. J. 68:251 (Feb. 14, 1898).

——. "Statistics Regarding the Gas Companies of America." Goodwin, William

BIBLIOGRAPHY.

United States—*Continued.*

———. W. Paper read before the American Gas Light Association, Philadelphia, Oct. 1886. 6 pp. ... 7

———. "Street Lighting, Cost of, in Different Cities in the United States." Engng. News June 28, 1890, p. 607.

———. "Street Lighting, Cost of. Unreasonable inequality of prices charged for illuminating the streets of American Cities." City Govt. 2:37 (Feb. 1897). ... 8

———. "Chaotic Condition of Our Street Lighting System as to Cost, etc." Hunter, D. Elec. Eng. 24:331 (Oct. 7, 1897), Prog. Age 15:465 (Oct. 15, 1897). ... 9

———. "Electric Street Lighting in American Cities." Cappelen, F. W. Mun. Engng. 15:276 (Nov. 1898); Finley, R. J. R. of Rs. 7:68 (1893). ... 10

"Liquor Laws, A Study of American." Eliot, Charles W. Atlan. 79:177 (Feb. 1897). ... 11

Mayor, Functions of. "Les Fonctions de Maire aux Etats-Unis." Chabanne, J. B. Revue Municipale 3:1627 (Oct. 14, 1899). ... 12

Municipal Control, Ownership, etc. "American Experiments in Municipal Control." (Reprinted from N. Y. World.) Mun. Rec. & Ad. Vol. 1, No. 23, p. 6 (Nov. 13, 1897). ... 13

———. "The Cost of Supplying Water, Gas and Electricity." Engng. Rec. 42:121 (Aug. 11, 1900).

———. "Municipal Electric Light Plants." (Bulletin No. 1, issued by the League of American Municipalities, New York City, Feb. 1898). ... 14

———. "Municipal Gas Works in the United States." Hollander, J. H. Independent Jan. 21, 1893. ... 15

———. "Municipal Lighting in the United States." Cappelen, F. W. J. Assoc. Engin. Soc. 18:313 (May, 1897). ... 16

———. "Municipal Ownership of Gas in the United States." Bemis, E. W. Am. Econ. Assoc. Pubs. VI:4 and 5 (1891). $1.00. ... 17

———. "Municipal Socialism in America." Chase, John C. Ind. 52:249 (Jan. 25, 1900); Maltbie, Milo Roy. Pp. 126-8 in "The Labour Annual for 1900." Edwards, Joseph, Editor. Wallasey, Edwards, 1900. 12mo, 176 pp. Cloth, 2s. ... 18

———. "Powers of Municipalities respecting Public Works." Goodnow, Frank J. Am. Econ. Assoc. 2:563 (1888). ... 19

———. "State Control of Corporations." Cahoon, James Blake. Am. Gas. Light J. 73:1047 (Dec. 31, 1900). ... 20

———. "The City in the United States—The Proper Scope of its Activities." Shaw, Albert. Pp. 59-73 in "A Municipal Program." New York, The Macmillan Co., 1890. 8vo, 246 pp. Cloth, $1.00. p. 82, Ind. Conf. See 6-18e. ... 21

———. "Water, Gas and Electric-light Plants under Private and Municipal Ownership." Fourteenth Annual Report of the Commissioner of Labor, 1899. Washington, 1900. 8vo, 983 pp.; criticism in Engng. N. 44:92 (Aug. 9, 1900). ... 22

Overcrowding. "Congested Districts in American Cities." Wright, Carroll D. Our Day 9:172 (1892). ... 23

"Parks and Squares in Cities of the United States." Eliot, Charles. Garden & F. 1:412 (1888). ... 24

———. "Park Movement in the United States." Garden & F. 6:221 (1893).

———. "Parkways and Boulevards in American Cities." Baxter, Sylvester. Am. Arch. Oct. 8, 1898. ... 25

"Paving, American Street." Engng. Rec. 37:29 (Dec. 11, 1897).

———. "Assessment of Cost of Pavement, the Practice of 27 American Cities." Pav. & Mun. Eng. April, 1895, p. 201. ... 26

———. "Brick Paving in the Middle West." Bain, H. Foster. Am. R. of Rs. 20:60 (July, 1899). ... 27

———. Street Pavements in American Cities. Gillham, R. Engng. News July 7, 1892, p. 2; Haupt, Lewis M. J. Frankl. Inst. Dec. 1889; anon. Engng. N. 23:292 (1890). ... 28

———. "Street Paving in Eastern Cities." Mchts. Assoc. R., Vol. 3, No. 35. p. 3 (July, 1899).

———. "Wood Paving in the East." Downing, M. A. California Municipalities 1:144 (Dec. 1899). ... 29

Police. Pp. 1016-1022, Encyc. Soc. Ref. See 1-3. ... 30

———. "Law of sheriffs, constables, marshals, municipal police and detectives." Warrum, Henry. Indianapolis, Warrum, 1895. 143 pp. $1.00. ... 31

United States—*Continued.*

——. " Limitations of Police Power in the United States, A Treatise on the." Tiedeman, Christopher G. St. Louis, F. H. Thomas Law Book Co., 1886. 662 pp. $6.00.   32

——. " Police Force in Eleven Principal Cities of the United States." Wheatley, R. Chaut. 7:197 (1893).   33

——. Prisons. " Our Penal Machinery and its Victims." Altgeld, John P. Chicago, McClurg, new ed., 1886. 8vo, 151 pp. Paper, 50c.   34

——. " Reformatory System in the United States, The." Reports prepared for the International Prison Commission. Barrows, S. J. Washington, Government Printing Office, 1900. Doc. No. 459, 56 Congress 1st session. 8vo, 240 pp.   35

——. " Statistics, Police Department." City Govt. 5:228 (Dec. 1898), 6:19 (Jan. 1899).

" Political Parties and City Government under the Proposed Municipal Program." Goodnow, Frank J. Pp. 129-145 in " A Municipal Program." New York, The Macmillan Co., 1900. 8vo, 246 pp. Cloth, $1.00.   36

——. " Our Political Methods." Field, David Dudley. Forum 2:213 (1886).   37

——. " Political Organizations in the United States and England." Bryce, James. No. Am. 156:105 (1893).   38

Referendum. (See under Direct Legislation above.)

Sanitation. " Boards of Health, The Powers, Duties and Limitations of." Patterson, S. A. Pro. 24th An. Meeting N. J. Sanitary Ass'n, 1898, p. 57.   39

——. " Defects of Municipal Sanitation in American Cities." Billings, John S. Forum 15:304 (1893).   40

——. History. " The Past and Present Condition of Public Hygiene and State Medicine in the United States." Abbott, Samuel W. Department of Social Economy for the United States Commission to the Paris Exposition of 1900. 8vo, 103 pp. Paper.   41

——. History. " Sanitary Science in the United States—its Present and its Future." Leeds, Albert R. Van Nos. Eng. M. 20:6 (1879).   42

——. " Manual for Boards of Health and Health Officers." Balch, Louis. New York, Banks, 1893. 242 pp. $1.50.   43

——. " National Government and the Public Health." Girdner, John H.; Doty, Alvah H., and Drake, C. M. No. Am. 165:733 (Dec. 1897).   44

——. " National Health Bureau in the United States, Need of a." Prudden, T. Mitchell. Hrprs. Wkly. 38:470 (1894).   45

——. " Department of Public Health for the United States." Sanitarian 38:442 (May, 1897).

——. " Quarantine System of the United States." Wyman, Walter. Sanitarian 39:418 (Nov. 1897).   46

" School System of the United States, The Public." Rice, J. M. New York, Century Co., 1893. 300 pp. $1.50. A summary in Forum 15:504 (1893).   47

——. " Centralizing Tendencies in State Educational Administration, Recent." Webster, W. C. New York, Macmillan, 1897. 8vo, 78 pp. 75 cents. (Columbia Univ. Studies in History, Economics and Public Law, Vol. 4.)   48

——. " City School Systems in the United States." Philbrick, John D. Circular of Information, U. S. Bureau of Education, No. 1, Washington, D. C., 1885. 207 pp.   49

——. " Compulsory Education in the United States." Shaw, W. B. Educa. Rev. 3:444 (May, 1892), 4:47, 129 (June, Sept. 1892).   50

——. " Free School System of the United States, The." Adams, Francis. London, Chapman & Hall, 1875. 300 pp. 9s.   51

——. " L'Instruction Primaire aux Etats-Unis." de Guer, Guerlin. Paris, Berger, Levrault & Cie., 1880. 8vo. 1fr.   52

——. " Legislation, Recent School, in the United States." Shaw, W. B. Educa. R. 8:258 (1894).   53

——. " Legislation for Cities, Recent School." Hinsdale, B. A. Dial 26:107 (Feb. 16, 1899).   54

——. " Public Schools of the United States." Hewes, F. W. Hrprs. Wkly. 39:1017, 1040, 1068, 1093, 1112, 1141 and 1164 (1895).   55

——. Reports of the Commissioner of Education. (From 1870 to present time. Statistics, descriptions, etc., of city schools in America and abroad.) Washington, Government Printing Office.   56

BIBLIOGRAPHY.

United States—*Continued.*

———. " Savings banks in the United States, School." Thiry. Reprinted in part in Report of U. S. Commissioner of Education, 1888-89, Vol. I, p. 655. — 57

———. Statistics of Enrollment, etc. Report of Commissioner of Education, 1894-5, Vol. II, p. 1170. — 58

" Sewage Disposal in the United States." (Containing a discussion of the principles and descriptions of the various methods, and of all the works in operation.) Baker, M. N., and G. W. Rafter. New York, D. Van Nostrand & Co., 1894. 598 pp. $6.00. — 59

———. " Federal Decision on Sewage Disposal Nuisances." Engng. Rec. 40:189 (July 29, 1899).

———. " Liability for Defective Sewerage, Municipal." Clark, Frank H. Central Law Journal 24:123 (1887). — 60

———. " Purification of Sewage in America." A series of articles in the Engineering News, beginning July 14, 1892. In book form: New York, Engng. N. Pub. Co., 1893. 196 pp. $1. — 61

———. " Sewerage of American Cities and Towns." Latrobe, C. H. Engng. News Dec. 3, 17, 1881. — 62

———. " Sewerage Systems in the United States and Canada." Engng. N. Aug. 23, 1890, p. 170.

" Statistics of Cities." U. S. Bulletin Dept. of Labor 3:625 (Sept. 1899), 5:916 (Sept. 1900), and to appear annually. — 63

———. " Census of 1900, Municipal Statistics in the." Engng. News 42:56 (July 27, 1899). — 64

———. " Municipal Statistics, the Census and Bemis." City Govt. 7:25 (Aug. 1899). — 65

———. " Mortality and Vital Statistics." Billings, John S. Washington, Government Printing Office. Part I, 767 pp. 1885. Part II, 803 pp. 1886. Tenth Census of the United States. — 66

———. " Municipal Statistics." Municipal Affairs 2:133 (March, 1898). — 67

———. " Report of Committee on Municipal Data." Brown, Charles Carroll. Mun. Engng. 19:174 (Sept. 1900). — 68

———. ' Social Statistics of Cities." Waring, Geo. E. Tenth Census, Washington, 1886. 2 vols, 915, 843 pp.; Billings, John S. Eleventh Census, Washington, 1895. 137 pp. Article by Wright, Carroll D. Pop. Sci. M. 40:607 (1892). — 69

———. Uniform Accounting and Municipal Statistics. Baker, M. N. City Govt. 9:61 (Sept. 1900), Mun. Engng. 19:210 (Sept. 1900); anon. Engng. N. 42:193 Sept. 1, 1900), 43:393 (June 14, 1900), 44:12 (July 5, 1900). — 70

———. (See also under **Census Reports**.)

" Street Cleaning Statistics for Forty American Cities." Rosewater, Andrew. Engng. News 43:136 (Feb. 22, 1900). — 71

———. " Cost of Street Cleaning in twelve American Cities." Engng. News April 11th, 1895. — 72

" Street Construction and Maintenance in American Cities, Laws regulating taxation for." Engng. News March 21, 1891, p. 281. — 73

———. " Taxation for Street Construction and Maintenance in American Cities." Engng. News March 21, 1891, p. 281. — 74

Taxation. (See above under Finance.)

" Telephone Charges, Power of Municipal Corporations to Regulate." McDougal, H. C. Am. Law R. May, 1896. — 75

———. " Directory, Johnston's Electrical and Street Railway." (Lighting, transit co's, telephones in United States.) New York, W. J. Johnston Co. Published annually, edition for 1897, 748 pp. $5. — 76

———. " Independent Telephone Association of the United States." (Anti-Bell Companies Organization.) Elec. Rev. 30:307 (June 30, 1897). — 77

Transit Facilities. " American Practice." p. 51 " Rapid Transit in Foreign Cities." Parsons, W. B. New York, 1894. — 78

———. " American Railways and American Cities." (Effect of discriminating rates on cities.) Fletcher, H. G. Atlan. 73:803 (1894). — 79

———. " American Tramway Notes." (A department in each number of the Ty. & Ry. World.) — 80

———. " A Trolley Trip from Boston to New York." Derrah, Robert H. St. Ry. R. 9:377 (June 15, 1899). — 81

United States—*Continued.*

———. "British Impressions of American Street Railways, Some." McCallum, Alexander. St. Ry. Jour. 13:20 (Jan. 1897). ... 82

———. "Cable and Electric Traction in America." Ry. World Dec. 1896, 8:58 (Feb. 9, 1899).

———. "Capitalization in America, Distribution of Street Railway Mileage and." St. Ry. J. 13:665 (Oct. 1897). ... 83

———. "Construction and Equipment, American Electric Street Railways, their." Hedges, Killingworth. New York, Spon & Chamberlain, 1894. 200 pp. $5. ... 84

———. "Directory, Johnston's Electrical and Street Railway." New York, W. J. Johnston Co. Published annually, edition for 1897, 748 pp. $5. ... 85

———. "Electric Traction in America." Bell, Louis. Ry. World 7:54 (Feb. 1898). ... 86

———. "Electric Traction in the United States in 1896." (Report of Messrs. Young and Clark to the Tramways Committee of Glasgow.) Electricity (London) Dec. 18, 1896, St. Ry. J. 13:28, 32, 36 (Jan. 1897). ... 87

———. "Electric Traction, American Statistics on." Ry. World 7:140 (May 5, 1898).

———. "Electric Tramways in the United States, The Early Future of." Ty. & Ry. World 8:399 (Oct. 5, 1899). ... 88

———. "Financial Practice and Engineering Methods of American Street Railways." Higgins, E. E. Elec. Eng. 23:403, 430, 447, 472 (April 14, 21, 28 and May 5, 1897). ... 89

———. "Financial Results of Cable and Electric Railway Operations in the United States." St. Ry. J. 13:209, 281, 409, 468 (April, May, July, Aug. 1897). ... 90

———. "Gross Receipts per Capita and per Mile of Track in the Principal American Cities." St. Ry. J. 15:227, 515 (April, Aug. 1899). ... 91

———. "Franchises in American Cities, Street Railway." Engng. News 43:13 (Jan. 4, 1900). ... 92

———. "Impressions of American Tramway Practice." le Rossignol, A. E. Mun. J. 9:749 (Sept. 21, 1900). ... 93

———. "Investments, American Street Railway." Higgins, E. E. (Supplement to the "Street Railway Journal," issued annually.) New York, Street Railway Pub. Co., 1899. 4to, 302 pp. Cloth, $5. ... 94

———. "Mail Matter on Interurban and Street Railways, The Carrying of United States." Dimmock, W. S. Mun. Rec. & Ad. 3:760 (Sept. 1898), Elec. Rev. 33:164 (Sept. 14, 1898), St. Ry. Rev. 8:613 (Sept. 15, 1898), Elec. Eng. 26:250 (Sept. 15, 1898), St. Ry. J. 14:639 (Oct. 1898). ... 95

———. "Power Stations of Electric Railways in America and the Economic Results of their Operation." Tandy, L. D. St. Ry. J. 13:18 (Jan. 1897). ... 96

———. "Rapid Transit in the Cities and the Census." Wright, Carroll D. Pop. Sci. Mo. 40:785 (1895). ... 97

———. "Rights of Street Railway Companies under the Constitution." Bonney, Charles L. St. Ry. Rev. 8:360 (June 15, 1898). ... 98

———. "Speed Ordinances in the Principal Cities of the United States." St. Ry. J. March, 1897.

———. Statistics. "Street Railway Mileage Cars and Capitalization in America." St. Ry. J. 15:100 (Feb. 1899). ... 99

———. "Statistics of Street Railways in the United States." (Reprinted from the St. Ry. J.) Engng. News 38:308 (Nov. 11, 1897). ... 100

———. "Street Railway Transportation." Pt. I, pp. 679-867 of "Transportation Business in the United States." Adams, H. C. Eleventh Census of the United States, 1890. ... 1

———. "Strikes, Recent Street Railroad." Gunton's 17:89 (Aug. 1899). ... 2

"Unemployed in American Cities." Closson, C. C. Q. J. E. 8:168, 453, 499 (1894). ... 3

———. "Labor Colonies Needed in the United States, Are?" Lowell, (Mrs.) Charles R. p. 77 "International Congress," vol. III, 1893. See 43-99. ... 4

———. "Labor Tests and Relief in Work in the United States." White, Alfred T. p. 87 "International Congress, vol. III, 1893, see 43-99. ... 5

———. "Movement of Unemployed in the United States." Pub. Opinion 15:499 (1893). ... 6

———. "Relief Measures for Unemployed in the United States." Closson, C. C. J. Pol. E. 3:461 (1895). ... 7

———. "Una Inchiesta sui Disoccupati negli Stati Uniti." Conigliani, C. A. Riforma Soc. 3:55 (1895). ... 8

Vacant Lot Cultivation. "Les Jardins Ouvriers aux Etats-Unis." Reviere, Louis. Ref. Soc. 5:956 (June 16, 1898). ... 9

United States—*Continued.*

——. "Eight Dollars from One." Powell, R. F. Pub. Imp. 3:313 (May 15, 1900). 10

——. "The Pingree Potato Patches." Gardener, Cornelius. Pp. 45-48 in "Proceedings of the American Park and Outdoor Art Association," Vol. 3, Pt. 3. 8vo, 56 pp. Pamphlet. 11

"Water-Front Engineering in American Cities." Holmes, H. C. Engng. Rec. 40:126 (July 8, 1899), 40:198 (July 29, 1899), 40:224 (Aug. 5, 1899). 12

Water Works. "Private Water Company, The United States Supreme Court on the Rights of a." Engng. Rec. 39:177 (Jan. 28, 1899). 13

——. "Courts, The Rate-Fixing Powers of." Engng. Rec. 41:1 (Jan. 6, 1900).

——. "Two Recent Legal Decisions Concerning the Sale of Water." Engng. Rec. 38:221 (Aug. 13, 1898).

——. "Franchises, Water Works." (Statistics of over one-third of the companies in the United States with discussion.) Engng. News Jan. 9, 1892, p. 37. 14

——. "Improvements in Water Works of America." Fteley, Alphonse. Mun. Engng. 15:147 (Sept. 1898). 15

——. "Pollution of Public Water Supplies in the United States, The." Fuller, George W. Engng. News 44:285 (Oct. 25, 1900), Mun. Engng. 19:337 (Nov. 1900). 16

——. Purification. "Sanitary and Chemical Purification of Water Due to Softening." Goldsmith, N. O. Pp. 61-68 in "Third 'Annual Report of the Central States Water Works Association, Cincinnati, O., Sept. 5-7, 1899." 17

——. "Purification of Water in America." Engng. N. Feb. 1, 8 and 22, 1894.

——. "Purification of Water in America, The Present Status of Methods of." Hazen, Allen. Engng. Rec. 42:442 (Nov. 10, 1900). 19

——. "Rates, Methods of Assessment and Collection of Water." Crandall, F. H. J. N. E. W. W. Assoc. 14:133 (Dec. 1899). 20

——. "Rates, Water, in the Larger Cities of the United States." Herrmann, August. Mun. Engng. 17:264 (Nov. 1899), City Govt. 7:110 (Nov. 1899), Fire & W. 26:411 (Dec. 9, 1899), 26:420 (Dec. 16, 1899), Eng. Rec. 40:459 (Oct. 14, 1899), Other Side, 1:267 (Dec. 9, 1899). 21

——. "Sources, Modes of Supply and Filtration of Public Water Supplies in the United States." Flynn, Benj. H. Engng. News 40:9 (July 7, 1898). 22

——. "Statistics of Financial Operation of Water Works." (Seventeen cities of more than 100,000 population in 1896.) Mun. Engng. 12:207 (April, 1897). 23

——. Statistics. "Capacity of Water Works Systems in American Cities." (Water Works Statistics for Seventeen Cities having more than 100,000 population.) Mun. Engng. 12:1 (Jan. 1897). 24

——. "Statistics of Municipal Water Works Plants." Mun. Engng. 12:359 (June, 1897). 25

——. Statistics. "Manual of American Water Works, Fourth Issue." (History and description of the source and mode of supply, pumps, reservoirs, stand pipes, distribution systems, pressure, consumption, revenue and expenses, cost, debt and sinking fund rates, etc., etc. of the United States and Canada). Baker, M. N. New York Engineering News Publishing Co., 1897. 8vo, 611 pp. Cl. $3. 26

——. Statistics. "Number and Ownership of Water Works in the United States and Canada." (Editorial, with interesting statistical tables). Engng. News 37:265 (April 29, 1897). 27

——. Statistics. "Ownership and Capacity of Water Works in American Cities." (Water Works Statistics for Cities of 50,000 to 100,000 population). Mun. Eng. 12:71 (Feb. 1897).

Uruguay. Local Administration. "La Administracion Local en el Uruguay." DePena, Carlos Maria. Revista Internacional 6:121 (Nov. 1897), 6:237 (Dec. 1897). 28

"**Utica, N. Y.,** Report on Municipal Ownership of Electric Street Lighting Plant for." Engng. N. May 7, 1896. 29

"**Utopias, Municipal.**" Spec. 64:364 (1890).

Vacant City Lots, Cultivation of.

See also Detroit, England, Germany, Hornsey, United Kingdom, United States.

"Allotments." Crespi, G. J. H. Good Words, Nov. 1898. 30

Vacant City Lots—*Continued.*

"City Farm Training Schools." Yale R. 7:95 (May, 1898). 31
"Cultivation of Vacant City Lots." Mikkleson, Michael A. Forum, May, 1896. 32
"Detroit Plan, The." Pingree, H. S. Our Day 14:254 (1895). 33
"Farming for the Poor, Free." Wilson, Rufus R. Hrprs. Wkly. 39:566 (1895). 34
"Pingree Plan, The." Lend a H. 14:404 (1895). 35
"Pingree Potato Culture and its Effects on Business." Robinson, Charles A. Arena 19:368 (March, 1898). 36
"Potato Patch, The." Lend a H. 16:362 (1896).
"Unemployed, Cultivation of Vacant City Lots by the." (Experience of a number of cities). New York, Association for Improving the Condition of the Poor, 1895. 47 pp. Discussion of this pamphlet in Garden and F. March 4, 1896. 37
——. "Successful Experiment for the Maintenance of Self-Respecting Manhood." Flower, B. O. Arena, March 1896. 38
"Vacant Lot Cultivation." Spiers, Frederic W.; Lindsay, Samuel McCune; Kirkbride, Franklin B. Char. R. 8:74 (April, 1898). 39

Vacation Schools. (See under **Schools.**)

Vagrancy, Tramp Problem in Cities, etc. (See Vagrancy under **Charities,** also under **Unemployed, The**).

"**Vancouver, B. C.,** Pavements in." Stuart, A. K. Tr. Can. Soc. Civ. Eng. 13:100 (1899). 40

Venal Voters in Cities. (See under **Bossism, Elections, Parties**).

Venice, Italy.
History. "The Venetian Republic." Hazlitt, W. Carew. New York, The Macmillan Co., 1900. 8vo, 2 vols. Cloth, $12. .... 40a
"Sociological and Ethnical Sources of the Greatness of Venice." Lombroso, Cesare. Forum 26:485 (Dec. 1898). 41

"**Veracruz,** Street Railways in." Pagés. Cons. Rep. 61:562 (Dec. 1899). 42

Versailles, France.
Electric Tramways. "Les Tramways Electriques à Versailles." La Revue Technique Feb. 10, 1897; Railway World (London) Feb. 1897. 43
Water Supply. "Les Eaux de Versailles." Thiteau, J. B., and Garlier, G. Ann. D'Hyg. Pub. 42:209 (Sept. 1899). 44

"**Vicksburg, Miss.,** History of." Simrall, H. F. See 1-4c. 45

Victoria, Australia. Direct Legislation. "Report of the Royal Commission on Constitutional Reform." 1894. Abstracted in U. S. Senate Doc. 340, 55th Congress, 2d session. 46

Victoria, B. C.
"City of British Columbia, The Queen." Durham, Julian. Canadian M. 12:207 (Jan. 1899). 47
"Sewerage of Victoria, B. C." Mohun, E. Tr. Can. Soc. C. Eng. 10:75. 48

Vienna.
"Baths at Vienna, The Municipal People's." Arch. & Buil. 30:115 (April 15, 1899).
——. "Die städtischen Volksbäder in Wien." Bernaneck, H. Zeitschr. d. Oesterr. Ing. u. Arch. Ver. March 25, April 1, 1898. 49
Buildings. "Wiener Bauten-Album." Wiener Bauindustrie Zeitung (Vienna), Jan. 28, 1897.
——. "Continental Town Halls: Vienna." Mun. J. 9:259 (April 6, 1900).
Charity. "Die persönl. Verhältnisse der Wiener Armen statist. dargestellt." v. Inama-Sternegg. Wien, 1892. 1m. 50
——. "Das sociale Elend der Grossstädte Wien u. Berlin." Deutsch, Ed. Wien, Mayer u. C., 1878. 51
——. People's Kitchens. "Wiener Volksküchen. Aufgabe, Beförderung, Verwaltung und Organisation." Kühn, Jos. Wien, Seidl u. Sohn, 1876. 2m. 52

BIBLIOGRAPHY.

Vienna—*Continued.*

———. " Poor Relief in Vienna and its Reform." Kobatsch, Rudolph. P. 241 " International Congress," vol. 1, 1893, see 43-99.   53
" Government of Vienna, Report on the." Kasson, John A. Foreign Relations Report for 1879.   54
———. " Gemeinde Verwaltung der Reichshaupt- und Residenzstadt Wien in den Jahren 1867-70, Die." Felder, Cajétan. Wien, Carl Gerold's Sohn, 1872. (Also for 1871-73). 24m. each.   55
" History of Vienna, Recent Events in the Municipal." Rowe, Leo S. The Citizen 1:282 (1895).   56
———. Past and Future. " Wiens Gegenwart und Zukunft." Norden, Hans. Breslau, Honsch & Tiesler, 1899. 8vo, 44 pp. 1 mark.   57
Housing. " Das bürgerliche Wohnhaus und das Wiener Zinshaus." Eitelberger, R., Ferstel, H. Wien, 1860.   58
———. " Der Verein für Arbeiterhäuser in Wien." Zeitschr. d. Oesterr. Ing. u. Arch. Ver. Feb. 19, 1897.   59
Lighting. " Die Stellung der Privaten Beleuchtungs-gesellschaften zu Stadt und Staat. Die Erfahrung in Wien, Paris und Massachusetts." Gray, John Henry. Jena, Gustav Fischer, 1893. 8vo, 167 pp.   60
———. " Acetylene Lighting at Vienna." Pro. Age 16:122 (March 15, 1898).
———. " Municipal Gas Fiasco in Vienna, The." Elec. Eng. 26:448 (Nov. 3, 1898).   61
Municipal Theatre. " Die Reconstruction des Burgtheatres." Prokop. Zeitschr. d. Oesterr. Ing. u. Arch. Ver. May 14, 1897.   62
Parks and Gardens. Haussmann. Allg. Bauz. p. 325, 1872.   63
" Play, Capitals at: Vienna." Robinson, B. Fletcher. Cassell's, p. 496 (April, 1898).   64
Prostitution. " Die Prostitution in Wien, in historischer, administrativer und hygienischer Beziehung." Schraub, Josef. Wien, 1886. 345 pp.   65
" Sewage Disposal, Vienna." Judd, Max. Cons. Rep. 47:240 (1895).   66
———. " Die Marschfeldbewässerung und Verwertung der Wiener Abfallwasser." v. Podhagsky, J. Wien, Civil Techniker, 1892. 8vo, 43 pp. 1m. 60 pf.   67
———. " Die Marschfeldbewässerung und Verwertung der Wiener Abfallwasser." Wodiczka, W. Wien, W. Frick, 1892. 8vo, 31 pp. 1m. 60 pf.   68
———. " Report of a Commission of Experts Concerning the Agricultural Utilization of Vienna Sewage." Pro. Am. Soc. Mun. Imp. (5th yr.) Pt. II, p. 28, Oct. 1898.   69
———" Collecting Sewer on the Right Bank of the Danube Canal at Vienna, The." Zeitschr. d. Oesterr. Ing. u. Arch. Ver. Jan. 28, 1898.   70
Statistics. " Statistisches Jahrbuch der Stadt Wien." Compiled by Stephan, Sedlaczek, Wilhelm Löwy and Wilhelm Hecke. Vienna, Verlag des Wiener Magistrats, published annually since 1882. Edition for the year 1896 appeared in 1898. 891 pp. (See also under **Austria**).   71
" Street Cleaning in Vienna." Judd, Max. Cons. Rep. 47:244 (1895).   72
———. " Street Dust and Street Cleaning in Vienna." von Schoen. Die Zeit May 13, 1899.   73
Street Improvements. " Ueber die Regulirung der Innern Stadt von Wien." Zeitsch. d. Oesterr. Ing. u. Arch. Ver. Feb. 19, 1897.   74
———. Plan. " Betrachtung über den Plan der Donaustadt längs der Regulirten Donau in Wien." Flattich, W. Zeitschr. des Oest. Ing. u. Arch. Ver. p. 1, 1877.   75
———. Plan. " Der Plan von Wien zur Zeit der zweiten Türkenbelagerung." Wellisch. S. Zeitschr. d. Oesterr. Ing. Arch. Ver. Aug. 11, 1899.   76
———. Prize Plan. " Der preisgekronte konkurrenz Plan zur Stadterweiterung von Wien." Föster, L. Allg. Bauz. p. 1, 1859.   77
———. " Die Regulirung des Stadttheiles vom Stadtparke bis zum Theatre a. d. Wien." Hudetz, Jos. Zeitschr. d. Oesterr. Ing. u. Arch. Ver. Oct. 22, 1897.   78
———. " Transformation of Vienna, The." Chapter VIII, p. 410, " Municipal Government in Continental Europe." by Albert Shaw. See 1-5.   79
———. " Wie soll Wien Bauen?" Fellner, F. Wien, 1860.   80
Transit Facilities. " Agreement with the Building and Operating Company for City Street Railways in Vienna, to be Organized in Vienna by the Firm of Siemens & Halske, Regarding the Transformation of the Existing Railway System of the Vienna Tramway Company for Electric Operation and Building of a Supplementary System." Translated from the German by Alderman Ernest F. Hermann, Chicago. 8vo, 28 pp. Pamphlet.   81

Vienna—*Continued.*

——. Building and Operation. " Der Prozess der Bau- und Betriebsgesellschaft für städtische Strassenbahnen in Wien vor dem österreichischen Verwaltungsgerightshofe." von Feistmantel, H. Ritter. Vienna, 1900. 8vo, 144 pp.   82

——. City Street Railway. Sonnenschein, S. Archiv. für Eisenbahnwesen, part V, 1894; Weinberg. Ueber Land und Meer Heft. 2; anon. Glaser's Annalen Dec. 1, 1897.   83

——. " Electric Traction in Vienna." Ry. World Feb. 1897, 7:367 (Nov. 1898).   84

——. Electric Traction. " Der Elektromotoren-Betrieb in Wien." Pere, Johann. Zeitschr. d. Oesterr. Ing. u. Arch. Ver. July 29, 1898.   85

——. Operation. " Der Betrieb der Wiener Stadtbahn." Gerstel, Gustav. Zeitschr. d. Oesterr. Ing. u. Arch. Ver. Feb. 25, 1898.   86

——. Track. " Der Oberbau der Wiener Stadtbahn." Koestler, Hugo. Zeitschr. d. Oesterr. Ing. u. Arch. Ver. 52:153 (March 9, 1900).   87

——, " Tramway Situation in Vienna, Austria." Ziffer, E. A. St. Ry. J. 13:663 (Oct. 1897).   88

——. " Tramways in Vienna." Jussen, Edmund. U. S. Consular Report No. 92, 1888, p. 97; anon. Ry. W. 7:411 (Dec. 8, 1898).   89

Water Supply. " Der Wasserversorgung Wiens, nach dem offiziellen Protokoll der k. k. Gesellschaft der Aerzte in Wien." Wien, A. Hölder, 1892.   90

——. A Comparison Between Vienna and Paris. " Einige vergleichende Mitteilungen über die Wasserversorgungs-Verhältnisse in Wien und in Paris." Sykora, Carl. Oesterr. Ing. u. Arch. Ver. July 1, 1898.   91

——. " Die Arbeiten der Wienthal-wasserleitung." Zeitschr. d. Oesterr. Ing. u. Arch. Ver. April 16, 24, 30, May 7, 14, 1897.   92

——. High Service. " Das Wasserwerk der wiener Hochquellenleitung." Bokowitz, Franz. Zeitschr. Oesterr. Ing. u. Arch. Ver. Aug. 19, 1898.   93

——. Pumping Station. " Das wiener städtische Schöpfwerk." Wiener Bauindustrie-Zeitung Jan. 14, 1897.   94

——. " The New Pumping Station and Water Tower at Vienna." Engng. Rec. 42:319 (Oct. 6, 1900).

——. " Das städtische Wasserwerk in Favoriten." Wiener Bauindustrie Zeitung June 21, 1900.   95

——. " Wasserwerk der Stadt Wien in X. Bezirk." Borkowitz, Fr. Zeitschr. d. Oesterr. Ing. u. Arch. Ver. 52:53 (Jan. 26, 1900).   96

Village Improvement, Articles on. Northrop, B. G. Forum 19:95 March, 1895); Robbins, Mary Caroline. Atlan. 79:212 (Feb. 1897); anon. Park & Cemt. 7:50, 74 (May, June, 1897).   97

Vincennes, Ind.

" Water Purification at Vincennes, Ind." Engng. News 43:291 (May 3, 1900).   98

——. " Mechanical Filtration, Vincennes, Ind." Engng. Rec. 41:419 (May 5, 1900).

" **Virginia,** Local Institutions of." Engle, E. H. J. H. Univ. Studies III:105 (1888).   99

Vital Statistics of Cities. (See **Statistics of Cities**).

Voters and Voting, Municipal. (See under **Bossism, Elections, Parties**).

" **Wallingford, Conn.**, Municipal Electric Lighting Plant." Perkins, Thomas C. Elec. W. & E. 35:391 (March 17, 1900).   100

" **Walsall, England,** The Sewerage of." Angel, R. J. Engng. Rec. 40:574 (Nov. 18, 1899).   1

Walworth [Eng.] (See under **London**).

Warsaw, Russia, Municipal Electric Plant. " Project für das Elektricitäts-Werk der Stadt Warschau." Lindley, W. H. Frankfurt-am-Main, August Oesterrieth, 1899. 8vo, 156 pp.   2

Wash Houses, Municipal. (See under **Baths, Laundries and Lavatories**).

BIBLIOGRAPHY.

Washington, D. C.

Government, General References.

City Government, Washington. Lee, M. N. Chaut. 22:39, 164 (1895); Meriwether, C. Pol. Sci. Q. 12:407 (Sept. 1897); Newcomb, S. Nation 18:407 (1874); Nott, C. C. Nation 15:328 (1872), 18:375 (1874), 20:5 (1875); Sedgwick, A. G. Nation 38:335 (1884). — 3

"Life in Washington, D. C." Curtis, William E. Chaut. 25:467, 579 (August, Sept. 1897). — 4

"Municipal Condition of Washington." Siddons, Frederick L. P. 358, Proc. Second Nat'l Conf. for Good City Govt., 1895. See 6-18b. — 5

"The Capital and the Capitol." Chap. XI. in "The Land of the Dollar." by G. W. Steevens. New York, Dodd, Mead & Co., 1897. 12mo, 316 pp. $1.50. — 6

"Washington, D. C." Ralph, Julian. Harper 90:657 (1895). — 7

"Washington: The City of Leisure." Low, A. Maurice. Atlan. 86:767 (Dec. 1900). — 8

Almanac. "The Washington Post Almanac." Washington. Published quarterly by the Washington Post. Edition for First quarter, 1898, 542 pp. 35c. per year. — 9

Art. "Competitive Designs for the Connecticut Avenue Viaduct, Washington, D. C." Engng. News 39:54 (Jan. 27, 1898). — 10

——. "Landscape in Connection with Public Buildings in Washington." Olmsted, Frederick Law, Jr. Engng. Rec. 42:624 (Dec. 29, 1900). — 11

——. "The Monumental Grouping of Government Buildings in Washington." Seeler, Edgar V. Engng. Rec. 42:599 (Dec. 22, 1900). — 12

——. (See also Streets below).

"Bridge Across the Potomac, The Memorial." Engng. Rec. 42:362 (April 21, 1900).

"Direct Employment of Labor by the Municipality." Ann. Am. Acad. Pol. Sci. 14:140 (July, 1899). — 13

Finance. "Tax Assessments in the District of Columbia, Report of Special Committee to Investigate." Johnson, Tom L. H. R. No. 1469, 52d Congress, 1st Session. — 14

"Franchises." West, Max. Ann. Am. Acad. Pol. Sci. 11:426 (May, 1898). — 15

"History of Washington, D. C." Vanderlip, F. A. See 1-4c. — 16

——. "City of Washington, The: Its Origin and Administration." Porter, John Addison. J. H. Univ. Studies III:11, 12 (1885). 66 pp. — 17

——. "Ring Rule, A Study of." Welling, J. C. Nation 42:47 (1886). (A criticism of John Addison Porter's "City of Washington, its Origin and Administration.") — 18

——. "Founding of Washington City, The: With some considerations on the origin of cities and location of national capitals." Spofford, Ainsworth R. Address read before the Maryland Historical Society, May 12, 1879. Baltimore, 1881. Printed by the Society. 62 pp. — 19

——. "History of the Government of the District of Columbia." Clephane, Walter C. Washington, 1892. 24 pp. 25c. — 20

——. "The Story of Washington." Todd, Charles Burr. New York, Putnams, 1889. 416 pp. $1.75. — 21

——. "Various Forms of Local Government in the District of Columbia." Bryan, W. B. 55th Congress, 2d Session, Senate Document 238, 1898. Pamphlet, 38 pp. — 22

History, Description and Statistics of Washington, D. C., in 1880. See Census. See 1-7. — 23

Housing. "Homes in Washington." Hitz, J. Am. J. Soc. Sci. 15:135 (1882). — 24

——. "Lodging Houses in Washington, The New Municipal." Warner, A. G. Char. R. 2:279 (1893). — 25

"Library in Washington, No Public." Bain, Geo. G. Hrprs. Wkly. 39:809 (1895). — 26

"Lighting Company of Washington, D. C., Electric, and its New Electrical Equipment, The United States." Hopkins, Nevil Monroe. Elec. Eng. 26:425 (Nov. 3, 1898). — 27

"Municipal Work in Washington, Recent." Engng. Rec. 39:235 (Feb. 11, 1899). — 28

"Parks of Washington." Am. Arch. 47:72 (1895).

"Pavements of Washington, D. C." Report of Engineering Department, District of Columbia, 1884. — 29

——. "Pavements and Vitrified Brick in Washington, D. C." Brick, May 1, 1900. — 30

Washington—*Continued.*

———. "The National Capital: Its Pavements and Parks, and its Form of Government." Mun. Engng. 15:205 (Oct, 1898).

"Sanitation of Washington." Billings, John S. Forum 15:727 (1893); Busey, Samuel C. Sanitarian 42:205 (March, 1899). 31

———. "Sanitary Drainage of Washington." Waring, G. E. Am. Arch. 8:77, 86 (1880). 32

"Sewerage of the District of Columbia." (Rudolph Hering, S. M. Gray and F. P. Stearns, Board of Commissioners). H. R. Ex. Doc. 445, 51st Congress, 1892. 33

———. "Sewage Disposal Project for Washington, The." McComb, D. E. Pro. Am. Soc. Mun. Imp. (5th yr.) Pt. II, p. 63 (Oct. 1898). 34

"Statistics, Vital, of the District of Columbia and Baltimore covering a period of six years ending May 31, 1890." Billings, John S. Washington, Government Printing Office, 1893. 241 pp. Eleventh Census of the United States. 35

"Street Cleaning in Washington." Engng. Rec. 39:470 (April 22, 1899). 36

Street Improvement. "Shepherd Improvements of the City of Washington, The." P. 573, John Addison Porter's "City of Washington." J. H. Univ. Studies III:11 and 12 (1885). 37

———. "Street Extension Plan for the Entire District of Columbia, A." Richards, William P. Pro. Am. Soc. Mun. Imp. (5th yr.) Pt. II, p. 138, Oct. 1898. 38

Transit Facilities. "Street Railways of Washington, D. C., The." Anon. St. Ry. J. Dec. 1894, St. Ry. R. 9:365 (June 15, 1899). 39

———. "The Displacement of the Cable by the Underground Trolley in Washington." Hopkins, N. M. Elec. Eng. 24:526 (Dec. 2, 1897). Another article, anon. Engng. N. 39:124 (Feb. 24, 1898). 40

———. "The Open Conduit Electric System of the Capital Traction Company." Elec. World 32:707 (Dec. 31, 1898). 41

———. "Work on the Capital Traction, Washington." St. Ry. Rev. 8:14 (Jan. 15, 1898). 42

"Tree Planting in the Streets of Washington." Richards, William P. Pro. Am. Soc. Mun. Imp. (5th yr.) Pt. II, p. 97 (Oct. 1898), Mun. Engng. 15:287 (Nov. 1898). 43

"Water Supply Problem in Washington, The." Engng. Rec. 37:313 (March 12, 1898). 44

———. "Filtration of the Washington Water Supply." Engng. Rec. 41:443 (May 12, 1900).

———. "Polluted Water Supply, Washington's." Busey, S. C. Sanitarian 40:385 (May, 1898). 45

———. "Purification Experiments at Washington, D. C., Water." Engng. News 42:373 (Dec. 7, 1899). 46

———. "Report on Water Purification Experiments at Washington, D. C." Engng. News 43:315 (May 17, 1900).

———. "Reservoir, The Brightwood, Washington, D. C." Engng. Rec. 41:193 (March 3, 1900).

———. "Waste and Use in Washington, Water." Gaillard, D. D. Engng. Rec. 42:277 (Sept. 22, 1900). 47

"What Women Have Done in Washington's City Affairs." Hosmer, Katharine. Mun. Aff. 2:514 (Sept. 1898). 48

Water Supplies of Cities.

See also Aberdeen, Albany, Allegheny City, Altoona, Amballa, Ashland (Wis.), Atlanta, Austria, Basle, Bellary, Berlin, Berwyn, Bilston (Eng.), Birmingham, Bombay, Boston, Brooklyn under New York, Budapest, Buffalo, Calbe, California, Cambridge (Mass.), Camden, Canada, Cardiff, Chatham, Chattanooga, Chicago, Chillicothe, Cincinnati, Cleveland, Colorado Springs, Columbus, Concord (N. H.), Constantinople, Cumberland, Danville, Dayton, Denver, Detroit, Dresden Duluth, Eastbourne (Eng.), Edinburgh, Erie, Florence (Colo.), Florida, Frankfort (Ger.), Galveston, Germany, Glasgow, Grand Rapids, Great Britain under United Kingdom, Halle, Hamburg, Harrisburg, Huddersfield, Illinois, Jersey City, Kettlewell, Khandwa (India), Kawloon, Landsberg on Wartha, Lancaster, Laodicea, Lawrence, Leighton Buzzard, Lexington (Ky.), Little Falls, Liverpool, London, Lorain (Ohio), Loughborough, Los Angeles, Louisville, Madison, Madgeburg, Manchester (Eng.), Massachusetts, Media (Pa.), Melbourne, Merthyr Tydvil, Milwaukee, Minneapolis, Mt. Vernon (N. Y.), Munich, Nashville, Newark, New Bedford, Newburyport (Mass.), New Jersey, New Orleans,

Water Supplies of Cities—*Continued*.

New York, Norfolk, North Carolina, North Tonawanda, Nyack, Ohio, Omaha, Orange (N. J.), Panama, Paris, Petrolea (Can.), Philadelphia, Pittsburg, Plymouth, Portland (Eng.), Poughkeepsie, Prenzlau, Providence, Provincetown (Mass.), Purleigh, Reading, Rhode Island, Rhondda (Wales), Richmond (Va.), Rochester, Rockford, Rome, St. Louis, St. Paul, San Francisco, Scutari, Simla, Skaneateles, Southampton, South Australia, Steubenville (Ohio), Syracuse, Toledo, Toronto, Torquay, Versailles, Vienna, Vincennes, Washington, White Plains, Williamsport, Wilmington, Zurich.

"Air Lift, The." Engng. Rec. 38:317 (Sept. 10, 1898).

"Analysis, Water." Wanklyn, J. Alfred, and Chapman, E. T. London, Trübner, 1874-79, 3d to 5th edit. 8vo. 5s.   49

——. "Examination of Water, Chemical and Bacteriological." Mason, William P. New York, Wiley & Sons, 1899. 12mo, 137 pp. Cl. $1.25.   50

——. "Some Results of the Systematic Examination of the Water of Public Supplies." Goodnough, X. H. J. N. E. W. W. Assoc., Sept. 1899.   51

——. "Standard Methods of Water Analysis." Fuller, George W. Engng. Rec. 42:397 (Oct. 27, 1900).   52

"Ancient Water Works." Mansergh, James. Engng. Rec. 42:517 (Dec. 1, 1900).   53

——. "Early Methods of Collecting, Storing and Distributing Water." Hill, William R. Mun. Engng. 15:12 (July, 1898), Fire & W. 24:257, 264 (Aug. 6, 13, 1898).   54

"Assessments for Water Mains." Engng. Rec. 37:533 (May 21, 1898).   55

"Bacteriology of Water Supply, The." Frankland, Edward. San. Rec. 19:595 (June 18, 1897).   56

——. "Bacteriological Examination of Water Supplies, The." Armstrong, Henry. San. Rec. 23:543 (June 23, 1899).   57

——. "On the Necessity of Cultivating Water Bacteria in an Atmosphere Saturated with Moisture." Whipple, George C. Reprinted from Technology Quarterly, Vol. 12, No. 4, Dec. 1899.   58

——. "Soil Bacteriology and its Relation to Water Supplies." Hunter, John. San. Rec. 20:1497 (Aug. 6, 1897).   59

Bibliography of Water Supply. "Litteratur des Gas- und Wasserfaches." Steude, M. München, R. Oldenbourg. 8vo, 78 pp. 2m.   60

"Bookkeeping for Water Companies, Model System of." Grimshaw, Robert. Mun. Engng. 12:76, 353 (June, Aug. 1897); anon. Mun. Engng. 12:149, 218, 292 (March, April, May, 1897).   61

"Capacities of Water Works Systems." Mun. Engng. 13:86 (Aug. 1897).   62

"Chalk, Water Supply from the." Builder Dec. 17, 1898.

"Consumption of Water by Cities and Towns." Ayres, H. W. Proc. American W. W. Association 8:46 (1888).   63

——. "Increase of Water Consumption." Fire & W. 26:370 (Nov. 4, 1899).

——. "Notes on Consumption of Water." Williams, G. S. Technic. (Univ. of Mich.), 1897.   64

——. "Rate of Water Consumption." Freeman, John R. Engng. Rec. 42:103 (Aug. 4, 1900).   65

——. "Waste of Water in Cities, Consumption and." Brackett, Dexter. Trans. Am. Soc. Civil Engineers 34:185 (1895).   66

——. "On the Water Circulation of Great Cities." Scottish R. 7:264 (1886).

——. (See Meters and Waste below).

"Contracts in Water Works Business, Special." Maury, D. H. Mun. Engin. 13:24 (July, 1897).   67

"Control of Public Water Supplies." San. Rec. 21:392 (April 15, 1898).

"Cost of Water Plants." City Govt. 4:61 (Feb. 1898).

"Difficulties in Obtaining a Water Supply, Some." Milner, Willis J. City Govt. 6:105 (May, 1899), Engng. Rec. 39:590 (May 27, 1899).   68

"Direct Pressure Water Supply, Relief from Violent Fluctuation in." Heim, John B. Mun. Engng. 13:27 (July, 1897), City Govt. 3:93 (Sept. 1897).   69

Electric Lighting Stations and Water Works combined. "Elektrische Beleuchtungszentralen in Verbindung mit Wasserwerken." Die Elektrizität Feb. 27, 1897.   70

Electrolysis. (See **Electrolysis**).

Water Supplies of Cities—*Continued.*

"Engineering, Water Works." Shields, W. S. Mun. Engng. 16:150 (March, 1899). 71

———. "Elements of Water Supply Engineering." Gould, E. Sherman. New York, Engineering News Pub. Co., 1899. 8vo, 168 pp. $2. 72

———. "Water Supply, Engineering." Folwell, A. Prescott. New York, Wiley & Son, 1900. 8vo, 562 pp. Cl. $4. 73

"European Cities, Water Supply and Sewage Disposal in large." Billings, J .S. Engng. Rec. Nov. 10, 1894. 74

———. "Water Supply of Various European Cities." Hazen, Allen. J. N. E. W. W. Assoc. Dec. 1894, J. Assoc. Engng. Soc. Feb. 1895. 75

———. "Water Works of Europe, European Continent." (Paris, Florence, Moscow, Vienna, Munich, Frankfort-a-M., Geneva, Zurich). Philadelphia, Commercial Museum, 1899. 8vo, 41 pp. Pamphlet. 76

"Fermentation, The Cause and Prevention of Water." McElroy, Samuel. Engin. M. 13:535 (July, 1897), Sanitarian 39:141 (Aug. 1897). 77

Filtration of Water Supplies, General Articles on. Clark, H. W. J. N. E. W. W. Assoc. Sept. 1899; Fuller, George W. Engng. Rec. 39:593 (May 27, 1899); Hazen, Allen. Mun. Engng. June, 1896; Hering, Rudolph. Engng. M. 11:627 (1896); Hooker, Samuel C. The Citizen 1:179 (1895); Hungerford, Churchill. Sci. Am. 77:68 (July 31, 1897); Knowles, Morris. Engng. Rec. 42:304 (Sept, 29, 1900); Smith, Edwin. Sanitarian 36:425 (1896); Weston, Edmund B. Mun. Engng. 13:199 (Oct. 1897), Engng. N. 38:239 (Oct. 7, 1897), City Govt. 3:155 (Nov. 1897); anon. Sci. Am. 79:310 (Nov. 12, 1898); J. Gas Light 76:217 (July 24, 1900); Engng. Rec. 39:241 (Feb. 11, 1899). 78

———. "Aeration, Water Filtration and." Charles, S. A. City Govt. 5:25 (July, 1898), Mun. Engng. 15:23 (July, 1898). 79

———. "Alum in Water Filtration, The Benefit of." Chapin, Charles V. Sanitarian 45:431 (Nov. 1900). 80

———. "An Improved Method of Filtration." (System in Operation in Worms, Kiel, Winterthur and other German Cities). Mason, Frank H. Consular Reports Feb. 1897. Extracts in the Sanitarian 38:289 (April, 1897), City Govt. 2:72 (March, 1897), and Arch. & Buil. 26:141 (March 20, 1897). 81

———. "Another large Filtration Scheme." City Govt. 6:114 (May, 1899).

———. "Europe, Filtration of Water in." Giles, William A. City Govt. 1:94 (1896). 82

———. "Experimental Water Filtration Plant, An: Its Design, Use, Economy and Value." Davis, Floyd. Mun. Engng. 19:320 (Nov. 1900). 83

———. "Filtration of Public Water Supplies, The." Hazen, Allen. (3d Edition). New York, Wiley & Son, 1900. 8vo, 321 pp. Cloth, $3. 84

———. Graded Filters for Large Quantities of Water. "Filtres Dégrosseurs pour Grandes Masses D'Eau." Peuch, A. Mem. Soc. d. Ing. Civils de France Nov. 10, 1900. 85

———. "Les Eaux de Rivères Filtrées." Hauriot. Ann. D'Hyg. Pub. 43:442 (May, 1900). 86

———. Mechanical Filtration. Bristowe, Frederick. San. Rec. 21:201 (Feb. 25, 1898); Mason, W. P. Mun. Engng. 15:23 (July, 1898); Weston, Edmund B. J. N. E. W. W. A. 14:333 (June, 1900); anon. Engng. Rec. 40:435 (Oct. 7, 1899), 41:223 (Mar. 10, 1900). 87

———. "Mechanical and Slow Sand Water Filtration." Engng. News 41:102 (Feb. 16, 1899).

———. "New Filtration Process." Ludwig, Charles V. F. Pub. Imp. 2:217 (Mar. 15, 1900). 88

———. "Plaque System of Filtration of Water Supplies, The." San. Rec. 20:307 (Sept. 17, 1897). 89

———. Sand Filtration. Fowler, Charles E. J. N. E. W. W. Assn. June, 1898; Lea, R. S. Sanitarian 42:289 (April, 1899), Trans. Can. Soc. Civ. Eng. 13:33 (1899); Ledoux, J. W. Pro. Eng. Club 16:108 (Mar. 1, 1899); anon. Engng. Rec. 37:343 (Mar. 19, 1898), 38:7 (June 4, 1898). 90

———. "Sand and Mechanical Filters, Relative Applicability." Fuller, Geo. W. J. N. E. W. W. Assn. Sept. 1899. 91

———. "Sand Filtration, Purification of City Water Supplies by." Firth, Frank J. Pamphlet, reprinted from Annals of Hygiene, U. of P. Press. 1896. Pamphlet, 12 pp. 92

———. "Surface Waters, Filtration of." Odling, William. London, 1893. 93

Water Supplies of Cities—*Continued.*

———. "Unfiltered Surface Water Unsafe Town Supply." Leffmann, Henry. "13th Annual Report of the State Board of Health * * * of Pennsylvania," p. 295. Harrisburg, 1898.   94

———. (See also Purification below.)

"Financial Management of Water Works, The." Kuichling, E. Pro. Am. Soc. Civil Eng. April, 1897. Mun. Engng. 13:207 (Oct. 1897).   95

———. "Financial Management of Water Works." (Statistics of Municipal Works only.) Coffin, Freeman C. J. N. E. W. W. Assn. Sept. 1897.   96

———. "Increased Revenue, Free Service Pipes and Filtration." Gwinn, Dow R. Mun. Engng. 13:28 (July, 1897), Fire & W. June 12, 1897, City Govt. 3:60 (Aug. 1897).   97

———. "Water Works Economy." Pater, Joseph J. City Govt. 6:29 (Feb. 1899).   98

"Fire Protection, Water Works, Hydrants, etc." Freeman, John R. J. N. E. W. W. Assoc. 7:49, 152 (1892); Abstract in Engng. Rec. July 16, 1892.   100

"Flow of Water over Dams, The." Engng. Rec. 41:591, 616 (June 23, 30, 1900).   1

"Free Water Supply." (Plan proposed by Hazen S. Pingree of Detroit, Mich). Engng. News Jan. 25, 1894.   2

"High Buildings, New System of Water Supply for." Huyette, W. S. Heating & Ventilation (New York), April 15, 1897.   3

"Hot Water from Street Lamps." Am. Gas Light J. 67:611 Oct. 18, 1897).

———. "Penny-in-the-Slot Hot Water." London 6:759 (Sept. 16, 1897).

"Hydrant Rentals, A Side Light on." Engng. Rec. 39:133 (Jan. 14, 1899).

"Investigation of Public Water Supplies." Davis, Floyd. Engng. M. 10:439 (1895); Newell, F. H. Mun. Engng. 14:76 (Feb. 1898).   4

———. "Investigation of Quality of Water for Public Use." Tuttle. A .S. Mun. Engng. 11:351 (Dec. 1896).   5

"Laboratories, Municipal Water Works." Whipple, George C. Pop. Sci. Mo. 58:172 (Dec. 1900).   6

"Law Relating to Water Supply." Pearmain, T. H., and Moor, C. G. San. Rec. 22:236, 264 (Sept. 2, 9, 1898).   7

———. "The Right to Shut Off Water." Engng. Rec. 37:489 (May 7, 1898).

"Lectures on Water Supply, Sewerage and Sewage Utilization." Corfield, W. H. London, Spon, 1874. Paper, $1.   8

"Locating a Public Water Supply." Mead, Daniel W. Engng. M. 10:876 (1895).   9

Mains. "Faulty Construction in Water Works Pipes." Cameron, W. L. Mun. Engng. 13:31 (June, 1897).   10

———. "Hydraulic Mains, A Difference in." Egan, P. Prog. Age 15:389 (Sept. 1, 1897).   11

———. "Laying Small Sized Water Mains." Heim, John B. Mun. Engng. 13:27 (July, 1897).   12

———. "Tables for Estimating the Cost of laying cast-iron water pipe." Weston, Edmund B. New York, Engineering News Pub. Co., 2d ed., 1896. Pamphlet. 8vo, 12 pp. 25c.   13

———. "Water Pipes on Metropolitan Water Works." Brackett, Dexter. J. N. E. W. W. Assoc. June, 1899.   14

"Management, A Lesson in Water Works." Croes, J. James R. Engng. Rec. 40:545 (Nov. 11, 1899); anon. Eng. Rec. 40:52 (June 17, 1899).   15

"Meters, Water." Rider, Joseph B. Fire & W. May 29, 1897.   16

———. "An Object Lesson." (Water Meters). Bolling, Charles E. City Govt. 6:105 (May, 1899).   17

———. "Consumption and Use of Meters, Statistics." Engng. News Jan. 16, 1892, p. 61.

———. "Popular Errors about Water Meters." Trautwine, John C. Paper presented to Engineers' Club of Philadelphia, 1899, pamphlet, 9 pp., City Govt. 5:195 (Nov. 1898).   18

———. "Prepayment Meters." Ross, R. Gas W. Aug. 13, 1898; Wilson, Andrew. Am. Gas Light J. Sept. 19, 1898, Gas W. Aug. 6, 1898.   19

———. "Present Day, Water Meters of the." Schönheyder, William. Surveyor 17:157 (Feb. 9, 1900).   20

———. "Progress of Water Meterage, The: Report from Harrisburg." Fire & W. March 6, 1897.

Water Supplies of Cities—*Continued*.

———. " Rates, Water Meters and." Heim, John B. City Govt. 4:207 (June, 1898), Fire & W. 23:209 (June 25, 1898), Mun. Engng. 15:17 (July, 1898). 21

———. " Waste, Value of Meters in Restricting." Case, L. N. Fire & W. June 26, 1897. 22

———. " Water Meters to Check Waste." Gemuender, M. A. City Govt. 2:71 (Mar. 1897). 23

———. " Water Meters in Municipal Supply." San. Rec. 22:566 (Nov. 25, 1898).

———. (See also Consumption, and Rates, above.)

Municipal Ownership. (See under **Municipal Control,** etc.)

" Municipal Water Works, Some Hints as to the Management of." Ulrich, C. F. pp. 160-164 in " Pro. of the 20th Annual Meeting of the American W. W. Assn. Richmond, Va., May 15-18, 1900." 8vo, 216 pp. Cloth, $1. (See also under **Municipal Control.**) 24

" Plain Talk from a Water Works Manager." Engng. Rec. 39:236 (Feb. 11, 1899).

" Pollution of Water and its Correction, The." Middleton, Reginald E. Mun. Engng. 14:137 (March, 1898); anon. Mun. W. 8:107 (July, 1898). 25

———. " An Injunction against Sewage Pollution of a California Steam." (Editorial.) Engng. Rec. 38:67 (June 25, 1898).

———. " Bacteriology of Soils with Reference to the Pollution of Water, The." Whipple, George C. Engng. Rec. 42:134 (Aug. 11, 1900). 26

———. " Contamination of our Municipal Water Supplies." Thornbury, Frank J. Chaut. 24:197 (1896). 27

———. " Detecting Impurities, Potable Water and Methods of." Baker, M. N. New York, Van Nostrand Co., 1899. 12mo, 97 pp. 50 cts. 28

———. " Incidental Pollution, Public Water Supplies Liability to." McKenzie, T. H. Sanitarian 45:428 (Nov. 1900). 29

———. " Legislation to Prevent Water Pollution, Proposed State." (Editorial.) Engng. News 41:169 (March 16, 1899).

———. " Locating and Removing Sources of Pollution from a Surface Water Supply." Sherrerd, Morris R. Mun. Engng. 13:278 (Nov. 1897). 30

———. " Manufacturing Wastes, Water Pollution by." Mun. Engng. 17:26 (July, 1899).

———. " Pollution of Water Supplies, Report of Committee appointed by the American Public Health Association." Proc. Am. Pub. Health Assoc., 1889. Pamphlet, 19 pp. 31

———. " Pollution of Water Supplies, Report on." Smart, Charles. Sanitarian Dec. 1896. 32

———. " Pollution of Public Water Supplies, The." Engng. Rec. 42:421 (Nov. 3, 1900).

———. " Prevention of Pollution of Streams and Rivers, The." Childs. Builder Dec. 31, 1898; anon. Engng. Rec. 38:243 (Aug. 20, 1898). 33

———. Protection of Water Supplies. Anon. City Govt. 8:2 (Jan. 1900); Sedgwick, W. T. J. N. E. W. W. Assoc. March, 1897. 34

———. " Public Water Supplies and the Prevention of the Pollution of the Same." Fuertes, James H. Proc. 24th An. Meeting N. J. Sanitary Assoc., 1898, p. 77. 35

———. " River Pollution." Dechan, Bailie. San Rec. 20:558, 613 (Nov. 19, Dec. 3, 1897). 36

———. Wells. " Sur la Contamination des Puits." Duclaux, M. Comptes Rendus 125:913 (Dec. 6, 1897). 37

" Present Tendencies in Water Works Practice." Engng. News 37:232 (April 15, 1897).

" Procuration of Water Supply, The." Sarles, W. T. San. Rec. 20:727 (Dec. 31, 1897). 38

" Public and Private Rights in River Waters." Engng. Rec. 40:576 (Nov. 18, 1899).

Pure Water. Austen, P. H. Engng. M. 1:95 (1891); Huston, C. D. City Govt. 7:113 (Nov. 1899); anon. Engng. N. June 4, 1896; City and State 5:374 (Dec. 15, 1898), 6:418 (June 29, 1899). 39

———. " Pure Water for Drinking and Cooking, a municipal problem of the very highest importance." Axtell, S. P. Engng. M. 11:67 (1896). 40

———. " The Purity of Water Supply." Hoppes, John J. Pp. 39-42 in " Second An. Conv. of the Central States W. W. Assoc., Springfield, O., Sept. 27-29, 1898." 41

Water Supplies of Cities—*Continued.*

——. " What is a Good, Pure, Wholesome Water?" Mason, W. P. City Govt. 6:106 (May, 1899). **42**

Purification of Water Supplies, Articles on. Cottrell, Henry E. P. Engng. (London) 66:253 (Aug. 26, 1898); Davis, Floyd. Engin. M. 2:819 (1892); Hazen, Allen. Engng. M. 15:249 (May, 1898); Kummel, W. Trans. Am. Soc. Civil Engrs. Nov. 1893; Leeds, Albert R. Cassier's M. Feb. 1897; Mason, W. P. Mun. Engng. 12:357 (June, 1897); Parry, W. Kaye. San. Rec. 25:27 (Jan. 12, 1900); Rohe, George M. Lend a H. 17:166 (1896), Sanitarian July, 1896; Thornburg, F. J. Chaut. 24:576 (Feb. 1897); Twelvetrees, W. N. San. Rec. 23:253 (March 24, 1899); Yaryan, Homer T. Eng. 35:55 (March 1, 1898); anon. Eng. 86:255 (Sept. 9, 1898); San. Rec. 22:96 (July 22, 1898); Engng. Rec. 42:313 (Oct. 6, 1900). **43**

——. " A Water Purifying Plant." Stillman, Howard. Engng. News 38:356 (Dec. 2, 1897), Trans. Am. Soc. of Mech. Engrs. Dec. 1897. **44**

——. " Aeration, Purifying Water by." Heysinger. Fire & W. 22:370 (Oct. 9, 1897). **45**

——. " An Outline of the Present Status of Water Purification." Fuller, George W. Mun. Engng. 16:377 (June, 1899), Fire & W. 26:240 (July 29, 1899). **46**

——. " Bacterial Purification of Water, The." Rideal, Samuel. Engng. Rec. 40:245 (Aug. 12, 1899). **47**

——. " Clarification of River Waters, The." Hazen, Allen. J. Frankl. Inst. 147:177 (March, 1899), Engng. Rec. 39:377 (March 25, 1899), Mun. Engng. 16:233 (April, 1899). **48**

——. " Metallic Iron, Purification of Water by." Chancellor, C. W. Am. Arch. June 5, 1897. **49**

——. " Nature in Purification of Water, Man's Imitation of." Swarts, Gardner T. J. N. E. W. W. Assoc. 13:1 (Sept. 1898). **50**

——. " Ozone, The Purifying and Sterilizing of Water by." Elec. Dec. 28, 1898. **51**

——. " Ozone, The Purification of Drinking Water by the Use of." Soper, George A. Engng. News 42:250 (Oct. 19, 1899). **52**

——. " Purification of Public Water Supplies, The." Hill, John W. New York, Van Nostrand Co., 1898. 8vo, 304 pp. Cl. $3. **53**

——. " Purification of Sewage and Water." Dibdin, W. J. San. Rec. 20:249 (Sept. 3, 1897). **54**

——. " Recent Progress in Water Purification." Fuller, George W. Pp. 76-80 in " Proc. of the Fourth General Conference of Health Officers in Michigan, 1899." **55**

——. " Water and its Purification, a Handbook for the use of local authorities, sanitary officers and others interested in water supply." Rideal, Samuel. London, Crosby, Lockwood and Son, 1897. 8vo, 292 pp. 7s. 6d. **56**

——. " Water Supply and Purification Works at Parkville and Bethany, Mo." Kiersted, Wynkoop. Engng. News 42:388 (Dec. 14, 1899). **57**

——. (See also Filtration above.)

Rates. " Abolition of Water Rates." (Editorial.) Mun. Engng. 17:162 (Sept. 1899).

——. " Basis of Water Rates." (Editorial.) Engng. Rec. 38:485 (Nov. 5, 1898).

——. " Comparison of Water Rates and Rules." Maury, Dabney H., Jr. Mun. Engng. 13:132 (Sept. 1897). **58**

——. " Meters versus Flat Rates." Schuchardt, R. F. Elec. Eng. 24:406 (Oct. 28, 1897), Am. Gas Light J. 67:732 (Nov. 8, 1897). **59**

——. " Selling Water by Meter Rates vs. Flat Rates." Smith, Frank C. Pp. 17-21 in "1st Rep. Central States W. W. Assoc., Columbus, O., Feb. 7-8, 1898." **60**

——. " Right to Sell Water by Meter Rates, The." Engng. Rec. 37:401 (April 9, 1898).

——. (See also Meters above.)

" Reports, Proposed Forms of Water Works." Pro. Am. Soc. Mun. Imp. (5th yr.) Pt. II, p. 191, 1898.

" Reservoirs, Cleaning." Gwinn, Dow R. Mun. Engng. 15:21 (July, 1898). **61**

——. " Cisternage and Constant Water Service." Alexander, Hugh. San. Rec. 24:389 (Nov. 3, 1899). **62**

——. " Compensating Reservoirs for Gravity Water Supplies in lieu of Compensation for Riparian Rights and its Legal Aspects." Babcock, Stephen E. City

Water Supplies of Cities—*Continued.*

Govt. 4:212 (June, 1898). 63

———. " Storage Reservoirs and Rainfall." Fox, William. San. Rec. 19:615 (June 25, 1897). 64

" Sanitary Problems connected with Municipal Water Supply." Mason, W. P. J. Frankl. Inst. 143:337 (May, 1897), San. Rec. 20:229 (Aug. 27, 1897). 65

———. " Control and Supervision of Public Water Supplies by Sanitary Authorities." Porter C. Sanitarian Nov. 1896. 66

———. " Death Rate in Cities, Influence of Sewerage and Water Supply on the." Smith, Erwin F. Supplement to the Report of the Michigan Board of Health for 1885. 168 pp. 67

———. " Impure and Unwholesome Water and Its Experimental Improvement." Davis, Floyd. Mun. Engng. 19:69 (Aug. 1900). 68

———. " Impure Water and Public Health." Davis, Floyd. Engng. M. 2:359 (1891). 69

———. " Is our Drinking Water Dangerous?" Hill, John W. Proceedings American Water Works Association, 1893. 70

———. " Sanitation of Drinking Water, The." Thornbury, Frank J. Arena 17:956 (May, 1897). 71

———. " The Water We Drink, Its Influence on the Health of the Community." Supplement to the Sanitary Record of April 30, 1897, p. 48. 72

———. " Watershed Areas and Sanitary Districts Coterminous, The Desirability of Making." Middleton, R. E. J. N. E. W. W. Assn. 13:199 (Dec. 1898). 73

———. " Watersheds of City Water Supplies, Dangers of Sanitary Neglect of." Mason, W. P. Sanitarian 38:385 (May, 1897). 74

———. " Water and Public Health." Fuertes, James H. New York, Wiley & Sons, 1st ed., 1897. 12mo, 85 pp. Cl. $1.50. 75

———. " Water Supply, considered principally from a Sanitary Standpoint." Mason, William P. New York, J. Wiley & Sons, 1897. 8vo, 504 pp. Cl. $5. 76

———. " Water Supply, considered mainly from a chemical and Sanitary Standpoint." Nichols, William Ripley. New York, Wiley & Sons, 1883. 8vo, 232 pp. Cl. $2.50. 77

" Sedimentation Basins for Water Works." Kiersted, Wynkoop, Engng. Rec. 40:506 (Oct. 28, 1899). 78

" Sewage, Water Supply and." Arey, C. O. Sanitarian 38:126 (Feb. 1897). 79

" Small Towns and Rural Districts, Water Supply of." Griffith, Percy. J. Gas Light (London) Jan. 26, 1897. 80

———. " Cheap Water for a Small Town." Engng. Rec. 37:452 (April 23, 1898).

———. " Financial Standpoint, Town Water Works from a." Hedenberg, W. L. Mun. Engng. 15:341 (Dec. 1898). 81

———. " Model Water Works for Small Towns." Moore, C. E. Cal. Mun. 1:9 (Aug. 1899), City Govt. 7:86 (Oct. 1899). 82

———. " Water Works for Small Cities and Towns." " Aquarius." Engng. Rec. 36:292, 492 (Sept. 4, Nov. 6, 1897); anon. Engng. Rec. 37:296, 496 (March 5, May 7, 1898); Goodell, John. New York, Engng. Rec. 1899. 8vo, 281 pp. Cl. $2. 83

———. " Water Supplies for Towns and Country Places." Palmer, Arthur W. City Govt. 5:222 (Dec. 1898). 84

" Sources of Water Supply and Disease, Notes on the Relation between the Geology of the." Manson, Marsden. J. Assoc. Engng. Soc. 24:321 (May, 1900), Mun. Engng. 19:11 (July, 1900), Cal. Mun. 2:175 (July, 1900). 85

———. " The Sources of Town Water Supplies, and their Bearing Upon the Public Health." Berrington, R. E. W. Jour. Gas. Lgt. June 14, 1898. 86

———. " Water and Public Health, the relative Purity of Waters from different sources." Fuertes, James H. New York, J. Wiley & Sons, 1897. 12mo, 75 pp. Cl. $1.50. 87

" State Supervision of Water Supply and Sewage Disposal, Proposed." Harmon, Jacob A. Ill. Soc. of Eng. & Surv. 1898. 88

———. " Duty of the State in Protecting Sources of Public Water Supplies." Probst, C. O. City Govt. 6:145 (June, 1899). 89

Statistics. " Handbook of Water Works Statistics and Fire Department Equipment." (U. S. and Canada.) New York, F. W. Shepperd, published annually, 18th year, 1897. 8vo, 458 pp. 90

Water Supplies of Cities—*Continued*.

"Transfer of the Watertown Water Works, The." Engng. Rec. 39:350 (March 18, 1899).

"Typhoid Fever and Water Supply." Benjamin, S. Sci. Am. Supp. June 11, 1887; Mills, Hiram T. J. N. E. W. W. Assoc. June, 1891, p. 149; anon. Engng. News April 2, 1893, p. 326. **91**

——. "Effect of a Pure Water Supply on Typhoid Fever in Newark and Jersey City, The." (Editorial.) Engng. News 38:217 (Sept. 30, 1897). **92**

——. "Les Eaux Sources et la Fièvre Typhoide." Thoinoit. R. Municipale 3:1931, 1947 (Feb. 24, March 3, 1900). **93**

——. "Statistics, Typhoid Fever, from large Cities of the World." Appendix A, p. 268, "Purification of Public Water Supplies." Hill, John W. New York, Van Nostrand, 1898. 8vo, 304 pp. $3. **94**

——. "Typhoid Fever and Water Supply in Sixty-six American and Foreign Cities." Hill, John W. Engng. News May 21, 1896. **95**

——. "Typhoid Fever Rates, Water Supplies of eight Cities in Relation to." Hill, John W. Sanitarian 38:531 (June, 1897). **96**

Underground Water, The Law of. Cecil, Robert. Engng. Rec. 40:632 (Dec. 2, 1899); Mansergh, James. San. Rec. 19:565 (June 11, 1897). **97**

"Valuation of Water Works, The." Engng. Rec. 37:298, 322 (March 5, 12, 1898).

——. "Valuation of Water Works Property." Kiersted, Wynkoop. Proc. Am. Soc. Civil Engineers March, 1897. **98**

——. "What is a Water Plant Worth?" Brown, Charles Carroll. Mun. Engng. 15:97 (Aug. 1898). **99**

"Waste, Water." Beardsley, Joseph. J. Assoc. Engng. Soc. 23:248 (Dec. 1899), Mun. Engng. 18:117 (Feb. 1900), Public Policy 2:332 (May 26, 1900). **100**

——. "British View of Water Waste, A." Engng. Rec. 41:150 (Feb. 17, 1900). **1**

——. "Causes and Corrections of Water and Gas Main Leakage." Sci. Am. Supp. 48:20048 (Dec. 23, 1899). **2**

——. "Leakage, Water." Bayles, James C. Public Imp. 1:26 (May 15, 1899). **3**

——. "Leakage from Street Mains, The." Croes, J. James R. Engng. Rec. 40:537 (Nov. 4, 1899). **4**

——. "Localizing and Preventing Water Waste." Croes, J. James R. Engng. Rec. 42:227 (Sept. 8, 1900). **5**

——. "Loss of Water from Pipes." Crandall, F. H. Mun. Engng. 14:193 (April, 1898); anon. Engng. Rec. 37:279 (Feb. 26, 1898). **6**

——. "Prevention, Water Waste and its." Case, L. N. City Govt. 3:163 (Nov. 1897). **7**

——. "Prevention, Waste of Water in Public Supplies and its." Hope, Wm. Proc. Inst. Civil Engineers 110:260 (1892). **8**

——. "Reduction of Water Waste, The." Sherrerd, Morris R. Engng. Rec. 40:458 (Oct. 14, 1899). **9**

——. "Relation between Cost of Water Wasted and Cost of Detection and Prevention of Waste." Jenkins, A. J. J. Gas Light. 76:88 (July 10, 1900), Surveyor 18:68 (July 20, 1900). Another article, anon. Engng. Rec. 42:81 (July 28, 1900). **10**

——. "Use and Misuse of Water." Berrington, R. E. W. Plumber and Decorator (London) Dec. 1, 1896. **11**

——. "Use and Waste of Water, The." Croes, J. James R. Engng. Rec. 42:196 (Sept. 1, 1900). **12**

——. "Water Famines and Water Waste." (Editorial.) Fire & W. 25:194 (June 17, 1899). **13**

——. "Water Waste in the Olden Time." Engng. Rec. 40:333 (Sept. 9, 1899). **14**

——. (See also Consumption and Meters above.)

Water Supplies, General Articles on. Bouscaren, G. Mun. Engng. 19:259 (Oct. 1900); Davis, Floyd. Engng. M. 3:227 (1892); Ficklen, John R. Ann. Am. Acad. Pol. Sci. 15:291 (March, 1900); Hering, Rudolph. Engng. M. 9:450 (1895); Hillyer, George. City Govt. 5:54 (Aug. 1898); McElroy, Samuel. Engng. M. 6:821 (1894); Mansergh, James. Surveyor 18:564 (Nov. 16, 1900); Ulrich, C. F. Fire & W. 26:256 (Aug. 12, 1899); Watson, W. M. Can. Eng. June, 1897; Wingate, Charles F. No. Am. R. 136:364 (1883); anon. City Govt. 1:139 (Dec. 1896); Eng. 89:654 (June 22, 1900); Fire & W. June 9, 1894; Engng. Rec. 41:73 (Jan. 27, 1900). **15**

Water Supplies of Cities—*Continued.*

——. "Water and Water Supplies." Thresh, J. C. London, Rebman Pub. Co., 1896. 8vo, 454 pp. Cl. $3.20.   16

——. "Water and Water Supply." Corfield, William Henry. New York, Van Nostrand, 1875. 145 pp. 50 cts.   17

——. "Water Supply." Mason, William P. New York, Wiley & Sons, 2d ed., 1899. 8vo, 512 pp. Cl. $5.   18

——. "Water Supply for Cities." Address before the Faculty and Students of the Univ. of Illinois. Hill, John C. 1896, pamphlet, 22 pp.   19

——. "Water Supply, Sewerage and Sewage Disposal." Mansergh, James. Surveyor 18:538 (Nov. 9, 1900).   20

"Wells, Public Water Supplies from Driven." Kuichling, E. City Govt. 8:96, 125, 152 (April, May, June, 1900), 9:15, 45, 71 (July, Aug. Sept. 1900).   21

Watford's [Eng.], Worries and Wants." Mun. J. & London 8:1163 (Oct. 27, 1899).   22

Weissenfels, Ger. Housing. "Aus zwei deutschen Kleinstädten, ein Beitrag zur Arbeiterwohnungsfrage." v. Mangold, Carl. Jena, Fisher, 1894.   23

"**Wellington**: A City of the Empire." Dolman, Frederick. Idler 15:166 (March, 1899).   24

West Ham, Eng. (See under **London**.)

Wharves and Docks. (See **Harbor Facilities**.)

Wheeling, W. Va., History, description and statistics of in 1880. Census. See 1-7.   25

White Chapel. (See under **London**.)

"**White Haven [Eng.]**, Some Public Works at." Brodie, J. S. San. Rec. 23:566 (June 30, 1899).   26

"**White Plains, N. Y.**, Water Works, The." Engng. Rec. 42:176 (Aug. 25, 1900).   27

"**Willesden [Eng.]**, Light and Traction." Mun. J. 9:584 (July 27, 1900).   28

"**Williamsburg**, History of." Tyler, Lyon G. See 1-4c.   29

"**Williamsport**, Water Supply at." Fire & W. 22:387 (Oct. 23, 1897).   30

Wilmington, Del.

"Garbage, Cremation of: The Methods used in Wilmington, Del." Phillips, Barnet. Hrprs. Wkly. 38:913 (1894).   31

"Gas Works of Wilmington, Del." Am. Gas Light J. 68:133 (Jan. 24, 1898).   32

"History of Wilmington, Del." Vallandigham, E. N. See 1-4b.   33

"Parks of Wilmington, Del." Leisen, Theodore A. Mun. Engng. 16:366 (June, 1898).   34

"Sewer, Wilmington's Intercepting." Hatton, T. Chalkley. City Govt. 1:90 (1896).   35

"Water Purification at Wilmington, Del." Eng. News 40:146 (Sept. 8, 1898).   36

Wilmington, N. C.

"History of Wilmington, N. C." Cheshire, J. B. See 1-4c.   37

History, description and statistics of Wilmington, N. C., in 1880. Census. See 1-7.   38

"**Wimbledon, Eng.**, the Sewerage of." Fuertes, James H. Engng. Rec. 37:232 (Feb. 12, 1898).   39

Winchester, Eng.

"The City of Winchester." Telford, John. Wesleyan Methodist Magazine Sept. 1899.   40

History. "Winchester." Kitchin, G. W. London, Longmans, 1890. Historic Towns Series. 8vo. 3s. 6d.   41

Wires, Underground vs. Overhead. (See **Conduits.**)

"**Wisby**: An Ancient Hanseatic Town." Hyams, Walter. Outlook 57:321 (Oct. 2, 1897). 42

Wisconsin.
"Charter and its Relation to Wisconsin Cities, The Model." Butler, John A. Proc. of the League of Wisconsin Municipalities, Bulletin No. 3, p. 10, June 26-27, 1899. 43
Elections. "Wisconsin Primary System." Monroe, Charles E. N. Y. Conf. on Practical Reform of Primary Elections, p. 133. Chicago, Hollister, 1898. 8vo, 150 pp. Paper. 44
"League of Wisconsin Municipalities." Sparling, Samuel E. Ann. Am. Acad. Pol. Sci. 14:272 (Sept. 1899). 45
"Legislation for Wisconsin Cities, The Need of." Douglas, A. S. Municipality p. 8 Oct. 1900. 46
"Local Government in Wisconsin." Spencer, David E. J. H. Univ. Studies VIII:2 (1890). 47
"Streets in Wisconsin Cities, Construction and Maintenance of." Buckley, Ernest R. Municipality, p. 1, April, 1900. 48
"Uniform Accounting for Wisconsin Cities." Sparling, Samuel E. Proc. of the League of Wisconsin Municipalities, Bulletin No. 3, p. 41, June 26-27, 1899. 49
——. "The Relation of the Simplified State Accounting System to Wisconsin Municipalities." Gilman, Stephen W. Public Policy 2:395 (June 23, 1900), Municipality Vol. I, No. 5, p. 19 (Dec. 1900). 50

Wolverhampton, Eng.
"Sewage Disposal at Wolverhampton, Eng." San. Rec. 23:417, 436, 458 (May 12, 19, 26, 1899). 51
——. "Wolverhampton Sewage Works." Berrington, R. E. W. Proc. Inst. Civ. Eng. (London) 110:289 (1892). 52

Women and their Relations to the City. (See also **Working Women and Settlements.**)
See also Boston, Chicago, Denver, Indianapolis, London, New Orleans, New York, Philadelphia, United Kingdom, Washington.
Female Suffrage. "L'Electorat municipal et provincial des femmes." Alix, Gabriel. La Reforme Social Nov. 1, 1896. 53
"Municipal Government from a Woman's Standpoint." Runkle, [Mrs.] C. A. p. 500 Proc. Second Natl. Conf. for Good City Govt., 1895, see 6-18b. 54
——. "Women's Work on City Problems." (A symposium. For articles see the individual cities.) Mun. Aff. 2:439 (Sept. 1898). 55
——. "Woman's Work in Municipal Housekeeping." Seward, Mary C. Our Country 5:180 (May, 1897). 56
"Reform, Relation of Women to." Welsh, Herbert. Printed by the Civic Club of Philadelphia, 1894. Pamphlet, 15 pp. 57
——. "Relation of Women to Municipal Reform." Mumford, Mary E. p. 135 Proc. Natl. Conf. for Good City Govt, 1894, see 6-18a. Also published by the Civic Club, Philadelphia, 10 pp. 58
Sanitation. "What Women have done for the Public Health." Thomson, Edith Parker. Forum 24:46 (Sept. 1897). 59
"Women's Part in Political Sins." Burleigh, Florence A. Am. M. Civics Dec. 1896. 60
"Women in Municipal Affairs." Nation 51:337 (1890). 61

Woonsocket, R. I.
"Sewage Disposal at Woonsocket, R. I." Engng. Rec. 39:250 (Feb. 18, 1899). 62
——. "Woonsocket, R. I., Results obtained with large Experimental Septic Sewage Tanks and Rapid Filtration at." Carpenter, George A. Engng. N. 44:435 (Dec. 20, 1900). 63
"Water Works Reservoir and Dam, Woonsocket." Cook, Byron I. J. N. E. W. W. Assoc. Sept. 1897. 64

Worcester, Mass.

"Sewage Problem of the City of Worcester, Mass., The." Sci. Am. Sup. 49:20287 (April, 7, 1900). 65

——. "Recent Changes in Sewage Disposal, Worcester, Mass." Engng. Rec. 41:242 (March 17, 1900). 66

——. "Sewage Works at Worcester, Mass." Engng. Rec. p. 258 (March 21, 1891). 67

——. "The Worcester Sludge Process." Engng. Rec. 41:370 (April 21, 1900). 68

——. "Worcester's Sewer System." Eddy, Harrison P. City Govt. 9:64 (Sept. 1900). 69

Working Women in Cities. (See also Women and their Relation to the City.)

"Condition of Wage Earning Women." Graffenreid, Clare de. Forum 15:68 (1893). 70

Housing of Women in Cities. (See Women under **Housing.**)

"Women Wage Earners." (Bibliography.) Campbell, Helen J. Boston, Roberts Bros., 1893. 303 pp. $1. (pp. 116 et seq. on "Women Wage Earners of Boston and New York.") 71

"Working Women in Large Cities." Fourth Annual Report of the Commissioner of Labor. Washington, Government Printing Office, 1889. 631 pp. 72

Wyoming.
Uniform Municipal Accounting in." Engng. N. 44:94 (Aug. 9, 1900). 73

Yonkers, N. Y.

"Bath, The Yonkers' Public." Engng. Rec. 37:567 (May 28, 1898). 74

"Electrolysis at Yonkers, N. Y." Knudson, A. A. Engng. Rec. 40:110 (July 1; 1899); Mun. Engng. 17:102 (Aug. 1899). 75

"Housing of the Working People in Yonkers." Bogart, Ernest Ludlow. Am. Econ. Assoc. 3:273 (Oct. 1898). 76

York, [Eng.]
(History.) Raine, James. London, Longmans, 1893. Historic Towns Series. 8vo. 3s. 6d. 77

York, Pa.

"Water Works of York, Pa." Birkenbine, John. Engng. Rec. 39:375 (March 25, 1899). 78

——. "Reconstruction of the York, Pa., Water Supply." Birkenbine, John. Pro. Eng. C. Feb. 1899. 79

Zürich.

Building Laws. "Zürcherisches Baurecht." Schneider, A. Zürich, David Burkli, 1865. 105 pp. 80

Burials. "Leichenverbrennung u. d. Crematorium in Zürich." (Especially question of cost and results.) Würmli, G. Zürich, Buchh. d. Schweiz. Grüthvereins, 1895. 16 pp. 30 pf. 81

——. "Zürcher Krematorium." Geiser, A. Schweiz. Bauz. Bd. XIV, Nr. 7 und 8 (1889); Heim, Albert. Schweiz. Blätter f. Gesund. Nr. 4 und 5 (1889). 82

Garbage Disposal. See 56-40b. 83

Gas Works. "Das neue Gaswerk der Stadt Zürich in Schlieren." Schweiz. Bauz. Oct. 28, 1899. 84

History. "Politische Wandlungen der Stadt Zürich." Treichler, J. J. Berlin, Carl Havel, 1885. 36 pp. 85

Housing. "Les Habitations Ouvrières dans le Canton de Zürich." Artibal, J. R. Municipale 3:1983 (March 17, 1900). 86

Municipal Government of Zurich. Demombynes, Vol. II, pp. 453-467. See 2-11. 87

Sewage Disposal. See 56-40b. 88

"Street Railway Engineering in Europe: The Street Railway System of Zurich, Switzerland." Zahn, G. H. B. Elec. Eng. 24:320 (Oct. 7, 1897). 89

Unemployment. "Ergebnisse der Arbeitslosenstatistik in Zürich." Lang, Otto. Sozialpol. Centralblatt June 26, 1893. 90

——. "Die Arbeitslosigkeit in Zürich in den Wintern von 1892-93 und 1893-94." Merk, Aug. Berne, 1894. 91

Water Supply. "Die Wasserversorgung von Zürich, ihre zusammenhang mit der typhus Epidemie d. J. 1884." Bericht der Wasserkommission. Zürich, Scherzerisches Antiquariat, 1885. 7 m. 50 pf. 92

——. "Water Filtration, Zurich, Switzerland." Fuertes, James H. Engng. Rec. 39:472 (April, 22, 1899). 93

AUTHOR LIST.

[Explanatory Note.—The number preceding each dash refers to the page, the number or numbers following refer to the titles on that page, which are denoted by the marginal numbers on the right of each page. Thus the reference written by A. C. Abbott is on page 240, title 57. In case there are two or more references upon one page, the page number is not repeated, but the title numbers are placed in order and separated by commas.]

A

Abbott, A. C. 240-57.
Abbott, Arthur V. 67-18.
Abbott, Samuel W. 241-73; 294-41.
Abel, L. 213-85; 216-63.
Abele, ——. 103-62.
Abella, D. F. 255-14, 25.
About, E. 210-13.
Ackworth, William M. 129-71; 132-59; 159-76; 284-3.
Acland, A. H. D. 285-35.
Acland, C. T. D. 274-42.
Acollas, Renè. 70-68a; 79-83.
Acton, William. 140-49.
Adams, ——. 227-51.
Adams, Alton D. 27-15; 117-59; 119-13; 120-51; 124-75; 125-81, 159-80; 165-11, 16; 166-50; 265-17; 266-42.
Adams, Alva. 5-93.
Adams, Charles Francis. 7-32; 29-61; 151-87; 231-39, 40; 233-97, 98.
Adams, Ernst A. R. 276-9.
Adams, Francis. 285-33; 294-51.
Adams, Henry C. 40-24; 44-29; 72-5; 158-45; 247-56; 296-1.
Adams, Herbert B. 15-25; 16-34; 116-46; 141-81; 171-57, 60; 248-67; 292-85.
Adams, J. C. 217-91.
Adams, S. A. 126-18.
Adams, S. H. 211-37; 249-84.
Addams, Jane. 26-77; 47-97; 48-18; 49-19; 50-38; 64-55; 247-47, 54, 56.
Addie, Peter. 105-27; 282-49.
Adickes, ——. 103-58.
Adickes, F. 88-59.
Adler, Dankmar. 36-33, 34.
Adler, Georg. 272-4; 273-20.
Adler, J. 272-190.
Ady, Clarence E. 143-20.
Affeld, A. O. 76-100.
Agar, John G. 161-5.
Agnew, S. H. 193-72; 218-12.

Aiken, William Martin. 12-35.
Albert, H. 62-13.
Albrecht, H. 89-81.
Albu, J. 22-77.
Alcorn, W. B. 223-45.
Alden, Percy. 8-57; 141-76; 247-53.
Aldrich, Allen. 232-83.
Aldridge, H. R. 100-71.
Alexander, H. C. 216-49.
Alexander, Hugh. 307-62.
Alessio, Giulio. 110-35.
Alford, Robert C. 99-48.
Alglave, E. 118-97.
Alix, Gabriel. 311-53.
Allan, Charles E. 281-37, 39.
Allen, Elizabeth A. 245-12.
Allen, Horace N. 246-36.
Allen, Kenneth. 16-36; 249-93; 250-6.
Allen, W. F. 151-83; 290-51.
Allen, Walter S. 151-94; 157-22, 24; 165-5; 168-79; 209-93.
Alling, Joseph T. 235-28.
Allinson, E. P. 223-54, 64; 224-68.
Allpress, R. H. 140-63.
Allsop, Robert Owen. 17-79.
Alongi, G. 110-43.
Alphand, A. 210-8.
Altgeld, John P. 294-34.
Alvord, John W. 53-100; 249-94; 286-41.
American, Sadie. 215-36, 45; 246-30.
Ames, George N. 269-26.
Ames, Herbert Brown. 156-2.
Ames, L. T. 106-40.
Amore, Nic. 170-26.
Amoretti, P. 111-48.
Amos, Sheldon. 146-86; 231-50.
Anderson, G. H. 9-86.
Anderson, Rowand. 11-26.
André, E. 213-66.
Andreas, A. T. 47-88, 91.
Andrews, Avery D. 181-77.
Andrews, Charles M. 55-33.
Andrews, E. Benjamin. 48-15.

Andrews, Elmer L. 252-58.
Andrews, George H. 174-20.
Andrews, H. A. 83-63a.
Andrews, Horace. 257-71; 266-49.
Andrews, William S. 193-77; 194-78.
Angel, R. J. 300-1.
Angell, Lewis. 105-12; 241-86.
Anschütz, Gerhardt. 85-4.
Anson, W. R. 141-77.
Ansted, D. T. 149-53.
Appleton, Joseph. 266-45.
Arago, Ch. 212-61.
Archer, W. 139-30.
Archer, W. H. 14-98; 203-40.
Archibald, E. M. 94-72.
Ardagh, Judge. 170-24.
Arey, C. O. 308-79.
Argyle, Duke of. 74-63.
Arkell, George E. 106-49.
Armand, Léopold. 244-65.
Armengaud, ——. 118-100.
Arminjon, Pierre. 275-58.
Armstrong, Albert H. 197-30.
Armstrong, C. M. 167-54.
Armstrong, F. C. 16-48; 108-83; 117-66; 148-27.
Armstrong, Henry. 303-57.
Arnaudon, G. G. 261-46.
Arnecke, ——. 61-100.
Arnold, F. 141-77, 81.
Arnold, Matthew. 285-34.
Arnold-Forster, H. O. 131-22; 281-36.
Artibal, J. 20-42; 21-48; 22-89; 86-26; 103-72; 144-41; 182-8; 229-88; 280-2; 312-86.
Artigues, George. 206-3.
Artom, Ern. 279-87.
Aschrott, P. F. 41-34a; 89-90; 277-38; 282-43.
Ash, Mark. 174-18.
Ashbridge, W. T. 146-88.
Ashby, Newton B. 62-11.
Ashley, Percy W. L. 129-90.
Ashley, W. J. 51-54; 280-8.
Ashman, Henri. 36-53.
Atkinson, Edward. 26-87; 35-22; 75-81, 95.
Atlee, Walter. 225-93.
Atterbury, Anson P. 193-57.
Atwood, Wm. G. 50-36.
Aucoc, Leon. 77-18.
Austen, P. H. 306-39.
Avebury, Lord. 164-80.
Avery, Elroy M. 53-4; 162-49.
Avery, Myrtilla. 244-77.
Avery, T. 24-34.
Axon, W. E. A. 4-56.
Axtell, S. P. 306-40.
Aydon, J. W. 75-84.
Aylward, John A. 290-59.
Ayres, H. W. 303-63.
Ayres, P. W. 44-23; 204-68.

B

Babcock, Kendric C. 161-19.
Babcock, Stephen E. 308-63.
Bache, René. 105-19.
Bachi, Riccardo. 110-40; 113-89; 276-89.
Backnoffner, R. 86-16.
Bacon, L. W. 181-73.
Baddelley, J. J. 134-22.
Baer, ——. 274-38.

Baer, John Willis. 50-43.
Baetjer, Edwin G. 15-26.
Bagwell, Richard. 274-54.
Bahrt, A. F. 244-63.
Bailey, Cyril. 141-81.
Bailey, George I. 75-91.
Bailey, Henry Turner. 244-76.
Bailey, T. Ridley. 285-25.
Bain, Geo. G. 301-26.
Bain, H. Foster. 293-27.
Baker, B. B. 145-51.
Baker, Charles Whiting. 159-84.
Baker, E. Burgoyne. 183-20.
Baker, Henry B. 154-57.
Baker, J. Allen. 143-21; 268-96; 270-29.
Baker, M. N. 5-95; 49-22; 71-86, 87; 165-99; 169-14; 198-53; 251-36; 295-59, 70; 297-26; 306-28.
Baker, R. S. 48-11.
Baker, Sir B. 142-92.
Balch, Emily Greene. 78-55, 56.
Balch, Louis. 294-43.
Balch, William R. 227-43.
Baldwin, A. S. 161-19; 240-55.
Baldwin, Elbert F. 221-12.
Baldwin, F. Spencer. 6-10.
Baldwin, Henry De Forest. 7-29; 175-37; 181-84.
Baldwin, W. C. 153-39.
Ball, Robt. S. 35-24.
Ballard, A. 280-10.
Ballod, Paul. 228-80.
Balmer-Rinck, J. 102-41.
Bamberg, C. 271-71.
Bancroft, C. F. 264-11.
Bancroft, F. J. 288-88.
Bank, A. B. 224-73.
Banks, E. L. 181-67.
Banks, Louis A. 100-61.
Banks, W. 270-30.
Barber, H. H. 116-38.
Barbour, Frank A. 150-70; 251-29.
Barbour, George M. 243-56.
Barboux, Henri. 76-5.
Barclay, Thomas. 25-48, 49.
Bardies, Ch. 207-20.
Barker, F. E. 165-99.
Barnard, Job. 158-44.
Barnes, C. E. 89-94.
Barnes, James. 183-34.
Barnes, L. C. 163-77.
Barnes, T. Howard. 152-29.
Barnes, William H. 261-56.
Barnet, A. A. 273-11.
Barnett, Canon. 101-7; 133-97.
Barnett, S. A. 141-81; 247-52; 248-70, 72; 273-34.
Barrally, T. W. 203-48.
Barré, L. A. 232-85.
Barrero, E. M. 148-24.
Barrett, John A. 195-98.
Barrow, E. G. 95-92; 251-32.
Barrows, John H. 9-65a; 170-23.
Barrows, S. J. 294-35.
Barry, John Wolfe. 143-8, 18; 144-29; 145-51.
Barry, Richard. 186-13; 194-95.
Barthélemy, A. 78-42.
Bartley, George C. T. 133-94; 278-39.
Barwise, Sidney. 249-80; 251-35.
Bashore, Harvey B. 243-39.

BIBLIOGRAPHY. 315

Bassell, Burr. 147-92.
Bassett, C. Ph. 62-19; 250-23.
Bastable, C. F. 279-71, 72.
Bates, Katherine Lee. 39-4a.
Batten, J. H. 8-49.
Battershall, W. W. 10-1.
Baumeister, R. 35-5; 249-89; 257-53, 61; 258-87.
Baxter, James Phinney. 9-64.
Baxter, R. Dudley. 279-90.
Baxter, Sylvester. 20-25; 26-79, 88; 27-13; 28-38, 40, 41; 29-56, 57, 59; 31-4; 113-92; 117-58; 151-89; 161-94; 170-20; 215-46; 216-52; 293-25.
Bayard, E. 211-34.
Bayles, G. J. 152-22.
Bayles, James C. 187-24; 309-3.
Bazalgette, C. M. 252-58.
Beach, Charles F., Jr. 5-99.
Beachcroft, R. Melville. 100-69; 105-33; 129-86.
Beal, B. L. 31-7.
Bean, L. S. 51-50.
Bean, W. Worth. 164-93.
Beardsley, Joseph. 309-100.
Beattie, H. S. 267-76.
Beatty, W. A. 239-36.
Beatty, William T. 220-79.
Beaumont, Irwin. 238-95.
Beaune, Henri. 147-9.
Bechard, Ferdinand. 97-12, 13, 14.
Bechmann, G. 211-28, 39.
Beck, Louis J. 182-14.
Becker, G. 112-77.
Beckett, J. 72-13.
Beeler, John A. 269-26.
Beer, E. 90-13.
Beggs, John I. 263-81.
Behm, E. 229-6.
Behrend, G. 118-86.
Beilby, George. 122-7.
Beitel, Calvin G. 222-25.
Beitzell, A. J. 246-19.
Belden, E. Porter. 185-83.
Bell, A. C. 173-100.
Bell, A. N. 173-2; 243-27.
Bell, Edward Hamilton. 13-64.
Bell, J. J. 220-82.
Bell, James. 91-18.
Bell, Louis. 266-35; 296-86.
Bellamy, Blanche Wilder. 184-62.
Bellamy, Francis. 4-60.
Bellamy, R. C. 122-13.
Bellangé, Charles. 77-32.
Bellet, D. 144-42.
Bellot, H. H. L. 39-99; 74-69.
Bellour, Maurice. 260-20.
Belmont, P. 73-29; 74-56.
Bemis, Alton A. 227-38.
Bemis, Charles H. 31-19
Bemis, Edward W. 7-32; 47-78; 48-14; 60-82; 73-32; 153-49; 158-43, 58; 159-64; 160-86, 93; 161-16; 162-38; 164-93; 165-21, 99; 166-34, 42, 48, 51; 168-82; 224-80; 289-24; 293-17.
Bender, Herm. 235-41.
Benedetti, F. 111-49
Bengough, W. 183-16.
Benham, Charles E. 54-16.
Benjamin, Anna N. 238-7.
Benjamin, S. 309-91.
Bennett, Alfred R. 167-58.

Bennett, S. H. 85-95.
Benzenberg, George H. 155-78.
Beraneck, Hermann. 211-32; 298-49.
Beret, Auguste. 103-61.
Bergh, Robert S. S. 93-54.
Berghoff, Ising 271-65.
Bernard, François. 81-29.
Bernard, W. C. 281-38.
Bernardi, Spirito. 76-8.
Bernheim, A. C. 176-67; 180-61; 181-76; 189-72.
Bernstein, A. 118-88.
Bernstein, Eduard, 282-44.
Berrington, R. E. W. 308-86; 309-11; 311-52.
Berry, Louis F. 38-94a.
Berryman, J. R. 5-2; 72-4.
Berthélemy, H. 73-25.
Berthold, G. 21-59.
Bertoglio, L. 78-44.
Bertram, Heinr. 22-79.
Bertrand, Louis. 19-9.
Besant, Walter. 44-31a; 131-44; 133-82, 95; 134-27; 135-32; 139-43; 142-95; 143-14; 228-83; 246-18.
Bettocchi, C. 24-22.
Betts, Lillian W. 107-58, 69; 192-56; 215-36.
Beveridge, A. T. Gordon. 101-1.
Beynon-Harris, George. 167-69.
Bibo, Nathan. 240-49.
Biddaer, ——. 19-3.
Biebel, H. M. 119-19.
Bienenfeld, Bernard. 219-48.
Bigelow, A. G. 37-56.
Bigelow, James F. 151-1.
Biggar, C. R. W. 205-82.
Biggs, Herman M. 192-36.
Bignami, Enrico 111-50.
Billings, John S. 15-32; 16-38; 29-72; 30-88; 40-18, 22, 25; 43-89; 188-54; 192-36, 37; 193-71; 224-87; 225-98; 240-61, 62; 250-8; 252-58; 294-40; 295-66, 69; 302-31, 35; 304-74.
Billings, R. C. 229-10.
Billows, F. H. 146-83.
Binney, Charles Chauncey. 65-71.
Binnie, Alexander R. 133-99; 212-64.
Bippen, Wilh. 32-38.
Birch, J. 99-60.
Birch, Walter de Gray. 135-34.
Bird, Albert A. 57-58; 64-43; 222-22, 41; 223-60; 224-86, 87; 225-1, 3.
Bird, George Frederick. 270-37.
Birkenbine, John. 312-78, 79.
Birkinbine, John. 224-67.
Birkmire, William H. 36-29.
Birtwell, Charles W. 116-41.
Bishop, Edwin F. 84-76.
Bishop, H. Collins. 120-34.
Bishop, J. B. 26-67, 74; 64-49, 57, 60; 65-74, 68a; 66-4; 174-21; 194-85.
Bisland, Elizabeth. 132-57; 139-43; 185-63.
Bitter, Karl. 13-68.
Bittinger, John L. 39-1.
Bivort, J. B. 18-97.
Black, Charles C. 172-74.
Black, G. Ashton. 182-93.
Black, H. C. 227-45; 242-9.
Black, Samuel L. 3-44.
Black, W. M. 264-100.
Black, William Nelson. 3-41; 183-28, 29, 32.
Blackall, C. H. 35-16; 100-92.

Blackford, Francis W. 218-19, 26; 235-47.
Blackmar, Frank W. 45-47; 239-20.
Blackwell, Robert W. 285-48.
Blades, F. A. 70-57.
Blair, D. E. 233-94.
Blair, James L. 181-74.
Blair, W. Nisbet. 141-98; 142-3.
Blake, H. B. 70-75.
Blake, Henry T. 172-70.
Blake, Lucien I. 67-20, 26; 112-66.
Blanc, Charles. 76-56; 79-82.
Blandin, E. J. 53-6; 204-63, 66.
Blas, D. Andres. 255-16.
Blas y Melendo, Andres. 255-19, 24.
Blaschko, ———. 21-73.
Blashfield, Edwin Howland. 13-64, 70.
Blashill, Thomas. 86-19; 105-34; 135-50; 281-42.
Blatch, Harriet Stanton. 69-54.
Bleicher, H. 82-55.
Bliss, W. D. P. 1-3.
Block, Maurice. 72-21; 77-20, 24, 33; 90-15; 206-99, 1; 207-10.
Blodget, C. W. 122-15.
Blomfield, Reginald. 213-78.
Blondel, Georges. 89-92.
Blood, John Balch. 270-31.
Blunden, G. H. 279-78, 86, 92.
Blyth, A. Winter. 241-95; 242-18; 252-58; 285-24.
Boardman, Albert B. 197-31.
Boase, C. W. 206-92.
Bocock, J. P. 76-12.
Bocock, Kempner. 107-64.
Bogart, Ernest Ludlow. 271-53; 312-76.
Bogart, John. 197-38.
Böhmert, Victor. 45-38; 61-4; 86-28; 259-10; 271-57.
Boileau, W. E. 55-21.
Bokelberg, ———. 96-94.
Bokowitz, Franz. 300-93, 96.
Boller, Alfred P. 177-36.
Bolles, D. H. 217-93.
Bollfe, J. 19-5.
Bolling, Charles E. 234-19; 305-17.
Bolsius, P. 98-30.
Bolton, C. E. 53-3; 54-13a.
Bolton F. 146-72.
Dompard, Raoul. 207-29.
Bompas, H. M. 100-91.
Bonaparte, Charles J. 15-9, 11; 44-25.
Bond, Edward A. 218-23.
Bond, Walter. 164-80.
Bondeman, Dallas. 111-63.
Böniches, F. 102-37.
Bonneau, Alex. 37-62.
Bonner, Hugh. 75-86; 182-3.
Bonney, C. Carroll. 290-40.
Bonney, Charles L. 296-98.
Bonomi, Ivanoe. 163-69.
Bonsal, Stephen. 15-13; 261-54.
Bonsfield, W. R. 273-34.
Boobbyer, Philip. 83-68.
Boos, Heinrich. 88-73.
Boose, J. R. 282-56.
Boot, Horace L. P. 120-46; 125-78, 82; 282-62.
Booth, Ballington. 179-39; 186-10.
Booth, Charles. 42-72; 106-49; 130-8, 9; 132-60; 136-65; 137-100; 141-77, 81; 143-11.
Booth, Henry J. 268-85.

Booth, Mary L 185-68.
Booth, Maud B. 105-28; 179-44, 186-10.
Booth, W. H. 278-64.
Booth, William. 51-51.
Booth-Tucker, F. de Latour. 44-28.
Borden, Philip D. 151-1.
Borias, Edmond. 121-64.
Borland, E. B. 264-4.
Bornhak, Conrad. 86-15; 88-68.
Bosanquet, Bernard. 40-33; 44-22; 51-52, 56; 105-9.
Bosanquet, Mrs. Bernard. 45-45.
Bosanquet, H. 44-22; 107-20.
Bosenberger, J. L. 268-86.
Botsford, Charles Hull. 123-34.
Bouët, H. J. 163-65.
Boulanger, E. 80-11.
Boulard, J. 118-97.
Boulden, Jane Long. 12-56.
Boulnois, H. Percy. 68-39; 100-67; 101-97; 102-27; 241-74; 285-26.
Boulter, Stanley. 281-33.
Boulton, H. E. 100-86; 136-52.
Bourcart, G. 69-51; 81-32.
Bourdeau, J. 81-40; 163-65.
Bourgeois, Léon. 81-34.
Bourinot, J. G. 39-99; 205-84.
Bourke, John Walton. 160-93; 164-88; 256-32.
Bourne, H. C. 132-62; 273-33.
Bournon, Fernand. 206-100.
Bouscaren, G. 309-15.
Boussard, J. 213-68.
Boutmy, Emile. 275-61.
Bouton, George T. 74-59, 70; 249-83.
Bowker, R. R. 24-15; 53-93; 100-85; 165-15.
Bowles, Samuel. 8-60.
Bowmaker, Edward. 100-64; 282-48.
Boyd, Carl. 291-81.
Boyd, John G. 157-27.
Boyd, Peter. 224-78.
Boyden, H. P. 70-71.
Boyeson, I. K. 8-48.
Boykin, James C. 244-80.
Boyle, James. 127-29; 285-49.
Boyle, John W. 168-88; 268-100.
Boynton, Edward C. 266-44.
Brabazon, Lord. 18-85; 213-80.
Brace, Charles Loring. 179-29; 191-16.
Brackenbury, C. E. 120-58; 121-74; 122-16; 124-59.
Brackenridge, James. 123-37.
Brackett, Dexter. 303-66; 305-14.
Brackett, Jeffrey R. 44-14.
Brackett, Mary Morrell. 190-93.
Bradford, Amory H. 259-3.
Bradford, Gamaliel. 3-28; 3-42; 26-86; 152-24; 289-8.
Bradley, J. P. 254-7.
Bradley, J. W. 285-21.
Bradshaw, M. 107-60.
Brady, C. E. 33-58.
Brainard, Erastus. 246-34.
Brainard, Owen. 36-28.
Bramhall, John T. 46-67; 48-5, 8; 49-27.
Brand, H. R. 135-42.
Brandau, L. 9-79.
Branson, Walter J. 66-99; 201-100; 223-62; 225-3.
Braun, Adolf. 21-55; 273-10.
Braun, Gustav. 15-7.

BIBLIOGRAPHY. 317

Braungart, R. 156-17.
Bray, F. C. 126-6.
Brearley, John Henry. 121-65, 66.
Breed, A. H. 38-82.
Breen, Matthew P. 201-18.
Brelay, Ernest. 103-66; 212-59.
Bremner, C. S. 131-43.
Brennan, John P. 204-70.
Breslauer, Bernhard. 20-35.
Brett, W. H. 54-9.
Bridgman, Henry H. 143-7.
Bridgman, R. L. 7-32.
Brierley, J. H. 101-8.
Brigden, W. W. 18-89.
Briggs, Josiah A. 220-89.
Brinley, Charles A. 64-45; 223-43.
Brisac, ——. 120-59.
Briscoe, M. S. 16-45.
Bristed, C. A. 209-79.
Bristowe, Frederick. 304-87.
Britton, John A. 124-50; 160-93; 164-84; 165-23.
Broadhurst, W. H. 219-49.
Broatch, W. J. 205-80.
Brocklehurst, F. 149-59, 62.
Brodhead, John Romeyn. 201-15.
Brodhurst, S. 276-7.
Brodie, J. S. 310-26.
Brodlique, Eva H. 48-18.
Brodrick, George C. 275-74, 75.
Brookman, F. W. 84-80.
Brooks, F. M. 66-100.
Brooks, J. G. 42-80; 89-89; 152-11; 271-55; 273-28.
Brooks, John P. 268-91.
Brooks, Robert C. 2-21; 20-42; 21-68; 23-9; 27-6; 87-32, 37, 38.
Brophy, William. 27-14; 75-83; 119-20; 265-19.
Bross, William. 47-89.
Brown, C. O. 35-21.
Brown, C. S. Vesey. 120-47.
Brown, Chas. Carroll. 68-28, 44; 74-71, 74; 108-94; 156-36; 163-51; 219-60; 258-80; 295-68; 309-99.
Brown, D. Walter. 292-3.
Brown, E. C. 292-99.
Brown, E. S. 188-50.
Brown, Edward Osgood. 74-51.
Brown, Frederick J. 16-39, 40.
Brown, G. E. 118-81.
Brown, G. P. 49-21, 22.
Brown, George Morgan. 7-32.
Brown, Glenn. 12-59.
Brown, Goodwin. 17-73; 18-86; 177-82.
Brown, H. 204-54.
Brown, Harold P. 58-66; 67-23.
Brown, I. B. 222-26.
Brown, L. W. 173-4.
Brown, Paul G. 47-74a.
Brown, S. Herbert. 33-50.
Brown, Thomas W. 60-82.
Brown, Wm. Adams. 193-63.
Browne, Frank Balfour. 283-73.
Browne, Junius Henri. 179-30; 272-92.
Browne, Thos. N. 147-11.
Browne, William W. 73-28.
Brownell, E. E. 67-16.
Bruce, W. W. 63-23; 104-82; 133-4.
Bruhl, Louis H. 39-16.
Brundage, Ben L. 220-86.

Brünning, ——. 205-87.
Bruns, F. 147-7.
Brusa, E. 109-7.
Brush, E. H. 34-92a.
Bryan, Clark W. 256-34.
Bryan, George J. 73-41.
Bryan, W. B. 301-22.
Bryan, Wm. H. 254-97.
Bryant, Henry F. 29-62; 55-29.
Bryce, P. H. 240-58.
Bryce, James. 64-50; 181-73; 217-2; 287-60; 289-4; 294-38.
Bucher, Karl. 16-52; 82-52; 103-60.
Buchtel, Henry A. 50-44.
Buck, Albert H. 242-24.
Buckley, Ernest R. 311-48.
Buckley, W. J. 118-94.
Budd, Henry. 217-82.
Buechel, Carl. 256-44.
Buel, C. C. 174-21.
Bugbee, J. M. 26-81; 75-88; 171-58.
Bugnottet, G. 140-55.
Bulla, John N. 38-82a.
Bullier, L. M. 117-70.
Bullit, John C. 223-54.
Buls, Ch. 12-52.
Bunce, J. Thackeray. 25-36; 276-85.
Buomberger, Ferdinand. 82-59.
Burbank, Emily M. 19-21.
Burdette, Everett W. 166-31; 168-90.
Burdette, Henry. 42-84; 43-88.
Burgess, C. F. 67-15.
Burgess, H. T. 14-100.
Burhans, J. A. 71-92.
Burke, M. D. 269-26.
Burke, Thomas. 127-40.
Burke, Ulick Ralph. 253-84.
Burleigh, Florence A. 311-60.
Burn, Robert Scott. 253-83.
Burnap, Charles E. 151-99.
Burnell, G. R. 206-2.
Burnet, Charles D 39-13.
Burnham, George, Jr. 223-54.
Burns, Clinton S. 253-78.
Burns, John. 129-74; 273-33, 34.
Burrage, Severance. 244-76.
Burrows, Montagu. 280-11.
Burt, F. P. 41-36.
Burt, Silas W. 200-93.
Burton, C. M. 53-8.
Buschmann, Nikolaus. 273-25.
Buse, Julien. 103-77.
Buseman, M. 20-23c.
Busey, S. C. 302-45.
Bush-Brown, H. K. 12-36; 176-79.
Bushée, Frederick A. 28-21; 29-66.
Busk, Alice E. 288-94.
Butler, George B. 174-22.
Butler, John A. 57-56; 155-81; 288-99; 311-43.
Butler, Nicholas Murray. 192-50.
Butler, William Allen. 185-86.
Butterfield, W. J. Atkinson. 121-73.
Butterworth, Irvin. 251-33.
Butts, Edward. 269-24.
Butts, I. 6-6.
Buxton, Noel. 126-16; 277-34.
Buxton, S. C. 278-56.
Buzelle, George B. 44-19.
Byles, W. P. 289-12.
Byrne, Austin T. 218-17.

Byrnes, T. 186-13; 226-30.

C

Cabeen. Mrs. F. Von A. 83-67.
Cacheux, Emile. 75-54; 88-78; 102-39, 45; 103-56; 244-67.
Cadet, A. 37-60.
Cadman, S. Parkes. 187-21.
Cadoux, Gaston. 208-52.
Cadwallader, Starr. 54-10.
Cady, Thomas. 190-95.
Caffin, Charles H. 13-64; 176-78.
Cahill, B. J. S. 239-21.
Cahoon, James Blake. 158-48; 157-26; 160-95; 161-16; 165-9; 266-41; 291-77; 293-20.
Calamandrei, Rod. 109-14.
Calderwood, John F. 263-78; 270-33.
Caldwell, Joshua W. 112-76.
Caldwell, W. 101-99.
Calkins, G. N. 285-28.
Callet, Albert. 79-87.
Cameron, Charles A. 62-7.
Cameron, G. 37-55.
Cameron, W. L. 305-10.
Cammann, Henry J. 178-23.
Camp, Hugh N. 179-23.
Campagnole, Edouard. 221-7.
Campbell, A. F. 44-30; 226-28.
Campbell, A. H. 84-82, 83; 280-4.
Campbell, A. W. 220-76; 242-7; 250-13.
Campbell, C. E. 109-97.
Campbell, Helen. 41-39; 105-32; 248-65; 312-71.
Campbell, M. James. 141-80.
Canby, Noble. 46-60.
Canfield, M. G. 158-49.
Cannan, Edwin. 163-58; 278-46; 279-77, 80.
Cannell, C. S. 252-58.
Canning, Thomas. 121-82.
Cannon, E. 229-97.
Canti, S. 235-36.
Cantlie, J. 140-54.
Capen, Samuel B. 6-17a; 29-51; 57-57.
Cappelen, F. W. 125-83, 85; 293-10, 16.
Cappelle, Ed. 117-72.
Capper, S. H. 36-36.
Carden, Edward. 61-2.
Carlier, A. 289-27.
Carlin, Eva V. 37-77.
Carnevali, Tito. 109-15.
Caröe, D. 258-93.
Carpenter, A. 250-13.
Carpenter, George A. 151-1; 311-63.
Carpenter, S. 123-23.
Carpenter, Thomas B. 83-63a.
Carr, C. E. A. 264-11.
Carr, Isaac. 72-16; 124-53.
Carr, William Wilkins. 225-3.
Carrera y Justiz, Francisco. 58-63.
Carret, James R. 152-7.
Carson, Howard. 152-4.
Carstens, C. C. 208-37; 212-60.
Carter, James. 288-79.
Carter, Luther C. 180-50.
Cary, Edward. 147-5; 194-85.
Cary, Thomas G. 239-39.
Case, L. N. 17-65; 306-22; 309-7.
Cassat, Alfred C. 204-63.
Castiglioni, L. 110-16.

Catania, C. 110-27.
Caulfield, John. 169-4; 238-2.
Caverly, C. S. 246-17.
Cawston, Arthur. 142-100.
Center, George L. 239-33.
Chabanne, J. B. 146-69; 293-12.
Chabrouillard, F. 286-52, 53.
Chadwick, Edwin. 99-52; 130-94; 274-47.
Chadwick, J. W. 37-55.
Challenger, Charles. 267-81.
Chalmers, M. D. 275-63.
Chalmers, Thomas. 50-42.
Chamberlain, Joseph. 3-31; 24-29; 27-89; 99-57; 100-81; 276-88, 91; 278-47; 289-29.
Chamberlain, W. G. S. 173-13.
Chambers, W. 41-35.
Chamen, W. A. 67-23.
Champagnac, Emile. 80-93.
Champernowne, Henry. 26-69.
Champlin, John W. 93-58.
Chance, George. 217-9.
Chance, G. Whitefield. 264-13.
Chance, W. 277-31.
Chancellor, C. W. 96-6; 211-37; 307-49.
Chandler, C. F. 292-98.
Chant, L. O. 42-78.
Chapin, Charles V.. 504-80.
Chapin, Henry Dwight. 146-85; 192-54; 255-88.
Chapin, L. E. 39-4.
Chapin, T. F. 245-8.
Chapman, E. T. 303-49.
Chapman, John Jay. 5-94a, 94b; 217-78, 85; 290-37.
Chapman, Sydney J. 279-88.
Charles, S. A. 116-85; 304-79.
Charnay, Maurice. 206-2; 209-91; 211-41.
Chase, Charles B. 258-74.
Chase, Harvey S. 29-68.
Chase, John C. 96-5; 293-18.
Chase, Philip A. 29-61.
Chassagne, ——. 208-42.
Chater, W. A. 133-7.
Cheetham, W. 112-78.
Cheshire, J. B. 310-37.
Chessman, James. 121-78.
Chester, John S. 156-7.
Chester, W. R. 121-70.
Cheysson, E. 90-100.
Chignell, R. 133-85, 92.
Child, G. W. 104-6; 241-85.
Child, Jacob T. 108-83a.
Child, W. D. 282-63.
Childs, ——. 306-33.
Childs, Stephen. 173-14.
Chipman, Willis. 39-2.
Chisholm, George C. 285-17.
Chittenden, L. E. 196-11.
Christian, George H. 167-55.
Chubb, H. 138-12
Church, S. H. 226-16.
Church, William G. 13-65.
Cicott, Frank X. 99-49; 203-39.
Cilleuls, Alfred. 80-12.
Clancey, John J. 274-49.
Clapp, Henry Lincoln. 245-96.
Clareti, J. 206-4.
Clark, ——. 296-87.
Clark, C. C. P. 65-70, 80.
Clark, Frank Humboldt. 268-84, 87; 295-60

BIBLIOGRAPHY.   319

Clark, Helen F. 182-15.
Clark, H. W. 114-12a; 151-2; 303-78.
Clark, John S. 165-99.
Clark, Walter 158-47.
Clark, Walton. 125-88a.
Clark, William A. 29-75.
Clark, Wm. J. 262-72; 266-38; 267-68.
Clarke, Christopher. 36-30.
Clarke, Eliot C. 30-81.
Clarke, Emmons. 192-41; 257-51.
Clarke, Francis E. 51-65; 66-96.
Clarke, Thomas C. 269-6.
Clegg, James. 84-80.
Clegg, Samuel. 121-88.
Clement, ——. 100-73.
Clement, F. 49-22.
Clephane, Walter C. 301-20.
Clevalier, Emile. 78-47.
Cleveland, E. C. 216-75.
Cleveland, H. W. S. 213-91; 214-10, 99; 215-24.
Clews, Elsie. 42-78.
Clews, Henry. 197-36.
Closson, C. C. 152-11; 296-3, 7.
Clough, John Lyle. 119-6, 7, 8; 164-90.
Cloverdale, W. H. 47-82.
Clow, Fred R. 70-76; 238-98.
Clowes, Frank. 142-89, 90; 249-84, 94.
Clifford, Frederick. 285-20.
Clifford, J. 244-79.
Cline, J. W. R. 125-92.
Coates, Foster. 176-73.
Cobb, A. G. 37-55.
Cobb, Albert Winslow. 27-95.
Cochin, Denys. 208-41; 209-89.
Cochran, Charles W. 59-63.
Cochran, T. 223-65.
Cochrane, Constance. 281-32; 101-14.
Cochrane, E. 104-5.
Codman, Henry Sargent. 213-90.
Codman, J. S. 120-36.
Coen, S. 109-3.
Coffin, Freeman C. 305-96.
Cogswell, Fredrick Hull. 172-64.
Cohn, E. 104-90.
Cohn, L. 79-74.
Coit, Stanton. 247-55; 272-2.
Colam, W. N. 63-28; 171-53.
Colbert, E. 47-85.
Colburn, Zerah. 138-14.
Colby, B. H. 49-22.
Cole, T. 25-41.
Cole, William I. 27-8, 10; 29-55, 65; 30-79a.
Cole, William J. 27-96.
Cole, W. W. 269-19.
Coleman, Chapman. 20-26.
Coleman, E. 162-31.
Coler, Bird S. 50-48; 71-98; 72-10, 12; 157-32; 162-46, 50; 174-19, 27; 175-43; 179-38; 182-90, 92; 183-31; 190-87, 98; 217-7; 289-6.
Collin, Charles A. 201-4.
Collingwood, Francis. 69-44c.
Collins, C. P. 249-96.
Collins, Patrick. 137-89.
Collins, Patrick A. 166-29.
Collins, W. J. 129-90.
Collis, C. H. T. 69-44b.
Colver, Henry Clay. 246-34.
Colyar, A. S. 170-30.
Combarieu, A. 210-1.

Commons, John R. 5-86, 87, 94; 8-58; 41-55; 47-78; 51-71, 72; 60-88; 65-87; 68-44a; 73-44; 98-44; 101-95; 113-83; 151-93; 159-70; 160-87; 165-20, 99; 223-65; 230-30; 231-43, 44, 48.
Compton, Lenox. 6-8.
Comstock, John M. 290-57.
Conant, R. W. 265-22.
Conaty, G. 264-11.
Conder, F. R. 3-33; 70-62; 136-59; 146-69, 71; 243-49.
Conder, J. B. Reignier. 278-65.
Conigliani, C. A. 296-8.
Conine, Martha A. B. 59-72.
Conkling, Alfred R. 3-30; 289-7.
Conner, Edward. 78-58; 209-90; 210-2; 211-33, 39; 212-59.
Connett, A. N. 82-46; 208-40.
Connor, R. 290-48.
Conrad, ——. 2-10; 103-57, 58.
Conradi, H. 82-49.
Conyngton, Thomas. 220-85.
Cook, Byron I. 311-64.
Cook, Clarence. 189-82.
Cook, F. A. 236-65.
Cook, J. 65-73.
Cook, Theo. A. 135-37.
Cook, W. W. 159-81.
Cooke, Frederick H. 4-71.
Cooke, George Willis. 55-26.
Cooley, C. H. 229-99.
Cooley, Stoughton. 3-43; 230-34; 231-43.
Cooley, Thomas M. 5-1; 74-58; 75-75.
Coolidge, Susan. 173-11.
Cooper, Edward H. 207-32.
Cooper, Ella H. 101-100.
Cooper, Frederick E. 144-42.
Cooper, H. S. 111-51.
Cooper, Sarah B. 245-6.
Cooper, Theodore. 196-13.
Cooper, W. J. 249-79.
Copeland, Guild A. 29-52.
Copley, I. C. 123-42.
Corbett, J. 136-76.
Corfield, Wm. Henry. 145-68; 250-24; 252-58; 253-85; 305-8; 319-17.
Cornaggia, C. O. 154-65.
Cornell, Robert E. 180-56.
Cornil, Georges. 271-63.
Corradini, F. 270-43.
Corthell, Elmer L. 149-57.
Coryell, J. R. 215-35.
Cosby, Frank Clark. 237-85.
Costello, Augustine E. 182-11; 191-19.
Costelloe, B. F. C. 134-12; 145-58.
Cottrell, Henry E. P. 307-43.
Cottrell, S. B. 127-41
Courcelle, Louis. 81-25, 43.
Court, W. R. 17-60.
Coutts, Baroness Burdett. 136-58.
Covert, John C. 79-88.
Cowan, Andrew. 216-71.
Cowan, R. 92-42.
Cowell, H. C. B. 272-3.
Cowen, John K. 8-56.
Cowie, Alexander. 39-7.
Cowper, Countess. 133-98.
Cox, E. 136-75.
Cox, Homersham. 275-62.
Cox, I. J. 238-13.
Coxe, A. C. 37-55.

Craft, Mabel C. 150-73; 240-44.
Craigie, F. G. 279-69.
Craik, H. 285-36.
Cram, J. Sergeant. 183-27.
Crandall, F. H. 297-20; 309-6.
Crandon, F. P. 6-7.
Crane, Albert S. 69-50; 250-16.
Crane, Walter. 12-34.
Crane, William H. 258-78.
Cranfield, Sydney White. 100-72.
Cranford, W. V. 68-41.
Cravath, J. R. 120-49.
Cree, Nathan. 61-89.
Crehore, C. F. 7-32; 64-47.
Creighton, Mandell. 39-12.
Cremnitz, M. 247-43.
Crépy, P. 34-74.
Crespi, Alfred J. H. 25-50; 277-21; 297-30.
Cridlan, J. J. 9-77.
Crimp, William Santo. 141-88; 251-45.
Cripps, H. L. 145-59.
Crissey, Forest. 48-100.
Crocker, Francis B. 119-32.
Croes, J. James R. 198-53; 199-77; 269-8; 305-15; 309-4, 5, 12.
Crofts, W. C. 163-74.
Croker, E. F. 182-4.
Croker, Richard. 194-85.
Crompton, R. E. 119-29.
Crooks, W. 228-60.
Crosby, Albert F. 71-97.
Crosby, Ernest H. 126-19.
Crosby, Howard. 176-57; 188-62; 191-15.
Crosby, William B. 33-60.
Cross, Judson N. 155-89.
Cross, R. A. 135-42.
Crothers, T. D. 43-98.
Crowell, Foster. 196-24; 250-10.
Crowell, John F. 270-46.
Crowley, Daniel N. 166-30.
Cruikshank, Alfred B. 189-76.
Cruppi, J. 208-44.
Cruveilhier, Jean. 80-8.
Cudworth, F. G. 265-17.
Culham, J. A. 290-39.
Cullinane, J. R. 117-61.
Cullings, T. C. 141-78.
Cumming, Alice L. 23-8.
Cummings, Edward. 126-15; 248-72.
Cunningham, Granville C. 107-73.
Curley, E. A. 3-34; 152-18; 188-45.
Curry, E. H. 139-43.
Curti, Theodor. 237-77; 259-16.
Curtis, Charles E. 72-17b; 168-88.
Curtis, William Eleroy. 34-77; 38-86; 285-46; 301-4.
Curtius, Ernst. 13-84.
Cutcheon, Lewis D. 93-61.
Cutler, Mary S. 2-20.
Cutter, Charles R. 151-1.
Cutter, John D. 65-79.
Cutting, R. Fulton. 162-40; 176-68.
Cutts, E. L. 54-17.
Czepelka, A. 267-73.
Czullik, A. 214-100.

D

Dabney, W. D. 157-34.
Da Cunha, Geo. W. 106-44.
Daft, Leo. 266-49.
Daley, Agnes. 187-37.
Dalla Vatta, Da Ricardo. 74-66.
Dallenbaugh, F. S. 76-98.
Dallinger, Frederick W. 63-35; 66-89.
Dalton, William. 198-53.
Damon, George A. 125-79.
Damon, Mary B. 107-65.
Dana, M. M. G. 141-81; 240-63.
Dana, R. H. 64-40; 65-68a.
Daniel, Annie S. 186-6; 188-50.
Dareste de la Chavanne, Antoine C. 79-90.
Darley, George. 115-20.
d'Arzago, A. de C. 154-64.
Dauvert, Paul. 80-7.
d'Avenel, Georges. 72-21a; 73-23; 77-25, 209-76.
Davenport, J. Aldersey. 251-49.
Davey, Henry. 25-50.
Davidof, L. 141-75.
Davidsohn, Rob. 76-6.
Davidson, Henry T. 107-72.
Davies, Dixon Henry. 160-98; 283-87.
Davies, E. A. 149-41.
Davies, Henry. 248-74.
Davis, A. 185-70.
Davis, A. H. 13-85.
Davis, Charles Henry. 263-88; 264-11; 266-44, 49.
Davis, E. H. 213--83.
Davis, F. A. W. 67-14, 26; 169-100.
Davis, Floyd. 243-50; 288-84; 304-83; 305-4; 307-43; 308-68, 69; 309-15.
Davis, Geo. H. 266-58.
Davis, Gherardi. 190-88.
Davis, Hartley. 194-85.
Davis, Horace. 52-88.
Davis, J. De P. 3-30.
Davis, W. M. 246-28.
Dawson, Philip. 264-11; 266-46, 48; 265-24.
Dawson, W. H. 212-59; 260-21.
Day, H. S. 278-58.
Day, Richard W. 265-15.
Deady, Matthew P. 290-52.
Dean, Sedgwick. 123-35.
Dearness, J. 246-19, 23.
Debell, Edwin L. 120-41.
de Calonne, Alphonse. 35-26.
de Castelleux, Comte. 81-28.
Dechan, Bailie. 306-36.
D'Echérac, ———. 207-23.
de Circourt, Comte A. 21-54.
de Coulanges, Fustel. 97-21.
de Courmelles, Foveau. 118-95.
de Crisenoy, J. D. 71-95; 79-76, 79.
Dee, Thomas G. 254-3.
Deery, John Jerome. 233-1.
de Ferron, H. 77-23; 275-82.
de Forest, Robert W. 104-100.
de Foville, A. 229-7.
de Franqueville, Le Comte. 77-36.
de Freund, E. 267-61.
de Gáes e Siqueira Filha, José. 234-21.
De Gand, Emmanuel. 78-64.
Degener, P. 250-14.
de Graffenreid, Clare. 101-94; 245-85; 312-70.
de Guer, Guérlin. 79-72; 294-52.
Dehaye, A. 276-100.
de Hornstein, Edouard. 37-63.
Dejamme, Jean 81-36, 38.

BIBLIOGRAPHY. 321

de Jong, E. W. 11-16.
de Kay, Charles. 21-60.
de Laborde, Alexander Louis Joseph. 209-67.
Delaire, A. 102-49.
De Land, Fred. 163-65.
de las Casas, William B. 29-61.
de la Sizeranne, Robert. 61-94.
Delaunoy, Léon. 81-44.
de Lautreppe, Lecoq. 207-21.
de Laveleye, Emile. 18-95; 98-26.
Delbrück, Hans. 272-97.
Dellwik, Carl. 124-69.
de Mailhol, D. 77-27.
de Malarce, A. 244-27.
De Marcère, Edouard. 79-67.
de Marco, De Viti. 110-38.
de Martinis, Ces. 110-19.
de Mattini, G. B. 159-76.
de Medeiros, J. J. Tavares. 230-23.
Deming, C. 65-69.
Deming, Horace. 52-88; 57-51; 288-1; 289-31.
Demmier, G. A. 246-31.
de Molenari, G. 97-15; 229-3.
Demombynes, Gabriel. 2-11; 14-2; 18-94; 23-4; 36-47; 58-67a; 77-37; 85-88; 85-100; 94-63; 98-24; 110-17; 203-50; 230-22; 236-57, 58, 60; 255-21; 259-7; 270-45; 275-84.
de Montmorency, J. E. G. 130-16.
de Morgan, John. 134-29; 135-35.
Dendy, H. 139-29.
de Néronde, C. 212-52.
Denham, Prierly. 84-76.
Denison, Geo. A. 256-33.
Denjean, G. 271-58.
Dennis, Nelson F. 10-4.
de Nouvoin, George. 80-99; 103-76.
Denslow, Van Buren. 194-85.
Densmore, George C. 195-3, 8.
Denton, J. B. 193-66.
Depasse, H. 210-100, 15.
De Pena, Carlos Maria. 297-28.
Deploige, Simon. 19-17; 259-14.
de Pontich, Henri. 78-40; 206-1; 207-15.
Derouin, H. 78-59.
de Rousiers, Paul. 160-91.
Derrah, Robert H. 263-83; 295-81.
de Saint Albin, Emm. 209-87.
de Sauvigney, A. Noirpoudre. 140-55.
Desbats, A. Gabriel. 79-78.
Deschanel, Paul. 79-66.
des Cilleuls, Alfred. 78-53.
de Segundo, Ed. C. 84-83.
des Marez, Guillaume. 97-19.
d'Esmenard, E. 33-65.
Desplanques, A. 72-20.
Després, A. 81-31.
des Rotours, J. Angot. 77-17.
de Tinguy du Pouet, J. 78-60.
de Toulza, Etienne. 77-19.
Deutsch, Ed. 20-38; 298-51.
de Variguy, C. 194-85.
Devine, Edward T. 44-35; 45-41, 46; 179-38.
Devine, James. 76-97.
Devlin, Thomas C. 7-34; 52-89; 65-72; 70-59.
Devonshire, Duke of. 159-76.
Dewart, Frederick W. 237-79.
De Weese, Truman A. 244-78.
Dewey, David R. 158-45; 168-91.

Dewey, Melvil. 116-36.
de Wiart, Carton. 18-1.
De Witt, W. C. 174-28.
de Wolf, Bradford Coit. 18-100.
De Wolf, John. 189-81.
d'Haussonville, Comte. 106-47.
Dialti, D. 109-3.
Dibble, F. L. 243-48.
Dibdin, W. J. 123-39; 145-67; 146-69; 248-84; 250-13; 251-32, 34; 307-54.
Dicenta y Blanco, D. Jose. 148-21.
Dicke, H. 124-68, 73.
Dickie, George W. J. 245-3.
Dickinson, C. A. 51-67.
Dickinson, W. H. 129-71; 146-69.
Diestelkamp, L. 89-82.
Dietrich, E. 216-64; 233-89.
Dieudonné, Emil. 212-49.
Diggle, J. R. 140-67, 68.
Dilke, Ashton Wentworth. 236-64.
Dilke, C. 14-98; 203-40.
Dilke, C. W. 4-54; 206-2.
Dill, —. 275-69.
Dillon, John F. 5-98; 71-90; 72-11.
Dimmock, W. S. 296-95.
Dittrich, —. 46-57.
di Verce, E. 110-31.
Doane S. Everett. 119-31.
Doane, William C. 126-10.
Dobbs, Archibald F. 145-58.
Docharty, Augustus T. 182-10.
Dock, Mira Lloyd. 213-79.
Dodd, Cyril. 285-19.
Dodd, E. Lawson. 101-15.
Dodd, J. Theodore. 278-40.
Dodge, W. C. 166-47.
Dodge, W. E. 224-80.
Dodson, G. R. 10-96.
Doehring, W. 21-49.
Doherty, Henry L. 122-2; 162-31.
Dohrmann, F. W. 110-18; 161-19; 206-9.
Dole, Chas. F. 64-44; 288-2.
Dole, S. Milo. 124-46.
Dolman, Frederick. 25-38; 40-31; 149-40; 153-32; 260-22; 284-90; 310-24.
Dommer, F. 117-63.
Domville, Percy. 95-91.
Donald, Robert. 17-77; 76-99; 77-35;100-93; 101-21; 130-15; 164-80, 83; 221-9, 10; 277-19; 284-5; 287-64.
Doniol, A. 82-47.
Dooley, M. A. 91-31.
Doran, —. 159-63.
Dorman, Lester M. 189-66.
Dorr, Julia C. R. 237-72.
Doty, Alvah H. 294-44.
Doty, Paul. 123-27.
Douglas, A. S. 311-46.
Douglas, Francis T. 29-54; 38-91.
Douglas, Henry W. 124-55.
Douglas, John. 283-74.
Douglas, Orlando B. 215-47.
Dow, A. W. 219-42, 56, 57.
Dow, Alexander. 120-37, 45; 164-95; 265-16.
Dow, W. A. 71-91.
Dowdall, Chaloner. 127-39.
Downes, Edward. 11-20.
Downing, M. A. 108-91; 221-96; 293-29.
Doyle, John T. 240-45.
D'Oyly, Claud P. 282-60.

Drage, Geoffrey. 274-35.
Drago, Raff. 85-93.
Drake, C. M. 294-44.
Drake, M. M. 34-88.
Draper, A. S. 192-45; 244-81; 245-10.
Drew, A. A. W. 245-4.
Drexel, Joseph W. 187-23.
Drexler, A. 272-98.
Dreyfus, F. 78-62.
Drohan, John. 55-25.
Droz, Numa. 259-16.
Drucker, —. 103-67.
Duane, Gen. 199-71.
Du Bois, James T. 89-91.
Du Bois, W. E. Burghardt. 69-55.
Duboisdenghien, L. 19-12a.
Dubsky, Alfred O. 34-74.
du Camp, Maxime. 207-11.
Duclaux, M. 306-37.
Ducroiq, Th. 77-29.
Dudfield, T. O. 102-29.
Dudley, Helena S. 30-80.
Duff, H. 104-98.
Duffy, C. N. 263-78.
Dufour, Pierre. 231-50.
Dumas, A. 212-52.
du Mesnil, O. 207-22; 209-70; 211-46.
Dumont, Hermann. 19-15.
Dunell, George R. 149-57.
Dunham, H. P. 169-19.
Dunning, R. 266-40.
Dupin, Claude François Etienne. 80-94.
Dupuy, Paul. 210-19.
Durand, E. Dana. 57-47; 74-55; 181-83; 184-60; 198-45; 292-93.
Durham, Julian. 298-47.
Duryea, E., Jr. 68-41.
Dwyer, —. 51-56.
Dyer, Francis J. 193-58.
Dykes, A. H. 125-95.

E

Earl, Robert. 200-87.
Earle, Alice Morse. 186-93.
Earle, E. Lyell. 182-13.
Earnshaw, Edward H. 124-62.
Easby, William, Jr. 286-38.
Easley, Ralph M. 63-34.
Eastlake, W. Delano. 111-56.
Eastman, T. W. 222-27.
Eaton, Dorman B. 3-30; 50; 52-86; 66-92; 176-65; 191-21; 194-85; 278-42.
Eaton, I. 114-6.
Ebelot, A. 34-77.
Eberstadt, Rud. 103-59.
Eberty, E. 20-45; 150-71.
Eckstein, —. 11-19.
Eckstein, Ant. 231-57.
Eddy, Harrison P. 312-69.
Edgecumbe-Rogers, S. 275-65.
Edgeworth, F. Y. 73-37.
Edwards, —. 100-73.
Edwards, Clement. 282-51.
Edwards, E. J. 194-85; 86, 87; 198-42.
Edwards, H. C. J. 253-88.
Edwards, H. S. 154-63.
Edwards, Joseph. 293-18.
Edwards, Percy J. 142-2.
Edwards, W. H. 19-22; 21-62; 67; 22-82; 86; 23-98, 2.

Egan, P. 305-11.
Egerton, William S. 214-21.
Egger, —. 271-60.
Egner, Frederick, 267-79.
Eheberg, K. Th. 70-70.
Eicholz, P. 32-40.
Eilvart, E. 107-61.
Einaudi, Luigi. 69-52; 159-79; 206-94.
Eitelberger, R. 258-88; 299-58.
Eldridge, W. K. 114-8; 214-13; 252-52.
Eliot, Chas. 29-59, 63; 215-32; 293-11, 24.
Eliot, Charles W. 52-88; 53-97; 245-1.
Eliot, Samuel A. 38-89a.
Ellert, L. R. 239-38.
Ellery, T. George. 10-91; 70-66; 215-28; 241-75, 76, 90.
Ellicott, Edward B. 47-76.
Elliott, A. C. 220-67.
Elliott, George Frederick. 8-40.
Elliott, J. L. 247-48.
Ellis, A. B. 70-68.
Ellis, Havelock. 227-31; 242-3.
Elsing, W. T. 44-31a; 187-21.
Elster, —. 2-10.
Elwell, P. B. 260-25.
Ely, Arthur H. 181-70.
Ely, R. T. 7-27; 9-65; 15-18; 19-21; 73-45; 85-95a; 160-85, 90; 163-54, 75; 273-34; 291-72.
Emack, Edward G. 264-100.
Embree, Frances Buckley. 47-96; 49-20.
Emerich, C. F. 228-67.
Emerson, Edwin J., Jr. 188-54.
Emery, Charles E. 177-88.
Emery, Jos. D. 52-77.
Emion, V. 207-20.
Emmet, J. T. 276-97.
Enderman, H. 219-41.
Engelmann, J. 236-62.
Engels, Fr. 102-51.
Engerth, Karl. 86-23.
Engle, E. H. 300-90.
Ensley, Enoch. 74-58.
Epps, William. 162-38.
Erdman, C. W. 32-41, 42; 89-93.
Erdmann, Wald. 89-95.
Ernouf, A. 214-7.
Ernst, —. 63-30.
Escard, Paul. 292-90.
Escudier, Paul. 208-61.
Estabrook, Harold Kelsey. 28-32.
Estes, Edith Perry. 31-13.
Etting, Theodore M. 8-55.
Eustis, William Henry. 152-26.
Evans, E. V. 57-46.
Evans, Forest L. 166-28.
Evans, F. V. 25-53.
Evans, N. 139-46.
Evans, Richardson. 10-93.
Evans, W. Arnold. 101-9.
Evarts, Wm. M. 200-86.
Evert, G. 87-36.
Everett, C. E. 159-62.
Eyre, Lincoln L. 217-83.

F

Faber-Madsen, V. 56-44.
Fahey, J. H. 31-17.
Faina, Annibale. 235-46.
Fairbanks, George R. 237-76.

BIBLIOGRAPHY. 323

Fairchild, C. B. 16-41; 30-100; 230-19; 269-17.
Fairlie, John Archibald. 60-80; 200-80; 292-87, 88.
Faisst, Rudolf. 271-68.
Fales, W. E. S. 191-12.
Falke, J. V. 214-15.
Falkenburg, Ph. 11-21.
Fall, Delos. 243-42.
Fanelli, Aug. 221-5.
Fanning, M. J. 54-13.
Fanshaw, E. L. 126-8.
Fanton, Mary A. 174-28.
Fardell, T. G. 129-77.
Farmar, A. 36-54.
Farnham, Irving T. 173-13.
Farrar, F. W. 227-53.
Fassett, Jacob Sloat. 6-13; 98-46; 198-57; 200-83.
Fatio, Guillaume. 259-18.
Faure, John P. 17-62; 177-82.
Fawcett, E. 188-50.
Fawcett, Henry. 44-26.
Fäy, Emile. 78-46.
Fay, Frank B. 41-62.
Fayès, Harriet. 107-80.
Fazi, Fr. 110-34.
Featherstonhaugh, J. D. 10-3.
Fee, William T. 26-59, 60.
Felder, Cajetan. 299-55.
Fellner, F. 299-80.
Felton, Charles R. 33-57.
Fergus, Andrew. 252-65.
Ferguson, F. L. 228-64.
Fernald, James C. 126-4.
Fernow, Berthold. 185-89.
Ferrand, Joseph. 77-34.
Ferraris, C. F. 272-74.
Ferree, Barr. 11-31; 12-43.
Férrero, G. 5-92.
Ferrière, F. 85-91.
Ferris, G. T. 257-54.
Fewtrell, W. T. 121-89.
Fiamingo, Guiseppe. 163-68; 273-31.
Ficken, John F. 45-53a.
Ficklen, John R. 173-6; 309-15.
Fiedler, Ottomar. 88-62.
Field, David Dudley. 7-32; 66-97; 294-37.
Field, John W. 283-72.
Fielde, Adele M. 176-58.
Fiellet, Paul. 207-24.
Finley, John H. 41-42; 291-72.
Finley, R. J. 104-89; 293-10.
Fiordispini, Biagio. 235-35.
Firth, Frank J. 304-92.
Firth, Joseph F. B. 129-89; 130-1, 3, 7.
Fischer, A. 20-39.
Fischer, Louis E. 119-18; 166-38; 169-97.
Fischer, Paul. 133-90.
Fish, Stuyvesant. 197-33.
Fish, Williston. 258-75.
Fisher, E. A. 220-89, 91.
Fisher, Francis. 65-78.
Fisher, Geo. E. 60-80.
Fisher, Lettice. 102-30.
Fisher, W. E. 91-20.
Fisher, Wm. R. 4-61.
Fisk, Harvey E. 17-82.
Fiske, Amos K. 6-12.
Fiske, Francis S. 112-69.
Fiske, John. 289-13; 290-49.

Fitch, Geo. Hamlin. 238-14.
Fitzgerald, John E. 22-93; 152-8.
Fitzgerald, T. J. 7-26.
Fitzgerald, W. H. 166-36.
Fitzpatrick, F. A. 192-48.
Flagg, Ernest. 35-9; 106-52; 187-21.
Flagg, J. Foster. 211-37; 252-58.
Flagg, J., Jr. 191-30.
Flakky, T. 270-44.
Flattich, W. 150-69; 299-75.
Fleming, J. A. 67-23.
Fleming, Owen. 100-74; 135-45.
Fleming, Rufus. 63-25.
Flesch, —. 82-51.
Fletcher, Banister F. 131-46; 282-53.
Fletcher, Elmer D. 249-90.
Fletcher, H. J. 228-71, 86; 295-79.
Fletcher, J. 138-25; 139-45; 141-88; 145-69.
Fletcher, Robert. 249-84; 253-74.
Fletcher, Wm. I. 116-37, 45, 47.
Fletcher, William Meade. 72-15.
Flinn, Alfred D. 31-15, 21.
Flinn, J. J. 46-58.
Flint, Weston. 116-49.
Flower, B. O. 28-29, 36; 33-61; 106-55; 158-50; 231-54; 298-38.
Flower, Lamorock. 251-43.
Flower, R. P. 174-21; 190-2; 217-92.
Flower, Walter C. 173-1, 4.
Flynn, Benj. H. 297-22.
Flynt, Josiah. 227-37; 273-14.
Folks, Homer. 41-37, 38, 53; 42-85; 43-6, 7, 8; 45-42; 179-31, 38.
Folsom, De Francais. 15-29.
Folwell, A. Prescott. 250-100; 249-91; 253-88; 304-73.
Folwell, Wm. W. 215-36.
Fonsalme, —. 272-75.
Fontaine, H. 118-91.
Foote, Allen Ripley. 13-79; 70-58; 124-74; 157-32, 33; 158-42, 57, 61, 62; 159-77; 160-93, 99; 161-12, 13, 22, 23, 26; 164-96; 189-74; 196-17; 204-65; 289-15.
Ford, A. H. 268-98.
Ford, John, 72-17; 201-1.
Ford, P. L. 188-55.
Ford, W. F. 70-63; 71-93.
Ford, W. H. 224-87.
Ford, Worthington C. 289-3.
Forel, Aug. 231-55.
Forman, —. 131-34.
Forman, A. 182-15; 186-18.
Forney, Matthias Nace. 230-37; 231-40, 45.
Forrest, J. D. 158-39.
Forstall, Alfred E. 167-52.
Forster, ——. 273-24.
Fortescue, Earl. 129-88.
Foster, D. B. 115-19.
Foster, E. 17-73.
Foster, Horatio A. 165-6; 263-76.
Foster, J. F. 216-49.
Föster, L. 299-77.
Foster, Maud B. 248-63.
Foster, Roger. 182-1.
Foster, Wm. E. 234-6.
Foster, Wolcott C. 83-63a.
Fothergill, John M. 243-44.
Foulke, William Dudley. 231-40.
Fournier, Marcel. 79-71; 81-27.
Fournière, Eugene. 7-25; 159-78.

324 MUNICIPAL AFFAIRS.

Fourquet, Emile. 273-15, 17.
Fourrey, E. R. 211-37.
Foveaux, F. 122-100.
Fowkes, Fanny. 41-47, 49.
Fowle, T. W. 277-32.
Fowler, Charles Evan. 30-95; 304-90.
Fowler, Gilbert J. 285-41.
Fowler, H. H. 283-81.
Fowler, W. Warde. 94-62; 235-34.
Fox, E. A. 48-7.
Fox, George L. 129-86; 172-69.
Fox, Hannah. 224-91, 92.
Fox, William. 308-64.
Foxcroft, Frank. 38-90.
Francis, Charles. 252-58.
Francisco, M. J. 151-97; 160-93; 161-416; 163-52; 164-93; 165-23; 166-24.
Francois, M. G. 284-92.
Frankel, Carl. 23-100.
Frankland, Edward. 303-56.
Frankland, Percy. 146-69.
Franklin, Benjamin. 36-38.
Franzioli, W. J. 195-2.
Freeman, E. A. 69-49; 274-39.
Freeman, H. F. 193-58; 248-72.
Freeman, John R. 76-3; 198-53, 56; 199-77; 303-65; 305-100.
French, Allen. 98-27; 110-21.
French, Lillie H. 13-64.
Freson, J. G. 33-71.
Freud, J. Richard. 2-25; 72-7; 239-17, 32; 240-49.
Freund, Rich. 21-56.
Friedberg, Robert. 87-50.
Friedrich, Adolf. 246-32.
Fryer, William J. 35-2; 178-13, 14; 182-9; 186-12; 187-33.
Fteley, Alphonse. 297-15.
Fuertes, James H. 9-89; 22-82; 23-98; 24-17, 18; 38-89; 50-39; 61-5; 62-6; 63-27, 29; 82-54; 92-39; 93-52; 112-73; 149-55; 150-64, 77; 156-20; 157-18; 204-53; 211-37; 234-10; 236-50; 252-58; 254-9; 280-3; 306-35; 308-75, 87; 310-39; 312-93.
Fuller, George W. 147-4; 297-16; 303-52, 78; 304-91; 307-46, 55.
Fuller, Henry B. 50-35.
Funck-Brentano, H. 208-58.
Fyfe, Peter. 101-10, 11; 92-36, 40; 240-60; 282-52.

G

Gache, Samuel. 34-78.
Gadsby, C. H. 268-4; 287-65.
Gage, Lyman J. 46-60.
Gager, Edwin B. 167-65.
Gaillard, D. D. 302-47.
Gale, James M. 93-52.
Gale, Peter. 281-21.
Gallarate, L. 110-16.
Gallatin, James. 187-40.
Galton, Douglas. 141-88.
Gamborg, J. 229-13.
Gannon, Mary Nevan. 106-52.
Garcke, Emile. 287-62.
Gardener, Cornelius. 297-11.
Gardiner, Florence Mary. 101-2, 3; 103-81; 106-51.
Gardner, E. C. 11-29; 12-38, 40; 243-34; 244-72.

Gardner, Edmund G. 76-7.
Gardner, Harry N. 24-19.
Gardner, Helen H. 178-20.
Gardner, Henry B. 70-73.
Gardner, Rathbone. 7-36.
Garfield, Harry A. 164-79.
Garfield, James R. 98-49.
Garfield, Joseph. 249-93.
Garibotti, Giuseppe. 162-45.
Garland, Caroline H. 205-72.
Garlier, G. 298-44.
Garnier, Léon. 80-7.
Garrelts, Fr. 16-55; 23-6; 237-77.
Garrett, Henry A. 262-67.
Garrett, J. H. 250-13.
Garrett, Philip C. 217-80.
Garrett, R. P. 33-59; 76-4.
Garrison, W. P. 3-30.
Gartner, J. 104-83.
Garton, W. R. 264-11.
Garvin, L. C. F. 7-32.
Gaupp, L. 86-18.
Gavett, A. J. 226-22.
Gavey, John. 261-41.
Gavin, Hector. 140-61.
Gavit, John P. 48-17; 51-70; 247-39, 42, 51.
Gay, Eben H. 71-94.
Gay, Ernest. 79-69.
Gay, Richard L. 151-81.
Gaye, A. 228-69.
Geïser, A. 312-82.
Gemünder, M. A. 70-72; 161-16; 162-36; 306-23.
Genis, M. Louis. 150-75.
Gennings, John. 137-96.
George, Henry. 187-21; 272-88.
George, John E. 48-3.
Georgievsky, H. 236-66.
Gerard, James W. 184-54, 185-82.
Gerhard, William Paul. 17-69; 43-92; 121-80; 122-3; 241-70, 81; 242-97; 243-33; 246-19; 249-85.
Germain, Eugene. 23-5.
Germain, Felix. 79-68.
Germinet, G. 122-99.
Geron, H. 287-57.
Geron, M. H. 269-15.
Gerry, M. H. 49-27; 264-11.
Gerstel, Gustav. 300-86.
Gerstfeldt, ——. 88-58.
Gevaert, Fierens. 209-69.
Ghent, W. J. 204-63; 261-50.
Gibbings, Alfred H. 166-32.
Gibbons, P. H. 121-83.
Gibbs, Phillip. 137-98.
Gibbs, William E. 118-74.
Gibson, F. M. 193-72.
Gifford, George. 259-13.
Gifford, O. P. 46-63.
Gigot, A. 132-62; 206-2.
Gilbert, William. 128-61.
Gilder, Joseph B. 185-74; 193-64.
Gilder, Richard Watson. 106-54; 187-26.
Giles, H. H. 44-32.
Giles, William A. 7-24; 64-54; 221-11; 245-39; 304-82.
Gill, Henry. 23-1.
Gill, J. P. 121-85.
Gill, Wilson L. 289-9.
Gillham, R. 293-28.

BIBLIOGRAPHY.

Gilman, Elizabeth. 86-27.
Gilman, Mrs. M. R. F. 248-67.
Gilman, Stephen W. 311-50.
Gilroy, Thomas F. 199-78.
Girdner, John H. 203-43, 44; 294-44.
Girling, G. E. 104-2.
Gladden, Washington. 3-30; 6-16; 7-21; 66-9; 162-39; 217-86; 272-95.
Glaister, John. 242-8.
Glasgow, A., G. 124-60.
Glazier, William. 107-75.
Glen, A. 285-23.
Glen, R. C. 132-47.
Glen, W. C. 132-47; 285-23.
Goadby, E. 126-5.
Godkin, E. L. 3-30, 51; 4-72; 7-28; 26-75; 57-45, 52; 66-1, 88; 152-20; 175-56; 176-59; 177-98; 190-99; 194-85; 198-42; 222-39; 233-96; 272-94; 278-52; 290-34.
Goes, Edmund. 154-73.
Goetz, Henry A. 35-14.
Goff, John W. 65-75.
Gollan, ——. 140-58.
Golde, (Mlle.), ——. 37-66.
Goldie, John. 43-3.
Goldsmith, N. O. 297-17.
Gomme, G. L. 4-53; 129-79; 130-95; 131-41; 133-5; 135-38; 137-5; 144-37; 274-57; 276-2, 95; 277-24.
Gondon, H. J. 60-80; 83-63a; 160-96; 238-95.
Gonzales de Junquitu, L. 255-12.
Goodale, Francis A. 43-1; 107-65; 248-66.
Goodale, W. H. 64-46.
Goodchild, F. M. 225-99.
Goodell, J. M. 249-89; 257-53.
Goodell, John. 308-83.
Goodhue, W. F. 68-38.
Goodnough, X. H. 303-51.
Goodnow, Frank J. 2-15; 6-5; 57-49; 86-10; 98-34, 37, 42; 158-45; 217-100, 1; 275-67, 73; 289-30; 290-36; 293-19; 294-36.
Goodnow, John. 253-90.
Goodrich, W. Francis. 83-65.
Goodwin, Maud Wilder. 184-61.
Goodwin, William W. 118-77; 292-100; 293-7.
Goppelsroeder, Friedrich. 37-69.
Gordon, Clarence. 51-70; 247-41.
Gordon, Geo. Brydon. 99-47.
Gordon, J. 243-29.
Gordon, J. E. H. 120-50.
Gordon, W. J. 91-17; 142-99.
Gordon-Cumming, C. F. 37-55.
Gordes, H. 268-90.
Gore, J. H. 98-28.
Gorst, John E. 273-26.
Gory, A. 78-59.
Goschen, G. J. 280-100.
Gossett, A. 104-7.
Gottgetreu, R. 157-19.
Gottwald, J. 56-38.
Goudy, H. 276-12.
Gould, E. R. L. 16-44; 35-4; 69-53; 100-65; 101-12, 23; 104-84; 105-18; 186-7; 222-23; 241-77, 94.
Gould, E. Sherman. 96-3; 199-66; 304-72.
Gould, S. B. 37-55.
Goument, Charles E. V. 11-14; 254-95.
Gowdy, John K. 210-10, 98.
Gowen, Charles S. 199-68.
Gower, F. Leveson. 228-73.

Grace, S. P. 60-81.
Grady, John. 28-20.
Graetz, L. 118-87.
Graham, A. H. 276-7.
Graham, H. G. 63-22; 91-28.
Graham, J. C. 280-1.
Graham, P. Anderson. 228-75.
Graham, Robert. 189-64.
Grahn, E. 90-12.
Grant, James. 63-21.
Grant, John H. 98-44.
Grant, Joseph D. 258-99.
Granville, Austyn. 48-99.
Graves, E. O. 246-33.
Gray, George G. 96-2.
Gray, John Henry. 28-42; 50-32; 151-91, 92; 162-49; 164-91; 167-53; 210-97; 299-60.
Gray, Samuel M. 225-4; 302-33.
Gray, W. N. 95-90.
Greathead, J. H. 145-50.
Green, ——. 161-18.
Green, Andrew H. 175-45; 180-48; 198-49.
Green, G. W. 64-37; 66-91; 71-93.
Green, John Richard. 247-44.
Green, (Mrs.) J. R. 281-26.
Greene, Francis V. 175-43; 218-18.
Greene, Thomas L. 291-67.
Greenlaw, Edwin A. 152-21.
Greenough, M. S. 122-90.
Greenwood, F. 44-33.
Greenwood, T. 116-44.
Greg, P. 135-42.
Gregorovius, Ferdinand. 235-43.
Gregory, C. Noble. 64-59.
Gregory, R. A. 139-43.
Gregory, W. D. 261-57.
Grelot, Felix. 77-28.
Greville, Lady V. 133-81.
Gribayédoff, V. 188-62; 191-24.
Gribble, T. Graham. 196-11; 269-6.
Grierson, Frank W. 145-65.
Griffin, Percy. 106-52.
Griffith, Percy. 283-75; 288-87; 308-80.
Griffiths, Arthur. 210-17; 227-35.
Griffiths, William Russell. 132-51.
Griggs, Julian. 55-24; 250-50.
Grimaldi, G. 109-99.
Grimes, George R. 219-61.
Grimm, Karl. 244-68.
Grimshaw, Robert. 22-87; 32-46; 211-42; 220-72, 78, 90; 221-100; 258-72; 303-61.
Grindling, C. H. 144-44.
Grinnell, Wm. F. 149-53.
Griscom, John H. 186-17.
Gross, Charles. 280-5, 18; 281-22, 23, 28.
Grosse, Karl. 115-28.
Grosseteste-Thierry, ——. 78-57.
Grosvenor, Edwin A. 56-34.
Grout, Edward M. 162-29; 189-74.
Grubb, E. B. 65-68a.
Grunsky, C. E. 98-32; 252-58.
Guastalla, Mich. 235-38, 39.
Gudger, ——. 206-97.
Guggenheimer, Randolph. 189-83.
Guichard, Charles. 94-66.
Guignard, A. 80-14.
Guillaume, Eugène. 82-48.
Gulick, Sydney L. 248-72.
Gulland, John W. 63-20.
Gumbleton, H. A. 181-80.

Gunkle, L. B. 204-60.
Gunn, O. B. 220-84.
Gunton, Herbert C. 25-56; 138-10.
Gurteen, S. Humphreys. 44-16.
Guthrie, E. B. 34-81, 94, 96; 68-36; 219-50; 269-26.
Guthrie, Geo. W. 226-10.
Guthrie, Ossian. 49-22.
Guyer, I. D. 47-90.
Guyot, Yoes. 130-5; 206-2, 7; 208-56; 227-33; 232-64.
Guzzi, Guis. 110-27.
Gwinn, Dow R. 233-95; 305-97; 307-61.

H

Haag, M. 212-52.
Hadden, —. 275-70.
Hadden, R. H. 132-73.
Haffen, Louis F. 177-96.
Hagen, E. 118-88.
Haight, A. S. 217-84.
Haines, R. 225-3.
Hake, A. E. 132-66.
Hale, C. 71-2.
Hale, Edward Everett. 3-30; 27-92; 28-23, 24, 37; 98-34; 176-64; 227-57; 290-45.
Hale, George W. 227-42.
Hale, R. S. 120-36.
Hall, Bolton. 105-29; 126-19.
Hall, C. C. 70-71.
Hall, Charlott C. 182-15.
Hall, Edwin T. 243-47.
Hall, Hans. 271-70.
Hall, Henry W. 144-44.
Hall, L. M. 107-64.
Hall, W. H. 214-9.
Halstead, Carolyn. 193-58.
Halstead, Leonora B. 2-16.
Halstead, Marshal. 25-44; 144-38, 42.
Halstead, Murat. 94-75; 177-98.
Hamilton, Annie. 235-43.
Hamilton, James H. 89-98; 229-90; 229-5; 260-29; 261-44.
Hamilton, Peter J. 155-98.
Hamilton, William Gaston. 18-83; 177-83.
Hamlin, A. D. F. 11-28; 36-35.
Hamlin, Leonora. 42-78.
Hamlin, Tennis S. 51-60.
Hammer, William J. 270-34.
Hammerton, J. A. 91-19.
Hammond, Jabez D. 201-17.
Hammond, M. B. 228-78.
Hammond, Robert. 282-59; 284-94.
Hampden, Guy. 167-64; 266-52.
Hampel, W. 214-16.
Hancock, W. Neilson. 274-52.
Hancock, C. 154-69; 156-11.
Hand, J. E. 7-22; 100-70; 141-74; 276-2; 278-40; 288-94.
Handcock, H. W. 125-95.
Hands, Alice J. 106-52.
Handy, William Matthews. 47-75.
Haney, James P. 244-74.
Hansen, Georg. 229-11.
Hansom, J. M. 248-64.
Häntzschel, W. 21-51; 22-84.
Harder, Julius F. 13-73; 258-81.
Hardesty, W. P. 59-71.
Harding, Burcham. 261-53.

Hardy, C. 103-68.
Hare, H. T. 157-21.
Hare, J. 130-98.
Hare, Thomas. 230-33, 35.
Harlow, James H. 10-9; 226-19.
Harmon, Jacob A. 308-88.
Harper, J. M. (W?). 52-81, 83.
Harrington, John W. 190-11.
Harris, D. L. 70-65.
Harris, Elisha. 242-20.
Harris, G. M. 120-47; 123-43.
Harris, H. Percy. 135-42.
Harris, J. A. 26-71.
Harris, Mary Dormer. 57-59.
Harris, Norfleet. 115-17.
Harris, T. William. 264-6.
Harris, Wm. T. 244-81.
Harrison, (Mrs.) Burton. 185-69.
Harrison, C. 128-50; 129-77.
Harrison, Carter H. 4-62; 6-11.
Harrison, F. 128-49; 129-84, 86.
Harrison, Frederic. 56-36; 64-51; 97-20; 131-25; 137-95; 208-64; 283-80.
Harrison, George A. 108-88.
Harrison, John. 164-80.
Harrison, L. 55-32.
Harkness, M. E. 131-20.
Harper, George H. 122-94.
Harrod, B. M. 173-4.
Harrod, M. D. 135-42.
Harston, Frederick. 41-61.
Hart, A. B. 39-5; 245-89; 291-82.
Hart, E. 132-63.
Hart, Edward James. 93-60.
Hart, T. N. 7-32.
Hartmann, von K. 117-65.
Hartwell, Alfred M. 17-76.
Hartwell, Edward M. 71-85; 256-35.
Hartwell, Frank N. 147-1.
Harwood, W. S. 155-90.
Haskell, John C. 152-15.
Haskins, Caryl D. 120-35.
Hassard, J. R. G. 178-21.
Hasse, Ernst. 115-29.
Hasson, W. F. C. 240-43.
Hastings, Charles W. 283-66.
Hastings, Elizabeth. 247-46.
Hastings, F. 136-79.
Hastings, L. M. 38-95; 68-43; 219-60; 249-98.
Haswell, C. H. 185-90.
Hatcher, E. N. 220-70.
Hathaway, S. J. 219-60.
Hatschek, Julius. 9-68.
Hatton, Joseph. 7-32.
Hatton, T. Chalkley. 310-35.
Haupt, Hermann. 264-99, 100.
Haupt, Lewis M. 68-40; 225-1; 223-86; 269-6; 293-28.
Hauriot, ——. 304-86.
Hauriou, Maurice. 78-39.
Hausen, P. Ch. 102-42.
Haussman, Georges Eugène. 208-62.
Haussmann, ——. 299-63.
Haussmann, Carl A. 81-19.
Haven, C. C. 270-38.
Haw, George. 136-68.
Hawley, Walter L. 182-100.
Hayes, George W. 220-77.
Haycraft, Thomas Wagstaff. 284-11.
Hayes, H. H. 12-37.

BIBLIOGRAPHY.

Hayter, Richard. 101-16.
Hazen, Allen. 10-2; 22-82, 83; 212-63; 225-3; 250-8; 297-19; 303-78; 304-75, 84; 307-43, 48.
Hazlewood, Arthur. 154-58.
Hazlitt, W. Carew. 128-66; 298-40a.
Headlam, Cecil. 204-55.
Headlam, Stewart D. 140-68.
Heath, F. G. 216-70.
Heather-Bigg, A. 114-2.
Hecht, E. 258-89.
Hecke, Wilhelm. 299-71.
Hedenberg, W. L. 250-19; 252-71; 308-81.
Hedges, Killingworth. 119-21; 120-52; 296-84.
Hegel, Karl. 88-65, 75, 76.
Hegner, Herman F. 248-76.
Heiden, E. 252-60; 253-87.
Heilprin, Louis. 196-11, 16.
Heim, Albert. 312-82.
Heim, John B. 148-17, 18; 169-3, 10; 303-69; 305-12; 306-21.
Heins, Maurice. 19-10, 11, 13; 133-1; 272-82.
Held, Otto. 89-96.
Heldt, P. M. 48-2; 215-26.
Hemming, A. 259-8.
Hemstreet, Charles. 185-84.
Henderson, Charles R. 44-10, 31; 50-42; 248-64.
Henderson, Harry B. 71-82.
Hendricks, Geo. B. 163-63.
Henman, William. 42-86.
Hennessy, Charles O'Connor. 197-37.
Hennicke, Jul. 150-74.
Henning, B. S. 267-80.
Henri, Albert. 19-4.
Henry, Frank R. 263-79.
Henry, John C. 265-21.
Henry, William Wirt. 234-14.
Henschel, Albert E. 175-47.
Hepworth, T. C. 119-25.
Herbert, William. 135-33.
Hereward, L. A. 180-47.
Hergner, Herman F. 48-17.
Hering, Carl. 266-39.
Hering, Rudolph. 13-86; 21-50; 68-37; 83-63a; 95-78; 225-94, 4; 249-84; 250-3; 252-58; 302-33; 304-78; 309-15.
Herkner, H. 271-68.
Herman, E. A. 251-32.
Hermann, August. 52-78; 291-69; 297-21.
Hermann, Ernest F. 299-81.
Herrfurth, L. 88-61.
Herrick, Albert B. 67-17, 22; 265-30, 31.
Herring, W. R. 122-92, 95.
Herschel, Clemens. 171-42; 218-31; 236-49.
Herschell, Lady. 207-27.
Hersh, Grier. 162-47.
Herzberg, E. 233-90.
Herzfeld, A. G. 125-2.
Herzfeld, Gustav. 175-46.
Herzog, Josey. 270-40.
Hesketh, Thomas. 125-80.
Hesse, A. 80-92.
Hetherington, F. A. 221-98.
Heulings, W. H., Jr. 263-91.
Heusler, Andr. 88-77.
Hewart, Beatrice. 131-31.
Hewes, L. F. W. 193-72; 294-55.
Hewett, Charles. 266-45.
Hewington, Frank A. 63-26.
Hewitt, Edward Ringwood. 184-40.

Hewitt, Mary Ashley. 184-40.
Hewson, Thos. 115-23.
Heyden, ——. 90-3.
Heyer, Edith. 48-18.
Heysinger, ——. 307-45.
Hibbard, George S. 228-85.
Hibbs, E. D. 269-16.
Hickenlooper, Andrew. 125-98; 166-49.
Hicks, W. L. 30-94.
Hickson, W. E. 128-63; 130-96; 276-96.
Hield, Willard J. 262-73.
Hiersemann, K. W. 214-3.
Higby, Clinton D. 289-14.
Higgins, Edward E. 168-75; 189-77; 264-10; 267-69, 71, 83; 270-35; 296-89, 94.
Higginson, Thomas Wentworth. 28-24; 138-21; 245-89.
Higgs, P. 118-3.
Hildreth, Arthur. 166-45.
Hill, A. Bostwick. 249-93; 250-22.
Hill, Alfred. 43-91.
Hill, C. T. 199-79.
Hill, Charles Shattuck. 49-23.
Hill, Florence D. 41-47.
Hill, George Everett. 35-3, 20; 83-63a; 96-4; 186-2; 252-58.
Hill, Hawthorne. 285-49.
Hill, John C. 310-19.
Hill, John W. 23-99; 95-88; 158-55; 159-74; 307-53; 308-70; 309-94, 95, 96.
Hill, Octavia. 100-78, 82; 104-92; 106-49; 135-42, 46, 51; 137-87; 214-97; 248-69.
Hill, William R. 169-9; 260-29; 303-54.
Hillyer, George. 13-89; 309-15.
Himmelwright, A. L. A. 35-8; 75-93.
Hinsdale, B. A. 244-81; 294-54.
Hinton, R. J. 179-38.
Hirsch, Adolph. 59-73.
Hirschberg, Ernst. 21-57; 273-30.
Hirschwald, A. 258-76.
Hirst, F. W. 70-71.
Hitching, Brooke. 138-18.
Hitz, J. 301-24.
Hoadley, G. 65-68a.
Hoare, Alfred. 134-14.
Hobhouse, Arthur. 74-63; 129-88; 130-96; 133-6; 136-57.
Hobhouse, Henry. 130-99; 275-80.
Hobhouse, Lord. 129-78.
Hobrecht, ——. 148-35.
Hobrecht, James. 22-81.
Hobson, J. A. 43-97; 44-22; 45-36; 223-2; 271-48; 272-81, 85.
Hodder, Frank H. 2-18, 19; 24-11, 11a; 46-71; 47-92.
Hodge, J. Aspinwall, Jr. 168-86; 201-3; 267-74.
Hofer, Thomas. 212-65.
Hoffman, E. F. 66-95.
Hoffman, Frank S. 85-1; 3-45.
Hoffman, Frederick L. 242-100.
Hoffman, Murray. 181-89.
Hofmann, E. 23-6a; 237-77; 259-9; 260-20.
Holbach, F. 12-55.
Holcomb, William P. 221-18.
Holden, Edward S. 116-40.
Holden, L. E. 214-12.
Holder, W. 281-40.
Holdsworth, W. A. 276-4.
Hole, James. 99-50.

MUNICIPAL AFFAIRS.

Holland, B. 139-38.
Hollander, J. H. 15-10, 21, 26; 52-77a; 293-15.
Hollingshead, J. 136-61.
Hollond, E. W. 132-76.
Holls, Fredcrick William. 64-52; 98-43.
Holman, H. 285-31.
Holman, M. L. 90-13; 237-93.
Holmes, A. B. 118-2.
Holmes, (Mrs.) Basil. 132-53.
Holmes, Daniel B. 264-3.
Holmes, F. M. 130-11; 132-61.
Holmes, G. J. 144-45.
Holmes, H. C. 297-12.
Holmes, Howard M. 37-61.
Holt, Byron W. 73-50.
Holthof, F. 118-85.
Holvoet, ——. 19-2.
Holyoake, M. O. 137-88.
Homan, George. 237-89.
Homes, Walton H. 263-84.
Homo, H. 45-54.
Honeyman, John. 100-74, 75; 281-31.
Honoré, F. 212-59.
Hooker, George E. 29-50; 49-24; 268-5.
Hooker, Samuel C. 225-3; 304-78.
Hoole, E. 100-79; 135-42.
Hooper, L. H. 208-38; 211-37; 221-7.
Hoopes, Maurice. 268-2.
Hope, Wm. 309-8.
Hopewell, Charles F. 120-53.
Hopkins, Albert Bassett. 128-53; 143-28.
Hopkins, Henry. 100-93; 112-67; 125-94.
Hopkins, John S. 65-85.
Hopkins, Nevil Monroe. 301-27.
Hopkins, William Rowland. 54-12.
Hoppes, John J. 306-41.
Horden, F. S. 37-58.
Horetzky, C. 252-58; 253-81; 262-64.
Hornaday, W. D. 14-91.
Hornaday, William T. 190-97.
Hornbrook, R. S. 69-48.
Hornby, John. 124-54.
Horr, Nelson T. 227-38.
Horsfall, T. C. 102-25.
Horstmann, L. 16-55; 23-6.
Horsley, J. W. 100-89; 102-32.
Horton, S. D. 231-43.
Hoskin, A. A. 289-11.
Hosmer, ——. 75-87.
Hosmer, G. W. 83-63a; 252-58.
Hosmer, James Kendall. 3-46.
Hosmer, Katharine. 302-48.
Hospitalier, E. 118-99.
Hoster, Wm. Johnson. 223-66.
Hotchkiss, Wm. Horace. 3-47; 98-34.
Hough, D. L. 227-52.
Hough, J. S. 225-97.
Houston, Edwin J. 266-37.
Howard, Charles Morris. 15-30.
Howard, Ebeneezer. 228-61.
Howard, George Elliot. 292-86.
Howard, George W. 15-23.
Howard, J. W. 218-27; 219-36, 37, 39; 221-92; 257-49, 50, 51.
Howard, William Willard. 93-57; 154-71; 155-87; 238-97; 246-34; 260-31; 261-49.
Howe, Frederic C. 291-74.
Howe, Irving E. 219-60.
Howe, Rufus. 194-85.
Howe, W. W. 173-97.

Howell, George. 100-77.
Howell, W. G. 266-49.
Howells, Anthony. 39-9.
Howes, Osborn. 165-99; 266-60.
Hoy, William Alexander. 186-96.
Hubert, P. C. 203-42.
Hubon, E. 117-71.
Hudetz, Jos. 299-78.
Hudson, Richard. 3-38.
Hügel, ——. 231-49.
Hughes, A. J. 108-87.
Hughes, B. 122-93.
Hughes, J. L. 261-59.
Hugo, C. 103-70, 74; 284-93.
Hulbert, Archer Buller. 218-21.
Hull, Charles H. 62-12; 135-30.
Hull, W. I. 41-44, 55.
Humphrey, Richard L. 224-75.
Humphreys, A. C. 123-24.
Humphreys, C. J. R. 117-55.
Humphreys, Mary G. 41-55.
Humphries, N. A. 285-14.
Humphrys, Norton H. 84-85; 120-55; 121-76; 122-11; 283-65.
Hungerford, Churchill. 58-64; 304-78.
Hunt, Fred W. 60-85, 85a.
Hunt, H. H. 265-34.
Hunt, John. 128-56. ·
Hunt, William. 33-55.
Hunter, D. 293-9.
Hunter, Dunlany. 261-47.
Hunter, John. 303-59.
Hunter, R. 42-79; 139-39; 214-98.
Hunter, Thomas. 284-99.
Hunter, Walter. 146-69.
Huntington, J. O. S. 104-93.
Hurd, Henry M. 43-89, 90.
Hurd, W. T. 164-94; 165-8.
Hurlbuts, H. H. 47-84.
Huss, George Martin. 35-9; 106-52.
Huston, C. D. 306-39.
Hutchinson, Joseph. 278-55.
Hutton, Lawrence. 188-54.
Hutton, William Holden. 56-35, 37.
Hutton, Wm. R. 177-95.
Huyette, W. S. 305-3.
Hyams, Walter. 311-42.
Hyatt, A. 215-34.
Hyde, Frank E. 147-11a
Hyslop, James H. 5-81; 44-17.

I

Iglehardt, F. C. 189-67.
Ilbert, Lettice. 101-13; 127-32.
Iles, George. 24-15; 195-96.
Ilgen, F. H. W. 120-57.
Imbart de la Tour, Jean. 78-65.
Ingals, E. F. 48-13.
Ingersoll, Ernest. 180-66; 190-8; 194-95; 196-26.
Ingham, J. A. 136-80; 229-98.
Ingham, W. 262-68.
Inglehart, Ferdinand C. 126-23.
Ingram, Arthur F. Winnington. 51-74.
Insley, Edward. 65-86.
Insull, Samuel. 60-82.
Irving, D. 67-11, 23.
Irving, Washington. 185-73.
Ivins, Wm. M. 3-30; 64-58; 65-81; 70-71; 217-94.

BIBLIOGRAPHY.

J

Jackson, J. 83-63a; 257-65.
Jackson, William. 29-69; 68-36.
Jacobus, D. S. 117-53.
Jager, H. 214-8.
James, C. C. 205-84; 256-36, 40.
James, Edmund J. 7-29b; 20-40, 43; 22-95; 46-69, 70; 87-43; 94-73, 74; 166-43; 212-52, 55; 228-86.
James, H. 278-56.
James, H., Jr. 209-86.
James, W. H. 132-73.
Jameson, J. F. 174-21; 185-81.
Janes, L. G. 4-73; 9-71; 171-56; 290-32.
Janin, George. 250-13; 251-32.
Janvier, Charles. 172-86.
Janvier, Thos. A. 184-59.
Jarvis, W. 154-68.
Jasper, William H. 182-96.
Jastrow, Ignaz. 87-34; 88-71.
Jay, A. O. 130-10; 133-91.
Jay, Raoul. 16-54; 237-77; 272-83.
Jean, Charles. 82-45; 212-56.
Jeannel, ——. 216-66.
Jebens, A. W. 86-6.
Jemot, ——. 69-45.
Jenkins, A. J. 309-10.
Jenkins, E. H. 67-14; 121-84.
Jenkins, H. M. 3-52.
Jenks, Edward. 203-37; 275-77.
Jenks, Jeremiah W. 64-61; 98-41; 231-40; 278-62.
Jenness, C. K. 239-24.
Jensen, Gerard J. E. 241-82.
Jernegan, Marcus W. 234-5.
Jevons, W. Stanley. 11-22; 116-38.
Jewett, F. G. 181-72.
John, J. B. 68-30.
Johnson, Alexander. 43-96; 45-38; 207-27.
Johnson, Edward H. 266-47.
Johnson, G. H. 269-6.
Johnson, Henry V. 160-93; 161-16.
Johnson, J. A. 74-73; 98-45.
Johnson, John Butler. 251-40.
Johnson, Lewis. 173-99.
Johnson, Thomas L. 204-67.
Johnson, Tom L. 301-14.
Johnson, W. P. 186-13.
Johnson, Woolsey McA. 96-97.
Johnston, Albert. 53-94.
Johnstone, Ralph W. 134-20.
Jolliffe, J. T. 125-97.
Jolly, L. 89-100; 245-92.
Joltrain, A. 211-31.
Jonary, Leon. 242-12.
Jonas, Charles. 238-5.
Jones, ——. 161-18.
Jones, Augustine. 214-93.
Jones, Beatrix. 213-67.
Jones, C. E. 169-12.
Jones, Charles S. 135-47.
Jones, Dwight A. 168-89.
Jones, Edward D. 45-49.
Jones, Ed. H. 95-89.
Jones, Harry W. 213-87.
Jones, Hugh R. 105-35.
Jones, L. H. 246-15.
Jones, John. 262-62.
Jones, M. Katharine. 24-16; 247-38.
Jones, Samuel M. 7-37; 159-64; 160-93; 261-51.
Jones, Wallace S. 235-48.
Jordan, David Starr. 3-30; 5-96; 105-98; 288-96.
Jordan, Edwin O. 49-22.
Jouanne, G. 118-76.
Jourdan, Gustave. 80-3, 5, 98; 81-35; 103-64; 105-24; 211-27; 242-96, 14.
Judd, Max. 299-66, 72.
Judge, Mark H. 126-22.
Judson, Frederick N. 155-97.
Judson, H. P. 5-80.
Judson, Wm. Pierson. 218-15.
Juillet, Saint Laeger. 79-70, 77.
Junger, O. 257-67.
Jürgens, R. 213-76.
Justo y Villanueva, L. 148-25.
Jutzi, W. 273-21.

K

Kähler, W. 88-57.
Kalle, ——. 35-99.
Kasson, John A. 7-32; 299-54.
Keasby, Edward Quinton. 120-54; 292-4.
Kedzie, Robert C. 154-60.
Keeler, Bronson C. 166-41.
Keeler, H. E. 159-66.
Keenan, George. 32-39.
Keene, W. F. 40-30.
Keller, John W. 179-38; 217-5.
Kelly, Daniel V. 239-25.
Kelley, Florence. 41-40, 58; 47-79; 48-18; 49-26; 179-26.
Kelley, Frank Bergen. 184-49; 185-67.
Kellogg, Charles D. 290-55.
Kelly, Edmond. 174-21, 23, 26; 176-64.
Kelsey, Albert. 11-27.
Kelso, W. W. 84-74, 76.
Keltie, J. Scott. 1-7a.
Kemmler, E. A. 219-60, 62.
Kemp, J. 95-93.
Kempner, Otto. 7-31.
Kempster, Walter. 59-78.
Kendall, Edward H. 192-35.
Kennan, George. 243-55, 56.
Kennedy, Alexander B. W. 143-22.
Kennedy, John L. 170-33.
Kennedy, H. Milton. 195-100.
Kennedy, Wm. M. 10-8.
Kent, Chancellor. 174-16.
Kent, Charles A. 59-75.
Kenyon, Clarence A. 221-98.
Kerr, Charles H. 81-41.
Kerr, James W. 239-17.
Kettell, T. P. 180-52.
Key, A. Cooper. 111-62.
Kibler, Edward. 204-64, 66.
Kickbusch, F. W. 256-41.
Kiersted, Wynkoop. 252-63; 307-57; 308-78; 309-98.
Kies, W. S. 66-94; 168-77.
Kilvington, Samuel S. 83-71.
Kimball, Geo. A. 68-35.
Kimball, W. M. 235-33.
King, A. B. 194-90.
King, Charles. 199-67.
King, F. W. N. 153-34.
King, George R. 215-22.
King, Grace. 173-94, 95.

King, Hamilton. 254-94.
King, Joseph. 141-76; 285-37.
King, L. M. 240-53.
King, Moses. 175-53.
King, William F. 199-69, 74.
Kingsbury, F. J. 229-93.
Kingsbury, Mary M. 193-65.
Kingsmill, Esther T. 41-48.
Kinkead, T. L. 179-38.
Kinnicutt, Leonard P. 249-86, 87; 285-38.
Kirchner, Otto. 153-53.
Kirk, Robert J. 56-42.
Kirkbride, C. N. 292-96.
Kirkbride, Franklin B. 17-72; 223-56; 298-39.
Kirkland, Joseph. 46-68; 47-95.
Kirkpatrick, E. A. 245-86.
Kirkpatrick, Samuel R. 223-61.
Kirtland, Edwin L. 98-33.
Kissam, George. 263-82.
Kitchin, G. W. 310-41.
Kitson, Arthur. 122-97.
Kittilsen, Edward. 84-76; 155-99.
Kittredge, A. O. 263-75, 78, 80.
Klapp, Eugene. 266-54.
Klasen, L. 102-38.
Kleinschmidt, F. 31-7.
Klickman, Wilfred. 144-42.
Knapp, A. 239-17.
Knapp, J. M. 248-71.
Knapp, Louis H. 34-96.
Knight, Charles W. 11-13.
Knight, Frank E. 265-32.
Knight, George W. 158-45.
Knight, Herbert. 274-45.
Knight, Maria. 239-40.
Knopf, S. A. 107-71.
Knott, G. H. 128-50.
Knott, W. W. 48-99.
Knowles, A. J. 144-44.
Knowles, C. M. 136-53.
Knowles, Morris. 226-21; 304-78.
Knox, E. F. Vesey. 287-54.
Knox, George W. 265-19.
Knudson, A. A. 67-13, 14; 111-58; 188-57; 233-100; 312-75.
Kobatsch, Rudolph. 299-53.
Koch, A. 106-37.
Koch, G. 95-80.
Koestler, Hugo. 300-87.
Kohl, J. C. 229-100.
Kohnke, Quitman. 83-63a.
Koller, Theodor. 84-84.
Kollman, J. 34-74.
Kollock, Henry. 200-88.
Koppe, ——. 86-29.
Koren, John. 125-3; 126-13, 20; 189-65; 202-22.
Körösi, Jos. 71-96.
Kotze, Otto. 85-5.
Kotzmann, A. 273-23.
Kramer, ——. 121-68.
Krannbals, Erich. 156-5.
Krieger, H. 22-91.
Kriehn, George. 12-53.
Kromayer, Ernst. 232-66.
Kropotkin, P. 42-81.
Krout, Mary H. 203-36.
Kruse, W. 228-82.
Kruseman, H. 103-73.
Kübler, William. 270-36.

Kuczynski, R. 229-96.
Kudlich, Herman C. 226-27.
Kuhn, Emil. 97-17.
Kühn, Jos. 112-75; 298-52.
Kühn, Julius. 231-52.
Kuichling, E. 169-5; 235-31; 305-95; 310-21.
Kummel, W. 307-43.
Kuntze, Osc. 244-61.

L

Labriola, Arturo. 163-57, 61, 71.
Lacava, P. 110-33.
Lackie, W. W. 119-17.
Laffitte, J. P. 230-36.
Laidlaw, Walter. 179-40.
Laing, J. B. 71-80.
Laird, John A. 237-93.
Lake, Edward N. 161-24.
Lakes, Arthur. 54-20.
Lalor, John J. 1-1; 65-84; 71-93; 97-15.
Lamb, Chas. R. 12-32.
Lamb, Frederick S. 12-54; 13-64.
Lamb, Martha J. 184-51; 185-69.
Lamb, W. H. 243-54.
Lambelin, Roger. 129-90; 289-28.
Lambert, Brooke. 132-72, 74.
Lambert, Carlton. 117-52.
Lammers, ——. 88-56a.
Lamson, D. F. 150-65.
Lanck, L. 242-16.
Lanciani, Rodolfo. 235-44.
Lander, H. C. 281-30.
Landis, Henry K. 122-91; 199-65.
Landon, Judson S. 244-70.
Lane, M. A. 47-80; 50-34.
Lang, A. E. 165-18; 168-84.
Lang, Evelyn M. 111-47.
Lang, Otto. 312-90.
Langbein, G. F. 180-54.
Lange, E. 260-20.
Lapworth, Herbert. 25-51.
Larcier, Ferd. 18-98.
Lardner, James F. 168-88.
Larocque, Jos. 4-78.
La Ruse, Benj. F. 252-58.
Laspeyres, E. 104-95.
Lass, Alfred. 145-60.
Lassar, O. 17-63.
Latham, Baldwin. 241-71.
Latham, Frank. 250-20.
Lathe, Agnes M. 15-27; 150-73.
Latimer, George D. 238-6.
Latrobe, C. H. 295-62.
Latrobe, F. C. 15-9.
Latta, James W. 165-99.
Laugel, A. 206-2; 208-47.
Laughlin, J. Lawrence. 160-1; 162-38.
Launay, ——. 211-39.
Laurent, Emile. 80-4; 105-25.
Laurent, H. 244-66.
Laurent, M. A. 210-11.
Laurent, M. H. 211-35.
Lauterbach, Edward. 201-99.
Lauth, Charles. 211-36.
Lavallée, Albert. 206-2.
Lavergne, F. 81-37a.
Lavergne, P. 78-61.
Lavery, James A. 113-90.
Laves, Kurt. 48-18.

BIBLIOGRAPHY. 331

Lavezzari, A. 267-77.
Lavollée, Rène. 102-46.
Law, Alice. 281-27.
Law, Henry. 250-16.
Law, Herbert E. 239-17.
Law, Herbert Henry. 249-88.
Lawrence, A. R. 182-99.
Laws, W. George. 171-54.
Lawson, Albert G. 50-47.
Lawson, H. L. W. 129-75.
Lawson, W. R. 265-28.
Lawton, Charles E. 176-63.
Lawton, G. W. 63-32.
Lay, Julius G. 255-17.
Lazare, Louis. 209-68.
Lea, Henry C. 4-63; 7-23; 223-44.
Lea, R. S. 304-90.
Leach, Orlando. 200-89.
Leake, Mrs. Percy. 107-77.
Learned, Henry B. 48-18.
Leas, C. A. 243-29.
Leavitt, John B. 176-59; 177-83; 191-24.
Le Bailly, A. J. 271-50.
Lebon, André. 77-22.
Leclerc, M. 86-9.
Le Cour, C. J. 140-50; 207-31; 210-22.
Ledoux, J. W. 23-7; 153-30; 304-90.
Lee, B. 242-98.
Lee, G. W. 273-34.
Lee, J. 113-97; 114-2.
Lee, M. N. 301-3.
Leeds, Albert R. 294-42; 307-43.
Lees, Herbert. 166-44.
Lefebre, G. 215-30.
Lefèvre, André. 78-49; 207-26; 213-70.
Lefevre, G. Shaw. 140-52; 142-4; 146-69.
Leffmann, Henry. 225-3; 305-94.
Legge, Hugh. 146-83.
Legoyt, Alfred. 228-72.
Legrain, ——. 80-10.
Lehmann, O. 216-61.
Lehr, A. 115-27.
Lehr, J. 103-57.
Leidig, Eugen. 86-14.
Leighton, Baldwin. 247-45.
Leighton, J. 128-51.
Leighton, S. 276-1.
Leipziger, Henry M. 188-51.
Leisen, Theodore A. 310-34.
Leitsch, W. C. 55-23; 70-77.
Le Morris, G. 141-79.
Leone, Enrico. 163-70.
Leporini, Gius. 111-45.
Leppington, C. H. de E. 44-12.
le Rossignol, A. E. 296-93.
Le Roy, P. A. 86-25.
Leroy-Beaulieu, Paul. 77-16; 208-54; 236-63; 272-86; 275-59.
Lescuyer, P. 77-31.
Leseure, E. K. 269-13.
Lespinasse, Geo. S. 210-3; 212-50, 57.
Letchworth, William P. 41-52.
Lethaby, W. R. 11-30.
Laugny, Georges. 212-52.
Leuthold, C. E. 86-21.
Levasseur, E. 229-12; 245-90.
Levermore, Charles H. 172-65, 66.
Levey, Edgar J. 182-95.
Levy, ——. 69-45.

Levy, A. 120-61; 122-1; 209-94.
Levy, E. C. 234-18.
Levy, J. M. 181-75.
Lewes, C. L. 214-94.
Lewes, Vivian B. 117-67; 124-71, 72.
Lewis, Alfred Henry. 197-30.
Lewis, Alice. 135-42.
Lewis, Austin. 239-31; 240-50.
Lewis, Charlton T. 158-56.
Lewis, Elizabeth Dike. 185-87.
Lewis, John C. 258-95.
Lewis, N. P. 74-65; 75-76; 219-45; 220-82, 83; 267-26.
Lewis, W. A. Aylmer. 205-89.
Lewis, Wm. D. 4-70; 224-80.
Lewisham, ——. 137-3.
Lexis, ——. 2-10.
Lexow, Clarence. 175-34; 191-22.
Liberty, W. J. 138-12.
Liebenam, W. 235-42.
Liesegang, Erich. 88-74.
Liger, François. 211-38.
Lightner, W. H. 238-95.
Lincoln, Alice N. 31-25.
Lincoln, G. W. 207-30.
Lincoln, Mary J. 29-48; 150-73.
Lindenthal, Gustav. 177-93; 197-30.
Lindley, W. H. 300-2.
Lindsay, Samuel McCune. 223-58, 59; 298-39.
Lindsley, A. V. S. 170-32.
Linton, Harvey. 11-12.
Lippold, H. 148-34.
Little, Archibald. 131-28; 221-15.
Little, J. T., Jr. 168-88.
Little, W. 127-46.
Littlejohn, Harvey. 9-78; 254-100.
Livache, Ach. 83-63a.
Livesey, George. 122-94.
Lloyd, Caro. 277-20.
Lloyd, Robert McA. 266-45.
Lobingier, Charles S. 205-81.
Loch, C. S. 44-18; 51-56; 99-55; 101-17; 132-69; 272-80; 277-30.
Locke, Franklin B. 93-56a.
Lodge, Henry Cabot. 28-26; 184-52.
Loeb, Morris. 56-43.
Loening, Edgar. 2-10; 36-41; 41-34a; 85-98; 89-97; 227-40.
Loew, Emil. 287-75.
Loewenstein, Franz. 17-71.
Loftie, William J. 128-68; 134-28.
Logan, Charles T. 15-8; 51-75; 226-11; 237-83.
Loliée, F. 209-72.
Lomas, Harold. 25-56; 287-53.
Lombroso, Cesare. 298-41.
Longstaff, G. B. 36-42; 285-16.
Lonsdale, Sophia. 277-37.
Loomis, Frank M. 34-82; 158-35; 217-96.
Loomis, S. L. 51-61.
Lopez, Charles A. 176-77.
Lord, James Brown. 176-74.
Loring, Charles M. 13-64; 258-95.
Loring, Florence Burton. 215-36.
Lossing, Benson J. 10-99; 184-55; 185-71; 291-80.
Love, Charles H. 132-52.
Lovegrove, James. 257-51.
Low, A. Maurice. 301-8.
Low, Seth. 4-64, 74, 75; 7-38; 9-73; 43-6;

332 MUNICIPAL AFFAIRS.

52-88; 98-34; 289-20; 290-38.
Low, Sidney J. 282-50.
Low, William G. 8-62; 177-100.
Lowcock, Sidney R. 251-32.
Lowell, A. L. 259-15.
Lowell, Francis C. 26-66; 27-91.
Lowell, Josephine Shaw (Mrs. C. R.). 44-24; 51-53; 176-66; 198-50; 227-58; 272-89; 296-4.
Lowles, John. 135-48.
Lowrie, Charles N. 216-58.
Lowrie, Sarah D. 223-56.
Löwry, Wilhelm. 299-71.
Lubbock, Gertrude. 44-34; 245-9.
Lubbock, John. 130-96; 145-58; 146-69.
Lucas, Ach. 78-43.
Lucas, Charles. 80-97.
Luchini, Odoardo. 110-26.
Lucipia, Louis. 78-51.
Ludlow, William. 96-3.
Ludwig, Charles V. F. 304-88.
Ludwig-Wolf, L. F. 87-39.
Lugilde y Huerta, M. 148-26.
Lukomski, T. 36-40.
Luks, W. 87-47.
Luloslawski, M. 236-69.
Lumley, W. G. 133-79.
Lundie, John. 269-6.
Lusk, H. H. 66-2.
Luten, Daniel B. 114-9; 219-58, 60; 220-67, 88.
Lymington, Viscount. 100-87.
Lynch, William. 281-20.
Lynch, William A. 161-21.
Lynn, John R. 121-72; 122-6.

M

Mabie, H. W. 260-35.
McAdoo, M. R. 263-92.
McAneny, George. 180-49.
McBriar, R. A. 125-99.
McBride, M. M. 179-33.
Macbride, Robt. J. 63-27; 115-34.
McCallum, Alexander. 296-82.
McCallum, M. 42-63; 277-36.
M'Cannel, W. J. 83-63a.
McCardy, J. J. 239-27.
McClintock, Charles T. 240-57.
McClintock, John N. 252-58; 253-89.
McClintock, Oliver. 226-10.
McClung, Hester M. 109-95.
McColl, Donald. 91-24.
McComb, D. E. 302-34.
McConachie, L. G. 66-100.
McConnell, John H. 155-94.
McCook, J. J. 65-67, 68; 96-1; 273-12.
McCormack, Ira A. 263-89; 270-32.
McCormick, Cyrus H. 214-18.
McCormick, S. D. 188-51.
McCracken, W. D. 61-96; 231-43.
McCullough, Ernest. 221-97.
McCullough, Richard. 263-93.
McDermot, George. 104-4, 94; 274-49.
McDermott, Edward J. 112-70; 147-97.
Macdonald, C. R. 246-22.
McDonald, Donald. 55-30.
MacDonald, J. 113-96.
MacDonald, J. A. 24-26; 272-85.
Macdonald, J. R. 186-14.
Macdonald, William. 277-15.

McDonald, W. 148-31.
Macdonnell, J. 278-53.
McDonough, John T. 200-96.
McDougal, H. C. 295-75.
Macé, G. 210-16.
Mace, Mrs. 141-73.
McElroy, Samuel. 304-77; 309-15.
McFarland, S. C. 204-54.
McFarland, W. A. 264-100.
McFarlane,——. 91-26.
McGann, L. E. 47-77.
McGinley, A. A. 51-70.
Macgowan, D. B. 23-96.
McGrady, Lord Provost. 62-18.
MacGregor, George. 91-27.
MacGregor, H. P. 269-20.
McGuinness, ——. 161-18.
McGuinness, Edwin D. 232-75.
McGuire, ——. 159-63.
McGuire, James K. 104-89; 157-29; 169· 11.
MacHarg, Martin. 10-2.
McIlhenny, John D. 123-28.
Mackay, ——. 273-34.
Mackay, H. C. 268-97.
Mackay, Thomas. 277-28.
McKellar, P. D. 252-58.
McKelway, St. Clair. 7-30; 217-87.
McKenzie, Anna. 108-93.
Mackenzie, Constance. 215-36.
Mackenzie, F. G. 126-12.
Mackenzie, J. J. 241-93.
McKenzie, T. H. 306-29.
McKeough, G. T. 246-19.
McKinley, A. E. 184-58.
McKisson, Robert E. 53-7; 158-59; 159-67.
M'Laren, J. 123-44.
McLaughlin, J. Fairfax. 194-88.
McLaurin, Donald D. 59-77.
MacLean, Annie Marion. 59-74; 107-79.
McLean, F. W. 73-34.
McLean, Fannie W. 107-65; 240-51.
McLean, George. 158-44.
McLean, S. J. 248-62.
McLoughlin, W. P. 187-29.
McMaster, John Bach. 292-84.
McMaster, R. Bach. 202-34.
McMath, Robert E. 98-34; 237-93; 251-46.
MacMorran, A. 275-69.
McMurray, T. S. 159-71.
Macnamara, T. J. 141-72.
M'Neel-Caird, Alexander. 276-14.
Macomber, J. K. 7-38.
Maconnachie, George. 282-47.
McTaggart, John. 32-27, 28.
MacVeagh, Franklin. 8-50; 46-61; 217-79.
McVeagh, Wayne. 224-78.
McVey, Frank L. 155-95.
MacVicar, John. 160-93, 99; 161-16; 163-51; 164-97; 165-7; 159-63.
M'Walter, J. C. 124-64.
Macy, Jesse. 85-89.
Madox, Thomas. 280-17.
Madden, M. B. 218-25.
Magee, Louis J. 90-11.
Maggiore-Perin, ——. 206-95.
Magie, B. C. 291-80.
Mahaim, Ernest. 19-14.
Mahany, Rowland B. 34-88a.
Maier, J. 119-30.

BIBLIOGRAPHY. 333

Maignen, P. J. A. 225-3.
Mailler-Kendall, Theo. 252-57.
Maissoneuve, S. 118-96.
Maitland, Frederic William. 38-87; 277-18; 280-9, 14.
Malachowski, Herm. 21-56.
Mallock, M. M. 234-4.
Malochee, H. J. 158-37.
Malone, James H. 153-38.
Maltbie, Milo Roy. 49-28; 82-60; 93-47; 131-23; 146-69; 164-78; 165-4; 167-71; 181-87; 225-3; 275-71, 81; 283-68; 284-96; 293-18.
Malzac, Miranda. 80-15, 16.
Mancini, I. 37-56.
Manega, Rudolf. 102-43.
Manfrin, Pietro. 109-9.
Mangenot, ——. 209-77.
Mangini, F. 147-10.
Manley, Henry. 31-2.
Mann, Wilbur E. 204-69.
Manning, H. E. C. 275-67.
Manning, Helen L. 30-78.
Manning, Warren H. 214-2.
Mansergh, James. 252-58; 288-89; 303-53; 309-15, 97; 310-20.
Mansfield, Howard. 205-80.
Manson, George I. 183-16.
Manson, Marsden. 308-85.
Mantova, G. 109-15.
Manville, E. 12-44.
March, H. J. 219-60.
Marble, A. P. 244-71.
Marburg, Edgar. 225-3.
Marechal, Henri. 124-77.
Maréchal, M. 209-95.
Marie, A. 208-36.
Marie, J. 78-50.
Marjolin, ——. 105-20.
Marks, Henry C. 39-14.
Markus, A. 16-56.
Marpaux, A. 60-86, 87; 81-39.
Marquardsen, Heinrich. 2-9; 18-96; 85-2; 86-18; 98-23; 255-23.
Marriott, W. T. 24-24.
Marrucci, C. 235-37.
Marryat, R. 242-10.
Marshall, Alfred. 135-42.
Marshall, Cloyd. 264-11.
Marshall, Edward. 137-84; 182-12; 187-21, 30.
Marshall, Matthew. 72-15; 159-72.
Marson, C. L. 44-11.
Marston, A. 252-58.
Martel, J. 72-19.
Martin, Arthur J. 249-84; 250-9; 253-79.
Martin, E. S. 180-59.
Martin, F. 37-65.
Martin, Henry. 22-90.
Martin, J. W. 137-99; 162-42; 246-29.
Martin, Rufus. 287-66.
Martin, William R. 5-89; 182-91.
Martinelli, Mass. 109-5.
Martyn, Carlos. 50-45.
Mascher, H. A. 9-80.
Maskery, ——. 253-86.
Mason, August Lynch. 161-25.
Mason, Charles. 84-75.
Mason, Edward G. 46-60.
Mason, Frank H. 82-53; 87-33; 118-83; 254-99; 304-81.

Mason, H. W. 38-80.
Mason, T. 137-4.
Mason, William P. 303-50; 304-87; 307-42, 43; 308-65, 74, 76; 310-18.
Mataja, Victor. 272-1; 273-32.
Mather, F. G. 65-77.
Mathews, J. Douglass. 102-26.
Mathews, Robert. 4-59.
Mathieu, A. 258-86.
Mattersdorff, W. 263-96.
Matteson, Andre. 9-69.
Matthews, Franklin. 50-37; 174-28; 190-8; 191-13, 24; 194-85.
Matthews, J. M. 185-88.
Matthews, Nathan, Jr. 26-82; 165-2.
Matthews, William. 288-91.
Matthiews, A. F. 189-78.
Mauran, John Lawrence. 237-84.
Mauri, Aug. 154-66.
Mauriac, Jean E. 26-63.
Maury, Dabney H. 67-25; 222-31; 303-67.
Maury, Dabney H., Jr. 307-58.
Mawson, Harry P. 100-88; 225-1.
Maxon, J. H. 117-60.
Maxon, W. D. 50-46.
Maxwell, Wm. H. 83-69; 84-72, 74; 192-44; 243-31; 250-11; 258-98; 285-43.
May, J. 9-85.
May, Max. 96-7; 103-69.
May, Max B. 52-79, 80.
May, O. 118-84.
Mayer, Julius M. 178-8; 188-45.
Mayo, Earl W. 197-30.
Mayor, L. 272-76.
Mayo-Smith, Richmond. 76-9, 10, 11, 13; 230-15.
Mazzocolo, Enrico. 109-10.
Mead, Daniel W. 305-9.
Mead, E. D. 5-85; 12-51; 237-73.
Mead, Mrs. Edwin D. 13-66.
Mead, Morris W. 165-12.
Mead, Whitefield. 51-62.
Meade, Charles A. 193-73.
Meade-King, W. O. F. 288-86.
Meade, Thomas De Courcy. 68-42; 101-4.
Means, D. M. 64-41; 73-38; 113-89; 228-86; 272-2.
Mearns, Andrew. 132-71.
Meason, M. L. 139-45.
Meath, Earl of. 129-86; 139-32, 34; 213-71.
Mechelin, L. 236-59.
Meehan, Joseph. 139-35.
Meeker, Claude. 32-31.
Meikle, William. 92-37.
Meiklejon, M. J. C. 135-39.
Meissner, Alois. 82-50; 103-65; 170-28.
Meissner, Gustav. 204-59.
Melendy, R. L. 48-3.
Mellen, Chase. 176-64.
Mendlik, A. 120-56.
Menger, ——. 14-1a.
Mercer, George Gluyas. 223-54.
Meredith, Ellis. 59-70.
Mereu, H. 206-93.
Merewether, H. A. 280-19.
Meriwether, C. 301-3.
Meriwether, Lee. 159-73; 162-38; 165-99; 167-67.
Merk, Aug. 312-91.

Merling, A. 118-88.
Merriam, John M. 27-5.
Merriam, Lucius S. 170-29.
Merriman, Mansfield. 241-68.
Merry, Andrew. 107-78.
Merwin, Henry C. 194-85.
Mesa E. 255-28.
Meunier, Stanilas. 212-61.
Meuriot, Paul. 228-87.
Meyer, E. 89-86.
Meyer, F. Andreas. 95-83, 87.
Meyer, Georg. 85-99; 213-69; 214-19.
Meyer, Louis F. 251-51.
Meyers, W. J. 48-1.
Michel, Georges. 272-87.
Micheli, Horace. 260-20.
Michie, T. J. 5-4.
Middleton, Reginald E. 146-69; 146-71; 306-25; 308-73.
Mikkleson, Michael A. 48-1; 298-32.
Miller, Alice. 48-18.
Miller, C. O. G. 121-67.
Miller, Geo. W. 181-70.
Miller, John. 184-53.
Miller, Joseph A. 232-73.
Miller, Joseph D. 98-34.
Miller, Kempster B. 260-37; 261-38.
Miller, O. T. 37-55.
Miller, Thomas D. 122-9; 261-43.
Miller, Warner. 126-24.
Milliken, Isaac T. 239-17.
Milliken, O. J. 48-15.
Millin, G. F. 143-27.
Millington, F. H. 99-59.
Mills, C. 181-79; 218-24.
Mills, F. J. 239-38.
Mills, Hiram F. 251-33; 309-91.
Milne, Peter. 198-53, 58.
Milner, Alfred. 247-68.
Milner, Willis J. 303-68.
Minett, R. 275-66.
Minot, Lawrence. 30-89.
Minot, Wm., Jr. 73-43.
Minshall, F. H. 58-62; 125-88.
Miotat, Eug. 211-29.
Miriel, Emile. 81-21.
Mischler, Ernst. 14-1.
Mitchell, Cornelius B. 258-95.
Mitchell, F. H. 243-45.
Mitchell, S. A. 252-58.
Mitton, G. E. 144-42.
Moeller, ——. 231-59.
Moffat, George. 269-7.
Moffat, W. 103-80.
Moffett, S. E. 4-65; 26-68; 231-47.
Mohun, E. 298-48.
Moireau, Auguste. 181-73.
Moireau, M. A. 81-37.
Moïse, Charles. 210-96.
Molitor, David. 291-63.
Molla, Pa. 109-99.
Monkswell, Lord. 143-20; 281-41.
Monod, Henri. 78-49a; 285-29.
Monroe, Charles E. 311-44.
Monroe, H. L. 119-27.
Monroe, Paul. 271-61.
Monstier, J. 13-82.
Montague, F. C. 193-62; 247-67; 275-78.
Montemartini, Giovanni. 110-37.

Montgomery, Caroline Williamson. 247-40.
Montpelier, J. A. 262-70.
Moody, Frank T. 155-94.
Moor, C. G. 305-7.
Moore, C. E. 308-82.
Moore, Chas. J. 60-80, 82; 158-45.
Moore, Clarence S. 168-88.
Moore, Dorothea. 48-18.
Moore, E. C. 48-3; 126-21.
Moore, E. C. S. 241-72.
Moore, F. W. 91-29.
Moore, H. E. 228-68; 272-77.
Moore, Helen. 107-65; 248-65.
Moore, M. I. 105-12; 241-86.
Moore, Robert. 68-36; 237-86, 91, 93.
Moore, Thomas Ewing. 148-29.
Moran, F. J. C. 114-2.
Mordecai, Augustus. 93-55.
Morgan, Edwin V. 185-92.
Morgan, J. 253-88.
Morgan, R. M. 178-12.
Morgan-Brown, H. 281-38.
Morgand, Léon. 77-30.
Morgensen, Peter. 73-27.
Morgenstern, Lina. 112-74.
Morier, R. B. D. 275-72.
Morison, Frank. 2-26.
Morris, Charles. 223-47.
Morris, Moreau. 17-73, 82; 18-83; 177-83.
Morris, William O'Connor. 274-49.
Morrison, W. R. 251-57.
Morse, Allen B. 91-30; 92-39.
Morse, A. D. 218-10.
Morse, Francis R. 41-59; 45-43.
Morse, W. F. 83-63a, 70; 84-80, 81.
Morss, Samuel E. 209-78.
Morton, Henry. 117-54.
Moses, B. 239-41.
Moss, Frank. 174-15; 184-36; 191-26; 227-44, 48.
Moss, Isaac. 186-13.
Mossa, Pietro. 109-11.
Moulton, J. Fletcher. 74-53; 279-74.
Mount, May Wilkinson. 173-10; 179-45.
Mountain, A. B. 167-61; 261-39; 284-95.
Mowry, Arthur M. 194-85.
Mowry, Duane. 155-76.
Mueller, Eugen. 232-68.
Mueller, O. N., Jr. 34-73.
Mühlke, C. 235-45.
Muirhead, James. 276-10; 285-13.
Muldaur, George B. 235-26.
Mulhall, M. G. 135-42.
Mullen, Ben H. 238-9.
Muller, ——. 156-9.
Müller, Alex. 253-87.
Muller, Emile. 102-39.
Mumford, Mary E. 8-62a; 224-88; 245-85; 311-58.
Munce, James. 18-91.
Munro, John. 146-69.
Munsell, Joel. 10-100.
Münsterberg, E. 94-77; 273-13.
Münsterberg, Th. 42-75.
Mure, W. J. 276-11.
Murlin, Edgar L. 180-64.
Murphy, Geo. H. 21-75.
Murphy, Shirley. 242-25.
Murphy, Walter. 222-20.

Murray, G. H. 279-76.
Muzzey, A. L. 48-18.
Myers, Cortland. 43-2.
Myers, Gustavus. 189-73, 75.

N

Nachtsheim, A. 267-78.
Nadal, E. S. 174-21; 176-70; 189-78; 198-42.
Napias, Henri. 207-33.
Narjoux, Félix. 207-18.
Nash, H. S. 51-66.
Nash, Vaughan. 145-62.
Nathan, Paul. 21-58.
Naville, E. 231-41.
Neal, Jane E. 127-38.
Negro, Luigi. 163-59.
Nelson, Henry Loomis. 290-53.
Nérincx, Alfred. 21-61.
Neumann, F. J. 87-45; 88-56, 60.
Newall, W. 130-98; 131-20.
Newbaker, C. A. 67-12.
Newberry, J. S. 190-4.
Newbigging, Thomas. 120-60; 121-89; 122-17; 283-67.
Newbigging, William. 124-56.
Newcomb, S. 301-3.
Newell, Wm. H. 105-11; 241-84.
Newland, F. W. 149-41.
Newman, A. S. 37-55.
Newsholme, Albert. 242-26.
Newton, T. M. 216-54.
Newton, Virginius. 234-17.
Nicholl, T. J. 219-35.
Nichols, George. 277-28.
Nichols, H. Bertram. 115-25.
Nichols, O. F. 195-3; 196-14.
Nichols, Wm. I. 3-37.
Nichols, William Ripley. 308-77.
Nicholson, C. N. 278-41.
Nicholson, W. 254-2.
Nicol, James. 92-41.
Nicolson, J. B. 276-11.
Nielly, ——. 207-23.
Niven, James. 149-44.
Nixon, S. Frederick. 202-26.
Noack, Fr. 205-73.
Noble, Andrew. 241-69.
Noble, John. 279-91.
Nöll, F. 87-46.
Norden, Hans. 299-57.
Nordhoff, Charles. 174-24.
Norris, H. M. 264-9.
North, E. P. 218-31; 221-93; 258-81.
North, F. M. 43-4.
Northcote, A. S. 65-66.
Northrop, B. G. 300-97.
Norton, C. E. 28-31.
Norton, George. 128-62.
Norton, Lord. 132-55.
Nott, C. C. 176-59; 301-3.
Nourse, Henry S. 151-90.
Novy, F. G. 24-57.
Nowroji, Hormusji. 19-19.
Noyes, Albert F. 31-22.
Nunn, T. H. 141-81, 87.
Nye, A. B. 38-78.

O

Oberbreyer, ——. 115-32.
Oberholtzer, Ellis P. 61-99; 98-36, 38; 291-61.
Oberholtzer, Sara Louisa. 246-24.
O'Brien, Edward C. 192-35.
Obrist, H. 13-76.
O'Callaghan, Edw. B. 186-98; 201-16, 19.
Ochs, George W. 46-56; 159-63.
O'Connell, Daniel. 240-55.
O'Conor, Charles. 198-48.
Odell, F. S. 153-39.
Odgers, William Blake. 275-64.
Odling, William. 304-93.
Oertel, O. 86-8.
Ogden, R. 160-88.
Ogden, William J. 15-16.
Ogle, W. 285-15.
Oldenberg, ——. 273-7.
Oldham, Edward A. 84-78.
Oldrini, A. 109-1.
Olin, Stephen H. 192-44.
Oliphant, F. H. 123-31.
Olive, Wm. Thomas. 149-53.
Olmsted, Frederick Law, Jr. 10-94; 29-58; 34-91; 190-85; 213-75; 215-48; 301-11.
Olmsted, John C. 215-25.
O'Meara, J. J. 73-44.
O'Neil, Thos. B. 256-43.
O'Neill, Henry. 152-28.
Onslow, A. W. 122-12.
Oosterbaan, G. 103-71.
Opet, O. 90-10.
Oppenheimer, F. 88-72.
Ordway, John M. 173-8.
Orr, Alexander. 197-30.
Orth, A. Leipzig. 256-48.
Orton, Edward, Jr. 220-68, 71.
Osborn, C. 105-31.
Osborn, H. V. B. 223-50.
Osgood, Fletcher. 31-22.
O'Shaughnessy, Richard. 274-53.
Ostrander, Dempster, 161-15.
Ostrander, S. M. 184-47.
Owen, Douglas. 134-26.
Owen, James. 205-90; 221-95; 247-84; 269-25.
Owens, R. R. 68-31.

P

Pagès, ——. 298-42.
Paige, J. D. 75-85, 90.
Paine, Robert Treat. 44-27; 100-80.
Paisley, A. Gardner. 100-66.
Paley, W. B. 144-30.
Palgrave, R. H. Inglis. 1-2; 16-50; 18-94a; 61-93; 73-44; 77-38; 80-13; 86-12; 97-8a, 11a, 11b; 104-86; 135-31; 228-70; 260-19; 279-85; 279-94; 280-13, 18.
Palmberg, Albert. 242-26.
Palmer, Arthur W. 308-84.
Palmer, Clarence S. 98-34.
Palmer, Emerson. 174-28.
Palmer, O. M. 190-5.
Panizza, Mario. 111-46.
Parent-Duchatelet, A. J. B. 210-21.
Parey, Karl. 20-32.
Parke, Roderick J. 160-93.
Parker, F. R. 278-60.
Parker, Francis J. 151-83.
Parker, G. A. 213-82.
Parker, Geo. F. 24-28.
Parker, J. 136-73.

Parker, R. D. 14-93.
Parker, William. 173-13.
Parkes, E. 9-82.
Parkhurst, Charles H. 6-9; 7-33; 174-21; 176-63; 191-24; 194-89.
Parkhurst, Henry L. 13-78.
Parmley, W. C. 251-26, 39.
Parry, W. Kaye. 251-32; 307-43.
Parshall, H. F. 92-45; 264-11.
Parsons, Frank. 53-96; 54-15; 60-87a; 63-31; 64-53; 98-34, 35; 159-82; 160-97; 161-14; 162-37; 164-93; 167-60, 68, 72; 168-82, 88; 231-40, 46; 262-65; 264-8.
Parsons, George Frederick. 126-19.
Parsons, H. de B. 76-96.
Parsons, James. 104-96.
Parsons, Samuel, Jr. 172-75; 215-35; 216-55.
Parsons, William Barclay. 16-43; 22-94; 50-29; 55-28; 93-49; 127-43; 144-35; 196-15, 18; 197-30, 38; 212-54; 295-78.
Parton, James. 3-30; 57-48; 152-23; 174-21; 198-44; 217-8.
Partridge, Newton A. 46-72; 50-32.
Partridge, William Ordway. 213-88.
Pascaud, Henri. 4-70a.
Pascoe, C. E. 130-96.
Pasquet, D. 129-90; 142-1.
Pasquier, Lucien. 79-74.
Pater, Joseph J. 305-98.
Paterno, P. A. 225-6.
Paton, James. 91-18; 162-38.
Patten, Simon N. 289-16; 291-68.
Patterson, C. Stuart. 52-88.
Patterson, S. A. 294-39.
Patterson, W. R. 210-14; 221-13.
Pattison, F. A. 35-18.
Patton, W. B. 62-16.
Paul-Dubois, L. 70-67; 79-81; 88-66; 280-16.
Paullian, Louis. 207-27.
Pavey, Frank D. 66-7; 174-21; 190-2; 217-6.
Payne, W. H. C. 146-75.
Peabody, Andrew P. 75-80.
Peabody, Francis G. 42-70; 43-94; 43-5; 61-3.
Pearmain, Alice Upton. 29-74.
Pearmain, T. H. 305-7.
Pearson, Chas. H. 227-54.
Pearson, F. S. 265-17.
Pease, Edward R. 126-14.
Pease, J. G. 276-8.
Pease, T. H. 53-99.
Peck, F. 133-83.
Peck, Hiram D. 204-61.
Peckham, S. F. 219-44, 52.
Peckham, Wheeler H. 175-35.
Peek, Francis. 243-47.
Peek, R. H. 82-63.
Peeters, L. J. 18-99.
Pegna, Marlo. 110-26.
Pelatant, Leopold. 81-22.
Pell, Albert. 73-36; 275-78.
Pellissier, Georges. 117-73.
Pennell, E. R. 130-96; 138-22, 24; 144-42.
Penniman, Jas. H. 245-87.
Penn-Lewis, W. 288-82.
Penrose, Boies. 223-54, 64; 224-68.
Pensa, Henri. 113-93.
Percy, G. W. 220-74.
Pere, Johann. 300-85.
Pérès, H. 260-34.

Périn, J. 36-40.
Perkins, F. B. 263-95.
Perkins, Thomas C. 300-100.
Perrine, F. A. C. 166-37; 248-61.
Perry, George R. 113-82, 83; 126-18.
Perry, J. Roy. 39-98.
Perry, Nelson W. 84-82; 120-42, 43; 264-11.
Persinger, Clark Edmund. 163-73.
Persse, T. B. 165-3.
Pesci, Ugo. 110-29.
Petch, Thos. D. 124-48.
Petrie, George. 156-1.
Petrovsky, A. G. 156-4.
Petsch, A. 221-99.
Pettigrew, J. A. 215-23.
Petty, William. 62-12; 135-30.
Peuch, A. 304-85.
Pey, J. B. 73-26.
Peytoureau, ——. 26-62.
Pfalz, F. 88-64.
Pfeffer, Walter. 255-29.
Pfingsthorn, Carl. 95-81.
Phelan, James D. 37-76; 38-83; 167-62; 239-29; 240-46.
Phelphs, L. R. 277-29.
Phelps, Charles E., Jr. 15-26.
Phelps, E. J. 46-72; 194-85.
Philbrick, John D. 294-49.
Phillimore, R. C. 135-49.
Phillips, Alfred E. 253-73.
Phillips, Asa E. 250-17.
Phillips, Barnet. 179-32; 198-53; 310-31.
Phillips, Ernest. 114-10.
Phillips, Geo. I. 287-59.
Phillips, H. A. 35-98.
Phillips, Hiram. 49-22.
Phillips, J. Roland. 279-93.
Phillips, Samuel. 172-79.
Pickard, C. E. 3-35; 228-77.
Pickard, J. L. 245-91.
Pickard, Samuel T. 230-17.
Pickering, J. S. 258-79.
Picot, Georges. 102-47; 209-73, 74.
Picton, J. A. 3-30; 276-94; 281-25.
Piequet, O. 236-56.
Pierce, Frank G. 161-16, 20; 166-39; 169-98.
Pierce, Frederick E. 187-27.
Pierce, Walter S. 83-63a.
Pierce, William T. 29-59.
Pierro, Luigi. 109-12.
Pierson, G. S. 252-54.
Pignant, P. 241-83.
Pilon, E. 80-9.
Pincus, Henry. 213-83; 214-1; 216-57.
Pine, John B. 185-76.
Pingree, H. S. 7-32; 59-76; 158-41; 160-93; 162-44; 167-63, 72; 298-33; 305-2.
Pini, G. 110-22.
Pitcairn, Hugh. 95-86.
Plehn, Carl Copping. 38-81, 81a; 71-99.
Plumb, F. 220-65.
Plummer, John. 14-96.
Pogson, J. 107-81.
Pöhlmann, R. 227-55.
Poindexter, Philip. 174-28.
Pokrovskaya, M. J. 104-97.
Polk, Jefferson F. 92-34.
Pomeroy, Eltweed. 61-90, 91, 95, 97, 98; 173-92; 238-99.

Ponsonby, E. 274-50.
Pooley, H. 121-77.
Poore, George Vivian. 100-68; 140-59; 242-13.
Pope, Franklin L. 125-96.
Poppenberg, Felix. 23-97.
Poppleton, William S. 267-64.
Porritt, Edward. 24-25; 26-70; 135-42; 137-90;
  176-59; 181-78; 273-48; 274-36; 276-90; 283-77;
  285-32; 287-73; 289-18.
Portal, Ethel M. 141-74.
Portalupi, Massimo. 161-27.
Porter, C. 308-66.
Porter, Dwight. 28-34; 68-36.
Porter, H. J. 221-6.
Porter, John Addison. 301-17; 302-37.
Porter, Robert P. 4-55; 32-30; 40-20; 70-78;
  72-6, 8; 92-35; 119-9; 161-11, 17; 164-87; 276-
  99; 284-4; 291-78.
Post, Geo. B. 258-81.
Post, James A. 59-79.
Potter, Alexander. 242-1.
Potter, B. 113-100; 114-3.
Potter, E. T. 187-21; 228-59.
Potter, F. D. 193-68.
Potter, Henry C. 141-81.
Potter, Henry Ingle. 100-72.
Potter, W. B. 266-51.
Potter, William. 224-78.
Potts, Alfred F. 162-41.
Powell, Gregory J. 205-76.
Powell, Lyman P. 1-3; 292-83.
Powell, R. F. 297-10.
Powers, Samuel L. 168-85.
Praft, J. W. 246-34.
Pratt, Mason D. 269-11.
Pray, W. L. 153-43.
Preece, Arthur H. 138-9.
Prendergast, Moret Y. 255-18.
Prentiss, John. 53-99.
Prescott, A. Ernest. 61-1.
Press, John. 52-84.
Pressly, Neill E. 260-33.
Preston, S. O. 172-63; 272-93.
Preston, W. C. 132-56.
Presutti, E. 109-4.
Preuss, Hugo. 90-6.
Price, E. C. 207-28.
Prichard, Frank P. 5-84.
Priestley, Joseph. 101-24; 243-32; 249-95.
Priestman, Arthur. 164-80.
Prince, Walter. 8-42; 172-68.
Prindle, H. B. 264-11.
Probst, C. O. 240-58; 308-89.
Probst; Friederick. 14-1b.
Probyn, J. W. 4-57; 77-36; 86-11; 98-26; 130-
  1; 203-40; 255-18; 274-42, 52, 53; 275-72, 74,
  75, 79; 276-85, 14, 15; 279-93.
Prothers, R. E. 129-74.
Prudden, T. Mitchell. 294-45.
Pruyn, Francis L. 199-64.
Pryor, James W. 57-55; 174-29; 181-70; 197-
  30; 200-94.
Puffer, F. E. 219-55.
Pugh, David F. 204-64.
Puibarand, Louis. 79-80; 279-81.
Pullen, Clarence. 23-59; 48-5.
Pullman, J. M. 44-13.
Pumpelly, J. C. 193-75; 257-69.
Purcell, Thomas P. 75-78.
Purdon, K. F. 94-76.

Purdy, Lawson. 73-35.
Purroy, H. D. 75-77.
Putnam, Elizabeth C. 41-50; 227-34.
Putnam, Harrington. 184-46,48.
Putnam, Herbert. 116-39.
Putnam, Ruth. 184-38.
Putzeys, E. 105-10.
Putzeys, F. 105-10.

Q

Quade, J. C. 112-72a.
Quick, J. H. 74-67.
Quilty, C. W. 161-9.
Quinby, Isaac N. 111-59.
Quincy, Josiah. 6-15; 17-61; 26-85; 27-90; 28-
  46; 29-53; 63-33; 94-67; 215-41; 289-17.

R

Rabbeno, Ugo. 273-27.
Rabot, M. E. 211-37.
Racine, ——. 262-69.
Raddin, Charles S. 49-22.
Rae, John. 74-60, 63.
Raemelin, C. 3-29.
Raffalovich, Arthur. 21-71; 33-54; 80-96; 102-
  50.
Rafter, George W. 111-61; 295-59.
Ragan, H. H. 98-25; 206-8.
Ragsdale, James W. 261-48.
Raine, James. 312-77.
Raines, J. 188-62.
Ralph, Julian. 24-21; 34-83; 46-66a, 72; 47-81;
  53-98, 5; 62-15; 155-87, 96; 172-89; 177-98;
  179-36; 180-49; 237-80; 238-97; 239-18; 301-7.
Ralston, W. R. S. 210-12.
Ramage, B. J. 255-11.
Ramalho, A. 80-91; 97-8.
Ramirez, D. B. Anton. 255-27.
Randall, C. D. 41-57.
Randall, E. O. 116-43.
Randall, John E. 119-28.
Randolph, Isham. 49-22.
Rankin, Norman S. 85-94.
Raper, G. A. 210-5.
Rathbone, William, Jr. 275-76; 279-89.
Rathowski, Math. G. 102-35.
Ratzel, Frederich. 229-8.
Rau, Albert. 86-22.
Rauch, John H. 48-6.
Rauchberg, Heinrich. 14-3a; 228-95.
Rawlinson, R. 99-56; 141-88; 242-90.
Raworth, J. S. 283-82.
Raworth, John. 157-28.
Raynor, C. H. 123-28.
Read, R. 253-88.
Reaney, G. S. 132-74.
Reason, W. 248-75.
Rebeillard, E. R. 207-35.
Reber, B. 37-64.
Réclus, E. 97-10.
Record, Geo. L. 66-97, 98.
Redmond, John M. 158-38.
Reed, Andrew. 285-12.
Reed, Charles Wesley. 161-19; 246-47.
Reed, Lyman C. 173-5.
Reed, W. B. 196-10.
Rees, William. 279-68.
Reeve, Fred'k C. 120-44.
Reich, Eduard. 231-52.

Reichardt, Erwin. 102-48.
Reichhelm, E. P. 122-5.
Reid, G. A. 13-69.
Reid, George. 250-12, 16.
Reid, H. G. 100-66.
Reid, Sidney. 178-2; 191-24.
Rein, Carrie. 44-20.
Reinherz, H. 107-76.
Remsen, D. S. 66-10, 93.
Renck, ——. 232-62.
Rendu, Ambroise. 230-38; 252-69.
Reno. J. W. 196-10.
Renouard, Alfred. 72-19; 221-7.
Reque, Lars S. 236-51.
Reuss, L. 81-30.
Reviere, Louis. 296-9.
Reynolds, Arthur R. 83-63a.
Reynolds, James B. 181-73.
Reynolds, J. Emerson. 62-9.
Reynolds, Marcus T. 22-9a; 109-62; 104-87.
Ricardo, Halsey. 12-33, 60.
Rice, C. Spring. 87-42; 90-1a.
Rice, George S. 199-74.
Rice, Allen T. 64-65.
Rice, Arthur L. 125-87.
Rice, Geo. S. 31-3.
Rice, J. M. 15-33; 29-73; 34-92; 48-15; 52-82; 108-92; 155-92; 192-44; 224-88; 237-90; 238-1; 245-14; 294-47.
Rice, W. 116-48.
Richard, Emile. 210-20.
Richards, Ellen H. 240-56, 66.
Richards, H. C. 146-75.
Richards, R. W. 260-24.
Richards, William P. 302-43.
Richardson, A. C. 34-87.
Richardson, Benjamin W. 9-84; 241-80, 88; 242-2.
Richardson, Charles. 52-87; 65-76; 159-64; 167-72; 217-88, 89, 98; 223-55.
Richardson, Clifford. 219-51.
Richardson, F. W. 32-31.
Richardson, Hester D. 193-58.
Richie, James. 54-11.
Richmond, Mary E. 42-82; 45-50.
Rideal, Samuel. 249-84; 251-32, 37; 253-4; 307-47, 56.
Rider, Joseph D. 305-16.
Ridgely, Benjamin H. 85-92.
Riding, William H. 189-69.
Ridpath, J. C. 48-9.
Riedel, J. 216-67.
Riedel, J. B. 98-31.
Rietschel, S. 88-70.
Riggs, H. F. 243-35.
Righter, G. Emil. 188-48.
Riis, Jacob A. 41-45, 46; 44-31a; 75-92; 105-16; 105-26; 106-41; 106-56, 57; 107-62; 176-59; 179-35; 186-5, 11, 15, 16; 187-19, 21, 22, 28; 188-42; 189-71; 190-8; 216-51, 53; 245-13.
Riordan, R. 216-72.
Ripley, William Z. 157-30; 228-84; 229-4.
Ritchie, Ryerson. 6-18.
Ritson, T. N. 282-63.
Ritter, John P. 178-22.
Robb, William Lispenard. 125-84.
Robbins, Mary C. 15-28; 48-5; 155-91; 214-5; 232-81; 238-100; 300-97.
Roberts, E. P. 120-48.
Roberts, George J. 121-87.

Roberts, H. 99-51.
Roberts, J. 140-58.
Roberts, James A. 201-7.
Roberts, W. E. 75-89.
Roberts, W. H. 51-55.
Robertson, R. F. 215-31.
Robertson, W. B. 144-31.
Robertson, W. Henry. 95-85.
Robin, André. 103-63.
Robins, E. C. 241-89.
Robinson, B. Fletcher. 94-68; 130-14; 131-36; 299-64.
Robinson, Sir Charles. 13-71.
Robinson, Charles A. 298-36.
Robinson, Charles Mulford. 12-61; 43-95; 63-63-24; 246-16, 30.
Robinson, H. 252-64.
Robinson, Henry A. 262-71.
Robinson, John Beverly. 12-39; 26-45; 178-7; 192-46.
Robinson, J. Clifton. 143-26; 265-18; 285-47, 48.
Robinson, J. R. 160-93; 161-16; 164-81.
Robinson, Wm. 210-6.
Robinson, W. L. 36-51a.
Robiquet, Paul. 209-66.
Rochetin, Eugène. 272-84.
Rockwell, Alfred P. 211-42.
Rodriguez, Pedro. 221-2.
Rodwell, A. 112-71.
Roebuck, J. A. 276-96.
Roechling, H. Alfred. 250-15.
Roechling, Herman. 22-82.
Rogers, Emma Winner. 9-70.
Rogers, G. Tracy. 269-23.
Rogers, John I. 224-80.
Rogers, Platt. 59-69.
Rogers, W. H. 192-35.
Rohe, George M. 307-43.
Rohts, C. 36-50.
Rollins, A. W. 107-60; 187-21.
Rollitt, Albert. 283-85.
Römer, ——. 148-23.
Roome, W. Harris. 7-31; 66-6.
Roosevelt, George W. 19-6; 33-63, 66.
Roosevelt, Theodore. 42-73; 65-84; 72-18; 96-7a; 185-66; 189-67; 190-1, 8, 9; 191-18, 28, 29, 34, 210-77, 227-32; 289-5, 21.
Roscher, Wilhelm. 229-1.
Roscoe, H. E. 149-52.
Rose, George B. 126-26.
Rose, John C. 228-65.
Rosencrans, W. H. 269-18.
Rosewater, Andrew. 205-77; 249-92; 250-17; 295-71.
Rosewater, Victor. 74-72; 119-22; 165-13; 205-79.
Ross, Edward A. 161-19.
Ross, James H. 66-3.
Ross, R. 123-28; 305-19.
Rosselli, Carlo. 110-26.
Rossi, Egisto. 110-25.
Rossiter, C. L. 267-62.
Rostand, Eugène. 80-2; 81-36a; 103-75; 271-59.
Rostron, Laurence W. S. 138-17.
Rothery, Guy Cadogan. 94-67.
Rothery, S. E. 260-32.
Rouanet, Gustave. 208-46.
Rouillet, A. 103-54.

BIBLIOGRAPHY. 339

Rounds, F. D. 266-59.
Routledge, R. 118-92.
Rowe, C. E. 67-27.
Rowe, Leo S. 2-22; 4-68, 69; 5-82; 20-47; 31-5; 46-72; 71-81, 83, 84; 81-42; 91-22; 97-22; 135-47; 137-82; 158-40; 174-29; 179-38; 180-49; 189-63; 194-95; 197-30; 208-48; 224-80; 229-92; 245-95; 288-100; 290-35; 299-56.
Rowntree, Joseph. 283-79.
Royer de Dour, Hippolyte de. 19-8.
Rudall, J. H. 71-90a.
Ruffin, John N. 206-98.
Rühlmann, Richard. 221-16.
Rule, Lucien V. 147-98.
Rümelin, Gustav. 229-14.
Runkle, Mrs. C. A. 311-54.
Ruprecht, Wilh. 137-94.
Russel, Ernest E. 105-17.
Russell, C. P. 121-86.
Russell, Charles Theodore, Jr. 53-2; 113-81.
Russell, George W. E. 7-29a.
Russell, James B. 242-23.
Russell, S. Bent. 237-93.
Russell, T. W. 62-7; 183-17; 282-46.
Rust, Charles H. 221-94.
Ryan, Harris J. 266-43.

S

Sachs, Edwin O. 75-79, 82.
St. Clair, L. M. 112-72.
Saintsbury, George. 149-37.
Sainz y Gomez, Miguel. 255-13.
Salazar, Fanny Zampini. 110-24.
Salisbury, Marquis of. 100-83.
Salmon-Legagneur, Paul. 79-89.
Saloma, G. Ricca. 163-65.
Salomon, Georges. 78-45.
Salomons, Henry H. 11-17.
Salter, W. M. 158-46; 272-85.
Saltsman, ——. 161-18.
Samuels, Mrs. A. 42-66.
Sanborn, A. F. 27-12; 28-28, 30; 151-84; 209-83.
Sanborn, Frank B. 55-27.
Sanders, C. 42-74.
Sanders, Dallas. 222-26; 268-88.
Sanders, Sedgwick. 140-56.
Sanford, Mary B. 193-57.
Sanger, W. W. 191-31; 231-51.
Sanlaville, Ferd. 79-75.
Sanne, Oscar. 214-95.
Sarcey, Francisque. 212-48.
Sargant, Charles Henry. 74-52; 279-73, 79.
Sargent, C. S. 13-64.
Sargent, J. H. 54-11.
Sarles, W. T. 306-38.
Sarrey, Paul. 207-19; 236-54.
Saunders, William. 136-56; 129-76.
Saunders, William F. 66-3a.
Savage, E. B. 253-75.
Sax, E. 102-34; 229-9.
Say, Horace. 209-65.
Say, Léon. 2-12, 13; 70-64; 71-95; 72-19; 78-47; 79-76, 79; 81-29; 207-23.
Sayers, H. M. 285-50.
Schaar, G. F. 122-18.
Schaeffer, J. H. 67-14.

Schaeffer, Nathan C. 245-85.
Schafer, ——. 148-32.
Schall, M. 156-10.
Schanz, Georg. 271-67, 69, 71; 272-6.
Schäppi, J. 272-99.
Scharf, J. T. 15-19; 224-72.
Schartlin, G. 23-6a; 271-68.
Schasler, M. 104-83.
Schauck, John A. 98-39.
Schellen, H. 118-90; 119-33.
Scherer, H. P. 83-63a.
Scheven, H. 230-27.
Scheyven, ——. 19-2.
Schieren, Charles A. 7-31.
Schikowski, John. 272-5; 273-9.
Schilling, ——. 118-5.
Schilling, George A. 50-33.
Schilling, N. H. 122-20.
Schimpff, Gustav. 270-36.
Schindler, Huber. 271-72.
Schindler, K. 23-3.
Schirmer, Carl. 156-13.
Schlesinger-Eckstein, Therese. 232-60.
Schloss, D. F. 113-84; 114-2; 282-55.
Schmid, F. 259-17.
Schmidt, C. D. 271-47.
Schmidt, Emil G. 123-45.
Schmölder, ——. 232-67.
Schmölke, J. 102-44.
Schnadhorst, F. 278-51.
Schneider, A. 312-80.
Schneider, K. 89-87.
Schoenhof, J. 283-69.
Schönberg, Gustav. 1-8; 16-51; 70-60; **89-97**, 100; 113-86; 245-92.
Schönfeldt, Gustav. 95-82.
Schönheyder, William. 305-20.
Schorrer, A. 271-69.
Schott, W. H. 119-16.
Schrader, A. C. 213-91.
Schrader, W. 165-17.
Schraub, Josef. 299-65.
Schuchardt, R. F. 307-59.
Schülke, Herm. 102-40; 104-8.
Schultz, A. 257-66.
Schulz, C. F. 54-14.
Schulze, G. A. 216-68.
Schurman, J. G. 44-15.
Schurz, Carl. 52-88, 90; 66-97; 68-29; **181-73**; 190-10; 217-81, 95.
Schuyler, E. 236-65.
Schuyler, Louisa Lee. 200-91.
Schuyler, Montgomery. 32-43; 36-31; **178-17**.
Schwab, John C. 182-2.
Schwanebach, P. 236-61.
Schwartz, J. C. 87-31.
Schwering, L. 156-8; 259-100.
Scidmore, Eliza Ruhamah. 221-14.
Scoble, H. T. 249-84.
Scott, Benjamin. 128-69; 130-96; **231-53**.
Scott, F. M. 68-36.
Scott, H. Y. D. 141-88.
Scott, W. J. 144-44.
Scotter, R. H. 287-61.
Scudamore, Amy L. 177-82.
Scudder, V. D. 193-58; 247-57.
Seager, J. Renwick. 129-91; 278-54.
Seaman, Louis L. 9-72.
Searles, Wm. H. 68-28a.
Sears, E. I. 174-21; 198-42.

Seavey, Fanny Copley. 237-87.
Sedgwick, A. G. 64-38; 181-69; 216-76; 301-3.
Sedgwick, W. T. 306-34.
Sedlaczek, Stephan. 299-71.
See, Milton. 13-72.
Seeger, Ferdinand. 199-100.
Seeler, Edgar V. 301-12.
Seeley, J. R. 88-69.
Seestern-Pauly, ——. 82-56.
Seguin, E. 190-90.
Seidel, Max. 90-2.
Seligman, E. R. A. 73-31, 33; 74-54, 62; 162-38; 201-3.
Sellers, Edith. 14-1c, 3; 20-37.
Senckel, Ernst. 246-25.
Senner, Joseph H. 76-14.
Sergeant, Charles S. 268-92.
Serra, Gius. 109-6.
Serrell, Lemuel W. 265-14.
Sewall, Frank. 12-45.
Sewall, William L. 39-1.
Seward, Mary C. 311-56.
Sexby, J. J. 139-36.
Seyffardt, L. F. 42-75; 57-60.
Shadbolt, R. G. 124-49.
Shadwell, Arthur. 146-69, 73.
Shafer, Sara Andrew. 11-24; 82-58.
Shaftesbury, Earl of. 104-99.
Shaler, Nathaniel S. 290-33.
Shand, A. J. 139-45.
Shapely, Rufus E. 224-84.
Sharpe, Reginald R. 135-36.
Sharpless, Isaac. 24-27; 149-39.
Shaw, A. C. 62-14.
Shaw, Albert. 1-5, 6; 3-30, 40; 5-91; 8-47; 18-99a; 24-23; 33-71; 52-88; 85-95b; 91-17; 95-84; 104-89; 108-84; 110-20; 130-96; 130-18; 139-44; 149-38; 160-94; 162-38; 174-29; 175-50; 183-35; 206-2; 207-13; 237-79; 239-31; 261-60; 272-90; 276-90, 92, 93; 289-23; 290-54; 293-21; 299-79.
Shaw, C. G. 276-13.
Shaw, Henry. 151-82.
Shaw, W. B. 294-50, 53.
Shea, John Gilmary. 184-53.
Sheahan, J. W. 47-94.
Shearer, William J. 245-7.
Shearman, August. 291-76.
Shearman, Thomas G. 72-46; 291 75.
Shedd, J. H. 68-36.
Sheffield, James R. 182-7.
Sheible, Albert. 125-78.
Sheldon, George. 58-67.
Sheldon, Samuel. 181-82.
Sheldrake, J. H. 125-89.
Shelton, Frederick H. 121-81; 123-22, 32, 33; 292-2.
Shenton, Henry C. H. 285-43.
Shepard, Edward M. 53-91; 152-17; 175-51; 197-31.
Shepard, F. J. 34-80.
Shepard, H. N. 152-25.
Shepardson, G. D. 160-2; 166-40.
Sherman, Alma Seymour. 41-43.
Sherman, Rogers. 64-56.
Sherman, Thomas H. 127-31, 42.
Sherman, W. J. 82-62.
Sherrerd, Morris R. 306-36; 309-9.
Sherwell, Arthur. 146-84; 283-79.
Shields, W. S. 304-71.
Shinn, Charles H. 239-17.

Shinn, G. W. 37-56.
Shoolbred, J. N. 118-93.
Shorey, Daniel L. 46-65.
Short, Sidney H. 54-13; 171-61; 195-2; 266-53; 286-48.
Shuey, Edwin L. 104-85; 213-86.
Shumann, Andrew. 48-10.
Siddons, Frederick L. 301-5.
Siegfriedt, Thorwald A. A. 109-96.
Sikes, Geo. C. 50-31.
Silbergeist, H. 148-28.
Silberstein, L. 23-96a; 144-43.
Silvernail, W. H. 174-25; 200-97.
Silverthorne, Arthur. 284-98.
Simon, John. 285-22.
Simonds, O. C. 214-14; 216-59; 258-91.
Simonetti, Lu. 235-40.
Simons, A. M. 81-41.
Simpson, ——. 129-89.
Simpson, D. F. 155-88.
Simpson, J. Alexander, Jr. 74-68.
Simrall, H. F. 298-45.
Sims, George R. 136-54.
Sinclair, A. H. 160-89; 262-65.
Sinclair, Graham M. 251-51.
Sioussat, St. George L. 15-22.
Sipione, Corrado. 109-13.
Sisley, R. 146-74.
Sisto, Gius. 110-28.
Sites, Clement Moore Lacey. 125-1.
Sitta, Pietro. 110-42.
Sitte, C. 258-84.
Skeel, Adalaide. 171-46.
Skinner, A. F. 172-72.
Skinner, Charles R. 245-83.
Skinner, Frank W. 49-22.
Slater, Edward T. 129-92.
Slater, J. W. 252-66.
Slater, P. F. 93-50.
Slater, T. 267-65.
Slicer, Thomas R. 51-68.
Sloan, A. M. 246-21.
Sloane, W. M. 230-29.
Slocum, F. L. 122-98.
Sly, Mary E. 48-5.
Small, A. W. 48-11.
Smalley, E. V. 49-22; 223-57.
Smart, Charles. 306 29.
Smart, William. 91-21; 92-33; 141-82; 159-76.
Smith, A. H. 50-41.
Smith, A. W. 220-66.
Smith, Alfred. 100-76; 103-79; 136-75; 138-26.
Smith, E. O. 24-35.
Smith, E. Shapnell. 257-58.
Smith, Edwin. 304-78.
Smith, Edwin F. 225-3.
Smith, Edwin Burritt. 46-64; 47-74; 48-12; 159-65.
Smith, Erwin F. 250-99; 308-67.
Smith, Frank C. 307-60.
Smith, G. H. 243-28.
Smith, Goldwin. 64-62.
Smith, H. 285-35.
Smith, H. Llewellyn. 141-69.
Smith, H. T. 163-51.
Smith, J. 5-97.
Smith, J. E. 128-58.
Smith, J. H. 37-59.
Smith, James Henry. 89-84.
Smith, Joel W. 49-22.

BIBLIOGRAPHY. 341

Smith, J. Toulmin. *4-58; 274-40; 276-3.
Smith, Katharine Louise. 104-88; 221-1.
Smith, Mary Roberts. 191-14.
Smith, Orlando J. 290-43.
Smith, Rufus B. 204-63.
Smith, S. 192-40; 241-91.
Smith, T. Carpenter. 162-32; 166-26.
Smith, Thomas E. V. 186-1.
Smith, W. C. 276-12.
Smith, W. S. 261-53.
Smyth, William R. 287-67; 288-78.
Snow, F. Herbert. 33-57; 113-83; 249-82.
Snow, J. Lippit. 232-80.
Snow, Marshall. 237-79.
Snow, R. W. 290-44.
Snowden, Yates. 45-53.
Snyder, C. B. J. 192-46.
Snyder, Geo. D. 258-73.
Snyder, John. 237-81.
Sodoffsky, Gustav. 236-67, 68.
Sohm, Rudolph. 88-75.
Solly, H. 99-58.
Somerhausen, ——. 19-3.
Somers, Richard. 280-15.
Sommer, Berthold. 183-33.
Sommerville, W. A. 136-63.
Sonneman, L. 90-14.
Soper, George A. 307-52.
Soper, J. P. H. 146-75.
Sospicio, Henri. 124-61.
Souden, Fred T. 146-69.
Southern, J. W. 116-42.
Souviron, Alfred. 77-15; 78-40; 207-15.
Soyka, I. 252-70.
Spahr, Jean Fine. 107-65.
Spalding, Fred P. 219-34.
Spalding, Henry. 100-74; 281-29.
Spalding, Thomas Alfred. 141-71.
Sparling, Samuel Edwin. 47-93; 71-89; 311-45, 49.
Speakman, Thomas H. 66-5; 217-90; 3.
Speare, S. L. 155-84.
Speed, John Gilmer. 50-30.
Speirs, F. W. 168-87; 224-80; 225-2; 271-54; 298-39.
Spence, C. H. 231-40.
Spence, Catherine H. 14-94.
Spencer, Anna Garlin. 42-64.
Spencer, David E. 311-47.
Spencer, Edward. 62-8; 99-54.
Spencer, Nelson S. 176-75.
Spencer, Walter B. 172-87.
Sperry, Henry M - 49-27.
Spielhagen, Fr. 19-21, 23.
Spindler, Will. 20-34.
Spofford, Ainsworth R. 301-19.
Spooner, W. A. 206-91.
Sprague, Frank J. 196-11; 197-40; 264-11; 269-6.
Sprague, Henry H. 26-80, 84.
Springer, Wm. N. 229-91.
Stallard, J. H. 224-80; 239-17, 26, 83; 240-52.
Staly, Cady. 252-54.
Stammhammer, Josef. 163-67.
Standiford, Charles W. 197-30.
Starr, Ellen Gates. 12-46; 51-69.
Starr, Merritt. 46-73.
Starring, Ford. 60-80.
Statham, H. Heathcote. 12-41; 36-43; 130-13; 140-51; 208-57.

Staub, A. 112-79.
Stayton, Geo. H. 139-42.
Stead, F. H. 46-62.
Stead, W. T. 46-66; 48-98; 50-49; 58-60a; 64-48; 131-27; 191-25.
Steadman, W. C. 136-69.
Stearns, C. K. 265-34.
Stearns, F. P. 151-100; 302-33.
Steele, John S. 180-57.
Steevens, G. W. 26-78; 46-59; 175-55; 188-43; 223-49; 301-6.
Steffenhagen, H. 85-3; 90-7.
Steffens, J. L. 35-27.
Stegman, R. 234-20.
Steiner, Ralph. 156-16.
Stephen, Archibald. 280-19.
Stephens, Henry C. 276-6.
Stephens, J. E. R. 105-22; 251-41; 285-39.
Stephens, Thomas. 182-97.
Stephenson, John. 184-41, 56; 190-86.
Sternberg, George M. 96-3.
Sterne, Simon. 4-66; 66-8; 145-49; 174-29; 181-73; 198-42.
Steuart, Sir James. 228-79.
Steude, M. 121-69; 303-60.
Stevans, C. M. 181-73.
Stevens, Alzina P. 47-96; 48-18.
Stevens, Charles E. 6-17.
Stevens, E. R. 169-95.
Stevens, Frank B. 75-94; 220-69.
Stevens, F. J. Warden. 125-86.
Stevenson, Mrs. Cornelius. 3-30; 223-52.
Stevenson, D. M. 272-78.
Stevenson, E. Irenaeus. 193-69.
Stevenson, F. W. 123-21.
Stevenson, G. E. 149-49.
Stevenson, Thomas. 242-25.
Stewart, A. J. 31-24.
Stewart, Alex. 253-88.
Stewart, D. H. 246-19.
Stewart, Ethelbert. 114-5.
Stewart, George. 233-93.
Stewart, Gilbert. 3-36; 204-66.
Stewart, Jane A. 17-67; 31-7, 33-60.
Stewart, Seth T. 246-30.
Stickney, Albert. 230-47.
Stieda, Wilhelm. 87-44.
Stiles, Henry R. 184-44.
Stiles, W. A 190-94.
Stilgoe, Henry E. 61-2.
Still, A. 283-70.
Stillman, Howard. 307-44.
Stimson, F. J. 291-65; 292-91, 92.
Stoddard, W. O. 191-17.
Stolp, Hermann. 89-85.
Stolz, Ferd. 237-77.
Stone, J. H. 276-8.
Stone, Melville E. 47-83; 49-18.
Stone, William L. 185-72.
Storer, J. J. 241-78.
Story, John. 115-24.
Storrs, Richard Salter. 175-41.
Story, John. 115-24.
Stott, H. 251-48.
Stout, Robert. 203-36.
Stoval, Pleasant A. 244-58.
Stover, Charles B. 193+62; 248-67.
Stowe, J. G. 10-95.
Strachan, James. 112-68.
Strachan, Robert C. 178-11.

Strache, Hugo. 124-57, 58, 63, 68.
Strachy, J. St. Loe. 61-92.
Stratton, F. S. 38-79.
Straus, Carl. 87-41
Straus, Nathan. 215-27.
Strauss, Paul. 42-83; 105-23; 208-43; 208-51; 242-19; 245-100.
Strecker, A. H. 123-28.
Streckfuss, Adolf. 21-53.
Strong, Josiah. 9-67; 42-69; 51-64, 73, 74.
Strong, Thomas N. 51-63; 230-20.
Strong, W. L. 7-32; 53-7.
Strutz, ——. 87-48.
Stuart, A. K. 298-40.
Stuart, Edwin S. 224-78.
Stübben, J. 9-74; 12-42; 13-63, 67; 54-18; 62-18a; 68-33, 34; 86-20; 103-55; 205-88; 211-45; 213-73; 216-65; 258-83, 96; 260-30; 269-22.
Stubbs, William. 280-12; 281-24.
Stürcke, Louis. 201-98.
Sturge, Elizabeth. 33-52.
Sturgis, F. R. 45-37.
Sturgis, R. Clipston. 259-2.
Stursberg, ——. 232-63.
Sugg, William. 122-4.
Sullivan, F. P. 267-72.
Sullivan, J. W. 61-88a; 259-11.
Sullivan, P. F. 168-75.
Sullivan, T. R. 28-41.
Sulzberger, M. 66-90.
Supan, Alex. 229-6.
Suplee, Henry Harrison. 118-78.
Swaab, S. M. 253-80.
Swaffield, Walter J. 28-35.
Swan, J. W. 122-10.
Swan, N. 85-94.
Swarts, Gardner T. 307-50.
Sweet, Ada C. 46-61.
Sweet, J. S. 169-99.
Swift, Lindsay. 28-41.
Swift, Lucius B. 108-90; 159-64.
Swift, Morrison I. 114-7; 240-59; 247-58; 248-78.
Swinton, A. A. C. 118-4; 119-23; 278-63.
Swoope, C. Walton. 224-77.
Sykes, John F. J. 101-5, 6; 105-14; 241-67; 242-22.
Sykora, Carl. 300-91.
Symmes, Frank J. 161-19; 240-48.

T

Tackels, C. J. 242-15.
Tafel, Gustav. 160-93; 161-16.
Taggart, ——. 159-68.
Taggart, Frederick J. 116-50.
Talbot, Arthur N. 249-84; 252-53.
Talbot, J. E. 31-7.
Talbot, M. 248-77.
Talcott, Mary C. 96-99.
Tammeo, G. 232-65.
Tandy, L. D. 296-96.
Taney, J. B. 18-92, 93.
Tanner, John R. 50-32.
Tarbell, Ida M. 209-84.
Tarnowsky, ——. 232-69.
Tattersall, C. H. 238-8.
Taüber, K. P. 244-69.
Taulier, A. 77-26.
Taussig, F. W. 291-66.
Tavernari, C. 221-4.

Taylor, A. 285-27.
Taylor, Benjamin. 92-44; 93-50, 51; 121-66; 284-3.
Taylor, Graham. 101-22; 192-56.
Taylor, Samuel M. 92-43.
Taylor, Warren. 194-85.
Teall, O. S. 7-32.
Tekulsky, Morris. 126-7.
Telford, John. 310-40.
Tenier, Charles. 33-68.
Tenius, Gustav. 89-88.
Terhune, Everitt Bogert. 33-71.
Terne, Bruno. 84-80.
Terrell, Ada K. 43-93.
Terry, Henry T. 53-99; 64-39.
Testart, A. 150-78.
Tetley, William C. 90-8.
Tew, J. S. 101-18.
Thacher, John Boyd. 10-97; 64-42.
Thaw, A. B. 179-43.
Thayer, George S. 166-33.
Thayer, H. 212-68a.
Theard, Alfred F. 173-4.
Thiele, L. 22-78.
Thiess, Karl. 273-8.
Thirlat, M. 81-24.
Thiteau, J. B. 298-44.
Thoinot, L. 211-37.
Thoma, ——. 42-75.
Thomas, Claude M. 150-76.
Thomas, E. 104-3; 222-20.
Thomas, J. F. 299-50.
Thomas, John Lloyd. 104-91.
Thomas, Karl. 118-80.
Thomas, Miss M. Carey. 245-99.
Thomas, Octavius. 234-9.
Thomas, Thaddeus P. 15-9.
Thomé de Gamond, A. 126-25.
Thompson, A. D. 68-28b; 108-85; 219-60, 63, 67; 222-32, 34; 251-28.
Thompson, Clifford. 76-2.
Thompson, Daniel Greenleaf. 194-91.
Thompson, David M. 232-70.
Thompson, Elihu. 119-10.
Thompson, G. F. 117-69.
Thompson, Gibson. 33-67.
Thompson, H. 37-55, 67.
Thompson, James. 280-6.
Thompson, R. E. 291-73.
Thompson, Seymour D. 5-3; 164-86.
Thompson, Silvanus P. 264-11.
Thompson, T. Kennard. 235-43.
Thompson, W. 276-86; 234-11.
Thomson, Edith Parker. 243-51; 311-59.
Thomson, Gilbert. 251-32.
Thomson, James. 62-17.
Thorlet, Léon. 78-48; 79-86; 81-26, 33.
Thornbury, Frank J. 306-27; 307-43; 308-71.
Thornbury W. 139-32.
Thorne, W. H. 174-28.
Thresh, J. C. 310-16.
Thring, Lord. 275-67.
Thudichum, George. 249-84; 251-32; 285-38.
Thurber, F. B. 198-53.
Thurston, Gates P. 170-34.
Thury, M. 271-49.
Tidy, C. M. 253-81.
Tiedeman, Christopher G. 227-41; 294-32.
Tieftrunk, F. 120-56.
Tilden, James A. 144-36.

BIBLIOGRAPHY.

Tilden, Samuel J. 198-46, 47; 201-10.
Tillson, George W. 218-33; 219-38, 40, 54; 220-80, 82.
Tiltman, Hessell. 17-80, 81.
Tite, W. 211-43.
Todd, ——. 161-18.
Todd, Charles Burr. 184-43, 49; 186-94; 193-56; 301-21.
Tolman, Wm. Howe. 7-32; 8-46; 17-66, 73; 18-83; 101-96; 106-48; 107-68; 176-60; 177-82, 83; 179-30, 41; 186-9; 192-39, 55; 194-84; 246-30.
Tomlinson, Thomas. 84-82.
Tomn, Lillian. 14-99; 203-38.
Tompkins, Elizabeth A. 188-49.
Tooke, C. W. 71-88, 100, 1; 72-3, 9; 74-64; 157-23, 25; 163-51; 251-44.
Tooley, S. A. 207-34.
Torrens, W. M. 130-96.
Torrents y Monner, A. 255-22.
Toulmin, George. 230-28.
Towle, Stevenson. 218-16.
Towner, Hiram. 195-3.
Townsend, Horace. 127-27.
Townsend, Mrs. John D. 41-51; 58-65.
Toynbee, H. V. 44-19; 145-57.
Tracy, Roger S. 228-86; 242-4.
Trani, V. 110-28.
Trask, Spencer. 184-42.
Trautmann, A. 90-4.
Trautmann, Mary E. 192-43.
Trautwine, John C., Jr. 225-3, 5; 305-18.
Treichler, J. J. 312-85.
Tremain, Henry Edwin. 161-6.
Trenholm, William L. 246-26.
Treub, M. W. F. 97-9.
Trevelyan, C. P. 259-14.
Treves, Claudio. 109-2.
Tribus, Louis L. 45-55; 76-1.
Trickett, W. 222-19.
Tricoche, George Nestler. 187-21.
Trollope, T. A. 278-48.
Tröltsch, Walt. 87-51.
Troske, L. 144-48.
Trotter, A. P. 117-56.
Truslow, Arthur. 215-43.
Tryon, Thos. 13-64.
Tsanoff, Stoyan Vasil. 215-38, 39, 42.
Tubbs, J. Nelson. 169-17.
Tucker, Preble. 176-64.
Tucker, R. S. 176-64.
Tucker, Wm. J. 30-79a.
Tuckerman, W. P. 214-17.
Tully, T. De Quincy. 177-1.
Turiello, P. 170-27.
Turnbull, Thomas. 243-46.
Turneaure, F. E. 148-16.
Turner, M. A. 258-90.
Turner, W. L. 224-88.
Turquey, Elie. 73-24; 80-17.
Tupper, E. Sherburne. 94-71.
Tuttle, Arthur S. 199-63; 305-5.
Tuttle, Leonard. 73-40.
Twelvetrees, W. N. 27-17; 144-44; 307-43.
Tyler, G. R. 130-17.
Tyler, H. L. 117-67.
Tyler, Lyon G. 310-29.
Tyng, T. Mitchell. 194-93.

U

Uebelacker, C. F. 157-31.
Ufford, Walter Shepard. 42-77.
Uhland, W. H. 118-86.
Uhle, John B. 242-5.
Ulbrich, J. 14-2a.
Unger, ——. 96-96.
Ulrich, B. A. 70-74.
Ulrich, C. F. 306-24; 309-15.
Uppercu, J. W. 262-74.
Upton, G. P. 47-94.
Upton, J. Kendrick. 40-28; 71-79.
Urbanitsky, A. 118-88.
Urdahl, Thomas K. 163-75.
Urquhart, W. P. 279-70.

V

Vacchelli, Giov. 110-23.
Vachee, Francis. 17-74.
Vacherot, ——. 62-6.
Vail, Anna Murray. 189-79.
Vaissière, M. 211-42.
Valentine, D. T. 186-99.
Valesh, Eva McD. 187-21.
Valframbert, Charles. 275-83.
Vallance, William. 133-77; 277-35.
Vallandigham, E. N. 310-33.
Valleroux, Herbert. 18-1b; 78-52.
Van Buskirk, W. F. 250-16.
Van den Heuvel, J. 19-17.
Vanderlip, F. A. 301-16.
Vandewalker, Nina C. 48-16.
Vandervelde, E. 158-53.
Van Gasken, ——. 224-74.
Van Geert, Prosper. 11-25; 18-1a.
Van Gilsie, J. A. 98-29.
Vanlaer, Maurice. 19-16; 81-20.
Van Pelt, Daniel. 175-48.
Van Rensselaer, (Mrs. Schuyler), M. G. 13-77; 175-49; 185-65; 185-77; 192-44; 244-75.
Van Vechten, Emma. 185-91.
Van Vloten, ——. 265-23.
van Wetter, R. 118-98.
v. d. Werra, F. M. 197-30.
Van der Weyde, N. J. 194-82.
Van Zandt, A. D. B. 60-82.
Van Zanten, J. H. 11-21.
Varney, Geo. J. 31-7.
Vassault, F. I. 65-68a.
Vaughan, Victor C. 105-21.
Vauthier, Maurice. 18-96; 275-60.
Vautier, Theodore. 123-40.
Veber, Adrien. 81-18; 113-87; 162-28; 163-65, 72; 170-21; 208-50, 55; 209-80; 73-26.
Veiller, Laurence. 107-60, 63, 70; 178-9; 184-35, 41.
Vencataratnam, Ganjam. 148-20.
Verdier, A. R. 237-79.
Vermeule, C. C. 172-85.
Vértess, Josef. 118-79.
Viallate, A. 194-85.
Vickers, George. 223-57.
Vidal, Georges. 126-11.
Viele, Egbert L. 223-86.
Vigoni, G. 154-62.
Vigouroux, Louis. 14-97.
Villain, Georges. 210-99.
Villard, Oswald Garrison. 186-100.
Vincent, Edgar L. 72-14.

Vincent, George E. 51-59.
Vincey, Paul. 208-59.
Vinck, Emilio. 19-12.
Vine, J. B. 274-55; 280-15.
Vischer, J. 46-64.
Vivarez, H. 118-1.
Vivian, H. 133-84.
Vogel, J. H. 252-67.
Volkmer, Volkher. 228-81.
von Below, G. 98-71.
von Bilinski, Leon Ritter. 87-55.
von Boenigk, Otto. 271-68.
von Brandt, Alexander. 97-16.
von Emperger, Fritz. 31-9.
von Feistmantel, H. Ritter. 300-82.
von Frankenberg, H. 271-64.
von Friedenfels, Josef Freih. 14-4.
von Gneist, Rudolph. 20-24; 87-35, 49; 129-93; 276-87.
von Heckel, Max. 16-54; 73-22; 287-74.
von Holst, H. 5-100.
von Inama-Sternegg, Karl Theodor. 14-4, 5; 298-50.
von Jagow, Eugen. 209-71.
von Kaufmann, R. 79-84; 291-70.
von Langsdorff, Karl. 253-87.
von Lenz, Richard. 271-68.
von Mangold, Carl. 153-41; 310-23.
von Maurer, G. L. 88-67.
von Nostitz, Hans. 287-71.
von Podhagsky, J. 299-67.
von Reitzenstein, Baron. 43-100.
von Reitzenstein, F. Frh. 70-60.
von Rosenberg, Wm., Jr. 14-93.
von Schoen, ——. 299-73.
von Soden, Herman. 21-52.
von Stengel, Karl Freih. 86-13.
von Wattenwyl, J. 273-29.
von Welck, A. 16-54.
Vreeland, H. H. 167-72; 168-75; 195-1; 196-27; 263-86.
Vrooman, F. B. 104-1.
Vrooman, Walter. 161-7; 190-91; 215-42.

W

Wade, G. A. 142-6.
Wade, H. T. 65-83.
Wade, James J. 251-51.
Wadlin, H. G. 28-33; 151-85; 152-6.
Wagner, —— 148-32.
Wagner, A. H. G. 87-52.
Wagner, Adolph. 70-69; 79-85; 87-40.
Wagner, Charles. 208-63.
Wagner, Herm. 229-6.
Wagner, Samuel Tobias. 225-93.
Wahl, Christian. 214-96.
Wait, H. H. 125-78; 119-15; 125-98.
Wait, J. C. 68-32.
Waite, Henry Randall. 5-90.
Wakeman, Antoinette van Hoesen. 48-4; 150-73.
Walbridge, C. P. 52-85.
Walcker, Karl. 88-79.
Waldo, Eveline A. 173-3.
Waldo, F. J. 105-15; 243-36, 37.
Waldron, Geo. B. 174-28.
Walford, Edward. 253-88.
Walker, F. A. 83-63a.
Walker, J. B. 228-86; 269-6.
Walker, Norman. 172-88.

Walkley, Arthur B. 143-16.
Wallace, J. M. 169-2.
Wallace, John. 16-46.
Wallace, Johnstone. 171-50.
Wallace, Lew. 56-34.
Wallbrecht, ——. 96-95.
Wallet, Paul. 244-60.
Walling, Geo. 191-20.
Wallis, W. E. 100-74; 136-71.
Walsh, Gertrude Ethelbert. 51-57; 264-11.
Walter, A. E. 267-63.
Walters, Lucy. 139-32.
Walthew, George W. 3-49.
Walworth, Ellen H. 243-57.
Wambaugh, Eugene. 159-76.
Wanklyn, Alfred J. 249-79; 303-49.
Ward, C. Osborne. 94-63.
Ward, Mrs. Humphrey. 141-85, 86.
Warden-Stevens, F. J. 84-72a.
Wardle, Thomas. 252-62.
Ware, James E. 106-52.
Ware, Thomas Webb. 14-98; 203-40.
Waring, George E. 1-7; 40-19a; 150-72; 153-39; 173-4; 175-44; 183-24; 186-2; 189-66, 68; 190-92, 7; 192-36; 193-72, 76, 77; 198-58; 215-40; 217-39; 228-74; 232-83; 240-64; 250-4, 5, 13; 252-58; 252-61; 257-51, 57, 59, 60, 62, 64; 290-33; 295-69; 302-32.
Warner, A. G. 301-25; 40-32; 45-39, 40; 44-21; 271-54; 272-79.
Warner, Brainard H., Jr. 115-31.
Warner, Geo. E. 165-1.
Warner, John De Witt. 10-92; 12-62; 30-93; 32-45; 49-25; 113-98; 168-75; 177-91; 188-45, 47; 189-77; 201-3; 225-100; 235-30.
Warner, Stutler. 257-55.
Warren, C. 139-45.
Warren, E. P. 143-10.
Warren, Frederick M. 211-47.
Warren, May Spencer. 138-23.
Warrum, Henry. 293-31.
Washburn, Albert H. 56-40; 89-99.
Waterlow, David, 136-67.
Waterlow, Sir Sydney. 102-28.
Waterlow, Sydney H. 106-43.
Waters, Theodore. 36-37.
Watson, Aaron. 171-48.
Watson, Edward W. 65-82.
Watson, Ellen. 226-25.
Watson, James. 32-33.
Watson, John. 224-70.
Watson, John F. 184-37.
Watson, W. M. 84-76; 95-92; 262-63; 309-15; 250-13; 252-55; 252-58.
Watt, Robert. 92-32.
Wattenberg, William. 159-76.
Watts, Franklin. 119-11.
Waugh, B. 41-41; 42-67.
Waurin, Louis. 85-87; 259-11.
Wauters, Alph. 19-7.
Way, T. R. 132-49.
Wayl, Th. 257-68.
Weakley, John B., Jr. 74-61.
Weaver, Emily P. 224-69.
Weaver, (Mrs.) E. A. 239-23.
Weaver, William. 258-92.
Webb, Herbert L. 55-31.
Webb, James Avery. 74-62.
Webb, Sidney. 103-78; 129-86; 130-6; 139-48; 274-56.

BIBLIOGRAPHY.

Webber, W. H. Y. 124-70.
Webber, Wm. L. 237-75.
Webber, William O. 93-56.
Weber, Adna Ferrin, 229-89; 259-1.
Weber, G. A. 106-45.
Weber, John. 227-39.
Weber, John B. 42-71.
Webster, George S. 225-93.
Webster, W. C. 294-48.
Weeden, William B. 232-78.
Weeks, Anna R. 116-51.
Wegmann, Edward. 56-39; 114-11; 199-72.
Weill, Friedrich. 256-46.
Weinstein, ——. 228-76.
Weinstock, Henry. 161-19.
Weise, A. J. 10-98.
Weissman, Henry. 188-44.
Weitzel, S. W. 239-22.
Welby, Sir Reginald Earle. 131-32.
Welch, Charles. 135-40.
Welch, J. H. 183-15.
Welch, William H. 241-10.
Welles, Henry J. 183-20.
Welling, J. C. 301-18.
Wellisch, S. 299-76.
Wells, D. A. 201-9; 73-48, 49; 70-61; 73-42.
Wells, J. 45-44.
Welsh, Charles. 107-74; 128-65.
Welsh, H. 64-64.
Welsh, Herbert. 7-23; 8-47a, 61, 63; 53-95, 1; 113-80; 223-46; 224-90; 311-57.
Wende, Ernest. 167-57.
Wentworth, John. 47-87.
Wernher, Adf. 36-49.
Westcott, J. T. 124-66.
Wescott, Thompson. 224-72.
West, E. L. 111-52.
West, Max. 73-30; 189-72; 301-15.
Westergaard, ——. 272-89.
Westergaard, Niels. 56-41.
Westgarth, William. 136-74.
Weston, Edmund B. 203-45; 304-47; 78; 305-13.
Wetherbee, George A. 151-1.
Wetherill, Edith. 223-52.
Wetmore, Jean. 119-24.
Wetzler, Joseph. 199-70.
Weyl, Th. 22-76.
Whale, George. 130-97.
Whalen, John. 197-30.
Whalen, Thomas A. 29-67.
Wheatley, Richard. 192-36; 190-8; 294-33.
Wheeler, D. H. 194-85.
Wheeler, Everett P. 45-51; 198-59; 5-88.
Wheeler, Wm. 13-80.
Wheelock, Webster. 238-95.
Whelan, D. P. 234-13.
Whelan, Frederick. 140-64; 132-75; 130-100.
Whinery, S. 218-20; 218-28; 218-22.
Whipple, Fred H. 117-64.
Whipple, George C. 303-58; 305-6; 199-60; 306-26.
White, Arnold. 133-80; 273-34.
White, A. D. 289-19; 245-89.
White, Alfred T. 198-58; 199-61; 296-5; 99-53; 100-90; 106-38; 106-42.
White, Francis H. 179-27; 41-60.
White, Gaylord I. 186-4.
White, H. C. 159-62; 44-19.
White, H. L. 215-37.

White, H. 15-31.
White, Henry. 114-2; 188-46; 243-53.
White, James H. 240-65.
White, Robert. 136-64.
White, W. Howard. 196-11; 83-66.
White, William A. 111-64.
White, William H. 121-79.
Whiteing, Richard. 207-12, 14, 17.
Whitelegge, B. Arthur. 242-17.
Whiting, Lillian. 28-27.
Whitlay, J. H. 94-70.
Whitman, Sarah W. 244-73.
Whitmore, C. A. 129-75; 129-71; 128-50; 134-13; 139-48.
Whitmore, Henry. 29-71.
Whitney, J. Eugene. 231-40.
Whitredge, Frederick W. 216-77.
Whitridge, F. W. 64-36; 65-84.
Whitten, Robert Harvey. 151-88; 292-94, 95.
Whitten, Robert H. 292-94, 95.
Whitten, W. H. 47-78.
Whittle, C. L. 151-86.
Wickett, S. M. 39-99.
Wieck, B. 258-82.
Wight, Chas. L. 267-66.
Wigmore, J. H. 65-68a.
Wilberforce, H. W. W. 285-19.
Wilbour, Joshua. 62-10.
Wilby, Chas. B. 8-59; 51-76; 52-88.
Wilcox, Delos F. 5-83; 13-83; 54-13; 153-50; 181-73; 202-27; 204-62; 288-98; 289-9, 10.
Wilcox, J. W. 258-77.
Wilcox, Walter F. 158-52; 163-56; 165-99.
Wilder, A. P. 4-76; 8-43.
Wilder, E. A. 234-23.
Wiler, C. 119-12.
Wiley, J. M. 26-64.
Wilhelm, Lewis W. 150-79.
Wilke, D. 236-70.
Wilkiemeyer, H. 125-91.
Wilkins, H. 280-98.
Wilkinson, James B. 205-74.
Wilkinson, John J. 120-62.
Wilkinson, Robert F. 200-90.
Wilkinson, Spenser. 133-89.
Will, J. S. 282-61; 258-76; 288-85; 288-90.
Will, T. E. 4-77; 7-32; 24-12, 15; 64-63; 215-37; 273-34.
Willebrand, J. P. 258-85.
Williams, Benezette. 233-92.
Williams, C. 190-8.
Williams, D. E. 55-22.
Williams, Fleming. 135-43.
Williams, Gardner S. 154-59; 303-84; 60-84.
Williams, H. S. 36-63a; 193-72; 211-42; 179-38; 192-38; 183-22; 42-68.
Williams, Henry W. 57-54.
Williams, I. P. 279-72.
Williams, J. H. W. 274-55.
Williams, J. J. 83-63a.
Williams, Jesse Lynch. 188-33; 194-81, 176-69.
Williams, Leighton. 4-67; 8-52.
Williams, Mary B. H. 17-68.
Williams, Robert. 137-83; 136-66.
Williams, Sylvester G. 57-53.
Williams, Talcott. 224-71; 194-85.
Williams, (Mrs.) Talcott. 224-89.
Williams, Timothy S. 72-17a.
Williams, William Klapp. 127-47.

Williams, W. M. J. 279-96.
Williamson, Emily E. 106-48; 172-71.
Willis, S. T. 192-49.
Willoughby, Edward F. 145-63; 242-21; 250-18.
Willoughby, W. F. 289-25; 271-56, 62; 80-6; 272-73.
Willoughby, W. W. 289-25.
Willcox, Francis W. 119-26; 122-14.
Willson, Arthur L. 261-58.
Wilmshurst, T. P. 94-69.
Wilson, A. J. 132-73.
Wilson, Andrew. 305-19.
Wilson, Anna T. 41-54.
Wilson, C. H. 163-55.
Wilson, Chester P. 254-96.
Wilson, E. D. J. 278-50.
Wilson, Edmund J. 101-19.
Wilson, F. Cortez. 117-67.
Wilson, George B. 232-79
Wilson, George G. 232-72.
Wilson, George R. 126-9.
Wilson, George W. 232-82.
Wilson, H. L. 263-77.
Wilson, James Grant. 185-80.
Wilson, John L. 183-16.
Wilson, Joseph M. 225-4.
Wilson, Philip W. 28-41.
Wilson, Rufus R. 298-34.
Wilson, T. M. 203-49.
Wilson, Woodrow. 1-7b, 2-14.
Winchester, A. E. 166-27.
Windmüller, Louis. 241-79; 216-60; 36-52; 178-19; 189-67.
Wines, E. C. 42-65; 227-49.
Wines, Frederick Howard. 227-46; 202-22; 189-65; 27-8; 11-18; 45-48; 40-17, 21; 126-13.
Wingate, Charles F. 309-15; 243-52; 241-87; 198-42; 192-36; 187-21; 113-95; 107-60; 105-13; 11-23.
Winkler, F. C. 154-74.
Winslow, F. E. 193-60.
Winsor, Anna Ware. 184-50.
Winsor, Justin. 28-25.
Winter, Alexander. 202-29.
Wintle, W. J. 144-42.
Wirminghaus, A. 229-94.
Wisner, Edward. 160-100; 161-8.
Wiss, Ed. 102-52.
Wist, Joh. 102-36.
Withington, W. H. 111-53.
Withrow, W. H. 262-66.
Witz, Gustav. 9-81.
Wodiezka, W. 299-63.
Wolcott, Mrs. Roger. 42-78.
Wolf, J. 273-22.
Wolff, Paul. 205-75.
Wollman, Henry. 50-40.
Wood, ——. 161-18.
Wood, Edmund. 171-44.
Wood, Esther, 141-79.
Wood, Frank, 250-1.
Wood, Henry B. 30-32.
Wood, Leonard. 243-56.
Wood, Octavius Grant. 101-93.
Wood, T. McKinnon. 129-73.
Woodburn, James A. 53-94.
Woodbridge, J. E. 94-64.
Woodbridge, S. H. 246-23.
Woodford, Arthur Burnham. 223-53.

Woodhead, G. Sims. 250-7.
Woodman, Alpheus G. 240-56.
Woodruff, Clinton Rogers. 9-66; 8-45, 54; 6-19; 7-23; 159-65; 173-98; 221-17; 222-21; 225-10; 225-3; 224-80; 223-48, 51, 53, 63; 239-31; 292-89; 290-41.
Woods, Henry D. 68-36; 211-25; 151-1.
Woods, R. A. 247-56; 247-49; 248-73; 247-59; 248-72; 51-58; 44-31a; 30-77, 79, 79a; 92-38; 142-94.
Woods, Robert P. 219-53.
Woodward, Frank E. 2-17; 23-10.
Woodward, W. A. 125-100.
Woodward, Wm. 140-62.
Woodward, W. C. 84-77; 84-79.
Woodworth, A. V. 272-96.
Wooley, Charles. 186-98.
Woolf, M. A. 179-37.
Woolsey, T. D. 227-36.
Wordingham, C. H. 149-47.
Worms, F. 78-59.
Wormsley, B. 276-98.
Worsley, Abby Howland. 42-87.
Worth, John Edward. 141-88.
Worthington, T. Locke. 100-63.
Wright, A. O. 45-52; 40-34.
Wright, Austin W. 158-51.
Wright, Carroll D. 100-65; 273-34; 229-10; 162-49; 295-69; 293-23; 296-97.
Wright, Geo. G. 38-92.
Wright, John Livingston. 31-7; 27-16.
Wright, John S. 47-86.
Wright, R. S. 130-99; 275-80.
Wright, Willis B. 153-44.
Wtoroff, Nicholas. 3-39.
Würmli, G. 312-81.
Wurster, ——. 159-63.
Würzburger, Eugen. 221-3.
Wylie, James R. 43-9.
Wyman, Walter. 294-46.
Wynkoop, Hubert S. 67-21; 67-19; 123-25, 26.

Y

Yager, Arthur. 158-45.
Yaryan, Homer T. 307-43.
Yerkes, Charles T. 169-93; 163-53; 267-82.
Yorke, E. H. 125-90.
Young, George H. 114-12.
Young, Henry G. 30-83.
Young, James. 285-30.
Young, James T. 78-63; 244-71.
Young, John. 92-46; 296-87.
Young, John F. 2-24.
Young, Peter. 121-71.
Young, S. G. 243-30.
Young, W. E. 3-32; 25-53; 57-46.

Z

Zacharias, J. 118-89.
Zahn, G. H. B. 312-89.
Zehnder, C. 231-58.
Zelle, R. 86-7.
Zeumer, Karl. 87-54.
Ziffer, E. A. 14-6; 268-93, 94, 95; 300-53.
Zimmer, ——. 83-56b.
Zimmern, Helen. 209-82.
Zradlowski, Ferd. 90-5.
Zuppinger, C. 237-77.
Zueblin, Charles. 48-5.
Zur Nieden, Walter. 89-86.

Augsburg College
George Sverdrup Library
Minneapolis, Minnesota 55404